Oracle Press™

Oracle Financials Handbook

David James
Graham H. Seibert

Osborne/ **McGraw-Hill**

Berkeley New York St. Louis San Francisco
Auckland Bogotá Hamburg London Madrid
Mexico City Milan Montreal New Delhi Panama City
Paris São Paulo Singapore Sydney
Tokyo Toronto

Osborne/**McGraw-Hill**
2600 Tenth Street
Berkeley, California 94710
U.S.A.

For information on translations or book distributors outside the U.S.A., or to arrange bulk purchase discounts for sales promotions, premiums, or fund-raisers, please contact Osborne/**McGraw-Hill** at the above address.

Oracle Financials Handbook

234567890 DOC DOC 90198765432109

ISBN 0-07-882375-7

Publisher
Brandon A. Nordin

**Associate Publisher,
Editor-in-Chief**
Scott Rogers

Acquisitions Editor
Jeremy Judson

Project Editor
Nancy McLaughlin

Editorial Assistant
Monika Faltiss

Technical Editors
The Oracle Financials Group

Developmental Editors
Amber Allen-Sauer
Lakshmana Rao

Copy Editors
Cynthia Putnam
Carl Wikander

Proofreader
Stefany Otis

Indexer
Valerie Perry

Computer Designer
Jani Beckwith

Illustrator
Brian Wells

About the Authors...

David James has been an information technology consultant for more than ten years. He has helped to implement Oracle Financials in a number of industry-leading corporations.

Graham Seibert is a financial consultant specializing in the implementation of Oracle Financials. He is the author of *Working with Oracle Development Tools* and *Oracle Data Processing: A Manager's Handbook.*

Contents

PART I
Getting Started

PART II
What Can the Package Do?

PART III

Managing and Customizing an Applications Environment

Acknowledgments

riting a book has numerous rewards, the greatest of which are the people you meet along the way. It has been a pleasure working with our publishers, Scott Rogers, Jeremy Judson, Ann Sellers, Monika Faltiss, and Nancy McLaughlin at Oracle Press.

A special mention must go to Amber Allen-Sauer, who, under impossible deadlines, performed a vital review of the entire manuscript and helped transform it into a book. Earlier on in the project, Lakshmana Rao contributed a significant amount of time and effort to a technical review of the work.

We are indebted to the Oracle Financials development team for their comments and advice on various topics. Specifically, Kelly Miller-Bailey, Jeanine Musch, and Virginia Caliguiran were the key players who shepherded the book's contents through the Oracle review process.

David James
Graham Seibert

My introduction to Oracle Financials was through Warwick Hill, a former colleague of mine at Price Waterhouse, and my good friend John Davidson. Both were instrumental in getting me involved with Oracle Financials at BP in Hamburg soon after I left London to join my wife in Germany. To both of them, I am very grateful. Unknowingly, they were the *sine qua non* of this book.

I would especially like to thank those whom I have worked with over the past many years, particularly Robert Martwich and Nick Morter, who worked on the ISP project at BP in Hamburg; Jim Bennett, Wolfgang Wurnig, and Alan Walder of Europcar; Val Gay at Post Office Property Holdings in London; and Jason Gan and Jon Edwards at Oracle UK.

I am deeply grateful to two friends whom I have relied on more than any others: Dean Priebee, an Oracle Applications expert, and Stuart Worthington, Financials DBA extraordinaire. Both have always been ready and willing to share their great expertise in a friendly and often humorous way.

My warm thanks go to Andrew Hollick and Erik Sisi of Oracle Middle East, who made available facilities and research material for the four months I was stationed in Dubai. During this time I wrote several early chapters, some of which were kindly reviewed by Stefan Harbermayer. I also wish to thank Vimal K. Gupta of Oracle for his review of Chapter 18 and all the SQL*Plus scripts, and James Walker of Blackwells for his comments.

Finally, I need to thank my wife Jane, for enduring with patience the lengthy book production process.

David James
London
April, 1999

Thanks first to Tom Harmon and Sue Jacox, who kept the business running while I worked on this book, and to my partners John Rodman, Mark Guiffre, Chris Willey, and Joe Costantino for their indispensable insights on Purchasing, Inventory, Order Entry, and Fixed Assets.

The Oracle Applications User's Group embodies the generous spirit of the true experts. Melanie Bock, who has worked with the Financials and the OAUG almost from its inception, continues to contribute advice over the online forum. She may recognize some of her wisdom repeated here. Maggie Coleman helped us learn the Manufacturing suite and contributes at every OAUG conference.

Micros Systems, Inc. is the kind of client consultants dream of, a rapidly-growing company lead by intelligent, goal-oriented managers on both the functional and technical sides. Thanks to the Information Systems management team: Rob Moon, Neil Smith, and Stan Wood; also to Joe Kirby, Rob Smith, and Joyce Healy; and to my functional-side clients, Donna Barron and Roberta Watson.

Special thanks to the people of Watkins Johnson Co., whose engineering mindset made Oracle Manufacturing and Seibert & Costantino look outstanding. Project Manager Scott Frager knew when to force the march, but also when to move the deadline. Systems manager Joe Dorsey assembled the best possible mix of employees and Oracle consultants for the job. Systems team lead Steve Stone taught us all the ins and outs of manufacturing, while Andi Drimmer, T.J. Caro, Dudley Wong, Phil Freemer, and Karen Oliver made WJ's ambitious customization plans appear, in retrospect, to be the only workable alternative. We were pushed by a great group of Superusers, including Doug Saar, Margie Marlow, Bill Paire, Anne Toffey, and Mike Staab.

I would also like to thank Wetzel Campbell, Michael Price, Ed Eichler, and Tom Traver of Oracle Corporation, as well as Ed Schaeffer, who has provided outstanding DBA support to so many of our clients; Dan Hinkle of the Information Systems Consortium; Bill Carr and Brian Belliveau of CAP Gemini; John Smith of Walker & Co.; Bob Bain, Phil Olphin, and Phil Ruberry of Black and Decker; Bill Super and Mike Goldman, who led the implementation at Mitre Co.; Dan Dunlap of CMSI; and lastly, Nancy Squires, who knows everybody in the Washington D.C. area who has Oracle skills.

Graham Seibert
Bethesda, Maryland
April, 1999

Introduction

Oracle Applications is a suite of more than 48 integrated software modules for financial management, supply chain management, manufacturing, project systems, human resources, and sales force automation.

Oracle Applications combines extensive functionality with state-of-the-art technology. The suite is fine-tuned to enable rapid implementation. Oracle Corporation has built its reputation in the database market. While the application suite has grown over the last decade, their purpose has remained unchanged. World-class business automation builds on the preeminent Oracle database using the full range of Oracle's own development tools. Application software is a cornerstone of Oracle's strategic direction.

Oracle Applications serves a broad market, ranging from small, PC-based organizations to Fortune 500 companies downsizing from rooms full of mainframes. Applications users and their data processing support staff have more in common. They appreciate the benefits that Oracle's immense power and flexibility can bring—and they almost always underestimate the amount of planning, preparation, and hard work required on their part to achieve those benefits.

This book focuses on those application modules which are oriented towards financial management. Our aim throughout has been to present three themes: the business functionality of these modules, the underlying technical aspects, and the management and organization of implementation projects. The book is split into parts to reflect these threads. In describing the functionality we have focused on the Oracle Financials modules. Despite this focus, the technology chapters and project management chapters apply equally to Oracle Manufacturing and Oracle Human Resources.

About This Book

The number of users who choose Oracle Financials as the logical way to handle their core financial procedures is growing rapidly. Many are moving from legacy administration systems to UNIX- or Windows 2000-based open systems—and implementing Oracle Financials as a standard company-wide accounting system. This book is aimed at people who are involved with implementation—people with inquiring minds who will want to get a synopsis of Oracle Financials and a preview of the complexities and pitfalls of implementing packaged software. Finance managers and systems personnel recognize that they can draw from the collective wisdom of the thousands of organizations that have already implemented Oracle Financials. The purpose of this book is to share much of the knowledge and hindsight that has been accumulated by all three authors during many years of successful Oracle Applications implementation projects.

Who Should Read This Book?

The data processors and the functional users have to pull in tandem to install the Applications. We have pitched this book to provide each with a broad understanding of the other's role. The Applications force an integrated view of the company. We have attempted to highlight the integration aspects of each Application.

"Beginning-to-intermediate" understates this book's utility. Almost every reader will be a beginner with respect to some of the topics we cover. While only the reference materials that Oracle itself publishes can provide the depth that specialists need in each functional area, this book will provide them, and their colleagues, the common frame of reference they need to work together on integrating the system. It offers the kind of outside perspective that Oracle could not provide with regard to conversion and integration.

We explain how to organize a successful implementation project, the essential concepts of Oracle Financials, and some of the underlying technical and accounting theory. The book is aimed at business people with a managerial accounting background and technicians with information technology experience. We have assumed that the business people have no specific technical skills and that the technicians have no accounting knowledge. A large part of the book's appeal, we think, will be interrelating business decisions and technical aspects in a way that both business people and technicians can understand. We do this by detailing specific information on the technical aspects of Oracle Financials for accountants, and providing guidance on the business functionality for implementers and developers.

This book is not an Oracle marketing brochure or a replacement for the reference manuals, but rather a pragmatic approach to understanding the Applications, and a practical manual for any implementation team. It should repay the time spent in reading many times over, and help you avoid costly mistakes.

Organization of This Book

This book is divided into three main parts:

- Part I contains an overview of the scope, the functionality, and the essential concepts underlying the Oracle Applications suite. This material is an overture to themes that appear later in the book. If you are totally new to Oracle Applications, you should read Part I first.

- Part II covers the function and the implementation issues involved with using the Applications. The chapters in Part II are included for your ongoing reference; they need not be read in order.

- Part III covers the technical and managerial issues that apply to all the Applications. Here you're introduced to the common building blocks that give the Applications their power and unity, the environment in which the Applications operate, and the Oracle programming tools that can help you customize the Applications to meet your specific needs. You'll learn about the organization and management of an Oracle Application implementation project, and the live-operation issues you must consider once you are up and running. This section is essential for anyone with management responsibility for an Oracle Applications implementation.

The material you'll find on the Osborne McGraw-Hill Website (**http://www.osborne.com**) is integral to this book. It contains extracts of the text, additional material, and some of the code fragments that you'll find in the book.

About Oracle Corporation

Oracle founder Larry Ellison is a visionary. The founding vision behind Oracle was similar to that of Microsoft. As the IBM monolith cracked, through evolutionary market forces aided by pressure from the Justice Department, major opportunities emerged in the technical community. Open alternatives to IBM, among them DEC, HP, and the nonproprietary Unix operating system, would provide enterprises with plentiful and inexpensive processing power. Ellison's vision was that a database would be essential to exploiting that power—and that the database could be proprietary.

Oracle Corporation experienced phenomenal growth, doubling its sales each year, for most of the 1980s. Each successive version of its database product offered more features and greater reliability. Oracle released powerful "fourth-generation" development tools to make it easy for programmers to use the database for data capture, reports, and ad-hoc queries.

The "fourth-generation" programming languages add significant value by making programmers significantly more productive. The greatest boon to programmer productivity, however, is not to program at all. At the same period during the '80s when Oracle was claiming its position as the dominant open-systems database, McCormick and Dodge, MSA, and American Software fought for dominance in the world of applications software. They worked primarily within the IBM world of proprietary operating systems and databases and the COBOL programming language.

By the late '80s Oracle's database and tools were robust enough to compete with IBM in supporting enterprise-level systems. Ellison, seeing the dramatic value Oracle could offer using its powerful database, tools, and development expertise to develop world-class applications, committed to building a financial software suite. Oracle, whose explosive growth presented a major need within the company for integrated software controls, served at its own test site.

Oracle Applications followed a different growth path than competing products. Oracle's competition embraced client-server computing, the model for enterprise computing that emerged along with the Windows desktop environment in the early '90s. PeopleSoft developed their suite of human resources, later financial and manufacturing software using that technology. SAP reengineered their mainframe-hosted R2 software to run in client-server mode. Oracle, however, saw the limits of client-server, and saw beyond it to the Internet. Their vision was correct; the Internet is a better architecture for delivering enterprise solutions. Unfortunately it proved to be uncomfortably far in the future.

Client-server systems have significant shortcomings. They impose a great deal of traffic on the network connecting client and server, which can hinder performance. They are difficult to manage; each user's desktop environment—usually Windows—is unique. Instead of managing applications centrally, system administrators often have to work at the retail level, fixing problems one user at a time. Some of these shortcomings have diminished over time. Processors, networks and databases, primarily the Oracle database itself, have evolved to the point that performance is acceptable. Network systems management tools, and the use of middle-tier network servers, have simplified configuration management. Nevertheless, client-server continues to make significant demands on computing, network and especially staff resources. The Internet is a better model.

Client-server's graphical user interface (GUI) proved to be so attractive that it overcame the architecture's shortcomings in cost and performance. Oracle's character-mode applications lost ground to their GUI-based competitors despite Oracle's superior performance and functionality. Meanwhile, Ellison's Internet vision experienced technical delays. Though he rightly predicted the exponential growth of the net, he appears to have underestimated the time it would take until network browsers became intelligent. Oracle's Internet Computing module requires Java applets to provide intelligence at the desktop level. Without Java, the number of exchanges with the Web and database servers would be prohibitive. Java was a longer time coming than Oracle expected. Only within the past year has Java on browsers become reliable enough to make Oracle's Internet Computing the best architectural choice for most users.

If it had been Oracle's goal to bypass the client-server phase in product evolution, timing thwarted them. They announced Smart Client, their client-server version, with Release 10.6 in 1996. 10.6 offered GUI functionality and several new products that were available only in GUI. Release 10.7 solidified the GUI product line and provided Year 2000 compliance. The growth of Oracle's software products slowed as their client-server offerings suffered in comparison with competitors' more mature offerings.

Oracle's Web tools grew robust in the time the Smart Client applications were maturing. Oracle Web Server is an industry leader. The Developer 2000 tools were upgraded to generate code for the Web. The Applications group released the Oracle Self-Service Applications as front-end, bolt-on modules to extend the functionality of their mainline Purchasing, Order Entry, Projects, and Human Resources products to anyone with Internet access who could benefit.

Oracle has been a pioneer in CASE (computer aided systems engineering) technology. Working within the Oracle product line, they have been able to offer the most extensive integration between upper CASE (analysis and design) and lower CASE (automatic program generation). Though CASE is a very powerful tool, using it successfully requires a high level of competence and commitment. It is ideally suited for use by software houses—such as Oracle in its role as the author of Oracle Applications.

The Internet Computing module brings all the pieces together. It uses Oracle's proven Web technology. It uses Developer 2000's Oracle*Forms 4.5 and Reports 2.5 code, which leverages the most significant portion of Oracle's Smart Client investment. Oracle has used CASE technology to generate the Applications, and offers CASE metadata to Applications customers. Internet Computing uses the cartridge technology released in Oracle8, placing application processing in the bosom of the database for efficiency and integrity. Oracle Applications, now including some 48 modules, is at the head of the pack in all significant technologies.

The Oracle RDBMS

Great software empires are often built on borrowed ideas. Microsoft parlayed a product they bought called QDOS (Quick and Dirty Operating System) into a desktop monopoly. Lotus borrowed heavily from Electronic Arts, and Apple from Xerox. Oracle is no exception. IBM saw the SQL language developed by the resident academics at their Santa Theresa labs as a promising concept but a threat to their dominant IMS database. Larry Ellison saw it as an opportunity.

The relational model was simply a better way of looking at data than the hierarchical and networked models it replaced. Initially, it was also less efficient and not much easier to program. Oracle has succeeded by consistently keeping its database performance at the head of the pack, increasing the utility of the base product by adding tools and applications, isolating the user from the operating system by building a lot of operating system functionality into its product, expanding the concept of an RDBMS to include concepts such as distributed processing and object management, and by cultivating a wide number of third-party business partners through its open architecture.

The RDBMS that lies beneath Oracle Applications manages the data, does backup and recovery, monitors its own performance, and provides a rich programming environment. It frees users to choose the underlying operating system on a commodity basis, because most of the discriminators are in Oracle itself. The remaining operating system questions concern reliability and scalability.

Version 8 of the RDBMS, which is required for Release 11 of the Applications, is object-relational. It has adapted object-oriented database management system (OODBMS) concepts into its relational architecture. Release 8's new *cartridge* architecture is an object-oriented programming device that places custom programming modules within the RDBMS, as close as possible to the data itself. It gives developers the ability to extend the basic functionality of the database itself to support such functions as geographical data, visual image data, time series, and context searching. Release 11's Workflow technology is one of several areas in which the Applications take advantage of cartridge technology.

Disintermediation—taking out the middleman—is one of the most significant benefits of the Internet. Not only does it cost money to have your employee give order status to a customer, but the customer would rather do it himself. Let him! Empower the customer to see his orders, and the vendor to see your upcoming needs. Oracle's Self-Service Web Applications are increasingly giving people outside the company the ability to reach in for information and to submit data, such as orders. Strong security features have been implemented in Oracle's Web products, the RDBMS, and the Applications themselves to allow global access without compromising confidential data.

Oracle Programming Tools

The Oracle RDBMS is a premier device for storing and retrieving transactional data, but it is not intended for end users. Programs have to accept data and queries from users and present results back to them. Programmers initially worked with Oracle the same way they worked with most of the databases of the early '80s, through compiled programs in languages such as COBOL and C.

Programmers access the database using the industry-standard SQL and PL/SQL languages for relational databases. The language specifications, set by industry committees, are in constant evolution. They always include features that the major vendors have yet to implement. Oracle's implementations have generally been as full as any in the industry.

SQL is the foundation language for Oracle and most other RDBMS systems. SQL's genius is that it is non-procedural. It is designed to deal with sets of records rather than individual records. The term "non-procedural" means that a programmer does not have to tell it how to proceed, that it, how to perform a query. A programmer uses the SQL language to describe the characteristics of the desired result. The intelligence to decide how to produce the result is programmed into the RDBMS.

PL/SQL is the procedural, or "programmable" extension to SQL. Despite the power of SQL, there are times when a programmer has to tell the computer exactly how to perform an operation, one record at a time, just as it was in mainframes. By their very nature many of the tools described below tend to deal with one record at a time. PL/SQL is the modern language for procedural programming, a vastly improved COBOL. It is common to most Oracle products.

Early in its existence Oracle recognized that programmers would be much more productive using products that had built-in features for accessing their database through SQL and PL/SQL. They created "fourth-generation" programming languages with built-in database interfaces for programmers and end users. The names of the programming tools have changed over time as their functionality has evolved, but the functional niches they fill are consistent. The tools, and their use in the Oracle Applications, are as follows:

- SQL*Plus is the simple, direct programming tool for the SQL and PL/SQL languages. It is intended for both programmers and end users. It is used by the Oracle Applications install and patch processes to create database objects for Oracle Applications. Oracle Applications can accept custom code written in SQL*Plus. It is a good tool for developing quick, simple reports, and batch processes.

- Oracle*Forms, previously SQL*Forms, is part of Developer 2000. It is exclusively a programmer's tool. Every part of Oracle Applications' terminal interface is written in Forms. Internet Computing and Smart Client are implemented in Forms 4.5. The character mode applications are written in Forms 2.4, the 1980s' product updated with Year 2000 and modern communications support. Though users can write their own Forms to extend the Oracle Applications, most find all their needs satisfied by the product as it is delivered.

- Oracle*Reports replaces the products previously named SQL*Reports and SQL*Reportwriter. It is part of Developer 2000. By design, Oracle*Reports supports both character mode and bitmapped (GUI) reports. Almost all Oracle Application reports are done in Oracle*Reports version 2.5. Oracle distributes most reports in character mode so they will be the same for all users, but it is easy even for character-mode users to convert them to bitmapped operation. It is common for Applications users to write custom programs using Oracle*Reports.

- Oracle Corporation uses their Designer 2000 CASE tool internally for development of the Applications. It generates code for Oracle*Reports and Oracle*Forms. Designer 2000K is intended to improve software reliability and boost productivity, especially in program maintenance. It can be a significant aid in writing large extensions to Oracle Applications. Oracle's delivery of CASE metadata for the Applications makes modifications to their code easier and more reliable in Release 11.

- Oracle provides several utility programs to support the RDBMS. Applications programmers make significant use of Oracle*Loader to load "flat" operating system files into Oracle tables for import into the Applications. The other utilities, such as export and import, are primarily of interest to database administrators.

The Oracle environment includes a number of software modules that, while they are not programming languages per se, require programming talent to set up and run. SQL*Net is the software layer that links servers to clients, and servers to servers in a distributed system. The backup, recovery and reorganization software is very sophisticated. There are complex modules to monitor and control database activity on a real-time basis. Oracle's Web Server supports the Internet. These tools are mostly within the province of the DBA.

Data Warehouse Directions
The SQL language and the Oracle RDBMS were originally intended to for decision support environments, that is, deriving meaningful management information from transaction data. The RDBMS evolved in a different direction. Customer demand and the architecture itself favored optimization for transaction processing. And, it turned out, an RDBMS is almost always optimized for certain access paths through the definition of primary keys

and indexes. Different technologies, tagged as "inverted list," "multi-dimensional," and "cubic," were better structured to support queries that make no assumptions about the data organization.

Oracle has adapted these concepts into its data warehousing offerings in several ways. Oracle Express is a multi-dimensional data warehouse. Oracle 8i, the latest RDBMS product, includes a number of features that enhance its use as a relational online analytical processing (ROLAP) engine. Oracle's data warehouse direction transcends both products. Their objective is to logically integrate data managed by all major vendors' RDBMS products, offering a common interface for online transaction processing (OLTP) and online analytical processing (OLAP) applications.

Oracle Express and Oracle Discoverer are the end-user tools designed to extract and present information from the data warehouse. They have powerful tabular and graphic data presentation facilities consistent with their intended use, supporting executive decisions and visually depicting alternatives in "what if" scenarios.

The Future Direction of Oracle Applications

Transaction processing has always been the strength of Oracle Applications. Oracle's latest products distill transaction data from many applications, including legacy and third-party systems, into information to support key business decisions. Some of the current and upcoming highlights of the Applications suite are:

- **Oracle Applications Data Warehouse** OADW gives users the power to quickly deploy a data warehouse that spans the Oracle Applications and other operational databases regardless of the Applications or RDBMS vendor. OADW includes the logical definitions (metadata) and programmed interfaces to extract data from the Oracle Applications, and the tools necessary to extract data from other vendors' packages. It provides access to this single logical repository using its Discoverer and Express analytical tools. OADW gives users the ability to drill down through the OLAP tools to the underlying transaction data. Though it has not yet been announced, one logical extension of this development would be for Oracle to announce data collection packs for other major applications vendors' packages, and other vendors' RDBMS products, making it possible to implement an off-the-shelf data warehouse solution in a multi-vendor environment.

■ **Business Intelligence System**   BIS is an Applications product to measure business performance by Key Performance Indicators (KPIs). It uses the standard Oracle products to form a data warehouse that may span the Oracle Applications and other systems. The KPIs distributed with the system ask the most essential questions about business operations: Should we outsource? Which products are most profitable? Which marketing programs have yielded the best results? BIS includes the metadata definitions and the extracts necessary to support the KPIs. It provides all the tools needed to modify KPI generation and to add your own KPIs. It provides exactly the tools you would want to deliver the data. Each decision-maker gets a home page with links to the processes that generate the KPI reports needed. They can be displayed in graphical or tabular form, and can be exported into spreadsheets or any other medium necessary for further consolidation and reporting.

■ **Activa**   This is Oracle's Activity-Based Management (ABM) system. You cannot measure the profitability of individual activities without detailed measurement of the resources they consume. Traditional systems have collected all costs into broad overhead categories in the General Ledger, and then used simplistic algorithms to allocate them to departments and products. The process hid those customers and products that cost more to service than they were worth. The data collection component of Activa makes you highly productive in defining the data elements to be measured and in implementing the collection mechanisms. It uses Oracle's data warehousing tools to store and present the data in the formats needed for Strategic Enterprise Management (SEM).

■ **Enterprise Data Management System**   EMDS is Oracle's application data integration product. It uses metadata definitions of data files in legacy and database formats to generate conversion and bridging code. EMDS speeds conversion to Oracle by reducing the programming burden. As enterprise-wide packaged software suites from Oracle and its competitors replace custom systems in more and more applications, EMDS may grow to become the medium for exchanging transaction data with other vendors' packages, much as the OADW handles consolidation for analysis purposes.

■ **Desktop Integration**   DI links Oracle Applications with spreadsheets and other desktop software. General Ledger is an early example: users can seamlessly import budgets developed in spreadsheets, and export actual balances for use in spreadsheet projections. The DI concept can be generalized across client-side software packages using industry-standard interfaces. In a less structured way, Oracle Applications can manage objects from voice applications, word processors, project management packages, graphics, and presentation packages.

■ **More self-service applications** Oracle's Workflow product makes it possible to offer, in Oracle's words, "universal access to untrained users" through front-end bolt-on products that interface with the Applications. The Workflow product provides users with the guidance they need to be successful. It protects Applications with security and encryption. It ensures data integrity by using the standard Open Interfaces to reedit the transactions as they enter the core Applications.

■ **More new applications** Oracle continues to release new applications at an accelerating rate. The powerful Designer 2000 CASE development tools and the rich baseline functionality common to all Applications makes it profitable for Oracle to create products for increasingly narrow markets.

■ **Mass customization** All package users today are constrained to some extent by package design. The strength of applications packages is that they include almost all of the functions that any user needs. A weakness is that they sometimes require all users to deal with design issues that affect only a few. Sometimes the architecture dictates that a user take several steps to accomplish a simple task because the software must also accommodate users for which the task is not so simple. By implementing the Applications in its own CASE technology and object-oriented programming techniques, Oracle may in the future enable customers to make customizations at the design level rather than through setup parameters.

■ **Delivery of the applications on a service basis** The Internet, operating over public and private networks, frees companies of the need to have a local data center. Oracle has announced a program to altogether remove the need for customers to have their own computers. Oracle itself will be able to host an instance of the Applications, set up as if it were to run at a company site, for use over the Internet. It will free customers of the need to buy hardware, staff database administrators, and deal with the issues of backups, disaster recovery, and applying patches and upgrades.

Open systems and the Internet are unifying themes throughout Oracle's product line. Oracle products have always been able to run on most hardware and operating system platforms. Oracle is developing the ability to operate in mixed environments at the database, tools, and applications levels as well.

Oracle's vision for the Internet is that whatever capabilities customers need on their desktop can be provided remotely. It has made that vision a reality for the Applications suite. Many functions, such as e-mail, are inherently network-oriented. Several software companies, among them Corel, Yahoo and IBM, are working on Java implementations of word processors and spreadsheets. When those applications go, they will take with them most of the rationale for having local storage and a large, configurable operating system on the desktop. Desktop users will have access to a library of programs as large as the Internet itself, but they will not have the responsibility of maintaining any of it. Oracle's database and network products have the openness, power, speed, and reliability to provide centralized management of data and programs to support this vision.

Reasons for Choosing Oracle Applications

Oracle's major competitors, SAP, PeopleSoft, and Baan, have used a mixture of third-party development, networking, and data warehousing tools in implementing their products. Each has woven them into a development platform that is available to their customers to use in writing extensions to the systems. The Oracle RDBMS and programming layers beneath the Oracle Applications are an essential part of their strength in comparison with other vendors' applications software. Enterprise-level software is an unusual purchase. The product is expensive, intangible, and impossible to fully understand. Buying the product means buying a story about the architecture and the vendor. Here is Oracle's story:

- Oracle Applications can be most efficient because they are wedded to the Oracle database. Other vendors forego the use of productivity features in Oracle's and other vendors' DBMS in order to support all of them. Portability among database vendors is not, however, of value to most software customers. Most companies stick with one

RDBMS vendor. When they do change, it is increasingly to Oracle, which is increasing its dominance in the RDBMS arena.

- The programming tools with which the Oracle Applications are written also benefit from being specific to the Oracle RDBMS. They are widely viewed as being highly efficient. In addition, they are widely used outside Oracle Applications. It is not nearly as difficult or expensive to find programmers to customize Oracle's applications as those that use proprietary languages, such as SAP or PeopleSoft.

- Oracle Applications' open architecture makes them easy to customize and integrate with other vendors' packages. Almost all application logic is available. Programmers can analyze it all, including those many modules that are best not to change, to get a thorough understanding of the system. The table structure is open, published, and accessible by linkage even to non-Oracle databases. Oracle's architecture makes it easier to bridge gaps between user requirements and the delivered functionality than other vendors' packages.

- Oracle's development tools are tightly integrated with the Designer 2000 CASE tool. This linkage makes it easy to develop custom extensions to Oracle Applications. It suggests that Oracle may at some point distribute Oracle Applications as metadata, which will make them even easier to customize.

- Oracle's AIM product, which captures the parameters for setting up Oracle Applications, can now automate setup by inserting them into the database. A user can expect that Oracle or third parties will write translators into and out of AIM, to facilitate integration and conversion among major applications vendors such as SAP, PeopleSoft, and Baan.

- The Internet is central to Oracle's overall product strategy. Oracle is developing robust tools such as the Oracle Web Server to support it. These tools are tightly integrated with Developer and Designer 2000, SQL*Net, and the rest of Oracle's product suite. Oracle has a significant advantage over less integrated vendors in moving its applications suite to the Web.

■ Economies of scale make consolidation a driving factor in the software industry. The amount of money a company has free for product development increases in direct proportion to its user base; the big keep getting bigger. Oracle has achieved a dominant position in the RDBMS market and appears to be in an excellent position to leverage itself into dominance in the Web and applications markets. At this writing the Oracle Applications are gaining market share from industry leader SAP.

■ Oracle's direction indicates that Oracle Applications will be interoperable with other vendors' applications. Its major competitors already use the Oracle RDBMS. Oracle is on the way to achieving data integration through its EMDS and OADW products. Oracle is the only vendor with enough control over its technology stack to protect its customers' applications software investments whatever the vendor.

The foregoing should convince you that Oracle is a sound long-term choice for meeting your business needs. The architecture offers a sound basis for long-term growth, and its openness suggests it will work cooperatively with other systems, or in the ultimate instance will be an accommodating system from which to migrate.

Using This Book for a Successful Financials Implementation

Although the steps involved in a Financials implementation echo those of traditional development, the process is altogether different. The development phase, which dominates a custom implementation, reduces to a few conversion and bridge programs in the Applications. Everything else moves in from the periphery: analysis, written procedures, setups, training, and testing. These all gain greater relative import.

Almost every step of an Applications implementation involves users to a greater extent than custom development. User input tends to be less visible to resource planners precisely because they have historically been secondary concerns. Chapter 16, "Project Organization and Management," addresses the unique concerns of an Applications implementation.

Establish a Plan

A Financials project typically involves a significant number of packages, people, and tasks. None of the tasks are huge, but many will be poorly understood or difficult to estimate even if you did understand them.

Make a plan despite your imperfect knowledge of what needs to be done. Accept the best available advice from Oracle, consultants, and your own staff. More important than creating the plan in the first place, commit to modifying the plan as your experience grows, even if it means moving deadlines.

Understand the Company's Business Practices

You must have an idea of how the business will operate as you set up the Oracle packages. Though the greatest benefits are to be realized by changing business processes, many companies decide to convert to Oracle first and then reengineer the business later.

Many users find that their current business processes are not well defined—especially the exceptions. Processes may be defined by personality, as in "Mary handles customer returns—ask her." Defaults are another broad area of exceptions. It may be that all new customers are accepted on a COD basis, with certain exceptions, or all customers have Net 30 payment terms, with exceptions.

Oracle's comprehensive design provides automated support for processes and exceptions. Even if you intend not to change your business rules at all, the Oracle setup will require that you define your current mode of operation in each application area. For companies whose processes are not already written down, this seemingly simple task almost always takes more time than is budgeted. Be sure to make a liberal allowance in the project schedule. Oracle or outside consultants who have implemented Oracle Applications before can be of great help both in building a project schedule and in defining your business processes to Oracle. Chapter 16 covers how you document business processes, where they fit in the project plan, and how they are expressed in your test scenarios and test scripts.

Understand the Applications Suite

Most people who have been through an Oracle Applications implementation have become experts in one or more areas. Ironically, just as an organization has cut over to Oracle Applications and needs experts badly, the implementers are gone. Companies obviously rely heavily on

Oracle consultants and independent consulting firms to bring in the expertise when it is needed. However, unless the organization's own staff is closely involved, they will lack critical knowledge of how the system was set up.

Product knowledge is significantly more important for package implementations than it is for custom development. With the Applications, one must proceed not knowing exactly how the code was written—only the externals of the "black box." Installing the Financials is not "development as usual" and cannot be handled as such.

This book itself provides a fast track to fill the product knowledge vacuum. Chapter 17, "Data Conversion, Training and Cutover," offers a comprehensive plan for Oracle and in-house training. In the short term, however, training is no substitute for experience. Almost every customer can benefit from using consultants to speed their Oracle Applications installation.

Get the Needed Level of Commitment from Users

Although the tasks in an Oracle Applications implementation echo those of traditional data processing development, it is the system users, not the MIS department, who must play the dominant role. The software works. The job is to decide how to use it. This is a job for people in the functional areas, and certainly not programmers.

The job is challenging and confusing. The users have to assume two jobs: keeping the business running with the old system and preparing for Oracle.

Many companies, especially smaller ones, are not in the practice of documenting the policies, procedures, and business practices supported by their automated systems. Oracle asks the users to apply systems engineering disciplines borrowed from the realm of data processing. They take time to learn and time to apply.

Almost every Oracle Application replaces another automated system of some kind. Users of those legacy systems ultimately own the data. Though the MIS department may help, the users have to be ultimately responsible for cleaning up and converting the data. It is hard work—gritty and unappetizing—but essential. "Garbage In, Garbage Out" starts with conversion.

Any new system takes training. Line-level users often need expert support, in the form of a help desk or a Superuser, for the first few weeks of operation.

Even though the MIS department may staff the help desk, it is the user departments that must ultimately support their own people as they use Oracle.

User departments, if they have not been through a major systems implementation, may not be aware of the scale of their involvement or the criticality of their commitment. The project plan, a joint product of the consultants, MIS department, and the users themselves, will make the level of effort required visible. Senior executives on the user side need to make sure that the personnel will be available.

Staff the Job Right, and Give It Time

Success requires a rich mix of expertise in the company business, the Oracle applications, data processing disciplines, and project management. The stakes are large, far beyond the visible costs of the packages, data processing equipment, consultants, and conversion.

The staffing objective should be to assemble the best possible group to meet all the project objectives, which include:

- Support for ongoing business operations during the implementation
- Appropriate package setup
- Complete and clean data conversion
- End user training and support
- A data processing and network infrastructure able to deliver the system to its users
- Trained staff to maintain, enhance, and upgrade Oracle Applications

People can come from the MIS department, user departments, Oracle consulting, large integration firms, and independent consultants. The hallmark of a successful project is flexibility: the ability to recognize the right mix of people, whatever the source, to assemble them, and to inspire them.

Be Pragmatic

The Oracle Applications include all the functionality that is common to most businesses. They do common functions well and completely. That notwithstanding, every company is individual. Sometimes a company has a novel mode of operation that gives it a unique competitive advantage.

Others have simply evolved their own particular, albeit successful, modes of doing business.

A purchaser of the Oracle Applications should plan to use them "Plain Vanilla" to the extent possible. You must, however, be willing to accept that there are occasions when it makes sense to write an extension to the system, or even modify Oracle's code. The project manager will do well to establish ground rules for performing cost/benefit analysis of such modifications, and to adopt procedures for managing such changes from the ideas in Chapter 15, "Customization and Modification."

How to Get Maximum Value from the Applications

Oracle Applications can transform your business. Or rather, they enable you to transform your business. They give you the ability to apply the best practices in industry to your business.

Though the returns are worth it, the price is significant. You have to be willing to continually reengineer your business to take maximum advantage of the Oracle features as your business evolves and Oracle functionality improves. Though many of the initial benefits of Oracle Applications are in cost avoidance, the most significant benefit is in expanding your ability to grow, to manage, and to serve customers.

Conclusion

Buying the Oracle Financials has put you in an excellent position now and for the future. Its built-in functionality will handle the vast majority of your business needs. It has been designed from the start for use over the Internet. It takes full advantage of Oracle's Web-oriented technology stack, the products themselves and the integration among them. Oracle's commitment to open systems, and the technology directions they have chosen for the Applications, will protect your investment both in the Oracle Applications and other systems, both legacy and third-party.

The benefit you derive from the Oracle Applications is proportional to the investment you make in them. They will, at a minimum, provide consistent financial accounting, resolve your Year 2000 problems, and integrate the operations of the departments that use the Applications. You can, if you wish, use the Applications to dramatically improve communications within and outside your company. You can implement policies through it that will cut your transaction costs, conserve your cash, let whole new classes of customers browse your offerings and buy on line, and make your suppliers into true partners. You can measure margins in far greater detail than before. Installing the Oracle Applications will make it possible for you to continually refine your operations.

Installing and operating the Oracle Applications is not like developing custom software. The mix of required skills, including those of the project manager, is altogether new. Although buying a package relieves you of the need to observe many traditional data processing methodologies, it brings a host of new requirements. Our hope in writing this book is to give you an understanding of what the packages can do and an appreciation of the steps required to install and operate them successfully.

PART
I

Getting Started

CHAPTER
1

An Overview of
Oracle Applications

hoosing and implementing a new software package can be a monumental and expensive task for your organization. When considering Oracle Applications, a number of questions present themselves: What are they designed to do? What are the benefits? Is buying them a good business decision? What strengths of the Oracle Corporation might cause you to favor their software over their competition? Once you've chosen Oracle, how can you succeed in installing the software, converting to it, and taking advantage of it to improve your business? Software is an intangible product, and Oracle Applications is a huge software suite, so answering these questions can be a detailed undertaking.

While Oracle Applications can satisfy almost all business needs, and does offer tremendous value for the money, it cannot be all things to all people. This is true with any of the "canned" software currently available. However, Oracle's architecture, documentation, and tools are designed to make their code uniquely easy to modify to meet your specific needs.

The Structure and Scope of Oracle Applications

Oracle Applications is a suite of more than 55 integrated software modules for financial management, supply chain management, manufacturing, project systems, human resources, and sales force automation. The modules vary in size and complexity from Oracle Inventory, the tables of which interface with a majority of the Oracle products and which affect many different departments within your company, to Cash Management, which serves primarily as a supplement to existing modules.

Oracle Applications combines powerful features with state-of-the-art technology, which is configured to enable rapid implementation. While the Applications suite has grown over the last decade, its purpose has remained unchanged. It offers world-class business automation built on the preeminent Oracle database, using the full range of Oracle's own development tools. Oracle's corporate structure recognizes two major product areas: databases, development, and Web tools, which has been the core of the company; and the Applications suite, which is the likely growth business of the future.

Oracle Applications serves a broad market, ranging from small organizations to Fortune 500 companies. Oracle Applications users and their data processing support staff often find that they have more in common than they originally thought. Both groups appreciate the benefits that Oracle's immense power and flexibility can bring, and they both almost always underestimate the amount of planning, preparation, and hard work required on their part to achieve those benefits.

This book focuses on those Applications modules that are oriented towards financial management. Our aim throughout is to cover three basic areas: the business functions of these modules, the technical aspects of the software, and the management and organization of implementation projects. This book is divided into strategic sections to reflect these threads. Our focus, of course, is on the Oracle Financials modules; however, most of the technology chapters as well as the project management sections apply equally to the Oracle Manufacturing and Oracle Human Resources product families.

The "Oracle Financials" components, which were the first modules released back in 1989, remain at the heart of the product line. Figure 1-1 shows the packages that have long been considered to make up the Oracle Financials suite. The ones in the inner circle handle money and generate General Ledger transactions. Purchasing, Inventory, and Order Entry, in the outer circle of the diagram, were usually included under the title of Financials because they generate transactions with financial implications. These original modules (which we focus on in Part II of this book) remain the most widely used of the Applications. They form the architectural anchor for the complete Applications product line, as illustrated in Figure 1-2.

FIGURE I-I.   *Oracle Financials—the core modules*

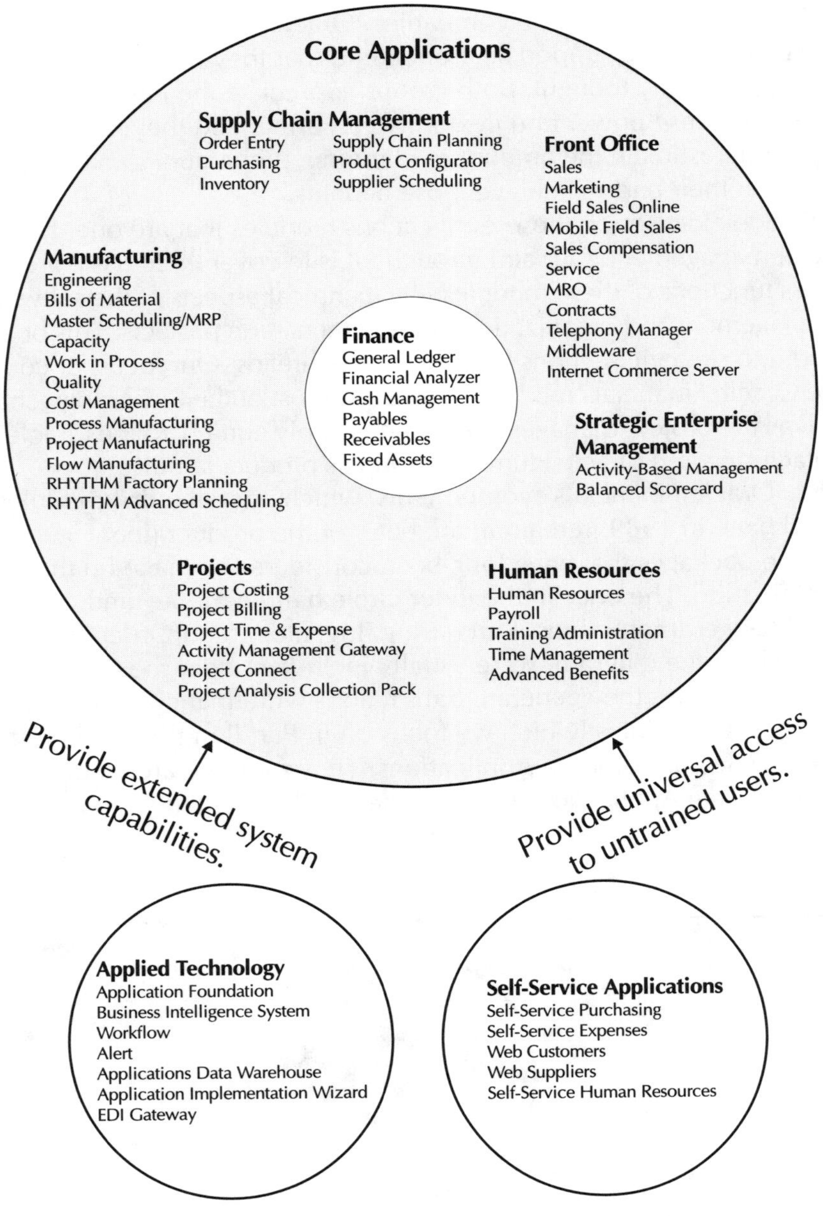

Core Applications

Supply Chain Management
Order Entry   Supply Chain Planning
Purchasing   Product Configurator
Inventory   Supplier Scheduling

Front Office
Sales
Marketing
Field Sales Online
Mobile Field Sales
Sales Compensation
Service
MRO
Contracts
Telephony Manager
Middleware
Internet Commerce Server

Manufacturing
Engineering
Bills of Material
Master Scheduling/MRP
Capacity
Work in Process
Quality
Cost Management
Process Manufacturing
Project Manufacturing
Flow Manufacturing
RHYTHM Factory Planning
RHYTHM Advanced Scheduling

Finance
General Ledger
Financial Analyzer
Cash Management
Payables
Receivables
Fixed Assets

Strategic Enterprise Management
Activity-Based Management
Balanced Scorecard

Projects
Project Costing
Project Billing
Project Time & Expense
Activity Management Gateway
Project Connect
Project Analysis Collection Pack

Human Resources
Human Resources
Payroll
Training Administration
Time Management
Advanced Benefits

Provide extended system capabilities.

Provide universal access to untrained users.

Applied Technology
Application Foundation
Business Intelligence System
Workflow
Alert
Applications Data Warehouse
Application Implementation Wizard
EDI Gateway

Self-Service Applications
Self-Service Purchasing
Self-Service Expenses
Web Customers
Web Suppliers
Self-Service Human Resources

FIGURE 1-2. *Logical organization of the Oracle Applications modules*

The Applications are primarily designed to manage operations. Financial data are mere by-products. Financial measures are certainly the best reflection of how the business is doing, but only a reflection. True business activity is in the operations that generate financial transactions: warehouse receipts, services delivered, and orders entered. Oracle Applications provides the operational controls needed to optimize financial results and capture financial transactions at a level of detail that supports rigorous measurement of operations.

Figure 1-2 shows the products that Oracle now calls the Financial Applications in the inner circle. The other Core Applications are grouped by functional areas in the larger circle surrounding the Financials. Each package is a set of processes and tables designed to support a distinct business function. The key feature of all the Oracle Applications modules, however, is data integration:

- *Master data is integrated.* All the applications share common files of customers, suppliers, employees, items, and other entities that are used by multiple applications.

- *Transaction data is integrated.* Oracle automatically bridges transactions from one system to another, as when Order Entry must decrement inventory to reflect a shipment or send an order line to Receivables to be invoiced.

- *Financial data is integrated.* Financial data is carried in a common format, and the implications of any financial transaction in one application are accurately transmitted to other affected applications. For example, Oracle ripples the implications of a price change through the Inventory, Work in Process, and Purchasing systems.

This level of cohesion brings major advantages over traditional "stovepipe" systems that address the needs of individual functional areas. Though integrated systems have long been a major objective of systems design, large-scale integration has rarely been achieved in custom-written systems. Businesses evolve so quickly that few ever agree on an enterprise-wide design, much less develop and implement a comprehensive data management system.

Oracle offers several additional Applications products that enhance the function of the Core Applications. The Applied Technology products grouped at the lower left in Figure 1-2 give the Core Applications additional messaging and analysis capabilities. The Self-Service Web Applications function as front-ends that give untrained end users—both inside and outside of the organization—the ability to query and submit transactions to the Core Applications under the control of Oracle Workflow.

NOTE
Figure 1-2 omits industry-specific applications. In addition, some of the applications may have undergone name changes since the printing of this book; their names are revised often.

Oracle incorporates best practices from the corporate, nonprofit, and government worlds in their software design. In buying Oracle Applications, you have purchased a very sophisticated integration model, broad enough to serve most businesses in most industries and flexible enough to be expanded to meet your individual needs.

Accounting Methods

Financial accounting satisfies the information needs of two major external audiences: investors and tax authorities. *Cost accounting*, also known as *management accounting*, is internal. It shows corporate management the financial workings of the enterprise in the formats best suited to supporting executive decisions. Though cost accounting works at a greater level of detail than financial accounting, both financial and cost accounting reports are derived from the same financial transactions. Oracle Applications uses the same databases to satisfy both the internal and external kinds of financial reporting requirements.

The transactions that drive financial and management accounting are in most cases just a by-product of corporate operations. Controlling those operations is the more significant function of Oracle Applications. Consider a company that has bought office equipment from a vendor, with the invoice received a while later. The operational issues to consider are:

- Does the invoice represent a real obligation?
- When should the invoice be paid, to take best advantage of the vendor's terms?
- Is there enough money to cover the draft?

The financial transaction is comparatively simple: credit the payables account and debit the office equipment expense account identified as the invoice was entered. In every package except the General Ledger itself, the financial reporting logic is subsidiary to operational control.

Cost and management accounts are generally intended for use by management. They are at a greater level of detail than statutory reports. They form the basis of informed management decisions. They can answer a number of questions: Which groups of customers have large outstanding receivables? Should we change payment terms? Which departments and product lines are most profitable? Which ones show the best improvement in gross margins? Should we reward those managers?

Operational Control

A company must control its operations to achieve optimal financial results. Control means satisfying customers: making commitments that satisfy customer needs and meeting the commitments. It means controlling assets, to get maximum use out of them. It means monitoring the performance of suppliers and people to keep their attention focused on supporting the company's mission.

Several requirements are common to control processes in various operations. These are the most frequent:

- **Defined routines, with defined exceptions**   Business must be handled by routine. It is vastly less expensive to handle transactions by rote than to invent procedures for each new case. There are, however, legitimate exceptions to almost every routine. Oracle modules are designed to minimize the effort involved in routine operations. They rely on a standard set of processes to bring exceptions to the attention of a human being as quickly as possible.

- **Workflow processing**   Many transactions, such as approvals and inspections, require moving a transaction and the associated paperwork from person to person within an organization, the exact path depending on the nature of the transaction and the outcome of prior steps.

- **Defaulting**   Oracle Applications makes processing decisions about individual records according to the value of field settings at that level. Payment terms are an example: should a given customer have to pay their bills in 30 or 45 days? Although it must be possible to set the terms customer by customer, they are much easier to administer if they are set for all customers, or at least by customer groups. Oracle makes broad use of defaulting hierarchies to allow you to control operations by setting field values for broad sets of records and to override them for subsets or individual records.

- **Capturing and editing parameters for batch processes**   Oracle Applications has been made very general to support a wide range of users. The trade-off is that most batch processes and reports require a series of parameters for exact control each time they are invoked.

Oracle uses more-or-less standard devices across all the Applications modules for these control functions. The system modules shown at the lower left in Figure 1-2 enhance the function of all the other packages. This standardization makes Oracle products efficient for their customers to learn and efficient for them to support, and it means that enhancements are available across all of the packages.

The Package Families

Oracle Applications has defied Oracle's best attempts at classification. Every year brings new packages and a new view as to the organization of the older packages. It is not that Oracle is indecisive. Rather, the packages are so well integrated that natural affinities exist between almost any two of them. Each time a new package enters the product line it shifts the relative importance of the integrated relationships. The following are some useful classifications that can be imposed on the applications shown in Figure 1-2:

- Enterprise Resource Planning, or ERP, is a term that covers the whole product line.

- The Financials Accounting products in the inner circle are closest to the money and to General Ledger reporting.

■ Supply Chain Management handles distribution, the business of getting materials from suppliers to customers.

■ The Oracle Manufacturing modules shown in Figure 1-2 are limited to those that affect product design and manufacture. The Supply Chain Management modules are often included under the concept of Manufacturing.

■ Oracle's Front Office applications are evolving rapidly. They deal with customers and sales people. Marketing is strongly linked with Order Entry, which actually accepts customer orders. Service is closely linked with the Manufacturing applications that create the items to be maintained.

■ The Human Resources product family obviously deals with people. They are also where information on organizations and hierarchies is maintained to support other applications such as Projects and Purchasing.

■ The Projects applications apply a project dimension to Purchasing, Payables, Order Entry, Receivables, and Inventory. Project Manufacturing links it with the rest of the Manufacturing suite. The project dimension serves both control and accounting ends. The project needs to stay on schedule. There is a financial need to see projects integrally, not period by period but inception-to-date, and, most importantly, to measure earned value and estimate profit and loss.

Though the classifications continue to evolve, each new module will only increase the level of integration and interdependence. Any business—your business—will benefit greatly by adapting this vast body of integrated features, then customizing it or integrating it with other packages to satisfy unique requirements. Many businesses will find that they can use most of the Oracle functions without changing them at all. In other cases, the effort made to install the packages will be minimal compared to the effort involved in developing those bits that must be unique. Therein lies the value of proprietary software.

What Are the Benefits? Reasons for Implementing Oracle Financials

While implementing Oracle Financials, you will be making many far-reaching decisions. To be able to make the right decisions for your organization you will need to fully understand the implications of the alternatives. You will also need to know why your organization is implementing Oracle Financials. The "why" behind the project is often crucial to distinguishing between many, otherwise similar alternatives. Every organization is different; your organization will have a variety and mix of different reasons for implementing Oracle Applications. It is always a good idea to identify the main reasons before you embark. These may include efforts to accomplish the following:

- Standardize on one global solution package throughout an organization.

- Enable your organization to conduct business over the Internet using Oracle's Self-Service Web Applications.

- Ensure that your systems are ready for the single European currency; this is a critical goal for businesses operating within the European Monetary Union.

- Ensure that your enterprise systems are Year 2000-compliant.

NOTE
Oracle Applications Release 11 is certified to be fully Euro-compliant; Release 10.7 and beyond are Year 2000-compliant.

- Decrease hardware and support costs.

- Improve productivity in the areas supported by applications software.

- Enable the business to improve operations and to continually adapt to changing requirements.

Identifying your particular business goals and then keeping them in focus will help your organization throughout the implementation process.

What Are Your Objectives? Setting Parameters and Expectations

Though taking full advantage of Oracle Applications can transform a business, most companies have more prosaic objectives. They need to be ready for Year 2000, to replace a few archaic systems that have become totally inadequate, to integrate their applications, or to implement a new chart of accounts structure.

Reengineer—Now or Later?

One of your first decisions as you implement Oracle Applications is whether to change your business procedures at the same time. Some companies opt for a two-phase approach. Phase I is to replace their legacy systems, function for function, with Oracle, and Phase II, usually in the indefinite future, is to use the features available in Oracle to reengineer the business. It turns out that just defining the current business processes involves more work than expected, but certainly much less than reengineering the business.

Reengineering the business *as you install* Oracle Applications can make a lot of sense. You are spared the effort of defining your existing business processes in Oracle, your users are only disrupted the one time, and you realize the full benefits of Oracle much sooner. On the other hand, reengineering is an even tougher job than software conversion. It takes lots more time, and it requires dedicated management to keep the staff inspired through the accompanying reorganizations, personnel actions, and retraining.

Oracle Applications is truly an enabling software product. Companies that fully exploit the features available in the Oracle modules put themselves at the forefront of modern business practice. The majority, those that merely convert to Oracle, realize significant tactical benefits in reliability, integration, and cost reduction. They also, for the first time in the history of data processing, put themselves in a position where inadequate software is no longer a major impediment to progress. In most cases, Oracle is ready to support improved processes as quickly as the organization can absorb them.

Which Oracle Architecture Should You Use?

Oracle's Internet Computing Model (formerly known as Network Computer Architecture, or NCA, or Applications for the Internet) is a compelling system. The full product line is implemented for the Internet, and it allows access via a thin-client browser. It is the only architecture available for the latest version of the Applications, Release 11. There is no reason to even consider a client-server implementation any more.

Character-mode installation may still be attractive to organizations that need to replace their legacy systems quickly and inexpensively to meet Year 2000 requirements. It is a short-term expedient, however; character mode will not be available for Release 11.

All the core financial Applications are available in character. Character mode usually does not require any change at all to desktop hardware or networks. Users overlook the fact that the interface is dated because it is fast, reliable, and full-functioned. It is a quick and inexpensive way to buy into the benefits of Oracle Applications, and it positions you to move into a full GUI implementation when time and resources allow.

Oracle has not promised to support the character-mode installations past the end of 2000 and will only offer limited support leading up to that time. The more significant factor is that all major development has been in GUI since about 1996. The new packages, and new features in the older packages, will never be available in character mode. Though character-mode systems will probably continue to work well, even after Oracle support stops accepting new bug reports, users who stick with character mode will stagnate. A company choosing character-mode operations as the quickest route to Year 2000 compliance must include a second conversion, to GUI, in their project plan.

Conclusion

Oracle Corporation, long the dominant vendor of database software, has increasingly emphasized applications software as the field in which it can offer the most value to its customers. Having developed its own database, programming tools, and Web support gives Oracle formidable advantages. Long known for their functional strength, Oracle's products have now become the industry leaders in their use of technology.

Every business is different. The question for you is not whether the Oracle Applications suite works—that has been proven—but rather how your company can best achieve its objectives using the Applications. Each company has a unique answer to this question. A successful implementation will require knowledge of the individual modules, the ways in which they work together, knowledge of how to adapt them, and a management plan. Those are the primary themes of this book.

CHAPTER 2

Implementing
Oracle Financials—
Essential Concepts

rganizations implementing Oracle Financials make important decisions on hardware configuration and application setup. Oracle Applications provides a vast array of features and business rules that can greatly improve productivity in your organization and enable your organization to conduct business in ways not previously possible. During implementation, you take advantage of its built-in flexibility by tailoring the standard features of the package to meet your specific requirements. Oracle Applications is quick to implement and easy to adapt. The speed and ease of the process, however, depend crucially on judicious decisions made early in the implementation cycle, and on the degree of customization you plan to make.

Do not allow shortsighted implementation decisions to hamper the long-term effectiveness of the software. Inappropriate decisions can be avoided if everyone involved in the planning process has an early understanding of the concepts essential for implementing Oracle Financials. This chapter introduces these concepts, highlighting decisions that will be difficult to change later on. Here you'll learn how to capture the level of financial information that you need, how to set up Financials within complex organizations, and how to meet the unique demands of the global business environment.

Capturing the Financial Information Relevant to Your Business

Oracle Financials can be configured to a remarkable extent without custom programming. All the forms and reports are designed to be flexible and to accommodate many kinds of business rules for a wide variety of situations. Along with the innumerable predetermined fields that appear on each screen, most screens can also accommodate the entry of additional information through the use of flexfields. This is an important feature for users of Oracle Financials. Flexfields are important building blocks in Oracle Applications: they allow screens and reports to contain data that is uniquely relevant for your organization. Each flexfield can be configured to capture and display the specific information you want.

Flexfields

There are two types of flexfields: Key and Descriptive. *Key Flexfields* are used throughout the Applications to uniquely identify information—General Ledger accounts, inventory items, fixed assets, and other entities that every business needs to keep track of. *Descriptive Flexfields (DFFs),* on the other hand, enable you to capture additional pieces of information from transactions entered into Oracle Applications. Descriptive and Key Flexfields share common features. They are multisegment fields; the number of segments and the length of each are totally under your control when you set up the Applications. When you navigate to a flexfield in a form, a pop-up window appears; you enter appropriate values for each segment or pick values off a pull-down list. The application validates individual segments according to value-set rules, and ensures that the combination of segments makes sense using cross-validation rules.

Descriptive Flexfields are recognized in most of the Oracle Applications database tables as *attribute* columns, while Key Flexfields are usually *segment* columns.

The Accounting Flexfield is the Oracle name for the account key used to record and report accounting information. The Accounting Flexfield is a Key Flexfield; it uniquely identifies General Ledger accounts and provides a flexible structure for any chart of accounts. You can set up the Accounting Flexfield to have any number of segments, up to a maximum of 30. Typically, an organization will need between five and ten segments. You should aim to design your chart of accounts to have as few segments as possible for ease of use; the 30-segment limit should be seen as a theoretical, not a practical, maximum. The more segments you have, the greater the range of segment reporting available to you. More segments, though, can mean extra effort to code and categorize financial transactions. There is a delicate trade-off between capturing and validating data on each and every transaction and the potential insight the extra data will give into your business.

The following examples are intended to provide an idea of the Accounting Flexfield. Chapter 3 explains in more detail how to design a suitable Accounting Flexfield for your organization. Most companies will use at least three segments: Company, Department, and Account. A typical organization may choose to set up the flexfield to have six segments called Company, Region, Cost Center, Account, Product, and Subaccount.

During data entry, the flexfield appears on your form as a pop-up window, as shown here, containing a prompt for each of your established segments:

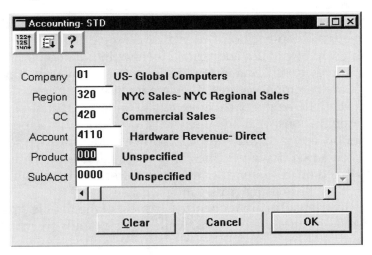

The data that you enter here will appear in the Account column of the Enter Journals form, as shown in Figure 2-1. When you generate reports, the Accounting Flexfield appears as shown in Figure 2-2.

A combination of segment values, known as an *account code combination,* uniquely identifies the Oracle General Ledger account. This is the finest granularity that Oracle General Ledger can record and report on. The management reports it produces present totals by code combination and accounting period. Transaction-level reports showing what went into a GL account balance must come from the systems that feed the General Ledger.

In Oracle Financials, monetary amounts are posted as debits and credits to account code combinations. Each account code combination has a balance at the end of each period. These balances form the basis of the balance sheet, profit and loss, and all other reporting in the Oracle General Ledger. These balances are readily available either from online inquires or on printed reports, or in some instances from the Web. The Accounting Flexfield segment structure determines the lowest level of detail for which account balances are held. You can readily consolidate up through the account hierarchy, using tools like summary accounts, parent accounts, and

Accounting Flexfield

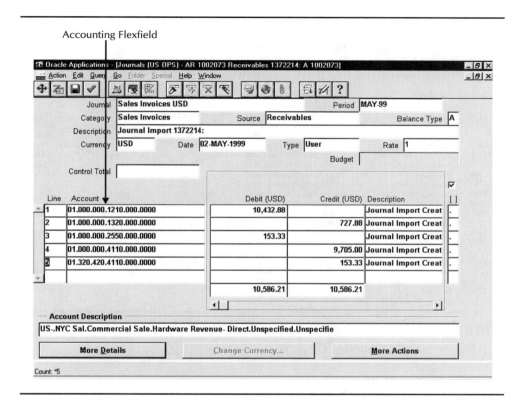

FIGURE 2-1. *The Enter Journals form showing the Accounting Flexfield*

rollup groups. The Accounting Flexfield is the lowest possible reporting detail attainable in General Ledger.

As mentioned, the Accounting Flexfield can contain up to 30 segments, and you are required to define a minimum of two segments (one qualified as the balancing segment and the other qualified as the natural account segment). The balancing segment is usually the legal entity or company that Oracle Applications uses to balance journals for each value of the segment. The natural account segment is classified with an account type of asset, liability, owner's equity, revenue, or expense. If you intend to use other modules, such as Oracle Assets or Oracle Projects, you need to assign an additional cost center segment. Cost centers indicate functional areas of your organization, such as accounting, facilities, shipping, and so on. You should also consider creating additional segments to anticipate future

				Period	

Currency: USD
Company Range: 01 to 01
Company: 01 US- Global Computers

Acct	Description	Accounting Flexfield	Beginning Balance	Period Activity	Ending Balance
1531	Buildings- CIP Cost	01.000.000.1531.000.0000	4,851,183.78	0.00	4,851,183.78
1531	Buildings- CIP Cost	01.110.110.1531.000.0000	31,000.00	0.00	31,000.00
1531	Buildings- CIP Cost	01.110.410.1531.000.0000	10,000.00	0.00	10,000.00
1541	Buildings- CIP Clear	01.000.000.1541.000.0000	(8,467,359.47)	0.00	(8,467,359.47)
1541	Buildings- CIP Clear	01.110.000.1541.000.0000	3,200.00	0.00	3,200.00
1541	Buildings- CIP Clear	01.110.110.1541.000.0000	978,722.20	0.00	978,722.20
1544	Machinery- CIP Clear	01.110.110.1544.000.0000	(700,000.00)	0.00	(700,000.0z0)
1550	Land- Acc. Depreciat	01.000.000.1550.000.0000	(506,805.58)	0.00	(506,805.58)
1551	Buildings- Acc. Depr	01.000.000.1551.000.0000	(4,409,599.52)	0.00	(4,409,599.52)
1552	Tenant Imp.- Acc. De	01.000.000.1552.000.0000	(2,099,245.69)	0.00	(2,099,245.69)
1553	Furniture- Acc. Depr	01.000.000.1553.000.0000	(3,038,271.76)	0.00	(3,038,271.76)
1554	Machinery- Acc. Depr	01.000.000.1554.000.0000	(8,036,158.07)	0.00	(8,036,158.07)
1555	Comp/Comm- Acc. Depr	01.000.000.1555.000.0000	(1,645,546.94)	0.00	(1,645,546.94)
1556	Vehicle- Acc. Deprec	01.000.000.1556.000.0000	(693,143.87)	0.00	(693,143.87)
1710	Intercompany Receiva	01.000.000.1710.000.0000	10,457.95	0.00	10,457.95
2110	Notes Payable to Ban	01.110.000.2110.000.0000	(29,522.00)	4,200.00	(25,322.00)
2210	Accounts Payable	01.000.000.2210.000.0000	(156,794,819.96)	(10,875.00)	156,805,694.96)
2210	Accounts Payable	01.110.110.2210.000.0000	1,950,000.00	0.00	1,950,000.00
2210	Accounts Payable	01.110.410.2210.000.0000	(125,000.00)	0.00	(125,000.00)

FIGURE 2-2. *A sample Detail Trial Balance report showing the Accounting Flexfield*

reporting requirements or organizational changes. The Accounting Flexfield is flexible enough to accommodate whatever the needs may be of your organization by allowing you to specify the number of segments you want, the length of each segment, and the name and order of the account code structure.

Before you begin setting up your Accounting Flexfield, you should carefully plan your organizational needs. It is easier to build flexibility into your account structure during setup than to try to change your account structure later. Consider future expansion and possible changes in your organization and reporting needs. Also consider the other Oracle Applications that you will be using now and in the future, because an incorrectly defined Accounting Flexfield can adversely affect your accounting data, chart of accounts structure, and other features. It is also difficult to change your Accounting Flexfield after it has been frozen and has been used to capture data through transaction processing. Changing your structures after-the-fact may create data inconsistencies that could impact the behavior of your application or require a complex conversion program.

As soon as you are satisfied, freeze your Accounting Flexfield structure to prohibit unnecessary modifications. You must freeze and compile your flexfield definition before you use your flexfield. If you have more than one flexfield structure, you must freeze, save, and compile each structure separately. Do not modify a frozen flexfield definition if existing data could be invalidated. An alteration of the flexfield structure once you have any flexfield data can create serious data inconsistencies. Changing your existing structures may also adversely affect the behavior of any cross-validation rules or shorthand aliases you have for your structures, so be sure to manually disable or redefine these rules and aliases to reflect your changed structures.

Key Flexfield Features

The combinations of a Key Flexfield, such as the Accounting Flexfield, uniquely identify a record in a database table. The philosophy of a relational database is that every table contains a group of columns, known as the *key columns,* that uniquely identify records in that table. Other examples of Key Flexfields are the Asset Key Flexfield, used for identifying fixed assets, and the System Items Flexfield, used for identifying inventory item numbers. There are 21 Key Flexfields in Oracle Applications; these are listed in Table 2-1.

All Key Flexfields share the same features. Indeed, the flexfield concept is fully generic, or "flexible" as its name implies. You can define shorthand aliases to speed up data entry tasks; you can define flexfield value security to ensure that particular users can enter only particular segment values; and you can define cross-validation rules to prevent users from creating new flexfield combinations that contain values that should not coexist in the same combination. You can allow, or intentionally prevent, dynamic insertion for any specific Key Flexfield. *Dynamic insertion* is the creation of a new valid combination from a form other than the Combinations form. For example, a user could create the combination representing "telephone expense for a new cost center" without leaving the Journal Entry form. Sometimes it may not make sense for the application to allow a user to create a new combination "on-the-hoof." A user should not be able to create a new product item while taking an order for product items using the Enter Orders form.

The Accounting Flexfield incorporates all the generic features of Key Flexfields plus some features that are not found in other flexfields:

Flexfield	Owning Application
Account Aliases	Oracle Inventory
Accounting	Oracle General Ledger
Asset Key	Oracle Assets
Bank Details Key	Oracle Payroll
Category	Oracle Assets
Cost Allocation	Oracle Payroll
Grade	Oracle Human Resources
Item Catalogs	Oracle Inventory
Item Categories	Oracle Inventory
Job	Oracle Human Resources
Location	Oracle Assets
People Group	Oracle Payroll
Personal Analysis	Oracle Human Resources
Position	Oracle Human Resources
Sales Tax Location	Oracle Receivables
Sales Orders	Oracle Inventory
Soft Coded Key	Oracle Human Resources
Stock Locators	Oracle Inventory
System Items	Oracle Inventory
Training Resources	Oracle Training Administration
Territory	Oracle Receivables

TABLE 2-1. *The Key Flexfields in Oracle Applications*

■ *Multiple rollup groups* are used to produce management summaries. You can define a hierarchy of parent and child values within each segment. When you report on a parent value, Oracle General Ledger automatically displays the total of the balances on all the children for that parent.

- *Summary accounts* provide online summary balances. Usually summary accounts are set up so that a total for each financial account is available irrespective of region, cost center, product, and so on. Summary accounts are useful for responding to questions like "what was our total revenue in the last period?"

- The Financial Statement Generator (FSG) allows you to easily build custom reports without programming. You can define reports online with complete control over the rows, columns, and contents of your report.

Accounting Flexfield Design

You should put considerable thought into the design and structure of your Accounting Flexfield before beginning your setup. Many companies put together a special project team to come up with a new chart of accounts structure prior to the systems implementation project. Companies use the implementation of Oracle Applications as a catalyst for introducing a new chart of accounts or a common chart of accounts across their entire organization. You should question up front if this is what your organization needs. Oracle Applications will support different Accounting Flexfield structures for each business unit in your organization that needs its own structure. You will still be able to use the native consolidation features in Oracle General Ledger to produce group consolidated accounts even if different parts of your organization use different Accounting Flexfield structures.

CAUTION

The upheaval in an organization when a new chart of accounts is introduced is similar in magnitude to that you'd expect upon introducing a new accounting system. Introducing both at the same time, then, can be particularly traumatic. Consider whether you can separate the two projects and minimize the risks.

The project team assigned the task of designing a new chart of accounts needs to consult widely within the organization to cover the reporting needs of all business areas. The team must be aware of the statutory accounting requirements and should be familiar with the mechanics of Accounting Flexfields within Oracle Financials. It is a mistake to think that the chart of accounts design is independent of the features of Oracle Applications. You should design your Accounting Flexfield to make full use of standard application features. Such features as journal allocations, the Account Generator, cross-validation rules, summary accounts, and rollup groups depend critically on the structure of your Accounting Flexfield. With a well-planned account structure, you will be better positioned to take full advantage of these built-in features. For example, several standard Oracle General Ledger reports use a range of accounts as a selection parameter. A report like the Oracle General Ledger Account Analysis, which takes a range of financial account codes as a parameter, will be considerably more useful if your account codes have been logically grouped into meaningful ranges. That way the report can be run from, say, account 2000 to account 2999 and retrieve a meaningful group of accounts, such as current liabilities. If there were no logic built in to the account codes and ranges, it would take considerably longer to obtain a list of all current liability accounts and would likely require custom report development at a later stage.

Logical grouping is one example of good Accounting Flexfield design. The design process is not an exact science, though a number of heuristic rules have built up to help with the design. These rules are described in detail in Chapter 3. A well-designed Accounting Flexfield is vital.

The finished design of the Accounting Flexfield is a milestone in the implementation of Oracle Applications. Before proceeding with subsequent phases of the implementation, ensure that the chosen design has the acceptance of people who will be working with it: the finance department, operational departments, and auditors. It is a good idea to ask Oracle Consulting Services or an experienced Oracle Financials consultant to validate the chosen design.

Workflow

Businesses thrive by acting on all sorts of information in a timely manner. Data must be delivered to people according to the type of data and the role of the individual. People act on the information and respond in a variety of ways. Purchase orders get authorized and are routed to the supplier. Customers pass a credit check and goods are supplied. Stock levels fall below a reorder level and are replenished. Processes can be triggered by goods arriving, a letter from a customer, a statement from your bank, and so on. Processes can result in financial transactions and journals being generated. Information can be routed to managers for authorization.

Business processes, seemingly always in flux, are many and varied. Oracle Workflow lets you automate and continuously improve business processes by routing any type of information to decision-makers, according to business rules. These key people can be internal or external to your organization. Oracle Workflow lets you model business processes using a drag-and-drop process designer. Perhaps company policy is changed so that purchase orders less than $100 no longer need manager authorization—you can redefine the purchase order approval activity in Workflow to approve low-value purchases automatically.

Until now finance systems have automated head office processes, but they have not reduced the burden of documentation sent by internal mail, faxes sent from one company site to another, and perfunctory telephone calls. Many workers nowadays are in decision-making roles where they have e-mail and Web access but no access to finance systems. The accounts payable people, for example, must chase a project manager in the field for a project code before they can process a purchase invoice. The billing department has to contact the account manager before assigning sales commissions to a salesperson. The accounting department needs to talk with the corporate tax department before deciding whether to capitalize an asset. By delivering electronic notifications, via e-mail or via a Web page, Oracle Workflow extends the reach of office automation beyond the finance department. Notifications are generated out of Workflow activities, and the responses are sent without intervention directly back into the Workflow process by e-mail, a Web browser, or the Oracle Applications Notification form. Finance and operational staff are relieved of the regular workload and are freed up to concentrate their time and expertise on out-of-the-ordinary events.

Accounting for Transactions

Oracle Workflow is also used in the Account Generator—a feature that constructs account code combinations automatically using user-defined criteria. The way Oracle Financials accounts for any particular event needs to be predefined during the setup of the system. To begin, you will need to catalog all the events in your organization that give rise to accounting entries. Typically, these are raising a purchase order, issuing a sales invoice, depreciating an asset, and revaluing foreign currency reserves at month-end. For each situation you need to understand in detail how account codes should be assigned. Accounting policies vary from company to company, and even within a company from time to time.

To allow for all eventualities and at the same time provide a packaged solution that does not need reprogramming, Oracle Financials provides a variety of different methods to derive the account codes. The user can enter codes directly, select them from a hierarchy of defaults, look them up based on transaction type, or find them with the AutoAccounting or Account Generator feature. The specific rules that Oracle Financials uses to assign accounting codes to transactions are described module by module in the chapters that follow. At an early stage in the implementation, it is important to realize that there are a variety of methods for the assignments; some are entirely under the user's control when the transaction is entered, while others are entirely under the implementer's control and hidden from the user when the transaction is entered. Getting the structure of the predefined codes right during the implementation phase is a major objective of your pre-implementation testing. Understanding the logic behind account assignments is part of mastering Oracle Financials.

Applications need to construct Key Flexfield combinations automatically for a number of reasons, primarily speed and accuracy. AutoAccounting and the Account Generator bring business logic and commercial rules-of-thumb to bear on account code derivation. These mechanisms reduce errors, speed up data entry, and provide coding consistency across the organization.

AutoAccounting

AutoAccounting is used in Oracle Receivables and Oracle Projects for generating default Accounting Flexfields for revenue, receivables, freight, tax, unearned revenue, unbilled receivables, finance charges, and clearing (suspense) accounts. AutoAccounting works on a relatively simple lookup table concept, but its simplicity does not preclude its effectiveness. Accounting Flexfields can either be defaulted as constants or be derived from one of several data sources related to the invoice:

- **Salesreps**   Account values associated with the salesperson are used.

- **Transaction Types**   Account values associated with the transaction type are used.

- **Standard Lines**   Account values associated with the standard memo line item or inventory item are used.

- **Taxes**   Account values associated with the tax code are used.

AutoAccounting allows you to default each segment for each account from a different data source if necessary. A revenue account may thereby be set up to default the natural account according to the type of sale (Transaction Type), and the cost center and region segments may be set up to default according to the particular salesperson (Salesrep).

The Account Generator

The Account Generator constructs account code combinations automatically using predefined criteria and is a generalized, more far reaching successor to the Release 10 Flexbuilder tool. In Release 11, Oracle Assets, Oracle Order Entry, Oracle Purchasing, Oracle Receivables, and Oracle Projects use the Account Generator to create combinations. The Account Generator obtains data from sources such as Key Flexfield segments, application tables, value sets, and constants; applies the customized business rules; and produces an appropriate account code combination.

Currently the Account Generator is used only for the situations described in Table 2-2. Used effectively, it is an extremely powerful tool, and will likely be steadily introduced for more situations within the Applications where Accounting Flexfields are needed.

Meeting the Varied Needs of Complex Organizations

Before you can embark on an Oracle Financials implementation you must plan how your computing power and accounting data are to be distributed among all the individuals who need access to financial systems. This is not a simple decision. The systems architecture has a subtle and pervasive impact

Application	Situation Calling for the Account Generator
Oracle Assets	Derivation of the depreciation expense account
Oracle Projects	Derivation of distributions for project-related purchase orders in Oracle Purchasing and invoices in Oracle Payables
Oracle Receivables	Derivation of the company segment for finance charges and foreign currency gain/loss
Oracle Order Entry	Derivation of the Cost of Goods Sold (COGS) account
Oracle Purchasing	Derivation of accounts for individual distributions made against purchase orders and requisitions

TABLE 2-2. *Use of the Account Generator Within the Applications*

on the features that can be readily delivered to users. A simple company will have only one set of books, for instance, and will not use Multi-Org functions. The following sections will help you determine how your company may fit into the Oracle Applications organizational model.

The Organizational Model Within Oracle Applications

Oracle Applications is designed so that it can be implemented in any organization, either commercial or nonprofit, and at the same time support all possible organizational structures. Because the range of possible organizational structures in actual organizations is limitless, the design of Oracle Applications contains a general organizational model that can be customized to fit any actual organization. Part of the process of implementation involves planning how your actual organizational structure maps to the general organizational model within Oracle Applications.

An organizational model is needed to support fundamental business requirements. Multi-Org is a feature that supports multiple organizations within a single instance of the database. You can set up multiple sets of books within a single instance, with each set of books having its own subledgers. The big advantage is the ability to support different logical business entities. With Multi-Org, you can sell and ship products across different legal entities spread across different sets of books. In addition, even within the same legal entity, users can be assigned to different operating units so that they cannot see or use data from other operating units, thus providing a high level of security. An enterprise must be able to perform the following functions:

- Record any number of organizations and the relationships between them, even if those organizations report separate sets of accounts.

- Support any number of legal entities, including jointly owned subsidiaries.

- Secure access to data so that users can access only the information that is relevant to them.

- Sell products from one legal entity and ship them from another legal entity, and automatically record the appropriate intercompany invoicing.

- Purchase products through one legal entity and receive them in another legal entity.

The multiple organization architecture determines how transactions flow through different organizations in Oracle Applications and how those organizations interact with each other. Organizations in Oracle Applications can be sets of books, legal entities, operating units, or inventory organizations. These terms are explained later. Some terms have an everyday meaning as well as a very specific Oracle Applications meaning. In particular, the term *organization* serves a double purpose. Its everyday meaning refers to a company, corporation, government agency, or charity. It also has a specific meaning in the Oracle Applications model. Do not expect *organizations,* as used in reference to Oracle Applications, to equate exactly to the everyday meaning.

Multi-Org is not required where subledger processing is centralized or where there is only one set of books. Similarly, Multi-Org is not required where one set of books has AP, PO, AR, OE and another set of books has none of these but only GL. Multi-Org requires only one installation of Oracle Financial Applications for an unlimited number of sets of books, thereby providing for viewing across multiple sets of books and easy administration of software related to upgrades. Multi-Org is defined by a hierarchy: A business group consists of *sets of books,* which are made up of *legal entities,* which are made up of *operating units*, which consist of *inventory organizations.*

The Set of Books

A set of books comprises a chart of accounts, a calendar, and a functional currency. Legal entities that share the same chart of accounts, accounting calendar, and functional currency can be accounted for in the same set of books. Consider an American corporation with a subsidiary in Germany. The German company must report statutory returns to the German authorities in the local currency (deutsche marks or euro). Because the corporation in the U.S. accounts in dollars, the German subsidiary has to be created in Oracle Financials as a separate set of books. Similarly, subsidiaries that use a different calendar or a different chart of accounts each need to be set up as separate sets of books.

The financial transactions and balances in Oracle General Ledger belong to one set of books. The user of one set of books sees only the journals that relate to that set of books. All other journals are hidden from the user on screens and reports. To access another set of books, the user would need the appropriate Responsibility privileges. The data within Oracle General Ledger is secured by sets of books. Within each set of books you may define one or more legal entities.

The Legal Entity

A legal entity is a company for which, by law, you must prepare fiscal or tax reports, including a balance sheet and a profit-and-loss report. In accounting terms, the legal entity is the smallest business unit for which you need to be able to produce a balanced set of accounts. For nonprofit organizations the legal entity is equivalent to a fund. Legal entities consist of one or more operating units.

NOTE
Release 10 provided only a few features for legal entities, such as intercompany invoicing and reporting of intrastate movement for the European Community.

The Operating Unit

Operating units represent buying and selling units within your organization. The operating unit concept is most apparent in Oracle Order Entry, Oracle Receivables, Oracle Purchasing, and Oracle Payables. The transaction data that these modules hold—purchase orders, invoices, payments, and receipts—are partitioned by operating unit. That is to say that one operating unit cannot see the purchase orders, invoices, payments, and receipts for another operating unit, even if the same vendor or customer is involved. The customer and vendor lists are shared across operating units. The address sites are partitioned by operating unit. Purchasing and selling give rise to liabilities and receivables that are balance sheet items. Consequently, all the transactions for an operating unit must appear on the balance sheet of only one legal entity. There is no reason to split the liabilities and receivables of one operating unit across two legal entities.

NOTE
The operating unit is a feature of the Applications' multiple-organization architecture (Multi-Org), which first became available with Release 10.6. Since Release 10.7, Multi-Org has become a standard part of the package. You will not find any reference to operating units in releases prior to 10.6.

The Inventory Organization

The inventory organization is a unit that has inventory transactions and balances, and possibly manufactures or distributes products. The inventory of an organization consists of the finished products that are ready for sale, all parts that are in stock waiting to be assembled into finished products, and all the assemblies of parts that are currently being assembled in the factory. A company's inventory changes continually as products are sold, new parts are purchased, and work progresses on assembly lines. Some organizations, such as banks, hospitals, and consultancies, do not have tangible inventories. They sell their services, expertise, and time.

The Oracle Manufacturing modules, including Oracle Inventory, are partitioned by inventory organization. From an accounting perspective, inventory is a balance sheet item and therefore belongs to one legal entity. You do not need to split an inventory organization across two or more legal entities.

The organizational model is a strict hierarchy. The minimum configuration is a server supporting one Financials database instance, with one set of books, one legal entity, and a single operating unit related to one

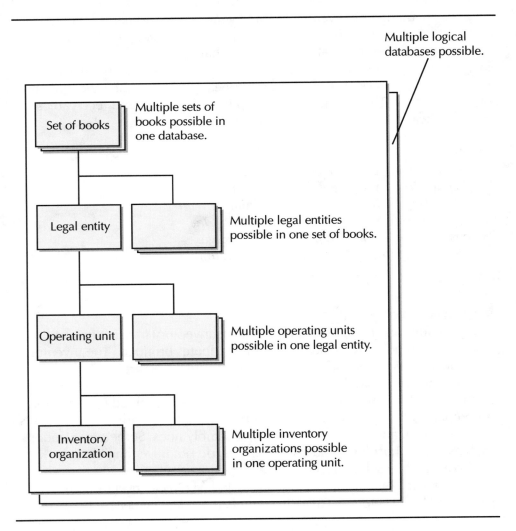

FIGURE 2-3. *The organizational model*

inventory organization, as shown in Figure 2-3. More complex organizations can be modeled by introducing multiplicity at any level.

The Logical Financials Database

Although not explicitly part of the Oracle Applications multiple-organization architecture, the number of logical Financials databases has a bearing on the intercompany capabilities that you will be able to deliver readily to the end users. Information held in the Applications is protected from unauthorized access. Access is restricted to authorized users, who are able to log in and work through an application's screens with their passwords. Each logical Financials database has a single list of authorized users. The repository for the user list, the Oracle Applications Object Library, is installed in the database once—as the first application module created when you install Oracle Financials—and it controls user access to all organizations within the database.

While it is possible to distribute the processing across nodes in a network system, Oracle Financials does not support databases distributed across machines. The distribution of the processing load provides fault tolerance in case one or more nodes fail. Oracle Financials databases are therefore essentially standalone database systems. They form islands of data. A global organization may implement one database instance for operations in America, a second database instance for Europe and Africa, and a third for Asia. The accounting setup, the user names, accounting calendar, and currencies will not be shared by those three database instances.

If you do decide to run multiple database instances, you may easily consolidate General Ledger transactions using the Release 11 feature Global Consolidation System (GCS). GCS caters to data collected from any source and any number of subsidiary accounting systems. These accounting systems do not need to be Oracle General Ledger systems. GCS can upload financial data from a spreadsheet as well as through a dedicated open interface. By using the GCS it is no longer necessary to organize a consolidation mechanism outside Oracle Financials. Even so, before choosing multiple financial databases or servers, consider the overhead of maintaining reference data, such as currency conversion rates, in separate databases.

Financials in the Global Businesses Environment

Hardware and network configurations can be complex. A large multinational organization with several operating units has finance users in many countries around the world. The corporation has a choice: either to run one centralized server and link all users by high-speed data connections (called a *wide area network,* or WAN) or to install smaller machines in each operating unit and connect the users by a *local area network* (LAN). Each option should be costed, because there is a trade-off between network communication cost (which is higher for a centralized server) and machine cost (which is lower for a centralized server). The hardware strategy has a subtle and pervasive impact on the software features that can be delivered readily to each user. Centralized servers are excellent for allowing regular and fast consolidation of financial data to produce group-wide accounts. In addition, a centralized server allows simplified creation of a common chart of accounts and common categories and classifications for all users. By contrast, local servers allow independent operating units a great deal of autonomy to run their business the way that suits them. Businesses have to adapt the hardware strategy to their corporate culture. However, local independence may be seen as a bad business practice because it can degrade the data being uploaded to corporate reporting systems.

The hardware configuration and the implementation of organizational structure are subtly related. The strategy for each should be chosen together, after you have fully researched the structure and needs of your business.

Creating a Model of Your Business

Before you implement Oracle Financials, model your entire business and determine your actual organizational structures. How many legal entities do you own? Where are your warehouses and manufacturing plants located? Are the finance, marketing, and personnel departments run at the group level, or by each business unit individually? Determine your reporting needs, as well as the levels of autonomy in your business. Keep in mind that reporting hierarchies may not match physical locations. The marketing manager for Asia and the Pacific, for example, might operate out of group headquarters in New York. The global effort can be broken down into smaller manageable chunks. A large multinational company, then, might choose to implement Oracle Applications in one business unit as a prototype, then later roll out the system to its other units.

Prototyping

The prototype may be a full implementation in a single business unit, or it may be a pilot implementation. Pilots can be implemented rapidly and used to validate new business processes and procedures. They allow managers, accountants, and implementers to build up confidence and understand how Oracle Applications works. From the start, the analysis of the business should consider all business units. All critical decisions about hardware distribution, organization, the structure of a chart of accounts, and other setup issues must suit the entire organization. Otherwise, limiting choices are made to fit the requirements of the prototype business unit, which severely hampers future implementations in other business units.

The final decisions about the hardware configuration and about organizational structure cannot be made independently of each other; both areas have to be considered together. The configuration is not determined by the size of your organization, but rather the complexity of your organization, its geographical spread, the level of autonomy that different parts of your organization have, and the similarity between their lines of business.

The Modeling Process

The modeling process can be likened to a process of mapping your actual organizational structure onto the implied organizational model of logical databases, each database catering to multiple organizations, and each organization consisting of multiple legal entities. If you are converting to Oracle Applications from an existing or legacy system, do not make the mistake of simply reimplementing your existing model.

Start the modeling process at the database level. Determine how many databases are needed to support your business. You can then model upward to decide how many servers are needed and which database instances will reside on each server. For each database instance you can model downward to determine the organizational structure implemented within each database.

Financial Reporting

The Accounting Flexfield segments support statutory and management reporting from the General Ledger (GL). There has to be a corporate-wide plan for financial reporting. Reporting needs that are not covered by a segment in the Accounting Flexfield have to be satisfied by a report from one of the other modules, or from a feeder system if the data is imported directly into Oracle General Ledger.

Each module provides several reports, each one detailing a specific type of financial transaction data. These standard reports can be requested by an authorized user at any time. Standard reports have a fixed format and layout, but their content can be focused each time the report is submitted by specifying selection parameters. The standard reports in Oracle General Ledger include Trial Balance reports, several Account Analysis reports, and Consolidation and Budgeting reports.

In addition to the standard reports, three other tools are associated with Oracle General Ledger for reporting financial data in a way that exceeds the intention of the standard reports.

The *Financial Statement Generator (FSG)* can be used for producing any financial report, such as a balance sheet or income statement. The FSG reports on account balance, either actual or budget, per Accounting Flexfield combination. It does not report on transaction detail. Refer to Chapter 3 for more information on defining FSG report formats.

Oracle Financial Analyzer is a separate module, with an OLAP multidimensional database at its core, which is used to produce complex analysis reports. Transaction data is exported out of Oracle General Ledger and imported into Oracle Financial Analyzer. It provides a complete set of tools for budgeting, forecasting, analyzing, and reporting corporate financial data.

The *Application Desktop Integrator* started life as a quick and simple way to import budgets and actual journals in Oracle General Ledger. It now includes the Request Center, a centralized report management tool from which you can submit, monitor, and publish any type of report to a variety of different formats—Web, spreadsheet, and text —all from a single user interface. Not only does the Request Center support publish-and-subscribe Web publishing, but it also allows you to download a spreadsheet version of the report-on-demand for analytical analysis.

Multiple Reporting Currencies

The Multiple Reporting Currencies (MRC) feature allows you to report and maintain accounting records at the transaction level in more than one functional currency. You do this by defining one or more reporting sets of books, in addition to your primary set of books. Companies need dual reporting currencies when they either operate in high-inflation economies or need to be able to report in both euro and a local currency.

Global Financial Applications

Oracle's globalization strategy is simple—to provide one global product that meets local, regional and global requirements. Business requirements for national and multinational users have been built into the Applications for 44 countries worldwide. The idea behind globalization is to put all features into the core product.

Oracle's earlier approach was to deliver the package in American English, with accounting features that closely corresponded to the Generally Accepted Accounting Principles (GAAP) of the United States, together with extensions—additional languages versions of screens and reports, extra software features, local statutory reports—that could be applied on top of the base package. Oracle called these extensions localizations. The same features are now developed, packaged and released centrally in one global Applications product.

National Language Support

The National Language Support (NLS) permits you to run Oracle Applications in languages other than American English. There are two distinct categories of NLS: the language *character set* that users are able to use when they key data into forms and the language *translation* of the fixed text on forms and reports. The character set available for user data need not correspond to the language of the fixed text on forms and reports. For example, the American English translation of the forms and reports can be used simultaneously with a data entry character set that allows local language characters to be entered.

TRANSLATIONS   The Oracle Applications forms and reports are available in over 29 languages in addition to American English. When you install Oracle Applications in a language other than American English, all the forms, menus, help text, messages, and reports appear in the selected language. If you have a need to view this information in more than one language (not including American English) within a single database instance you may install Multilanguage Support (MLS). This feature allows users on the same system to view fixed text, appearing on screens and in reports, in different languages according to their user setup designations.

FOREIGN CHARACTER SETS Choose a character set that includes all the printable characters you are likely to need. Character sets are grouped according to the number of bits and bytes needed to uniquely identify each character. Regular ASCII is a seven-bit character set. If you want to work in German you need an eight-bit character set to store extra characters such as ä, ü, and ß. The Japanese character set requires 16 bits (two bytes).

You can always store data in American English with any of the available character sets. However, you may use only one character set on any given database instance, a limitation that could be a determining factor in the number of database instances you end up installing at your site. For example, currently you could not store both Japanese and German in the same database, since they both use different character sets. Future releases will allow you to do this through the use of the UTF8 character set. Your DBA will need to know which character set you intend to use before the database is created. The default character set is WE8ISO8859P1.

Address Styles

Oracle Applications lets you enter customer, supplier, bank, check, and remit-to addresses in country-specific formats. For example, if you have customers in Germany, you can enter German addresses in the format required by the Bundespost, while you can enter addresses for customers in the United Kingdom in the format recommended by the Royal Mail. The data will still be stored in the same database columns, but the input screens format and syntax will be specific to your country instead of always reflecting the United States Postal Service requirements.

Localizations

Localizations are designed to meet the specific needs of certain territories or countries. Most localizations are necessary because the local laws or accounting practices differ from those that are common in the United States.

For example, most countries have their own special formats for checks and electronic correspondence with banks. The electronic payment formats for each country are also included in the localizations. Unlike translations, where one language must be chosen as the base language, it is possible to install the localizations for several territories. This would be necessary for a Dutch company that intends to use electronic payments with both French and German banks.

Each territory that has localization modules belongs to one of three regions: Asia Pacific; Europe, the Middle East, and Africa (EMEA); or the Americas (Canada plus Latin America). An additional region, called *Global*, is for localizations that apply to territories throughout the world. For example, localizations used in both Europe and Latin America are classified in the Global region.

The effects of localizations vary widely—some could only have a minor effect on one module, while others may have wider reaching effects. As a general rule, if a process is a generally accepted practice or is government-required, it will probably be included in the localization for your country or territory.

NOTE
Translations and localizations are separate from and independent of each other. Suppose, for instance, that you were to install the French localization software, but not the French translations. You would then be able to issue commands in French, but all your screens and reports would remain in English. Or, suppose you wanted all screens and reports in Italian, but none of the Italian localizations. Both of these configurations are possible and common, especially within multinational companies.

Conclusion

This chapter has provided an overview of the essential concepts involved in implementing Oracle Financials. These concepts are described and explained in more detail in the chapters that follow. As you progress through the rest of the book, you will recognize which aspects of the information presented here are going to be of particular importance for your Financials implementation. You may want to pay particular attention to these aspects and concentrate your research on those implementation decisions that, once made, are difficult to change later.

PART II

What Can the Package Do?

CHAPTER 3

Oracle General Ledger

racle General Ledger is the collection point for all financial transactions. It is a tool for integrating subledger activity, consolidating group-wide accounts, and producing the statutory financial reports.

The Heart of Your Accounting System

General Ledger is at the heart of any accounting system. It is the central repository of all subledger activity, maintaining the highest summary level of financial information from the transaction details supplied by its subledgers. All events that have a financial or monetary impact are ultimately reflected in General Ledger.

Oracle General Ledger is a comprehensive financial management solution that enhances financial controls, data collection, and financial reporting throughout an enterprise. For businesses operating in a global environment, Oracle General Ledger handles currency conversion rates, offers support for the euro, and tracks and reports balances in multiple currencies. To track transactions and account balances in multiple currencies, you can automatically replicate journals from your primary functional currency set of books into one or more foreign currency sets of books used for reporting purposes. Oracle General Ledger enables rapid implementation, easy adoption from legacy systems, accurate and timely transaction processing, improved enterprise decision support, and increased operational efficiency with quick closing procedures.

Anything that has a financial impact on the company has to be accounted for. Normally, transactions are entered into Oracle subledgers. For example, a customer invoice is entered into Oracle Receivables after Oracle Shipping has notified Receivables that a product has been shipped to the customer. To purchase office equipment, a purchase order is recorded in Oracle Purchasing. When the equipment arrives and the invoice is received, the purchase order is closed and a liability is recorded in Oracle Payables. Finally, Oracle Payables sends information to Oracle Assets to capitalize the equipment and initiate depreciation. The data in all of these subledgers is then transferred to Oracle General Ledger through a standard transfer program. Oracle Applications is built on the principle that such events, or financial transactions, are entered only once, whether in General Ledger or its subledgers.

Transactions that are not entered into any other subledger can be entered directly into Oracle General Ledger using the Enter Journals form. See Figure 3-1 for sample journal entries. Companies must ensure that all financial transactions are represented only once in the ledger. A control mechanism outside the accounting system should be in place and maintained to ensure that accounting entries are entered and not duplicated. Not all companies implement all the Financials modules. One company may choose not to implement a particular module, such as Oracle Assets, and will have to enter all asset additions, disposals, and depreciation information directly into Oracle General Ledger. A company using Oracle Assets would key the asset information into Oracle Assets, and Oracle Assets would prepare a journal entry that gets transferred into Oracle General Ledger.

On the other hand, a company using Oracle Assets and Oracle Payables would have asset information already available in Oracle Assets if an invoice was created in Oracle Payables. The Mass Additions feature in Oracle Assets

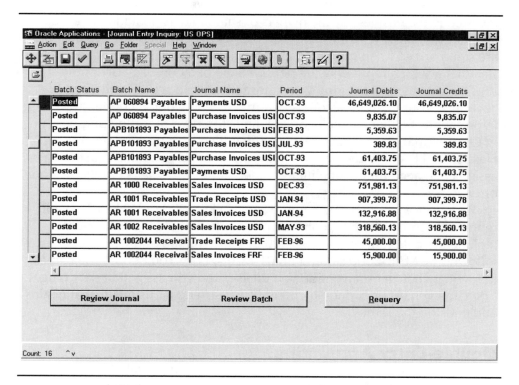

FIGURE 3-1. *Sample journals shown in the Enter Journals form*

allows you to transfer asset information from any feeder system, such as Oracle Payables and Oracle Projects, into Oracle Assets. Then, from Oracle Assets, you can send asset journal entries to Oracle General Ledger. One way or another the financial transaction finds its way into Oracle General Ledger.

Overview of General Ledger

Most people are familiar with their own bank statement, which shows an opening balance, transactions that occurred throughout the period, and a closing balance. That statement is a snapshot of your account at a particular point in time. A company keeps an account, like the records the bank keeps of your bank account, for every organization or customer that the company does business with. The balance sheet summarizes accounts and financial activities in three broad categories: assets, which represent all the things that the company owns; liabilities, which show how much money the company owes to others; and capital/retained earnings, which show the total cash invested in the business by the owners or shareholders. In addition, accounts are kept for all the revenues and expenses of the company. These accounts are summarized in an income statement, also called a profit and loss statement, which represents the performance of a company over time.

The first step in capturing your transactions is to set up your chart of accounts. Your chart of accounts determines how your accounting information is collected, categorized, and stored for reporting purposes. In Oracle Financials, all accounts are identified by a unique Accounting Flexfield (AFF) combination, which is your chart of accounts structure. You assign each account the qualifier of *asset, liability, owner's equity, revenue*, or *expense*.

Periods are identified by names such as FEB-2000 or WEEK12-98 and represent non-overlapping consecutive date ranges. FEB-2000 would include the date ranges 01-FEB-2000 to 29-FEB-2000 and would be followed by MAR-2000 starting on 01-MAR-2000. You choose the names, following whatever convention you devise, and you assign the date ranges. You can even set up a one-day period for year-end adjustments that begins and ends on the same day.

Double-Entry Accounting

Double-entry accounting requires constant symmetry; total debits must equal total credits. Every accounting transaction results in one or more debits and credits that always remain in balance. For example, a $5000 purchase of office equipment would result in an increase to the asset account as well as an increase to a liability account. In Oracle Financials, the account number is referred to as the *Accounting Flexfield* (AFF), which is used throughout all of Oracle Applications whenever a transaction is entered into the system. The Accounting Flexfield consists of multiple segments, such as those for company, cost center, and account. One full Accounting Flexfield is called a *combination.* Each journal entry line is tagged with an Accounting Flexfield combination. For expense transactions, the AFF usually identifies who incurred the cost (for example, which company or department) and what the cost was for (for example, travel expense). If you want more detailed information, such as which region, cost center, and product incurred the cost, you can design your AFF structure to include that information as well. Because total debits must always equal total credits in every transaction, Oracle General Ledger requires that all journals balance. If you try to enter an unbalanced journal, Oracle General Ledger will either reject the transaction or force the transaction to balance by posting the difference to a suspense account.

Multiple Charts of Accounts

Companies that operate globally may require the use of multiple charts of accounts. For example, a company with subsidiaries in different geographical regions may have to adapt to different account structures based upon various laws for that region or base currency requirements. Oracle General Ledger allows you to define as many charts of accounts as desired all within a single installation of the product.

Accounts and Periods

You can enter transactions only in an open period. Many times, several periods are open at once to allow for prior period transactions and future period transactions. Once you know that you no longer need to keep the period open to enter transactions, you should close the period to prevent accidental entries into that period.

The transaction is dated in the accounting system according to when it actually occurred, not according to when it was entered into the system or processed. This is in contrast to the way Online Transaction Processing (OLTP) systems tend to work. Transactions in an OLTP system are dated with the day and time when they were created. In an accounting system, today's date and time is not so important. (In fact it is stored in Oracle

Financials as part of the audit trail.) The accounting period in which a financial transaction falls is likewise determined by the date when the transaction actually occurred, and not when it was entered into the accounting system.

Finance and accounting departments often have targets for the prompt closure of accounting periods. An important role delegated to the system administrator or a key person in the finance department is opening and closing the accounting periods. A one- or two-week time scale is a reasonable closing schedule for companies that operate on calendar month periods. However, the number and timing of the periods can be chosen to suit your company's local accounting practice. Various common accounting calendars are shown in Table 3-1. The accounting periods in Oracle Financials can start and finish on any day of the year, and the start and end days can differ from year to year, but the number of periods each year must remain constant. This limitation is required in order to produce year-to-year comparisons. The financial year can also end on any chosen day. Common year-ends are December 31, because it fits in with the calendar year; March 31, because it fits with the United Kingdom's fiscal year, which runs from April 6 to April 5; September 30 for the U.S. government fiscal year; and June 30, which is favored by auditors, who otherwise have a resource problem dealing with all the companies with December 31 year-ends.

Posting is simply the process of updating the account balances of your detail and summary accounts. Posting can be done at the time of journal entry, at a later time to post a group of journal batches, or automatically using AutoPost. AutoPost uses criteria sets that are a combination of journal sources, journal categories, balance types, and periods. When you run this program, it selects the journals that meet the criteria and posts them automatically at specific times and submission intervals defined by you. Each time you post journals, the system keeps a record of the total debits and the total credits posted to each account in the period and uses these totals to keep a running total of the account balance for each period. The following formula shows how the account balances are calculated:

Account Closing Balance = Opening Balance + Total (debits)
– Total (credits)

Account Opening Balance for One Period = Closing Balance for the
Previous Period

Calendar	Number of Periods	Duration of Each Period	Usage
Quarter	4	13 weeks	Rarely used except by low-transaction, dormant companies.
Month	12	Calendar month	Standard business calendar. Financial year ends on December 31, or any other chosen day.
4-4-5	12	Each quarter is three periods of four, four, and five weeks each.	Alternative to calendar month. Provides equal-length quarters, giving better quarter-to-quarter comparisons. Users normally put odd days into the first and last weeks of the year, so fiscal years are directly comparable.
Week	52	52 periods of one week each	Favored by retail companies that require rapid feedback on sales figures. A month is too long to wait for critical figures. Odd days at year-end are usually swept into the dead time around the holidays.
Day	260 ± 25	Each trading day is a separate period.	Favored by banks, which have to show day-end balances for regulatory compliance.

TABLE 3-1.   *Common Accounting Calendars and Usage*

These two rules determine how the balance of each account develops over a period of time. An example of this is shown in Figure 3-2. Box 1 shows the account balances, Box 2 shows the posted journal, and Box 3 shows the updated account balances. The journal in this case is simply a salary payment to employees from a bank account with some other administration cost.

1. Opening Balances

Natural Account	Debit	Credit
Cash and receivables	137,000	
Other current assets	140,000	
Plant and equipment	120,000	
Land	40,000	
Investments	76,000	
Liabilities		60,000
Common stock		250,000
Other contributed capital		47,000
Sales		1,290,000
Investment income		3,000
Other revenue		2,000
Salary and wages	65,000	
Cost of goods sold	900,000	
Exchange rate losses	5,000	
Depreciation and amortization	47,000	
Administration	3,000	
Provision for bad debt	119,000	
Grand Totals	**1,652,000**	**1,652,000**

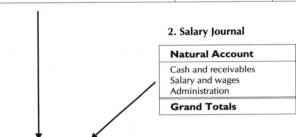

2. Salary Journal

Natural Account	Debit	Credit
Cash and receivables		37,000
Salary and wages	35,000	
Administration	2,000	
Grand Totals	**37,000**	**37,000**

3. Closing Balances

Natural Account	Debit	Credit
Cash and receivables	100,000	
Other current assets	140,000	
Plant and equipment	120,000	
Land	40,000	
Investments	76,000	
Liabilities		60,000
Common stock		250,000
Other contributed capital		47,000
Sales		1,290,000
Investment income		3,000
Other revenue		2,000
Salary and wages	100,000	
Cost of goods sold	900,000	
Exchange rate losses	5,000	
Depreciation and amortization	47,000	
Administration	5,000	
Provision for bad debt	119,000	
Grand Totals	**1,652,000**	**1,652,000**

FIGURE 3-2. *Account balances develop over time as journals are posted*

There is a variation on the second rule for revenue and expense accounts at year-end. Revenue and expense accounts are part of the profit and loss for the company. The definition of *profit* (or *loss* if the profit is negative) is:

Profit = Total Revenues – Total Expenses

At the end of the financial year, the profit or loss for the year is calculated and transferred to the balance sheet as retained earnings. The revenue and expense accounts start the new financial year with a balance of zero.

NOTE
Oracle General Ledger calculates the profit figure and transfers it to the account designated as the retained earnings account for that set of books. The calculation takes effect when you open the first period of the new accounting year, and it is based on the account type defined for each Accounting Flexfield combination. For this reason it is important to set up the account types in Oracle correctly when the segment values for each account are defined. Mixing profit and loss accounts (revenue and expense) as balance sheet accounts (asset, liability, and owner's equity) or vice versa will inevitably result in an incorrect profit figure carried forward into the next financial year.

The two rules, plus the variation of the second rule at year-end, completely describe the processing logic encoded into General Ledger. The mechanics of a ledger system has its origins in paper-based lists of accounting records, known as *ledgers*. The processing logic needed to run a computerized ledger system is not complex. Small companies and sole traders can run a perfectly adequate general ledger system on a spreadsheet. Oracle General

Ledger has significant advantages for larger organizations, which need several users to access the system at the same time. Large organizations must be able to perform the following tasks:

- Process high volumes of data

- Provide transaction processing through journal approvals and secured access to journal posting and reversal

- Create custom and standard reports using Oracle General Ledger's reporting tool, the Financial Statement Generator (FSG)

- Account for multiple currencies

- Create and maintain budgets

- Consolidate groups of companies or subsidiaries

- Provide a spreadsheet interface for entering journals, creating budgets, or creating and analyzing reports using the Applications Integrator (ADI)

- Provide Online Analytical Processing (OLAP) capabilities using Oracle Financial Analyzer to further analyze information and expand reporting capabilities in a multidimensional environment

Auditing and Security

Oracle General Ledger maintains an audit trail for every financial transaction to allow you to go back to the original entry for purposes of reconciliation and auditing. This audit trail helps accountants validate their reports and ensures data security. Tampering with accounts and figures is much more difficult with proper controls in place.

Journal Entries

Journals can be entered into Oracle General Ledger using various methods: manual entry, subledger entry using the Journal Import interface, and spreadsheet entry using the Applications Desktop Integrator. The following illustration shows a typical journal entry.

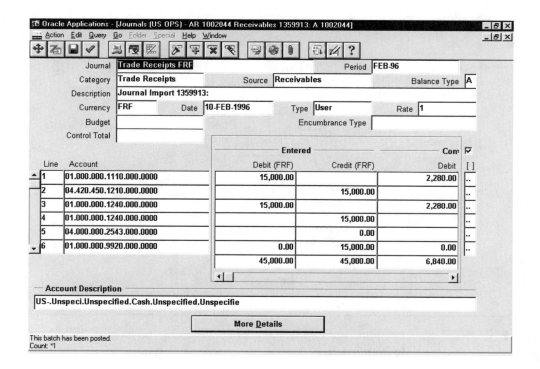

Integration with Other Financials Modules

Unless you opt for a manual solution using only General Ledger, you will inevitably need to import data from your subledgers. The Journal Import interface is the common tool for importing transactions into Oracle General Ledger. When you transfer data from Oracle subledgers, the system automatically populates the database table called GL_INTERFACE, from which the journal import process captures its data.

The Journal Import Interface

Journal transactions may originate in the subledgers or in an external feeder system. Each Oracle subledger that transfers transactions prepares the journal entry records, inserts them into the GL_INTERFACE table, and starts the journal import process. Figure 3-3 shows the main accounting transactions that flow from the Oracle subledgers and a few symbolic external feeder systems.

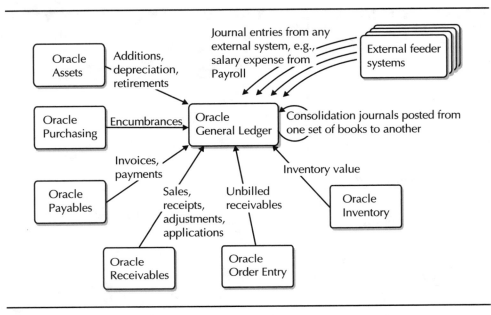

FIGURE 3-3. *Integration of Oracle General Ledger using the Journal Import interface*

The Journal Import interface uses the GL_INTERFACE table as a bridge between external systems and the Oracle General Ledger base tables where journals are stored. For each journal line that needs to be imported, a single record is inserted into the GL_INTERFACE table. The journal import process is started and an execution report shows what has processed. In the event that journals are not imported successfully, the errors are listed in the execution report. Each of these errors needs to be corrected using the Correct Journal Import Data window, and then the journal import process must be restarted. Alternatively, if the journal data set is beyond repair, all records must be deleted using the Delete Journal Import Data window, and the data must be prepared again from the feeder system. Figure 3-4 diagrams the process. For transfers initiated from Oracle subledgers, the system automatically populates the GL_INTERFACE table, and then starts the journal import process. The journal data transferred from Oracle subledgers seldom shows data errors. Although errors are rare, they do happen, and so it is advisable to check each and every process to ensure it has completed successfully. The most common and easily rectified error is attempting to import into a closed period. To correct, open the period and rerun the import.

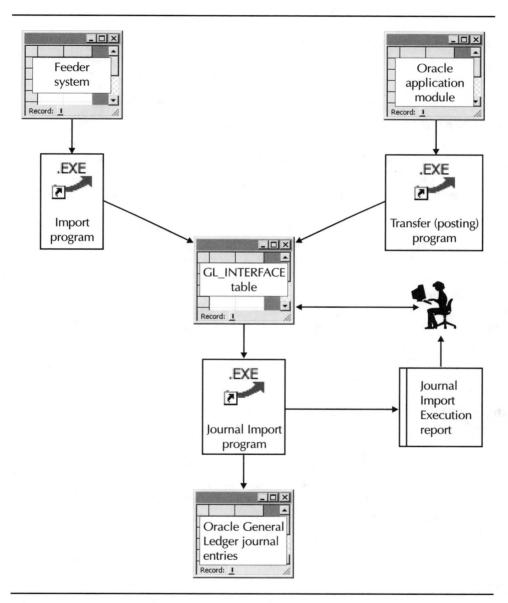

FIGURE 3-4.   *The journal import process*

Alerts, managed from Oracle Alert, are a good device for performing checks such as these, precisely because they advise users when exceptions occur. You can write an alert to send a simple e-mail to the accounting manager (or whoever is in charge) when a process such as this, which is expected never to fail, actually does fail.

JOURNAL IMPORT VALIDATION   The Journal Import interface performs validation on all journals. This is intended to ensure that all journals entered into Oracle General Ledger are right and proper. Journal Import validates batches, journal entries, and journal lines. The data attributes of the journals are checked in detail, ensuring that all the accounts are valid and that attributes like the journal category are appropriate. The period into which you are importing needs to be open and the journal needs to balance. Error codes are printed in the Journal Execution report next to the GL_INTERFACE data that is in error. A list of all the error codes and their meanings can be found at the end of the Journal Execution report. The validation ensures that all accounts, sources, categories, and dates are valid. Oracle uses the journal source to identify the subledger (such as Oracle Payables); the category represents the type of transaction, such as Adjustments. The Journal Import program allows you to select what you want to import by the source. If there are errors in your import process, you can review the error codes in the Journal Execution report.

IMPORTING FROM EXTERNAL SYSTEMS   Importing financial transactions from external systems is very simple. Data records are inserted into the GL_INTERFACE table, and then the journal import process is started. You can use SQL*Loader, an Oracle utility to insert data read from files directly into a database table, or you can use more complex import programs written using any programming language that supports embedded SQL. Whatever the mechanism for inserting the records, the GL_INTERFACE columns shown in Table 3-2 must be populated.

The interface program that populates the GL_INTERFACE table can also submit the concurrent request to run the journal import process. Doing this is particularly useful for regular or overnight imports from feeder systems. Programmers can initiate concurrent programs by calling the submission routines from the operating system, PL/SQL, or Oracle Forms. Each time the routine is called, the appropriate parameters, such as the name of the concurrent program, and the parameter values should be passed. Refer to the *Oracle Applications Object Library Reference Manual* for more details.

Column	Purpose
SEGMENT1 through SEGMENT30	Identifies the Accounting Flexfield segment values of the journal
CODE_COMBINATION_ID	Used as an alternative to the SEGMENTxx values
ACTUAL_FLAG	A for actual amounts
REFERENCE1	Used to create a journal batch name of the format <REFERENCE1><Request ID><Actual Flag> <Group ID>
REFERENCE4	Used to format the Journal Entry name
ACCOUNTED_DR	A debit amount
ACCOUNTED_CR	A credit amount
ACCOUNTING_DATE	Determines in which accounting period the journal appears
STATUS	The value NEW
SET_OF_BOOKS_ID	Determines in which set of books the journal appears
USER_JE_SOURCE_NAME	Determines which source the journal has
USER_JE_CATEGORY_NAME	Determines which category the journal has
CURRENCY_CODE	Determines which currency the journal has

TABLE 3-2.   *GL_INTERFACE Data Needed by Journal Import*

TRANSFERRING FROM OTHER MODULES   The journals from each module are clearly identifiable according to their batch name and journal name. Each subledger transfer is tagged with a unique identifying number, as shown in Table 3-3.

When you submit the Journal Import program, or any of the transfer programs from the subledgers, you must specify whether the import should operate in summary mode or detail mode. Summary mode produces one journal entry line per distinct Accounting Flexfield combination (for example, company, department, and natural account). Conversely, detail mode imports the journal with as many journal entry lines as there are transaction lines in the GL_INTERFACE table. Summary mode reduces the size of journals, the amount of disk space required, and the time it takes to retrieve the data.

Batch Name	Journal Name	Transactions Included
user-ref Payables	Payments *CUR*	Payments transferred from Oracle Payables. (*CUR* is the currency of the payments and *user-ref* is the reference given to the transfer by the user who started it.)
user-ref Payables	Purchase Invoices *CUR*	Purchase invoices transferred from Oracle Payables.
AR *control-id* Receivables	Sales Invoices *CUR*	Sales invoices transferred from Oracle Receivables. (*control-id* is a sequential number assigned to each transfer by the system.)
AR *control-id* Receivables	Trade Receipts *CUR*	Trade receipts transferred from Oracle Receivables.

TABLE 3-3. *Naming Conventions for Journals Transferred from Subledgers*

Summary mode is good for performance, but the direct one-to-one correspondence between General Ledger and the subledger is lost. In order to retain the audit trail back to the subledger, details taken from the imported journal lines can be retained in the GL_IMPORT_REFERENCES table. By default this feature is deactivated, but it can be activated from the Define Sources window. Provided this feature is activated, several drill-down inquiry screens are available to trace transactions back to the subledgers. Activating this feature increases the clarity and visibility of the audit trail and is strongly recommended. The mechanics of the drill-down are described in more detail in Chapter 18.

OTHER USES FOR JOURNAL IMPORT   Journal Import is used internally by the standard consolidation process to transfer account balances or detail transactions from one set of books to another. If you have chosen to implement multiple instances of Oracle Financials, use Journal Import to consolidate account balances from the remote databases into one central database that holds a consolidated set of books. Journal Import can load or convert opening balances from a legacy system when you first go live with Oracle General Ledger.

Journal Import can be used to import budgets or encumbrances. To do this, enter the value *B* or *E* in the ACTUAL_FLAG column and the appropriate budget version ID in the BUDGET_VERSION_ID column or the appropriate encumbrance type ID in the ENCUMBRANCE_TYPE_ID column of the GL_INTERFACE table.

The import process is often useful for statistical journals. For example, the manufacturing system may control the units-of-production figures that GL needs for allocations. Common practice would be to write a simple script to generate a statistical journal to post to the ledger. The same would apply to head counts from Human Resources, billable hours from Projects, and of course statistical journals can be imported from non-Oracle subledger systems as well.

Posting

After importing your journals, you can post them in Oracle General Ledger to update the account balances. When you post to an earlier open period, actual balances roll forward through the latest open period, budget balances roll forward through the end of the latest open budget year, and encumbrance balances roll forward through the end of the latest open encumbrance year. If you post a journal entry into a prior year, General Ledger adjusts your retained earnings balance for the effect on your revenue and expense accounts. You can automate your posting process by scheduling the Automatic Posting program to periodically select and post batches.

You can also set the criteria for the Automatic Posting program to post transactions based on journal source (such as fixed assets), journal category (such as manual year-end adjustments), and effective date combinations at different intervals for different transaction groups. With the Journal Approval System, you can require that journal entries from any source be approved before posting. Oracle General Ledger offers security to control which users can post and reverse journals.

The Closing Schedule

At the end of an accounting period, all companies go through a closing process to close the period and produce final financial reports. These reports are considered final because once the period is closed, the figures for that period can no longer be changed.

Some companies allow for closed periods to be reopened to add any missed journal entries. However, this practice should not be taken lightly. If your company's policies and procedures allow for the reopening of closed periods, you can do so in Oracle General Ledger using the Open and Close

Periods form. However, you should restrict access to this form to select individuals in order to protect your accounting data. New transactions posted to a reopened period will invalidate subledgers and cause you to re-create financial statements and consolidation reports. Most companies have strict closing procedures that prohibit the possibility of reopening closed periods. Instead, companies use current-period journals to make prior-period corrections.

The following list outlines the events required to process transactions and close your period. The tasks do not have to be performed in the exact order described.

1. Set the status of the first accounting period in the new fiscal year to Future Entry.
   (Optional) If your business rules require you to create reversing entries at the beginning of every period, generate and post accruals from the prior period now.

2. Transfer data from all of your subledgers and feeder systems to the GL_INTERFACE table.

3. Run the Journal Import process to populate the GL_JE_BATCHES, GL_JE_HEADERS, and the GL_JE_LINES tables. This can be done automatically from the subledger systems, or manually from Oracle General Ledger.

NOTE
If you allow suspense posting in your set of books, you can choose a Journal Import Run Option that will post any journal import errors to a suspense account. If you do not choose this run option, Journal Import will reject any source/group ID combination that contains account errors.

Posting from the subledger systems transfers data to the General Ledger interface and journal entry tables, but does not update general ledger balances. You must run the posting process from General Ledger to update the GL_BALANCES table.

4. Review the Journal Import Execution Report to check the status of all imported journal entries.

5. Delete any error journal entry batches. Determine the cause for these error batches, and retrieve the run ID from the Journal Import Execution Report. If you encounter a small number of errors, make the necessary corrections in the GL_INTERFACE table using the Correct Journal Import Data window. If you encounter a large number of errors, delete the Journal Import data from the GL_INTERFACE table, correct the information in the feeder or subledger system and run Journal Import again.

6. Close the period for each subledger. This prevents future subledger transactions from being posted to General Ledger in the same period.

7. Review and post the imported journal entries. You can review them online or in reports. The following reports will be usefull at this stage: Journal Batch Summary Report; General Journal Report; Journal Entry Report; Journal Line Report; Journal Source Report; Journals by Document Number Report (when document sequencing is used); Unposted Journals Report.

8. Perform reconciliations of subsidiary ledgers by reviewing and correcting balances. The following reports are useful to help you reconcile: Account Analysis with Payables Detail; Account Analysis with Subledger Detail; General Ledger Report; Posted Journals Report; Journals Report with Subledger Detail; Accrual Reconciliation Report.

9. Generate all recurring journals and step-down allocations. (Optional) If you did not generate and post your prior period reversals at the beginning of this period, be sure to generate reversals now.

NOTE

Although it is customary to post reversing entries at the beginning of a new period, many companies will leave this step as a period-end procedure.

10. Revalue balances to update foreign currency journals to your functional currency equivalents.

11. Post all journal entries, including: manual, recurring, step-down allocations, and reversals. Be sure to generate and post the step-down allocations in the correct order.

12. Review your posting results. The following reports are helpful: Posting Execution Report; Error Journals Report.

13. Update any unpostable journal entries and then post them again. Common reasons for unpostable batches include control total violations, posting to unopened periods, and having unbalanced journal entries.

14. All errors in the journal entry batches must be corrected and resubmitted for posting.

15. Run General Ledger reports, such as the Trial Balance reports, Account Analysis reports, and Journal reports. It is convienient to group period-end reports in a report set to maintain a consistent audit trail.

16. Translate balances to any defined currency if you need to report in foreign currencies.

17. Consolidate your subsidiary sets of books if you have multiple companies.

18. If you are performing a year-end close and your accounting calendar includes an adjusting period that represents the last day of the fiscal year, close the current period and open the adjusting period.

19. Create and post adjusting entries and accruals in the adjusting period.

20. Run Trial Balance reports and other General Ledger reports in the adjusting period after adjustments are made.

21. Close the last period of the fiscal year using the Open and Close Periods window.

22. Open the first period of the new fiscal year to launch a concurrent process to update account balances. Opening the first period of a new year automatically closes your income statement and posts the difference to your retained earnings account.

The period-end reports include a balance sheet, income statement, and statement of cash flow. In addition, companies produce a suite of management reports showing actual sales against budgeted sales and any other key indicators that managers need. These reports, whose layout and content are specific to your organization, are not available as standard reports in Oracle General Ledger; they must be defined as Financial Statement Generator (FSG) reports or possibly defined in Oracle Financial Analyzer if you are using this tool. It is important to manage and rationalize the number and volume of reports produced at period-end. If managers had their wish, you would probably have to produce three or four distinct reports per manager. The sheer volume of report output for a large organization would be overwhelming. Some big organizations, including Oracle, are migrating rapidly from a *push* organization, in which FSG reports are distributed to managers, to a *pull* organization, where managers look in a data warehouse to retrieve the figures they need.

Financial Reports

The trial balance ensures that total debits equal total credits. This is the basis of the double-entry bookkeeping system. It tells you whether or not your accounts balance. A simplified trial balance is shown in Table 3-4. The Grand Totals line at the bottom shows that the debits do indeed equal the credits. The figure itself, $1,652,000 in the example, does not have any useful significance for the company or its managers.

The balance sheet is a snapshot of the financial position of a company. It is one of the key reports included in regulatory reporting. Like most financial reports, it is used for external purposes by investors, customers, and creditors. The balance sheet demonstrates the following accounting principle:

Assets = Capital + Liability

Whereas the content is similar, the format and layout of the balance sheet vary from company to company. The essence, though, is to show all assets of the company with a total, and to show all capital and liabilities of the company with a total. The simplified trial balance shown in Table 3-4 has been recast as a balance sheet in Table 3-5. That there is not much difference between the two reports in this example is a consequence of the over-simplification of the layout. The totals on a balance sheet, in contrast to those shown on a trial balance, have major significance to the business and its managers.

Natural Account	Debit	Credit
Cash and Receivables	100,000	
Other Current Assets	140,000	
Plant and Equipment	120,000	
Land	40,000	
Investments	76,000	
Liabilities		60,000
Common Stock		250,000
Other Contributed Capital		47,000
Sales		1,290,000
Investment Income		3,000
Other Revenue		2,000
Salary and Wages	100,000	
Cost of Goods Sold	900,000	
Exchange Rate Losses	5,000	
Depreciation and Amortization	47,000	
Administration	5,000	
Provision for Bad Debt	119,000	
Grand Totals	**1,652,000**	**1,652,000**

TABLE 3-4. *A Simplified Trial Balance for a Manufacturing Company*

The Retained Earnings line, shown in Table 3-5, is usually included as a current period net income. As described earlier, the retained earnings are calculated at the end of the financial year by calculating the profit (or loss) for the year. The income statement, or profit and loss report, is the worksheet used by accountants to perform the following computation:

Profit = Total revenue – Total expense

A very basic income statement is shown in Table 3-6.

	Debit	Credit
Assets		
Cash and Receivables	100,000	
Other Current Assets	140,000	
Plant and Equipment	120,000	
Land	40,000	
Investments	76,000	
Total Assets	**476,000**	
Liabilities		60,000
Common Stock		250,000
Other Contributed Capital		47,000
Retained Earnings		119,000
Total Capital and Liabilities		**476,000**

TABLE 3-5.   *The Balance Sheet for the Same Manufacturing Company*

Accounting Methods

There are two main accounting methods. The *accrual method* records revenues and expenses when they are incurred—not when payment is received. For example, a sale on account would be recorded as revenue even though the customer has not paid the bill. The *cash basis method* records transactions when payment occurs, regardless of when the transaction takes place. For example, when the company receives the customer's check, revenue is recorded even though the goods were shipped two months earlier.

Generally Accepted Accounting Principles (GAAP) require companies to use the accrual method for financial reporting purposes; it is considered a more accurate depiction of a company's income and expenses. However, different companies may account for transactions using different accounting methods based on their own countries' laws and regulations. Oracle Financials have been developed to meet GAAP requirements as well as the special needs of different countries. For example, in Oracle Payables you can choose whether to record journal entries for invoices and payments on an accrual basis, a cash basis, or a combined basis. With combined basis

	Debit	Credit
Revenue		
Sales		1,290,000
Investment Income		3,000
Other Revenue		2,000
Total Revenue		**1,295,000**
Expenses		
Salary and Wages	100,000	
Cost of Goods Sold	900,000	
Exchange Rate Losses	5,000	
Depreciation and Amortization	47,000	
Administration	5,000	
Provision for Bad Debt	119,000	
Total Expense	**1,176,000**	
Profit		**119,000**

TABLE 3-6. *A Basic Income Statement, or, Profit and Loss Report*

accrual, journal entries are posted to one set of books, and cash basis journal entries are sent to a second set of books.

Average Balance Processing

General Ledger can automatically maintain average balances on an account-by-account basis for all balance sheet accounts. Averages are calculated from actuals, and are needed by some financial institutions for regulatory reporting. Average balance processing can be enabled for each set of books, and the average and standard balances can be stored in the same set. General Ledger stores Period Average-to-Date, Quarter Average-to-Date, Year Average-to-Date, and End of Day balances for every day. Average balances are updated each time journal entries are posted.

You can translate average balances to any reporting currency and consolidate average balances between accounting entities. Average balances can be reviewed online or in standard reports, and the General Ledger Financial Statement Generator (FSG) can be used to easily create custom financial reports that comply with the Federal Reserve's statutory reporting requirements. You can also reference average balances in formula journals, such as recurring journals and MassAllocations, and archive and purge average balances for any range of accounting periods.

General Ledger Setup

With Oracle General Ledger and the suite of Oracle Financials applications, you do not need custom programming to tailor your applications to reflect your enterprise's operations and policies or to keep pace with your changing business needs. All of this can be accomplished through standard setup of the application. You can, for example, create an unlimited number of charts of accounts to reflect the way you do business, use General Ledger's Account Hierarchy Editor to reorganize account structures with drag-and-drop ease, take advantage of user-definable flexible data fields to add new types of information to your database, and make your windows reflect the way you do business—all without programming. In addition, any changes you make are preserved through subsequent software upgrades—automatically.

The *Oracle Implementation Manual* is an essential source of information to help you implement Oracle Financials. It explains all the mandatory and optional steps, including those with dependencies on other setup steps. Also, every company ought to have an *Accounting Procedures Manual* that spells out how to create manual journals, accruals, and allocations. It should also explain the period closing process and year-end activities. Needless to say, the manual must be intimately tied to the Oracle processes. You should continually modify a draft of the manual throughout the setup process. It is especially important in testing. As part of cutover, make sure there is test data to check every procedure in the manual.

Open and Close Accounting Periods

Once you have defined the calendar with accounting periods, you are invited to open an accounting period. Be aware that once you have opened the very first period, you can never open a prior period. A common mistake is to open the current period during the setup, and then attempt to convert historic balances into prior periods. Unfortunately, by that stage it is too late to open any prior periods. To avoid this pitfall, get agreement on the earliest period that is ever likely to be used. Open that period, and then open all subsequent periods up to and including the current one. Then close all the prior periods to prevent accidental entry into a prior period. When the conversion of history is ready to take place, the pertinent prior periods can be reopened, and journals can be imported or keyed in. When the GL period remains "future-enterable," manufacturing, for example, has no problem transacting against it. If accounting accidentally opens, and then closes the period, manufacturing can no longer transact. This is an extremely important point, and great care should be taken to ensure that accounting be very careful not to open/close a period prematurely.

Setting Up Parents, Rollup Groups, and Summary Accounts

Value sets can be more than one-dimensional validation tools, especially in General Ledger. The user can define hierarchies of values through parent-child relationships. The Financial Statement Generator (FSG) and the Global Consolidation System (GCS) use the concept of rollup groups to simplify reporting. Unlike parent-child relationships, rollups go across all segments of the Accounting Flexfield.

Management reporting is the ultimate objective of General Ledger. It must be succinct—top management needs only the aggregate numbers. Oracle General Ledger uses several different devices to adapt its relational database, essentially flat in structure, to companies' hierarchical reporting needs. Figure 3-5 depicts the relationships graphically.

The sequence needed to define rollup groups is:

1. Define the flexfield segment format.

2. Define value sets for the flexfield values.

3. Define parent-child relationships over the individual segments within the Accounting Flexfield, to as many levels as appropriate.

4. Set up your set of books.

5. Determine what summaries will be required for reporting and online inquiry purposes. This is essential. The Oracle structures will support almost any reporting requirements that have been defined, but Oracle cannot be structured to anticipate requirements that have not been defined.

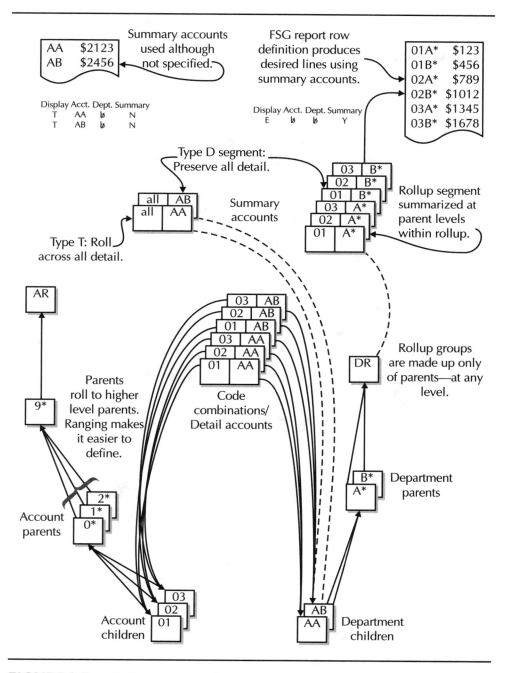

FIGURE 3-5. *Rollup group mechanics*

6. Ideally, assuming the reporting requirements are known in advance, define rollup groups before defining key segment values. See the discussion of parent-child relationships and rollup groups in the *Flexfields Reference Manual.*

7. Define summary accounts as required for the rollup groups. They are needed to support online inquiry and for performance purposes.

8. Define FSG reports. All report definitions use Accounting Flexfields, not rollup groups. The Accounting Flexfield may include parent segments, which fit the Accounting Flexfield structure. However, they take advantage of the summary accounts that have been defined via rollup groups and wildcards.

It is a user's responsibility to define parent-child relationships and rollups because they are wedded to the account and department number data, which users own.

Several independent hierarchies may be laid over the department structure. Three are shown in Figure 3-6.

Each hierarchy serves a different purpose:

■ Divisions are used for sales analysis. Many departments belong to the default division, 00, which is to say *no* division.

■ Locations equate to plant locations. Every staffed department belongs to a location. The location hierarchy is used to consolidate and compare plant operations.

■ Companies represent the formal structure of the corporation. Each department belongs to only one company. For that reason, companies can be used for balance sheet as well as profit-and-loss reporting.

■ Legal entities are one matrix rollup of companies. This rollup is useful for tax purposes.

■ Management is a second rollup of companies, representing the management structure at higher levels. Reports produced within this hierarchy are used for management purposes.

Figure 3-7 shows the parent-child and rollup groups defined on the account segment. These first-level parents roll into second-level parents

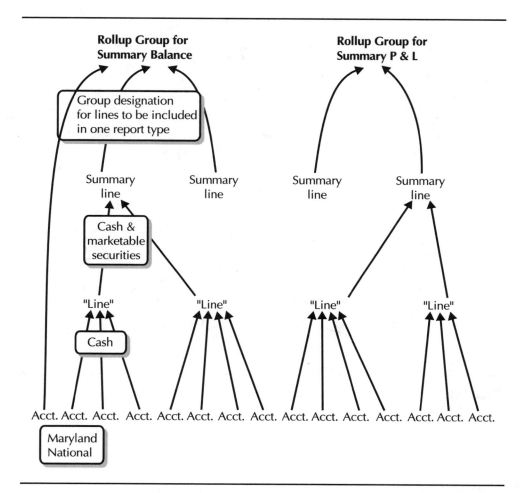

FIGURE 3-6.   *Account parent-child rollup*

used for more summary reports. First- and second-level parents may be combined in any combination into rollup groups, which may be used in specifying summary accounts. FSG reports can be set up to print only summary accounts within the account range specified for reporting. Doing this reduces the effort involved in specifying certain reports.

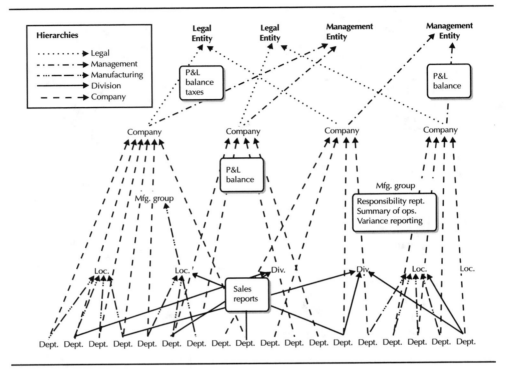

FIGURE 3-7. *Department segment, parent-child, and rollup groups*

Currency

For businesses operating in a global environment, Oracle General Ledger handles currency conversion rates, supports the euro, and tracking and reporting of balances in multiple currencies. You can enter daily conversion rates between any two currencies, regardless of your functional currency. To track transactions and account balances in multiple currencies, you can automatically replicate journals from your primary functional currency set of books into one or more foreign currency sets of books used for reporting purposes.

Accounting Flexfield Design— Best Practice

The accounts tracked by General Ledger are collectively referred to as the *chart of accounts.* The chart of accounts defines how your accounting information is categorized, collected, and reported. The first step in implementing Oracle General Ledger is setting up your chart of accounts. The design and use of your chart of accounts is crucial. It should fit the needs of your organization and allow for meaningful analysis. For example, if your company is small, a simple account structure with only two segments—one for account and one for department—may suffice. However, if you are a large corporation with multiple products and sales organizations, you need a more robust structure that includes additional segments for company, product, and region. When defining your chart of accounts, consider the following suggestions:

- Define a flexible account structure that accommodates your current organization and anticipates the way you will run your organization in the future.

- Define an account structure large enough to reflect the important aspects of your organization, but small enough to be manageable and meaningful.

- Define an account structure that accommodates and properly classifies information from your other financial information sources.

- Create an account structure that provides a logical ordering of values by grouping related accounts in the same range of values. Additionally, create an account structure that allows for expansion and development of new categories.

What to Consider

To arrive at an optimal design for your organization, there are many aspects to consider. Some of these aspects are discussed in the following sections. The discussion is intended as a road map, so that you may assess which areas are of relevance to your situation and focus further research on these topics. The *Oracle Applications Flexfield Manual* is a good source for detailed instructions. If you have not worked with Oracle Applications before, you are strongly advised to seek help in the initial design and implementation of your Key Flexfield. This task should be taken on by an experienced Oracle Financials functional consultant.

Reporting Needs

The setup of flexfield segments should support your reporting requirements and be part of a corporate-wide plan for financial reporting. Remember this major principle: Do not include segments that do not get fed from most subledgers. Also consider the corollary to this principle: Determine in advance which reporting will be done in subledgers and which will be done in Oracle General Ledger.

Organizational Structure

As mentioned in Chapter 2, the chart of accounts belongs to the set of books level in the organizational structure. Each set of books has only one Accounting Flexfield structure. That is to say, when you set about designing an Accounting Flexfield, you will already have in mind the legal entities, operational units, and inventory organizations that the Accounting Flexfield is going to support. So whether you are considering the entire enterprise or a subset of it, the important point is that you know in concrete terms which parts of the enterprise you are analyzing. Unless you know this you are liable to vacillate between the planned use of the organizational features in Financials and the proposed Accounting Flexfield. You will bounce back and forth without any objective way of choosing between alternatives. It is far better to get agreement on the planned use of the organizational features, and the number of servers and number of databases, and then venture forward from this solid foundation to design the Accounting Flexfield for each set of books.

Security

Often you will want to restrict which accounting transactions users can see and the range of accounts that they can post to. The primary level of data security within Oracle Financials is the Responsibility. Once a user chooses a Responsibility, he or she will only see the accounting transactions for the operating unit connected to that Responsibility. This takes care of which accounting transactions a user can see, in a way that does not depend on the design of the Accounting Flexfield. The segment level security feature is intended to restrict the range of accounts that users can post to. Security rules define ranges of account code combinations that are excluded, and then the rules are assigned to a Responsibility. All users of that Responsibility are restricted from entering or viewing that range of accounts. A common use is restricting the salary and wages accounts to the personnel department. Doing so ensures that confidential payroll data is not freely available to all users. Another use is for companies that have one chart of accounts but many sets of books or legal entities. These companies want to ensure that users do not inadvertently make a cross-company posting by using the wrong company code. A security rule can be set up for each Responsibility, restricting the range of company codes that can be entered to the companies that belong in that set of books. See Chapter 14 for more on flexfield validation and security.

As mentioned earlier, you can require that journal entries from any source be approved before posting with the Journal Approval System, and you can also control which users can post and reverse journals in Oracle General Ledger.

Code Combination Validation

Not every Accounting Flexfield (AFF) combination makes sense. For example, it may not make sense to put a department number on an asset account, because assets are owned by companies, not departments. It may not make sense for an overhead department, such as plant security, to post to a revenue account.

You set up cross-validation rules in Oracle to prevent creation of AFF combinations that do not make sense. The rules block out permissible and impermissible ranges of numbers. For asset accounts, the typical range of allowed departments is 000 to 000 (that is, none). It makes a simple rule.

Complex cross-validation rules can be an early warning sign that your proposed flexfield design is not optimal. Suppose you have two segments: one for sales region and another for Canadian province department. You would need complex rules to indicate that the combination of British Columbia and Eastern Region was invalid. Moreover, the rules could change. Your Central region could split into the Quebec and Ontario regions. In a good flexfield design, each segment (other than dependent segments) is reasonably independent of the others.

Values that Change over Time

The Accounting Flexfield is the basis for year-to-year comparisons. Change it and the comparisons become invalid. Plan your natural account segment so that it changes little over time. Accommodate change in this area through reporting devices and consolidations, not in the ledger itself. However, for all your planning, some reorganization is inevitable. Plan your departments in such a way that the rollups can be used for year-to-year comparisons even as the organizations within them are redefined.

Some segments have a limited life span, such as those for project, program, and funding. There are two ways to take an existing account code combination out of use. When you disable a segment value, Oracle will no longer create code combinations using that value, though you can still post to combinations that have already been created using it. For instance, when a project ends, you may assume it would be an error to create new code combinations using that project, though it could be proper to post adjustments for a while. You disable posting on a combination-by-combination basis. If you want no activity against a project, set the Disabled flag for every combination using that project value.

Plan how you will take segments and code combinations out of use. There are many places in the system where you specify default segment values to be used by Automatic Account Generation. It creates significant difficulties for your users if you disable one of these default values.

Summarization

Summarization can be accomplished with the Accounting Flexfield using several different mechanisms; assuming your analysis of reporting needs has revealed some need for summarization, you must decide which mechanism to use. Top management needs only the aggregate numbers to make their decisions. Because management reporting needs to be succinct, summarization plays a very important role in Oracle General Ledger. The following five mechanisms are available for summarization:

- Dependent segments
- Parent segment values
- Summary accounts
- Rollup groups
- Explicit calculations in FSG reports

Only the first of these, dependent segments, needs to be decided upon at the time the Accounting Flexfield is set up. However paradoxical as it may seem, do not restrict your attention to dependent segments, but rather plan how the other techniques are going to be used while you design your Accounting Flexfield. The reason for this is that parent segment values can often provide a more straightforward way of achieving the same result as dependent segments. To understand this, some explanation of the five mechanisms is needed.

A *dependent segment* is a segment whose meaning depends on a previous segment. A common example of dependent segments comes from airplane seat numbers. Airlines number the seat rows and allocate letters to designate window, center, or aisle seat. That way, Seat 14A is unique on the aircraft—row 14, window seat. In Oracle terminology 14A is two segments; the "seat" segment depends on the "row." A designation of *seat* alone is not sufficient to mark out a single seat on the aircraft. One could give a unique number to every seat on the plane, but then passengers would have no easy way of verifying if they have a window, center, or aisle seat until they board the plane. Seat 14B (coach) is a center seat, whereas 1B (first class) is on an aisle. Dependent segments are useful in this respect because they convey more meaning than an arbitrary numbering scheme. Use dependent account segments when you want a context-sensitive segment whose values have different meanings when you combine them with different values of the primary segment. A common use for a dependent segment is account and subaccount. Table 3-7 shows a basic chart of accounts using a subaccount dependent segment.

Subaccount 30 is both the Royal Bank of Scotland and Office Furniture. Which of these two meanings is relevant in any particular circumstance is given by the account code. The total Cash at Bank is the balance on the account 2800; the total Fixed Assets is the balance on the account 3060. The summarization is implicit in the scheme.

Dependent segments are the only form of summarization that reaches into the subledgers. Dependent segments are an integral part of the Accounting Flexfield, and if you use a dependent segment you must enter it at any point that you enter an account code combination. If you need reporting summarization within a segment value from a subledger, having a dependent segment is an elegant way of achieving it.

Often the dependent segment approach works well for some segment values but not for all. Some accounts fall neatly into the hierarchy of account and subaccount, but other accounts do not. It becomes laborious to enter

Account Code	Description	Subaccount Code	Description
2800	Cash at Bank	29	Standard Chartered Bank
2800	Cash at Bank	30	Royal Bank of Scotland
2800	Cash at Bank	31	ING Bank
2800	Cash at Bank	32	Citibank
3060	Fixed Assets	10	Machinery
3060	Fixed Assets	20	Buildings
3060	Fixed Assets	30	Office Furniture
3060	Fixed Assets	40	Vehicle Fleet

TABLE 3-7. *The Account Codes, with a Dependent Subaccount Segment*

the dependent segment value when in fact no value is appropriate. Reporting segments such as regions made up of many districts, or projects composed of subprojects, are more likely to be successful candidates for implementation as dependent segments. Unless the segment/subsegment hierarchy can be applied rigorously to all segment values, do not use dependent segments. The same effect can almost always be achieved using a single segment and parent accounts.

NOTE
A dependent segment can always be redesigned to avoid using the dependent segment feature of the Accounting Flexfield. Increase the length of the primary segment and incorporate the dependent segment into the primary segment.

The account and subaccount schema shown in Table 3-7 has been recast as an amalgamated account code in Table 3-8. Structured keys with hidden

Amalgamated Account Code	Description
280029	Cash at Standard Chartered Bank
280030	Cash at Royal Bank of Scotland
280031	Cash at ING Bank
280032	Cash at Citibank
306010	Fixed Assets – Machinery
306020	Fixed Assets – Buildings
306030	Fixed Assets – Office Furniture
306040	Fixed Assets – Vehicle Fleet

TABLE 3-8.   *Account Codes Designed without a Dependent Segment*

meanings such as these are frowned upon by relational design purists. From a practical point of view, users prefer structured codes, and there is no overriding reason from an application-implementation point of view to avoid building structure into a list of segment values. The codes are easier to learn and they convey a meaning—before too long accountants and users no longer need to see the description to recognize the account. Common sense tells us that only pairs of segments with a similar meaning are amalgamated. Account and subaccount segments are good candidates for amalgamation, whereas cost center and project are not.

The problem with dependent segments is their all-or-nothing hierarchy. You cannot switch it on for some values and switch it off for others. This capability, though, is exactly the forte of parent segment values.

Parent segment values, and their children, form a hierarchy within a segment. Parent segment values are like any other segment value, except they have other values defined as their children. The hierarchy is maintained in a simple drag-and-drop form called the Account Hierarchy Editor, as shown in the following illustration. Account Hierarchy Editor is accessed through ADI.

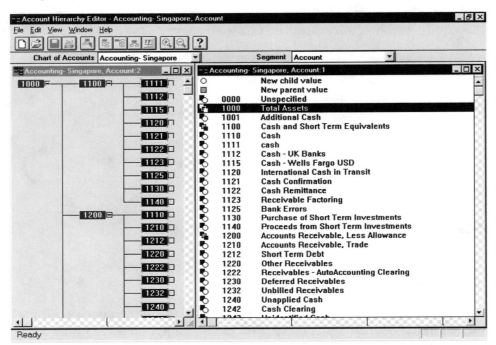

Table 3-9 shows how parent accounts might be introduced into the account code segment. Parents can be defined with any child value or range of child values. The child values do not need to be consecutive, and they do not need to be ranges. If the segment values have been assigned according to some logic, they will already contain an implicit structure, and the child ranges, as in this case, will fall neatly into consecutive ranges.

The balance on a parent account is equal to the sum of the balances on all its children. Be aware that a child value can belong to several parents, and that a parent itself can have a parent. The hierarchy can be as deep as you like. Oracle General Ledger does not store the balance of a parent account; the balance is calculated each time it is needed. For this reason the account balances of parent segment values are not available for online inquiry. This shortcoming of parent segment values is overcome by summary accounts.

Account Codes with Parents	Description	Child Range
280000	**Cash at Bank (Parent)**	**280001-280099**
280029	Cash at Standard Chartered Bank	
280030	Cash at Royal Bank of Scotland	
280031	Cash at ING Bank	
280032	Cash at Citibank	
306000	**Fixed Assets (Parent)**	**306001-306099**
306010	Fixed Assets – Machinery	
306020	Fixed Assets – Buildings	
306030	Fixed Assets – Office Furniture	
306040	Fixed Assets – Vehicle Fleet	

TABLE 3-9.   *Account Codes with the Introduction of Parent Accounts*

Summary accounts are account code combinations. You cannot post to summary accounts; the account balances associated with them are calculated by the system during posting to be the sum of other account code combinations. Exactly which accounts are summarized is determined by the summary account template; the template specifies whether to summarize all segment values into one value (which appears as *T* for Total) or whether to retain the detail for each segment of the Accounting Flexfield. A company with the Accounting Flexfield defined as *Company-Account-Department* could set up a summary account template *Total-Detail-Total.* The system would then maintain one summary account for each separate value of the Account segment. That way it would be possible to inquire about the balance of the summary account T-2800-T online, which would be the total Cash at Bank for all companies and departments; or the summary account T-3600-T, which would show the total Fixed Assets for the entire enterprise.

Summary account templates can be created or removed at any time, and there is no limit to the number that you can maintain at any one time. In contrast to parent segment values, summary accounts do have stored balances in the system. Whereas parent segment values encode a hierarchy within a segment, summary accounts create a hierarchy of flexfield combinations. Because summary accounts have stored balances, processes like generating FSG reports or generating consolidation batches can be processed faster if summary accounts have been used.

A *rollup group* is a collection of parent or child segment values. Rollup groups are a shorthand entry for a particular group of accounts.

Table 3-10 shows a comparison of features provided by the different methods of summarization.

Application Features

The Accounting Flexfield pervades Applications. Many application features add value to a particular Accounting Flexfield design. Your ability to use these features easily is closely related to your Accounting Flexfield design.

Three qualifiers single out three segments for special treatment by the Applications. As mentioned in Chapter 2, three different segments have to be qualified as the balancing segment, natural account segment, and cost center segment. The balancing segment is reserved for the segment that holds your company code, legal entity, or fund. General Ledger ensures that all journal entries balance for each value of the balancing segment that is referenced. Many reports, such as the General Ledger Trial Balance reports, either break on the balancing segment or have the balancing segment as a parameter. The year-end process that calculates retained earnings does so once for each value of the balancing segment.

The natural account qualifier determines which segment is categorized as asset, liability, owner's equity, revenue, or expense. Here again, many reports make hidden use of the natural account qualifier—the Trial Balance reports use it to determine which segment to report on; dozens of reports have an account segment range in their list of parameters.

It is not only the segment qualifiers that have a distinctive effect on application features. There are many mechanisms for generating default values for Accounting Flexfield segments. The effectiveness of these mechanisms hinges very often on the design of the flexfield. AutoAccounting is used in Oracle Receivables to automatically assign Accounting Flexfield codes for transaction accounts, such as receivables, freight, or revenue. The Flexbuilder tool can be used in an increasing number of circumstances to intelligently generate Accounting Flexfield values. Anyone planning to use these features should be aware of the implications while designing their Accounting Flexfield.

	Dependent Segments	Parent Segment Values	Rollup Groups	Summary Accounts	Explicit Calculations in Reports
Is the feature only visible in GL?	No	Yes	Yes	Yes	No
Is reorganization of the hierarchy possible?	No	Easy	Easy	No	Not without reprogramming
Are summarized numbers stored in GL?	Yes	No	No	Yes	No
Is posting possible at all levels of the hierarchy?	Yes	Yes	No	No	No
Are account balances available by online inquiry?	No	No	No	Yes	No
Are account balances available using FSG?	Yes	Yes	Yes	Yes	Yes
Are account balances available in Allocation formulas?	No	Yes	No	Yes	No

TABLE 3-10. *Comparison of Various Mechanisms for Summarization*

Legacy System Analysis

You should consider which data was collected by the old system. Was it adequate or were there gaps that prevented certain sales analyses? What gaps were there? Gaps in the old system should be filled by reporting segments in the new system.

An Externally Imposed Chart of Accounts

Some countries, like France, impose a chart of accounts, or at least an account numbering scheme, for reporting purposes. Whereas a French company might want to use the nationally imposed chart of accounts throughout its organization, a multinational company with its own chart of accounts frequently needs to meet the reporting requirement of the host nations where it conducts business. Most reporting requirements can be satisfied by Oracle General Ledger in the following way: two sets of books are set up—one with the company's own chart of accounts and one with the statutory French chart of accounts. All accounting entries are made and processed in the first set of books. After period-end, the balances are transferred to the second, statutory set of books, using Oracle General Ledger's Global Consolidation System (GCS). The statutory reports are then produced from the second set of books, based on the statutory chart of accounts. You can use the GCS to consolidate between any chart of accounts structure. However, if some reports can be satisfied only from the subledgers, then those subledgers must have a sense of the French accounting structure. Since it gets its AFF structure from the ledger, you must support it with a French-structure General Ledger chart of accounts. You would post to the French set of books, produce tax reports from the French books, and then consolidate to another set for management reporting.

After completing your consolidations, you can review consolidated balances online and drill down to the subsidiary balances that you consolidated. The Consolidation Hierarchy Viewer displays multilevel consolidation structures in an expandable hierarchical format, enabling you to immediately visualize and analyze the entire consolidation structure, no matter how many intermediate parents it contains.

Good Design Principles

It is easier to build flexibility into your account structure during setup than to try to change your account structure in the future. After considering the preceding topics, you are in a good position to start designing your Accounting Flexfield. The design will be complete when you have finalized the number of segments, their order and length, the valid values for each one, and the separator symbol to appear between them.

The Number of Segments

Commercial businesses all face similar accounting and management challenges, so it is reasonable to expect that the same sort of business dimensions will apply to different companies. You may find that the classifications are different from company to company, but the underlying dimensions are the same. Nonbusiness organizations operate in similar if not identical circumstances. They need to track the same sorts of things, but often name them differently. Table 3-11 lists common business dimensions for both business and nonbusiness organizations. Each of these dimensions will become a separate segment in the Accounting Flexfield.

The Order of Segments

The order you assign the segments of the Account Flexfield will determine their order of appearance on reports and screens. Segments that are frequently defaulted should appear towards the end of the flexfield. This will increase data entry speed.

Some claims have been made that the order of the segments has an effect on performance. This may be true but only in a badly tuned application database. In a well-tuned application the order of the segments should make no difference to the application performance. Application tuning is a large topic that falls outside the scope of this handbook. Note, however, that the following tuning parameters should be set within the application before a DBA tunes the database by creating new indexes and such:

■ In Oracle General Ledger you should run the Optimizer after you create a large number of segment values or add or delete summary templates. The Optimizer stores statistics and creates indexes, and improves the performance of long-running programs like the FSG, Posting, and MassAllocations.

■ You can tune Journal Import control parameters in the Define Concurrent Program Controls window.

Dimension	Business	Nonbusiness
Legal entity	Company	Fund
Natural account	Account	Account
Responsibility	Cost center or department	Program
Sales analysis	Product Distribution channel	
Geography	Region or district	
Intercompany	Intercompany	
Project	Project	Funding vehicle
Fiscal reporting	Tax code	Appropriation year

TABLE 3-11. *Common Segments in Business and Nonbusiness Organizations*

Length of Each Segment

Consider the structure of values you plan to maintain within the segment. For example, you might use a three-character segment to capture project information and classify your projects so that all administrative projects are in the 100 to 199 range, all facilities projects are in the 200 to 299 range, and so on. If you develop more than ten classifications of projects, you will run out of values within this segment. You might want to add an extra character to the size of each segment to anticipate future needs.

If you anticipate frequent restructurings, which require you to disable values and enable new ones, you should allow for enough digits to avoid having to recycle values. For example, if you disable old cost centers and enable new ones frequently, you will "use up" cost center values quickly. You should therefore use a larger maximum size for your cost center value set, so that you can have more available values. For example, three digits would allow you to create 1,000 different cost centers (numbered 000 to 999).

Defining Valid Segment Values

Is a value required for a segment? Even if a particular dimension cannot be assigned a value, it is usual to implement the segment with the validation *Value required = Yes,* and to create a segment value of zeros, *00000,* meaning

None or *Not Specified.* It is unwise to allow a Not Specified value for either the segment you specify as the natural account or the company (balancing) segment. Such values allow users to post to a ghost account in a ghost company, which sooner if not later would have to be explained.

For each segment you must define a value set, which restricts the valid values that can be entered. The value set can be either numeric or alphanumeric. You should set up alphanumeric value sets, because summary accounts use the value *T* to represent Total. However, the segment values you actually use should be numeric, if at all possible. Numeric segment values can be keyed far faster than alphanumeric values. It is also much easier to specify ranges with numbers than with letters, and ranges are extremely useful in rollup groups, parent-child relationships, and FSG reports.

To reduce maintenance and maintain consistency between sets of books, you can reuse value sets when defining multiple charts of accounts. Using the same value sets allows two different sets of books to reference the same segment values and descriptions for a specified segment. For example, the values in your natural account segment, such as 1000 for Cash and 2100 for Accounts Payable, may be equally applicable to each of your sets of books. Ideally, when you set up a new set of books you should consider how you will map your new Accounting Flexfield segments for consolidation. When a common natural account segment is used between sets of books, it is easier to map account balances from your subsidiary sets of books to a consolidating entity.

Cross-Validation Rules

Not every Accounting Flexfield combination makes sense. For example, if your organization manufactures both computer equipment and trucks, you might want to prevent the creation of "hybrid" part numbers for objects such as "truck keyboards" or "CPU headlights." To prevent users from entering invalid combinations of segments, Oracle General Ledger allows you to set up cross-validation rules. Cross-validation rules define whether a value of a particular segment can be combined with specific values of other segments.

The Separator

The choice of a suitable symbol to separate the segment values is not trivial. For quick data entry, choose numeric segment values followed by a period ("."; *full-stop* in British English). That way the entire Accounting Flexfield can be entered from the numeric keypad on the keyboard. For example, the numeric account code combination

```
01.320.420.4110.000.0000
```

is significantly faster to enter than an alphanumeric combination such as

```
USA/NYC/420/4110/NON/NONE
```

Maintenance

Your account structure and Accounting Flexfield must be maintained as your business grows and changes. Oracle General Ledger reduces the effort of maintenance through the Mass Maintenance Workbench, which allows you to move balances from one account to another, or merge balances from multiple accounts into a single account, while maintaining financial integrity between Oracle General Ledger and its subledgers. You can also automatically create new account combinations based on existing combinations. In addition, Oracle General Ledger allows you to create new mass allocations and mass budgets by copying existing definitions and then making incremental modifications.

What to Avoid

Good design is like elegance and beauty—it is hard to define but everyone recognizes it when they see it. It is easier to be specific about what contributes to a bad design. The following pitfalls should be avoided.

Accounting Flexfields That Are Too Long

The theoretical maximum length of the Accounting Flexfield is a massive 7,229 characters (30 segments × 240 characters + 29 separators). A practical limit is much smaller, as a long Accounting Flexfield becomes unwieldy and tiresome to enter. Some reports in Oracle General Ledger report only the first 30 characters of the Accounting Flexfield. If the length of your flexfield (all the segments plus the separator between the segments) is longer than 30 characters, these reports will be less useful to your organization; therefore it makes sense to define your Accounting Flexfield to be fewer than 30 characters.

Two Segments Used for the Same Thing

Group similar business dimensions into one segment. For example, you need only one segment to record and report on both districts and regions. Because regions are simply groups of districts, you can easily create regions within a district segment by defining a parent for each region, with the relevant districts as children. Use these parents when defining summary accounts to maintain account balances and when reporting hierarchies to perform regional reporting. This method accommodates reorganizations. If you want to move Berlin into the East German region, you simply redefine your parents so that Berlin rolls up into the East German region. This method also avoids excessive cross-validation rules.

Poorly Defined Segment Usage

Ensure that the use and meaning of a segment is well understood. Check that people are referring to the same thing when they say "Southern region" or "headquarters cost center." This concern may seem trivial, but confusion can lead to a rapid decline in the usefulness of stored data. Consider geographic location. What exactly is being recorded? Is it the location of the salesperson who made the sale or the location of the customer? The two may not be the same. For example, a salesperson for Gas Turbine Limited (GTL) based in the U.K. makes a sale to a customer in the Middle East. The U.K. regional sales manager will want to see total sales for all salespeople, irrespective of customer location. There has been a recent Middle East marketing campaign. The marketing manager will want to see the effectiveness of the campaign by monitoring sales by customer location. The marketing manager will not see the expected increase in Middle East sales if that sale is accounted for as U.K. revenue. Suppose that the company that bought the gas turbine calls the local representative office of GTL in the Middle East for engineering support. The cost of providing the support is allocated to the Middle East region. The revenue is accounted for against the U.K., and the maintenance costs charged to the Middle East. It would be very difficult to determine if conducting business in the Middle East is a profitable venture for GTL. Insight into the business is lost by the lack of clarity in the segment definition.

In the GTL example, staff had not realized that they were dealing with two geographic splits—salesperson location and customer location. Look for early warnings that a segment definition is unclear or ambiguous. Does the choice of segment value seem arbitrary or are there two equally good choices and no objective way to choose between them?

Two segments that genuinely represent the same dimension should be combined into one segment. Two distinct business dimensions should never be combined, however, even if they appear superficially to be the same. The design and use of the Accounting Flexfield is crucial. Failure to optimize the structure of the Accounting Flexfield is a primary reason implementations do not deliver the benefits that were originally envisioned.

General Ledger Reporting

Oracle General Ledger increases your decision-making capabilities by ensuring that the right business information reaches the right people at the right time. Oracle provides sophisticated operational and financial reporting tools that include proven, high-volume reporting capabilities, interchangeable report components, desktop extensibility for customizing standard reports, and powerful server-based processing.

A rich range of reporting techniques can be brought into action in concert with Oracle General Ledger. In addition to a suite of standard reports, Oracle General Ledger has its own integrated report generator: the Financial Statement Generator. There are many standard reports, including Trial Balance reports, General Ledger reports, Journal reports, Budget reports, and Consolidation reports. There are no predefined balance sheet or income statement reports. If your organization demands "what-if" reporting or forecasts, the native reporting features of Oracle General Ledger will probably not be powerful enough. You can consider exporting data to Financial Analyzer, which provides multidimensional financial analysis that is beyond the intended scope of Oracle General Ledger, or you can try downloading balances to a spreadsheet via the Applications Desktop Integrator (ADI).

Financial Statement Generator

The example balance sheet in Figure 3-8 is typical of the style of report that the Financial Statement Generator (FSG) can produce. This is an end user report generator. Business people should be able to define and run their own finance reports without intervention from the MIS department. At the same time, FSG security prevents users from viewing data for accounts to which they have no access.

```
                        U.S. Operations      Date: 02-JUL-1999 11:28:35
                         Balance Sheet                     Page:    1
                      Current Period: JUN-99
```

(Currency: USD)

	JUN-99 Actual	DEC-98 Actual
ASSETS		
Current Assets		
Cash and short-term equivalents	995,787	840,908
Accounts receivable, less allowance	899,942	1,084,858
Other current assets	169,995	171,560
Inventory	168,919	187,139
Total Current Assets	2,234,643	2,284,465
Long-term cash investments	15,039	41,963
Fixed assets, less depreciation	731,565	685,754
Other assets	98,962	99,072
Intercompany assets	250,408	245,989
Total Assets	**3,330,617**	**3,357,243**
LIABILITIES & EQUITY		
Current Liabilities		
Notes payable	5,795	5,623
Accounts payable	165,820	169,895
Income taxes payable	125,051	181,999
Accrued compensation & benefits	474,634	434,435
Other current liabilities	566,715	663,012
Total Current Liabilities	1,308,015	1,454,964
Long-term debt	853	897
Other long-term liabilities	22,012	21,726
Deferred income taxes	3,884	9,207
Total Liabilities	1,364,764	1,486,794
Shareholders' equity		
Common stock	1,995,853	1,870,449
Total Equity	1,995,853	1,870,449
Total Liabilities & Equity	**3,330,617**	**3,357,243**

FIGURE 3-8.   *A sample FSG report*

The FSG is built on two premises: it reports only on data in General Ledger, and it provides granularity only down to the account balance per Accounting Flexfield combination. Within the bounds of these two premises, you can define almost any report data and layout you want. That said, report generation with the FSG is not as simple as using PC desktop tools, and the final result may not be as elegantly formatted. For this reason the FSG often falls short on the original promise to be a business manager's tool. If report presentation is a major concern, then the Applications Desktop Integrator (ADI) is a more appropriate tool. ADI's report wizard provides a spreadsheet-based interface to the FSG.

Why Use the FSG?

Oracle realizes that it would be impossible to design one version of the financial reports that would meet the needs of all its customers. Some accountants include in the cost of a fixed asset not only its net invoice price, but also its acquisition and installation expenses. Others do not. These fine distinctions could not be covered by one or two standard balance sheets. Instead, Oracle has provided the FSG, a complex and powerful report generator that can produce tabular reports of almost any data. You will not find a balance sheet or income statement in the list of standard reports within Oracle General Ledger, but such reports can be produced with FSG.

FSG report output is not always the most attractive and sometimes it is important for reports to look good. The alternatives to using the FSG are to export data to Oracle Financial Analyzer and use the reporting tools that Oracle Express provides, to program custom reports in Oracle*Reports, or to use ADI to apply format themes to your reports and publish them to a Website or spreadsheet.

Each of these alternatives has its disadvantages: Oracle Financial Analyzer and spreadsheets involve the overhead of transferring data and keeping a duplicate copy; Oracle*Reports programs have to be written from a zero start point, and all the business logic, accounts to summarize, and accounts to show in detail are often stored in the program and not as data. That means that modification can be a programmer task and not an end user task.

FSG Components

The components of an FSG report are similar to spreadsheet rows, columns, and formulas. Report generation proceeds in a two-step process: define the report components, and then run the report. The next time you need the same report layout, you do not need to define the report components again; you can simply run the stored report definition for a new accounting period. The way report components can be recycled and reused is a big advantage that FSG has over custom programming. A report includes the following independent components:

- Row set
- Column set
- Content set
- Row order
- Display set

The simplest reports are defined by a row set and a standard column set. Optionally, you can define your own custom column set. Also, you can add a content set, row order, or display set to enhance the report or refine the information in the report.

Reporting with the FSG is a mix-and-modify, recycle-and-reuse activity. A new report can be defined simply by mixing an existing row set with an existing column set. If what you need is similar to what you had previously, but you now want comparison-to-the-budget figures as well as actuals, then simply copy the column set and modify it to include a column for budget and a column for variance. The new report layout reuses the old row set without any extra effort by you.

The FSG Concept

The Financial Statement Generator is a tool for reporting on account balances by period. It cannot report on individual journal entries in General Ledger. Accounting data can be visualized as an array of cells, as shown in Figure 3-9. The array is like a large pile of dice, each one holding an account balance according to its position in the structure. The three dimensions that make up the array are the Accounting Flexfield, accounting periods, and the type of balance. In FSG terminology, the Accounting Flexfield dimension becomes a row set, while the type of balance is encoded into the column set. The reporting period is supplied by the user at run time.

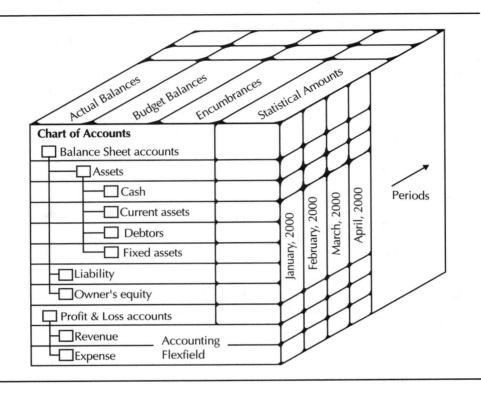

FIGURE 3-9. *Visualization of the three reporting dimensions*

Reports generated with the FSG can cut, slice, sort, and summarize the dice in all ways imaginable. However, the FSG cannot show more detail than allowed by the three dimensions: Accounting Flexfield, accounting periods, and the type of balance. None of the dice can be broken down into smaller units, such as individual journal transactions within a period. Account balances are balances, and no transaction detail is available. Periods cannot be split into weeks or days, and the chart of accounts cannot be split by attributes that are not contained as segments.

Defining Reports

Many users commit the error of approaching FSG the same way as custom report development with a regular programming tool. After an extensive effort to analyze all user requirements across the company, a finite number of reports are designed with a fixed layout and purpose. Intended to meet as many user requirements as possible, the reports are created as FSG reports and made available for the users.

Inevitably, such reports will not satisfy all the users, because compromises had to be made during the design, and, as the business develops and grows, the reports are either never used or fall slowly into disuse. A better approach, for which the FSG is ideally suited, is to provide adequate training to end users and delegate the responsibility for defining reports to the people who actually work with the report output. To prevent users from going off on their own and duplicating each other's work, some central coordination can be provided for allocations and standard row sets.

A report is defined by specifying the report objects FSG should use to build the report. Once you define and save a report, you can use it any time— to run the report, define a report set, or copy and save it as a new report.

Running FSG Reports

To run an individual report, follow these steps:

1. Navigate to the Run Financial Reports window, shown in Figure 3-10.

2. Choose Individual Reports, Single Report Set, or Multiple Report Set from the pull-down list.

3. Enter the name of a predefined FSG report.

4. Specify the report parameters, such as Period, Currency, Segment Override, and Rounding Option.

5. Press the Submit button.

The report is submitted as a job on the Concurrent Manager request list. If you press the Define Ad Hoc Report button, you can specify a row set and column set to be used to generate a report, without first having to link these two as a predefined FSG report.

REMEMBER
Define ad hoc financial reports, as necessary, to meet one-time reporting needs.

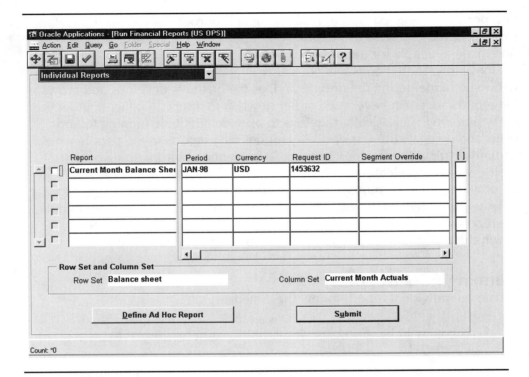

FIGURE 3-10. *The Run Financial Reports window*

More on FSG Techniques

Building a basic FSG report is straightforward. The tools used can be extended to produce delimited output that can be transferred directly to a spreadsheet. If you build new FSGs regularly, you will want to reuse report components like row sets, and, to avoid needless duplication of calculation, you will want to build the business logic into parent values and not FSG formulas. These advanced techniques are explained next.

PRODUCING SPREADSHEET-COMPLIANT OUTPUT   You can download FSG report output into a spreadsheet on your personal computer. When you define the report, or when you run the report, choose Spreadsheet as the output option. FSG produces the report in a tab-delimited format, so that report columns get interpreted as spreadsheet columns when you load the report file into a spreadsheet. Once imported into a spreadsheet, the numbers can be made visually distinctive using the text formatting tricks and graphics that are available in a spreadsheet but not in the FSG. The ADI request center has further simplified the process of publishing report output to the Web or a spreadsheet.

REUSING ROW SETS   Row sets contain knowledge and logic about your company in a way that other components such as column sets and content sets do not. This attribute derives from the fact that the row set specifies which accounts appear and in which sequence and which detail accounts are summarized into headings. If you have many row sets, each containing the same logic, you increase the maintenance workload that kicks in when your business logic changes. This creates unwanted opportunity for your reports logic to miss segment values in calculated aggregate results, even though the underlying numbers are correct. For this reason, it makes sense to reuse each row set in as many report definitions as is feasible. Define a row set for each distinct report family: balance sheet, income statement, cash flow, contribution analysis, source and application of funds, and so on. But avoid the temptation to have several balance sheet row sets, all of which are similar but not identical. You can still generate several different balance sheet reports—by combining the single row set with different column sets, or specifying that parent values should be expanded at run time, or overlaying a content set to produce a balance sheet for each cost center.

This might seem to contradict earlier advice to delegate the report definition task to the end users, inviting them to do whatever they like. But normally what happens is that a single financial accountant will probably be in charge of the balance sheet row set; a treasury manager will be responsible for the cash flow report row set; and a cost accountant will be taking care of contribution reporting. They are all masters of their own sphere of interest.

WHERE TO STORE BUSINESS LOGIC   Maintainability is key. If business logic changes, it only needs to be changed in one place. The logic available in parent values is available for all reports without having to be repeated in each row set definition. Therefore, business logic should be built into parent values and not contained within the FSG setup. On the other hand, the math capability behind each row of a row set can legitimately be used for calculating report totals, variances between actual and budget, or percentage figures. These formulas cannot be put into parent accounts, which cater only to summation, and not subtraction or division.

FSG TRANSFER Any Financial Statement Generator report object, report, or report set can be copied between databases. This capability eliminates the need to rekey report definitions in multiple databases. For example, you can define FSG reports in a test system while implementing General Ledger, then automatically transfer those reports to your production system.

FSG-RELATED PROFILE OPTIONS Three user profile options control the behavior of the FSG:

- FSG: Allow Portrait print style
- FSG: Expand Parent Values
- FSG: Message Detail

FSG: Message Detail can be useful if your report did not produce the output you were expecting, and you want to figure out why and fix it. Initially, a visual check of the report components might be enough to identify the problem, which might be an incorrectly specified range of accounts or a wrong calculation. If you have examined the report components and still cannot find the problem, you can access the FSG: Message Detail profile option. This profile option controls the degree of detail that appears in the message log file while your report runs. The default value for this profile is Minimal, which prints only the error messages in the log file. If you change the profile option to Full, you get detail memory figures, detail timings, and SQL statements, which are useful for report debugging.

REPORT LISTINGS ON FSG COMPONENTS A range of report listings of FSG components helps you debug and fine-tune report definitions. For example, the Where Used report shows where specific segment values are used in row sets, column sets, and content sets. If you are considering changing the use of an account code or redefining a parent value in the account segment, you can use this report to quickly tell you which predefined FSG reports will be impacted, and then use this information as the basis for modifying these reports, if necessary.

Oracle Financial Analyzer

Oracle Financial Analyzer is an online analytical processing (OLAP) tool used for planning, analyzing, and reporting corporate financial data. It uses a multidimensional data model that is ideal for online analysis. With the Oracle Express multidimensional database at its core, Oracle Financial Analyzer lets you set up a customized system that reflects your corporation's unique organizational structure and facilitates the management of your financial data at all business levels. It handles organizational consolidations across multiple hierarchies and automatically performs line item and time aggregations. The Financial Analyzer uses a separate database from the Oracle General Ledger database, an arrangement that necessitates the overhead of periodically transferring the data and creates the possibility of the two databases getting out of sync. This overhead has to be weighed against the advantages of the additional tools. Financial Analyzer provides some very powerful functions for analyzing and presenting financial data capabilities that are beyond the intended scope of Oracle General Ledger. Oracle Financial Analyzer's budget features are mentioned in Chapter 4.

Whereas data in Oracle General Ledger is cataloged according to Accounting Flexfield segments and accounting period, segments and periods in Oracle Financial Analyzer become dimensions. Dimensions and the different values that dimensions may take on are referred to as *meta data* in Oracle Financial Analyzer. When you first install Financial Analyzer there are no dimensions or dimension values defined. The Financial Analyzer meta data is transferred from Oracle General Ledger automatically when you first transfer account balances. The elegance of Financial Analyzer comes from its ability to treat all dimensions as equal. Oracle General Ledger can relatively easily produce a report with accounts down the left-hand side and different periods across the top. Imagine you need to produce an inverted report with periods down the page and account codes across the top. This type of work is where Oracle Financial Analyzer begins to shows its strength. Similarly, the normal time comparisons in Oracle General Ledger are year-to-date, or current period versus preceding. Imagine an industry that is cyclical but has a natural rhythm that is something other than a straightforward yearly cycle. An oil industry executive may well want a like-for-like comparison with a previous period when the crude oil spot price was at the same level. An income statement comparison of the periods April 1994 and January 1998 (when oil was about $16 per barrel, even though it rose to over $26 in between) would be quick and simple with Financial Analyzer. Yet again, the dimensions can be further aggregated using hierarchies and models in Oracle Financial Analyzer.

The integration between Oracle General Ledger and Oracle Financial Analyzer has been improved in Release 11. You can now transfer summary balances, average balances, encumbrances, and statistics as well as detail balances.

The Applications Desktop Integrator (ADI)

The ADI gives users an alternative spreadsheet-based front end to perform full cycle accounting. Most functions can be performed in a disconnected mode. You can create budgets and use a flexfield pop-up window to enter and validate new budget accounts. Segment value security is enforced for accounts included in your budget worksheet. You can record transactions and define and publish reports from any application to a Website, a spreadsheet, or a standard text document. ADI includes theme formats you can apply to your reports as well as custom formatting you can apply to individual cells in both spreadsheet and Web report output. After reports are completed, you can perform data pivoting and account drill-down to analyze your financial results in a multidimensional user interface.

Oracle General Ledger Data Model

This section contains a brief description of the transaction tables in the Oracle General Ledger module. If you need to write custom extract scripts or GL reports, you should have an understanding of the GL database layout and how the accounting data is stored.

Table 3-12 lists the transaction tables in Oracle General Ledger and their contents. Journals are stored in the three tables GL_ JE_BATCHES, GL_ JE_HEADERS, and GL_ JE_LINES. A journal batch is a group of related journals that are posted together. The period in which the journals belong is

Table Name	Contents
GL_ JE_BATCHES	Journal batches
GL_ JE_HEADERS	Journals
GL_ JE_LINES	Journal lines
GL_BALANCES	Balances for every code combination, currency, and period

TABLE 3-12. *Transaction Tables in Oracle General Ledger*

stored at batch level. Each journal in a batch gives rise to a separate record in the GL_ JE_HEADERS table.

TIP
Whereas GL_JE_BATCHES are called journal batches *on the Oracle General Ledger forms, and GL_ JE_LINES are referred to as* journal lines, *the records stored in GL_ JE_HEADERS are simply referred to as* journals *on the application forms.*

A *journal* is a group of journal lines that balance. The sum of the debits is equal to the sum of the credits. The currency code is stored at journal level. The GL_JE_LINES table holds a record for each journal line. The lines record the accounted amounts, either debit or credit, and the account code combination that the amount will be posted to.

Chapter 2 explained how a set of books is defined as an Accounting Flexfield, a currency, and a calendar. In Figure 3-11 you can see the intricate relationship between a set of books and the GL_BALANCES table. A record in the GL_BALANCES table is the balance for a specific account code combination for a specific period and currency. Balances, therefore, belong to a set of books.

FSG reporting as well as much of your own custom reporting is driven by balance rather than transaction data. Here again, the table structure is simple. Table 3-13 lists the major tables you need.

Table Name	Contents
GL_SETS_OF_BOOKS	A row for each set of books
GL_PERIODS	A row for each calendar period
GL_CODE_COMBINATIONS	All the Account Flexfield segment values
FND_CURRENCIES	A row for each currency
GL_BALANCES	Balances for every account code, currency, and period combination

TABLE 3-13. *The GL_BALANCES and Related Tables*

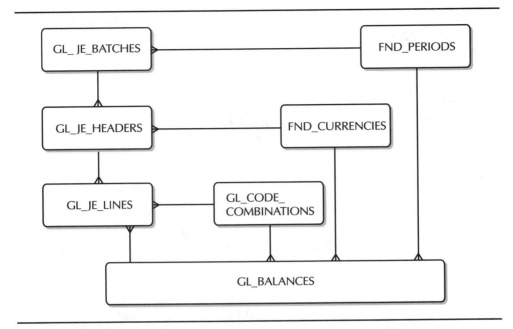

FIGURE 3-11. *Oracle General Ledger data diagram*

The first four tables help you select what you need out of GL_BALANCES, the repository where the actual balance numbers are held.

The Posting Process

The posting process takes a journal batch and updates the account balances in GL_BALANCES according to all the individual debits and credits that are contained in the GL_ JE_LINES tables belonging to that journal batch. Once the journal batch has been posted, the attribute GL_BATCHES.POSTED is set to Yes, so that it cannot be posted a second time.

Each of the balances stored in GL_BALANCES has been calculated from summing the relevant records in GL_ JE_LINES. The GL_BALANCES table is used to improve performance. Many processes, such as standard reporting and all FSG reporting, require the use of account balances that are contained in the GL_BALANCES table.

Without a balances tables the system would have to recalculate the balance each time it was needed by summing the journal lines. Calculating the balance once and then storing the value provides a much better use of CPU processing power.

Conversion from Legacy Systems

The strength of Oracle's General Ledger and the Oracle Applications lies in their superior technology and software architecture. Oracle products are built according to open industry standards that provide flexibility, high performance, and extensibility. You can easily migrate from your legacy system to Oracle Applications, or you can integrate Oracle Applications with your existing third-party products via numerous open interfaces.

Unless you are using Oracle General Ledger from day one of operations, you will have some form of conversion to perform—for example, transferring account balances or transaction history from a legacy system. Your conversion plan needs to recognize the requirement to retain an audit trail of prior years' data. So, before you perform your conversion, make sure you have an audit trail of prior years' data, such as hard-copy journal reports and archived copies of the legacy system files. It may be useful to put them into spreadsheet or desktop database systems to help accountants access them more easily.

Though prior-year budgets can be converted as easily as balances, it is uncommon to bring them forward via automated conversion scripts. Most users are content to import what they need into Oracle from the spreadsheets in which they are developed.

Converting Historical Data

There are three basic options as to how much balance history to convert: none, back to the start of the financial year, or back through prior years. Be guided by your reporting needs. However, bear in mind that once you have a program in place to convert any historical period, you can pretty much convert as many periods as you want. A conversion program uses legacy data to generate one journal per accounting period. Complexities arise if there are multiple sources of legacy systems (both a legacy financial system and a legacy cost accounting system, for example). Conversion will need to merge both systems. The base data in all cases is an account trial balance from the legacy systems. You may need to map accounts between legacy and new systems. If you are really lucky, the accounts will map one-to-one, or many-to-one—in which case it is simply a matter of sorting and summing to produce the new account balances. If the mapping is one-to-many (as is the case if the new chart of accounts carries more detail and finer graduations than the old), you must inject some logic into the conversion to split the balances. It is not always possible to split them precisely in half; most end users will be pragmatic about this. The following techniques are for mimicking a one-to-many mapping:

- Posting legacy balances to parent accounts, when parent accounts in Oracle are a closer one-to-one match to the legacy accounts.

- Injecting the splitting rules into the conversion by allowing users to explicitly enter a splitting factor in transit between the legacy and new system.

- Coding the logic into the conversion programs, using whatever extra data or algorithms that are necessary.

The maximum extent of transaction conversion is usually this: the user will want to translate and repost current-year journals in Oracle. It is useful to have a whole years' journals available under a single system.

Balances versus Transaction Detail

Most users convert little or no transaction history. It is only really useful when the Oracle system will post in detail, when there are subledgers to exploit drill-down, and when transactions can be converted for the subledgers as well. This combination will almost never happen. Exceptions exist, of course. Clearing accounts, for example, will need their detail transaction history in order to be useful after conversion. For the vast majority of situations, transferring balances is sufficient, and users do not need the transaction history.

Opening Balances and Movements

Whether you are transferring balances or transaction history, the same method is used: you import journals via the Journal Import interface. To that extent, even if you are loading balances, nothing is loaded directly into the GL_BALANCES table (there is no interface for that); the balance amounts are cast into the form of a journal and loaded and posted in the normal way. The balances journal is constructed to have a journal line for each distinct Accounting Flexfield that you intend to load. The amount for a line within the journal is the current period balance less the prior period balance (called the *movement*), so the year-to-date numbers are always right. The exception is the first period that you choose to convert. Into this period you must post an open balance as well as a movement. Open balance plus movement is equal to closing balance, so you can also choose to post only a closing balance into the first period and a movement in all subsequent periods. Either way, the ledgers will balance because the legacy ledger was balanced.

TIP
Clean up the data in the legacy system as much as possible before a conversion. At least, make sure that the legacy ledger balances and reconciles internally. Turn off suspense accounting temporarily and continue attempting to import your conversion journals until you are confident that all segment values are defined and the cross-validation rules permit creation of the needed combinations.

Bridging—An Extension of Conversion

Until now, we have considered conversion as a one-off process at the point of cutover from legacy to Oracle systems. A phased cutover, where Oracle General Ledger goes live first and subledger modules are cut over some time later, introduces the need to have *bridging programs*—conversion programs that run on an ongoing basis translating account postings from legacy subledger systems into Oracle General Ledger. Whether you consider these programs as bridging conversion programs or full-blown interfaces depends on how long you plan to use them. The function they perform is identical; however, an interface should be elegant and robust, as it will probably need to be maintained at some stage in its life. A conversion program is a one-off, throw-away piece of code—it needs to work and no more. It makes no sense to build it to the same quality standards as an interface.

Either way, bridging programs and interfaces need a more permanent lookup table to hold the account mappings. Implementing the mapping in a table makes it easy to maintain the mapping, make corrections, or add new mappings if new codes are created in the legacy system.

Other Methods for Loading Legacy Data

Another method to transfer balances and transactions from legacy systems involves using Oracle General Ledger's Global Consolidation System. Even though GCS was created to perform consolidations, you can use this feature to load transactions or balances contained in a legacy set of books to a new set of books in Oracle General Ledger. GCS provides exceptional flexibility in allowing you to transfer data across any chart of accounts structure, any source, any calendar, any currency, and any level of detail. Because GCS offers an open interface, including a spreadsheet interface, it can be accessed by non-Oracle systems through programs that load data from legacy systems. GCS does this by providing sophisticated features for mapping data between accounting entities. For example, you can automatically map source accounts from the legacy system to destination accounts in the new system.

You can also use the Mass Maintenance Workbench to automatically create new account combinations based on existing combinations.

Coordination with Subledger Conversion

General Ledger conversion has to be carefully coordinated with other subledger conversions. Open items imported into Payables and Receivables are treated by Oracle Financials as fresh transactions, and these will post to General Ledger. Left unchecked, the fresh transactions could give rise to journals that duplicate legacy journals or account balances imported directly into Oracle General Ledger. There are three common strategies for avoiding duplication:

- After performing the subledger conversion, transfer subledger balances to General Ledger and then reverse the resulting journal batch in General Ledger. Care must be taken to ensure that this batch contains only conversion items.

- Segregate the chart of accounts into GL accounts and subledger accounts; ensure that the GL conversion references only GL accounts and the subledger conversions reference only their accounts. A complete and watertight segregation is not as easy as it might sound.

■ Fudge the open item conversion in the subledgers so that, when posted to General Ledger, they create a net movement of zero. This can be achieved by coding Payables invoices with the same account code combination for the liability account as for the expense distribution account. Likewise, for AR invoices the Receivables account code combination is used for both the receivables account and revenue account.

Be especially careful that the same account mapping is used for General Ledger and subledger translations. In particular, receivable account balances converted to General Ledger will, in the fullness of time, be reduced to zero by postings from Oracle Receivables. A mismatch between the translation mappings could cause problems for many months to come.

Loading and Copying Segment Values

There may be thousands of natural accounts and thousands of organization codes for General Ledger. The accounting staff almost always pulls them together in a spreadsheet. As most organizations use the Oracle installation as an occasion to change their chart of accounts structure, the spreadsheet may also include a column for the old account value. It usually includes parent-child relationships as well, showing the reporting hierarchy or hierarchies.

Transcribing all this data from the spreadsheet to Oracle even one time is a major job. But once is never enough. While the data processing staff is working to bring up the Financials environment, the accounting staff is invariably engaged in the never-ending task of perfecting their account structure. The same can be said for other flexfields: item numbers, fixed assets, locations, and jobs. For the sake of accuracy, all these values need to be loaded fresh at conversion time. That, in turn, means they need to be loaded for each dry-run of the conversion process.

The desktop integration feature of Oracle's Smart Client implementation provides the spreadsheet integration to address this long-standing need. It is now possible to use standard Applications features to mass-load value sets.

Generations of character-mode users facing this requirement developed scripts to insert values directly into Oracle Applications. Because of the flexibility they offer, such scripts may still be valuable in a Smart Client environment. A sample script (upload12.doc) to load from a spreadsheet is available on the Osborne-McGraw-Hill Website (**www.Osborne.com**).

A Novel Way to Create New Account Code Combinations

The GL interface will create code combinations dynamically if they are needed. To enable this feature, check the Allow Dynamic Insertion box in the Key Flexfields Segments window. That done, you can prepare a journal import that has all the new code combinations that you need to create and zero amounts everywhere. Once this has been loaded, the code combinations will have been created. The dummy journal can be deleted later. The same principle can be applied with the GL Desktop Integrator.

Conclusion

Oracle General Ledger is the heart of your accounting systems and allows your business to respond proactively to changes in today's business climate. Oracle Applications provides quick and easy implementation, painless migration from existing financial systems, accurate and timely processing of all your transactions, improved decision support through better reporting and analysis, and quick, automated closing procedures. It can greatly increase the operational efficiency of your business—an advantage crucial to success in today's fast-moving corporate arena.

CHAPTER
4

Budgeting and Allocations

ifferent groups within your organization require various levels of detailed information regarding performance. And while *financial accounting* is well-defined and commonly used, it cannot always address the informational needs of day-to-day processing. *Management accounting,* also referred to as *cost accounting,* is an optional accounting discipline used by internal managers to help manage assets, reduce company costs, perform financial analysis, and plan for future goals.

This chapter will describe the differences between financial and management accounting, detail the budgeting and cost allocation functions of management accounting, and explain how Oracle Financials can help you perform those functions efficiently and effectively.

The four main branches of accounting are *financial accounting, management accounting, tax accounting,* and *nonprofit accounting.* Public companies are required to implement financial and tax accounting to report results of their operations to outsiders. Nonprofit accounting, also called *fund accounting,* is used by colleges and universities, hospitals, and governments. Terms such as *encumbrances, budgetary control,* and *available fund balance* are common in nonprofit and government organizations.

Differences Between Financial and Management Accounting

Financial accounting information is used primarily by external users, such as investors, creditors, customers, and government agents, who are far removed from the day-to-day activities of an organization. These users rely on financial reports to help them make decisions. For example, investors use financial statements to determine if they should buy, sell, or hold their investments in a company. The main purpose of financial accounting is to record and report on the economic transactions of a company in a consistent and objective fashion. All public companies are required to issue regular financial statements that conform to *Generally Accepted Accounting Principles* (GAAP).

Management accounting is used by managers and other internal users who are involved with the day-to-day activities of an organization. It addresses management's need for current, detailed internal operating information, such as unit of production costs or sales by department.

Because financial accounting is regulated (by the Securities and Exchange Commission in the U.S. and the Registrar of Companies in the U.K.), and management accounting is unregulated, most corporations pay more attention to quarterly and annual financial reporting requirements than to management accounting or reports.

The Limitations of Financial Accounting

You cannot run a business relying on financial accounts alone. Financial reports are prepared after the close of an established period, and tend to look backward through time. They provide information about economic events that have already transpired and are highly aggregated, showing very little detail about any particular product line or inventory item. For example, in a typical income statement, there is one Cost of Sales line item that may represent ten different product lines. This information is of little use to managers who want to know which product line incurs the most costs or what the unit costs of each product are. Managers need this detailed information to help them analyze the profitability of each product line for making decisions on setting prices, switching suppliers of raw materials, or improving the assembly process. Managers cannot wait several days after the close cycle to obtain this information; they require detailed, up-to-the-minute information to help them make daily, even hourly, operating decisions.

Different Types of Reports

The underlying numbers and the fundamental transactions for both management accounting reports and financial accounting reports are basically the same, the difference being that the reports themselves show different levels of detail. The two sets of reports can be seen as two different windows on the same data. There is no Oracle "Management Accounting" module, but simply the ability to design and construct a variety of different reports, each one taking into account the divergent business rules of financial and management accounting. The Financial Statement Generator, included in Oracle General Ledger, is just one tool that helps you build and customize reports for your financial and management accounting needs.

The first step in designing an effective reporting framework is to carefully design your chart of accounts. A well-constructed chart of accounts can provide meaningful reports. For companies just starting out, an account segment that specifies whether it is an asset, revenue, or expense account is usually sufficient. However, if you want to be able to track costs by department and by the products produced by each department, you need a more sophisticated account structure that includes a Department and Product segment in your chart of accounts. Of course, as your company grows and your reporting gets more sophisticated, the more complex your chart of accounts becomes. The term that Oracle Applications uses to refer to your chart of accounts is the Accounting Flexfield. The combination of account, department, product, and so on is called the Account Code Combination. From the Accounting Flexfield, Oracle General Ledger can produce both your management and financial reports with as much detail as you require. When you start your analysis of financial and management reporting requirements, keep the following in mind: financial accounting reports reflect the results of the business as a whole, while management accounting reports tend to break down a business into its constituent parts, such as costs by company, cost center, department, and/or product.

Bridging the Gap

Companies that operate separate systems for financial and management accounting are operating inefficiently. No matter how strong your financial accounting system is, it is not a substitute for effective management accounting. Just collecting data and issuing highly aggregated reports are insufficient for running your business. In order to operate your business efficiently, you must implement both management accounting and financial accounting and integrate them with one another.

Oracle Financial Applications can replace disparate systems with an integrated financial solution, capable of supplying both financial and management figures.

Budgeting

Two key functions of management accounting are planning and budgeting, both of which help companies establish goals, set direction, and identify potential problems and opportunities in a timely fashion. Plans and budgets are also powerful control tools that set milestones for measuring progress, allowing managers to track the variance between actual results and planned results.

A budget can be thought of as a planned level of expenditure. In the U.K., the Institute of Cost and Management Accountants has defined budgeting as "a plan quantified in monetary terms prepared and approved prior to a defined period, usually showing planned income to be generated and/or an expenditure to be incurred during that period and the capital to be employed to obtain that objective."[1] A budget should reflect the goals that an organization plans to attain in a future period by means of expenditure.

A budget always refers to a specific time period, such as one year or five years. With Oracle Financials you can define your budget periods as months, quarters, half-years, or full years. Generally, your budget periods should coincide with your accounting periods to ensure proper matching of budget balances with actual balances.

The Budgeting Process

Some companies conduct a formal budget approval process, while others take a more relaxed approach. The number of managers involved in the budget process can also vary. Budgets can be set at the board level as part of a high-level business strategy or developed by shop floor managers to help them control their own operational spending. The range and style of budgets defies simplistic description. A great strength of Oracle Financials is that it does not constrain the methods and techniques of budget approval and entry. The wide range of methods for entering and modifying a budget in Financials matches the limitless variety of methods used to derive and approve budgets.

Whichever budgeting process you choose, Oracle Financials give you the freedom and flexibility to set your own rules. A wide array of methods and tools are offered to help you enter, modify, approve, analyze, and report on budgets in whatever way you see fit. You can mix and match budgeting methods to accommodate different needs by different departments or managers.

---

[1]From *Principles of Cost Accountancy* by Alan Pizzey (Cassell, 1987).

Ongoing Budget Review

Simply collecting budget data and issuing the final budget report is meaningless unless there is a continual review process that takes place inside your organization. Managers must continually review budget targets to ensure that they are close to actual amounts. If not, corrective action should be taken. Again, in many organizations this is a formal review process, and actual versus budgeted expenditures are often used to judge the performance of individual groups within the organization.

Budgets are used in the following ways:

- As day-to-day operational tools to control spending

- As yardsticks to measure actual performance against planned performance

- As warning signs that allow you to act quickly (for example, to change the direction of a particular business unit or product line that is not meeting its targets)

Budgetary Control for Nonprofit Organizations

A topic related specifically to budgets in nonprofit organizations is *budgetary control.* Budgetary control refers to the process of recording budget data and tracking encumbrance, and actual data against a budget.

Budgetary control is a major concern of nonprofit and government organizations, because laws mandate that such groups spend only what has been allotted or budgeted. These organizations work for the public and operate without a profit motive, so there are limitations on the funds they have available. Often, a donor to a public organization will designate a specific purpose for the donated funds, such as building a library or a new hospital. In such cases, the law requires that the organization spend only the amount of money that has been assigned to that particular expenditure. A nonprofit group, for instance, is not allowed to use money from the hospital fund to complete construction of the library; money for the two projects must be maintained and used separately.

NOTE
With Oracle Financials, you can track budget or encumbrance data using budgetary accounting or encumbrance accounting.

Funds checking is a feature of budgetary control that verifies available funds online before processing a transaction, thus helping to prevent overspending. With funds checking, you can verify transactions online against available budgets, immediately update the funds available for approved transactions, and control expenditures at the detail or the summary level.

Budgetary Control in Oracle Subledgers

When you enable budgetary control and enter a purchase order or an invoice, Oracle Purchasing and Oracle Payables check to ensure that there are sufficient funds available. The system then displays a status message: either Passed Funds Check or Failed Funds Check. If the transaction passes funds checking, the funds are set aside until they are expended.

You can implement budgetary control in Oracle General Ledger to check funds for manual journal entries. You can run budgetary control in two modes: Advisory or Absolute. Select Advisory if you wish to receive a warning message when a transaction exceeds its budget limit but still want the ability to save your work. Select Absolute if you want the program to prevent you from saving transactions that exceed their budget limit.

Types of Budgets

There are several types of budgets that are used by companies: the *operating budget, capital budget* (for fixed assets), *master production schedule* (for manufacturing companies), *variable budget* (for example, percentage of production), and *time-phased budget* (for capital projects).

Budgets are derived from Oracle General Ledger balances. The following is a list of balance types used by General Ledger:

■ Actual balance

■ Encumbrance balance (used by nonprofit organizations)

- Average balance (used by financial institutions)

- Statistical balance (such as headcount or square footage)

Oracle Financial Applications provide three different methods for entering and reviewing budget amounts:

- You can enter budget amounts or budget journals using Oracle General Ledger.

- You can use the Budget Wizard, a budgeting tool within the Oracle Applications Desktop Integrator, to enter budget data within an Excel spreadsheet. The Budget Wizard automatically builds a budget spreadsheet based on the budgets you define in Oracle General Ledger. Budget balances can be downloaded from Oracle General Ledger or uploaded from the spreadsheet. The spreadsheet interface allows you to automatically graph your budgets, and then to use the graphs for comparing budgeted costs against actuals.

- You can use Oracle Financial Analyzer, a distributed application for financial reporting, analysis, budgeting and planning, to enter new budget data or update budget amounts already created in Oracle General Ledger. With Oracle Financial Analyzer, you can easily analyze any financial data already collected by Oracle General Ledger using state-of-the-art OLAP (Online Analytical Processing) tools.

Budgeting with Oracle Financials

Oracle General Ledger provides a variety of powerful and flexible budgeting tools to help you facilitate better planning and control without the drudgery often associated with budgeting. With Oracle General Ledger, you can spend your valuable time analyzing budgets, not just entering and capturing data. Oracle Financials provides many features designed to help you perform budgeting in your organization.

UNLIMITED BUDGET VERSIONS   You can have as many versions of your budget as you want. You can use any budget version in any report, and even compare different versions of your budget. This allows you to create multiple "what if?" budgets and use them to plan business strategies.

DECENTRALIZATION To decentralize the budgeting process within your organization, you can define a budget organization along department, division, or cost center lines. Or, you can centralize the process by having only one budget organization. In either case, you have the power and flexibility to determine who enters budget data by assigning passwords to budget organizations within your enterprise.

FLEXIBILITY You can enter budgets according to your planning needs: weekly, monthly, quarterly, or annually. You can create budget journal entries to provide an audit trail for your budget.

SPREADSHEET INTEGRATION The Budget Wizard tool in Oracle Applications Desktop Integrator (ADI) provides a spreadsheet-based budget entry screen that facilitates simple data entry and modeling in a disconnected environment. You can enter your new budget balances manually, use budget rules, or use formulas and models. The spreadsheet can be saved on your desktop and worked on at any time. When you are satisfied with your budget, you can upload the new balances into Oracle General Ledger. If you prefer Lotus 1-2-3 as your spreadsheet interface, you can enter amounts in Lotus 1-2-3 and then transfer actual and budget data from your spreadsheet into Oracle General Ledger.

BUDGET FORMULAS AND ALLOCATIONS Budget formulas enable you to build a complete budget using any combination of fixed amounts and account balances, including actuals or budget amounts. For example, you could draft an entire budget using the previous year's actuals for overhead costs and applying a 15-percent increase in sales revenue. Then you can use allocations, called MassBudget, to distribute the budget amounts across departments, divisions and so on. The formulas used in MassBudget can be simple or complex, and you can allocate to parent accounts without having to enumerate each child value separately.

BUDGET TRANSLATION You can translate foreign currency budget balances as well as actuals. This capability allows you to create budget-versus-actuals reports in your reporting currency using the Financial Statement Generator.

ORACLE FINANCIAL ANALYZER INTEGRATION Oracle General Ledger's integration with Oracle Financial Analyzer lets you easily identify, analyze, model, budget, forecast, and report on information stored in your general ledger. You can use the sophisticated budgeting capabilities of Oracle Financial Analyzer (OAF) to develop your budgets within a multidimensional analysis framework. Once you have completed your budgets in OAF, you can automatically write your budget amounts back to Oracle General Ledger. You can either enter your data into a new budget in General Ledger, separate from the original budget, or store several versions of a budget for comparative reporting purposes.

Allocations

Another function of management accounting is allocations. Allocations spread costs or revenues from one source to other sources. This function allows a more granular estimate of the true cost or revenue source. For example, a typical cost allocation might be to spread overhead costs, such as utility costs, across departments or products, based on square footage or number of employees.

There are two mechanisms within Oracle General Ledger that allow you to create allocations: MassBudget for allocating budget amounts, and MassAllocation for allocating actual or encumbrance amounts. Both features require that you create batches that contain one or more formula entries. One formula may generate allocation journal entries for a group of cost centers, departments, divisions, and so on. For example, you can allocate total benefit costs to all cost centers based on headcount. You can allocate a pool of marketing costs to several departments based on the ratio of department revenues to total revenues.

Allocation Formulas

MassAllocation uses a generic formula to calculate allocation amounts:

cost pool × (*usage factor* / *total usage*)

In each MassAllocation formula that you define, you specify fixed amounts, fractions, or general ledger accounts for the cost pool, usage factor and total usage. In addition to the formula, you must enter a target account and an offset account. The target account specifies the destination of your allocation; the offset account is used to post the offsetting debit or credit entry from your allocation. Extremely sophisticated allocations can be set up quickly and simply, using parent accounts and the looping feature. The looping feature visits all child accounts of a specified parent and calculates the appropriate allocation using the generic formula just shown.

An Allocation Example

Assume there are three departments in your company: Departments 101, 102, and 103, which occupy 45 percent, 30 percent, and 25 percent of the company's floor space, respectively. These departments are children to the parent Department 100 which is used as the offset account. If rent expense for an accounting period is $100,000, you will produce the following allocation journal:

Type	Account	Debit	Credit
Target	Rent Expense - Dept 101	$45,000	
Target	Rent Expense - Dept 102	$30,000	
Target	Rent Expense - Dept 103	$25,000	
Offset	Rent Expense - Dept 100		$100,000

The allocation feature is a powerful accounting tool, and it can be used with actual or encumbrance journal batches. Nevertheless, MassAllocation does require some initial setup and planning efforts to ensure proper implementation. With recurring journal entries and allocation formulas, you can perform many types of allocations:

NET ALLOCATIONS   Net allocations are made on an incremental basis over previous allocations. The allocated amounts reflect changes in the cost pool. Rather than reallocating the entire revised amount, a net allocation allocates only those amounts that update the previous allocation. Net allocations allow you to rerun allocations, without overallocating, as many times as you want to in the same period.

STEP-DOWN ALLOCATIONS   Step-down allocations occur in groups, and cascade in such a way that the target of one allocation becomes the cost pool of the next. For example, you might first allocate a portion of your overhead costs to the Finance department, then allocate total

Administrative costs to other departments (after including in the Finance department cost its portion of the overheads).

RATE-BASED ALLOCATIONS   These are made using location formulas based on current, historic, or estimated rates. For example, bad debt may be budgeted at 1 percent of turnover.

USAGE-BASED ALLOCATIONS   Usage-based costs are allocated according to statistics such as headcount, units sold, square footage, number of deliveries, or computer time consumed. Rent, for instance, is typically allocated on square footage usage per department.

STANDARD COSTING ALLOCATIONS   In standard costing, allocations are based on statistics such as sales units, production units, number of deliveries, or customers served. For example, you might want to calculate your cost of sales according to this formula:

number of units sold × standard cost per unit

Conclusion

Management accounting is not a byproduct of financial accounting; it is a separate discipline that deserves much attention. Without a sound management accounting system in place, managers cannot make thorough internal decisions regarding business operations. Long before the end of any accounting period, managers need detailed, timely reports that act as early warning signs of any potential cash crunch or inventory shortage. Financial reports only provide a scorecard of the past results. Managers want up-to-the-minute, customizable reports that can be obtained from Oracle General Ledger's Financial Statement Generator.

Oracle Corporation's suite of financial applications seamlessly integrates your management and financial accounting systems without the need for double maintenance or duplication of effort. Oracle General Ledger, coupled with the ADI's Budget Wizard, allows you to perform the budgeting process using a familiar spreadsheet environment to create and modify your budgets. The budgets are based on the same chart of accounts and accounting calendar used for your financial accounting information. The integration of Oracle General Ledger and Oracle Financial Analyzer allows you to quickly identify, analyze, model, budget, forecast, and report on information stored in your general ledger without rekeying information. Oracle General Ledger's MassAllocation and MassBudgeting features allow you to perform allocations by defining formulas that you can reuse again and again.

CHAPTER
5

Oracle Payables

payables system is the last stage of supply-chain management. It allows companies to pay suppliers for merchandise and services. There are several opportunities in Oracle Payables for automation, since the terms and conditions are known at the purchase order (PO) stage and, assuming that the goods are accepted, payment follows at a later, fixed time.

The goal of supply-chain management is keeping stock levels low but having sufficient stock to meet demand. Stock sitting in a warehouse equates to money tied up unproductively—but only if you have paid for that stock. The goal of payables management is to postpone payment as long as possible while ensuring that invoices are paid by their due date.

Receiving goods and paying for them weeks later amounts to an interest-free loan from your supplier. Supermarkets are champions at using the good terms offered by suppliers. Supermarkets may be operating on wafer-thin margins, but they regularly sell their stock days (if not weeks) before they pay for it. They have a surplus working capital, which they invest for profit. Supermarkets are an extreme exponent of investing other people's money wisely; but managing suppliers' payment terms is a business practice that all commercial organizations can benefit from.

Purposes of a Payables System

The purpose of a payables system is to help you manage your procurement cycle, allowing you to process high transaction volumes and keep control over your cash flow. It also gives you the ability to better manage your supplier relationships and price comparisons. Oracle Payables can be configured to save your company money by enforcing your payment policies, such as:

- Paying suppliers on time, but no earlier than necessary
- Taking discounts when prudent
- Preventing duplicate billing/invoice
- Avoiding overdrafts of your bank accounts

Since payables is only part of a complete cycle, it must be integrated with other modules. Oracle Payables shares purchase order information with Purchasing so that you pay only for goods you ordered and received and do not pay more than the price quoted by the supplier. It shares receipt information with Purchasing so that you do not pay for items that are faulty, broken, or substandard. Oracle Payables is fully integrated with Oracle Assets in a way that allows you to account for fixed assets purchased. It is integrated with Human Resources to ensure that employee expenses are paid efficiently and with Oracle Cash Management to enable you to reconcile your payments against a bank statement.

Innovative Uses of Oracle Payables

Many software features that were once considered "bells and whistles" are increasingly becoming standard business requirements. Oracle has responded to this trend by adding functionality to payables and by creating some completely new modules that interact with payables. These include Web-enabled commerce, electronic data interchange (EDI), evaluated receipt settlement (ERS), and procurement card integration.

Web-Enabled Commerce

Web-enabled applications give access to any user with a Web browser and the appropriate security clearance. Oracle has termed this application *self-service,* as it allows users access to data directly instead of, as previously required, filling out a paper form and then having a payables clerk do the actual data entry. Using a standard Web browser and the Self-Service Expenses application, described in more detail in Chapter 13, employees can enter their own expense reports. Mobile employees can use the Expense spreadsheet to track expenses offline in *disconnected mode,* then upload their expense records into the Self-Service Expenses application to submit for approval. Once an expense report is submitted using Self-Service Expenses, Oracle Workflow routes the report for approval and automatically enforces company policies and business rules. Oracle Payables then processes the expense report and issues a payment to the employee.

Electronic Data Interchange (EDI)

Electronic data interchange (EDI) is a process for using electronic messaging to communicate with trading partners. Instead of printing paper documents such as purchase orders, invoices, and remittance advisories, Oracle Applications uses the Oracle EDI Gateway to send these documents to your trading partners. Oracle Applications uses International standards X12 and EDIFACT to ensure that recipients will be able to read the message, regardless of whether they are using Oracle Applications or not. These two standards are commonly used; X12 is sponsored by ANSI and used in the United States, and EDIFACT is sponsored by the United Nations and primarily used in Europe. The Oracle EDI Gateway extracts the data from Oracle Applications and delivers it in a common format to an EDI translator. The translator converts the common format supplied by Oracle Applications to either X12 or EDIFACT.

The actual mechanism for transferring the electronic document to the other party is not prescribed. In the same way that a paper document can be faxed, mailed, or sent by courier, electronic messages can be sent in a variety of ways:

- Via modem links across phone lines
- Across the internet
- On floppy disk sent through the postal service

EDI transactions can be either inbound (data coming in from a partner to be loaded into Oracle Applications) or outbound (data that's been extracted from Oracle Applications and is now being sent to a partner). Support for new transaction types is continually being added; an outbound purchase order EDI has been available since Version 1 of the Oracle EDI Gateway product, and Release 11 of Financials introduced support for inbound invoices. While you can write custom programs to fulfill any EDI need, the EDI transaction sets currently available for use in combination with Oracle Payables are shown in Table 5-1.

The outbound application advice (824/APERAK) can be used to inform a supplier of a duplicate invoice or an invoice that does not refer to a valid purchase order. It can be used to notify a supplier of invoice data rejected for any reason or to confirm that you have accepted an invoice.

Evaluated Receipt Settlement (ERS)

Traditionally, payment has been based on receipt of the supplier's invoice. Recent innovations in workflow, however, have led to evaluated receipt settlement (ERS). The receipt of goods drives payment under ERS; no paper invoice is sent to the accounts payable department. Evaluated receipt

Transaction	X12 Standard	EDIFACT Standard	Direction
Invoice	810	INVOIC	Inbound
Payment Order/Remittance advice	820	PAYORD REMADV	Outbound
Application advice	824	APERAK	Outbound
Shipment and Billing notice	857	No equivalent	Inbound

TABLE 5-1. *EDI Transaction Sets in Oracle Payables*

settlement (ERS) enables a user to automatically create standard, unapproved invoices for payment of goods. The invoices are based on receipt transactions that have been processed through Oracle Purchasing. Creation of an invoice may be triggered by an Advance Shipment Notice (ASN) from the supplier (processed by Purchasing/Receiving under Oracle Purchasing) or a third-party receiving process. Invoices are created using a combination of receipt and purchase order information; this process eliminates duplicate data entry and ensures accurate and timely data processing. Evaluated receipt settlement is also known as *payment on receipt* or *self-billing.*

Under the ERS system, you choose which suppliers participate, and you enforce matching rules to ensure that the proper payments are made to your suppliers. The system creates invoices with multiple items and distribution lines, and automatically accounts for sales tax. The amount on the invoice is determined by multiplying the quantity of items received by each item's unit price on the purchase order. The payment terms on the invoice default to the purchase order payment terms. The payment currency defaults from the supplier site. Sales tax is calculated based on the tax codes on each line of the purchase order.

The ERS process prevents the supplier's expense of generating invoices, and yours of matching invoices to receipts and processing payments. It imposes a measure of control in doing so. As the customer, you must be careful to accurately record what is received. Your business processes must absolutely minimize discrepancies between the purchase order and the receipt. The supplier must be equally vigilant in comparing your remittance advice with its shipments to you.

Procurement Cards

To simplify the administration of employee expenses, companies may offer their employees use of a corporate card, which can be used to make purchases on the company's behalf. With the procurement card integration feature, new in Release 11, you can import the transaction detail from statement files provided by the card issuer. Employees are notified automatically of any transactions appearing on their card; then, they can use Oracle Self-Service Expenses to verify those transactions and override default transaction accounting. Once the transactions have been verified, invoices will be automatically created that represent the employer's liability to pay the card issuer.

Procurement cards reduce transaction costs in several ways:

■ Obligations to many suppliers are consolidated into a single payment to the card issuer.

■ The transaction description is already automated, to some degree, in the line detail provided by the card issuer.

■ The employee is identified automatically.

■ The accounting distribution can often be fully determined by identifying the employee and the supplier. If not, the number of choices is usually quite limited.

This process can empower employees to buy what they want and when they need to. In essence, it enables them to be more productive without creating additional paperwork or bypassing the business approval and audit procedures.

Attachments

You can link invoices to nonstructural data, such as images, word processing documents, spreadsheets, and video files. These attachments are stored within the Oracle Database and are accessible through the Payables screens. This new feature allows your payables department to build a better profile of your suppliers and trading partners, and makes the information readily accessible.

For example, you could attach to an invoice a scanned image of the original supplier's invoice. Doing this would allow you to archive the paper copy and rely entirely on the application data and the image stored in Payables to resolve any future queries. This method is particularly suitable if you use a paper-based procedure for invoice approval and account coding. The invoice image can be scanned after it has been forwarded to the buyer for approval and account coding.

An Overview of Payables in Your Business

As soon as a company agrees to purchase goods or services from a supplier, it has an encumbrance—whether the company chooses to account for it or not. As the goods or services are received, the encumbrance converts to a liability to pay the agreed price for the goods. The liability remains on the company's balance sheet until the goods or services have been paid for.

Payment terms will have been agreed upon at the purchase stage, and the supplier should quote these terms when sending an invoice for the goods. Typical payment terms might be 30 days net; better terms would be 90 days net or a one-percent discount. The latter means the full amount is due by the 90th day, but there is a one-percent discount if the invoice is paid earlier. There is no limit to the range of possible payment terms; terms are separately negotiated either supplier-by-supplier or by purchase order. Having waited as long as possible before sacrificing the discount or going into default, you pay the invoice. Payment can be made by check, bank-to-bank electronic funds transfer (EFT), or any of a range of cash and noncash payment methods. Once the invoice has been paid, the liability in the balance sheet is reduced to zero.

To explain the figures that appear on the balance sheet, you need to be able to list how much money is owed to each supplier and prove that the total money owed equals the liability shown on the balance sheet. This reconciliation of the Payables subledger with General Ledger (GL) should be performed regularly—at a minimum the end of each accounting period. To start the reconciliation, compare the standard Oracle Payables Trial Balance report with the payables liability account line in the appropriate Financial Statement Generator (FSG) balance sheet report.

Timing Your Liability

Companies differ on when liability is first measured. Some companies record their liability from the day the invoice arrives or the date on the invoice, not from the day the goods were received. The invoice due date has no bearing on the eventual liability; the due date is for operational control, not accounting. Organizations that automate purchasing and payables processes are in a better position to record liability for goods ordered but not received and for goods received but not invoiced. However, if you use payables without the purchasing system, the best approximation is to record the liability when the invoice is received. Bear in mind that the decision on when to recognize a liability is a commercial accounting decision, and it should not be driven by system considerations.

Companies with a backlog of purchase invoices at period end will calculate the total amount owing from all the invoices that have not been keyed, then enter this single figure as an accrual journal in General Ledger. This allows the accounts to show an accurate liability figure and the accounting period to be closed on time. Once the backlog of invoices has been individually keyed into Payables, the accrual journal has to be reversed in the following period.

The Payables Workflow

Oracle Payables is tightly integrated with Oracle Purchasing and Oracle Cash Management. The close integration is dictated by workflow: purchase orders in Purchasing give rise to invoices in Payables, and invoices give rise to payments, which will show as bank statement entries in Cash Management. If necessary, Payables can be installed on its own without Purchasing or Cash Management, but you may not be able to take advantage of the full range of automation that would otherwise be available.

If you are not using ERS, suppliers will send you an invoice for the goods you have received. These invoices will be processed by your accounts payable department, which ensures that the supplier is known and that the price, quantity, and payment terms match those on the original purchase order. Your business processes should specify how to deal with invoices from suppliers who are not in the system. This occurs commonly, even with a purchasing system in place. Many obligations, including withholding tax and property tax payments, originate without a purchase order. In these cases, the user may have to do either one or both of these extra steps:

- Identify and set up a supplier record in Oracle Payables.

- Determine which expense account codes the items should be charged against.

Once entered and approved, the invoice is available for payment. Physical payment can take place in many different ways, including the following:

- Automatic or manual checks

- Wire transfers

- Electronic funds transfer (EFT)

From the payables point of view, the invoice is considered paid and you have reached the end of the payables cycle. The payment will eventually appear on the company's bank statement, and at that stage it should be reconciled within Oracle Cash Management. Reconciling the payment removes it from the list of payments issued but not yet cleared. Cash Management's reconciliation feature is powerful because it enables you to handle queries from suppliers much more effectively. You can bring up a record of the supplier's account online and identify previous invoices, their due dates, and their actual payment dates. If the check has been presented, you can see the date it was reconciled. Sometimes suppliers mistakenly believe that a particular invoice has not been paid. Having crucial information at your fingertips (that is, the payment date, the check number, and the date on which the check was cleared by your bank) is a powerful way to quickly set the record straight, avoid making duplicate payments, and maintain better supplier relations. Since Release 10.7, the bank reconciliation functionality has been part of Oracle Cash Management. Cash Management creates postings from a cash clearing account to correspond to the reconciled payments. Prior to Cash Management, an early version of payment reconciliation was available within Oracle Payables. Bank reconciliation is described in more detail in Chapter 7.

Oracle Payables posts accounting transactions to Oracle General Ledger. It also integrates with Oracle Purchasing for invoice matching, with Oracle Fixed Assets for tracking fixed asset purchases, and with Cash Management for enabling checks and payments issued out of Oracle Payables to be reconciled with your bank statement. In addition, expenditures can be transferred to Oracle Projects for project accounting, tracking, or billing. An overview of the integration is shown in Figure 5-1.

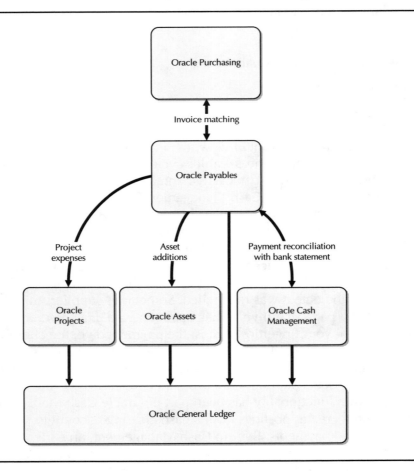

FIGURE 5-1. *Oracle Payables integration*

The Payables Cycle

All payments pass through the same four-step Payables cycle, as shown in Figure 5-2. An objective of your Payables setup is to reduce overhead costs by automating the cycle to the extent possible, while still keeping all your controls in place.

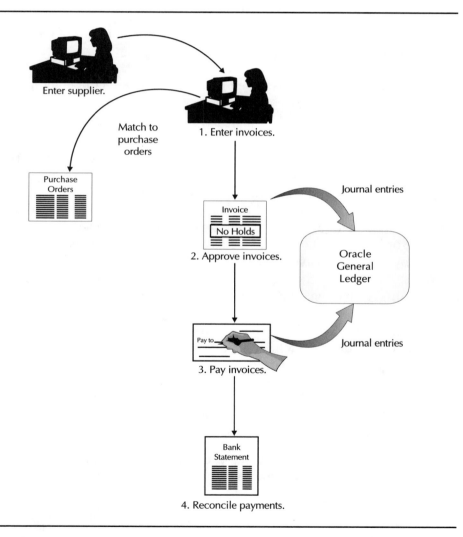

FIGURE 5-2. *The Oracle Payables cycle*

The Payables cycle consists of the following four steps:

1. Enter invoices. (This process may or may not include matching each invoice to a purchase order.)

2. Approve invoices for payment.

3. Select and pay approved invoices.

4. Reconcile the payments with the bank statement (part of Oracle Cash Management).

The first three steps are discussed just ahead. Bank reconciliation is described in more detail in Chapter 7.

Step 1: Enter Invoices

Invoices are entered in Oracle Payables using the Invoice Workbench. This form is at the heart of accounts payable processing, allowing you to process all types of invoices while maintaining accuracy and control over what you pay. There are many different fields contained within the Invoice Workbench; some are required for approval, others are derived or defaulted from supplier purchase order information. Other fields are purely optional and may never be used by some companies. The details of the form—the data that must be entered and the cross-validation of related data—depend on the type of invoice you are entering. The various types of invoices are listed here:

- **Standard**   A regular supplier invoice. The invoice usually includes line-item details, including a description and price.

- **Credit Memo**   An invoice you receive from a supplier representing a credit for goods or services purchased.

- **Debit Memo**   An invoice that notifies a supplier of a credit you recorded for goods or services purchased.

- **Expense Report**   An invoice you enter to record business-related expenses for employees. The employee is the supplier.

- **PO Default**   An invoice for which you know the matching purchase order number. Payables fills out as much information from the purchase order as possible: supplier name, supplier number, supplier site, and the currency.

- **QuickMatch**   An invoice that you want to match automatically to a specified purchase order and all the shipment lines on the purchase order. Oracle Payables completes the match automatically for each shipment line where the quantity ordered is greater than the quantity already billed against that shipment line.

- **Mixed**   A standard or credit/debit memo invoice that you want to match to a purchase order, another invoice, or both. You can enter either a positive or negative amount for a Mixed invoice.

- **Prepayment**   An invoice used to make advance payments for expenses to a supplier or employee. In this case, you may not have actually received the goods or services yet.

NOTE
Once you have saved an invoice with the type of PO Default, Mixed, or QuickMatch invoice, Payables will change the invoice type to Standard. You cannot later search and find PO Default, Mixed, or QuickMatch invoices in the Invoice Workbench.

INVOICE MATCHING   Payables provides extensive purchase order matching features to ensure that you pay only for goods and services you ordered, received, and accepted.

If a discrepancy appears between the figures on the supplier's invoice and your figures, the invoice should be put on hold and not paid until the difference has been clarified with the supplier. The matching process is highly integrated with Oracle Purchasing. If you are populating the purchasing tables with imported data, you must also populate the invoice and line-level match flags that allow the invoice to be paid.

When you match during invoice entry, you indicate whether you want to match to the purchase order shipment or to specific purchase order distributions. You then choose the shipment or distribution you want to match to and the quantity and price you are matching. Then Payables performs the following for each matched shipment:

- Updates QUANTITY_BILLED and AMOUNT_BILLED in PO_DISTRIBUTIONS.

- Updates QUANTITY_BILLED in PO_LINE_LOCATIONS.

- Creates one or more AP_INVOICE_DISTRIBUTIONS, which records the QUANTITY_INVOICED, the UNIT_PRICE, and the PO_DISTRIBUTION_ID, in addition to other Payables information.

You have the option of setting up two-, three-, and four-way matching to ensure that you pay only for goods and services that have been ordered, ordered and received, or ordered, received, and accepted. Purchase invoices must be matched to a purchase order and, optionally, receipts and inspections, before they can be approved for payment.

Oracle does not currently provide an open interface for purchase orders, but you could take advantage of matching by importing pertinent PO information from another purchasing system into the following tables through customizations:

- PO_HEADERS

- PO_LINES

- PO_LINE_LOCATIONS

- PO_DISTRIBUTIONS

- PO_DISTRIBUTIONS_AP_V (view of PO_DISTRIBUTIONS)

- PO_RELEASES (blanket purchase orders)

- PO_LOOKUP_CODES

CAUTION

If you use Oracle Purchasing, you should not import purchase order information into these tables for use in AP invoice matching. The data constraints necessary for operating AP invoice matching successfully are much less restrictive than the data constraints necessary for Oracle Purchasing to correctly pick up and process the data you import.

INVOICE IMPORT   The Invoice Import process allows you to create Payables invoices through an automated process. You would typically use this feature for established suppliers with a large business volume, for interfacing with external systems you may have or for the initial data conversion to Oracle Payables. The Import captures descriptions and prices at a line level. It can include either the accounting distribution or the information needed to have Automatic Account Generation determine the distribution. It can capture and carry supplier-specific information in Descriptive Flexfield (DFF) attributes.

Step 2: Approve Invoices

Invoices must be approved before they can be paid. For efficiency, Payables can be set up so that most invoices flow straight through to payment. Holds, which require someone to act before the invoice can be paid, should be the exception and not the rule. Otherwise, a large number of invoices would require manual intervention at a stage in the cycle where it was not necessary to do so.

An invoice may be approved one of two ways, through online approval or the Approval Process. Online approval is done on an individual invoice basis and initiated from the Invoice Workbench screen. This is best used if you have a particular invoice that needs immediate approval and payment. The Approval Process is a concurrent program that scans all payable invoices and reassesses the system holds on each invoice. It produces a report showing which invoices have new holds placed and which invoices have holds released and is usually set up to run in the background or run manually immediately before the payment process.

During approval, validation occurs for matching, tax, period status, exchange rate, and distribution information for invoices, and holds are applied to exception invoices. The approval procedure applies system holds to invoices. For new invoices, the approval procedure assesses whether any holds are needed; if so, the holds are placed on the invoice. For existing invoices with holds, the procedure assesses whether the existing holds are still appropriate and whether any new holds are necessary as a result of changes that have been made to the invoice. For example, when a tax variance hold is corrected, the tax hold is released. But if, after that change, the invoice lines no longer add up to the invoice total, the approval process places a distribution variance hold. Clearing invoice holds on a batch of invoices is an iterative process, but user holds are always left unaffected and must be removed manually.

HOLDS   Holds are placed by the system or a user on invoices that are not approved. Some holds prevent the invoice from being transferred to General Ledger. Users can place holds for any reason. System holds are used to enforce certain data integrity and business reality checks. An invoice cannot be paid or posted if the sum of its invoice lines (called distributions) does not equal the total invoice amount (DIST VARIANCE is nonzero) or if the tax for a line does not equal the net amount multiplied by the tax rate (TAX VARIANCE is nonzero). The approval process inspects all new invoices or invoices with holds and places new holds or removes holds that are no longer relevant; it can be run either as a concurrent program (called Payables Approval) or online for each invoice. If you are using Batch Control, you can also run Approval By Batch by using the Approval button on the Batch Control header window.

TIP
For sites with a high volume of invoices, set up the Payables Approval process to run two or three times during the day, or once during the night, on new invoices. Doing this relieves invoice entry staff of approving each invoice one-by-one online.

Holds are categorized according to the general reason for placing the hold. Table 5-2 gives an example for each of the different types of holds. The complete list of holds along with their suggested actions can be found in the Oracle Payables reference manual.

Whenever you have an invoice with a hold, you must remove the hold before the invoice can proceed to the next stage in the cycle. Certainly, all invoices with holds that prevent them from being transferred to General Ledger have to be cleared, and the invoices posted, before the accounting period can be closed.

Type of Hold	Example	Reason	Remedy
Account	DIST ACC INVALID	Invoice distributed to an invalid account.	Change the transaction or make the account valid.
Funds	NONSUFFICIENT FUNDS	Invoice distribution amount exceeds funds available.	Manually override the hold or put more funds into the account.
Invoice	AMOUNT	Invoice amount exceeds amount specified for the supplier site.	Approve payment manually.
Matching	QTY ORD	Quantity billed exceeds *quantity ordered* × (1 + *percent of tolerance*).	Wait for the match to be satisfied, or approve payment manually.
Variance	DIST VARIANCE	Sum of distributions is not equal to the invoice amount.	You must resolve the discrepancy before the invoice can be paid.

TABLE 5-2.   *Types of Holds and Examples of Invoice Problems*

TIP
*Oracle Alert can be integrated effectively with
Payables to streamline the approval process.
For instance, an alert can be programmed to
e-mail the buyer if there is a matching hold.
The buyer can then research the hold and
release it, if appropriate.*

Step 3: Pay Approved Invoices

Once the invoice has been entered and approved, it must be paid in a
timely manner to take advantage of available discounts and retain good
relations with your suppliers. In Oracle Payables you initiate payment runs
on a regular basis, say weekly or every second working day. The pay run
will select all invoices that need to be paid, according to your criteria, and
generate the appropriate payment documents. A single payment will be sent
covering all a supplier's invoices that are due to be paid. You can optionally
choose the Pay Alone feature to make sure that only one invoice is paid per
payment document. This approach can be important for tax authorities, for
example, who demand a one-to-one correspondence between payments
and paperwork.

The five steps in the pay run are listed here:

1. **Select**   Invoices are selected if they fall due on or before the "pay
   by" date you specify and they meet all the other criteria you specify
   (such as pay group, method of payment, and currency).

2. **Modify**   You can optionally prevent payment to a supplier, prevent
   payment of a particular invoice, or add an invoice that Payables did
   not originally select.

3. **Format & Print**   The selected invoices are formatted either as checks,
   in which case Payables produces a print file containing remittance
   advice information and the formatted check information, or as an
   electronic payment file, in which case a data file containing the
   payment information is formatted according to a particular bank or
   EDI format. Checks are printed onto the company's check stock
   stationery, or a bank file is transmitted to the bank over a modem link.

4. **Confirm**   You confirm to the system that each check has been paid. Confirmation releases a concurrent process that records the invoices as paid and marks the payments to be transferred to General Ledger.

5. **Deliver**   Checks are posted to the supplier, or a bank file is delivered to the bank.

At any time independent of your regular payment cycle, you can issue a manual payment (generated wholly outside the system but entered into Oracle Payables to ensure the correct accounting entries are generated) or a Quick Payment (a one-off payment for a single supplier generated within Oracle Payables). Either method is useful, for example, if you are late with your payment, and the supplier is pressing for payment prior to the next regular payment run. On the whole, manual checks and Quick Payment should be discouraged because the administrative costs associated with a single payment are far higher than for payments issued in a regular payment run. Oracle Applications recognizes that there will be circumstances when a manual check is needed, and the applications are flexible enough to cope with these exceptional situations.

PAYMENT METHODS   There are a number of possible payment methods, including printed checks, printed transfer slips, and electronic documents like EFT or EDI. The aim is to choose a payment method that the supplier accepts and that is inexpensive to operate, as your bank may impose different charges for various payment methods. The two most commonly used are:

- **Checks**   Although check payment is readily accepted, it is also relatively expensive considering the fees and the time and material required to print, mail, and reconcile checks. In addition to the payment document itself, Payables can be configured to generate remittance notices. A *remittance notice* is a letter informing the supplier of an imminent payment; it includes details of the invoices that are being paid.

- **Electronic Funds Transfer (EFT)**   Consists of a formatted file with payments information sent to your bank so it can disburse the payments directly into each supplier's bank account. Some countries have well-established EFT standards that are accepted by all its banks. In the United Kingdom and United States, the BACS (Bank Automated Clearing System) is commonly used; in Germany, the Deutsche Bank DTA (Datenträger Austausch) format is widely accepted. Many country-specific formats are provided by Oracle, but if your bank uses one that is not supported, you will need to write a customized EFT payments program to generate the appropriate file layout. If the layout differs only slightly from a standard layout, it can be relatively simple to copy the standard program, re-register it under a different name, and make the necessary layout changes in the Oracle Reports designer. You will need to work with your bank to determine the required format.

General Ledger Transfer (Posting)

All subledger modules have a program that reviews all new or changed transactions (such as invoices, debit memos, and payments) and creates a batch of journal entries in the interface table that is ready to be imported into General Ledger as a journal. These programs are called Transfer To General Ledger.

The journals created from Payables are clearly identifiable in General Ledger according to their batch names and journal names. The logic behind the batch names is shown in Table 5-3, where *CUR* is the currency of the payments and *user-ref* is the reference given to the transfer by the user who started it.

When you use accrual basis accounting and submit the Payables Transfer To General Ledger program, Payables can transfer accounting information for both your invoices and payment transactions to the Payables

Batch Name	Journal Name	Transactions Listed
user-ref Payables	Payments *CUR*	Payments transferred from Oracle Payables
user-ref Payables	Purchase Invoices *CUR*	Purchase Invoices transferred from Oracle Payables

TABLE 5-3. *Payables Journals in General Ledger*

General Ledger interface table. When you submit the program, you can choose to transfer invoice, payment, or all (both invoice and payment) transactions. The accounting distributions for an *invoice* typically debit the expense or asset accounts and credit the AP liability account of an invoice. The accounting distributions for a *payment* typically debit the liability account and credit your cash or cash clearing account. When you create payments, Payables may also create distributions for discounts taken and foreign currency exchange gains or losses incurred between invoice and payment time.

Supplier Data

The supplier data is made up of your list of suppliers and their address and bank information, referred to as *sites*. These suppliers are uniquely identified by a supplier number (which can contain characters as well as numbers) and are associated with any number of supplier sites. A site is basically an address from which the supplier conducts some or all of its business. Sites are classified as Purchasing sites, RFQ Only sites, and, most importantly for Payables, Pay sites. A Pay site is where you send payment for an invoice. You cannot enter an invoice for a supplier site that is not defined as a Pay site. The supplier master tables (often termed *vendor master tables* at the database level) are shared with Purchasing. Chapter 9 addresses the considerations involved in converting supplier information when you go live with Oracle Applications.

A schematic diagram of the supplier master tables is shown in Figure 5-3. Only the most important fields have been shown here; many more exist. Defaults are held at supplier level and supplier site level to speed up invoice entry. Incidentally, defaults are also held in the Payables Options form; these defaults are used when you define a new supplier. The defaults held at supplier level are used when you create a new site. The defaults at site level are used when you create a new invoice.

If you enable the Use Multiple Supplier Banks Payables option, you can enter your suppliers' bank account information in the Banks window and then assign bank accounts to your suppliers and supplier sites. If you do not enable this option, you can continue to enter a single bank for each supplier or supplier site in the Suppliers and Supplier Sites windows.

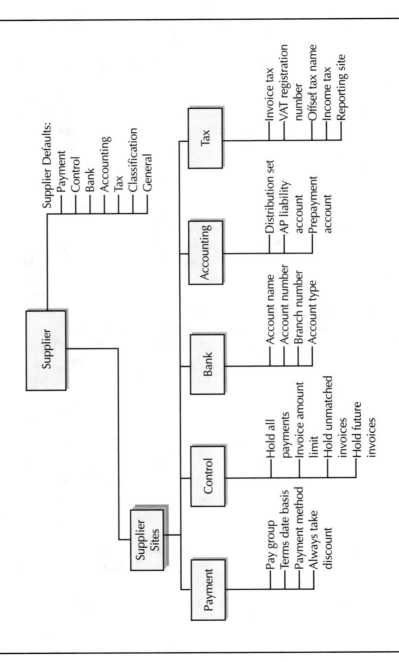

FIGURE 5-3. *The supplier master tables*

CAUTION
The defaults held at supplier level are used when you create a new site. The defaults at site level are used when you create a new invoice. This arrangement may become confusing if you change the supplier's bank details at supplier level and then pay an invoice for that supplier. When you create an electronic payment, the system will upload the bank details from the site level, which will show the original, unchanged bank details.

The Supplier Account

Each supplier in the supplier database has an account. The account is a record of all the transactions (such as invoices, prepayments, debit memos, and payments or payment reversals) that affect that supplier. The supplier accounts have little to do with the accounts stored in Oracle General Ledger or the Accounting Flexfield. The supplier account balance is calculated as follows:

> *Inv* (invoices for this customer)
> + *DM* (debit memos)
> + *CM* (credit memos)
> − *Pre* (prepayments)
> − *Pay* (payments)
> ─────────────────────────
> *Resulting account balance*

You can view the supplier's account balance on paper by running the Invoice Aging Report, which can be submitted for a single supplier. Alternatively, the Accounts Payable Trial Balance Report shows the account balance separately and in total for all suppliers. A snapshot of the supplier's account is available online from the Find Invoices window. Choose the Calculate Balance Owed button to see how much you owe a supplier and how many unpaid invoices you have in the system for the supplier.

Accounting Methods

When you set up Payables, you choose a primary and an optional secondary accounting method in the Payables Options window. The accounting method determines the number and nature of the journal entries Payables creates when transactions are transferred to General Ledger. There are three available accounting methods:

- **Cash** When you purchase an item, you recognize the expense (or, if it is a fixed asset, the increase in asset value) when you have paid for the item. You post only payments to General Ledger, not liability information for invoices. The payment distributions typically debit an expense (or asset) account and credit the cash or cash clearing account.

- **Accrual** When you purchase an item, you recognize the expense (or, if it is a fixed asset, the increase in asset value) when you receive an invoice from the supplier. At that point you also record a liability to pay the invoice. You post accounting distributions for both invoices and payments. The invoice distributions generally debit an expense (or asset) account and credit a liability account.

- **Combined** You maintain one set of books for cash accounting and another for accrual accounting. You choose which will be your primary set of books and which will be your secondary set of books. Invoice distributions are recorded in your accrual set of books, and payment distributions are recorded in both your cash and your accrual set.

Accrual basis accounting is used most often. The remainder of this chapter assumes that accrual basis accounting is being used.

CAUTION
Once you have posted transactions, you cannot change your primary accounting method. To make such a change, you would have to define a new Accounts Payable organization and start over.

Accounting Entries for Payables Transactions

There are two main events in Payables that give rise to accounting transactions: entering an invoice and issuing payment. Other activities such as adjusting invoices, creating expense reports, and processing prepayments also trigger accounting transactions. The following sections describe the accounting entries that are generated for different transactions entered in Payables. In addition, there is an explanation of how Oracle Financials assigns account codes to the various accounting entries. During posting, entries are created as journal lines and batches; they are then placed in the GL_INTERFACE table, ready to be imported into Oracle General Ledger. Be aware that, while transactions in Oracle Payables update the supplier's account within Payables immediately, they impact GL account balances only after you have run the Payables transfer process and posted the resulting journal within Oracle General Ledger.

Prepayments

A prepayment is a payment of a certain amount before you have received an invoice from the supplier. A prepayment could be sent with the purchase order as a deposit for goods or services. When you apply the prepayment to an invoice, you reduce the amount due on the invoice. For prepayments, Payables creates distributions that debit your prepayment account and credit the supplier's liability account. Here are the journal lines that would be generated by a $20 prepayment:

Account	Derivation of the Accounting Flexfield	Debit	Credit
Liability	Defaulted from the supplier site; can be overwritten during invoice entry.		20
Prepayment (asset)	Defaulted from the supplier site; otherwise entered during invoice entry.	20	

Invoices

An invoice increases the supplier's account balance by the invoice amount. Invoices are entered in Oracle Payables either through the Invoice Workbench window or through the Invoice Open interface (Imported), where you will be required to choose an expense (asset) and tax accounts for each invoice line. Once the invoice is completed, the corresponding journal entries will be posted to General Ledger in the next GL transfer. Here are the entries that would be created if an invoice amount of $235 were entered:

Account	Derivation of the Accounting Flexfield	Debit	Credit
Liability	Defaulted from the supplier site; can be overwritten during invoice entry.		235
Expense or Asset	Can be defaulted from the purchase order; otherwise, entered during invoice entry.	200	
Tax	Defaulted from the Tax Name setup; can be overwritten during invoice entry.	35	

NOTE
There may be multiple expense (or asset) accounts on an invoice if the invoice contains many invoice distributions.

The nature of accounting transactions for an invoice depends on whether you have posted liability for goods received and, consequently, whether you have used Oracle Purchasing to initiate the invoice. The invoice will trigger accounting transactions, the net result of which is a liability to pay the supplier and a debit distribution to stock, fixed asset, or expense, depending on the nature of the purchase. If the purchase order and receipt were processed in Oracle Purchasing, there will be a liability for goods received related to the purchase as well, and the liability for goods received will be replaced by an invoiced liability. Since it is not required to use Oracle Purchasing with Payables, this transaction may not always take place.

Credit Memos and Debit Memos
A memo decreases the supplier's account balance by the memo amount. Credit memos and debit memos both have the same effect from an accounting point of view: they reduce the amount that you owe the supplier. Both credit memos and debit memos are used to record a credit against an invoice for goods or services purchased. Credit and debit memos are netted with the original invoice at payment time, resulting in a payment being issued for the reduced amount. Reductions to invoice amounts are distinguished according to their origin, either received from the supplier or created internally.

- **Credit Memo** Negative amount invoice created by a supplier and sent to you to notify you of a credit

- **Debit Memo** Negative amount invoice created by you and sent to a supplier to notify the supplier of a credit you are recording; usually sent with a note explaining the reason for the debit memo

Although the distinction between these two types of transactions is a reasonable one, the terminology is counter-intuitive and confusing. Both transactions post a debit entry to the supplier's liability account and should perhaps be more correctly called *external debit memo* and *internal debit memo*. External debit memos are called credit memos because, as far as the supplier is concerned, they are credit memos in his or her accounts. Once entered to Oracle Payables, there is no difference between credit memos and debit memos, and both are processed in an identical fashion. In broad terms, their effect is opposite that of an invoice. Here is a comparison of sample entries that might be generated for a $47 credit memo and a $47 debit memo:

Account	Derivation of the Accounting Flexfield	Debit	Credit
Liability	Defaulted from the supplier site; can be overwritten during memo entry.	47	
Expense or Asset	Entered during invoice entry or defaulted from the invoice if the memo is matched to an invoice during entry.		40
Tax	Defaulted from the Tax Name setup; can be overwritten during invoice entry or defaulted from the invoice if the memo is matched to an invoice during entry.		7

Payments

A payment decreases the supplier's account balance by the payment amount. Payments can be generated in a variety of ways depending on the urgency of the situation and whether you want to computer-generate the payment document or initiate payment outside of the Financials system. The available methods are summarized in Table 5-4.

Method Used to Enter the Payment	Method Used to Generate the Payment	Advantage
Automatic, in a payment batch	Computer	Mass payment of all suppliers who are owed money.
Manual, from the Payment Workbench	Check is hand-written or typed, or bank transfer is initiated by wire.	Flexibility to record payments initiated and completed outside of Financials.
Quick, from the Payment Workbench	Computer	Ability to make immediate payments when speed is important.
Quick, from the Invoice Workbench	Computer	Convenience. Most payment information is entered for you, and you skip the invoice selection step needed in the Payment Workbench.

TABLE 5-4.   *Methods Available to Pay Invoices*

No matter how the payment is generated or entered into Oracle Payables, the postings it gives rise to when it is transferred to General Ledger are the same. It credits bank cash or cash clearing, and it debits the liability account associated with the invoice being paid. Paid invoices show a liability of zero. Here are sample journal entry lines generated by a $235 payment:

Account	Derivation of the Accounting Flexfield	Debit	Credit
Liability	Taken from the invoice(s) being paid.	235	
Bank cash account	Derived from the bank associated with the chosen payment document.		235

Payments do not give rise to tax postings. If, for instance, the preceding sample payment were based on the sample invoice entries described earlier, the two liability accounts would now be the same, and the balance on this account in General Ledger would be zero. The invoice would now be paid, and there would no longer be a liability to that supplier, assuming that this were the only activity on this account. (In any real situation, there would be other supplier liabilities posted to the same GL account, and it would be unlikely that the account would balance to zero.)

Integration with Other Financials Modules

This chapter has already discussed Payables integration with Oracle General Ledger and Oracle Cash Management in detail. Payables is integrated with several of the other Oracle modules in order to complete the flow of the procurement cycle and prevent duplicate data entry. This interaction and sharing of information is what allows Oracle Applications to be a full working "application" instead of several standalone modules. Data and processes flow into payables from other modules and then back out of payables into still other modules.

Integration with Oracle Purchasing

Payables shares supplier information with Oracle Purchasing. You can enter a supplier in either application, and then use that information to create purchase orders in Purchasing and invoices in Payables. The two modules completely share the database tables PO_VENDORS and PO_VENDOR_SITES, although Purchasing is the actual owner of the tables. There is no duplication of data, and any changes made to the supplier details in one module are immediately available for use in the other module.

Once you have created and approved purchase orders in Purchasing, you can match Payables invoices to one or more purchase order shipments or purchase order distributions. When you do this during invoice entry, Payables creates invoice distributions using the purchase order distribution accounting information.

Though it has no logic to compute them, Payables can discharge payment obligations for amortized loans. When you must account separately for the principal and interest elements of loan payments, the standard approach is to generate the payment stream in another system, then load the Invoice interface table with appropriate distributions.

Lease payments, with an unchanging distribution, are easier to handle. Payables will accept and store future transactions, known as *recurring invoices,* to enter into the payment cycle as they are due.

Integration with Oracle Self-Service Web Applications

The Self-Service Applications allow users to view and update data from a Web browser. The Applications often simplify these processes; in the case of Web Suppliers, for instance, your trading partners will actually become "users" of the application.

Web Suppliers gives your trading partners controlled access to review the status of Payables information within your database, including invoices and payments. Application security allows you to control access based on supplier or supplier site

Self-Service Expenses enables employees to do their own data entry for expense reports. The information they enter online is entered directly into the AP_EXPENSE_REPORT_HEADERS and AP_EXPENSE REPORT_LINES tables. Workflow ensures that these expense reports are approved and routed according to the business rules that you define. For example, you can set up Payables to require a justification for specific expense types (for example, entertainment). You can also use Payables to review, audit, adjust, and approve expense reports.

Integration with Oracle Receivables

Trading partners who have a reciprocal relationship with you—meaning that along with selling you goods or services, they also purchase goods or services from you—are considered both suppliers and customers. In the Oracle Applications these are treated as two completely separate entities. The customer entity is managed through Oracle Receivables and has almost no exposure to the supplier entity. If information regarding this type of trading partner needs updating in Oracle Financials, you will need to do so in two separate screens.

A Customer/Supplier Netting Report is provided, but exact naming, currency, and tax codes must exist for both the customer and supplier side before Oracle considers them to be the same trading partner. This is often not the case, so this process is usually handled manually or through custom development.

Integration with Oracle Projects

Project-related information can be entered in payables during invoice entry at the header or distribution level. Oracle Projects can also be used to pass charges from suppliers through to customers, a process that is a recurring task in business. Many companies are explicitly in the consignments or brokerage businesses, and other companies pass along some of the costs of providing service. Oracle Projects identifies recoverable expenses at purchasing time, captures the payment transaction, and passes the expenses on to Receivables. It has extensive logic for applying markups, accruing and grouping recoverable expenses, and presenting such charges on an invoice. Oracle Projects is a major system unto itself, and it is usually not worth the effort of installing it simply to rebill recoverable expenses.

Instead, you may institute a simple, straightforward customization that will work with any release of the products. You can structure a Descriptive Flexfield (DFF) to capture the customer data, such as the order number, as you process either a purchase order in Purchasing or a customer invoice in Receivables. From that point you can write a script to populate the interface tables for import by Receivables' AutoInvoice process.

Other Integration

There are additional processes that can conceivably be integrated with Payables, depending on your business needs. These processes may be incorporated into future releases of Payables; current need, however, is generally not compelling. Transaction volumes are typically small enough that they can easily be processed manually.

Oracle Fixed Assets computes the obligation for property taxes. Oracle Payroll withholds money for income tax, insurance, retirement, and other outside payees. Other systems, such as those used to compute corporate income taxes, usually present the payment obligation in report format. A common approach for paying the taxes is to set up the taxing entity as a supplier, generate an invoice for the amount due, and let Payables generate the check.

The Oracle Payables Data Model

Oracle Payables maintains data in a large number of tables. The data can be categorized as either reference or transaction data. *Transaction data* refers to invoices, credit memos, adjustments, and payments—the data that makes up the supplier's account. *Reference data* refers to supplier information, a large number of lookup codes, and static information. The purpose of this section is to describe the transaction tables and how the accounting data is stored and processed.

Figure 5-4 depicts the main Payables transaction tables and their relationships to one another. The transaction tables fall into two groups: the Invoice Group, which stores all the data entered through the Invoice Workbench, and the Payment Group, which corresponds to payments raised either through the Payment Workbench or by an automatic payment run.

AP_INVOICES stores invoice header information; it has one row per invoice, credit memo, or debit memo. As you would expect, AP_INVOICES carries the VENDOR_ID and the invoice AMOUNT. The invoice lines, including tax lines if there are any, are in AP_INVOICE_DISTRIBUTIONS. Each distribution carries an amount and an account code-combination ID. AP_PAYMENT_SCHEDULES holds one row per invoice unless the invoice is due to be paid in installments, in which case there will be one row per installment. Each installment is characterized by a due date and an amount.

The AP_CHECKS table holds payment documents, including checks, EFT payments, or wire transfers. There is one row per document; the table stores information about the supplier who received the payment (VENDOR_ID, VENDOR_NAME, and so on), the bank account that was drawn on (BANK_ACCOUNT_ID), and the AMOUNT and CHECK_DATE.

The AP_INVOICE_PAYMENTS table holds a permanent record of all payment documents that have been issued to pay invoices and invoice installments. If you need to account for a payment that is less than the total amount, you must create additional invoice installments in the

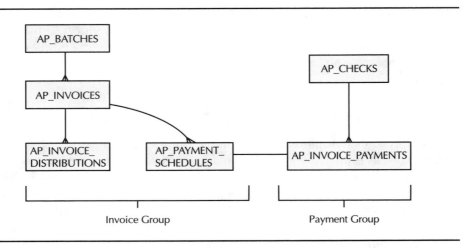

FIGURE 5-4. *The main Payables transaction tables*

AP_PAYMENT_SCHEDULES table. Once a scheduled payment has been made, there is a one-to-one relationship between AP_INVOICE_PAYMENTS and AP_PAYMENT_SCHEDULES. The AP_INVOICE_PAYMENTS table holds the AMOUNT of the payment, the ACCOUNTING_DATE, and two account code-combination IDs. These are the asset account related to the bank account on which the payment is drawn and the accounts payable liability account of the invoice that is being paid.

Technical Overview of the Automatic Payment Process

The payment process described earlier has five stages: Select, Modify, Format & Print, Confirm, and Deliver. Two important concurrent processes underlie these steps: the standard Build Payments program and a Formatting program. The Build Payments program is called several times during the cycle, and its behavior at each stage is different.

Oracle Payables handles the first four stages of the payment process, as diagrammed in Figure 5-5. It keeps track of each payment batch by updating AP_INV_SELECTION_CRITERIA.*status.* The status lifecycle progresses from NEW through BUILT (after the Build Payments program has built the payment batch), to FORMATTED (after the format program has generated the payment documents or checks), and finally to CONFIRMED. The Build Payments program generates the Payment Register report, either Preliminary or Final depending on the stage in the cycle.

SELECT   You initiate each step from the Payment Batch Actions window. When you create a payment batch, the BATCH_NAME is entered into the AP_INV_SELECTION_CRITERIA table, along with the selection criteria you specify and the payment limits for the batch. The Build program is submitted in order to build the payment batch. *Building* means the following:

- Selecting the invoices and invoice installments for payment. (These are inserted into AP_SELECTED_INVOICES.)

- Calculating how many documents are needed.

- Allocating document numbers to each selected invoice. (Document information is inserted into AP_SELECTED_INVOICE_CHECKS.)

- Generating the Preliminary Payment Register report.

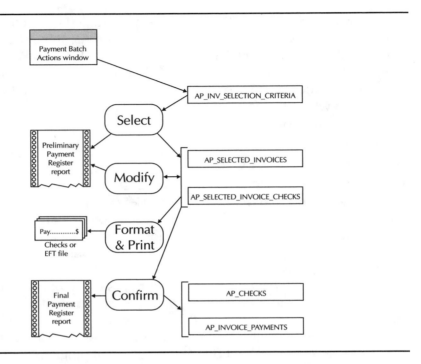

FIGURE 5-5. *The automatic payment process in Oracle Payables*

The processing logic to assign document numbers determines whether or not you have specified one document per invoice. During a check run, if a single check is issued to pay multiple invoices, the build process ensures that the maximum number of invoices that can appear on the remittance advice area of the check is not exceeded. If the remittance advice area is full, the check is voided and the excess invoice details are printed on the next check. The final check for each supplier carries the full amount of the payment.

MODIFY At any time before formatting, you can optionally modify the payment batch. You can prevent payment to a supplier, prevent payment of a particular invoice, change the invoice amount, or add an invoice that Payables did not originally select. After the batch has been modified, the Standard build program is resubmitted to reallocate document numbers.

FORMAT & PRINT   When you format your payment documents, Oracle Payables calls the program associated with the payment format you have chosen. Oracle delivers several payment format programs with Oracle Payables; you can also write your own. Each program will format checks to be printed or generate an EFT text file containing the payment information. You can choose from many check layouts and several bank file formats. Oracle can accommodate all the major international standards for both check layouts and EFT formats. The formatting program takes invoice and check information from AP_SELECTED_INVOICES and AP_SELECTED_INVOICE_CHECKS.

The output file is stored in the Payables output directory. Its name is created by appending a period and the Concurrent Manager request number to your Application Object Library user ID (for example, OSBORNE.1824).

CONFIRM   Confirmation is the last step performed within Oracle Payables. This step is very important because it generates the document and invoice payment records, which later get posted to Oracle General Ledger, and updates the payment history of invoices paid in a payment batch. If you have any unconfirmed payment batches, you cannot close a period or use the same payment document for any other payments until you confirm the payment batch. The Confirm program is submitted from the Payment Batch Actions window to confirm a payment batch. It takes invoice and document information from AP_SELECTED_INVOICES and AP_SELECTED_INVOICE_CHECKS and inserts confirmed documents and invoice payments into AP_CHECKS and AP_INVOICE_PAYMENTS, respectively. A batch can be CANCELLED at any stage up to CONFIRMED.

Technical Overview of General Ledger Interface

Transaction records that give rise to General Ledger journal postings show a telltale footprint. They all have a currency, an amount, a date, and a corresponding code-combination ID. For invoices, credit memos, and debit memos, the two relevant tables are AP_INVOICES and AP_INVOICE_DISTRIBUTIONS. In accounting terms, the total supplier liability is held in AP_INVOICES, and the expense, asset, or tax distributions are found in AP_INVOICE_DISTRIBUTIONS.

For payments, AP_SELECTED_INVOICE_CHECKS carries both the bank account code-combination and the accounts payable liability account code-combination.

The GL transfer process (registered as APPOST in the Concurrent Manager) is a Pro*C program that searches the AP_INVOICES, AP_INVOICE_DISTRIBUTIONS, AP_SELECTED_INVOICE_CHECKS tables for new rows that have not yet been posted to GL. For each new transaction, journal entry lines are inserted into the GL_INTERFACE table. APPOST updates each transferred transaction as posted and automatically submits the GL Journal Import process. If you have any unposted transactions, you cannot close a period.

Conclusion

The payables system is responsible for the payment of trade creditors. It is the last link in the supply chain. The importance of an effective payables system derives from its key position both in traditional cost control and in management accounting. Two trends in commerce are making payables even more central to a business: the growing dominance of supply-chain management in manufacturing industries, and the gradual shift of commerce away from a static, supplier-customer model to an open, global, networked economy, in which trade is initiated on the Web and conducted by means of electronic commerce. As both of these trends strengthen, Oracle Payables will prove itself an invaluable core application.

CHAPTER
6

Oracle Receivables

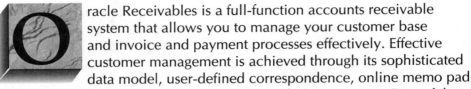racle Receivables is a full-function accounts receivable system that allows you to manage your customer base and invoice and payment processes effectively. Effective customer management is achieved through its sophisticated data model, user-defined correspondence, online memo pad for tracking customer interactions, and comprehensive reports. Powerful cash application tools and strong invoicing controls allow accurate processing of high transaction volumes with minimal manual data entry. In addition to supporting every Oracle module that generates customer payment obligations, notably Order Entry, Projects, and Customer Service, its open design supports non-Oracle systems and customer extensions within the Oracle product line.

Oracle Receivables and Your AR Business Processes

Most companies' policy is to take on new customers only after their accounts receivable department completes a satisfactory credit check. They also review established customers' credit in the process of accepting new orders. After the order has been satisfied, the receivables function includes invoicing customers for sales and following up to ensure prompt payment. The Oracle Receivables workflow is shown schematically in Figure 6-1.

Companies sell their products either for cash (immediate payment in the form of a check, credit card, or notes and coins) or as invoiced sales on credit with specific payment terms. Invoiced sales create a *receivable* in the balance sheet (General Ledger), which represents the money due to the company. The financial health of a company depends on keeping track of its customers and ensuring prompt collection of the money owed.

Receivables produces three legal documents to notify customers of their obligations:

- An *invoice* is usually sent shortly after a sale has been made. It states the obligation and provides details.

- A *statement* is a summary of the transactions over a period of time. It shows all open transactions. It may also show payments made within the period.

- A *dunning notice* informs the customer of past-due obligations.

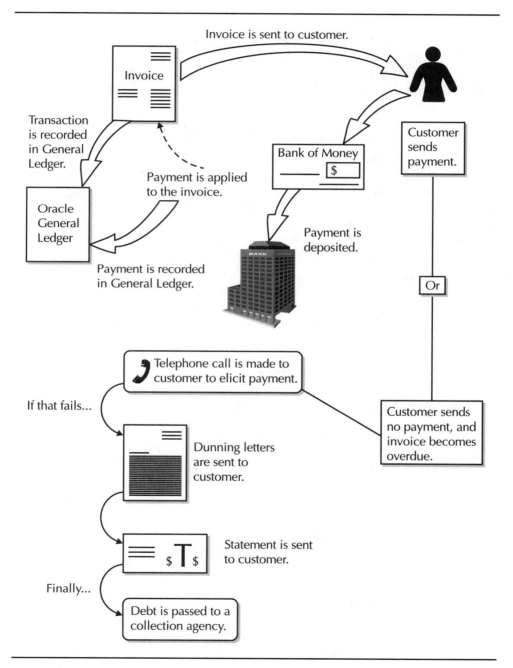

FIGURE 6-1.   *An overview of the Oracle Receivables workflow*

Companies can choose not to use both statements and dunning notices. However, because they are legal documents, most companies retain the ability to produce all three document types in a paper format. In the interests of efficiency, however, many now send invoices by EDI, fax, or e-mail, and they may agree with established customers to rely exclusively on electronic documents.

The customer can choose to pay the invoice in a variety of ways: by check or bank transfer, direct debit, or bill of exchange. When payment is received from the customer, you apply the cash to the customer account, reducing the amount owed and generating journals in GL. A partial payment will reduce the amount owed, but not to zero. The amount owed by each customer can be seen on the Aging Report and Account Detail screen.

Company policy establishes the steps to take when customers do not pay on time. Companies need to balance the risk of losing customers against the risk of being unable to collect debt. The process usually begins with a telephone contact, followed by dunning letters. Statements of a customer's account can be sent out periodically, and as a last resort, if the debt remains overdue, finance charges may be applied and the account can be referred to a debt collection agency or the company's legal department.

Creating and Managing the Customer Database

Accurate and up-to-date customer information is essential to many aspects of running a business: marketing, sales, and customer services as well as receivables. The Oracle Receivables customer repository can hold and share an extensive range of customer data. Oracle's sophisticated data model handles the many forms in which a company can relate to its customers. The customer is associated with any number of site addresses, and each address can have a list of contact names and telephone numbers. Each site can be designated for one or more functions, such as marketing, shipping, invoicing, and collections. You can designate contacts for each function. The overall customer data scheme is shown in Figure 6-2.

As customers are entered into the system, each is given a customer profile. The customer profile is an essential concept in Receivables. Default data values are taken from the profile during data entry, and many of Receivables' reports use customer profiles as a selection parameter.

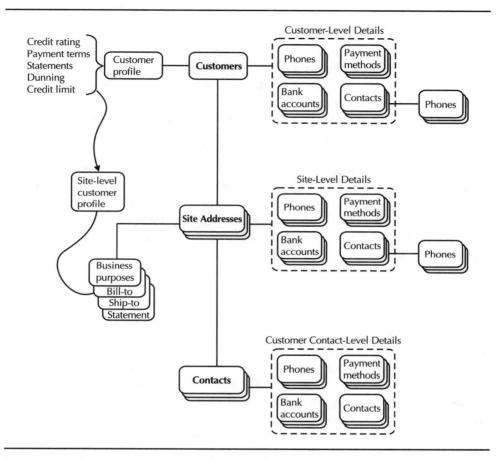

FIGURE 6-2.   *Customer data*

Customer Profiles

Customer profiles let you categorize customers into groups, known as *profile classes.* A profile class reflects several characteristics of each customer, including credit rating, payment terms, whether finance charges are calculated on overdue invoices, whether statements or dunning letters are sent, and the customer's credit limit.

While you should maintain a small, manageable number of profile classes, it is clear that each customer is unique, and a specific customer may not necessarily fit exactly into any one of the profile classes that you have set up. You can alter the characteristics of a particular customer's profile without modifying the profile for all the customers in the same profile class. When you make a change to a customer's profile and save your changes, the system asks you whether you want to apply the change to only this customer's profile, to all customers in the same profile class, or to all customers in the profile class who have not had their profile individually modified.

Customer profiles can be assigned at either customer level or customer bill-to address level. Because the credit limit is defined in the profile, it can make a significant difference whether you monitor credit compliance at customer level or customer bill-to address level. Although it is not enforced by the structure of Oracle Receivables, which is completely flexible, it makes organizational sense to establish a policy of tracking customer profiles at customer level or customer bill-to address level, but not a mix of both.

The Customer Account

Oracle Receivables enables you to search for customer information using the customer name or various other criteria. Using the Find Customers window, you can look up a customer on the basis of a phone number or view all customers within a given city, state, county, province, country, postal code, or area code. Each customer in the customer database has an account. The customer account in Oracle Receivables is not the same as the financial accounts stored in Oracle General Ledger. The customer account is a record of all the transactions—invoices, receipts, and so forth—that affect that particular customer. The account balance is calculated as follows:

> *Inv* (invoices for this customer)
> + *DM* (debit memos)
> + *Adj* (positive adjustments)
> − *CM* (credit memos)
> − *Rec* (receipts)
> − *Adj* (negative adjustments)
> _____
>
> *Resulting Account Balance*

You can view the customer account on paper by running a statement or the Aging Report, or you can view it online with the Account Details window, as shown in Figure 6-3.

Transactions in Receivables have an impact both on the customer account and on the financial accounts in General Ledger. There is no straightforward connection between the effect of a transaction on the customer account and on the postings to financial accounts. Some transactions, like the application of an on-account receipt to an invoice, have no effect on the customer's balance but do alter financial account balances in the GL.

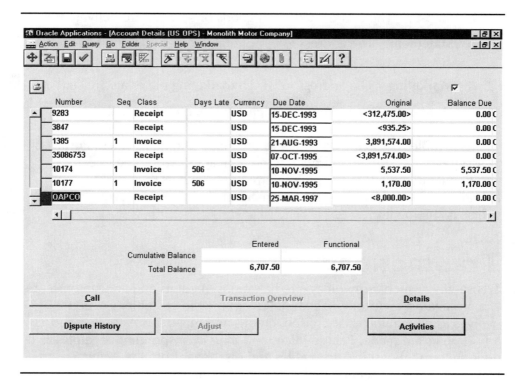

FIGURE 6-3.   *The online Account Details window*

Business Purposes

Business Purposes identify the role played by each of the customer sites. A customer could be ordering goods or services from many different offices, for delivery at several other locations. Customers can ask for the invoice to be sent to any address they choose. Some have centralized accounts payable and offer one invoice address irrespective of the delivery address, while others want invoices sent to the relevant local administrative office. Credit control, statements, and dunning letters can all be produced at either customer level or customer bill-to address level. Oracle Receivables provides the following predefined Business Purposes.

- **Bill-to**   The address to which invoices are sent
- **Ship-to**   The address to which goods or services are delivered
- **Statement**   The address to which statements and dunning letters are sent
- **Marketing**   The address to which marketing materials are sent
- **Dunning**   The address to which reminder letters are sent

Receivables offers the flexibility to define additional Business Purposes to assign your customer addresses. One typical use would be to carry additional addresses for shipping information, such as the freight forwarder, customs agent, systems integrator, or in-country agent for an overseas shipment.

Transactions

Transactions, such as invoices, credit memos, receipts and adjustments, are entered against a customer account. Over time the customer's account evolves as new invoices are raised, credits and receipts are applied and adjustments are made. Paid invoices and their corresponding receipts are of no long term interest in Receivables and disappear from the Aging Reports. However, each transaction will be posted to General Ledger and will have contributed to the receivables, revenue, tax, and cash balances.

Invoices

Each invoice lists what the customer has received and explains how the total invoice amount, which may include tax and freight charges, has been calculated. The standard printed invoice, while containing all the pertinent data, is commonly customized to alter the format and layout. Law dictates that certain data must appear on invoices—in the United Kingdom, a company's invoice must state the company name, its registration number, and its registered address. Tax requirements have to be observed, and certain customers may demand that you quote the purchase order number on their sales invoice.

Invoices are entered in Oracle Receivables through the Transactions window or the Transactions Summary window, or they are imported through the AutoInvoice open interface. You must provide the customer number and bill-to address, the receivables account and freight account, and revenue and tax accounts for each invoice line. An invoice increases the customer's account balance by the invoice amount. Here are the accounting entries that would be created for a sample invoice amount of $125:

Account	Derivation of the Accounting Flexfield	Debit	Credit
Receivables	Defaulted from the transaction type; can be overwritten during invoice entry.	125	
Revenue	Defaulted from the item; can be overwritten during invoice entry.		100
Tax	Defaulted from the specified tax rate; can be overwritten during invoice entry.		15
Freight	Defaulted from the transaction type; can be overwritten during invoice entry.		10

TIP
*You can use batch controls to ensure accurate
data entry, and you can enter sales credit
information to compensate the salesperson.*

An invoice often has multiple revenue account lines. For example, an
invoice from a hardware reseller for a PC server and installation shows two
separate lines on the invoice. The PC sale and the installation service are
posted to different revenue accounts.

Recurring Invoices

Recurring invoices are useful for situations where you regularly deliver the
same goods or services to a customer. You might need to bill for insurance
premiums, a maintenance contract, or lease repayments once a quarter for
three years, but you do not want to manually create a new invoice every
time. You can quickly create a group of invoices that share the same
characteristics using either the Transactions Summary window or the Copy
Transactions window. All of the dates for the copied invoices (for example,
transaction date, GL date, and due dates) are determined using a copy
rule. You may specify any one of the following copy rules: Annually,
Semiannually, Quarterly, Monthly, Bimonthly, Weekly, Single Copy,
or Days.

The Single Copy rule creates one copy of your model invoice for the day
you enter in the First Invoice Date field. The Days rule creates invoices at a
fixed interval of days, based on the number of days you specify.

Tax Considerations

Tax is relevant in Oracle Receivables as companies must bill their customers
tax on sales, collect the tax, and then pay the tax to the local fiscal authority.
You can set up Receivables to use one of two basic types of tax: value
added tax (VAT) or sales tax. The two methods of tax calculation are not
interchangeable, so once the setup has been performed you cannot
calculate and process the other tax type. VAT is a fixed percentage rate and
is primarily used in the European Union and parts of Asia (e.g., Thailand and
Singapore), while sales tax is levied in the United States and is based on the
location of the customer. Both types of tax can be set up so that specific
items or customers are exempt.

Oracle Receivables also provides a flexible tax defaulting hierarchy that you can define at the system options level. This hierarchy determines the order in which Receivables derives a default tax rate when you manually enter transactions or import them using AutoInvoice. Though Oracle Receivables includes logic to compute taxes, the calculation may be performed in other packages. Order Entry shares the Receivables tax tables. It has the capability to display taxes in customer quotes and orders. You have a choice of letting Receivables compute taxes or importing tax lines through the AutoInvoice import function.

TIP

If you need to process both sales tax and value added tax, set up Receivables for sales tax and define VAT rates. Then choose the appropriate VAT rates when you enter invoice lines.

Value-Added Tax

VAT is imposed on the value added to goods or services at each stage of their supply. The VAT charged on a customer invoice is referred to as *output tax*; it is calculated by multiplying the value of the goods or services by the appropriate tax rates. Any VAT paid on a vendor invoice is referred to as *input tax*. The amount due each period, monthly or quarterly, is calculated as follows:

Amount Due = Total Output Tax – Total Input Tax

VAT becomes due when the sale is invoiced, irrespective of whether the customer has paid the invoice or not. Depending on the payment terms you offer your customers, you may well end up paying the VAT to the tax authority before you have collected the money from your customer. Such sales have a short term negative impact on your cash flow; you pay the government before the customer pays you. There is a provision to reclaim VAT if the customer persists in not paying and the debt is written off.

Whereas Oracle Receivables provides standard reports showing the total tax charged, the liability to pay the tax to the fiscal authority is not created in the Oracle Payables module. This liability should be entered manually in Payables, a task that is normally done at fixed intervals, that is, one Payables invoice is created monthly or quarterly.

VAT rates vary from country to country, and each country has exceptions for exempted sales, for example, zero-rated and low-rated. The rate is based on the type of goods sold, with low rates frequently targeted to support social ends. In the U.K., for example, books are zero-rated, while children's clothing and heating fuel are low-rated. You use the Tax Codes and Rates window to define appropriate tax codes and rates.

Sales Tax

Sales tax is based on the location of the customer receiving your goods or services. The calculation of sales tax is based on the state, county, and city components of the customers' addresses and the tax rates assigned to each of these components. You can override any tax rate through customer and product exemptions, and you can compile periodic sales tax returns using the U.S. Sales Tax Report. Many jurisdictions have different sales tax rates for different types of goods as well. Groceries, for instance, are often taxed lower than other consumer goods, and to encourage the use of natural gas, the state of Maryland exempts gas appliances from sales tax.

Oracle provides a full schema for tax rate structures. However, the process of keeping it populated with accurate data is truly onerous. It involves all kinds of taxing jurisdictions: states, counties, cities, and special jurisdictions. U.S. companies that do business on a national basis usually find it well worth the price to subscribe to a service such as Vertex to obtain automatic updates. These vendors usually provide scripts to automatically post their data to the Oracle tables. Alternatively, you can use the Sales Tax Rate interface (described later in this chapter).

The tax information service should be one of the Superusers' earliest considerations. It typically takes about three months to select a vendor and install the software. Usually it is best to use a single service for property tax rates (fixed assets), payroll tax rates (HR/payroll), and sales tax rates (AR). It is not a secondary matter. Oracle Receivables provides a flexible tax defaulting hierarchy that you define at the system options level. This hierarchy determines the order in which Receivables will derive a default tax rate when you manually enter transactions or import them using AutoInvoice.

Revenue Recognition

Accounts receivable is designed to be the single source of revenue transactions for the General Ledger. It simplifies the accounting. A single set of numbers—amounts actually invoiced and received—drives the General Ledger, sales analysis, sales compensation, and marketing compensation.

Receivables may be set up with an aggressive revenue recognition policy, billing orders as they are accepted and accruing revenue upon billing, or it may be set up with a conservative policy of not recognizing revenue until the money is in hand. Some businesses call for even greater restraint. Universities collect tuition in advance of delivering instruction, and a landlord may collect rents well in advance. The wisest policy for these companies is to debit advance payments to a separate account, to be journaled into earnings at the time services are actually delivered.

Automatic Account Generation (AutoAccounting and Flexbuilder)

Assigning Accounting Flexfield combinations to financial transactions is a major function of all the Financials packages. The assignments must be accurate for the financial reports to be meaningful. However, keying a multisegment Accounting Flexfield for every transaction would be incredibly time-consuming. Through Version 10.7, Receivables uses AutoAccounting, the Oracle Receivables forerunner of Flexbuilder and Automatic Account Generation. AutoAccounting provides a mechanism for generating default Accounting Flexfields—for revenue, receivables, freight, and tax—based on other parameters associated with the invoice you are entering. Elsewhere in the applications, Flexbuilder performs exactly the same role, but in a more flexible and generally better way. AutoAccounting and Flexbuilder are not interchangeable. Flexbuilder cannot be used in place of AutoAccounting in Receivables to generate default accounts for revenue, receivables, freight, and tax. Flexbuilder is used in Receivables, but for the fairly minor task of assigning the correct company segment value for realized exchange gain-and-loss journal entries.

Oracle Receivables uses Flexbuilder to generate the appropriate balancing-segment values for finance charges and exchange rate gain-and-loss accounts. For example, if you assess finance charges for an invoice that has a receivables account with a company segment value of 20, and the balancing segment of your finance charges account is 10, then Flexbuilder sets the balancing segment of the finance charges account to 20. Doing this ensures that finance charges that belong to Risky Insurance Offshore Ltd. do not end up accounted for as income for Risky Insurance

Corp. The finance charge account and the exchange rate gain-and-loss accounts are set up only once, in the System Options form, so it is not possible to set up different accounts for each company that is handled within one installation of Receivables.

While setting up AutoAccounting, you indicate whether to use a constant value for each of the account segments or to look up the value from another table. The range of lookup tables is limited to Salesrep, Transaction Types, Standard Lines, and Taxes. Here are some examples of standard AutoAccounting table assignments:

Account to Be Generated	Table
Receivables	Transaction Types
Revenue	Standard Lines
Freight	Transaction Types
Tax	Taxes

Remember that each segment of each account can be generated according to a different rule. This is useful, for example, if you want the natural account for revenue to default from the Standard Line, but you want the cost center to be derived from the Salesrep. Although there is the flexibility to generate each segment from a different table, there is rarely any need for this.

Limitations of AutoAccounting

AutoAccounting does not allow you to use rules to derive the company segment. Imagine you are the Financials Controller of Risky Insurance, and you manage two separate operations within one installation of Oracle Receivables: Risky Insurance Corp. which has company code 10, and Risky Insurance Offshore Ltd. with company code 20. Because the majority of business is conducted by Risky Insurance Corp., you set up the Transaction Types and Standard Lines with the default company code 10. As you enter an invoice for Risky Insurance Offshore Ltd. you overwrite the company segment of the receivables account with a rarely used but perfectly valid company code 20. When you come to the revenue lines for that same invoice you should post the revenue to company 20, but the Accounting

Flexfield will have been generated from the AutoAccounting rules as 10. There is no possibility to cascade the company code from the receivables account you have just entered into the revenue account.

AutoAccounting is limited to deriving the Accounting Flexfield values for revenue, receivables, freight, tax, and the less frequently used AutoInvoice clearing, unbilled receivable, and unearned revenue accounts. These are all the accounts required during invoice or debit memo entry. You cannot use AutoAccounting, or Flexbuilder for that matter, to generate accounts used during receipt entry, such as unapplied receipt, unidentified, on-account, and so forth.

Logic in newer packages such as Order Entry overcomes most AutoAccounting limitations. Release 11, with Automatic Account Generation, totally does away with them. Users can overcome the limitations of Release 10.7 and earlier by programming the necessary segment selection logic into an interface instead of leaving it to AutoAccounting.

Printing Transactions

The following three programs are used for printing Accounts Receivable transactions:

- **RAXINV_SEL**   Prints selected invoices, based on parameters you enter.

- **RAXINV_NEW**   Prints all transactions that have not been printed previously.

- **RAXINV_BATCH**   Prints a batch of invoices.

The standard layout is intended to be a template, as there is no possible way Oracle could build one invoice that would satisfy all its customers. You will likely need to alter the layout to fit your organization's specific needs. Since the standard report already prints nearly all data that is relevant for these transactions, your customization will probably include removing elements you don't wish to print and changing the layout. Be sure to use a programmer experienced with Oracle*Reports, as the data model and functioning of the software is quite extensive.

TIP

If possible, use the bitmapped version of Oracle*Reports, and program the invoice print program to print your company logo and the invoice boilerplate text with a TrueType laser printer. Your invoices look smarter, and the programmer will avoid the time-consuming problem of lining up printed text on preprinted stationery.

Debit Memos

Oracle Receivables handles debit memos the same way it handles invoices. A debit memo increases the customer's account balance by the debit memo amount and is used to bill a customer for additional charges in relation to a previously invoiced sale. There is a whole range of situations where such additional billing is necessary. A debit memo would be handy, for example, when the freight cost has been left off of an original invoice because it was not known at the time of the earlier billing.

A debit memo is a legal document that you send to the customer, and it must comply with the same legal and tax requirements that are relevant for an invoice.

Credit Memos

A credit memo (CM) is used to alert a customer to a reduction in charges related to a previously invoiced sale. An on-account credit memo is a reduction in charges that is not tied to a specific previous invoice. There are many situations in which this is necessary. You create a credit memo when a discount is given at the end of a quarter for customers who have bought in excess of a discount threshold. Whenever possible, however, it is important to tie the CM back to the original invoice. That way you can assure that the proper account will be hit and you will maintain a better audit trail. A credit memo is also a legal document that you need to send to the customer.

A credit memo decreases the customer's account balance by the credit memo amount. Here are the accounting entries that would be created if a sample credit memo of $11.50 were applied to an invoice.

Account	Derivation of the Accounting Flexfield	Debit	Credit
Receivables	Same receivables account as the related invoice.		11.50
Revenue	Same revenue account(s) as the related invoice.	10.00	
Tax	Same tax account(s) as the related invoice.	1.50	

Here are the accounting entries that would be created for a sample on-account credit memo of the same amount:

Account	Derivation of the Accounting Flexfield	Debit	Credit
Receivables	Defaulted from the transaction type; can be overwritten during CM entry.		11.50
Revenue	Defaulted from the item; can be overwritten during CM entry.	10.00	
Tax	Defaulted from the tax rate; can be overwritten during CM entry.	1.50	

Receipts

Cash, checks, bank transfers, and other forms of payment received from a customer are called receipts. A receipt is entered via the Receipts window or the Receipts Summary window, or it is imported through the AutoLockbox interface. The acid test that all receipts have been correctly accounted for is the bank reconciliation.

Accounting for receipts depends on the extent to which the receipts can be identified. The ideal situation occurs when the customer clearly identifies the invoice or invoices being paid. Such receipts are entered and applied to the respective invoices, and no further research is necessary. These receipts are called *applied receipts.* When it is not possible to establish the invoice numbers, but it is clear which customer has sent the money, the receipt is entered and applied to the customer's account, but not to specific transactions in the account. Such receipts are referred to as *on-account* or *unapplied.* Lastly, if it is not possible to determine which customer made the payment, the receipt is entered without specifying a customer account. These are known as *unidentified receipts.* The quantity, in terms of both number and value, of unidentified and on-account receipts should be kept to a minimum. With unidentified receipts, a continued effort is made to find the customer and record this in the system. On-account receipts are also researched to determine which invoices the customer had intended to pay, and then the receipts are applied to those transactions.

Enter Receipt Actions

Oracle Receivables provides a powerful feature that lets you create item-level actions while you enter and apply your receipts. With item-level actions you can create adjustments, issue chargebacks, and apply receipts to your credit memos and on-account credits to reduce your customer's balance.

Applied Receipts

An applied receipt decreases the customer's account balance by the applied amount. Here are the journal entries that would be generated by a sample applied receipt for $125:

Account	Derivation of the Accounting Flexfield	Debit	Credit
Cash or Bank Asset account	Taken from the payment method; cannot be overwritten during entry.	125	
Receivables	The receivables account(s) of the applied invoice(s).		125

On-Account or Unapplied Receipts

An on-account receipt decreases the customer's account balance by the receipt amount. Here are the journal entries that would be generated by a sample on-account receipt for $125:

Account	Derivation of the Accounting Flexfield	Debit	Credit
Cash or Bank Asset account	Taken from the payment method; cannot be overwritten during entry.	125	
Unapplied	Taken from the payment method; cannot be overwritten during entry.		125

Unidentified Receipts

Unidentified receipts have no effect on customer account balances because the customer is not known.

Until the customer is known, the possibility remains that an unidentified receipt was sent in error and that the money may have to be paid back. This is represented by showing a liability in the balance sheet equal to the value of the unidentified receipt. Here are the journal entries that would be generated by a sample unidentified receipt for $125:

Account	Derivation of the Accounting Flexfield	Debit	Credit
Cash or Bank Asset account	Taken from the payment method; cannot be overwritten during entry.	125	
Unidentified	Liability account taken from the payment method; cannot be overwritten during entry.		125

Receipt Reversals

Oracle Receivables lets you reverse receipts when your customer stops the check or when your receipt comes from an account with insufficient funds.

You can also reverse a receipt if you want to re-enter and reapply the receipt to another debit item. To reverse a receipt, you can create either a standard reversal or a debit memo reversal. When you create a standard reversal, Oracle Receivables automatically updates your General Ledger and reopens the invoices you closed with the original receipt. When you create a debit memo reversal, all previous receipt activity remains unchanged, but the customer account is charged with another receivable.

Application of On-Account Receipts

Receipts that were on-account when they were entered should be applied to their invoices once it is clear which invoice the customer wishes to pay. The Applications window can be used to apply a receipt to an invoice or several invoices—or any combination of invoices, debit memos, and credit memos that belong together. The credit posting is always to the receivables account of the invoice that is being applied. The debit posting hits the account that was previously posted in credit. This ensures that once a receipt reaches its final resting state as fully applied, the postings generated are always the same: a debit to the cash or bank asset account, and a credit to the receivables account of the applied invoice. Whichever route the receipt has taken through being unidentified or unapplied, the unidentified or unapplied account is debited to cancel the credit that was posted when the receipt was originally entered. Here are the journal entries that would be generated by a sample on-account receipt for $125

Account	Derivation of the Accounting Flexfield	Debit	Credit
Receivables	The receivables account(s) of the applied invoice(s).		125
Unapplied or Unidentified	The unapplied or unidentified account from the payment method; cannot be overwritten during entry.	125	

Miscellaneous Receipts

The term *miscellaneous receipt* refers to cash received in respect to revenue that has not been invoiced. Typically this is revenue such as investment income or bank interest. Miscellaneous receipts are accounted for on a cash basis, the revenue is recognized when the money is received. To enter a miscellaneous receipt, navigate to the Receipts window and choose the Misc receipt type. There is no need to enter a customer account for miscellaneous receipts. The accounting for miscellaneous receipts is determined by the payment method and receivables activity you choose from a list of values. You can enter any receivables activity that has previously been defined as a Miscellaneous Cash receipt type.

NOTE
An unidentified receipt should not be entered as miscellaneous simply on the grounds that the customer number does not need to be entered. If it is originally entered as a miscellaneous receipt, you will not be able to apply the unidentified receipt once you determine the customer and invoice number.

Here are the postings that would be generated by a sample miscellaneous receipt for $342:

Account	Derivation of the Accounting Flexfield	Debit	Credit
Cash or Bank Asset account	Taken from the payment method; cannot be overwritten during entry.	342	
Revenue	Taken from the receivables activity selected during entry; can be overwritten.		342

Automatic Receipts

Automatic receipts are either bills of exchange or direct debits. Direct debits are a method of payment in which the customer authorizes you to debit the amount due directly from his own bank account. You do this by sending your bank a datafile, on tape or disk or via the Internet, which the bank processes. Bills of exchange are processed in the same way as direct debits, except there is an extra authorization step. Before you debit your customer's bank account, you must notify the customer that you intend to take a certain amount in respect of certain invoices. Once the customer has provided authorization, you can debit the bank account in the same way as for direct debits. To a certain extent, bills of exchange and direct debits rely on trust; if you habitually take too much money, or take money before it is due from a customer's bank account, the customer or the bank will withdraw your authority to directly debit the account.

Bank File Formats

The transfer of funds occurs when your bank processes the remittance datafile you send to them. The format of the electronic file has to be agreed upon with your bank. Each country tends to have its own standard for bank files; a U.S. Treasury Format is in use in the United States; the United Kingdom uses BACS (Bank Automated Clearing System); Germany uses the Deutsche Bank DTA (Datenträger Austausch). Many more formats are in use around the world and an increasing number of these are covered by Oracle's Globalizations.

Multiple-Invoice Applications

You must be able to create complex cash applications that involve many transactions and that have the capability to either fully or partially apply to each transaction. Oracle Receivables provides this powerful ability, and thus allows your staff to be more efficient. To apply customer receipts to a group of transactions at once, navigate to the Receipts window, query or enter the receipt to apply, and then click Mass Apply. The customer's open items appear in a window. To apply the receipt, check or uncheck the Apply check box next to each transaction. The Applications window is shown in Figure 6-4.

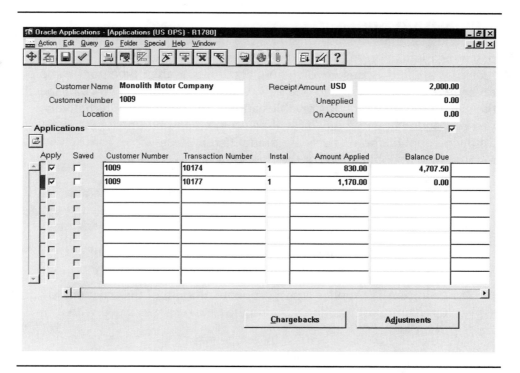

FIGURE 6-4. *The Mass Apply window for applying receipts to multiple transactions*

Cross-Currency Receipts Application

In Release 11, Oracle Receivables allows you to apply a cash receipt in one currency against one or more invoices in different currencies. You can also apply multiple payments in any predefined currency to a single invoice. Companies that invoice or receive any of the euro currencies need to manage cross-currency receipts. Receivables supports the processing requirements of currencies that are fixed-rate denominations of the euro. Cross-currency applications between two euro currencies do not generate exchange-rate gain or loss postings.

Application Rule Sets

Oracle Receivables Release 11 supports a user-defined hierarchy of payment application rules. You can define a set of rules to control how the receipt is applied against invoice line, according to their type (for example revenue line, tax, freight and charges). Within each rule set, you can specify the exact order in which Receivables applies the payment. Alternatively, you can define how the receipt will be prorated among line types. The following application rule sets are predefined in Receivables for use with manual receipt applications or the Post QuickCash program:

- **Line First - Tax After** Applies payment to the open line amount, and then the remaining payment amount to the associated tax amount.

- **Line first - Tax prorate** Applies a proportionate amount of the payment to the open line and the tax amount for each line.

- **Prorate All** Applies a proportionate amount of the payment to each open amount (e.g. line, tax, freight, charges) associated with a debit item.

QuickCash

QuickCash lets you enter your receipts quickly, with a minimum amount of information. QuickCash receipts are temporarily stored in two interim tables called AR_INTERIM_CASH_RECEIPTS and AR_INTERIM_CASH_RECEIPT_LINES. Batches of QuickCash receipts must be posted to transfer them from these interim tables to the regular receipt tables within Oracle Receivables. Posting QuickCash batches updates the customer account balances and causes the receipts to appear on reports and inquiry forms within Oracle Receivables; it also realizes the applications specified during receipt entry. Once QuickCash batches have been posted, the relevant invoices will appear as closed in Oracle Receivables. The two interim cash receipt tables are used by the AutoLockbox interface when receipts are imported from a bank file.

TIP
*Because records are continually being inserted
and deleted from the two interim QuickCash
tables, QuickCash online entry may slow down
as the tables become fragmented. This may be
a driving factor in setting your DBA's schedule
to periodically rebuild these two tables, taking
care to keep all the records in the tables at the
time of the rebuild.*

AutoCash Rules

AutoCash rules are used by the Post QuickCash program to determine how
to automatically apply cash receipts against open customer transactions.
Oracle Receivables offers five receipt application rules that you can use to
create AutoCash rule sets:

- **Apply oldest debit items first**   This rule matches receipts to debit
  items, starting with the oldest debit item first.

- **Apply receipts to past-due items**   Money received goes to overdue
  bills first.

- **Clear the account**   Post QuickCash uses this rule only if your
  customer's account balance exactly matches the amount of the
  receipt. If it does, the receipt is applied to all open transactions on
  the account.

- **Clear past-due invoices**   This rule is similar to the preceding "clear
  the account" rule because it applies the receipt to your customer's
  debit and credit items only if the total of these items exactly matches
  the amount of this receipt. However, this rule applies the receipt
  only to items that are currently past due.

■ **Clear past-due invoices grouped by payment term**   This rule is similar to the preceding "clear past-due invoices" rule, but it first groups past-due invoices by their payment term, and then uses the oldest transaction due date within the group as the group due date.

■ **Match receipts with debit items**   This rule applies the receipt to a single invoice, debit memo, or chargeback that has a remaining amount due exactly equal to the receipt amount.

The rules you select affect the ease with which your receivables staff can apply cash and finance charges for your customers. For example, matching receipts to debit items tends to minimize the number of open items, making life easier for your accounting staff. On the other hand, a customer who just paid a recent bill might see finance charges for an old item that would not appear if the money had gone to the old item first.

It is well worth spending time on designing your AutoCash rule sets during the implementation of Oracle Receivables. The more applications that can be performed automatically, the less tedious work for your staff. In addition, fast and accurate application of cash dramatically reduces the number of payment inquiries from your customers.

Adjustments

Adjustments are alterations to debit items (invoices, debit memos, and chargebacks). You can separately adjust the tax, freight, lines, or receivables amount of a debit item, and the adjustments can be either positive or negative. You do not need to inform the customer about adjustments; they are internal corrections that do not materially affect the legal documents—invoices and debit memos—that have already been sent to the customer. Adjustments are commonly made for the following reasons:

■ Correcting a data entry error

■ Writing off a receivable item

■ Adjusting sales revenue credit to your salespeople

You create an adjustment in the Transactions Summary window by querying the transaction, selecting it, and then clicking the Adjust button.

Adjustments have to be approved. The person entering the adjustment can approve it, provided their authorization limit exceeds the value of the adjustment; otherwise adjustments are authorized later by another user whose limit is sufficient. Unapproved adjustments do not get applied to the customer balance or transferred to General Ledger. The postings generated by an approved adjustment depend on what was adjusted—tax, freight, revenue lines, or receivables—and the contra account supplied by the user when the adjustment is entered. An unpaid invoice of $125 that was being written off as a bad debt would generate the postings shown here:

Account	Derivation of the Accounting Flexfield	Debit	Credit
Receivables	The receivables account of the adjusted invoice.		125
Adjustment	Taken from the receivables activity entered by the user; can be overridden.	125	

Writing Off Small Amounts During Receipt Entry

Often the receipt amount that the customer has paid does not exactly equal the invoice amount. This can result in either an underpayment or an overpayment. In the case of a substantial underpayment, the invoice is left open for the customer to pay the remainder. In the case of an overpayment, the difference is refunded to the customer. A common cause of overpayment is the customer paying the same invoice twice—such double payments should always be refunded.

If the overpayment or underpayment amount is small (in the subjective judgment of the person accounting for the receipt) the difference can be written off. Some common causes of small differences are listed here:

■ The customer rounds the amount down to the nearest whole number.

■ The customer remits the wrong amount by mistake.

- The customer pays a foreign currency amount that does not exchange to the required amount of the invoice.

- A bank or correspondence bank has taken a handling fee for a bank transfer.

Experience shows that underpayments are more common than overpayments, so a degree of restraint should be instituted before underpayments are written off. However, there is a cost associated with chasing every last cent, and most companies accept that it is not economical to pursue small underpayments.

In receivables, you handle these small differences by making adjustments and chargebacks against transactions to which you are applying a receipt. You create chargebacks and adjustments against each transaction, for positive or negative amounts, by clicking the Adjustment and Chargeback buttons from the Applications window.

Finance Charges

The Statement and Dunning Letter programs apply finance charges to past-due amounts. You set the finance percentages in each currency and give your rules for grace periods.

Finance charges are a frequent bargaining chip in collections and, as such, a frequent subject of adjustments. Many collectors will waive finance charges in exchange for prompt payment of past-due amounts. Setting up finance charges is an important aspect of setting up Oracle Receivables.

Commitments

A customer commitment takes the form of either a deposit or a guarantee. A *deposit commitment* occurs when the customer agrees to pay a deposit for goods that they have not ordered yet, while a *guarantee commitment* is a contractual guarantee of future purchases. Both of these are handled by Oracle. They give rise to unbilled receivables and unearned revenue account postings. Within Receivables, a separate commitment balance is maintained. Analogous to the account balance, it ebbs and flows according to customer commitments and transactions. The customer commitment balance is available in several places within Receivables and is also available if you are using Oracle Order Entry. You can see the balance for a particular commitment when entering an order (if you are using Order

Entry), a manual invoice, or a credit memo against a commitment or by running the Commitment Balance Report. All transactions that reference a commitment or reference an invoice that references a commitment affect the balance of that commitment. The general formula for calculating the balance of a commitment at any given time is as follows:

> *Com* (original amount of commitment)
> − *Inv* (invoices against commitment)
> − *CMI* (credit memos that reference invoices that reference commitments)
> + *CMC* (credit memos against the commitment itself)

Resulting Commitment Balance

If you were to enter a deposit of $1000, Receivables would create the journal entry shown here:

Account	Derivation of the Accounting Flexfield	Debit	Credit
Receivables (deposit)	Derived using AutoAccounting structure.	1000	
Unearned Revenue	Derived using AutoAccounting structure.		1000

If you were entering an invoice against this deposit, Receivables might create these sample journal entries:

Account	Derivation of the Accounting Flexfield	Debit	Credit
Receivables (invoice)	Defaulted from the transaction type; can be overwritten during invoice entry.	1100	

Account	Derivation of the Accounting Flexfield	Debit	Credit
Revenue	Defaulted from the item; can be overwritten during invoice entry.		900
Tax (if you charge tax)	Defaulted from the tax rate; can be overwritten during invoice entry.		100
Freight (if you charge freight)	Defaulted from the transaction type; can be overwritten during invoice entry.		100
Receivables (deposit)	Taken from the commitment.		1000
Unearned Revenue	Taken from the commitment.	1000	

When you apply an invoice to a deposit, Receivables creates a receivable adjustment against the invoice. Receivables uses the account information you specified in your AutoAccounting structure. If cash were received against the preceding deposit, Receivables would create the journal entry shown here:

Account	Derivation of the Accounting Flexfield	Debit	Credit
Bank Cash Account	Derived from the payment method.	1000	
Receivables (deposit)	Taken from the commitment.		1000

Finally, if you were to enter a guarantee, Receivables would create this journal entry:

Account	Derivation of the Accounting Flexfield	Debit	Credit
Unbilled Receivables	Derived using AutoAccounting structure.	1000	
Unearned Revenue	Derived using AutoAccounting structure.		1000

Entering an invoice against a guarantee and applying cash to a guarantee work in the same way as deposits; the receivables (deposit) account is replaced with the unbilled receivables account.

Customer Follow-Up

Collectors work constantly to collect debt promptly, to ensure the customer accounts balances in the system are up to date, and to chase past-due invoices. Within Oracle Receivables customer phone calls can be tracked and logged, statements can be generated and sent to customers (so that they can check their records against yours), and reminder letters can be sent to chase past-due invoices.

Customer Calls

The Customer Calls window is used to record the results of your conversation with customers. Customers may tell you that their invoice was wrong, that they dispute some of the charges, that they did not receive the goods, or that they have already sent payment for the invoice. You can enter follow-up actions on the basis of what you agree with your customer. While you talk to the customer, you can quickly review all customer information and verify that the customer's record of the open transactions agrees with your record. It is good business practice to encourage a "one-stop" approach to customer service. That is, customer calls should be logged and the appropriate action determined at the time of the original telephone conversation. Any department that relies on written memos of the conversation or a procedure for passing action to other people within the organization is inherently inefficient, error-prone, and slow to respond to customers.

Dunning Letters

Dunning letters are sent to remind customers of overdue invoices. A dunning run is submitted in one step in the Reports-Collections window, but the dunning letters are produced in two stages. The first of these, the Dunning Letter Generate program (ARDLGP), determines which customers should receive a dunning letter and indicates the invoices that should appear on the dunning letter. The second, the Dunning Letter Print program (ARDLP), produces a letter for each of the customers selected in the first step. The layout of the letter and the text that appears on it can be customized as described later in the chapter. That way you can control the severity and content of each dunning letter. The first dunning letter might simply say, "These invoices are now overdue. Please remit your payment as soon as possible," whereas the third letter may say, "Invoices that are more than six weeks overdue will be passed to our legal department for collection. Until your account is settled, we are unable to supply any further products to your company."

Creating Dunning Letter Sets

Having determined that a customer will receive a dunning letter, the Dunning Letter Generate program next determines which level (1, 2, or 3) of dunning letter the customer should receive. Oracle Receivables can use two methods to determine which letter to send:

- Days overdue
- Staged

Using the days overdue dunning method, Oracle Receivables looks at the oldest debit item for the customer and compares the number of days it is past due with the date ranges of each letter in the dunning letter set, as shown in Table 6-1.

Dunning Letter	Days Overdue Low	Days Overdue High
First letter	10	20
Second letter	21	30
Third letter	31	999

TABLE 6-1. *Letters in a Days Overdue Dunning Letter Set*

Using the staged dunning method, you assign a dunning-level range to each letter in the set. The dunning level of a debit item is the number of times it has appeared on a dunning letter. The Dunning Letter Generate program increments the dunning level of each debit item it selects. You also assign a minimum number of days that must pass before a transaction can appear again on a dunning letter. Oracle Receivables looks at the oldest debit item for the customer and compares the dunning level of the transaction with the dunning-level ranges of each letter in the dunning letter set, as shown in Table 6-2.

The Dunning Letter Generate program sieves out customers who need reminder letters. The program identifies the overdue items for each customer and selects an appropriate letter to send them. Once customers and their overdue items are identified, the Dunning Letter Generate program inserts appropriate records into the two tables AR_CORRESPONDENCES and AR_CORRESPONDENCE_PAY_SCHED. These tables form the link between the generate program and the print program, as shown in Figure 6-5. The

Dunning Letter	Dunning Level Low	Dunning Level High	Minimum Days Before Reselection
First letter	0	1	15
Second letter	2	2	5
Third letter	3	999	5

TABLE 6-2. *Letters in a Staged Dunning Letter Set*

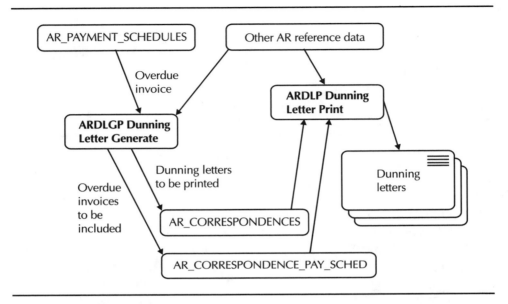

FIGURE 6-5. *The dunning process*

Dunning Letter Print program produces a dunning letter for each record in AR_CORRESPONDENCES that has the REQUEST_ID of the generate program request ID.

With Release 11, implementations of Oracle Receivables that are set up with multiple organizations can create centralized statement and dunning sites for customers.

Dunning Letter Customization

Many aspects of dunning letters can be customized without programming. A dunning letter is constructed of header text, body, and footer text. With Release 11 the letters can be created in the Dunning Letter window. In prior releases, the header and footer text could be edited using a regular text editor. For example, to enter body text for the dunning letter USER1, you edit the file $AR_TOP/srw/ardl1b.txt.

Within the text you can embed field variables, which get interpreted and replaced with the appropriate information when the dunning letter is printed. Receivables can interpret the four field variables shown in Table 6-3.

With Release 11, you can create an unlimited number of dunning letters, each customized with your own header and footer text. The three sections of a standard letter—header, body, and footer—are shown in Figure 6-6. The body of the dunning letter contains a list of customer transactions. The selection criteria for choosing which transactions are shown and whether a letter is sent at all were described in the preceding sections. The exact logic that is applied can be modified by using switches defined as part of a dunning letter set. The switches determine whether unapplied receipts are included, whether all customer transactions are included or only those that are overdue, and whether disputed items are included.

A dunning letter set is simply a group of three dunning letters. The seeded dunning letter set called STANDARD consists of three dunning letters of increasing severity. The dunning letter set also controls when each letter is sent, whether the letters have to be sent in sequence, and a host of other control parameters, each of which can be individually set, as shown in Figure 6-7.

Field Variable	Value	Example
&F_collector_name	Collector name	Mrs. Jayne McGraw
&F_collector_telephone	Telephone number of collector	555-1860
&F_customer_name	Customer name	Monolith Motor Company
&F_customer_number	Customer number	1009

TABLE 6-3. *Field Variables in Dunning Letter Text*

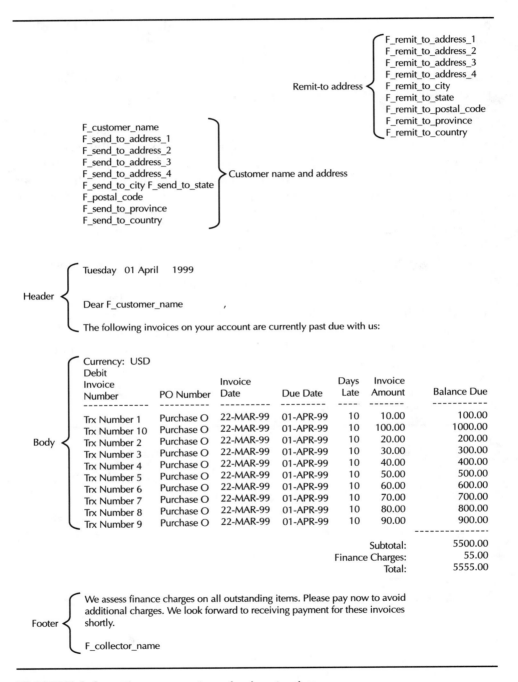

FIGURE 6-6. *The construction of a dunning letter*

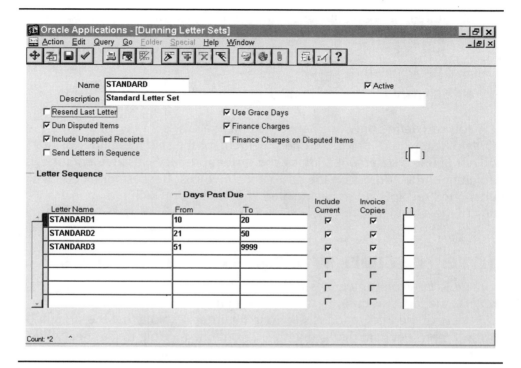

FIGURE 6-7. *The Dunning Letter Sets window*

Statements

A customer statement shows all account activity in a particular time frame, since the last statement. Statements are often sent as an alternative to dunning letters, although some companies send both statements and letters.

The statement differs from a dunning letter in that it shows all account activity (invoice, debit memo, chargeback, commitment, receipt, on-account credit, credit memo, and adjustment) and not just the overdue items that appear on letters.

The following components of the statement can be customized:

- **Statement cycles**   Determine the frequency with which particular customers receive statements.

- **Statement-aging buckets**   Show how much of the debt is overdue and by how many days. The buckets are date ranges, such as 0-15 days, 16-30 days, or over 31 days and can be set according to your preference.

- **Standard messages**   Printed text on the bottom of the statements.

You can define only one active statement address for each customer. Oracle Receivables produces one statement for the statement address. If you do not define a statement address, the system produces a statement for each different bill-to address on the customer's invoices. Because on-account or unapplied receipts are not associated with a site, they will not appear on any of the statements.

Integration with Other Modules

Oracle Receivables integrates with several other modules in a way that reflects the fact that customers are at the center of your business. An overview of the integration is shown in Figure 6-8. (Note that the straight arrows represent data that is interfaced from one module to another, while the curving arrows indicate common data that modules share by referencing each other's tables.)

Receivables shares customer data with Order Entry, Projects, and Services. The same customers are available in all modules, and they can be maintained from any modules. Updates made in one are immediately available in Receivables.

Order Entry

The shipping process within Order Entry records products shipped to customers and updates the inventory. Shipment information, such as quantities, selling prices, payment terms, and transaction dates, are transferred into Receivables via the AutoInvoice interface. AutoInvoice creates the invoices for the sale in Oracle Receivables and accounts for the sales revenue. Invoices that originate in Order Entry are printed in Receivables.

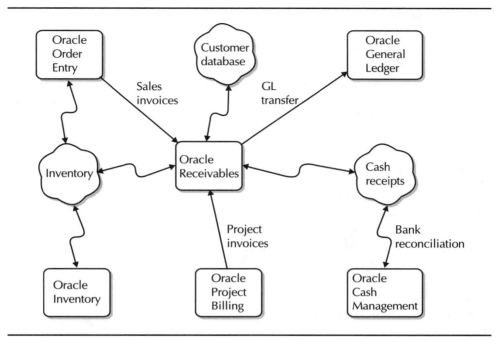

FIGURE 6-8. *An overview of Oracle Receivables' integration with other modules*

Creating Invoices from Orders

The AutoInvoice interface is a one-way process; there is no interfaces to post Receivables transactions back into Order Entry or Projects. The sales records don't reflect discounts, write-offs, and other adjustments made in the collection process.

Set out your business processes to require that reversing transactions originate in the same place as the original transaction. Customer returns need to be entered into Order Entry as RMAs (Return Material Agreement) to handle the inventory and sales compensation and other implications.

Despite the fact that it is a one-way passage, Receivables maintains somewhat informal links back to Order Entry through the open AutoInvoice interface. AutoInvoice requires that you use a 15-column Descriptive Flexfield (DFF) to uniquely identify invoice headers and lines in the import process. The line columns have to include those for the header. Each line identifier has to be unique; each unique combination of header DFF segments represents one invoice.

The content of these columns is totally up to you. However, if you plan to use Oracle's standard invoicing programs, it is best to make the fields consistent with the fields in Oracle Order Entry. The standard invoicing programs link back to the Sales Order tables through INTERFACE_ LINE_ATTRIBUTE6, which is used for the sales order line ID, and INTERFACE_LINE_ATTRIBUTE7, which is used for the picking line ID.

Projects

Project invoices are imported into Receivables via the AutoInvoice interface. All of the data Receivables needs to create PA_INVOICES is supplied by Oracle Project Billing, and is then processed by AutoInvoice to create invoices in Receivables. A further process then runs to tie back the invoices in Receivables to the original invoice in Project Billing. This is to ensure that all the project billing invoice data is loaded successfully into Oracle Receivables. For successfully transferred invoices loaded into Oracle Receivables, the tieback process updates the project accounting data to reconcile invoices in Oracle Projects to Oracle Receivables. Rejected invoices remaining in the Oracle Receivable interface tables are updated so you can correct them and transfer them again to Oracle Receivables.

Inventory

Inventory items are necessary in Order Entry to identify what has been sold. All Oracle products that reference inventory items do so by referencing the System Item Flexfield. The sales invoices imported from Order Entry into Receivables also share the inventory information.

General Ledger

The GL transfer process reviews all new transactions in Receivables and creates the appropriate journal entries in Oracle General Ledger. These journal entries are imported to General Ledger via the Journal Import interface. The GL transfer process must be started by a human operator, as it cannot be automated. When it is submitted, the operator must choose to post in detail or summary mode. Summary mode produces one journal entry line per distinct Accounting Flexfield combination. Detail mode creates at least one journal entry for each transaction in your posting submission. The operator should choose either one mode or the other, as a mix of summary and detail creates confusion for users. The benefits of each have been discussed in Chapter 3.

Receivables Open Interfaces

Oracle Receivables provides four standard open interfaces:

- **AutoInvoice**   Used for loading invoices, debit memos, credit memos, and on-account credits.
- **AutoLockbox**   Used for loading bank receipts.
- **Customer**   Used for loading customers, addresses, contacts, telephones, and profiles.
- **Sales Tax Rate**   Used for loading tax rate information.

The first interface, AutoInvoice, is used by other standard Oracle modules to import data into Receivables. But the other three are designed to allow you to build ongoing interfaces with external systems or for initial data conversion.

AutoInvoice

The AutoInvoice interface lets you import invoice information from financial billing systems or invoices from Oracle Order Entry and Oracle Project Billing. This interface is extremely powerful and complex, allowing the import of credit memos and debit memos as well as invoices. Since you can import only at the transaction level, grouping rules are used to determine which lines will be placed together on the same header level transaction once they have been imported.

Customer Interface

The Customer interface lets you import new and update existing customer data from any feeder system and ensures that the data that you import is accurate and valid within Oracle Receivables. The Customer interface is essential during cutover for high volume data conversion. The interface can be used on an ongoing basis when custom or third-party systems are the first to collect data on customers. Members of organizations such as labor unions are often customers in that they buy subscriptions or supplies. It is convenient to let the membership system collect member data and then import it into Oracle Financials as needed to support customer billing.

AutoLockbox

The automatic Lockbox interface is used to load receipt information in Receivables. The primary purpose is to provide an automatic interface for receipts communicated to your organization electronically by your bank on a Lockbox tape or file. The interface is quite general, and AutoLockbox can be coaxed into use for importing receipts from any external system, even if the data is not strictly a bank lockbox. You can define payment application rules to control how the receipt is applied against line types (tax, freight, and invoice lines) and to predefine a sequence for closing transactions. You choose among a variety of rules, such as matching the oldest invoice first, matching on amount, or matching any user-defined hierarchy of rules. Application rules can be assigned to each transaction type, allowing you the flexibility to apply credit card sales by exact match on amount, while applying customer cash receipts on an oldest first basis. The use of the automatic Lockbox interface to boost the hit rate of receipt applications is described in Chapter 18.

Sales Tax Rate Interface

The Sales Tax Rate interface lets you load sales tax records—new locations and tax rates—into Oracle Receivables from a sales tax feeder system. You insert records into the AR_TAX_INTERFACE table and then run the interface to validate and transfer the records to the underlying Receivables tables. The interface program lets you load one or more tax rates for the same location that cover different date ranges and postal codes. The records that you load into Receivables through the Sales Tax Rate interface program update your existing sales tax rates with the most current tax rates for each location. The Sales Tax Rate interface program can adjust the active date range of existing tax rates as new tax rates are loaded into Receivables. Oracle Order Entry also uses the Sales Tax Rate interface.

The Receivables Data Model

This section briefly describes the transactions in the Oracle Receivables module. The purpose of this section is to provide a high-level overview of the data structures and processing used by Oracle Receivables. Refer to this section if you are planning to write custom reports based on the Receivables data, or if you want to define alerts against actions or events triggered in Receivables. You should not plan to update or insert data, unless you do so via one of the standard interfaces.

The data model in Receivables has to cope with the conflicting needs of posting to General Ledger and providing customer account balances. The transaction tables and their usage are listed in Table 6-4.

Table	Purpose
AR_ADJUSTMENTS	Storing adjustments to invoices. The amount of each adjustment, the activity name, and the accounting information is held in this table. When an invoice is adjusted, the AMOUNT_DUE_ REMAINING in AR_PAYMENT_ SCHEDULES is updated.
AR_BATCHES	Grouping individual receipts; this table is optional. If used, a batch holds information about the batch source used, the bank account, and control totals.
AR_CASH_RECEIPT_HISTORY	Storing the current status of a receipt, receipt history, and receipt reversals. Receipts go through a cycle of steps that include confirmation, remittance, and clearance. Each step creates rows in this table. The CODE_COMBINATION_ID column stores the accounts that are debited and credited as part of these steps.

TABLE 6-4. *The Transaction Tables in Oracle Receivables*

Table	Purpose
AR_CASH_RECEIPTS	Storing one row for each receipt. Invoice-related receipts have payment schedules and applications, while miscellaneous receipts (not related to the invoice) have distributions stored on AR_MISC_CASH_DISTRIBUTIONS.
AR_MISC_CASH_DISTRIBUTIONS	Storing all the accounting entries for miscellaneous cash applications. Miscellaneous cash is income that does not relate to a customer, such as stock dividends or bank interest.
AR_PAYMENT_SCHEDULES	Storing two types of records: invoice-related and receipt-related. The table contains one record for each invoice installment, or one row per receipt. Different transaction types are identified by the CLASS, which can be invoice (INV), debit memo (DM), credit memo (CM), deposit (DEP), guarantee (GUAR), chargeback (CB), or receipt (PMT).
AR_RECEIVABLE_APPLICATIONS	Linking the receipts applied to invoices with the credit memos applied to invoices. This table holds the amount applied, the status, and the accounting distribution for the application.
RA_BATCHES	Storing information such as the batch source and control totals. Invoice batches are optional.

TABLE 6-4. *The Transaction Tables in Oracle Receivables* (continued)

Table	Purpose
RA_CUST_TRX_LINE_GL_DIST	Storing all accounting records for a transaction. These are distinguished by the ACCOUNT_CLASS designation, which can be freight, receivable, revenue, tax, unearned revenue, unbilled receivable, or charges. The ARGLTP program uses GL_DATE and AMOUNT to post the correct amounts to GL for each transaction.
RA_CUST_TRX_LINE_SALESREPS	Storing sales credit assignments for invoice lines.
RA_CUSTOMER_TRX	Storing header information for invoices, debit memos, credit memos, chargebacks, deposits, and guarantees. Each row includes general information such as customer, transaction type, and printing instructions. This is a fundamental table in Receivables.
RA_CUSTOMER_TRX_LINES	Each transaction line relates to just one transaction in RA_CUSTOMER_TRX. Lines may be either revenue item lines, tax lines, or freight. Each row records the quantities ordered, invoiced, and credited, as well as unit prices.

TABLE 6-4. *The Transaction Tables in Oracle Receivables* (continued)

At first sight the data model seems complex. It is based on a transaction view of Receivables and not an accounting or customer reporting view. The accounting information is spread across five distinct tables, which have a double bar as shown in the data model in Figure 6-9.

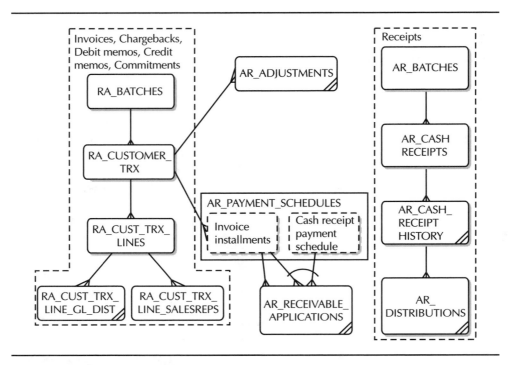

FIGURE 6-9. *The Receivables data model*

The Receivables Aging Report, which is the central Receivables report, is large and complex, reflecting the fact that the AR_PAYMENT_SCHEDULES table is used for two distinct purposes: invoice installments and cash receipt payment schedules. It is a single table created from two subentities. The AR_PAYMENT_SCHEDULES table is used for many things, the most important of which is the record of the customer account. As noted earlier, the Oracle Receivables module does not store the customer's account balance anywhere. Instead, the balance is calculated whenever it is needed. The sum of the AMOUNT_DUE_REMAINING for a customer for all confirmed payment schedules gives the current customer balance.

Technical Overview of the Application Process

Application is the process in which you match debit transactions with credit transactions. Debit transactions increase the customer's balance, while credit transactions decrease the customer's balance. Refer to Table 6-5 to see how transactions are classified into debit and credit transactions.

Application is the term for matching credit transactions to debit transactions in order to create a group of transactions that taken together have a zero effect on the customer's balance. The normal situation is for a receipt to be applied to an invoice. Both the receipt and the invoice are for the same amount, and together they cancel each other out. More complex applications involving multiple receipts, invoices, and credit memos can also be envisaged. The rule for determining a valid application is simply

$$\Sigma \, (Inv + DM + Chargebacks + Deposits - Rec - CM) = 0$$

You can apply all or part of a receipt or on-account credit to a single debit item or to several debit items. When an invoice-related receipt is first entered, a row is created in the AR_RECEIVABLE_APPLICATIONS table with a status of UNAPP and an application type of CASH. Each subsequent application creates two new rows, one with APP status for the amount being applied, and another with UNAPP status for the negative of the amount being applied. When a credit memo is applied, a row is created in the

Debit Transactions	Credit Transactions
Invoices	Receipts
Debit memos	Credit memos
Chargebacks	
Deposits	

TABLE 6-5. *Classification of Transactions as Either Debit or Credit*

AR_RECEIVABLE_APPLICATIONS table with a status of APP and application type of CM.

The rows in AR_RECEIVABLE_APPLICATIONS are a link between the transaction you are applying and the transaction to which you are applying. The PAYMENT_SCHEDULE_ID column links the receipt or credit memo to its payment schedule in the AR_PAYMENT_SCHEDULES table. The CASH_RECEIPT_ID column stores the receipt ID of receipt transactions, while the CUSTOMER_TRX_ID column stores the transaction ID for credit memo transactions. The APPLIED_PAYMENT_SCHEDULE_ID and APPLIED_CUSTOMER_TRX_ID columns reference the transaction to which this record applies. The AR_RECEIVABLE_APPLICATIONS table resolves the many-to-many relationship between receipts and transactions, as well as the many-to-many relationship between credit memos and invoices.

ON-ACCOUNT RECEIPTS AND AR_RECEIVABLE_APPLICATIONS

On-account receipts are handled in a special way by Oracle Receivables. When an on-account receipt is entered, a row is created in AR_RECEIVABLE_APPLICATIONS in the usual way. However there is no payment schedule to link the record to. On-account receipts do not relate to any particular transaction. There is a seeded shadow row in AR_PAYMENT_SCHEDULES identified by *PAYMENT_SCHEDULE_ID = –1*. All on-account receipts are linked to this shadow row.

TIP
If you write reports on receipt applications, do use an outer join to link AR_PAYMENT_SCHEDULES tables with the RA_CUSTOMER_TRX table. Otherwise none of the on-account receipts will be selected. There is no record in RA_CUSTOMER_TRX that corresponds to the PAYMENT_SCHEDULE_ID = –1 rule in AR_PAYMENT_SCHEDULES.

Technical Overview of the GL Transfer

The GL transfer process reviews all transactions in AR and creates the appropriate journal entries in General Ledger. Accounting distributions are stored in RA_CUST_TRX_LINE_GL_DIST, AR_DISTRIBUTIONS,

AR_RECEIVABLE_APPLICATIONS, AR_ADJUSTMENTS, and AR_MISC_CASH_DISTRIBUTIONS (this table holds the accounting distributions for miscellaneous cash). Transaction tables that give rise to GL journal postings all have a currency, an amount, a date, and a corresponding code combination ID.

The GL transfer process (registered as ARGLTP in the concurrent manager) searches for new transactions that have not been transferred previously (POSTING_CONTROL_ID = –3). For each new transaction, journal entry lines are inserted into the GL_INTERFACE table. ARGLTP updates each transferred transaction as posted (by populating POSTING_CONTROL_ID, GL_POSTED_DATE) and optionally submits the GL Journal Import process. POSTING_CONTROL_ID uniquely identifies in which GL transfer the record was transferred, and the time stamp in the GL_POSTED_DATE column signifies when the record was transferred. Interestingly, if you request summary posting from AR to GL, the summarization is performed by the Journal Import program, and not by the ARGLTP.

Advanced Features

Receivables accounting periods control the dates that can be transacted, but do not affect how transactions appear in the General Ledger. The GL date given for each transaction determines the GL period into which it falls. Invoices also have a transaction date, the date that appears on the top of the invoice. The transaction date determines when the invoice shows up in the customer account.

CAUTION
Because the transaction date is used for the customer account, and the GL date is used for postings to General Ledger, you should ensure that these two dates are always identical; otherwise customer balances in Receivables will not equal the accounts receivable balance in General Ledger.

There are no account balances stored in Receivables. Account balances are calculated each time they are queried, either online or in reports. Online account balances are always as of today's date, whereas standard reports work on an as-of-date-supplied parameter. One advantage of receivables working on a daily basis is that it is possible to request customer account reports for any day of the year, not just for period-end balances. Without this capability all statement and dunning cycles would be restricted to an accounting period cycle.

Customer account balances are not calculated at period-end and brought forward to the next period. Oracle Receivables uses the same accounting periods that General Ledger uses, but it has no month-end process. Period statuses in Receivables can be opened and closed independently of General Ledger. A transaction cannot be entered unless the Receivables period is open. The period cannot be closed unless all transactions have been transferred to General Ledger.

The Customer Account and Balance Due

The following formula is used to calculate a customer's account balance at any point in time:

$$Inv + DM \pm Adj - CM - Rec$$

The calculation uses the original full amount of each transaction, whether it is an invoice, debit memo, credit memo, adjustment, or receipt. Throughout Oracle Receivables you find another amount alongside the original amount; it is called the *balance due*, *outstanding amount*, or *amount remaining*. These three terms are synonymous. Look again at Figure 6-3, which shows the account details for the Monolith Motor Company. The rightmost column shows the balances due, some of which are zero.

As noted earlier, accounts receivable departments spend considerable time researching and applying receipts. They need a way of knowing when a transaction is complete. The balance due tells them when a transaction is fully applied: either the obligation has been paid in full, or the credit has been totally applied to other obligations or refunded. There is another powerful reason for working with balances due rather than original amounts. If you replace the original amounts throughout the formula $Inv + DM \pm Adj - CM - Rec$ with the outstanding amount, the result does not change. Customer account balances can be calculated from either the original amount or the outstanding amount of individual transactions.

In Figure 6-3, Monolith Motor Company has two open invoices: one for $5537.50 and one for $1170; the balance is $6707.50. The balance due for both of these invoices is the same as their original amounts. Suppose that Monolith then sent us a check for $2000. We might assign the receipt a reference, R1780, and enter it initially as unapplied. Here is how the customer account would now appear:

Number	Class	Original	Balance Due
10174	Invoice	5537.50	5537.50
10177	Invoice	1170.00	1170.00
R1780	Receipt	2000.00	2000.00
Monolith Motor Company Account Balance		4707.50	4707.50

The new account balance would be $4707.50, which is the old balance minus $2000. Note that the balance due for each transaction is the same as its original amount. If at some stage we established that the $2000 receipt were intended to fully pay invoice 10177, and the remaining $830 to partially pay invoice 10174, we would enter the receipt applications in the Applications window. The customer account would now appear as shown here:

Number	Class	Original	Balance Due
10174	Invoice	5537.50	4707.50
10177	Invoice	1170.00	0
R1780	Receipt	2000.00	0
Monolith Motor Company Account Balance		4707.50	4707.50

Notice that none of the original amounts has changed; they never do. The receipt R1780 has been fully applied, the $2000 has been "used up" paying invoices, and the balance due on the receipt is shown as zero. Invoice 10177 has been fully paid, which is reflected by the zero balance due. The remaining $830 has been used to partially pay invoice 10174, which is left with a balance due of $4707.50. You have perhaps noticed that the account balance has not changed as a result of the receipt application; the sum of the original amounts is the same as the sum of the balance due column. Applications are customer-account neutral.

Transactions with a balance due of zero are referred to as *closed;* otherwise they are *open.* Closed transactions do not contribute to the customer balance. The work in a receivables department is directed towards reducing the balance due on all transactions to zero and closing each transaction. However, closed transactions can be re-opened if, for example, applications are deleted (a check bounces) or if a closed invoice is adjusted. Table 6-6 summarizes the effect of various receivables transactions on the customer's account balance.

Reconciliation

There are three types of reconciliation in addition to the bank reconciliation mentioned earlier. The types, which are distinguished according to what is being reconciled with what, are referred to generically as external reconciliation, internal reconciliation, and GL reconciliation.

- **External reconciliation** The process of ensuring that all invoices have been correctly imported from feeder systems. The total revenue reported from your sales systems must equal the total revenue reported out of receivables for any comparable time period.

- **Internal reconciliation** The process of ensuring that the customer balance for each customer is the same irrespective of whether it is calculated using original amounts or outstanding amounts. Remember, the formula $Inv + DM \pm Adj - CM - Rec$ would give the same result whichever amount was chosen.

Increase Balance	Decrease Balance	Neutral
Invoice	Credit memo	Unidentified receipt
Debit memo	Applied and on-account receipts	Application of a receipt

TABLE 6-6. *The Effect of Different Transactions*

■   **GL reconciliation**   The process of ensuring that the transactions in Receivables have been accounted for correctly and of verifying that the journal entries in General Ledger that have come from the subledger are all present and correct. A complete Receivables to General Ledger reconciliation is normally replaced by the reduced scope of a receivables "control" account reconciliation. That is, the subledger receivables total is reconciled to the receivables accounts in General Ledger.

The timing of these reconciliations can be problematic. The logical sequence is to do the external reconciliation first, followed by the internal reconciliation, and then the GL reconciliation. If performed in some other order, any corrections you make will force you to repeat one of the previous reconciliations. For example, if you do the internal reconciliation first, before doing the external reconciliation, and then you identify an Order Entry invoice that belongs in the period but has not been imported, you will have to import it into Receivables, and that will force you to repeat the internal reconciliation. Although the logical sequence is clear, the timing is not so obvious. It makes no sense to start the external reconciliation until the external feeder systems have completed their period end. Otherwise, further invoices can be generated after you start the reconciliation. However, you must keep Receivables open during the reconciliation, so that if discrepancies are found they can be corrected in the period in which they belong. That means that all three reconciliations should be completed after closing the feeder systems, but before closing Receivables. Not all companies are prepared to hold Receivables open long enough to rigorously complete all three reconciliations.

TIP
If you want to close the period to prevent further data entry, "soft close" the period by changing the period status to Close Pending, which is similar to Closed but does not validate for unposted items.

The Purge Feature

Oracle Receivables includes an archive and purge feature. The purge is to recover disk space by archiving closed transactions. The archive process satisfies legal requirements imposed by various taxing authorities that accounting documents must be kept for a certain number of years before being disposed.

If disk storage were unlimited and machine processing power arbitrarily fast, no one would need to purge data at all. But, presently and for the foreseeable future, machine capacity is limited; after a certain amount of time your disk will be full and response times will suffer—no matter what size system you have. This is when a purge is needed. Space is more often a problem in Receivables than the other modules, because each transaction in Receivables eats up more space than a comparable transaction in the other modules—for example, a journal in General Ledger or an invoice in Payables. Another reason is that companies tend to have a higher volume of Receivables invoices than other business transactions.

Before implementing the archive and purge process, assess if you really need to do so by balancing the cost of buying more hardware with the cost of implementing and testing the purge. Users prefer having transaction history online, and it is difficult to put an economic value on the extra procedural effort needed to research an archived transaction compared to an online transaction.

The purge works by removing records of historic transactions—receipts, invoices, credit memos, debit memos, chargebacks, adjustments, and commitments—from the database. These can be copied onto tape or any other storage device, and then deleted from the online database. Removing the records releases disk space for current data.

Groups of interrelated transactions are purged if all transactions in the group are closed, and if the youngest transaction is older than a certain age. You might want to purge all closed transaction groups that are older than one year. The ground rule for purges is that after the purge, none of the customer account balances will have changed; therefore, the group of records that is purged must have the following property:

$$Inv + DM \pm Adj - CM - Rec = 0.$$

Receivables Conversion Issues

Conversion strategy is a trade-off between the effort involved and the completeness of the converted data. The minimum effort is no conversion:

Customer accounts are "run-down" or "run out" in the old system. Customer receipts for old invoices are entered in the old system; and new invoices are keyed into Oracle Receivables.

No Conversion

Not converting has serious drawbacks for users. The customer's actual balance at any point in time has to be assimilated from both systems. This means that statements or dunning letters cannot be produced throughout the duration of the "run-down." Running two systems concurrently is particularly difficult if you cross a year-end, as all financial accounts will have to be summarized from the two systems.

Eventually you will want to switch off and archive your legacy system. At that point you will inevitably have some open items, and you need to decide what to do with them. A "no conversion" strategy often turns into a "minimal conversion" strategy. With this in mind, you may as well anticipate doing some sort of conversion when you go live; then at least you'll have the benefit from day one.

Minimal Conversion

A minimal conversion involves converting only outstanding balances. After the last month-end in the old system, a list of customer balances is generated from the legacy system and used to create data for the Customer interface. A customer is created in the Oracle Receivables system, with one open invoice to show the outstanding balance for that customer.

Minimal conversion has the advantage that you can stop data entry into the old system immediately and switch all entry tasks over to the new system. The disadvantage is that there is no detailed accounting information in the new system, so no aging of debt is possible and the customer statements and dunning letters will contain no history.

Open-Item Conversion

The next step up is to convert open items. After the last month-end in the old system, a list of open items—invoices, credit memos, or receipts—is generated. Each open item is then transferred into the new system. The customer should not be able to detect that you have migrated from one system to another. Statements and dunning letters will show all open items with the correct reference numbers and outstanding amounts.

Open-item conversion is the authors' preferred conversion strategy because it is transparent to the customer and provides more detail than a minimal conversion.

Full Conversion

The last option is to convert all transactions from the old system. This involves doing a full conversion of all transactions (open and closed), and then reapplying receipts and credit memos to close items and re-create the account history. The extra effort required to bring across the closed items and the history is seldom worthwhile.

Choice of Mechanism—Manual, Interface, or Mix

The choice of mechanism is independent of your decision on what to convert. You can decide to convert any particular data element either manually or via an interface, using a custom-built data load program. Consider the effort required for each route: Manual conversion costs (*time needed to manually key one data record*) × (*number of data records*); program conversion takes the total effort involved in programming, testing, and running a migration from old to new. Manual conversion works well when dealing with a low volume of transactions, while programmatic conversion is justified with high volumes.

The more detail and history you decide to convert, the more interfaces you will need to program and test. Table 6-7 shows exactly which interfaces you will need to implement depending on the range of data that you want to convert. You need not choose between an entirely program-based or manual conversion. For example, what if you wanted to convert only open items? Suppose your old system has a large number of customers and open invoices, but a low number of receipts and credit memos (as would be quite normal). You can convert customers and invoices using a program, and you can convert receipts and credit memos manually.

Interface Needed Data	Customer Customer	AutoInvoice Invoice	Credit Memos	Auto- Lockbox Receipts	Applications
No conversion					
Convert only customer balances	✔	✔			
Convert only open items	✔	✔	✔	✔	
Convert open items and history	✔	✔	✔	✔	✔

TABLE 6-5. *The Range of Interfaces Depends on What You Choose to Convert*

NOTE

Make sure you convert the receivables account for each transaction correctly, according to an agreed mapping between old and new systems. Although the transactions themselves do not need to be posted within Receivables, any applications that reference converted transactions automatically give rise to GL postings to their receivables accounts. An inaccurate conversion of Receivables accounts can cause headaches long after the conversion is completed.

Customer Conversion

Customers are the heart of corporate life, and life goes on during conversion preparation. The least disruptive approach to customer conversion usually involves some mixture of cleaning up data in the legacy system beforehand, and using automated scripts to simplify the conversion process. The following factors are best addressed by knowledgeable people in advance of conversion:

■ Dividing customer records into customers and customer locations. The legacy system may not make the distinction.

■ Defining the activities at different locations, such as bill-to, ship-to, marketing, collections, and so on.

■ Defining which customer locations belong to each operating unit in a Multi-Org implementation.

■ Entering address and contact data. The customer database is remarkably flexible; it can associate contacts with the company, with a site, or with a function. The same is true with addresses and telephone numbers. Doing this will force you to express relationships that are implicit in your legacy system.

Automated scripts can handle or at least support the following kinds of conversion activities:

■ Converting to upper- and lowercase. Using upper- and lowercase makes more attractive invoices and order confirmation letters for your customers.

■ Validating postal codes, getting the full code (ZIP plus four in the United States), and getting the names of the towns spelled completely and correctly. Third party mailing list data is helpful for this task.

■ Standardizing your use of salutations (Dr., Mr., Mrs., Ms., M., Mlle., Srta., Sra., Herr, Frau, and so on).

As noted, the Oracle Customer Interface process is remarkably flexible. It can import the same data into a number of different table structures. It is wise to choose a few representative customers to import repeatedly into the Conference Room Pilot instance, to confirm that the data is being stored as you expect. The interface allows you to create new customers, addresses, contacts, and phone numbers and also to update existing data.

The legacy system will almost invariably include some data items that do not appear to map to Oracle. You may not know immediately what they are for, but it is unwise to leave them behind. Consider, as a strategy, sticking them in a comma-delimited format into one of the many Descriptive Flexfield attributes (Attribute *n*) that you will not need for use with a real DFF. The import process handles this with ease. Then the data will be available for reference or as the source for SQL scripts if you need it in the future. You can always set the items to null when you are sure they won't be needed.

Conclusion

Oracle Receivables is a worldwide best practice tool that improves your cash flow and handles all your invoicing needs. Its powerful online collection tools help you track, monitor, and collect your receivables, thereby reducing your delinquent accounts. Transaction efficiency with high payment volumes is promoted with cash application features like AutoLockbox, automatic receipts, and EDI. Seamless integration with other systems allows you to use Oracle Receivables independently of the Oracle Applications integrated suite of business solutions.

CHAPTER
7

Oracle Cash Management

he purpose of Oracle Cash Management is to help you manage and control the cash cycle of your enterprise in order to ensure liquidity and improve profitability. The key benefits of this module include enterprise cash forecasting, efficient bank reconciliation, extensive multicurrency capabilities, and cash balance information that is always up-to-date. Cash Management is an enterprise-wide solution, providing comprehensive integration with other Oracle applications as well as open interfaces for integration with external systems. Cash Management supports two distinct but related business functions:

- Bank reconciliation
- Cash forecasting

Bank reconciliation determines whether the balance on your bank accounts in Oracle Financials is equivalent to the balance shown on your bank statements; cash forecasting uses the results of this reconciliation—a known and proven cash position—to predict your balance for next week, next month, next quarter, and so on.

The Cash Management module has gone through a rapid evolution. It was first introduced in Release 10 and, unlike the other applications, it is available only in GUI. When first introduced, Cash Management dealt primarily with bank reconciliation; it consolidated a range of banking features, from Oracle Payables and Oracle Receivables, and made them available in one place.

Cash Management has been enhanced and extended throughout the product cycle of Release 10. The cash forecasting features were introduced in Release 10.7 with Prod 16 Smart Client. Release 11 has been expanded not only to include expected cash outflow based on payroll payments taken from Oracle Payroll, but also to enable cash forecasts that draw on relevant financial transactions from external systems on local and remote databases. International companies that have several Oracle Financials databases around the world are no longer constrained to local cash forecasting; a company-wide forecast can now be compiled within a distributed database environment.

NOTE
The character mode versions of Oracle Payables and Oracle Receivables include bank clearance capabilities. Character mode users can either continue using these features or migrate to the bank reconciliation features in the GUI version of Cash Management. However, character mode installations using Release 10.7 Multi-Org or Oracle 8 must use Cash Management for bank reconciliation.

The Need for Cash Management

Treasury managers are continually monitoring cash flow details to ensure that the net cash inflow will cover the company's cash requirements. Managing cash in this way offers several benefits:

- **Improved overall profitability**   Surplus cash is quickly located, and can then be invested.

- **Reduced risk of currency exposure**   Currency imbalances are quickly detected, and thus can be promptly resolved.

- **Prevention of finance charges**   Insufficient cash flow situations are anticipated ahead of time, allowing for prompt adjustment.

Early predictions of insufficient cash flow give managers time to react. There are a variety of ways to steer a company away from a cash crisis—herein lies the expertise of the treasury department—but no department can respond appropriately or swiftly without having a sophisticated liquidity analysis tool to prepare accurate cash forecasts quickly. Organizations that trade internationally have to manage their currency exposure by balancing their future inflow and outflow currency by currency, period by period. Large currency imbalances must be avoided in order to prevent exchange losses.

The starting point for an accurate cash forecast is a proven cash position. The accounting process used to prove a cash position is bank reconciliation.

Bank Reconciliation

Bank reconciliation is an audit requirement; bank accounts are an asset of the company, and you must be able to explain all balances on the balance sheet. Bank reconciliation goes further than an audit and can reveal fraud as well as errors. To ensure that your transaction records match and that neither you nor the bank has made an error, you should reconcile your bank accounts each time you receive a bank statement.

Reconciliation is the process of explaining the difference between two balances. There are legitimate reasons for two balances to be different—for example, timing differences—but once the legitimate differences have been eliminated, the balances should be the same. Basically, bank reconciliation uses the following formula to ascertain that the balance on the bank accounts in Oracle Financials is equivalent to the balance shown on the bank statements:

> *Bank account balance in Oracle Financials*
> + *Items on bank statement, but not in Financials*
> − *Items in Financials, but not on bank statement*
> _____
>
> *Bank statement balance*

At the most basic level, bank reconciliation is an exercise in comparison. We take an extract of the bank account in Oracle Financials and compare that to the statement provided by our bank. All transactions that appear the same on both lists are checked off. These are the reconciled transactions. We are then left with two sets of entries: bank statement entries that are not listed in Financials and Financials entries that are not listed on the bank statement. Both sets of entries require analysis to determine whether the source of the discrepancy was an error or a legitimate difference. This distinction is important; errors must be corrected.

The best method for dealing with entries that require correction is determined by the circumstances, but the essential purpose is to reverse the original (error) transaction and to enter a new transaction. Errors on the bank's behalf must be reported to the bank and corrected. New in Release 11 is the capability to reconcile bank corrections against the original bank errors.

Legitimate differences occur when the Cash Management bank account differs from the actual bank statement for the following reasons:

- Timing differences due to checks in transit or other uncompleted items

- Bank charges and items that are unknown until they appear on the statement

- Fees for currency conversion

- Transactions that haven't yet been processed, such as payroll deductions from a service bureau

The differences have to be eliminated; you do this by making appropriate account entries to explain them. The reconciliation process is diagramed in Figure 7-1.

The Reconciliation Process

Oracle Cash Management is a collection point for bank transactions, regardless of where in the system they may have been entered. Bank transactions entered directly into Oracle General Ledger or generated from Payables, Receivables, or Payroll can be reconciled within Oracle Cash Management. Payments made to suppliers and recorded through Oracle Payables generate credit entries in the bank account, while customers' receipts entered in Receivables post debit entries. Salary payments to employees are recorded in Oracle Payroll, and other bank transactions that may have been initiated from external systems, such as an EPOS (electronic point of sale) merchandising system, may also be stored in Cash Management. Transactions may then be reconciled either manually or automatically using the Reconciliation open interface.

Oracle Cash Management distinguishes between clearing and reconciling. You clear a transaction as soon as you have documentary evidence from your bank that it has processed the transaction and the funds have been moved into or out of your account. You reconcile a transaction once it has appeared on your bank statement. Reconciliation itself implies clearance. When you reconcile a transaction, the transaction is first cleared (the statement itself is the documentary evidence) and then matched to a bank statement line.

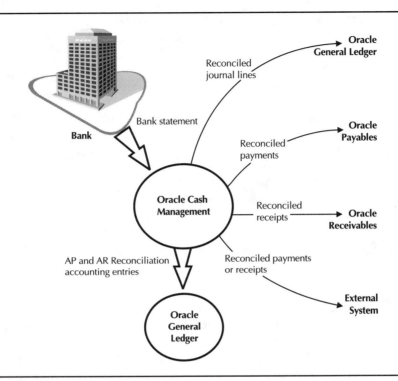

FIGURE 7-1. *An overview of bank reconciliation*

Loading the Bank Statement

You can reconcile transactions manually, or you can load an electronic bank statement directly into Oracle Cash Management, where the bank statement lines are reconciled automatically. The automatic reconciliation looks for certain "match" criteria to determine whether a transaction and a bank statement line are indeed one and the same. When using the Bank Statement open interface, flat file statements are uploaded into the Cash Management tables quickly and easily.

Reconciling Journal Entries

Some of the journal entries in General Ledger did not originate from another module, but instead were entered directly into General Ledger. These transactions can be reconciled to your bank statement with Cash Management. The AutoReconciliation program will match the transaction if the journal line description matches the statement line transaction number.

REMEMBER
This matching rule should be observed when entering data into General Ledger journals; otherwise the AutoReconciliation program will not make any matches. It is especially important to load the correct data into journal line descriptions when converting legacy bank account lines into Oracle General Ledger.

Reconciling Payments
Supplier payments entered in Payables can be reconciled to your bank statement lines. When you reconcile payments using Oracle Cash Management, the payment status is updated to "Reconciled." If you enable the Allow Reconciliation Accounting option, Payables will also create accounting entries that debit the cash clearing account and credit the cash account of the bank account that you used to pay the invoice.

Reconciling Receipts
Receipts created in Receivables may also be reconciled to bank statement lines. Cash Management updates the status of the receipts to "Reconciled" and creates appropriate accounting entries to be transferred to Oracle General Ledger. Payables and Receivables can generate reconciliation accounting entries for cash clearing, bank charges, and foreign currency gain or loss.

Reconciling Other Transactions
Some transactions that will appear on your bank statements are not initiated from the Oracle Applications. Such is the case when you are charged bank charges or receive interest, or when the bank applies a specific exchange rate on foreign currency transactions, or when a customer receipt is returned due to nonsufficient funds (NSF). Oracle Cash Management is the primary point of entry for these transactions. Used in this way, Oracle Cash Management becomes a subledger in its own right.

Cash Forecasting

Cash Management helps you analyze liquidity across the entire business. You can quickly prepare accurate cash forecasts and analyze your currency exposure, enabling you to make informed financing and investment decisions. You can forecast in any currency, across different organizations in your enterprise, and for multiple time periods. Cash forecasting is integrated with General Ledger, Receivables, Order Entry, Payables, Payroll, and Purchasing, as well as with external systems through the Forecasting open interface. Figure 7-2 charts a cash position forecast.

Accurate cash forecasting depends on up-to-date banking information and relevant information from operational systems. The audience for the cash forecast is the treasury manager. The forecast is just that—a forecast; therefore it does not form part of the statutory accounts of the company.

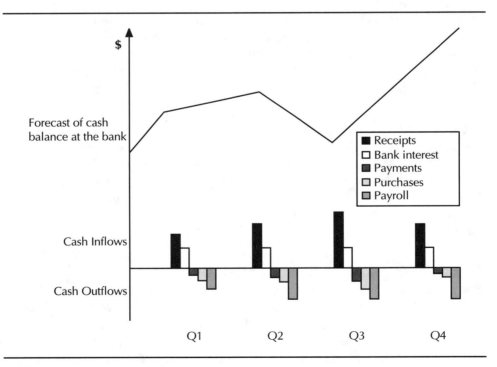

FIGURE 7-2. *A sample cash position forecast*

Cash forecasting takes today's cash position and attempts to roll the balance forward to a future period by adding predicted cash inflow and subtracting predicted cash outflow. The cash inflow and outflow figures are derived from the various sources shown in Table 7-1.

When producing a forecast, bear in mind the limited scope of the future-dated transactions stored in any accounting system. The money due from customer invoices over the next month can be judged accurately by looking at due invoices in Oracle Receivables. However, future sales that have not yet been invoiced will not appear in Receivables, and a six-month forecast should include a sales forecast generated either from revenue budgets in General Ledger or from outside the system. You can base your forecast on future transactions, such as orders and invoices, or historical transactions, such as payments, receipts, and payroll.

Cash Inflow	Cash Outflow
Customer invoices due in the intervening period (Oracle Receivables)	Liabilities due in the intervening period (Oracle Payables)
Receipts (Oracle Receivables)	Payments (Oracle Payables)
Sales orders that have not been invoiced (Oracle Order Entry)	Liabilities for goods ordered but not invoiced (Oracle Purchasing)
Budgeted revenue (Oracle General Ledger)	Unordered requisitions (Oracle Purchasing)
Inflow from external systems	Expense budgets (Oracle General Ledger)
User-entered inflow	Encumbrances (Oracle General Ledger)
	Payments (Oracle Payroll)
	Outflow from external systems
	User-entered outflow

TABLE 7-1. *Cash Inflow and Outflow*

You can use the Forecasting open interface to view cash flows from external systems. Remember to include outflow generated by repayment of loans. Typically, this sum can greatly exceed the normal accounts payable balances, but it is not tracked and accounted for in Oracle Payables because the lender is not considered a trade creditor. In addition, look for capital expenditure that has been approved by directors but has not been put out to contract yet.

Forecasting is built around cash forecast templates. A template determines whether to forecast by days or General Ledger periods, specifies which sources are included, and determines the level of detail. You generate periodic cash forecasts by projecting the cash position for each template. The forecast itself can be in any currency, and once generated, it can be modified or exported to a spreadsheet application. In a multiple organization environment you can also forecast across organizations.

Cash Management Interfaces

A great deal of routine and time-intensive work can be avoided by using the Cash Management interfaces. Interfacing bank data into Financials is a priority because a high volume of transactions regularly passes through your main bank accounts.

The Bank Statement Open Interface

If your bank provides statements in a flat file format, such as BAI or SWIFT940, you can use the Bank Statement open interface to load this information directly into Cash Management. This interface validates the bank account and currency code in the header information, and you can optionally use control totals. Statement lines with errors can be corrected in the Statement Interface window. This feature can save hours of manual data entry and error correction. It is highly recommended that you negotiate a flat file statement with your bank if you plan on reconciling your accounts within Oracle Cash Management.

The Reconciliation Open Interface

The Reconciliation open interface is a powerful feature for enterprise-wide reconciliation. You simply define a database view or a table that Oracle

Cash Management can use to access the payments and receipts in your external system. The Reconciliation open interface is also extensible. Oracle Cash Management executes your custom reconciliation logic when reconciling your external transactions.

The database view CE_999_INTERFACE_V forms a bridge between Oracle Cash Management and data held in an external transaction system. During implementation you redefine this view to point to the payment or receipt transaction table in the external system. Each view column has to be mapped to the corresponding data field. You can use the reconciliation logic in the interface even if the external system data cannot be viewed dynamically across SQL*Net. To do so, create a table called CE_999_INTERFACE_V in the Financials database, and then use SQL*Loader to populate the table with payment and receipt transactions from the external system.

The Forecasting Open Interface

The Forecasting open interface supports cash forecasting in a distributed database environment, allowing you to combine relevant transaction information from both local and remote databases.

The Cash Management Data Model

For bank reconciliation, Cash Management uses receipt and payment information held in Oracle Receivables and Payables. Bank statement headers and lines are held in the two tables described here:

Table	Purpose
CE_STATEMENT_HEADERS_ALL	Holds one row for each separate bank statement.
CE_STATEMENT_LINES	Holds one row for each line on a bank statement.

When payments or receipts are cleared or reconciled, Cash Management updates the flags in tables owned by Oracle Payables and Receivables. Refer to detailed chapters on Payables and Receivables to view their data models.

Conclusion

Through the last several releases of Oracle Financials, Cash Management has evolved from a single screen in Oracle Payables to a full-blown module of its own. It manages bank data entered in General Ledger, Payables, Receivables, and Payroll, along with information from external systems, via multiple open interfaces. Oracle's Cash Management module provides multicurrency cash management for worldwide organizations. It serves the need of all businesses to reconcile their bank statements, and it uses the proven cash position of reconciliation as a springboard toward predicting cash flow and upcoming Fiscal requirements.

CHAPTER

8

Oracle Assets

ixed assets constitute the durable capital base of an enterprise, traditionally the "property, plant, and equipment" necessary to deliver products and services. The concept has expanded over the past decades to include investments in nontangible assets, such as software.

Asset management encompasses three primary activities: physical upkeep, asset tracking, and financial administration. Issues concerning the physical upkeep of assets include asset location, the condition of existing assets, and assignments of asset management responsibility to various individuals within an organization. Tracking functions run the gamut from controlling leased, loaned, and consigned items from acquisition through return to administering periodic asset maintenance. Financial administration issues involve asset value, depreciation, and taxation.

Oracle Assets has always been a robust product. Users familiar with earlier releases will be pleased to find that it is now a complete asset management system. Bar code support for physical inventories makes it easy to reconcile the books with physical reality. The use of bar codes with Asset Warranty Tracking makes it much easier to take full advantage of the service due on a product, even as it moves from department to department.

The types of items tracked in Oracle Assets often require specialized financial consideration. Laws from different jurisdictions dictate how you can depreciate them, what investment tax credits apply, how you treat them in corporate reorganizations, and how you bring construction-in-progress (CIP) items onto the books. Oracle Assets allows you to attach notes in the form of spreadsheets, scanned documents, and other images to asset records. It is the best possible way to associate the online system with your offline business processes.

An Overview of Depreciation

Capital assets such as buildings and machinery typically lose value over time. The loss of value during any given period is called *depreciation,* and it is charged as an expense in that period. The value of the asset at any point in time—usually the cost minus depreciation taken to date—is called the *net book value.*

Markets ultimately determine the value of any asset, but it would be impractical to survey the market every year to determine what each asset is worth. When an asset is acquired or built, accountants generally assign an initial book value, an economic life, and a formula to determine the value of the asset at each period during that economic life. An asset may have a *residual value* beyond which it will not depreciate. A car, for example, is always worth a hundred dollars as scrap.

Each period's depreciation is booked as an expense in that period. At the end of its economic life, the initial cost of the asset (less residual value) will have been expensed. The depreciated book value appears on the balance sheet as an asset. The asset is taken off the books when it is sold. The difference between the price received and the book value at the time of sale is posted to a Gain or Loss on Sale income account.

Depreciation is a "funny money" expense that lends itself to accounting tricks. Taking depreciation quickly has the effect of not only understating the value of assets, but also decreasing stated income (and hence income taxes). Stretching it out can make a company's book value appear unnaturally healthy. For these reasons, governments and national accounting standards committees (the Financial Accounting Standards Board, or FASB, in the United States) have standardized the ways in which companies recognize depreciation. The primary objectives of these groups include ensuring fair taxation and enabling shareholders to make meaningful comparisons between companies.

Business Taxes and the Need for Multiple Sets of Books

Many government bodies tax business assets. These bodies may have their own assessors—which is common for agencies dealing with property taxes applied to real estate and fixed plant assets—or they may allow the business itself to compute the tax based on a legislated formula. The taxing entities accept the company's own records (which are audited by outside auditors and, if necessary, by the taxing authorities themselves) as the basis for computing tax liability.

These government entities regulate and monitor the way in which assets are depreciated. The longer the life of an asset, the more the government will receive in tax revenue. Moreover, the less depreciation expense a company takes, the more revenue will be subject to income taxes.

Governments set their own rules as to the depreciable life of different categories of assets and the depreciation formulas that apply to them. Not surprisingly, different taxing entities demand different depreciation schedules.

Oracle Assets helps you compute the most favorable taxation in areas over which you have some discretion. It has the capability to carry one asset in multiple tax depreciation books for different taxing jurisdictions. The purpose is usually to carry varying net asset value figures in accord with the different sets of laws, though depreciation and investment tax credits may figure in as well.

It would be impossible to achieve consistency between depreciation deductions (and the resultant net asset values) in one set of books and property tax computations in another set. If the depreciation schedules are different, the asset values will also differ. In the United States, most jurisdictions follow the federal government's lead regarding depreciation computations; otherwise, it would be much more difficult to reconcile state and federal tax returns. This arrangement means that it is usually adequate to maintain two depreciation books: financial and federal. States, counties, and cities are less concerned with whether the asset reports and property tax filings they receive agree in value with the company's income tax filings, as long as the two filings can be reconciled and each jurisdiction gets the tax computed by the formulas it dictates.

Ledger Accounting

The depreciation expense from each Oracle Assets depreciation book flows to a single General Ledger (GL) set of books. The flexfield combinations for the various asset, liability, and depreciation expense accounts are in the Accounting Flexfield structure corresponding to that set of books. The relationship is many-to-one: Many Assets books can be associated with one GL set of books.

There is an advantage to keeping the relationship one-to-one. Oracle Assets can easily handle transfers of assets between organizations when those organizations are in one Assets book. It generates intercompany journals to move the assets and associated liabilities between balancing segments within the one General Ledger set of books.

To move assets from one asset book into an associated tax book, you can run a process called "Mass Copy" that will automatically migrate all assets and their associated transactions. You can avoid a lot of work by keeping all assets in a single asset book. During the setup of your book, define your various flexfields in such a way that you can create the necessary reports and journal postings through native Oracle Assets functions. As you weigh your various reporting requirements against keeping separate sets of books, be sure to favor the data over rigid adherence to a "pure vanilla" use of Oracle Assets. You will minimize maintenance effort if you keep the data structure simple and keep all of your records in one asset book.

Oracle Assets is usually not a factor in the design of the Accounting Flexfield (AFF). Assets are usually associated with the organizational elements of the AFF, company, and department. If depreciation expense is charged out by other segments, such as product line or project, it is usually better handled by allocation within the GL than by settings within Assets.

Tagging with Asset Identifiers

Oracle Assets associates four unique identifiers with each asset. Their names, uses, and sources are shown in Table 8-1.

Identifier	Optional?	Use	Source	Purpose
Asset Number	No	External; forms and reports	User-assigned or generated; may be imported. If generated, it is the same as the Asset ID.	Identifies the asset in Oracle Assets forms and reports.
Tag Number	Yes	External; bar codes	User-assigned; usually imported.	Provides bar code tracking of assets.
Asset ID	No	Internal	Generated	Links asset records with depreciation and other transactions.
Serial Number	Yes	External	User-assigned	Provides an additional asset identifier; usually assigned by the manufacturer.

TABLE 8-1. *Unique Identifiers for Various Types of Assets*

It is useful to affix physical property tags to items for the purposes of asset control. Making items scannable saves a lot of time if assets are to be counted, moved, or maintained with any frequency. The master record in Oracle Assets carries both your unique physical tag and the Oracle Asset Number. Either can serve as a reference in the Transfers form.

The tag number relates items controlled by Oracle Assets to legacy and external systems. Oracle imports, accepts, carries, and reports on the tag number but does not generate or otherwise process it. There are several tagging systems. Scannable tags can be preprinted and positioned in the receiving area to be affixed to items as they arrive. Choosing scannable tags requires a business procedure to get the tag number into the asset record. Alternatively, you may develop a system to print bar code tags. If you have that luxury, it may be advantageous to use the asset number as the tag number.

Either alternative will require a moderate amount of third-party or bespoke (custom) code. If you are using preprinted tags, consider putting a scanner "wedge" on the receiving area terminal. As they affix the tag during the receiving process, staff members can scan the tag number to a Descriptive Flexfield, the asset addition interface in Oracle Assets. A small bespoke program can get the tag number from there to the Mass Additions table. Going the other way, it is only a minor programming effort to pull the asset number or tag number out of the system and send it to a bar code printer.

Release 11 includes full support for scanning bar-coded assets, including the capability for reports to reconcile scanned assets to those in the system. The process can drive additions, transfers, and retirements to bring the assets book in line with reality.

Major capital items often include components that need to be separately tracked and depreciated. For example, suppose a building includes an HVAC system (heating, ventilating, and air conditioning) which, in turn, includes compressors and generators. Oracle Assets can carry each device for depreciation purposes, but it will not record any configuration data. When planning your asset management system, keep in mind that some trackable and depreciable items may be enclosed in or covered by other items—that is, their tags may not be visible.

The Asset Key Flexfield

The Asset Key Flexfield supplements the asset number with descriptive information that can be used to meet your organization's individual needs. While the Asset Number uniquely identifies an item, the Asset Key Flexfield groups assets by nonfinancial identifiers. Company, Account Number, Department and Product are some examples of identifiers that can be tracked in the flexfield segments.

The Asset Key Flexfield can include up to ten segments. As with any Oracle flexfield, you define the number of segments and the name, format and length of each of them. By taking advantage of Oracle flexfield validation features, you simplify and refine your data entry process. If the Asset Number and Tag are sufficient for physical tracking, you can reduce the Asset Key Flexfield to a token one-segment flexfield.

The Asset Key Flexfield plays no role in financial reporting, but is often used as the basis for custom reporting. It is designed to be used with the Descriptive Flexfield for storing information that will be used in custom reports. The standard forms support the complex functions of data capture and validation without the necessity of specific knowledge of the data. This leaves you the relatively simple task of preparing custom reports in the format that best supports your unique needs. Applications Desktop Integrator (ADI) gives you the ability to create custom reports for a number of Financials packages, including Oracle Assets. It lets you choose the columns to be displayed and used for selection and sorting in its variable format reports. The Asset Key Flexfield provides an ideal framework for your custom ADI reporting. It has as many segments as you are likely to need, and the way in which you define it is not constrained by any predefined uses within Oracle Assets.

The Category Flexfield

An asset's category determines its financial treatment within Oracle Assets—that is, the way in which the asset is depreciated. The derivation process is illustrated in Figure 8-1.

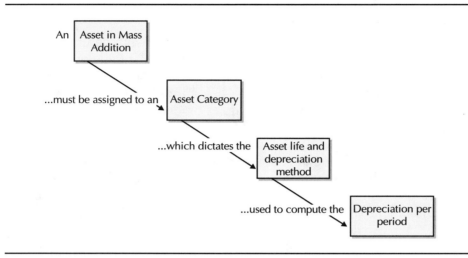

FIGURE 8-1. *Derivation of depreciation amounts*

Depreciation computations depend on such factors as the type of depreciation (life, units of production, or flat rate), the depreciation life, and the depreciation method. Flat rate depreciation is implemented as a straight percentage of cost, with no regard to depreciation life. As you can see in Figure 8-1, the full lifetime depreciation treatment of an item can be established by the cost of the item and the Asset Category assigned to it as it enters the system.

The Asset Category specifies a default depreciation method to be used with an asset. You will usually want to set up categories in such a way that you do not need to override the defaults they establish; this way, items can enter the system through Mass Additions without your having to deal with them individually. You can preassign the Asset Category for any item you buy regularly.

The Asset Category specifies the General Ledger accounts to be used for the following:

- Asset cost and Asset clearing accounts
- Construction-in-progress (CIP) cost and CIP clearing accounts

- Depreciation expense and depreciation reserve accounts
- Revaluation reserve and amortization accounts

Oracle Assets combines the account information provided in the Asset Category setup with various business rules to generate the General Ledger journals. In Release 10.7 and earlier, Oracle Flexbuilder was used to automatically derive account combinations for certain transactions. However, Oracle Workflow Builder and Account Generator now allow you to create, view, or modify any business process with simple drag-and-drop operations while the system automatically derives the proper account combinations.

Oracle provides up to seven segments for the Category Flexfield. You can use separate segments for concepts such as depreciation type, depreciation life, and method, or you can put them all together in a single segment. For example:

Segment 1: Vehicle | Segment 2: Owned–Luxury

or

Segment 1: Vehicle–Owned–Luxury

The advantage of multiple segments is that each segment can be validated independently as new categories are created. However, most companies do not have so many different depreciation plans that this is an issue. It is quite likely that the major effort in defining Asset Categories will take place at conversion, after which new categories will rarely be added. As editing new segment values is not a significant problem, some users may find that a single segment works best

The Location Flexfield

The Location Flexfield is used for recording the physical location of assets and for property tax reporting. Its segments usually include the country, state/province/department/land, county, and city in which an asset is located. To facilitate asset moves, you may want to add the addresses of facilities within a city. For example, you could define a Location Flexfield with these segments:

COUNTRY | STATE | CITY | STREET

A data record for one of your assets might use those segments to store the following values:

USA | CA | Los Angeles | 107 Chester Avenue

Oracle allows you to define up to seven segments. The number you decide is final, so you should be generous with your designation. Decide how Oracle's reports will support your property tax business operations. Consider your business processes for physically tracking assets. Plan for the future and define as many segments as you will ever need. You should include the following factors in your decision:

- **Your Outside Tax Rate Services**   Get the tax package at the same time you buy Oracle. Make sure that the geography you define maps to the data you will integrate with Oracle.

- **Your Company Locations**   How closely will you track assets? To the city? To a campus? A building? A floor? A room? Your business processes have to achieve a balance between the value of being able to locate assets and the cost of recording their movements.

- **Segment Edits**   You will want lookup table edits of country, state, and county. Which other segments will you want to edit? You probably will have names for your campuses, but can you anticipate every possible room number?

- **Cross-Validation Rules**   It would be painful to compile and write out the rules for numerous valid combinations of county, country, and state. Unless you can buy these rules through a service, having them all available is probably not worth the effort. On the other hand, it is generally easy and useful to write cross-validation rules for your own business locations. For example, Micros Systems headquarters must be in Beltsville, Prince George's County, Maryland, U.S.A. The cross-validation rules on a company-specific segment can force valid geographic data into other segments for the purposes of property taxes.

Merger and Acquisition Considerations

Tangible assets are a major factor in valuing corporate reorganizations. Assets that are changing ownership need to be fully identified by item, cost, and remaining depreciation. Because it is independent of financial factors, the Asset Key Flexfield is useful for grouping assets to be transferred. Once grouped, their value can be reported and agreed upon.

Oracle Assets carries all the data required to generate Mass Additions into a new system. In other words, the Oracle Assets module serves as a very accessible legacy system. Custom scripts to extract data for export are easy to write. The acquiring firm will find all the essential data whether or not it uses Oracle Assets.

Tax books shadow the actual asset books. Thus, the export procedure for deacquired assets (those that have been sold, scrapped, or transferred out) must ensure that the same assets appear in the financial and tax books after a reorganization. Tax books require a separate export/import process using Mass Copy, however, since tax book depreciation is independent of financial depreciation.

Taxes

Property tax is the major tax reporting requirement addressed by Oracle Assets. The concerns are the location of each item and the item's value in the eyes of the taxing authorities. The second major tax issue, income tax, is handled by General Ledger, which uses asset value and depreciation figures from Oracle Assets. Oracle Assets also carries the data to support other types of taxation, such as lease tax and use tax. Minor taxes can be handled by linking spreadsheets to asset records, but the system lends itself to custom-coded extensions where they are needed.

Property Tax Calculation

Oracle Assets supports real and personal property tax calculations through tax books and the Location Flexfield. The Property Tax report shows assets within a given geography. Real and personal property are distinguished by the property class assigned to the asset. You can use the desktop interface to pull these assets into a spreadsheet to compute tax liability.

Spreadsheets play a major role in most Oracle Assets property tax computations. Though the rules are complex—different states and counties have their own rules for property classes and depreciation—the data is not highly volatile. It works well to have Oracle serve as the repository for these handmade processes as well as for the data that drives them.

In Release 11, Oracle is fully integrated with three specialized third-party property tax preparation services. You send them data from Oracle Assets in their format: a Location Flexfield in the layout they dictate, identifying data for the taxable property, and your valuation data. The service will prepare property taxes for all applicable filing jurisdictions. It is simple to use and accurate, and saves significant amounts of time.

Income Tax Calculation

Tracking depreciation is the primary means by which Oracle Assets can help you calculate your income taxes. Depreciation reduces taxes by reducing taxable income. Gains and losses on sales can be viewed as adjustments to depreciation. Investment tax credits, a tax policy device used in the United States to favor certain types of business investments, affect the tax itself rather than taxable income.

Depreciation

Depreciation is an instrument of public tax policy; depreciation regulations are designed to encourage investment. Allowing a company to front-load depreciation schedules (that is, to take more depreciation early in an asset's life) reduces the tax liability that results from a capital investment. The tax is made up in later years when less depreciation remains to be taken. Table 8-2 shows the effect that straight-line depreciation would have on a $5000 investment for a firm in the 40 percent tax bracket. Table 8-3 shows the effect of accelerated depreciation on the same loan.

In both cases the after-tax cost of the investment is $3000, which represents 40 percent off the initial cost. The difference, however, is timing. With straight-line depreciation, the cost reduces to $3000 after five years; with accelerated depreciation it gets there in three. Figures 8-2 and 8-3 present the same information graphically. Figure 8-2 shows that although the total depreciation deductions are the same under the two methods, they come much sooner with ACRS. Figure 8-3 shows the effect on total costs: asset cost net of tax savings from depreciation goes down faster with ACRS.

	Year 1	Year 2	Year 3	Year 4	Year 5	Total
Investment	−5000	0	0	0	0	−5000
Depreciation	1000	1000	1000	1000	1000	
Net cash flow before taxes	−4000	1000	1000	1000	1000	
Income tax benefit @ 40%	400	400	400	400	400	2000
After-tax cash flow effect of investment	−4600	400	400	400	400	−3000

TABLE 8-2.   *Cash Flow Under Straight-Line Depreciation*

Because tax depreciation does not accurately reflect the true worth of an asset, the company's financial books show depreciation and net asset value differently than do the tax books. Frequently, there are several tax books, each with different figures.

Your company may maintain its tax books in General Ledger. If so, you can post tax journals directly to the GL set of tax books. You can then

	Year 1	Year 2	Year 3	Year 4	Year 5	Total
Investment	−5000	0	0	0	0	−5000
Depreciation	1250	1900	1850	0	0	
Net cash flow before taxes	−3750	1900	1850	0	0	
Income tax benefit @ 40%	500	760	740	0	0	2000
After-tax cash flow effect of investment	−4500	760	740	0	0	−3000

TABLE 8-3.   *Cash Flow Under Three-Year ACRS*

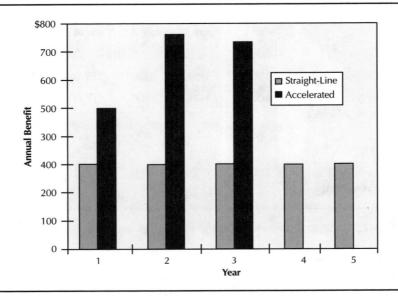

FIGURE 8-2. *Comparison of cash flow under straight-line and accelerated depreciation*

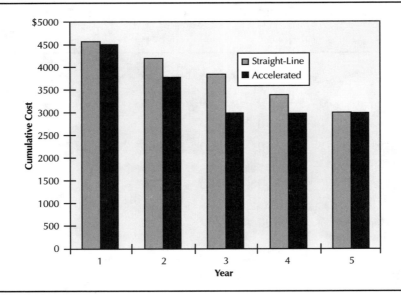

FIGURE 8-3. *Cumulative after-tax cost under straight-line and accelerated depreciation*

reconcile the tax books with the financial books, and compute taxes entirely within General Ledger.

Whether or not you maintain tax books in General Ledger, the real-money implications of tax book numbers must ultimately flow to the GL financial books. To account for the differences in depreciation recognized between the two books, follow these steps:

1. Within Oracle Assets, post depreciation from Assets' financial books to the set of financial books in General Ledger. The postings should look something like these:

Account	Debit	Credit
Depreciation expense	20,000	
Depreciation reserve		20,000

2. Use the tax books with Assets to compute the depreciation allowed for tax purposes. Subtract the depreciation listed in the financial books from the depreciation listed in the tax books to determine additional allowable depreciation expense. Suppose it is $5000. To take additional depreciation in the current year but show that it must be paid back in future years, create manual journal entries like these:

Account	Debit	Credit
Net depreciation expense adjustment	5000	
Deferred depreciation expense		5000

3. Create a manual journal entry for the tax implications of the accelerated depreciation. If the rate were 40 percent, the entries would look like these:

Account	Debit	Credit
Income tax payable adjustment	2000	
Deferred income tax		2000

With these steps, General Ledger's financial books fully reflect the impact of tax book depreciation. Current expense is increased and current tax liability is correspondingly decreased, but the deferred depreciation and tax accounts reflect the fact that these current benefits will be reversed sometime in the future.

Recoverability Ratio

Recoverable cost is the total amount of investment that can be recouped through depreciation over an asset's lifetime. Both the financial and the tax books carry recoverable costs.

When the recoverable amounts in the tax and financial books are the same, usually the price of the asset minus its salvage value, there is no problem in computing depreciation. The total lifetime depreciation flowing from the tax books will equal the total flowing from the financial books. Accelerated depreciation will be recaptured within the asset's lifetime.

If the recoverable cost in the tax books exceeds the recoverable cost in the financial books, the full depreciation from the tax books could exceed the price of the item. Tax authorities do not allow this. The Oracle Assets topical essay entitled *Calculating Deferred Depreciation* suggests the following steps for handling this situation:

1. Run the Oracle Assets Recoverability report to compute the lifetime recoverable cost in the financial and tax books.

2. Compute the ratio between the two: corporate (financial) recoverable cost to tax recoverable cost. This recoverability ratio should be less than one.

3. Multiply the tax depreciation in each period by the recoverability ratio. This will force the total recoverable cost on the tax side to equal the total corporate recoverable cost. Financial depreciation will still have the shape of the tax depreciation curve, usually front-end loaded, with more depreciation in the early years. Each period's depreciation will just be proportionately less, so the total depreciation just equals the allowed amount.

Investment Tax Credit

An investment tax credit (ITC) is independent of depreciation. The taxing authority allows a company to reduce its tax obligation by a fixed percentage of a qualifying capital investment. The downstream considerations come into play when the asset is sold or retired. If the asset has not been in use for the prescribed period of time, the company may be liable for ITC recapture upon its sale.

Leased Assets

The physical handling of leased assets is similar to that of owned assets. The major difference is the need to track when the lease will expire, so that the lease can be extended or the item returned. Lease expiration dates and lease terms must be carefully monitored.

Financially, leased items are more an issue for the accounts payable department than for managers of fixed assets. The accounts payable department makes the periodic payments. Capital leases, however, have an amortization structure with principal and interest elements. Release 11 carries and displays amortization data, which allows you to view the amortization schedule on a capital lease. The distinctions between an operating lease, which can be expensed, and a capital lease, which is treated as a sale or purchase from an accounting standpoint, are subtle. Oracle Fixed Assets applies an FASB13 test to leased assets in order to determine how they would be accounted under U.S. tax law. You can override Oracle's determination, however, if your tax rules are different.

The Asset Additions Cycle

Most fixed assets enter the system in batch mode through Mass Additions. You can use custom scripts at cutover to populate the table with legacy data, or you can use the Create Assets feature to prepare the additions in spreadsheets, then use the Applications Desktop Integrator to validate your additions. After cutover the data flows through existing integration from Oracle Purchasing and Oracle Payables. You can have Oracle Projects make entries into the Mass Additions interface as construction is completed on capital projects.

Set up Oracle Inventory and Oracle Purchasing to meet the requirements of Oracle Assets: You may want to assign inventory item numbers to things you buy on an ongoing basis. You can then give them an Asset Category that will flow through to Oracle Assets.

You can assign items to a GL asset account as you enter invoices in Oracle Payables. The association actually takes place at the GL distribution level to account for the possibility that the expense for one invoice line may be distributed to multiple organizations.

Run the Create Mass Additions process in Oracle Payables periodically to send additions over to Oracle Assets. After they have been imported, use the Prepare Mass Additions form to fill in missing data, including the location, an Asset Category if the item is not defined to inventory, and depreciation particulars.

TIP

If you can codify the business rules you use to assign locations and categories, you can save some work by automating this function. The purchase order number and the AP Invoice Distribution line are available within Oracle Assets. A programmer can follow these items back to Descriptive Flexfield entries in the Purchasing or Payables system and then use those DFF entries to fill in the required location, category, and depreciation information. You can make the system capture fixed asset data from the best possible source, whether you are the requisitioner, buyer, AP clerk, or Oracle Assets administrator.

The Create Assets feature supports a disconnected environment, one in which the assets are not fed from the Oracle Purchasing, Accounts Payable, Inventory, and Projects systems. Create Assets builds an Excel spreadsheet based on the needs of your Oracle Assets implementation. It validates your entries against your lists of values and gives you the flexibility provided by Excel data-entry shortcuts such as forms and macro logic. You can route data files from legacy and feeder systems into the spreadsheet to complete and refine the data before passing it to Oracle Assets.

Capital Budgeting

Capital budgets are projections of capital expenditures and the depreciation expense flows that recapture those expenses. Oracle Assets includes reports to compare budgets and actual expenses on a yearly basis. Reports of projected depreciation are useful for General Ledger budgeting purposes as well.

Oracle Assets budgets follow Asset Books and Asset Category groupings. This arrangement offers a finer level of control than General Ledger budgeting, which must be done within the Accounting Flexfield structure.

Converting to Oracle Assets

Converting your assets correctly is a major challenge in cutting over from your legacy system to Oracle Assets. Testing—through repeated trial conversions—is the key to success. The critical determinants are whether the asset figures (original cost and depreciation reserve) and the future depreciation stream are correct. Your conversion test plan should accomplish the following goals:

- *Establish criteria for success at the balance-sheet level.* Start by comparing the legacy asset and depreciation reserve accounts stored in General Ledger to the legacy system figures stored in Oracle Assets. Because some legacy assets and ledger systems are independent of one another, the figures may not match. Oracle, on the other hand, keeps the two in absolute agreement. You need to plan for a one-time accounting adjustment to bring assets and the ledger in line at conversion. The standard criterion for success in converting assets is that the totals of asset value, depreciation reserve, and residual value in Oracle match the total in the legacy system. The test plan will specify that reports from the two systems match.

- *Establish criteria for success at the depreciation-expense level.* The standard criterion for success here is that the future depreciation cash flows are the same in Oracle as in the legacy system. Again, specify the reports that should match between the two systems.

- *Define depreciation methods and categories to accommodate legacy assets.* Each asset that enters Oracle through Mass Additions will be identified with a category and, through the category, a predefined depreciation method. You cannot import a depreciation flow with an item; you must use an Oracle-assigned method.

■ *Establish a strategy for assets that have remained on their original depreciation schedules.* These are the easy ones. Oracle can correctly establish the net book value and remaining depreciation flow given the original cost, current cost, recoverable cost, depreciation plan, and date the asset was placed in service. Your plan should call for importing these values; you can use them to run depreciation for the subsequent years. Throw away the ledger journals, because the legacy ledger balances already reflect the acquisition and the prior year's depreciation. The Oracle Assets book should reflect the same values as the legacy book, and it should generate the same depreciation going forward.

■ *Establish a strategy for assets with depreciation schedules that have changed over time.* Taking a simple example, suppose a $10,000 asset goes into service on a five-year depreciation schedule, but is changed after three years to a ten-year life, with the adjustment to be amortized. Give it zero residual value. Figure 8-4 shows the asset's lifetime depreciation, and Figure 8-5 show's the residual value at the end of each year.

If the asset is imported into Oracle at the end of the sixth year, it will have a residual value of $2283 and see depreciation of $571 per year. These figures ($10,000, $2283, and $571 per year) are the original cost, residual value, and depreciation flow that would apply in the last three years of a $10,000 item depreciated over 17.5 years. The numbers in Oracle would be exactly correct if the in-service date were pushed back by 7.5 years, and the asset were depreciated on a 17.5 year straight-line plan.

However, this approach poses some difficulty. First, the in-service date might be important in the future; changing it misrepresents reality. More significantly, there is no standard depreciation schedule for a 17.5-year life. Oracle only deals with integers of years for asset life. The asset would require a handmade, one-of-a-kind depreciation plan. So would every other asset that changed plans or saw an amortized adjustment anywhere over its life.

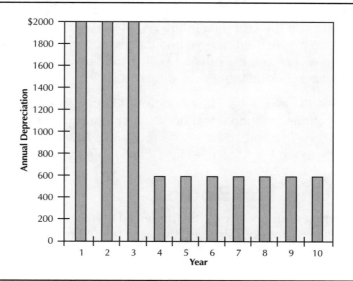

FIGURE 8-4. *Depreciation schedule reflecting a changed asset life*

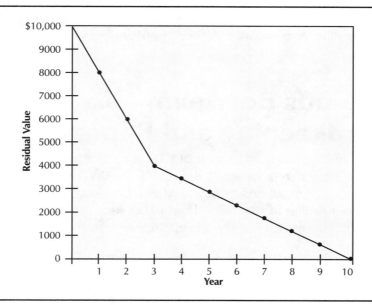

FIGURE 8-5. *Annual residual values of the same asset*

- Oracle provides the tools you need to enter revalued assets directly. As you enter the cost data in the FA_MASS_ADDITIONS table, also enter the revaluation reserve and the revaluation amortization basis. Oracle will record the original cost in the books, but compute future depreciation using the revalued figures.

- Release 11 provides a Mass Additions Upload feature in the Applications Desktop Integrator. You can purify and prepare your assets data in a spreadsheet, and then have ADI load the data directly to the FA_MASS_ ADDITIONS table.

Converting Tax Books

When converting your tax books, the preferred method is to repeat the tax book depreciation process. First, add the item to the financial books. Next, move it to the appropriate tax books. Then, run depreciation against both the financial and the tax books.

The converted tax books may tie in to a set of tax books in General Ledger, but not all companies keep multiple ledger books. The conversion plan must include procedures for generating balance reports in the Oracle and legacy assets tax books to show that both sides agree on the amounts being transferred within tax books. These amounts include acquisition cost, depreciation plan, accumulated depreciation, and residual value for tax purposes.

Trade-offs Between Recordkeeping and Reporting

The one parameter common to most of Oracle's standard reports is the Asset Set of Books. Several reports group items by Category and Location, and only a few group items by Asset Key Flexfield. Unless you use desktop functions, your design of reports and sets of books must take into account two conflicting design points: *report structure* and *asset transfers*.

- **Report structure**   Because most reports accept only a few parameters, reporting is easiest with multiple sets of asset books, each with relatively few entries. The easiest way to report on groups of assets within one General Ledger set of books is to keep them in separate Asset sets of books.

■ **Asset transfers** Because the only way to transfer items between sets of books is to remove them and then add them back in, the system structure favors fewer, more inclusive Asset sets of books within a General Ledger set of books.

The General Ledger interface is straightforward, whether there are few or many sets of asset books. The issue in deciding how many sets of asset books to maintain is primarily one of record-keeping versus reporting. Assets performs both functions, but the recordkeeping is arguably the most essential—and favors keeping fewer and larger financial books.

Oracle Assets provides the necessary master record of which items the company owns and where they are. The master record is the thread that ties the systems together for audit purposes: The ledger agrees with the Oracle Assets books, and all Assets books carry the same assets.

The more than one hundred standard reports in the Oracle Assets system are indicative of the variety of information needs. Even a thousand could not satisfy all users, and yet each installation uses only a small fraction of those provided. Variable Format Reports, which you can access through ADI's Request Center, is a new feature that works with Oracle Assets. You can extract Assets data to be manipulated with whatever desktop tool you favor. Spreadsheets are the most common. You can also go to the Internet via HTML. Defining how to extract data for use in standard variable format reports is a setup and programming task. From that point on, creating reports is strictly up to the Oracle Assets users.

The alternative to using desktop tools is to modify the standard Oracle reports, primarily adding additional selection criteria. Doing this is a much easier and less expensive task to manage than fragmenting the assets among many financial books.

Conclusion

Oracle Assets provides the essential record-keeping features for property, plant, and equipment, combined with the processing logic required to support almost every conceivable depreciation schedule. It will help you maintain accurate financial records of assets for financial and income tax reporting purposes, and its design ensures the integrity of the journals it sends to General Ledger.

Improved integration with other systems, notably Projects and Payables, now gives Oracle Assets more physical asset management functions, along with the ability to handle leases and warranty information. You can take advantage of Oracle's partnerships with tax information providers to compute your property tax filings automatically. The open design of the module allows you to easily capture and work with custom data. You can add processes to manipulate and report on fixed-assets data through spreadsheets linked to the database, third-party software built to work with Oracle, or your own custom routines.

CHAPTER
9

Oracle Purchasing

urchasing is an integral part of the corporate supply chain. Among other things, it replenishes your inventory, fulfills customer demand, and helps control outside processing. Manufacturing and inventory departments base their purchasing recommendations on what goods are being requested and what goods are on order, as well as when they will arrive. The Oracle Purchasing component works at the transaction level.

Purchasing Overview

Purchasing is usually considered the first phase in the supply chain cycle. Its major functions are sourcing, requisitioning, purchasing, and receiving. The strength of the process lies in supporting operational rather than management decisions. For example, it can help personnel determine whether or not to approve an order or how much of an item to replenish, but it does not address such strategic questions as which suppliers should enjoy long-term contractual relationships. Oracle's Business Intelligence System (BIS) product completes the picture. It provides all levels of users with answers to questions across all Oracle modules, including Purchasing. Information can be accessed directly from the transaction system or from a central repository, such as a data warehouse.

Purchasing handles all acquisition activity within a company: goods and services, raw materials, services, capital goods, expendable supplies— everything the company needs. It captures task and accounting information that will be needed downstream by Project Accounting, Fixed Assets, Payables, and eventually the General Ledger. People and systems throughout the company use requisitions to tell the purchasing department what they need. Purchasing orders the requisitioned goods from suppliers, and receiving accepts delivery of items and delivers them internally to the requisitioner or stocks the item in inventory.

Approval policies are applied to all purchasing documents before the system acts on them. The document will be routed through the appropriate approval chain according to the source of a document, the amount ordered, the type of material, and other criteria you may apply. Oracle Purchasing efficiently determines the accounting distribution for each purchasing line by applying sophisticated defaulting logic to the input provided by the requisitioner or buyer. The Workflow engine used to guide transactions through the routing and accounting distribution processes provides the users with excellent guidance and makes it possible for you to adapt the processes as necessary.

Requisitions

The requisition form begins the procurement process. It says, "I want it." The requisition process has traditionally been a manual one, with a trail of paper forms and written approvals. Because they had to be relatively simple, the manual approvals procedures were frequently inappropriately loose or restrictive for the requisition in question.

Although this process works satisfactorily for some, a manually structured business process misses the advantages of integration. Oracle Purchasing is flexible enough to support all kinds of business procedures. The objective of the requisition form is to efficiently capture everything up front, from the eventual user. This user is the best source for defaulting the following information:

- **Requisitioner's identity and organization** With Oracle Purchasing, capture of this data is automated, though the user has the option to override the defaults.

- **Description of the needed goods** With an online requisition, the user can either choose the right item from an online catalog or enter descriptive information and a suggested buyer and supplier for nonstock items and services.

- **Information on account(s) to charge for the purchase** Depending on your setup, most accounting information will be derived automatically on the basis of the identity of the requisitioner and the item being requested. The requisitioner is a better source for additional data than are people farther downstream, such as the buyers and the payables clerks. Also, the requisitioner is the one who will know and care most about his or her budget situation. For users with lengthy Accounting Flexfields or significant project and task information requirements, capturing accounting data at requisition time is the only way to make sure the input is accurate.

The Web is a natural vehicle for requisitioning. "Empowering employees" is a mantra of our generation, and a wise one. Giving employees the ability to get the materials they need to do the job—without a lot of fuss and by-your-leave from management—certainly makes them more productive. The Web, over an intranet or the Internet, can push this capability to all corners of the organization. Requisitioning under Web Employees, described in Chapter 13 is fully integrated with Oracle Purchasing and other Oracle modules. It delivers true self-service.

Oracle has incorporated requisitioning functions using its workflow technology. It provides flexible, rules-based processes that you can tailor to meet specific business needs. It can, for instance, approve requisitions automatically and create purchase orders directly, on the basis of factors such as the cost, item category, and requisitioner. It can automatically route requisitions through an approval cycle and prompt approvers to act. It can handle technical as well as financial approval cycles. It can communicate via e-mail, the Web, or directly through the applications.

With Release 11, Oracle Web Employees offers several powerful features to reduce hassles in requisitioning. Procurement cards (P-cards) bypass requisitioning altogether. Employees use their procurement card to make a purchase. Oracle Payables derives the accounting information from data imported from the card issuer. Employees can verify their transactions, change the accounting data, and challenge any transactions on the statement that they did not make. In the future, the requisitions features within Web Employees will be able to impose an approval process on procurement card purchases. The requisitioner will put the P-card number on the requisition. Once the requisition is approved, the purchase will flow through on the P-card without the need for purchase order or release transactions.

The Inventory and Material Requirements Planning modules compute requirements by balancing demand (a combination of orders and forecasts) against supply (what is on hand, on order, and being manufactured). These systems can create requisitions to fill the difference between supply and demand. The generating systems populate all of the required data fields, and these requisitions are usually converted to purchase order releases that you can set up to pass straight to the suppliers without buyer intervention.

Approval policy for requisitions is defined at setup. Controls are imposed according to what is being ordered, who is ordering it, and how much it costs. These factors also determine which people appear in the approval chain or hierarchy. Even though just as many people may have to approve a requisition, the paperless approval process is usually quicker. Where a paper requisition might sit in an in-box for a week, Oracle Purchasing actively "pushes" actions awaiting approval to the approvers' attention when they log in. The automated system can have variable routing depending on who is available. As a last resort, Oracle Workflow and Oracle Alerts can automatically generate e-mail to nudge along actions that seem to be hung up along the way. In theory, all this automation and notification should speed up the requisitioning process.

Requisition Templates can also be set up to streamline the entry of requisition lines. Your Item Master may contain thousands of part numbers, yet most groups within your organization only order from a small subset of that large list. Requisition Templates can be created from a list of frequently ordered items or even from an existing requisition, saving your employees the time and preventing the mistakes involved in searching the entire Item Master for the parts they need.

Suppliers

Successful buying entails satisfying the needs of the company at the lowest overall cost. This is often not the same as getting the lowest price. Buyers' time costs money, and unreliable suppliers can cost a company in terms of lost production, lost sales, and the paperwork involved in such tasks as inspections, returns, credit memos, and invoice adjustments. Supplier relationships are a key element in purchasing strategy, and Oracle is designed to manage these relationships.

Suppliers need to be set up before a buyer can create a purchase order. The essentials of supplier setup include name and address, site, terms of payment, and type (i.e., outside supplier, employee, or other types you have set up). Many other information items may be entered at the supplier level, saving keystrokes at the transaction level later on. There is usually a preferred ship-to address, bill-to address, mode of shipment, and so on associated with a supplier. Information entered for the supplier will become the default for all purchase orders entered for that supplier. Other data elements satisfy government tax and statutory reporting requirements. Payables and Purchasing share the same supplier and vendor files, and supplier maintenance screens can be made available in either or both of these applications. (Supplier access should be a secured process within any organization). Responsibilities and business procedures should be in place to ensure that the supplier update process is coordinated and that only approved suppliers are entered and any duplication avoided.

Supplier Relationships

Both buyers and sellers find it most efficient to set up long-term purchasing relationships. Sellers get business they can plan on, and buyers get the advantages of negotiated low prices, minimal paperwork, and the reliability that can only be achieved by sharing planning information with trusted suppliers. Both sides find it worthwhile to invest in establishing these relationships, and Oracle Purchasing provides several features that will help you manage them.

Contracts

Purchase orders and purchase agreements are the contractual vehicles recognized by Oracle. Purchase orders (POs) are one-time affairs, complete unto themselves: They specify what to deliver, when, and where. POs may be adequate for all procurement activity in smaller organizations, and the 90 percent of the suppliers who account for 10 percent of purchasing volume in larger organizations. Long-term supplier relationships, however, usually involve purchase agreements.

There are two types of purchase agreements. The more basic, a Blanket Purchase Order (BPO), specifies items and prices as negotiated with the supplier. A BPO usually applies for a given period of time; it may also stipulate minimum and maximum unit and dollar order amounts. Purchase Order Releases, referencing the BPO, are created as required to tell the supplier what to ship and where.

A Contract Purchase Agreement, the second type of purchase agreement, is really only an agreement to agree. It specifies terms and conditions but no items; other types of POs can reference a Contract Purchase Agreement. A Contract Purchase Agreement can also support competitive solicitations. First, there has to be an approved quotation through the Request for Quotation (RFQ) process, which is described later in this chapter. Then, buyers create Purchase Order Releases referencing both the Contract Purchase Agreement and the approved quotation under it.

Planned Purchase Orders (PPOs) establish a vehicle to satisfy projected material and services needs over a period of time. They mix features of standard orders and BPOs. Like a standard order, PPOs specify accounting distributions for each line item. Like BPOs, the lines are only tentative; a release is required for actual delivery. A PPO can be used to reserve funds under encumbrance accounting. For example, a school system, not knowing exactly how much heating oil it will require for the year or when it would be delivered, can use a PPO to protect that line of the budget with an encumbrance.

These one-, two-, and three-step processes (contract, optional bid, and optional release) are designed to cover all ordering, from the basic to the most demanding procurement processes. They are structured for material and for most services purchases. Purchases of services usually specify a monetary amount rather than an item quantity. Purchasing provides line types for each, and it allows you to define any other line types that make sense. You may want to consider Oracle Project Accounting for managing truly complex services contracts, such as erecting a building or constructing a software system.

Solicitations

The process of establishing a relationship can be formal or informal. The United States federal government sets the standard for formal procurements. Its process also represents a maximum investment in establishing a supplier relationship. It is worth identifying each of the steps in the full process to see where Oracle's features can be useful.

1. A department within the company or agency drafts a requirements document, specifying what and how much is needed, and when it is needed.

2. The buyers use their fund of experience and outside databases to assemble a list of potential suppliers.

3. Purchasing sends Requests for Information (RFI) to the identified suppliers. It may publish the solicitation as well. U.S. public agencies use the newspapers and *Commerce Business Daily*.

4. Purchasing decides whether or not to do a formal procurement. If not, it skips to Step 7 of this list and enters into negotiations with one or more suppliers.

5. For a formal procurement, purchasing writes a Request for Proposal (RFP) or a Request for Quotation (RFQ). The RFP restates the requirement and specifies the format for a response. It may dictate some terms and conditions (T&Cs) and specify the format for adaptable T&Cs that must be stipulated in the bid. The request often spells out the criteria that will be used in evaluating the proposal. Purchasing sends the bids to all qualified parties who have expressed an interest and follows up with a bidder's conference.

6. Purchasing evaluates supplier proposals.

7. Purchasing asks the top bidders for Best and Final Offers (BAFOs). The suppliers' BAFOs typically firm up terms and conditions.

8. The two parties complete a contract incorporating the RFP and BAFO documents.

Oracle is continually adding support for the solicitation process. It now handles RFQ, quotations, and RFQ-only suppliers. (These features exist solely to support the bidding process.) It supports solicitations both with and without a prior purchasing agreement. Online quote analysis supports the selection process. Oracle Web Suppliers is designed to distribute notice of your requirements early and broadly.

The Purchasing RFQ process starts at Step 5—with an RFP/RFQ. If the RFI needs to be communicated to a large audience, it could begin at Step 3 by posting the requirement through Oracle Web Suppliers. Seen from another perspective, the RFQ itself serves as an RFI. It alerts suppliers to your need. The Approved Suppliers List (ASL) that Purchasing uses can carry source and price information item by item. An RFQ involves identifying a few suppliers from whom to request quotes on items that may or may not have been defined yet in the Inventory Item Master. (Items such as nonproduction purchases may never become part of the inventory system.) Purchasing provides forms for defining the RFP and entering bids. Once an award is made, the buyers cement the link between the procurement and the existing purchase agreement. They can then use Oracle's Approved Suppliers List and Sourcing Rules to indicate, by item or commodity, which contracts to source from.

A Supplier Quotation List is a predefined set of suppliers who can be referenced when putting together an RFP. A company may have Contract Purchase Orders with Staples, Office Max, and Ginn's Office Supply. To save time, it could put those three suppliers on a list called, perhaps, "Office Supply." Putting together an RFQ for print cartridges would involve simply naming the item and the supplier list.

A competitive procurement can require a lot of time, which of course is not free. There are opportunity costs associated with the elapsed time, as the business may not be able to move until procurement is complete. Unless the business' policies absolutely require a competitive process, the purchasing manager may want to apply a cost-benefit analysis and limit RFQs to larger procurements. By posting solicitations on the Web, Oracle Web Suppliers can decrease the time and cost involved in a competitive buy.

Approvals

Separating the authority to initiate and to approve expenditures is a fundamental accounting control observed by most organizations. The security controls define which types of approvals apply to each document type and which people can view and modify each document type.

A setup parameter determines whether approval goes by individual (supervisor) or by position (hierarchy). Either way, approval uses human resources tables, which are present whether or not you have Oracle Human Resources installed. If it goes by supervisor, the system looks at the supervisor link in a person's record. If it goes by position, the system finds the position each person occupies, links to the position hierarchy to find which position is next in the pecking order, and then links back to find the incumbent in that position, as shown in Figure 9-1. However it is set, the system eventually routes approvals through people, not positions. Security is enforced by login accounts and Responsibility parameters—and it is people who have login accounts. The approver uses an "electronic signature," which amounts to a login name and password.

The approval hierarchy process is rather complex. It takes a close reading of the *User's Guide* to fully understand its mechanics. Some Oracle customers have simply interfaced to an existing signature matrix for their approval routings. The incorporation of Oracle Workflow into this process in Release 11 gives you the power to modify the Oracle logic described next.

The overview presented here introduces the approval architecture and gives an idea of what can be done with the product's existing features. The discussion follows the setup sequence recommended in the *Installation Guide*. It ties in to Figure 9-2, which shows the major tables and the processes that populate them.

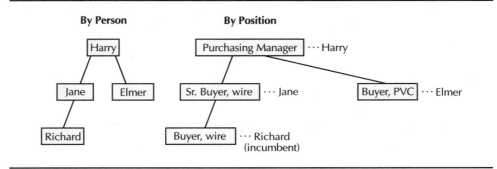

FIGURE 9-1. *Supervisor versus hierarchy approval structures*

You must coordinate Purchasing with Oracle Human Resources if you are using both systems. When both systems are used, the following steps may be performed as part of HR setup:

1. **Define jobs** A *job* is a set of responsibilities, such as those performed by a buyer or a receiving clerk. The people who create and approve purchasing documents have jobs. You need to define only those jobs that will be referenced in your approval process. Selecting requisition approvals can involve most of the company, whereas purchase order approvals are pretty much confined to the purchasing department.

2. **Define positions** This step is necessary if you are defining approvals by position hierarchies rather than supervisors. A *position* is a job slot—a job within an organization at a location. (Organizations and locations have to be defined earlier in the setup process.)

3. **Define the hierarchy approval chain** Use the Define Position Hierarchy screen to indicate how the positions relate to one another.

4. **Enter employees** Once you've defined jobs and positions for your employees, it's time to enter their names into the system. It helps to go from the top down if you are using the supervisor approval approach, so that the supervisors are already defined when you need to reference them as you set up the employees who report to them.

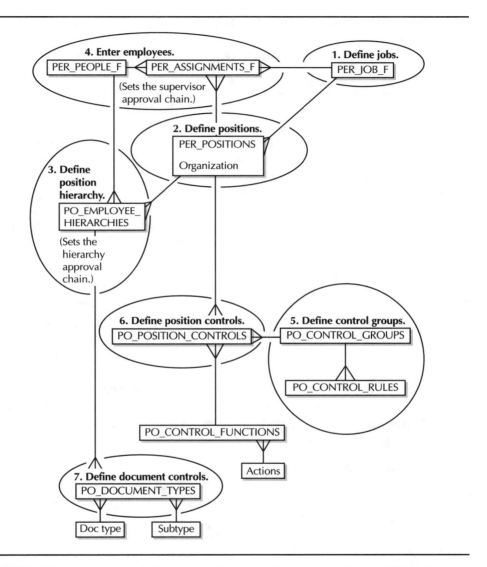

FIGURE 9-2. *Relationships among the major forms procedures and database tables in the approval process*

After you have defined the relationships among your employees through these setup steps, you define their actions and authority levels through a series of setup steps in Oracle Purchasing:

1. **Define control groups**   Use this function to give names to groups of attributes of things that need control, like "Documents associated with Department XYZ for equipment lease expenditures over $1000." A set of rules identifies all types of things in the group. Each rule can use a combination of total document amount, General Ledger accounts, item category, item, and location. The groups will be used later on to establish what needs to be approved and who can approve how much. Each group has an approval amount limit. Groups can overlap in instances in which larger orders require more approvals than smaller ones. Higher approval amount groups will be associated with higher-level positions.

2. **Define position controls**   This step associates your control groups with either jobs or positions. Positions are required if you are using hierarchies, but not if you are using supervisor approvals. This screen establishes which positions can perform which functions (also called *actions*) on documents within a control group. The actions are Approve, Approve & Reserve, Reserve, Accept, Submit, Forward, Reject, and Return. To clarify the nomenclature, Reserve means to reserve or obligate funds; Accept means to accept a prior approval. Both Forward and Submit pass the approval action up to the next level.

3. **Define document controls**   This step associates a document type with an approval hierarchy. Document controls establish who can see the document, who can change the document, and what kinds of changes are allowed. Document controls link to positions through the hierarchy, and the position controls indicate the approval authority associated with each position. This brings together all the information as to who can do what: the people, the pecking order, the accounting information, the item information, the monetary amounts, and the action types.

This approval structure is extremely powerful and flexible, and represents a great design effort on Oracle's part. It is also quite involved to set up and debug. Any company planning to make serious use of electronic approvals will need to plan and test the setup extensively. The processes will be widely visible within the company, with correspondingly high risks if the setup is not done correctly. Organizations that plan to cut over to Oracle on a short deadline (and who doesn't?) and don't already have electronic approvals should stick with their existing procedures through cutover, and then implement electronic approvals by phases, first for POs and later for requisitions.

Globally Approved Supplier Lists

The Approved Suppliers List (ASL) relates items to your suppliers and the manufacturers who provide your suppliers, while providing information about the relationship between you and the supplier. For instance, ASL will answer the following: Who is the preferred supplier? What agreements are in place? Which suppliers have been debarred and can no longer be used? The ASL carries practical information, such as vendors' part numbers and units of measure.

Large businesses do much of their purchasing at a global level, negotiating agreements that all operating units within the business can share. The process brings a number of efficiencies. Company-wide agreements offer better prices, and negotiating at a macro level cuts the overhead costs involved in buying.

Vendor Part Numbers, Substitutes, and Cross-References

Each supplier has its own part numbering scheme and will likely use its own part number on invoices and shipping documents. Some suppliers may, as a courtesy, include your part numbers as well as the manufacturer's name and part number. You may also want to record this information for various reasons. You may store the vendor part numbers, for instance, on requisitions, purchase orders, or quotations. Oracle Inventory keeps a cross-reference of manufacturers' names and part numbers. The Approved Suppliers List (ASL) helps the buyer to select a supplier and use the appropriate vendor part numbers and vendor units of measure on the PO.

Frequently, a supplier will want to substitute one item for another. Whether you allow the substitution depends on the context. In your business, you may be able to substitute Kleenex for Scott Tissues. The distributor cannot, but might be able to substitute boxes of peach-colored

Kleenex for boxes of blue-colored Kleenex. The manufacturer, Kimberley-Clark, obviously cannot substitute one color for another. Substitution may be one-way or two-way. You can substitute bottled water for tap water, but not the other way around. Certain substitutions may be allowed only for a given period of time or for certain purposes. It would be logical to allow substitutions on issue but not on receipt.

The most elemental question when dealing with substitute items is whether to assign separate item numbers. If there is only one item number for Kleenex, peach- and blue-colored Kleenex will all be jumbled together on the shelves, with no separate accounting. When they have separate numbers, you can use the Define Item Relationships form to define substitution relationships. Inventory produces reports that may be useful in receiving, though there is not much logic to support substitution. These are simplistic examples, but they represent the need to distinguish between similar goods within your organization.

Purchasing offers a more general cross-reference feature for users to apply as they wish. A company that buys through distributors often has several part numbers to deal with—one for the original manufacturer and others for the intermediate suppliers. Add to that the fact that these sources may make substitutions upon occasion, such as satisfying an order for a five percent tolerance resistor with an order with only a one percent tolerance resistor, because that is what they have in stock. The generic cross-reference function is a great foundation for custom code. Oracle provides the data capture screens and some basic reporting. You can apply the relationships any way you need to meet your unique business requirements. This feature is often used to store the item's legacy part number, if your Item Master was converted.

Purchase Agreement and Catalog Import

When you purchase at a global level using ASLs, your supplier may have as much to do with the items on a purchase agreement as you do. When Dell Computer or Staples gives you a corporate discount, they provide a catalog of the items they cover. You offer your employees and customers what the supplier offers you.

In Release 11 you can use the Purchasing open interface to import prices and define the items to your system—either through electronic data interchange (EDI) transactions or by loading them directly from a flat file.

You can automatically add the items to your price and sales catalogs, Approved Supplier Lists, and Sourcing Rules.

This facility can leverage productivity tremendously. It cuts the administrative effort involved in using multiple suppliers and in changing suppliers. It integrates with Oracle's quotation process, so the successful bidder's offerings can be incorporated quickly and smoothly into your business.

Communicating with Suppliers

Big money is involved in your communications with your suppliers. Having a product available where customers need it and when they want it will bring you a good price. Goods that cannot be sold or used are a liability. Information about what you can offer your customers may be the difference between success and failure. Oracle Purchasing is designed to get complete information to and from suppliers quickly.

Electronic Data Interchange (EDI)

EDI is a protocol for exchanging machine-readable transactions between buyers and sellers. There are standard transaction formats for orders (including headers, lines, and shipping information), order changes, order cancellations, order confirmations, and every other common transaction. EDI transactions parallel the transactions available in Oracle Purchasing, and the elements (header, line, and shipping) map closely to Oracle's data structure.

Business entities that participate in the exchange of EDI information have unique routing identifiers. Instead of having to initiate one-to-one communications with each seller, a buyer submits all EDI transactions to a network. The network sorts and forwards them according to the routing code. This role has heretofore usually been filled by value-added networks, though the Internet is evolving as the preferred medium of exchange.

Automatic-Faxing

Faxing directly from Oracle Applications to your trading partners represents an intermediate level of automation: electronic on the sending end, paper on the receiving end. It accommodates suppliers whose internal processes depend on paper, yet it achieves the speed and cost benefits of electronic delivery. While automatic faxing is not currently included as a standard feature of Oracle Applications, it can be accomplished through minimal customizations and with Alliance Partner software. At a minimum, it will require customizations to the external document (the Purchase Order, Requisition, etc.) that you wish to fax, as well as a fax server that is set up within System Administration as a printer queue.

Oracle Web Suppliers

Web Suppliers is an Internet tool that provides your suppliers a controlled view of different aspects of their dealings with your organization. For example, you can post solicitations for your suppliers to review or you can let them preview your internal plans so they can provide you maximum service. Chapter 13 provides further details about this module.

Drop Shipment Communications

Drop shipment eliminates the time and expense of routing goods through your warehouse en route to a customer. Although drop shipment enables you to offer better prices and service, you become dependent on your supplier and customer for information about the transaction, such as when to invoice. Oracle Purchasing has incorporated support for transactions that facilitate drop shipment. Drop shipment is further described in Chapter 11.

An Advance Shipment Notice (ASN) from your supplier lets you know that an order has shipped. In a drop shipment environment, a shipped order may trigger an ASN to your customer and/or send an invoice.

Supplier Acceptances acknowledges that the supplier has accepted the order and committed to a delivery date. This feature lets you know whether the supplier can meet your customer's needs. Use an Alert to notify the buyer if there is no supplier acceptance within a predetermined period of time. You may want to have Order Entry forward the information as an acceptance to your customer.

Suppliers under Multi-Org

Suppliers are best maintained in a global perspective. If Ford Motor Company were to negotiate a worldwide contract with Silicon Graphics, every Ford division would need to recognize Silicon Graphics as the same supplier, and the corporation would need to monitor total purchasing. Suppliers, therefore, are global within Oracle Purchasing and Payables, though supplier sites may be specific to an operating unit. Ford of Germany may do business with SG's office in Germany, but the system will recognize that office as part of SG's global organization.

Inventory organizations within a company are connected by a transportation web. Factories or distribution centers ship to sales locations, or one sales organization that is long on product may support another that is short on product. Chapter 10 describes how to define freight carriers to the system, how to handle freight invoices, and how to account for the cost of freight.

The Implications of Multi-Org

Multi-Org functions make it possible for one installation of Oracle Purchasing—one set of software and tables—to handle multiple organizations. Oracle supports multiple organizations at the set of books, business group, legal entity, balance book, operating unit, and inventory levels. The four higher-level organizational structures are important primarily from an accounting standpoint. The last two affect Purchasing operations:

- **Operating unit**   This structure is associated with login Responsibility. It defines the scope of Purchasing activities available through a single user of the system.

- **Inventory organization**   This structure resides within an operating unit. It limits receiving to shipments destined for a specific inventory location within the operating unit.

Multiple Organizations in Inventory

Purchasing includes the Inventory screens necessary for creating and maintaining inventory items. This is an essential detail. Purchasing usually precedes Inventory in a phased implementation. Many attributes are associated with every item in a company's inventory. Some of these, such as description and size, are immutable. Most large companies allow other attributes, such as whether the item can be stocked, manufactured, or ordered, to differ between inventory locations within an operating unit. Not all inventory sites will need to store, or even need to see, every item of inventory.

Each operating inventory location, those that handle transactions, can be associated with a master inventory organization. The master organization carries the definition of every inventory item available to the operating inventory locations associated with it. It provides a common reference for shared item numbers, and it carries values for item attributes that are the same across all organizations.

In the simplest installations the master is the only inventory organization; otherwise, the operating inventory organizations each have some subset of the master inventory, with local settings for those attributes that are controlled at the organization level. The master organization can be shared as widely as needed within a company to ensure a common definition of parts and products. The only proviso is that every organization using the master has to have a common set of books. This is because several attributes, such as Expense Account, Encumbrance Account, Sales Account, and Cost of Goods Sold, are Accounting Flexfields. They only make sense within the context of a single set of books.

One installation of Purchasing (that is, one login Responsibility) can order items for any inventory organization within its operating unit. Each shipment must be made to an inventory organization for which the item is defined. The Enter Receipts screen operates one level down, at the Inventory Organization level. A receiving clerk can receive only shipments due into his or her location. Purchasing Responsibilities frequently include forms that operate at both the Operating Unit and Inventory Organization levels, so your users will need to use the Change Organization form with some regularity to define item attributes or perform receipts at the different inventory locations available to them.

Receiving

Receiving is the function of accepting goods from a supplier and delivering them to their destination within the company. It usually involves checking the receipt and goods to make sure the quantity is correct and the quality is satisfactory, and then passing the information to Payables to use as the basis for paying an invoice. If you have enabled three- or four-way matching, then the receipt of an item will be required before an invoice can be paid.

Oracle Purchasing continues to add features that reduce the amount of labor involved in receiving. In Release 11, Advance Shipment Notices (ASNs) received through EDI prepare the loading dock to process a receipt automatically. Oracle's Payment on Receipt option generates an automatic invoice, saving the vendor the effort of creating it and you the effort of processing it for payment. Drop shipments to support Order Entry eliminate the need for your warehouse to handle goods that would only have to be reshipped. If you are using Web Suppliers you may also receive Purchase Orders via your Internet browser with just a few clicks of the mouse,

Exceptions

Most of the time a packing slip references the order number. The people on the dock can compare the packing slip with the items received and the order. They enter the quantities received of each line item. The complexity is in the exceptions.

To help when there is no packing slip, Oracle lets the receivers scan by supplier, item number, and supplier part number to look for a matching order.

Quantities received don't always match quantities ordered, and the receipt date may not coincide with the required date. Purchasing uses a series of defaults—at the system, supplier, and purchase order level—to set tolerances for these variables. Purchasing enforces the business rules for dealing with exceptions, whether to reject the order or accept it with notification to the buyer that there is an exception. On a practical note, many receiving operations move so quickly that there is only a moment on the receiving dock for accepting or rejecting an order. A warning note is not much use to purchasing; it is more effective to write an alert that e-mails the buyer when the company accepts an out-of-tolerance shipment. The system needs to know when an order is closed. Most of the time Oracle's native logic handles the situation. Once all lines are closed, the entire order will be closed. Lines, then, are the issue. What if eleven units of an item were ordered, ten were received, and an invoice arrives for ten? There is a set of tolerance parameters to decide whether that line should remain open to receive one last item, or whether to assume that no more are coming. There are more tolerance parameters on the Payables side to reconcile prices and quantities invoiced to what was ordered and received.

Purchasing only applies the fuzzy logic of tolerances to order lines; you will need to define processes to handle orders themselves. When do you close a PO with one line that has never been received? How about one with a line that was 80 percent received three months ago? Sometimes these matters take human judgment. Use Oracle Alerts to notify the appropriate buyer of POs that remain open but appear inactive, so they can decide whether to contact the supplier regarding the remaining items or simply close the PO.

You may set up Purchasing to allow suppliers to ship substitute items, if the ordered item is out of stock or is unavailable. A default chain establishes whether the system will accept recognized substitutes for any given line item on an order.

Sometimes a receipt cannot be matched to a purchase order. The PO may already be closed, the items may have been order without a PO, or the supplier may have made a mistake. The setup parameters specify whether to accept such shipments or return them to the supplier.

Receipt Routing

Each Purchase Order line specifies one of three ultimate destinations for the item: Inventory, Expense, or Shop Floor. Business procedures establish the path that received items follow leaving the loading dock. They may go right to their destination, or they may be inspected first.

A *receipt traveler* provides information regarding items in transit within the company in the same way a packing slip represents a supplier shipment. It indicates what the item is and where it is going. Inventory needs that information to stock items correctly. It helps people who order expensed items to reconcile what they get with what they requisitioned, and it informs inspectors what to do with an item after they accept it.

Drop Shipment Receipts

A *drop shipment*, by definition, is never physically received in your warehouse. Therefore, it may be difficult to record information that would normally be picked up at the receiving dock: what was received, how many, and in what condition. The processing requirement depends on whether you or one of your customers is the recipient. Your customer is the recipient when you use the Customer Drop Shipment feature of Oracle Order Entry. As the recipient, your customer takes the lead in resolving the quality issues. You may assume the shipment has been received when the supplier sends you an Advance Shipment Notice, or you may confirm the receipt by telephone. The customer is responsible for notifying you if the materials received are not those specified in the shipping notice or invoice that you have sent. The resolution between you and the customer is handled by Order Entry; Purchasing handles issues between you and the supplier.

Oracle Web Employees handles drop shipments to recipients within your own organization, for example, construction material delivered to a building site. These shipments are like receipts of expense items at your warehouse, except the receiving and inspection process is delegated to people at the site. They can handle it through the Desktop Receiving functions in Oracle Web Employees. Otherwise they will usually confirm the receipt by telephone and let the warehouse record it in Oracle.

Productivity versus Security

Until recently, receiving has been a fairly labor-intensive operation. Companies with established supplier relationships often find that formal receiving does not add enough value to justify its cost. They may let the supplier replenish inventory, and take the supplier's word for how much was sent. This offers maximum efficiency. Periodic audits and inventory out-of-stock conditions will tell over the long term whether the suppliers' claims for quantities delivered are accurate.

Oracle continues to incorporate improvements to streamline communications with suppliers. It offers the following new features:

- *Web confirm receipts* (Release 10.7) allows employees to confirm the receipt of shipments to company sites other than your warehouse.

- *Receiving open interface* (Release 11) accepts scanned receipt data or receipt transactions prepared in an outside system.

- *Advance Shipment Notice* (Release 11) lets suppliers prepare you for a receipt of a shipment with an electronic packing slip, so your receiving dock can process an entire shipment with a single confirmation. The ASN is designed for use with bar code scanning. The receiving dock can use hand-held RF (radio frequency) scanners to record pallets or parcels being received.

- *Kanban purchasing* (Release 11) treats the presentation of a Kanban card, or just an empty container, as an order to a supplier. The transaction is usually captured by a bar code scanner. The system is most often set up to trigger an automated payment through Oracle Payables, and the transaction costs are minimal. Chapter 10 describes the use of Kanban in inventory and manufacturing systems.

These electronic processing alternatives give you the ability to control receiving at a minimal cost per transaction. Oracle continues to offer several levels of receipt control in a document-oriented environment:

- *No receiving* is a very simple option. For services and Kanban purchasing, the invoice alone may be adequate.

- *Express receiving* works on an exception basis. The receiving clerk notes that the transaction is an express receipt. Other than the entered exception lines, an express receipt takes the amount received to be the open amount for every line on the order. The process saves time by placing more responsibility on the receiving clerks. Finding what is missing takes more brainwork than finding what is there.

- *Standard line-by-line receipt confirmation* lets personnel check the quantities received against the packing slip and then enter quantities into Oracle from the marked-up packing slip.

- *Blind receiving* offers maximum control—and a maximum of work. Because receivers do not know how much of each item to expect, it is impossible for them to dispose of a shipment quickly by just keying in the open amounts. It forces the receivers to count every item. This approach is most useful in operations with low volumes of expensive materials.

Integration with Other Modules

Purchasing, being the initial process in the procurement cycle, is tightly integrated with several of the other modules. This integration serves as the foundation for the more extensive material management that is available through Inventory, Order Entry, Manufacturing, and Project Accounting. Because of this, purchasing analysts usually need to handle their implementation as part of a global vision.

Payables Integration

Purchasing and Payables share supplier data and generally work with the same transactions. As far as transactions go, most business that results in accounts payable is done through contractual vehicles established in Purchasing. Payables looks to Purchasing to validate payment obligations through a two-, three- or four-way match process.

- A *two-way match* confirms that an invoice matches a purchase order. This way the company does not pay for items it did not order. Two-way matches are appropriate for purchases of services and other intangibles that do not result in receipts of material goods. Rent and phone bills are two good examples.

- A *three-way match* requires that an invoice be matched to a purchase order and that the purchase order be physically received, all prior to payment. This prevents payment for items that were ordered, but for some reason were never received by your company.

- A *four-way match* adds inspection to the process. Not only were the goods received, but they were accepted as well. Inspection is largely a matter of timing. Some items, such as electronic equipment, may take a while to check. The company does not want to pay for the equipment until it has confirmed that the items meet their quality specifications.

The Payment on Receipt feature consolidates the receiving and payables functions. It relieves the supplier of the need to invoice, and you of the burden of processing the invoice. Instead, Oracle Purchasing creates an invoice automatically upon completion of the receiving, inspection, and/or delivery process. It uses the payment terms and conditions set up for the vendor and automatically creates the match to the purchasing document. The supplier will have created an open receivable without ever issuing an invoice. Both parties use the price lists and financial terms in the governing purchasing agreement. The high level of trust in this business arrangement pays major dividends, significantly reducing paperwork for both buyer and seller.

Projects Integration

Oracle Projects initially captured project and task data for expensed items only. Project Manufacturing, new in Release 10.7, carries project identification through inventory and manufacturing. Purchase Order lines can include project and task data regardless of the destination: expense, inventory, or shop floor.

As far as a project is concerned, money is as good as spent once a requisition goes to Purchasing. It can't be spent twice. The Purchasing system gives Projects the information it needs to commit funds within the project budget. It provides Projects with up-to-date status and cost data as a purchase advances through the requisition, purchase, and receipt phases. Payables finalizes the cost when the invoice comes through.

Order Entry Integration

User requisitions for internal stock items never go to suppliers. These requisitions are routed to Order Entry, via the Order Import Open Interface, as internal orders to be satisfied from inventory once the requisition has been approved. Internal Orders will then proceed through the order cycle—Pick Release, Ship Confirm, and Inventory Interface—in a manner similar to that of an external customer order. Just as for requisitions that are satisfied through POs, Purchasing closes the requisition when the item is delivered to the requisitioner.

Inventory Integration

Many items handled by Purchasing must be identified by item numbers because the numbers are required for manufacturing, selling, and stocking items. However, Oracle Purchasing can handle orders for anything, whether or not it has an item number. Using item numbers in situations where they are optional offers a number of advantages:

- **Points of reference**   Each item is known by one designation throughout the company.

- **Consistency**   Suppliers always see the same description for orders of the same item. If they fill the order correctly once, they can be expected to do so again.

- **Recording usage**   Item numbers make it possible to track usage automatically.

- **Streamlining of accounting processes**   Each item number has an associated cost; this simplifies the processes of budgeting and paying invoices.

Purchasing needs the ability to create item numbers, or have them created, because they are essential to even the most basic purchasing operations. It is equally important to maintain central control in assigning part numbers, to ensure that they adhere to standards, to avoid duplicates, and to make sure that all the essential data about an item is captured as the number is set up. Chapter 10 suggests procedures for item number assignment.

As mentioned earlier, many attributes are associated with an Inventory item—far more than are just needed for Purchasing. Oracle sets attributes of all kinds as items are created; some of these attributes cannot be changed later, and many depend on other settings. The purchasing analysts need to anticipate downstream uses of Inventory item data in their implementations. On a transaction basis, receipts of stock items from the Purchasing system bump inventory balances up. Purchasing puts records of open orders in the MTL_SUPPLY table to help Inventory plan its replenishment requirements. Requisitions for Internal Orders place a demand on items that is later relieved by Order Entry once the item has been shipped.

Units of measure conversion is another powerful feature of Inventory that makes it possible to buy an item by one measure, store it by another, and issue it by yet a third. See Chapter 10 for a fuller discussion of the inventory integration considerations.

Accounting Issues

Purchasing has limited communication with the General Ledger, but as the first link in the supply chain it is the ultimate source of a great deal of accounting data. It prices requisitions based on the frozen costs in Inventory, and then uses those extended costs to determine what approvals are needed to encumber funds, to accrue receipts, and to establish an expected price for Payables.

Average and Standard Costing

Oracle Applications allows you to choose between average and standard costing. *Average costing* is intuitive. If you have ten baseballs in stock at $5 each, and then you receive another ten at $7, your average price is $6. End of story. It is simple and it works.

Standard costing is the alternative. Under standard costing, you would put the $7 baseballs into stock at $5, keep the price at $5, and post the difference to a variance account. Then somebody would have to look into the variances to see what went awry. Who wants to do that?

Standard costing, it turns out, makes more sense than it would appear. Until recently it was the only option allowed for use with Oracle Manufacturing, and it is highly advantageous for distribution operations as well. Chapter 10 explains this further. In short, average costing is not a true average. It averages only one thing—the price on the Purchase Order. There is still variance between the purchase price and the invoice price. Average pricing means that the price changes all the time, making it harder for the tolerance process to highlight price changes. Most important, average costing supports the notion that purchase cost represents the total cost of an item, when the full cost actually includes purchasing, handling, storage, inspection, shipping, and a host of other activities involving the item.

In terms of accounting, there is always a need for an invoice price variance account. A purchase price variance account is necessary under standard costing. Management's objective is the same whatever the mechanism: to make sure that the company is paying what it expects to pay and that it pays a fair price. This concept is fundamental in dealing with suppliers and in product pricing. Chapter 11 describes how costs serve as the basis for setting sales prices.

Accrual Accounts

A receipt of goods represents an obligation to pay, whether or not the invoice is yet in hand. Receiving posts an expense to an accrual account, which Payables relieves when it actually pays the bill. Inventory receipts are accrued immediately, and a setup option governs whether receipts of expensed items are accrued immediately or at month end. Chapter 5 includes an accounting model that demonstrates how this works.

The process computes the accrual amount by extending the quantity on the receipt by the line item price from the purchase order. It is only an approximation. Payables deals with discrepancies using its own tolerance logic. It posts acceptable differences to the invoice variance account.

Accrual accounting is an improvement on cash accounting in that it recognizes an expense when the items are received. That is not early enough for some entities, especially governments, which must adhere rigorously to their budgets. Encumbrance accounting goes this one or two better. An encumbrance picks up expected expenses at the time a department makes a requisition or when the purchase order goes to a supplier. These encumbrances are called, respectively, *commitments* and *obligations.* Encumbrances are posted to the ledger to represent money obligated to be spent. The Financial Statement Generator reports in General Ledger can report on encumbrances as a separate line, or net them with accruals and actual expenses against the budget to see how much is left. Receipts relieve encumbrances—the actual obligation replaces the expected obligation.

Automatic Account Generation (AutoAccounting and Flexbuilder)

It is convenient, as in the preceding paragraph, to say that receiving posts to "the" accrual account. It is usually a single account in the chart of accounts structure, but it may exist in a great many Accounting Flexfield combinations. Oracle uses the accounting distributions from the purchase order line to get the other segments.

It is worth discussing where those segment values originate. The requisitioner or buyer may enter them directly, segment by segment, though doing so is a lot of work. The originator of the transaction may use a one-field shorthand code for a full accounting distribution. Additionally, there may be defaults associated with the supplier or item. The system may use Automatic Account Generation (new in Release 11; formerly called AutoAccounting and Flexbuilder) to apply user-specified rules to derive segment values from some combination of the requisitioner's department, item category, supplier, project, or other available data.

The mechanisms described earlier are all used to generate individual flexfield combinations. Users often want to split the costs of a purchase over two or more combinations. Purchasing provides multiple accounting distributions for this purpose. Determining whether it is easier to do the distribution in Purchasing or in the General Ledger using allocations is a significant business process decision.

Although Purchasing itself makes rather limited use of accounting data, Payables and Projects depend on the accounting data that is collected here. You can always demand that the users key in a full multisegment distribution, but a key task in setup is to devise a scheme that takes advantage of all Oracle's devices for automatically populating flexfield values, thereby minimizing manual keying and maximizing both productivity and accuracy.

Implementation

Some users will bring up all the packages at the same time in a "Big Bang" conversion. The alternative is a phased approach. Though there is not a mandatory sequence for installing Oracle Applications, in general Purchasing builds on Payables, which builds on General Ledger. This sequence of dependencies is based on accounting information. On the materials side, Inventory builds on Purchasing, and the Item Master usually comes up as part of the Purchasing conversion (see Chapter 10 for detailed information on converting the inventory master). The scope of the Purchasing conversion depends on what has been done in previous phases.

Converting the Vendor Master

Expect the legacy vendor master file to be cluttered with duplicate suppliers and ones that haven't been used in years. You can also expect users to advocate converting the file as-is because the schedule does not allow time to clean it up prior to conversion. This may or may not be true, but you can be confident that the users will never find time to clean up the data after it goes into Oracle Purchasing. Oracle does not allow deletions from some of its master tables, and it is quite exacting for those that are allowed—the master record being purged usually cannot have open, or even recent, transactions against it. Users will see the same stale and duplicate suppliers and incorrect data forever unless they cull them at conversion. Take the time to make sure you are converting clean data.

Once you have extracted a list of suppliers from your legacy system, spreadsheets are a great tool to use for cleaning up supplier data. Most companies find that their supplier data fits comfortably within the 16,000 rows and 256 columns available in a spreadsheet. Sorts are useful for finding duplicate suppliers, and the word processing features can be used to convert cases, translate abbreviations, and make other global changes.

Old mainframe systems did not deal well with lowercase letters. Keypunches and printers had a hard time with them. However, GOING TO UPPER- AND LOWERCASE LETTERS MAKES A HUGE IMPROVEMENT IN READABILITY. It makes a better impression on suppliers, and it makes it far easier for them to read purchase documents. Lowercase letters and proportional spacing also make it possible to fit much more information into your notes.

Oracle can assign vendor numbers automatically or accept user-generated ones A common approach is to keep the old numbers for suppliers that are converted, and then make the new Oracle vendor numbers one digit longer. After conversion, Oracle's number generator is set one past the highest number of the old scheme. If legacy used five-digit numbers, the first new Oracle-assigned vendor number would be 100000.

Purchasing and Payables share the vendor tables. A lot of the master data, such as payment terms, is more for use by the Payables system, though the screens are available in the Purchasing setup menu tree. In any case, the Payables setup has to be thought out prior to supplier conversion.

There is no "vendor open interface," so a custom program is required to load the vendor and site information. Therefore, you will need to determine whether to manually enter your vendor master or proceed with a customization The process is relatively straightforward and not terribly risky if you follow the guidelines presented in Chapter 15. The script needs to load the PO_VENDORS_ALL and PO_VENDOR_SITES_ALL tables.

Converting Transactions

Runout, manual conversion, and programmed conversion are the main alternatives for dealing with open transactions in the cutover to Oracle Purchasing. Because different types of transactions have different life cycles, a combination of methods is often most effective.

Requisitions are easy to run out. They are not automated in most legacy systems, and if necessary, the company can forcibly clear the legacy system before cutover. Requisitioners are in-house; you can tell them to hold their requisitions for a week or so, whereas it would be tough to tell suppliers not to send confirmations nor deliver their goods.

The Requisitions open interface provides an easy migration path for users converting from a system that already uses automated requisitions. You can write an extraction program to read the requisitions from legacy files and load them to the interface. The state of the requisitions is an issue: you should complete all the requisitions on which activity has started, so that Purchasing can treat the imports as new transactions.

Purchase orders and PO releases are open until your suppliers satisfy them, which can take an indeterminate period of time. It may be possible, depending on the interfaces involved, to run out your POs and PO releases by using the legacy purchasing system in parallel with Oracle. If so, you can continue to receive under the legacy system while placing new orders in Oracle. The viability of this approach depends on the related systems: can Receiving identify shipments as being legacy or Oracle, and can Payables match its invoices with POs and receipts from two sources?

Another alternative is to start entering orders into Purchasing before cutover, but not receive any goods or make any payments until afterwards. This strategy will hold the volume of open orders at cutover to a manageable number, which can be rekeyed into Oracle after legacy shuts down. This approach requires that supplier data be converted early, with a manual process to coordinate supplier data updates until cutover.

 REMEMBER
Purchase agreements are usually valid for long periods of time. Open agreements have to be rekeyed into Oracle in any runout scenario.

The last alternative is to write automated conversion scripts. Converting open Purchase Orders requires writing directly to the Oracle tables, as there is no "purchase order open interface." To keep the conversion as simple as possible in Purchasing, you may want to convert partial receipts into open receipts for the remaining quantities, then let the Payables section manually reconcile invoices against receipts in the two systems.

There are significant accounting implications in an automated conversion. The accounting data often has to be translated from a legacy accounting structure into Oracle. The accounts may be different under Oracle. Lastly, Oracle accrues upon receipt, expecting Payables to reverse those accruals. The automated conversion process has to generate the accruals accurately or the ledger will be thrown off.

Converting Purchasing History

Auditing requirements demand that records of closed purchasing activities be available for several years. It is almost never worth the effort to convert this data into Oracle. The rather minimal advantages—supplier performance tracking and online query into old transactions—can be had more easily outside the Purchasing application. The reasons not to write conversion scripts for live data are given earlier in this chapter. Historical data is still more daunting, as it may incorporate old suppliers and accounting data, and require significant purification, translation, and normalization into Oracle's data schemas.

There are several more pragmatic ways to store and access your historical data:

- Microfiche or hard-copy transactions will suffice if the volumes are small. However, the time it takes to riffle through bankers' boxes of old transactions can mount up quickly.

- Use standard query tools. Put legacy transaction data into a custom database on a PC or in Oracle, and then access it using a standard tool such as Microsoft Access or Oracle Browser. This allows users to search by part number, supplier name, contact, and other useful data fields.

- Put historical data in simple Oracle tables. Put a bespoke form on the Applications menu so users can navigate to it easily. A simpler approach, if you don't need the access management afforded by the Applications, is to write a small program to deliver query results in HTML though the Web server.

Testing

Testing can verify that your setups will make Oracle Applications support your business procedures. Chapter 16 describes the testing process in detail. For Purchasing, you need business processes for most or all of the following tasks:

- Requisitioning expensed items, inventory replenishments, and capital goods.

- Creating purchase agreements.

- Performing RFQs.

- Creating purchase orders for different types of suppliers and products.

- Creating accounting distributions using distribution sets, shorthand accounts, defaults, and automatic account generation.

- Ordering goods under purchase agreements.

- Receiving goods under all possible exception conditions, including incorrect quantities, substitute items, unexpected receipts, unknown suppliers, and damaged goods.

You need test scenarios for the business processes, and you need test data to support the scenarios. When you are satisfied that the test scenarios work within Purchasing, you must perform integrated testing with Payables, General Ledger, Inventory, Projects, Order Entry, and any other systems with which Purchasing is integrated.

REMEMBER
Take the time and energy to plan thorough tests. To repeat the theme of this book: the Applications work. The question is whether you have made them work for you.

Customization

Documents that go outside the company should represent the company well. Most companies add a company logo and return address to the purchase order print program. Change orders and RFQs usually need the same type of modification. The alternatives for hard-copy documents are to adapt your purchase orders to preprinted forms, have a vendor provide a flash overlay for a laser printer, or create a bitmapped report that uses a PostScript printer.

Oracle provides about 100 standard reports with the system. Many of these are highly parameter-driven, producing output in a number of different formats. Though the packaged reports may not be exactly what users would design, they satisfy most basic data requirements.

Besides external documents, the following are the most common custom reporting requirements:

■ Adapting high-volume internal documents, such as requisitions and receipt travelers, to precisely meet the company's needs.

■ Adding Descriptive Flexfield columns to reports. For example, defense contractors may accept a priority rating in a DFF, and then print it on the purchase order.

■ Displaying vendor and manufacturer part numbers on reports, along with the Oracle item number.

Purchasing is a powerful module designed to support a business area that varies little from company to company. Most users will not find much of a gap between what they need and what the package does.

Conclusion

Oracle Purchasing improves all aspects of the process of acquiring goods and services. It manages what to buy through its links with Inventory and Material Requirements Planning (MRP). Inventory maintains the definitions of purchasable items and services and works with MRP in determining when and in what quantities to replenish stock items.

Electronic requisitioning and approval requires approvals consistent with the cost and nature of a user's request and prompts approvers to move requisitions through the system quickly. Oracle's sourcing rules in most cases make vendor selection totally automatic. Routine replenishments should require no user intervention.

There are many avenues available to inform vendors of your needs, including paper documents, the Web, EDI, and fax. Oracle Purchasing can manage complex solicitations and awards. It can use sophisticated sourcing rules to automatically select a vendor for each purchase.

By validating accounting and project data as it captures each requisition and purchase order, Purchasing ensures that the financial implications of its activity will flow accurately through Projects, Accounts Payable, Inventory, General Ledger, and Fixed Assets. Two-, three-, and four-way matching protect you against making erroneous disbursements through Oracle Payables.

Conversion is a major factor in installing the Purchasing module, especially since Oracle has yet to provide open interfaces for the Vendor and Purchase Orders conversions. Purchasing is often the first financial system with broad visibility throughout a company to go in. It requires a well-conceived access security plan. Online requisitioning and approvals, when used, demand extensive planning and testing.

By automating purchasing decisions that can be reduced to rules, Oracle Purchasing frees your staff to concentrate on more strategic objectives, such as building the best possible relationships with your suppliers. The full and timely information you can now provide may allow your suppliers to offer better prices and service.

CHAPTER
10

Oracle Inventory

nventory is at the heart of almost any business and is central to the planning process. The considerations in setting it up are at least as complex as those for any other single application. Commonly, Inventory will be installed during the implementation of Order Entry, Purchasing, Manufacturing, or Supply Chain Management but it is an extremely complex module in its own right with several important setup considerations.

Overview of Inventory

An inventory system provides physical management of a company's stock until it is either used up or sold. It also performs a logical, cataloging function. This stock is referred to by its item number and has many attributes that affect the transactions that the modules can process against the item.

Every other module within Oracle Applications that needs to name types of objects looks to the Inventory Item Master for details regarding an item. These objects include products ordered through Oracle Order Entry, items invoiced through Oracle Receivables, items purchased through Oracle Purchasing, items paid for through Oracle Payables, items maintained through Oracle Service, and items charged against projects in Oracle Projects. Every module in the Manufacturing suite (Engineering, Bills of Material, Work in Process, Master Production Schedule/Material Requirements Planning, and Cost Management) deals with items named in Inventory. Because many other modules need to access data in the Inventory Item Master, the Define Items form is found in the menu structure of most of the modules.

Inventory's ability to maintain items can extend further than its management of physical assets. Intangibles like magazine subscriptions or labor hours carry inventory names. The company can sell these items along with physical objects. Assemblies that are never stocked can also be defined in Inventory. A *phantom item*, for example, represents an intermediate step in manufacture, an assembly that is never stocked in inventory because it is used immediately in a higher-level assembly. A *planning assembly* represents a statistical average of parts requirements.

The stock management function is unique to Oracle Inventory, as it manages physical instances of items that are available for sale, distribution, or internal consumption. Oracle Inventory's on-hand balance is increased when an item is bought or made. Inventory relinquishes control and decreases its balance when items are sold or put to their final use within the company. Pads of paper in the stock room are inventory; the same pad of paper on somebody's desk is not—as far as the company is concerned, it is already used. A new desk in the warehouse belongs to inventory; a desk in somebody's office is no longer in inventory. Many major purchases, such as plant and equipment, never have an on-hand balance because they are put to their final use as soon as they are bought.

NOTE

Oracle Inventory is not a property management or asset tracking system. It is not well suited to keeping track of who currently has furniture, computers, or other assets that are in use within your company or on loan to customers. Oracle Assets is the package for managing such "inventory" of expensed and capital items. You can, however, track capital items that have been returned to your warehouse awaiting reuse within the company in both Assets and Inventory.

The assets in inventory would not be worth tracking if they had no economic value, and Oracle Inventory recognizes that the purchase price is only part of the entire cost. There are additional costs associated with receiving, inspecting, manufacturing, storing, transporting to your other inventory locations, shipping to customers, and counting assets. Inventory is one of several systems that capture such costs. Wherever assets come from and however they are derived, Oracle Cost Management can store values for these cost types with each inventory item. Its cost rollup function can sum the different cost types for purposes of analysis or to set a realistic frozen cost to use as a basis for pricing.

The science of managing inventory involves having what is needed, when it is needed, and having no more than is needed. Oracle Inventory provides a number of different algorithms for projecting material requirements into the future. It has the ability to use these rules to compute future requirements, then recommend when, what, and how much to buy to satisfy the need. It coordinates with Manufacturing for parts required to build products. Supply-chain management software coordinates with external suppliers to ensure availability of raw materials.

Large enterprises will have a number of physical warehouses stocking different items for different purposes. Setting up multiple inventory organizations that share one item master will provide the balance between global and local item definitions. Doing this allows local manufacturing and distribution center managers to control the operations they manage, while giving vendors and customers a common view of your company.

Integration with Other Modules

In the Oracle Applications scheme, modules other than Inventory are responsible for getting materials into and out of Oracle Inventory's custody. Purchasing and Work in Process are the primary sources of materials, which are either bought or made. Order Entry and Work in Process are the primary consumers; material is either sold, used internally, or put into products. These modules refer to Inventory master tables as they generate transactions that affect Inventory, notably receipts and issues. They perform their own work and then provide Oracle Inventory with the transactions needed to update balance records after the fact. This is important to conceptualize. Inventory does not issue stock to be sold. Instead, Order Entry takes the material (via the pick-release process) and then notifies Inventory that the material is gone. Inventory does not receive stock. Purchasing brings it in, and then notifies Inventory to increment its records accordingly.

Internal to the company, these systems work as a *troika.* Even if a warehouse manager needs a chair from his own inventory, the transaction needs to go through three systems to ensure proper accounting and replenishment. He submits a Requisition to Purchasing, which sends an Internal Purchase Order to Order Entry, which cuts a Pick Slip, and then ships the chair with a Pack Slip. Purchasing picks up the item with a Receipt, and then delivers the chair to the requester in the warehouse. This process may seem complex, but is necessary in order to retain control and record the proper accounting transactions.

Most transactions are processed in batch mode though open interface tables. Timing is critical. The concurrent processes must run frequently enough that the Inventory records are kept sufficiently accurate to support the target service levels.

Oracle's design anticipates integration with non-Oracle systems. Two tables, MTL_DEMAND and MTL_SUPPLY, provide Inventory with the information it needs to support replenishment processing. Outside systems as well as the Applications feed these tables. The only requirement is follow-through. The systems have to be conscientious about closure—relieving demand, for instance, when an order is canceled or shipped.

Item Setup

Inventory items are widely used throughout the Oracle Applications product suite. You often have to set them up to be independent of the Inventory package itself. In fact, many users who need items will never use Oracle Inventory Responsibilities at all.

Item Numbers

You are probably surrounded by item numbers as you read this book. Look at the bottom of your keyboard, your mouse, your telephone, or your stapler. The numbers you find there uniquely identify types of items—parts, supplies, and products—to a company and its customers.

Part numbers can be made up of several segments, separated perhaps by dots, slashes, or dashes. One segment may identify the class of product (say, a modem) and another may specify the type of modem (56KB external). Segmented part numbers like this are called *intelligent keys.* They tell you something about the item in addition to uniquely identifying it. Oracle handles segmented identifiers through its Key Flexfield feature.

Choosing the System Item Key Flexfield scheme you will use to identify items is one of the first tasks you face in setting up Oracle Inventory. The scheme should be broad enough to cover every type of inventory in the company. A supermarket chain may have separate legacy systems to handle headquarters' stockroom inventory, produce division resale inventory, and produce manufacturing inventory for the store-brand pasta plant. Oracle Inventory will need to track them all.

Legacy inventory numbering schemes were often constrained by design limitations from the era in which they were conceived. One notable limiting factor was the 80-column punched card. Designers often held part numbers of eight to ten characters so the remainder of the card would have room enough for a complete transaction. Often the original intelligent-key features in such short numbers have become obsolete. For example, if a company established a system in which the first character of a part number indicated the product in which it is used, that designation will have lost its meaning when the company grew beyond 26 products. When the intelligent key structure breaks down and the part number itself does not inform the user about the part, company operations become dependent upon people who know the numbers by heart.

Oracle item numbers have overcome several early design problems. Productivity in keying in a part number is no longer an issue: Oracle can complete the number automatically or present a short pick list based on the first few keystrokes. Self-checking numbers[2] are of less use now that operators can visually verify a description on the screen.

The Oracle part number should satisfy the following criteria:

- It should be unique across all operations within the company that uses item numbering. Often the easiest way to put this into effect is to let one segment of the new part number indicate what legacy system it came from or what group within the company defined it.

- It should have an intelligent link with the legacy system. People who know the legacy numbers should be able to use Oracle without memorizing anything new.

- It should be short enough to fit conveniently into displays and reports. Although Oracle allows up to 20 segments of 40 characters each, for a theoretical total of 800 characters, three segments and 15 characters, including separators, is a reasonable maximum. Otherwise, users may have to scroll field contents in screens, and part number fields may wrap on reports. Most users get by with one segment.

- It should not hinder performance or be difficult to support with bespoke (custom) code. Multiple segments add to the complexity of user-written reports and forms.

---

[2]A *self-checking number* contains its own validity check. The simplest technique is to choose part numbers that are divisible by some prime number, like 11. A keypunch machine had enough logic to validate self-checking numbers before they even got to the computer. It could tell that 107063 is a valid part because it divides evenly, and that 107064 is not. Needless to say, self-checking adds length and makes the numbers harder to assign.

■ It should anticipate reporting requirements. Many processes, in Inventory and other modules, have the ability to address ranges of items. Order Entry maintains price lists by item range. Plan to take advantage of this as you lay out the first (or only) segment of the item number.

■ It should anticipate flexfield security requirements. You may set up rules, in the same format as Accounting Flexfield cross-validations, to limit users to predefined ranges of items associated with their assigned Responsibilities.

■ It should have some sort of validation plan. In a multisegment item number you may want to confine every segment but one to a limited set of values. Most systems leave the last segment unconstrained so it can be chosen to make the number unique.

■ It should have consensus. People identify with item numbers. You can expect resistance, rational or not, if the "headquarters MIS guys" impose a new numbering scheme without user buy-in.

Expect to spend a fair amount of time resolving the seemingly simple issue of what the stock number will look like. The process presents a good opportunity to air everyone's expectations of the new system.

As you design the part numbering scheme, give some thought to the business process for assigning numbers. Implementing a global part number standard can bring major benefits, but it also requires discipline. It is usually necessary to have a centralized cataloging operation that assigns numbers throughout the organization. Because there is no mechanism in Oracle Inventory to make mass changes to established items, it is best if all the master-level attributes for the item are set as the item is created. It is reasonable to limit the ability to create new part numbers to only one responsibility, and only assign one person and a backup to that responsibility. Establishing a "Request for New Part Number" document will help make this process more formal and to ensure adherence to numbering and description standards.

Manufacturers and distributors have their own part numbering systems, which are very significant in the Purchasing and Payables applications. Chapter 9 covers manufacturer part numbers, substitutions, and cross-references. Customer part numbers and commodity codes are new in Release 10.7.

Attributes

The Inventory master table, MTL_SYSTEM_ITEMS, is one of Oracle's largest master files in terms of the number of columns and rows. Some of the columns provide characteristics unique to the item, such as the Key Flexfield that identifies the item, its weight, and its volume. Most columns categorize the item in various groups: Is it hazardous material? Does it need to be cycle counted? Can it be sold?

Columns equate to attributes in database terminology. A column in the MTL_SYSTEM_ITEMS table corresponds to an attribute of the item defined by a row in the table. For example, a Hazardous Material class might be an attribute of the item Turpentine. Attributes are organized in groups. The Define Item and the Update Item forms group attributes by business areas such as Purchasing, Order Entry, Inventory, MRP, Service, and so on. This system allows a user to review the settings of related attributes as a group. Attribute groups also support security. A Responsibility can be restricted to updating only attributes within specified groups.

The setup of an item's attributes is critical to how that item will be transacted and processed throughout all the modules that access the Inventory Item Master. Several attributes cannot be changed once they have been set and transactions have run against them. This fact is particularly important for companies that implement Oracle Applications in phases. If, as is often the case, a company brings up Purchasing and Payables first, it may not appear to matter which way the Pick-to-Order or BOM-enabled flag is set. These settings become important as Manufacturing and Order Entry are used. Getting them right when Purchasing is installed avoids the time-consuming and risky task of directly updating the database with SQL when new Applications come online.

Setting hundreds of attributes individually for each item would be a daunting task and would be likely to yield inconsistent results. The use of templates and user-defined statuses allow you to set these attributes *en masse* for like items. Custom conversion scripts can extend this same leveraging logic across all items being added as a group. It is essential to plan these group operators, templates, and statuses as an integral part of the inventory conversion process.

REMEMBER
Try to handle as many attribute settings as possible in the initial Item Master conversion—even for applications that will come up in later phases.

Attributes Within Inventory Organizations

Some attributes, such as item name and description, belong to the item itself. Others, such as whether the item is purchased or made, depend on the item and the inventory organization in which it is being used. You specify in setup which attributes will be controlled at the Item level and which at Item/Org (item/organization). Attributes set to Item-level control will have the same value across all Inventory organizations. Attributes set to Item/Org-level control may have different values across the organizations. For example, Micros Systems manufactures its point-of-sale terminals in Beltsville, Maryland but distributes them worldwide. Its 3700-series workstation is stockable in Beltsville, Los Angeles, Boston, Chicago, and many other cities; however, it can only be built in Beltsville. The Stockable and Build-in-WIP flags are both set at the Item/Org level.

It is essential that all organizations within a company share a common Inventory master. Otherwise, there would be duplication of effort, with multiple part numbers for the same item and possibly multiple items with the same part number. Though it is not mandatory, you usually associate every Inventory organization within one set of books with one common master organization. This association does not require Multi-Org, nor is it restricted by organizational hierarchies defined in Multi-Org.

The master organization is usually not an operating organization. It does not maintain stock or execute transactions. It functions merely as a reference. It includes a record for every item used in any of the operating inventories as well as for intangible items used in Purchasing and Order Entry that never appear in operating inventories.

Oracle specifies certain attributes that must be controlled at the master organization (Item) level and a few that must be managed at the organization (Item/Org) level. The control level of the remainder of the attributes, a majority, is for you to determine at setup. Accounting fields provide an example of the way you determine the control level. If your Automatic Account Generation takes only the natural account segment from the Cost of Goods Sold account, it may be that one account will be sufficient for the item throughout the company. If, on the other hand, you need it to provide product line or organization data, you might establish it as an Item/Org attribute.

Templates

Templates are used to set the attributes that determine how various applications will handle an item. Although it is possible to set the attributes individually when defining an item, the standard approach is to name the item, then identify one or more templates to set the item attributes. A template does not have to set all attributes. If only ten specific attributes are defined in a template, applying the template leaves the other attributes unchanged. Used online, a template sets the attributes only in the Define Item screen, not in the database. If you apply several templates to one item, the settings overlay one another. The Define Item screen logic checks all the attributes at once, just before it saves them, to make sure they are consistent. The Item Open Interface can accept only one template name. The templates you define for conversion, therefore, each need to set every attribute that is not unique to the item and organization.

REMEMBER
Be sure to debug your templates before putting them into use. To do this, use the template to create a phony item in a test instance. The Define Item screen will present an error if the attributes are inconsistent.

Oracle offers the Copy Item function, which is an alternative to using templates. This function copies all attributes of one item to those of another. It can be easier than using templates, but it risks compounding any existing errors. The best way to ensure consistent attribute settings is to make sure you have a well-planned, stable set of templates, then use those templates every time you set up an item. Address the risks of copying as you write business procedures for creating items.

You need templates at two levels for each type of item you will be defining: a master-level template to create a new item in the master organization, and at least one lower level template to add the same item types to operating Inventory organizations. The master level templates are the only source that will be used for attributes controlled at the Item level. To avoid conflicts, only Item/Org attributes should be enabled in operating level templates.

There are several reasons to keep your templates in a spreadsheet as you develop them. You need to coordinate your master and operational level templates. You frequently need to compare attribute settings in different templates and make across-the-board changes; for this reason, you will want to print your templates in a succinct form. If is often worth the effort to write code that automatically loads the templates from a spreadsheet, thereby ensuring that your templates remain identical across all environments.

Many users put the template name in the Item Type attribute. Though templates are designed in such a way that you can use many of them in creating one item, in practice you should use only one. That is all the Open Item Interface will accept. If you ever need to update item attributes after the fact using SQL, it is essential to know which template was used to create each item.

TIP

Your templates are not automatically updated when Oracle adds new attributes to the item master, such as those added in 10.7 to support departure planning and Oracle Service. If your templates appear to work differently after an upgrade, check to be sure that the defaults Oracle generates for new attributes you do not set are consistent with the attributes already in your template.

Unit-of-Measure Conversions

Warehoused items are stocked under units of measure (UOM). There are several possible conversions for Oracle to deal with:

- Your suppliers may deal in different units of measure than your company.

- Your external customers may use different units of measure than you use in stock.

- Your internal users may order merchandise by different units of measure.

Some conversions are universal, but others are item-specific. A gross is always 144 of an item, and a dozen is always 12. However, a unit name may mean more than one thing. For example, a case of soft drinks contains 24 cans, but a case of motor oil contains 12. What is the conversion between *case* and *each*? And although a half-pound of butter equals one fluid cup, the same is not true for water.

Oracle's conversion logic appears in the Inventory, Purchasing, and Order Entry applications. The default for Purchasing is the Primary Unit of Measure, and the default for Issue is the Unit of Issue. However, most screens present the user with a quick-pick of values to override the default. The quick-pick entries are the values within a UOM class. A UOM class is made up of related measures. Fluid measures would include milliliter, ounce, centiliter, teaspoon, tablespoon, cup, pint, quart, liter, gallon, barrel, and so on. Similarly, weights would run from microgram through ton and long ton; lengths would run from perhaps microns to meters. There is a base unit in each UOM class to which all other units are related. The base units are the basis for interclass conversions as well. To convert a tablespoon of butter into kilograms, the logic would find the equivalent measure in the base unit for volume, perhaps fluid ounces; then convert ounces to the base unit for weight, maybe grams; and, lastly, convert to kilograms.

CAUTION
UOM conversions often work better in theory than in practice. They must be set up carefully, because technology can be more sophisticated than the people who have to use it. The U.S. Army Depot in Long Binh, Vietnam, for example, once received enough telephone poles to build a log cabin city due to a unit-of-measure gaffe. A clerk had thought that the unit of measure was each, when it was actually something like a carload.

Used in combination, Oracle's Applications impose checks that help validate unit conversion. It should be apparent when the unit is wrong on an order—the extended price for the order line will be way off. This check is absent for Oracle Inventory users who don't use Oracle Purchasing. The Inventory system will just as readily accept ten pallets of copy paper as ten sheets, and the problem may not be recognized until there is an out-of-stock condition or a wild variance in stock valuation.

The Inventory and Purchasing Superusers need to put a lot of planning into the UOM conversion plan. The first step is research to determine which measures are in use, then to set up appropriate UOM classes. After the classes are in place, planners need the right combination of business procedures and training to make sure that the requisitioners, buyers, and order entry clerks are alert to the way conversion works and understand the units that are applicable to their operations.

You should usually choose your smallest common unit to be the Primary Unit of Measure. This is ordinarily the Unit of Issue, or retail unit. Purchasing can place orders in the units most convenient to the supplier, and they will be converted to stock units upon receipt.

Oracle does not allow you to change the Primary Unit of Measure for an item. To do so would render historical transactions meaningless and change their accounting implications. That being given, it is worth the effort to fully understand units of measure and get them right in the initial inventory conversion. Figure 10-1 depicts the Oracle tables that are involved in UOM conversions.

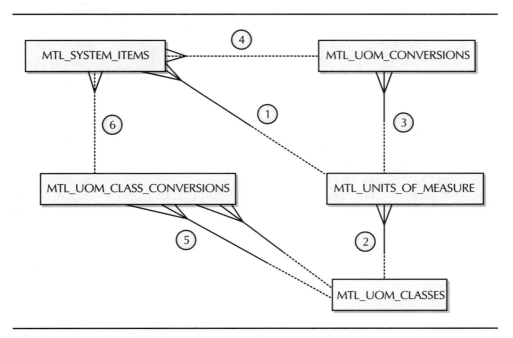

FIGURE 10-1.   *Tables involved in unit-of-measure conversions*

The lines in the drawing represent the relationships between the tables, which are as follows:

1. Every item must have a Primary Unit of Measure.[3] It is a mandatory field in the interface table.

2. Each unit of measure must belong to a UOM class. A class is made up of units of the same kind of measure. Inches, feet, and meters would belong to the length class. Each, dozen, gross, and ream would belong to the count class. Each class has a base unit of measure.

3. Every unit of measure other than the base unit has to be convertible into the base unit. If the base unit is *each,* then a dozen is 12 times *each,* and a gross is 144 times *each.*

4. Optionally, the relationship can be made to apply only to a given item. Within the count class, if the item is *egg,* then a carton is 12 times *each.* If the item is *soft drink,* then a carton is 24 times *each.*

5. There may be conversions between UOM classes, and

6. These conversions may be item-specific. If the item is *butter,* for instance, then one pound (weight) equals two cups (volume). Oracle would use this conversion, plus two UOM conversions, to figure out what a tablespoon of butter weighs in ounces.

SETTING UP THE UOM CONVERSION FOR YOUR INVENTORY

Start by writing a script to find all of your legacy units of measure and their conversion factors. Draft your Oracle Unit of Measure setup procedures based on that list, correcting for whatever shortcomings you know to exist in the legacy system. Find out what manual computations purchasing/receiving and order entry/invoicing have to do under the legacy systems, then set up Oracle to handle them automatically.

---

[3]In Entity-Relationship diagrams, the solid bar from the item's end means *must,* the dotted line from the UOM end means *may,* and the crows foot means *many.* What this means in Relationship 1, for instance, is that each UOM record may be referenced by zero to many Material System Items records. A UOM class may have class conversions; class conversions must have a UOM class.

REMEMBER
The only opportunity to correct ill-chosen legacy units of measure is upon conversion of the Item Master. The scripts that load the Item Interface table have to be coordinated with the ones that load the Transactions Interface to pick up on-hand balances, the Purchasing Interface, and the Sales Order Interface

Status Codes

Inventory processes refer to eight status attributes to determine which processes can operate on an item within a given organization. These correspond roughly to master-level attributes that define whether the process is even applicable to the item. For example, an obsolete product may be an inventory item but not currently enabled for stock. On the other hand, a Pick-to-Order item could never be enabled for purchasing, because it has no physical reality. It is no more than a number given to a set of items that may be ordered together as one.

Table 10-1 shows the eight status attributes. Where one exists, it identifies the base attribute prerequisites for setting the flag to enabled status.

The value you enter for item status in the Open Item Interface overrides values you provide for the eight status attributes. You usually want to use the following strategy at conversion time:

1. Define master and operating level templates for your different item types, including settings for the eight "enabled" attributes.

2. Define a separate status code for each combination of the eight attributes. There may be ten to twenty different combinations.

3. Enter the name that represents the appropriate combination of "enabled" attributes as the status code attribute in the template.

This approach simplifies conversion. All you need to do is associate a master-level template with each legacy item and an operating-level template with each item in an operating inventory organization. The eight item-status attributes are set according to the status code in the template.

User Status Name	Meaning	Enabled Attribute	Base Attribute
Stockable	Item can be stored in inventory.	STOCK_ENABLED_ FLAG	INVENTORY_ITEM_ FLAG
Build in WIP	Item can be built by manufacturing.	BUILD_IN_WIP_FLAG	n/a
Transactable	Transactions can be performed on the item in Order Entry, Purchasing, and Manufacturing.	MTL_TRANSACTIONS_ ENABLED_FLAG	n/a
Purchasable	Item can be put on a Purchase Order.	PURCHASING_ ENABLED_FLAG	PURCHASING_ITEM_ FLAG
Internal Orders Enabled	Item can be ordered for use within the company. This affects Inventory, Order Entry, and Purchasing.	INTERNAL_ORDERS_ ENABLED_FLAG	n/a
Customer Orders Enabled	Customers can order the item.	CUSTOMER_ORDER_ ENABLED_FLAG	CUSTOMER_ORDER_ FLAG
Invoice Enabled	Item can appear on an invoice in Oracle Receivables.	INVOICE_ENABLED_ FLAG	INVOICEABLE_ITEM_ FLAG
BOM Allowed	Item may appear in a Bill of Materials, either as an item to be built or as a component on a bill.	BOM_ENABLED_FLAG	BOM_ITEM_TYPE

TABLE 10-1. *Inventory Item Statuses*

Using status codes provides more control than updating the eight attributes individually. The fact that you must name a predefined combination protects you from entering inconsistent settings. Item statuses give you the ability to plan and apply changes for groups of items at the same time via a batch process. It gives you the ability to ensure consistency among your organizations and within your product lines.

Updating statuses through the combinations you establish in the Define Status form is a two-step operation. Users enter pending statuses for items via the Define Pending Status screen, then apply them using the Update Item Status concurrent process. Business procedures usually require that groups of related items, and items in multiple organizations, change status simultaneously.

Statuses are highly interdependent. Relatively few status combinations make sense in an organization, and individual items will go through a characteristic life cycle, such as from prototype to active to pending deletion. Plan to deal with statuses as a group using the Define Status screen to give your own name to combinations of all eight statuses.

Revisions

Manufacturers change their products over time. They may change the components or the manufacturing process to reduce costs, improve the product, or reflect a change in suppliers. Identifying a revision level with the product helps move older versions out of inventory and allows customer service to provide better warranty and maintenance support to buyers.

You can update revision levels directly through Inventory screens. However, revision is usually handled through Oracle Engineering, part of the Manufacturing product suite. A revision usually corresponds to a change in the Bill of Materials for an item. Oracle Manufacturing associates item revisions with the Engineering Change Orders (ECOs) that implement changes in the bill structure. The manufacturing plan coordinates parts and processes so that as of the ECO implementation date, everything is in place and the stock of no-longer-used components is exhausted or returned to suppliers.

Bills of Material

Inventory and Order Entry use the manufacturing concept of bills of material, even if you do not have Oracle Bill of Materials (BOM) installed. Bills play a role in the following situations:

■ **Pick-to-Order (PTO) Bills of Material** PTO items are defined to sell a number of items as a group. A computer retailer will carry monitors, keyboards, and system units as separate inventory items, but they may find it convenient to give a separate inventory number to a complete system, to ease the order entry process. The system will sell at a discount to its component parts, and the system will generally ship as a unit.

- **Assemble-to-Order (ATO)**   ATO items require a manufacturing step to create the ordered item. There is a Work Order associated with the order line, with a Bill of Materials to specify the components in the assembly. The assembled item goes from manufacturing into inventory to be held until it ships.

- **Configure-to-Order (CTO)**   Options are carried in the bill of materials for the saleable item. Order Entry requires that users make all appropriate option selections before the order can be booked. CTO option selection applies to Pick-to-Order as well as manufacturing Assemble-to-Order operations.

- **Inventory replenishment**   Material Requirement Planning, with or without manufacturing, can use the Bill of Materials to determine what to reorder.

- **Costing**   Costs of the individual components within the Bill of Materials (material, overhead, and so on) are rolled up to arrive at a proposed cost for a manufactured item.

- **Item revision levels**   A change in the Bill of Materials for an item, usually corresponding to a new revision level.

Bills of materials are essential to manufacturing operations. Pick-to-Order bills are surprisingly relevant for smaller internal and resale inventories. Many companies carry preassembled kits in inventory because they do not have PTO capability. Bill conversion adds a significant degree of complexity to inventory planning and setup.

TIP
Take an in-depth look at Oracle Bill of Materials features if you are planning to use Order Entry. Most users have just enough kitting, subscriptions, and Pick-to-Order activity that they need it. It is far easier to implement Pick-to-Order initially than to convert later.

Grouping Items

A large inventory must be managed as much as possible through mass rather than individual actions. *Categories* are the mechanism for grouping items according to the way they will be handled internally. *Catalogs* group items by how they appear externally: what they look like, how they function, and how they are used. Leverage through groupings is one of the keys to Oracle Inventory's power.

Categories and Category Sets

A category set represents one way in which to divide items into categories. There is usually more than one category set because it is useful to divide items up in different ways. Oracle's internal processes use categories in reporting within seven functional areas for which an item may be enabled: Inventory, Purchasing, Order Entry, Service, Engineering, Costing, and Planning.

The Purchasing category set is useful to buyers. It splits all items up by their purchasing categories, which may include electronic components, commodity items, capital equipment, and packaged goods for resale. These categories would be useful for purchasing activities such as assigning buyers and tracking vendors. The Engineering category set, on the other hand, might divide items up according to the responsible engineering group.

Oracle's standard forms and reports in the seven applications just mentioned accept categories as input parameters. For example, Order Entry accepts a category as a parameter in its pricing, scheduling, and backlog reporting processes. Categories give the sales department the power to discount computers differently from computer printer ribbons. Oracle Applications forces a category for every enabled item subject to reporting within a functional area via a two-step process:

1. As part of setup, users must specify a default category set for each of the seven previously named functional areas.

2. Each category set must designate a default category.

Users who do not want to take immediate advantage of categories— more probably, those whose conversion schedule does not allow for

improving the business process at the time of cutover—can
specify the same one or two category sets as the defaults for all seven
functional areas.

The Open Item Interface process currently assigns default categories as it
loads items. The ability to import categories will be available soon under
Release 11. In the meantime, if there is any category information to be
preserved from the legacy system, users should take the following measures:

- Pass category names associated with each item into Oracle
  Financials via user-defined attributes in the Open Interface table.

- Use the online forms to define categories and category sets
  corresponding to the category information in the item import
  just mentioned.

- Write a custom script to read the categories associated with
  each item, look up the appropriate CATEGORY_ID and
  CATEGORY_SET_ID, and insert MTL_ITEM_CATEGORIES rows
  appropriate to each item.

Figure 10-2 shows the foreign-key relationships that have to be
maintained as you add categories. The relationship between category sets
and categories is complex. The most common usage is to choose your
categories so that each category belongs to only one category set, and to
make an exclusive definition of which categories are within a category set.
Doing so divides everything cleanly: Every enabled item gets assigned to
one of the specified categories within a category set. However, Oracle
allows categories to belong to multiple category sets and permits category
sets to be nonrestrictive.

Categories are identified by flexfields, and the flexfield formats can be
different for different category sets. This degree of flexibility makes sense.
The concept behind category sets is that the many different ways to group
items have little to do with one another. In practice, most category schemes
can be satisfied by single-segment flexfields. Table 10-2 shows three
categories that might be established if the item in question were a computer
processor. Notice that two of the categories, Purchasing and Inventory, have
two-segment flexfields.

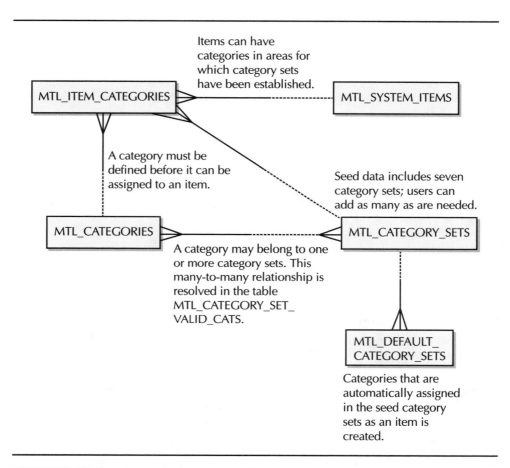

FIGURE 10-2. *Simplified category relationships*

Category Set	Category Set Flexfield		Category Flexfield	
Purchasing	Usage	Material class	Computer	CPUs
Order entry	Order category		System components	
Inventory	Storage type	Control level	Fragile packaged	High dollar

TABLE 10-2. *Sample Flexfield Formats for Itemizing a Computer Processor*

TIP

Even though you may use only one or two structures for your categories (a typical shop would have one- and two-segment structures), it is a good idea to define a separate structure for each category. Doing so provides you with a context field for any Descriptive Flexfields (DFFs) associated with the category. You might, for instance, want to carry the name of the person responsible for setting prices as a DFF for each Order Entry category. The flexfield structure will tell the Define Category form to automatically present the appropriate DFF pop-up window; for other categories there could be a different DFF, or none at all.

The catalog scheme can be extended infinitely. Oracle Inventory often supports custom-written subsystems, which may have to categorize items in unique ways. For example, the Institute of Electrical and Electronics Engineers (IEEE) carries subscriptions as inventory items. One orderable item equates to a certain number of issues, or all issues of a publication for a certain time period. The IEEE has a custom-written subscription fulfillment system that uses Oracle Order Entry and Receivables as a front-end. It could, for the purposes of subscription management, develop a category set to categorize subscription items by periodicity: monthly, bimonthly, quarterly, semi-annual, annual, and as required. Oracle's extensible functionality can minimize the amount of custom code needed in custom subsystems.

Catalogs

Catalogs serve as indexes to inventory items. They help sales people, customers, buyers, and engineers locate things by description. Each item can be cataloged by any number of characteristics appropriate to its type. A catalog group, defined as part of setup and associated with the item through the Define Items screen, establishes which descriptive elements apply to the item. Each item is assigned to only one catalog group. Catalog entries for an item are free-form—that is, they are not required and are not validated against any list. They are in a table rather than a flexfield structure. Catalogs are non-intrusive and can be quite useful.

The Search Items inquiry screen handles catalog searches. You query using the catalog group name and some combination of values and wildcards for the descriptive elements associated with that group. The form returns items that match the search criteria. Other forms, notably Delete Items and Item Cross References, allow you to link to the Search Items screen to pick items. A number of reports are able to select and sort information on the basis of catalog entries. Purchasing and the Manufacturing applications also take advantage of catalog data carried in the Inventory Master.

Issues of Volume

Inventory manages voluminous data in many ways. There are large numbers of items. There are large volumes of transactions against those items. There are a great many attributes associated with each item and transaction. There are a great many different groupings of items. There are often many locations, costs, prices, vendors, and so on associated with an item.

Oracle Inventory is designed to minimize the human effort associated with tracking the vast amounts of data associated with individual items and transactions. The power of its design is in the leverage that the following shortcuts provide:

- **Templates**   Used as items are being created, to assign large numbers of attributes as a group.

- **Categories**   Used for dividing items into functional groups for internal use and for organizing processes that address items by category.

- **Mass edits**   Helpful for updating attributes that need frequent maintenance.

- **Multiple organizations**   Control the many attributes that are common throughout all operating organizations at the item level, while letting attributes that affect site-level inventory operations be addressed by location.

- **Default chains**   Provided in all Oracle applications; used for broadly applying general rules while allowing specific exceptions.

- **Open interfaces**   Embed transaction logic in outside systems and import the results into Inventory. The design of the master table itself anticipates custom processes to update attributes when the standard mass edit logic is not applicable.

The U.S. Bureau of the Census, which performs a small-scale manufacturing operation, is an example of the use of Oracle's open architecture and transaction import. The Bureau presses CD-ROMs of census data on a make-to-order basis—a process too simple to justify the use of a manufacturing software suite. To recognize the cost of manufacture, it customized Order Entry to have it create a miscellaneous receipt of the ordered item in response to each customer order. That way, Order Entry has something to ship from inventory, at an appropriate cost, but Inventory shows it as stock-on-hand only for the brief period between order entry and the time the warehouse picks the order for shipping.

Physical Storage and Management

Physical storage of items is laid out to serve operational needs. The same type of item may appear many places within the system. Oracle defines a hierarchical storage scheme, which breaks down as follows:

- *Inventory organizations* have different missions (for example, manufacturing versus sales) and different geographical locations.

- *Subinventories* reflect different storage areas within a geographical location. They are usually defined by the physical location and the nature of the items being stored.

- *Stock locators* are the addresses of storage locations within the warehouse. They are optional by subinventory.

Inventory Organizations

An Inventory organization within Oracle runs its own show. Although a single installation of Oracle Inventory can maintain Item Master records for an entire company, the people within each organization within the installation are responsible for managing their own stock. As indicated previously, many attributes of an inventory item can be different in different inventory organizations. Oracle Inventory moves stock between organizations by way of internal orders, using Purchasing on the demand end and Order Entry on the supply end. Material does not move across organizations unless the people in the organizations allow it to do so.

Purchasing can support multiple Inventory organizations. A single Purchase Order can handle deliveries to multiple locations. Its receiving operations support only one location at a time. People working at a loading dock only need to deal with receipts for their warehouse.

Manufacturing is oriented towards plants, which are associated with their own Inventory organizations. A manufacturing plant draws raw materials from, and sends finished goods to, a single Inventory organization.

Order Entry has a customer's perspective. Just as customers hope to deal with the company without having to be conscious of that company's internal operations, Order Entry maintains a global view. It accepts product orders on behalf of the whole company or operating unit, using customer data that is shared and consistent regardless of the organization. Order Entry's concern with organization has to do with satisfying an order. It determines the plants or warehouses that will be used to make and ship products, and it provides for each operating unit to have separate customer addresses and contacts.

Individual employees normally belong to one organization, defined in their user profile and the Responsibilities available in their login menu. Oracle Applications hides its complexity from them. They see items, purchase orders, and other activity in light of their responsibility in a given transaction, which handles movements between organizations using internal orders. Oracle Purchasing, which is associated with one organization, passes a requisition to Oracle Order Entry. Oracle creates an internal order to fill the requirement from the source organization designated for the item in question. It is visible to the requesting Inventory or Purchasing organization in the same way a supplier order would be. The organization can see its open request for the item, and it can see the item as due into its organization.

Multiple inventory organizations serve different locations, corporate organizations, and purposes. Oracle can handle many kinds of relationships among them. You may create a structure in which material flows in one direction, such as plant to distribution, or in both directions. If the locations are close, you can have the system decrease stock in the source and increase stock in the receiving organization in the same transaction. If not, you can have the system track in-transit inventory. You can have Oracle manage all aspects of your shipping operations.

The cost of an item may vary in different inventories. A markup can represent value added in freight, handling, or within the company. Oracle can compute this transfer charge as a flat rate or a percentage. Or, you may use a manual business procedure or custom software to establish costs in different sites, in which case the difference will be posted to a variance account.

Subinventories

The subinventory determines the uses to which an item can be put. For example, returned items awaiting inspection cannot be shipped to a new customer. The following questions should be considered when setting up subinventories:

- Does the system track quantities for the subinventory? (Whether the quantity can be allowed to go negative is established at the organization level.)

- Does the system track locations for the subinventory?

- How available is stock within the subinventory to customers? Is it nettable against demand? (In other words, can it be shipped as product?) Is it reservable against customer orders? Should it be considered in Available-to-Promise (ATP) calculations?

- Are items in the subinventory considered inventory assets, as opposed to expensed items?

The answers are generally *yes* for the major subinventories that support customers and manufacturing operations. They track quantities, have locations, are nettable, "ATPable" and reservable, and are carried as assets.

Minor subinventories are convenient holding places for material in transit, such as returned goods or received goods awaiting inspection. Planning the major subinventories is an important part of setup. Make sure you split asset inventory into appropriate subinventories upon conversion, because it can be troublesome to redefine subinventories (and locations) after conversion. It is easy to add minor subinventories as required, as long as you do not have to move balances into them.

Subinventories are a useful tool for managing consignment goods. They can be associated with ledger accounts in a way that recognizes that consignment "assets" are offset by the liability that consignment goods belong to another firm. The native functionality of Oracle Inventory lends itself to custom extensions to handle the requirements associated with consignment goods.

Locators

Warehouse locator codes usually include segments for aisle, rack, and bin corresponding to aisles on the long dimension of the warehouse, rows of racks across the warehouse, and stacks of bins from floor to ceiling. Large organizations may want another segment or two for building and room number.

Stock locators are a natural use of flexfields. Choosing your location numbering scheme is part of setup. Oracle allows a large number of segments and characters. Short and concise is best, as in this example:

Building	One character
Aisle	Two positions
Rack	Two positions
Bin	One position

You can build the whole aisle-rack-bin structure into a single segment or split it into multiple segments. The benefits of a multisegment approach are modest. Using value sets to limit the valid entries in a given segment allows for expansion of any individual segment if a longer location code is needed. On the other hand, maneuvering through data entry screens is faster with one-segment flexfields. Most companies combine all elements of the locator into a single segment.

Your location numbering plan has to cover all types of storage. You might have to compromise, say, between an aisle-rack-bin scheme for packaged products, a rotating bin scheme for small electronic components, and a yard-storage scheme for lumber or quarry stone. Remember that Oracle, perhaps unlike legacy systems, will manage your entire inventory.

To allow for growth and promote ease of understanding, your numbering scheme must reflect an appropriate balance between brevity and content. Brevity is most important in data entry. It does not matter much if you scan most of your location codes, but it matters a lot to anyone who has to key them in. This example points up the need for a holistic approach to the applications—the need to plan setup, business procedures, and hardware at the same time.

Stock locators must be unique within an organization. Although some subinventories may not require locator codes, the numbers themselves are independent of the subinventory.

Locators may be specified or dynamic: either there is a preassigned place for everything, or you choose from available locations as items need to be stocked. In subinventories that use locations, each stock number may have a default location from which it is to be picked for shipment and another, possibly different, default location where it should be put upon receipt. Where the items are actually stored is quite independent of where they ought to be—Oracle Inventory records both. There may be multiple locations for a given stock number, each with a balance of individual units. Oracle Inventory can also track items by serial or lot number within each location.

TIP
Accounting considerations make it difficult to move stock locators from one subinventory to another. If you must do this, use miscellaneous transactions to bring the balances to zero, deactivate and then rename the locations in the old subinventory, define them in the new subinventory, and then pick up the balances through miscellaneous receipts. It is a good job for an SQL script.

Lot Processing

A *lot* is a group of units of a single type assumed to have the same attributes and to be controlled as a group. Lots are usually manufactured together and subject to the same quality controls and handling. The major attributes of a lot are the lot number and expiration date.

Lots are useful in managing goods with limited shelf life. In general, the oldest merchandise not having reached its expiration date should be consumed first. There should be business procedures or subsystems to deal with stock that has passed its expiration date.

Lot numbers are associated with transactions affecting lot number-controlled items. Lot numbers provide an audit trail through the system. Purchasing can receive items with lot numbers, Inventory can accept items with lot numbers from manufacturing, and Order Entry can pick and ship by lot number. This audit trail is essential in resolving problems such as finding where flawed components may have been used in manufacturing. Lot control must be a factor in planning business processes for discrete manufacturing. It demands a push-type inventory management system that records parts usage before the fact.

Serial Number Processing

Tracking of serially numbered items can start at several points within the Inventory process: when the items are received into inventory, when they are received out of manufacturing into inventory, or as they are shipped. You decide item by item whether to use serial numbers and at what stage to start tracking them. Your choice will have a significant impact on the labor and processing involved in material movement transactions, and will depend on how much detail you need to track about each item.

Transactions for serially numbered items have to reference all of the individual item numbers. The only economy available for data entry is that transactions can be entered by serial number range. The labor impact of this requirement will depend on the level of automated data capture within the warehouse. Capturing movements through a bar code scanner is, of course, more efficient than keying transaction data in through Oracle Inventory's online forms. However, there are costs involved in implementing bar codes that should be weighed against the added benefits.

Oracle Service and custom extensions to Oracle Applications often take advantage of serial numbering. Service can associate Original Equipment Manufacturer (OEM) warranty terms and conditions with components sold to customers. Test and inspection results are associated with serial numbers. Oracle Order Entry controls RMAs (Return Material Authorization; for more on RMAs, see Chapter 11) of serially numbered items by serial number. That serial number may be useful in custom systems that track the costs of warranty support.

Configuration management, the tracking of serially numbered components within serially numbered assemblies, adds two more dimensions to the dilemma. The first dimension is depth. The system needs to track serial numbers at each level of nesting within the final product. The second dimension is time. Serially numbered components may be swapped in and out of an item. This can happen before shipment, in test and inspection, or through field upgrades and maintenance. An engineering change may change the structure, substituting one item for two, for instance. Configuration management is a widespread requirement, and one that differs significantly from industry to industry. Any Oracle Applications user with such a requirement should fully investigate Oracle's product and enhancement plans in the Manufacturing and Service areas before developing custom code for this complex application.

Balances

Oracle Inventory provides inquiry forms for the various ways you need to look at item balances. View Item Quantities shows what is on hand, by subinventory and location and revision level, lot number, and serial number data. View Subinventory Quantities and View Locator Quantities give you inventory balances from a warehouse storage perspective.

View Item Supply-Demand Information addresses a more interesting question: whether or not the warehouse can satisfy demand. It shows quantities on hand, due in by Purchase Order, due in from Manufacturing, and reserved and due out on Sales Orders.

Inventory derives the quantity on hand from Views instead of storing the information as a column in a table. MTL_ITEM_QUANTITIES_VIEW and MTL_SUBINV_QUANTITIES_VIEW sum across lots and serial numbers, and over receipts and issues, to present the figure of interest: how many of the item are available. The quantity can be used to satisfy customer orders if you have specified in setup that assets in the subinventory are nettable against demand.

An entry in the Define Organization Parameters form controls whether or not negative balances are allowed. Though it may be counterintuitive, allowing negative balances often improves accuracy. The premise is that Oracle Inventory's balance is not expected to be 100-percent accurate, but it should be accurate enough to assure a target level of support. The reasons for the discrepancies between what is actually in your warehouse and what is being reported in the application, are timing and the economics of recordkeeping. Warehouse personnel may not record a transaction as it happens, but possibly hold paperwork until a certain time of day, or even day of the week. Additionally, Oracle Inventory processes some transactions in batch mode, another element delaying the process. Also, as described in the following section on inventory counts, the cost involved in achieving and maintaining complete accuracy is usually not justified.

NOTE
There may be accounting reasons for running a negative inventory. For example, during conversion, Micros Systems needed to make its legacy inventory available to be picked and shipped from Oracle's Order Entry. Micros could not allow Oracle to value the inventory, however, because its legacy system already accounted for assets on hand. The solution? They set up two offsetting subinventories in Oracle: one with positive balances from which they could ship and capture the cost of goods sold, and an offset with negative balances. The result was an Oracle Inventory that could be used for shipping and would accurately record the cost of goods sold, but which appeared in the General Ledger as an asset with zero value.

Counting

The gap between ideals and reality can cause credibility problems in Inventory. The simple view is that the automated system should know exactly how many grommets, for example, are on the shelves. An answer like "3285.32 grommets" will not make sense. How could there be .32 grommets?

It is a problem of volume. An operation of any size cannot be assured of knowing exactly how much it has of any item at any time. It does not pretend to try. It asks a more sophisticated question: How accurate does the data have to be to get the job done? Oracle supports this statistical view. How accurate do the balances have to be?

Similar considerations apply in managing your checking account. You do not have to know exactly how much money you have at all times; you only need to know enough to make decisions. Can you afford the new suit? Do you have to draw on the credit union to make the mortgage payment? And, you need enough control to make sure nobody else is writing checks on your account and the bank has not made any mistakes. The bottom line is that you need to know more or less what you have at all times, and you need to reconcile every now and then. You weigh the effort of keeping the balance totally up-to-date against the cost of an occasional bounced check, and decide what level of accuracy is optimal for you.

Inventory balances have to be accurate enough that the warehouse finds sufficient quantity on hand when the automated system says to pick the item—not all the time, but a very high percentage of the time. Conversely, counting inventory costs money, often more than the items are worth. Management is the art of striking the right balance. Cycle counting with ABC analysis—counting the most important stock most frequently—gives the highest level of inventory performance for the counting effort invested. Cycle counting and ABC analysis will be discussed in more detail in the upcoming sections.

Manufacturing Inventory Counts

Manufacturing operations assume that counts are approximate. Most of them do not actually count parts as they go into assemblies. Instead, they compute part usage by taking into account the number of items produced, the bill of materials for the items, and attrition factors built into the bills to cover waste. As mentioned earlier, *backflushing* is the process of updating inventory after the fact by this kind of deduction.

Attrition factors can yield fractional inventory balances. If 1 tube breaks for every 10 TV sets made, inventory should go down by 11 after a lot of 10. What about after 5? With rounding, 2 lots of 5 would reduce inventory by either 10 or 12, both inaccurate. The answer has to be to reduce inventory by 5.5 tubes after a run of five, despite the fact that tubes only come in integer quantities. The next inventory count will reconcile this estimate to the actual quantity on hand.

Physical Inventory

A physical inventory is a count of all items in some portion of an inventory. Oracle Inventory takes a snapshot of the balances as they exist at a point in time. Using the snapshot as a baseline, Oracle prints inventory count tags for the warehouse staff, accepts its counts, and then requests recounts or makes adjustments. Your business procedures may allow inventory activity to continue throughout the count. Oracle does all its comparisons against the frozen snapshot. Allowing operations to continue, however, means that the counters have to allow for activity between the freeze and their count.

Though Oracle offers full support for physical inventory counts, most organizations find that cycle counting according to an ABC analysis is the most effective way to achieve their objective on a regular basis. The fact that Oracle lets you have both systems in use at once eases the transition to cycle counting.

ABC Analysis

ABC analysis divides stock into categories to be managed with different levels of intensity. There are typically three categories, though Oracle allows any number. Category A stock is high-value, mission-critical, and/or high-volume. Category B is in the middle, and Category C is low-value, low-action, and low-volume. It is worth a high investment of labor to keep the counts accurate for Category A items. Category B and C items merit proportionately less effort.

Oracle lets you categorize your parts by on-hand quantities or on-hand item value; historical usage quantities, value, or number of transactions; forecast quantity or value; MRP demand quantity or value; or adjustment amounts. In the end, you can choose only one method to have Oracle automatically assign categories to your items. Run the analysis three or four ways to see which one appears to work best and note the exceptions. You may find that major end items represent the greatest high-dollar values but that the biggest adjustments are in items that regularly get broken or are subject to theft. Take the Oracle Inventory category assignments as a starting point, then use manual reassignments to take care of the exceptions.

Oracle provides two reports to help categorize items based on cost and activity in a given period. The ABC Descending Values sorts items in descending order by the level of activity (monetary value, transactions, or quantity) and provides a cumulative total at each line. In other words, it highlights the items for which activity and cost show the most need for tight control. The Define ABC Assignments form assigns ABC classes to items; all you have to do is specify the cutoff points. Then, use the ABC Assignments list to show your assignments.

Many other criteria may be used to assign ABC categories. Users can buy third-party software or take advantage of Oracle's open design to write their own ABC stratification logic. Standard cycle-count functionality will handle the assignments you have made using custom algorithms.

Cycle Counting

Cycle counting has replaced "wall-to-wall" counts as the preferred technique for managing warehouse stock. Shutting down operations just for a count is disruptive in small organizations and impossible in large ones. On top of everything else, complete inventory counts may be less accurate. People with little inventory experience are pulled in just for counting, and there is tremendous time pressure to finish and get back to business.

Cycle counting uses the ABC groups to establish how often items get counted. Users might specify that *A*s get counted once a month, *B*s quarterly, and *C*s yearly. In setting up the count, the system divides the number of items to be counted by the number of workdays available to count them, so warehouse personnel count roughly the same number of items every day. The warehouse usually schedules an hour or two per day for counting, at a time when receiving and picking activity are low.

When the entered counts disagree with the computer count and the discrepancy is within a user-prescribed tolerance, the entered count is taken to be accurate; otherwise the system will request a recount. As with the physical inventory process, although transactions can still be done during the count, they will complicate the process. Your business procedures should allow time for a count and a recount in a period when the items are physically inactive.

Cycle counting keeps average accuracy in the warehouse high and consistent. Management can devise reports (again, usually custom or third party, using Oracle transaction data) to monitor warehouse accuracy as measured by warehouse denials, stock shrinkage, and other parameters.

Many organizations converting to Oracle have not implemented cycle counting. It represents a significant change in philosophy and business procedures, and it is usually best left until the Oracle system is running smoothly. A gradual cutover is recommended, starting with the Category A items. The warehouse knows the process is working when the number of recounts falls to an acceptable level, indicating that most counts agree with the automated records. Some items—and some subinventories—can continue under the old counting methods while cycle counting is being implemented.

Replenishment Counts

Inexpensive, expendable items may not be worth counting at all for financial purposes. If they are essential for the operation, however, they do need to be replenished. Oracle supports *replenishment counts,* in which the counter may either directly enter the quantity to be ordered, or enter a count so Oracle can perform MIN-MAX computations to determine what to order, as described in the following section.

MANAGING STOCK REPLENISHMENTS   Inventory is responsible for the big picture of overall material requirements. In addition to its balance records, it maintains a MTL_SUPPLY table to record all items expected to be received into inventory. These include items on order from suppliers, items being manufactured, items in transit from other company locations, and items due back from customers. Inventory keeps a parallel MTL_DEMAND table with records of all material requirements for customer orders, manufacturing raw material needs, and requisitions for internal use. Inventory is only the custodian. Purchasing, Order Entry, and Work in Process (among other Applications) maintain data in these tables to reflect their operations.

Inventory replenishment logic compares future demand against what is on hand and on order to determine what needs to be ordered. If there are customer orders for six of an item, and two are on hand and two on order, the replenishment logic has to order more. It creates and sends a requisition to Purchasing.

Determining what to order is complicated by the time factor and ordering considerations. Suppliers and internal manufacturing operations need time to ship or make inventory items, and efficiency demands that items be ordered in rational units, like boxes or pallets. Using the actual need as a basis, the replenishment logic figures out how much to order and when.

Inventory uses forecasts to compensate for the fact that it cannot get materials instantaneously. It adds forecast quantities to actual demand to compute the most realistic estimates of requirements at each future point in time. The purchase requisitions it generates take into consideration the following lead time factors:

- The time it will take to turn a requisition into a purchase order and get it to a vendor

- The time it will take a vendor to ship the item
- The time it will take to receive, inspect, and deliver the item to its destination

Oracle Manufacturing plans the production of manufactured items to meet firm and forecast demand. In addition to the preceding factors, it takes into account the time it takes to make items.

MIN-MAX PLANNING   Stock items may be coded for replenishment by reorder point (ROP) or by MIN-MAX logic. MIN-MAX logic is the simplest. It can base the replenishment decision solely on the amount of stock on hand and on order, or it can take demand into account as well. It takes minimum and maximum values from the min_minmax_quantity and max_minmax_quantity attributes in the MTL_SYSTEM_ITEMS record for the item.

MIN-MAX includes expected receipts (supply) and existing orders (demand) out to a cutoff date you specify. If the quantity on hand and on order falls below the specified MIN, it orders up to the MAX, as shown in Figure 10-3.

Demand data may at times be excluded altogether. It is not useful when lead times are longer than delivery schedules; in that case parts could not be ordered from vendors in time to meet user needs. In addition, demand data may not be worth the effort for inexpensive items that experience steady consumption, such as paper clips or solder.

Looking forward using demand and forecasts information and analyzing matching supply against demand by time period will usually provide a more accurate picture of requirements than will MIN-MAX point-in-time projection. Reorder point replenishment, as shown in Figure 10-4, uses future demand plus safety stock to compute requirements.

REORDER-POINT PLANNING   Safety stock is a "fudge factor" to protect against the risks of a change in demand. Oracle Inventory supports two statistical methods for computing safety stock. It can use a straight percentage of forecast demand. Alternatively, if there is enough history on the item, Oracle can compute safety stock as a factor of historical usage and the desired service level. Service level expresses, in statistical terms, the amount of time an item should be available when it is requested. It takes more stock to support a 99.9 percent satisfaction level than a 99 percent

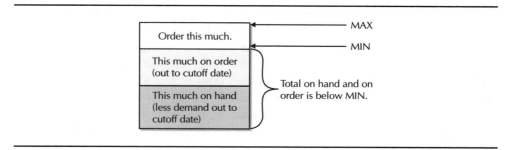

FIGURE 10-3. *MIN-MAX reorder calculation logic*

level. Businesses have to decide, by item, the trade-off between the cost of carrying stock and the cost of being unable to satisfy customers.

ROP incorporates the concept of an Economic Order Quantity (EOQ). The EOQ formula balances the one-time costs of processing an order (cutting the purchasing order, receiving, and so on) against the ongoing carrying cost of keeping stock in the warehouse (cost of money, occupancy, overhead, and shrinkage). The item manager factors in the standard units for ordering and handling material (case, pallet, and so on) in setting the Fixed Order Quantity and Fixed Lot Size Multiplier attributes for the item. When the ROP replenishment logic determines that more stock is needed, it creates a requisition for some multiple of that adjusted EOQ.

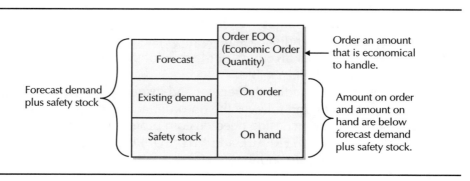

FIGURE 10-4. *ROP replenishment logic*

Time is an important factor in balancing supply with demand. A carload of grapefruit next month does not satisfy shoppers tomorrow. You specify time buckets (days, weeks, or periods) within which Oracle matches supply and demand. You set the parameters up item by item to meet your business needs. For a hospital, a can of Spam due in this week will satisfy cafeteria demand next month. Milk due this week will not. If you are using weekly time buckets, you would say that the supply and demand for milk must match one another within each time bucket, whereas with Spam the demand in one time bucket can be satisfied by supply in any previous time bucket. You also specify how future supply may satisfy current demand. A pair of skis due next month may satisfy demand this week if the customer is willing to wait. Your company has to set the rules.

MATERIAL REQUIREMENTS PLANNING   The Material Requirements Planning (MRP) application handles material planning across items and across organizations, using purchasing and manufacturing as sources for the items. Inventory handles replenishments at the item level only. In making its computations, it looks at supply due from purchasing or manufacturing and demand for that item itself or as a component of a Pick-to-Order order line. In a manufacturing operation, however, the system needs to translate demand (in terms of shippable product) into requirements (in terms of components). MRP uses bill of material explosions to determine those parts requirements. MRP can also compute requirements across an organization, determining how much each factory must produce, and each warehouse must ship, in order to meet company-wide demand. MRP and inventory replenishment both calculate what is required and generate requisitions for Purchasing. Purchasing follows its setup rules to act on the requisition. It finds a source—either another organization within the company or a vendor—and places the appropriate internal or external purchase order. It advises Inventory of the state of the requisition through postings to the MTL_SUPPLY table.

Oracle Purchasing handles the receipt and inspection of items. It adjusts the inventory balances and relieves the on-order amounts appropriately. Users without Oracle Purchasing need custom programs to populate the MTL_TRANSACTION_INTERFACE and MTL_SUPPLY_INTERFACE tables with appropriate records to show purchasing activity.

Forecasting and Demand

Each installation needs to establish its own policies for recognizing demand and making forecasts to be used by the Oracle Material Requirements Planning application. Order Entry is the primary demand driver. Establishing order cycles is a major part of Order Entry setup, and the Demand Interface is part of the cycle. In other words, a demand can be made visible to Inventory at several points in the cycle between the time an order is first entered and the time it ships. The earlier the demand is recognized, the higher the demand satisfaction will be; however, carrying costs will also be higher as a result of items held for orders that never firm up.

Demand, which is associated with *actual* customer requests, is firmer than forecasts, which are *estimates* of future requests. Forecasts have to be done by item, and they have to allow appropriate algorithms and parameters for each item. The algorithms take into account historical demand, trends, and seasonality and use mathematical smoothing techniques. You can make intuitive projections when past demand is nonexistent or would be a poor guide.

Actual demand places a reality check on a forecast. The forecast of what will happen has to be adjusted for what is actually happening. In inventory terms, demand *consumes* forecast. Subject to some exceptions, each order for an item lowers the forecast demand as it raises the actual demand. The exceptions follow:

- A given order that dwarfs the average is called an *outlier.* Suppose a Christmas tree lot forecasts selling 500 trees a week, one at a time. If it receives one order for 300 trees, that does not mean that the best guess is only another 200 will be sold. On the contrary, the best guess is that the order for 300 is a fluke and perhaps 495 more will be sold, one at a time. In Oracle, the lot managers could reflect this by setting the outlier update percent to 1, meaning that no single demand can consume more than 1 percent of a forecast.

- After correcting for outliers, if the forecast for a period can fully consume the new demand, it is consumed. Demand goes up, forecast goes down. Forecasts may be kept by demand class—groups of customers and types of orders. Oracle then follows rules for consuming by demand class. For example, Schlage Lock may not want OEM orders for deadbolts to consume the forecast for its wholesale distribution arm. In other words, if OEM sells twice as many as expected, it will require more manufacturing instead of taking the pressure off the dealer sales force. Replenishment will buy the parts to make more deadbolts.

If the forecast for the period cannot fully consume the demand in that period, Oracle follows the rules given for demand consumption. It may use up the demand by consuming forecast within a specified number of periods preceding the demand period, consuming forecast within a number of periods after the forecast, or "overconsuming" forecast in the current period. Overconsumption effectively ignores the impact of excess demand in one given period on the forecast. The replenishment algorithms use all the real demand, including that in the period of overconsumption, and add to it the forecasts for other periods that would have been diminished if the overconsumption had been applied to them. Overconsumption results in higher replenishment orders.

Different sources of demand require separate forecasts. Schlage's forecast for deadbolts will be the aggregate of direct sales forecasts in the states and countries in which it markets, plus what it may manufacture for private-label sales. The forecasting system uses forecast sets to combine multiple forecasts into aggregate figures to plan manufacturing.

A *forecast set* is a group of forecasts that combine to give a complete forecast, as illustrated in Figure 10-5. A forecast must belong to one and only one forecast set. There may be more than one forecast set, each representing a different business scenario. You can have and maintain any number of forecast sets. A given run of the Inventory Reorder Point Planning Report or of MRP, however, has to use a single forecast set (or forecast) to calculate material requirements and create requisitions.

Multiple forecast sets are useful for "what if" projections. You can model different economic scenarios or determine what would happen if you acquired new customers or expanded your marketing territory. You can compare the results of different MRP runs. MRP runs do not order items; they simply create requisitions. Planners can look at different requisition

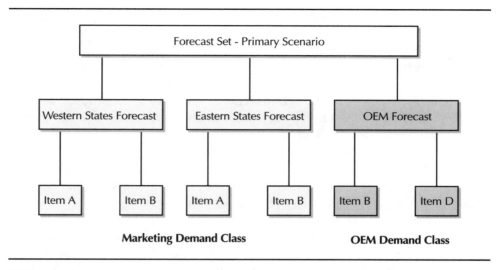

FIGURE 10-5.   *A sample forecast set: three forecasts divided into two demand classes*

quantities based on different forecasts and decide what to order. Once an order has been placed, the supply it represents will be taken into account by all MRP runs.

Forecast sets need to be consumed only if they are used in the replenishment process. Oracle can consume more than one set, if you want to consistently generate material requirements for multiple scenarios.

Kanban

Kanban, which means *card* in Japanese, is a term applied to a group of supply and inventory business procedures for moving materials through a production organization. It is characterized by speed and simplicity. Kanban is best suited for *flow manufacturing,* assembly-line operations that produce similar items on a continuous basis.

The production process is broken down into processing units (PUs). Each PU takes in raw materials, adds value to create an output, and passes the output to another PU. A Kanban card, or even just an empty container, signals one PU to resupply the next one up the line. Presenting the card takes the place of a requisition or a delivery order, depending on whether or not it goes outside the company.

The number of cards in circulation controls production; a PU is not allowed to make its product without a card. The simplicity of the system minimizes the cost of capturing transactions. It is easy to record that a Kanban container passed from one station to another. A bar code scanner is the preferred method, but a hand tally will suffice for most organizations.

Oracle accepts Kanban as an alternative to setting a Release Time Fence for MPS/MRP within an organization. You have to define a pull sequence for every Kanban item, showing the sequence of Kanban locations (that is, the processing units or PUs) that models the replenishment network. The replenishment network includes locations on the shop floor, outside suppliers, other production lines, and non-Kanban organizations. Because the PUs are represented by locations, Oracle allows the use of stock locators for purposes of Kanban definition, even if locator control is not in effect for the organization, subinventory, or item.

The pull sequence provides Oracle with the information it needs to automatically create Kanban cards for each item, subinventory, and locator. Each card is uniquely identified by a generated Kanban number. You have the option to ignore the pull sequence and manually generate Kanban cards using numbers of your own choosing.

Automated support enhances the simple manual Kanban concept. Bar code scanning accurately captures shop floor movement at very little expense. You can have Oracle create non-replenishable Kanban cards to handle spikes in demand, and you can have Oracle temporarily take cards out of circulation to hold down supply.

Conversion Issues

Oracle Inventory provides many open interfaces to assist with ongoing interfaces and initial data conversion. This section covers issues related to conversion, such as the item, transactions (opening balances), and location conversions.

Item Master Conversion

Oracle Inventory provides the Item Open Interface to enable you to load new items into the Inventory Item Master. This program processes records that you have loaded into the MTL_SYSTEM_ITEMS_INTERFACE table, which has columns corresponding to those in the MTL_SYSTEM_ITEMS table. The load process crosschecks to ensure that the attribute settings are consistent with one another.

When converting from a legacy system to Oracle Inventory it can be difficult to map all the item attributes one-to-one, or even come close. Legacy items do, however, usually fall into groupings such as those defined by Oracle templates. The recommended approach to conversion is as follows:

1. Define templates that can be used to set up every type of item in the organization. The Item Open Interface can apply only one template to set attributes for an item.

2. Associate a master-level template with each legacy item. If possible, expand the legacy schema to carry the template name, so you can prepare for Oracle conversion as you maintain the legacy system.

3. Load the interface table with records in which the item-specific attribute columns (item number, weight, units of measure) are populated, and name a template that will fill in all other needed attributes in the master organization. Typically, more than half the attributes will remain null; your testing will indicate which attributes need values.

4. Import the master items into Oracle.

5. Populate the interface table with organization-level records. These usually include little more than the item number, the organization, and the organization-level template to apply. The organization-level template must be compatible with the master-level template. You may find it useful to define the templates such that the name of one can be derived from the other.

6. Import the organization-level items into Oracle.

Using templates does more than just simplify the conversion. It ensures that new items created after cutover will have the same characteristics as legacy items brought over during conversion.

TIP

The Attribute Names in the Define Item screen and the Define Item Template screen are not the same as the column names in the interface table. Use the following SQL routine to create a list of the correspondence between internal and external attribute names:

SELECT attribute_name, user_attribute_name
FROM mtl_item_attributes
ORDER BY attribute_name;

Oracle can carry multiple values for certain attributes that legacy systems define as unique to an item, such as cost, sales price, catalog, and category data. The interface program does not load these values. However, the Oracle tables are relatively straightforward. Plan to write SQL*Plus or PL/SQL scripts to populate them as part of the conversion.

There is no open interface for batch updates of items. It is critically important to choose the right template at conversion. Make sure your test plan includes transactions from every business area, particularly Inventory, Purchasing, Order Entry, and Manufacturing—that will use the attributes you set.

Transaction Conversion

Once the items and locations are in place, you can use the Open Transaction Interface to bring in balance data as miscellaneous receipts. The process is straightforward. The balances will be debited to the material account associated with the subinventory. The accountants need to tell you where to post the credit.

Making the accounts balance between the legacy system and Oracle Applications takes some effort. The accounts will balance only if both the inventory balances and the item costs agree. Set up the Open Item Interface to bring in the frozen standard costs of each item. Reconcile the legacy inventory valuation that existed prior to conversion with the Oracle valuation. After you get the inventory-to-inventory conversion to balance, it should be a small matter to reconcile to the General Ledger. There should be no adjustment at all if the legacy inventory agrees with the legacy ledger.

Costs are more volatile than items themselves. Oracle provides an online mechanism to update them. You use the Update Costs form to assign the new cost to the Pending cost type, then run Update Standard Costs to have Oracle apply the change and compute the accounting implications. Although you must let Oracle apply the changes, it is quite easy to write your own script to create Pending cost type records. Use Oracle's utility to delete Pending costs, insert your new Pending values into CST_ITEM_COSTS and CST_ITEM_COST_DETAILS, and then run the update. Oracle does the complex work of revaluing stock, in-transit inventory, and work in process.

Location Conversion

As of Release 10.6, users can convert items and import balances via the open interfaces, but you still need custom scripts to set up stock locators. You set them up first because stock locators have to be present to accept balances.

There are usually so few subinventories that you create them manually. The major issue, deciding which subinventories to define for asset items, can remain unresolved well into setup. One of the first jobs in conversion will be to populate the location tables. Figure 10-6 shows how these tables relate to each other and the sequence of conversion within each organization. The tables with heavy borders are populated manually at setup. Those with medium borders are populated in the first automated conversion steps, and those with light borders are populated in the second phase of conversion.

MTL_SYSTEM_ITEMS master records need to be converted independently of locations and prior to loading any balance or location information for items. Load them through the Open Item Interface, as described earlier in this chapter.

FND_FLEX_VALUES may be used to validate some segments in the Location Flexfield, though usually not all. If you are going to limit the values

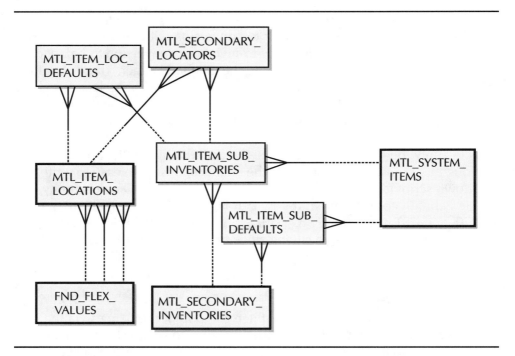

FIGURE 10-6. *Relationships among location tables in Inventory*

a segment may assume, you have to set them up in advance. Most organizations develop a mass load utility for flex values as part of General Ledger setup.

MTL_ITEM_LOCATIONS defines locations within the organization. These locations are independent of the items stored in them. There is no open interface to import these records. Write a script to create them from legacy location data. The script will perform the following tasks:

  1. Create a master list of item locations from legacy files.

  2. Perform the required translation from the legacy system into the Oracle Location Flexfield format.

3. Insert records directly into the MTL_ITEM_LOCATIONS table. Chapter 15 describes the process of analysis and programming. Be sure to do the following:

   ■ Validate the segments against any flex value sets you may have defined for the Location Flexfield.

   ■ Use the legacy data to select a valid subinventory for the location. Subinventories can be assigned according to the type of item currently in the location, but inventory management is generally easier when physically adjacent locations belong to one subinventory. Recognize, however, that this may force some trade-offs between re-warehousing and assigning a less than optimal subinventory scheme.

   ■ Populate any other columns for which data is available from the legacy system, so that nothing is lost. Leave no legacy attributes behind. Map them into unused Attribute 1...30 columns if Oracle does not have a place for them.

   ■ Populate the WHO columns with the date and the user id of the author of the load script. Or, better yet, create a conversion user and run all conversion programs from that account. Then, even years later, everyone can clearly identify records that were created during initial conversion.

   ■ Use the Oracle-provided sequence MTL_ITEM_LOCATIONS_S to generate unique LOCATOR_ID values.

4. Test the validity of the conversion script by querying created locations and assigning items to them in the test instance.

Balance and location data are usually available in the same legacy file. Depending on the legacy system's sophistication or lack thereof, the data may be in the extract used to populate MTL_SYSTEM_ITEMS. Your first step is to write a custom script to populate the tables, shown at the top of Figure 10-6, that join to both items and subinventories. You add the balances after you have defined places to put them.

Chances are that Oracle Inventory admits more complexity than the legacy system. Your algorithms will have to define not only where items are, but also where they go when they arrive and where to look for them first. MTL_ITEM_SUB_INVENTORIES, MTL_SECONDARY_LOCATORS, and MTL_ITEM_SUB_DEFAULTS are simple tables. Generate entries for the mandatory columns and populate the others to the extent that legacy data is available.

Accounting Entries for Inventory Transactions

Inventory accounts for items and their costs. Its financial accounting is automatic; few organizations would bother to track items that have no monetary value. The money side flows to the General Ledger, where the financial operations of the whole enterprise are recorded and reported. Reporting follows the Chart of Accounts, shown in Chapter 2.

Inventory is carried on a company's books as an asset. The most fundamental accounting requirement is that the value of all the items in inventory sum to the amount carried on the General Ledger books. There can be more than one set of books, and more than one Inventory organization within each set of books, but they all need to balance.

In addition to the summary reports required by law, the ledger provides the detailed information to support business decisions. The following types of decisions are made in Inventory:

- What is the real cost at sale of an inventory item, figuring in the purchase cost, handling costs, storage, and everything else?

- How can inventory costs be reduced? What are the optimal trade-offs?

- Ultimately, what products are profitable for the company to manufacture or sell?

The Oracle Inventory setup requires many ledger accounts. These accounts are the basis for ledger reporting, of which the material managers will be the biggest users. They need to work with the accounting department and the software setup team to make sure that the accounts will serve their own information needs.

Shaking down the accounting setups is a major part of the Inventory installation process. Setup would be simple if users knew how Oracle Applications worked and what they needed in the way of reports; unfortunately they usually don't have this information. Deciding what they want in light of what Oracle can do is a matter of trial and error. There is a big difference between keeping the books in balance and producing information needed to manage the business.

Accounting models are an essential device for planning and communication. They show what information will flow to the ledger. The model is a kind of "financial flowchart" that accountants, functional experts, and the MIS staff can share in setting up the Oracle Inventory parameters.

The following accounting model is simple and accurate—but very incomplete. It exemplifies how to get the process started.

Step 1. Finance an inventory company by putting cash into the company for an inventory account:

Account	Debit	Credit
Cash	100	
Equity		100

Step 2. Use $60 to buy some inventory:

Account	Debit	Credit
Inventory Assets	60	
Cash		60

Step 3. Sell the inventory for $80:

Account	Debit	Credit
Cash	80	
Inventory Assets		60
Profit		20

Balance sheet statements after each of these transactions would show the financial state of the company at that time:

After Step 1				After Step 2				After Step 3			
Assets		**Liabilities**		**Assets**		**Liabilities**		**Assets**		**Liabilities**	
Cash	100	Equity	100	Cash	40	Equity	100	Cash	120	Equity	100
				Inventory	60					Profit	20

Additional Accounting Transactions

The preceding model is overly simplistic, but it is financially accurate in that it balances, while not providing much useful information. The following paragraphs introduce some of the accounts that Purchasing and Inventory setup require. They make the accounting model and financial reporting more complicated, but they do a better job of reflecting the actual state of the business.

Most companies operate on an accrual rather than a cash basis. Their books show expenses as they are due, rather than when they are paid. They show income when it is earned rather than when the money is paid. Step 2—buying inventory—becomes two steps.

Step 2(a). Buy the assets and incur a liability to pay for them:

Account	Debit	Credit
Inventory Assets	60	
Accounts Payable		60

Step 2(b). Pay for the purchased assets:

Account	Debit	Credit
Accounts Payable	60	
Cash		60

The balance sheet statement after Step 2(b) would look the same as that shown in the first example. After Step 2(a), it would show the liability for accounts payable as follows:

Assets		**Liabilities**	
Cash	100	Equity	100
Inventory	60	Accounts Payable	60

Introducing the accounts payable account increases the utility of the financial statement by adding new information. It tells management that there is $100 in the bank, but $60 of it is owed to suppliers. Oracle Payables requires at least one accounts payable account.

This model still does not reflect how business really works. The verb "buy" in Step 2(a) is too simplistic. Buying is really a process in which ordering, receiving, and paying the bill are separate steps. The company will issue a purchase order to the vendor. The vendor will ship the product, then send an invoice separately. The company actually owes for the goods when they arrive, regardless of when the invoice arrives. This calls for a Receipt Accruals account. Sometimes the company wants to know how much (in monetary terms) has been ordered or even requested to be ordered, so it doesn't spend the same money twice. Still assuming that the exact cost of the assets are known start to end, the accounting model would include the following steps:

Step 2(a). Order the assets:

Account	**Debit**	**Credit**
Assets on Order	60	
Purchase Obligations		60

Step 2(a). Receive the assets.

Account	**Debit**	**Credit**
Purchase Obligations	60	
Assets on Order		60
Inventory Assets	60	
Receiving Accrual Account		60

Step 2(a). Process the invoice:

Account	Debit	Credit
Receiving Accrual Account	60	
Accounts Payable		60

Step 2(a). Pay the bill:

Account	Debit	Credit
Accounts Payable	60	
Cash		60

Oracle Inventory uses all the accounts just mentioned, in addition to others, to account for such things as materials that have been received but not yet inspected. In addition to showing how an accounting model works, this example shows how accounts are used to show the detail necessary to manage business operations.

Variances

Prices and costs are subjective. By convention, the term *price* applies to the seller's side of a transaction and *cost* applies to the buyer's side. Your supplier's price is your cost. Price and cost vary over time, and there may be several in effect at one time. In the course of a routine purchase there may be slightly different amounts at each step in the process:

■ The amount the internal requisitioner expects an item to cost

■ The supplier price that the purchasing department enters on the purchase order

■ The invoiced price from the supplier

■ The standard cost of the item within the inventory system

Differences in price require adjustments in most of the steps shown in the accounting model used earlier as well as in many other places within manufacturing. The adjustments, called *variances,* are posted to variance accounts. Here is what happens to the buying segment of our accounting model when the system sees three different prices: $55 (standard cost), $60 (purchase order price), and $58 (invoice price):

Step 2(b). Receive the assets.

Account	Debit	Credit
Inventory Assets (at standard cost)	55	
Purchase Price Variance Account		–5
Receiving Accrual Account		60

Step 2(b). Process the invoice:

Account	Debit	Credit
Receiving Accrual Account	60	
Invoice Price Variance Account		2
Accounts Payable		58

Passing the differences to variance accounts buffers the system from constant small changes in price. It is probably true that no two Ford automobiles rolling off the assembly line cost exactly the same amount to make. Ford, however, plans and prices as if they do. The company sets a standard cost, watches the variances closely, and then periodically adjusts the standard cost to bring variances back down.

Managing inventory and manufacturing processes is a matter of managing variances. They have to be kept small through periodic adjustments to standard prices, a process that brings them in line with actual costs for purchasing and handling.

Average versus Standard Costing

Costing provides a system for judging success in many areas. At the highest level, margin on a product is the difference between price and cost. You analyze elements of cost and patterns of change to evaluate the performance of your purchasing, inventory, and manufacturing organizations. The choice of either average or standard costing is ultimately a business decision—Oracle Inventory can perform both.

Under *average costing,* Oracle recomputes item cost with every receipt. Under *standard costing,* the inventory asset account is charged for each receipt at standard cost, with the difference posted to the Purchase Price Variance (PPV) account.

The similarities between standard and average cost are significant. Both cost methods recognize an Invoice Price Variance account (IPV), in Payables, for differences between the purchase price and the invoice price. IPV picks up prompt-pay discounts and other charges and credits that affect the ultimate cost of purchased materials. Material is only one of the five cost elements for which average costing is an alternative. The other four, discussed in the following section on standard costs, are treated the same under either system.

A change in the frozen cost of an item ripples through a number of inventory, purchasing, and manufacturing processes. Each issue to manufacturing is costed at the average cost in effect at the moment of the issue. The adjustments the system makes as you change the frozen cost are ultimately posted to variance accounts you have defined in inventory, purchasing, and manufacturing setups.

CAUTION
Converting from one costing method to the other is difficult. Take the time to determine your long-range needs as you initially install Oracle Inventory.

Nonmaterial Expense Collection

Manufacturing collects expenses associated with producing individual products. Even in a manufacturing organization there are a number of overhead expenses that cannot be pinned to one item of inventory. However, there is no tool provided for non-manufacturing organizations to track expenses by item. Overhead expenses such as warehouse management generally have to flow to the ledger and be allocated back to individual items. Overhead costs associated with running an inventory system follow these paths into the ledger:

- Overhead labor charges may be collected by a labor distribution system; they flow from payroll to the ledger.

- Overhead resource charges (utilities, and so on) are captured by Payables; they flow to the ledger.

- Overhead costs (occupancy, and so on) are captured by Payables and as depreciation flows from Fixed Assets and other sources; they flow to the ledger.

- Expenses associated with Inventory operations flow to the ledger using Accounting Flexfields defined in Inventory setup. Because the item number does not flow to the General Ledger, you need an allocation formula to distribute the ledger amounts to individual items.

The ledger postings are differentiated according to Accounting Flexfields associated with the items and the organizations, subinventories, and categories that apply to the item. The GL might capture, for example, inventory shrinkage for office supplies into one GL account. You can develop your own formulas to spread such overhead expenses over actual inventory items.

What you do with inventory overhead depends on the needs of the organization. If inventory is a major part of your operation and is held for resale, it makes good sense to compute the costs of purchasing, receiving, and managing it into the price at which an item is carried in inventory and eventually sold. If the inventory is for internal use, it may be adequate to absorb the cost of managing it as corporate overhead or use a high-level allocation to spread overhead to the organizations it serves.

Setting Standard Costs

Costs are usually set at two levels: *buy* and *make*. The cost of *buy* (purchased) items is easier to establish. The simplest figure is the average price recently paid to suppliers. The cost of *make* (manufactured) items equals the cost of the component items plus the labor, overhead, and outside processing that goes into them.

For users who need to establish costs precisely, Oracle defines five cost elements for each item:

- Material (the average purchase price)
- Overhead (resource and department overhead)
- Material Overhead (also called *burden*)
- Outside Processing
- Resource

The total cost of an assembled item is computed as the sum of the five cost elements for the item itself and of the lower-level assemblies within it. In Oracle's terminology, total cost is the *rollup* of the costs associated with the five *this-level* cost elements (those associated with assembling the item from its components) and the five *prior-level* cost elements (those same five cost elements applied to the creation of the lower-level items that make up the assembly).

Users who take advantage of these cost elements usually break down costs even further by defining cost subelements unique to the organization that rolls up to the cost. For example, the resources that go into the manufacturing of a part may include labor and utilities. Material overhead may include costs of purchasing and receiving.

Oracle automatically computes and assigns the average cost of purchased items if you elect to use average costing. It collects the raw figures you need to compute all other types of costs, for both *buy* and *make* parts, but assigning them is up to you.

Oracle specifies five steps for setting standard costs:

1. Define pending costs.

2. Roll up pending costs.

3. Print and review pending costs.

4. Update pending costs.

5. Print new standard costs.

The end of the process, applying costs in Steps 3 through 5 after you know what they should be, are straightforward. The art of pricing is in the first two steps, establishing pending costs.

Define Pending Costs

Pricing starts at the bottom, meaning the cost of an assembly depends on the cost of the components. The first step, therefore, is to establish costs for the lowest-level items: those you buy from outside suppliers. These items usually have the planning_make_buy_code attribute set to "buy." You can, however, have a bill of materials for a *buy* part and specify that the cost be derived by a rollup in the next step.

To manually copy the frozen item costs into pending, use Copy Costs, and then use the Define Costs screen in Oracle Cost Management to enter or update pending item costs. You enter costs at the level of the five cost elements just described; the form displays the total as the pending item cost.

A large number of items and frequent changes would make a manual approach to setting pending costs impractical for most manufacturing organizations. If your organization cares only about material costs, Oracle's average costing will satisfy your requirement. Otherwise you can write custom SQL scripts to insert pending costs into the CST_ITEM_COSTS and CST_ITEM_COST_DETAILS tables. Use the following guidelines:

- Define the costs of parts by user instead of basing them on rollup.

- Insert costs only for the elements you use. There is no need to insert zero values for cost elements you don't need.

- Tag the costs as being for *this level. Prior level* costs would come from components, which a purchased item does not have.

CAUTION

Never insert frozen cost types (cost_type_ id = 1) directly. Doing so will change the cost without adjusting the General Ledger, destroying the financial integrity of the applications. Instead, always create pending costs, and have Oracle's Cost Update process convert them to frozen.

Use these guidelines above to apply the pending costs once you know what they are. The Oracle Financials capture and carry a significant amount of data to help you compute the five cost elements, but they leave it to you to write the equations to derive them.

Material cost, the price you pay for an item, is available from Oracle Purchasing. Oracle's average costing sets the cost to a weighted average: the total on-hand quantity multiplied by the average cost equals the amount paid for stock on hand. It uses the purchase order price, not the invoice price. You may want to use a different method, such as using the most recent price. You may want to use actual invoice prices. Or, you may want to use an outside source, such as commodity prices from the Internet.

Material overhead costs are associated with the item type, not individual instances of an item. They can include the costs to procure, ship, receive, and warehouse an item. You can compute a figure from Oracle Purchasing's records of purchases and Oracle Inventory's records of stock movements. You need your own algorithms. The cost of receiving and warehousing 100 sacks of cement, for example, depends on the time it takes and the cost of labor, neither of which quantity Oracle Inventory captures directly. Although you know it costs more to handle cement than nails, your company has to judge whether it is worth the effort to assign each item a material overhead cost or simply charge all warehouse operations to overhead.

Overhead costs represent the cost of running a materials operation. Many companies do not bother to allocate them down to the item level. They collect the costs of the purchasing, warehousing, and shipping operations in the General Ledger and set margins high enough to cover them. If you have multiple locations, some more efficient than others, it may be worth allocating the overhead to provide a truer picture of cost-of-sales.

Resource utilization is usually not a factor for purchased parts. In discrete manufacturing, Oracle Manufacturing captures resource utilization costs, including labor, by work order. Its reports show the standards and variances. You can use the work-order level data to compute new standard resource utilization.

Outside processing is also not commonly associated with purchased parts. It is captured by Oracle Purchasing on a Work in Process job when a manufacturing operation is performed by an outside contractor. The cost is associated with the item being assembled through the WIP job.

In net, unless you use average costing, you always need a formula to compute the material costs of purchased parts. To reflect the differences among items and among warehouse operations, you may want to assign material overhead and overhead costs. Manufacturing organizations use the data captured by Oracle Work in Process to compute costs for the resource and for outside processing cost elements.

Roll Up Pending Costs

The cost of an assembly is the cost of its components plus the cost of building the assembly itself. *This level* costs include the resources and outside processing that go into manufacturing the assembly, the material overhead costs of handling the completed assemblies, the overhead costs of the inventory operation, and at times a material cost for shop stock, such as cotter pins, solder, and other materials that are not carried on the bill of materials. *Prior-level* costs are the totals of the five cost elements for the component parts of the assembly. If all you care about is a component's total cost, you may have Oracle roll up all prior level cost elements into the material cost.

Oracle Cost Management's rollup process computes new costs for items flagged as "based on rollup." To roll up Pending costs, follow these steps:

1. Create Pending cost type records for the items to be rolled up in CST_ITEM_COSTS and CST_ITEM_COST_DETAILS. This step can be accomplished by using the copy feature, then updating the records through the Define Costs form. The alternative is to write scripts to update or insert the records directly. You need to set the based-on-rollup flag for the item to have Oracle perform the rollup. You define *this level* values for the five cost elements for manufactured items yourself. The rollup process itself will extend the standard cost of

resources you specify on the Bill of Materials, following the links shown in Figure 10-6.

2. Configure Inventory to calculate component costs. You usually specify Frozen as the default cost type in the Define Cost Types setup for the Pending cost type. This instructs the rollup process to use frozen costs for an item for which no pending costs have been defined. In other words, use the old costs when you don't have new ones.

3. Run the rollup process. It uses the Bill of Materials to compute the prior level costs for the assembly. A one-level rollup uses just the costs of the components on the bill, whether they are *buy* or *make*. A full rollup computes the costs of all intermediate level assemblies starting from the buy parts. In either case the rollup creates CST_ITEM_COST_DETAILS records for every cost element in use. It adds the *this level* and the *prior level* costs to get total costs by cost element, and it adds the five cost elements to get a pending item cost.

Print and Review Pending Costs

Oracle provides a costed, indented bill report that shows how the rollup cost of an item was derived. The report's detail is very useful in debugging your rollup procedures, though its size makes the report cumbersome for monitoring the whole costing process. You may want to use simple SQL*Plus scripts to analyze items with unexpectedly large differences between the old and new prices.

Update Pending Costs

The Update Standard Costs procedure is at the heart of costing. The Frozen item cost is the single figure used for valuing inventory as well as the cost of goods sold and the default cost in purchasing.

Update Standard Costs copies costs and cost elements associated with the Pending cost type to the Frozen cost type. At the same time it creates all the cost adjustment transactions needed to make the General Ledger's asset balances equal to the extended value of material on hand, in transit, and on the shop floor in WIP.

Print New Standard Costs

The last step is to distribute these new costs within your organization via standard Inventory reports.

The Costing Tables

Figure 10-7, complex as it may appear, is a highly simplified illustration of the data relationships involved in capturing and carrying manufacturing standard costs for labor and resource utilization.

The cost that is used throughout the Applications for a given item is carried in the CST_ITEM_COSTS record for frozen costs associated with that item. Other columns in that table, and CST_ITEM_COST_DETAILS, show how the cost was derived. Oracle seeds two other cost types, Average and Pending, both of which have assigned uses within the system. The rollup process will support any additional cost types your organization may add. The other tables in Figure 10-7 show where standard costs are carried and actual costs are collected in the manufacturing process.

Routings define the sequence of operations involved in making a product. Each operation may use any number of resources, among them labor, machine time, and commodity items like electricity. Which resources are used, and standard usage for them, are defined as part of the routing steps. The associated BOM_RESOURCES record gives a current cost for the resource.

Routings represent standards, or expectations, of how an item is supposed to be built and what resources it is supposed to take. In discrete manufacturing, these standards go into each job as a sort of budget. Then, over the course of manufacturing, the job records (shown in the upper-right of Figure 10-7) capture what actually happens. The Shop Floor Transactions screen captures utilization figures associated with each resource used in each step of each job to produce one inventory item. This is far more detailed than most users can afford to enter by hand; most will capture it automatically, or not at all.

Direct Jobs within Oracle Work in Process capture the cost of actually producing products. Oracle Manufacturing can set up overhead jobs to capture indirect labor and resource usage. Users can exploit the job data captured by Manufacturing to update standard resource utilization in the routings based on actual work order experience. The cost rollup process will

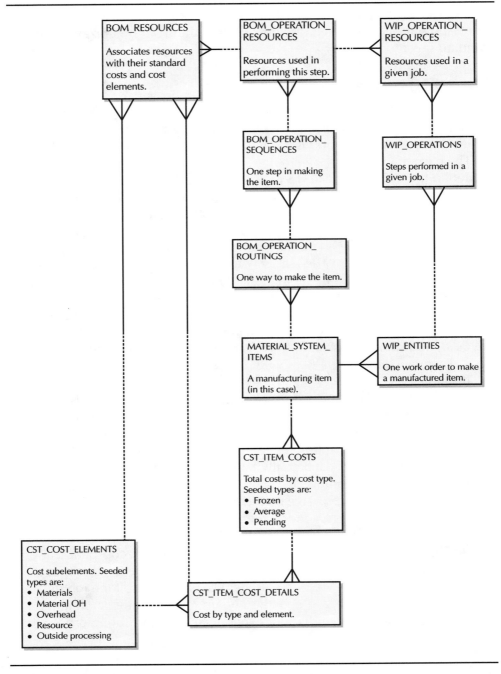

FIGURE 10-7. *Capture and application of costs in Oracle Manufacturing*

extend the standard resource utilization by resource unit costs to derive Pending values for the resource cost element and subelements.

Determining Sales Prices

Oracle Order Entry manages sales prices through the use of price lists and discounts as described in Chapter 11. The frozen standard cost is the most common basis for setting prices and the only one for which there is automated support. The mechanism favors a system that computes list prices, and uses them as the basis for creating different price lists for different customers.

Full knowledge of the cost factors involved in handling an item is essential to successful pricing. Order Entry users need to plan their pricing operations with an understanding of the power of Inventory's item cost processes. This pushes back, pyramid-style, into manufacturing. It is impossible to know the cost of an assembly without accurate costs for the subassemblies. Oracle provides a robust mechanism to compute and maintain accurate item costs; and its cost system is the most convenient basis for computing sales prices.

Project Manufacturing

Oracle Projects casts a project-and-task perspective on your business activities. Whereas accounting budgets focus on accounting periods, a project budget takes a lifetime view of the tasks that make up a project. A project budget can assess *earned value*, weighing progress made against expenses incurred. The tasks within a project may be seen as milestones, not just steps to making a product. A project view can also put profit and loss into sharper focus.

As of Release 10.7, Oracle Inventory lets you issue, receive, and track inventory quantities by project. It collects costs from Inventory for transfer to Oracle Projects. Project Manufacturing has a parallel capability to account for manufacturing expenses at a project level. Oracle Purchasing and Payables have long been able to manage project expenses. These packages combined give you the ability to maintain accurate records on the costs of prototype projects or work done for others on an outsourcing basis.

Activity-Based Costing

Activity-based costing, the second ABC acronym in Inventory, is not to be confused with the ABC analysis used to support cycle counts. Activity-based costing "assigns cost to activities based on their use of resources, and cost to cost objects based on their use of activities."[4] Activity-based costing in Oracle Inventory means using the features of all the Applications to capture the actual costs of doing business at a detailed level, taking advantage of the cost mechanisms shown in Figure 10-7 to carry granular cost data and bringing standard costs in line with actual costs as often as required.

Only a minority of users will implement activity-based costing immediately upon converting to Oracle. However, if you manage inventories of goods for sale it may be a good idea to include ABC in your long-range plans. You want to optimize your margins at the lowest possible levels, and you cannot know your margins without knowing your costs. Analysis tools such as Oracle's Business Intelligence System enable you to put ABC data to good use in support of management decisions.

Planning and Debugging Cost Transactions

The Oracle Inventory Reference Manual includes long, useful essays on average costing and standard costing. Diagrams show the debit and credit implications of many standard transactions. These diagrams are essential to your planning, but not sufficient. The diagrams do not begin to cover all cases, and the simple debit/credit T-bar diagrams apply only to the natural account segment of the Accounting Flexfield. Your setup process has to ensure that the other segments—organization, product line, and the like—are also being generated correctly.

The situation calls for a common-sense testing scenario. After the accounting department has established a Chart of Accounts structure, you should run the following type of test in one of the early development environments:

1. Establish proposed natural account values for inventory.

2. Set up test subinventories. They will need values for some or all of the following, depending on whether the installation includes manufacturing: material accounts, material overhead accounts, overhead accounts, outside processing accounts, and encumbrance account entries if you have specified encumbrance accounting.

3. Set up Automatic Account Generation (Flexbuilder prior to Release 11) to generate the flexfield combinations for material expenses in Oracle Purchasing and the Cost of Goods Sold account in Order

---

[4]Peter B. Turney, "Common Cents, the ABC Performance Breakthrough," *Cost Technology,* 1992.

Entry. These will use segments from the code combinations carried in Oracle Inventory to derive the segments used for the eventual General Ledger postings.

4. Set up one standard item of each major type in inventory. This would include consumable supplies, manufactured, resale, consignment, nonstock, and whatever other categories make sense to the business. They may equate fairly closely to your templates. Assign account values for cost_of_sales_account, encumbrance_account, expense_account, and sales_account, consistent with your setup in Step 3. Put them in the appropriate subinventories. If you are including Order Entry and Receivables in the test, you may need to set up the AutoAccounting rules that will use segments of the sales account in creating the flexfield account to which it credits orders.

5. Set up or select master item records for other transactions, such as customers and vendors.

6. Refer to the *Inventory User's Guide* to set up default accounting information through the Define Organization Parameters screen. Specify Transfer Detail to General Ledger so you will be able to tie back any implications in General Ledger of a transaction to the transaction itself for the purposes of this testing. Note that you will almost certainly want to change this setting in production.

7. Create a list of transaction scenarios to be tested. These should include entries such as:

   - Cost change
   - Inventory adjustment
   - Cycle count
   - Complete from manufacture
   - Replenishment
   - Internal orders
   - Sales order; pick-release
   - PO receipt, inspection, and release

The remaining steps of the test follow the plan set forth in Chapter 16. Once the test scenarios are laid out, you create test data for each transaction in the scenario, open a test accounting period, and run the test transactions (and only those test transactions) through the system in the chosen accounting period. You can examine the Accounting Flexfields as they appear in the MTL_MATERIAL_TRANSACTIONS table.

This catalog lists only essential steps. You need to elaborate on it, keeping in mind that thorough testing is the key to success in data processing in general, and especially in Oracle Applications. To repeat this book's central theme, the issue is not whether Oracle's code works, but whether you have made it work for you. The only way to know is to test your transaction types, using your business procedures and your setups.

Operation of Oracle Inventory

Responsibility for running the Oracle Inventory system is best vested in one individual within a company, with operations within each Inventory organization delegated to a person within that organization. Manufacturing concerns often give the responsibility to a Materials Management Group, sometimes shared with Purchasing. Distribution companies may see it as part of operations. Whoever has the task, the system usually has more indirect users, through all the other Applications that depend on Inventory, than direct users.

Responsibilities

Defining jobs and limiting system access to the requirements of individual jobs are essential parts of Inventory setup. Chapter 14 describes how Oracle Applications uses Responsibilities to control access. The Responsibilities that Oracle delivers with the package are "user-friendly," rather than "manager-friendly," in that they offer a minimum of frustration by allowing a maximum of access. You will generally want to define your own, more limited Responsibilities, along the following lines:

- The Superuser has access to every process and every organization.

- Master Item Managers can create, update, and delete items and item attributes. They usually cannot set up catalogs, categories, or templates, but they can apply them to items. Business processes need to establish policy for deleting items and changing item numbers.

- Organization Item Managers in decentralized operations have the ability to add items and change attributes at the organization level.

- The Warehouse Manager can define subinventories, set up cycle counts, and manage the adjustment process.

- Line-level warehouse staff can assign locations, move inventory, and initiate and enter cycle counts.

- A Purchasing responsibility has the ability to update Inventory Master attributes in the Purchasing Group, such as lead-time.

- An Order Entry Responsibility has the ability to update items, subject to the same limitations as Purchasing.

- Accounting or the Warehouse Manager has the authority to do the closing.

Although each attribute associated with an inventory item belongs to a certain attribute group, the Define Items form provides access to all attributes. Use the Function Security feature to restrict users' access to those attributes for which they are responsible. Use flexfield security as well if different part number ranges belong to different organizations.

Interface Manager Processing

Inventory, like all of the Applications, has online screen operations and batch reporting. It has an intermediate layer, invisible to users, of *workers* that update Inventory transaction tables after the fact. These concurrent processes, executing in the background, are a concession to efficiency. What they do is conceptually real-time, depending on the resubmission intervals you set up, but it would slow down the interactive processes if they were executed online. Instead, the online process writes the process to an interface table, and the workers take it from there. This has the added benefit of providing a natural interface into which user-written routines can insert their transactions.

The MTL_TRANSACTIONS_INTERFACE table is the major source of input for the Material Transaction Worker. It can be populated by user-written code as well as the standard Oracle online Applications. Oracle's architecture anticipates integration with custom and third party systems. The Cost Worker checks a flag in MTL_MATERIAL_TRANSACTIONS to see whether a transaction needs to be costed.

At setup time, users can choose whether the transaction worker will run periodically as a concurrent process or immediately as a concurrent process. The greater the volume, the greater the advantage in periodic concurrent processes. The downside of periodic processing is that records are not totally up-to-date. It may take a minute or two for a pick or a receipt to be reflected in the database, raising (however minimally) the chance of a stock-out or unnecessary backorder.

Use the Request Interface Managers form to start the background processes and specify how often they should run, how many can run, and how many transactions they should process at a time. It is more efficient to process a larger number at one time, but each process completes more quickly if the number is small. Whatever the number, as a concurrent process is initiated, it will spawn itself enough times to handle all the pending transactions. The workers behave like any other concurrent job, resubmitting themselves each time they complete, so there is always at least one active or pending job for each worker.

Because they work as background processes, it often takes a while to notice when the workers stop working. Inventory balances stop getting updated, or transactions stop being costed. Sometimes the workers are idle because the DBA has shut down the concurrent manager to which it is assigned. Occasionally a pending concurrent process gets put into standby status and never starts.

The interface managers update transactions with error messages if they cannot be processed. You can view transactions that are in error through the View Pending Interface Activity form. Because errors are the exception, it takes discipline to remain in the habit of checking. The most common errors are caused by periods being closed within an organization before all the transactions were completed. However, there is the potential for numerous errors to occur, as these interfaces serve many different functions.

Periodic alerts are convenient for monitoring potential error conditions. They are easy to set up and efficient to run. Many users write alerts to check for an excessive number of records or the presence of error records in the MTL_TRANSACTIONS_INTERFACE table.

Archiving and Deleting Data

The Inventory system generates transactions at a tremendous rate. The Purge Transaction History process (an online form, initiating a concurrent process) deletes all transaction data prior to the given date. The only restriction is that the date must be in a closed period. Period purges are absolutely essential to holding down processing times and disk storage requirements to acceptable levels.

Purged data is no longer available for any reporting purpose. Business needs define by policy what data, if any, must be kept for historical or audit purposes. They can likely satisfy any archiving requirements by running a concurrent process to generate detail-level transaction reports, which can then be copied from disk to a high-volume offline medium such as tape or optical disk.

Deleting item records from the master is another matter. Items are the foundation of the inventory system. INVENTORY_ITEM_ID is a foreign key that permeates the whole suite of Oracle Applications. The first step towards deleting an item is to disable it for Purchasing, Manufacturing, and whatever other system might use it. Allow time for all the transactions that reference the item to be flushed through the system. After the item is no longer likely to appear in reports, it may be useful to change the item identifier to tag the item as awaiting deletion. For example, Watkins Johnson puts a "Z_" prefix on inactive items. Finally, the item can be deleted using the Delete Item Information form.

NOTE
Assemble-to-Order manufacturing generates one custom item and Bill of Materials for each Final Assembly (FAS) work order. These one-time items are usually most in need of deletion. They are also among the easiest to identify, because their item numbers have a characteristic infix. Such items are usually associated with one sales order and one point in time.

Advantages of an Open Design

One characteristic that distinguishes Oracle Inventory is the ease with which it can be extended using custom code. Oracle Corporation takes a keen interest in such user extensions. Its consulting arm, Oracle Consulting Group, will make such enhancements on a contract basis. If there is a broad enough community of interest, Oracle will incorporate the extension into its standard product. The Oracle Applications Users Group (OAUG) maintains an Enhancements Committee that works closely with Oracle on such requests.

NOTE
See Chapter 14 for details on the Oracle Applications Users Group.

Oracle's RMA (Return Material Authorization) processing is an example. The Order Entry functions are fairly full-featured; they can get the material back, put it into inventory, and issue a replacement or a refund. The RMA process does not extend to disassembly and restocking of configured Assemble-to-Order items. Users may need to develop their own business processes and custom routines to record the fact that configured items have been stripped to their components and to receive them back into the warehouse.

Conclusion

Part of the Inventory system is global, available to users of any product that uses items. Purchasing, Payables, Order Entry, and Manufacturing need that function to define inventory items, to give them prices, and to assign them to categories and catalog groups. The part that is unique to Inventory, that you have to buy, has to do with running a warehouse. It includes subinventory and location management, warehouse counts, unit-of-measure conversions, and replenishment.

Most users need to define Inventory items earlier in the implementation cycle than they need Inventory itself. They need to look ahead to the total requirement, because some attributes cannot be changed. Inventory attribute settings and unit-of-measure logic require close attention.

Oracle Inventory includes powerful devices for helping users cope with large numbers of items and transactions. Item templates, catalogs, categories, manufacturer's part numbers, customer part numbers, and cross references all make it easier to locate items of interest and to deal with groups of items at one time.

Warehouses occupy a unique niche at the lowest level of Oracle's Multi-Org hierarchy. Inventory gives users the ability to manage activities in the areas of receiving, shipping, item cataloging, and warehouse operations at whatever level is most appropriate, from company-wide to highly local.

The cost data carried in Inventory supports Order Entry pricing. It takes all costs into account; purchase cost is only the beginning. It can also carry cost elements for resource usage, overhead, handling, and many other cost elements. Although you can sometimes capture these costs directly at the item level, they are most often captured in the General Ledger, from which they must be allocated to individual items. Since margins drive profit, this planning is fundamental to most businesses. The best time to start is at initial item conversion.

CHAPTER
11

Oracle Order Entry

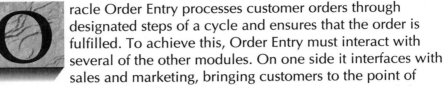

racle Order Entry processes customer orders through designated steps of a cycle and ensures that the order is fulfilled. To achieve this, Order Entry must interact with several of the other modules. On one side it interfaces with sales and marketing, bringing customers to the point of placing an order. On the other side it interfaces with Inventory, and through Inventory to Manufacturing, to fulfill orders. Release 11 adds a direct link with Purchasing to handle for drop shipments. Order Entry is closely linked with Oracle Receivables, which handles customer payment for the orders, and with Oracle Sales Compensation, Oracle Service, and Oracle Product Configurator.

The focal point of Order Entry is one very complex form, which has evolved in Release 11 into a group of related forms called the Orders Workbench. It can capture the detail needed in a multiline, multishipment order for a configured manufactured product as well as a simple requisition for pencils from the stockroom. The setups and default logic enable users to move quickly through the form while performing all the necessary checks. The *Order Entry User's Guide* states as a major design objective that "...you should be able to enter orders with a minimum of keystrokes." The entry form, despite its complexity, achieves this objective.

Requests for maintenance and service (in Oracle Service) tie in to the orders under which the items were shipped and to maintenance agreements. Return material processing has long been part of Order Entry.

Fulfillment completes the Order Entry process. It creates pick slips to instruct warehouse personnel to pull items from stock and packing slips to accompany shipments to the customer. The relational design takes into account the many conditions that can arise, such as partial shipments, warehouse denials, backorders, and consolidated shipments.

Oracle Web Customers can empower your customers to enter their own orders and check on the status of existing orders. Some customers don't need traditional salesmanship—they know exactly what product they want or are able to determine what they want from your catalog or Web page. The self-service store function of Oracle Web Customers is fast and accurate, and it saves you the cost involved in entering customer orders. Chapter 13 describes this feature in more detail.

Customer Relationships

Ongoing customer relationships are reflected in Order Entry customer and agreement records. Customer records carry address, contact, tax, credit terms, and other items of information that tend to be constant from order to order. Chapter 6 describes the concept of customer data. Customer agreements represent a set of negotiated terms for doing business with a customer; they can apply to specific products during a specific time period.

To serve the conflicting goals of productivity and completeness, a Quick Customer screen is available in addition to the detailed Enter Customer Information form. The first of these, the Quick Customer screen, captures the minimum information needed to serve a one-time customer, whereas the Enter Customer screen captures all the data needed to support a long-term relationship. They both populate the same tables.

Customer data supports both sales and marketing. The sales process involves individual transactions—accepting, shipping, and billing orders. Marketing seeks to address the broader issues of who is buying and what is being bought. Some customer data, such as SIC code,[5] order type, and customer class, is not used extensively in Order Entry reports but is very valuable in data warehouses or datamarts. You need to look at the downstream as well as the immediate uses of data as you write business procedures for setting up customers.

The ways in which customers may be related are so complex as to defy rigid classification. Instead of attempting to show hierarchies or any such scheme, the Order Entry system allows you to record that a relationship exists and whether it is reciprocal. The relationships you define may make it possible for one customer to have the terms and conditions established for another. They allow a sales order's sold-to customer, ship-to customer, and bill-to customer to all be different—a feature that is very useful in government and subcontractor sales—thus eliminating the need to duplicate addresses under multiple customers. The structure also helps Receivables apply payments; one customer may pay another customer's bills.

---

[5] *Standard Industry Classification*, a four-digit code used by the U.S. government to categorize businesses.

Agreements

Long-term agreements with your customers give both parties the benefits of a stable flow of business, predictable pricing and delivery terms, and decreased transaction costs. Order Entry does not demand agreements—it handles one-time orders quite smoothly—but using agreements makes the order entry process significantly easier for established customers. Associating an order with an agreement automatically defines the following parameters:

- The customer or customers covered by the agreement
- The price list
- The terms (when Receivables expects payment, and what prompt payment discounts apply)
- The invoice rule (when and how Receivables invoices the customer)
- The accounting rule (when Receivables is to recognize revenue)

The discounts associated with a price list may reference an agreement; an order placed under the agreement may get a more favorable discount than would apply otherwise.

Customer agreements should be part of the business plan for most companies. They are a convenient vehicle for offering preferential treatment to steady customers, decreasing your workload, and preventing errors in data entry.

Orders

Application users spend most of their time working in the Orders Workbench screens where productivity is of paramount importance. The GUI forms, which have more data per screen and can have displays customized using folders, represent a significant step forward from character-mode operations. You can enter, view, and update sales orders using the Sales Orders window. You can also adjust pricing, assign sales credits, record payment information, attach notes, schedule shipments, enter model options, query material availability, and make material reservations all in one form.

The Order Types and Order Cycles features let you tailor the process to meet your business needs. They require you to perform all the steps appropriate to an order type and avoid any unnecessary steps.

Oracle regards a customer as belonging to the whole enterprise. Policy is pretty much company-wide. For Order Entry, Multi-Org functionality is primarily a matter of convenience, cutting the clutter and the number of decisions to be made at data entry time. It defines the people and locations with which a given operating unit deals.

Order Types

Oracle Order Entry requires that every order be assigned an order type. The order type is fixed once the order is entered. The order type affects your navigation through the Sales Orders windows, and it establishes the order cycle.

Order Entry maximizes your productivity in completing the form by tailoring default field values and order cycles based on the order type you defined. Order types also provide a useful means of grouping orders for reporting. It extends to revenue reporting out of Oracle Receivables, because the order type links to an invoice (transaction) type. Order types are often grouped along major sales groups, such as federal, commercial, international, and domestic.

Holds and Approvals

Holds represent exception conditions that require human judgment. All types of holds can be applied manually. Holds can prevent a specific cycle action from occurring until the hold is released; for example, a hold can prevent pick release until all export documentation is completed. Holds can be applied automatically to all current and future orders for a particular customer, item, or site address. Credit check violations and GSA (the federal government's General Services Administration) violations are other types of automatic holds.

The Order Entry system lets you advance orders through their assigned order cycle with a minimum of work, except for the holds you build in explicitly for problem resolution and approvals. The International Brotherhood of Electrical Workers (IBEW) sells blank forms, T-shirts, hats, and other promotional items to union locals. The amounts are relatively modest, and the IBEW's relationship with the locals is long-standing. It wants orders to flow through the system unimpeded so that merchandise gets from the warehouse to its customers as quickly as possible. Micros Corporation, on the other hand, often deals with large orders from new customers. The corporation needs to confirm its ability to ship before it can accept an order, and acounting needs to approve the credit terms.

Order Entry implements credit checking through the use of credit holds. These are primarily designed for business-to-business credit operations and are intended to ensure that a new order will not put a customer's outstanding balance over the credit limit.

Approvals add further human checkpoints at various stages of the order life cycle. You may want your engineering department to review orders for equipment prototypes so it can confirm that the price and delivery can be met. You may want the purchasing department to confirm that it can satisfy an order. Some product types may need a review for export controls. You may use approval steps as integration points for custom-written or third party software that analyze orders. Approvals are built into your order cycles as prerequisites to other cycle actions. Unlike with Purchasing, there are no approval hierarchies. To implement an approval chain similar to those in Purchasing, you would need to set up multiple approval actions.

Items in Order Entry

Order Entry handles orders for tangible and nontangible goods, services, and configurable items. Whether or not the item is physically in the warehouse, anything that can be ordered is in the inventory master table. An orderable item may be a radio, a subscription, or an hour of labor. Chapter 10 covers how you set up items and their attributes that define what is orderable.

Order Entry handles transactions other than sales that provide a product to a customer. Some obvious examples are leased items, promotional materials, and demonstration and loaned items. Oracle Sales and Marketing and Web Customers, for example, can accept requests for product literature to be fulfilled through Order Entry.

Assemble-to-Order items are manufactured as needed. Either it doesn't make sense to build for Inventory, or each unit is configured to order, incorporating customer-selected options. For example, you can usually select the modem speed, hard disk size, multimedia features, and memory when you buy a PC. An orderable item is defined as one item in Inventory, with a bill of materials (BOM) describing how to build it. The bill structure includes option groups and optional items within the groups. Order Entry presents these choices on the order screen and won't book the order until the item is fully configured. At that point the customer order is linked to a Final Assembly work order to have manufacturing create what the customer ordered.

Oracle's Product Configurator expands the validation possibilities and extends configuration capabilities to untrained users over the Internet. Its indented-list presentation guides the user through the selection process. The user can click to a single-level view for a complete description of the option choices at that level.

While native Order Entry is driven by table-based rules, the Product Configurator provides APIs to let you plug in custom-written PL/SQL code. It can manage whatever level of complexity exists in your business. It can configure groups of order lines that are identified as full systems. It can even handle upgrades to configured items that are already installed. By applying its rules to the current product configuration in Oracle Service, the Product Configurator is able to determine which upgrade orders it can accept for an item.

Pick-to-Order (PTO) provides a convenient shorthand for combinations of products. Your company may sell cribs, mattresses, sheets, and mobiles to hang over the crib, each with its own part number. You may also sell these items together, as an ensemble, probably at a lower price than you'd charge when selling the same items separately. This *ensemble,* or *kit,* would have its own part number. Order Entry translates the Pick-to-Order part into its components and places a demand on Inventory for real items—the components— instead of the kit.

An Assemble-to-Order (ATO) item is a product that is custom-built out of standard components for each order. The system carries a bill of materials that defines how to make the product and how much time it will take to assemble. ATO order lines become linked to the Final Assembly (FAS) work order created to have the item built under Oracle's Work in Process system.

Both ATO and PTO items can also be Configure-to-Order (CTO). A CTO item can be customized by selecting options. When you buy a new car, for example, you may select a larger engine or a deluxe audio system. Some options may have suboptions. What speakers do you want with the audio system you've selected? Or, now that the new parents have chosen blond wood over white finish for their nursery ensemble, do they want the pink, yellow, or blue fabric trim?.

The structure of PTO and ATO products, options and all, is carried in Oracle Bill of Materials. An Inventory item with the Assemble-to-Order or Pick Components (that is, PTO) attribute will have an associated bill of materials. The bill is in the Order Entry organization, which—in a Multi-Org environment—is usually not the same as the warehouse organizations.

The bill associated with a standard (without options) PTO or ATO item identifies its components. A PTO item may include other PTO items as components, as shown in Figure 11-1. An order for the top item is recorded as an order for all the "real" items that make up the bill.

The bill for a configured item may include optional items or option groups. The exact configuration has to be defined before the order can be booked. In Figure 11-2, the bill for Option Group C will have a rule for optionally selecting Item E and Item F. Suppose the rule says that only one of the two items can be specified. The order can be booked only when the customer has specified whether or not Item D is present, and has chosen either Item E or Item F.

Suppose the customer wants Item A with optional Item E. If Item A is Pick-to-Order, this line will result in shipping Items B and E. If it is Assemble-to-Order, it will result in a manufacturing job to assemble Item A from Items B and E.

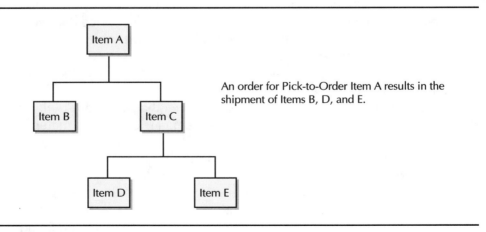

An order for Pick-to-Order Item A results in the shipment of Items B, D, and E.

FIGURE 11-1. *Bill explosion for a PTO item*

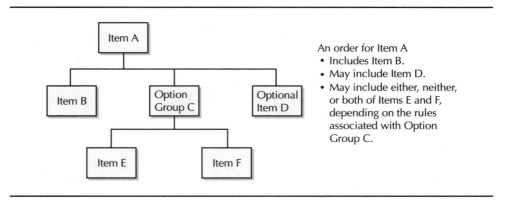

An order for Item A
- Includes Item B.
- May include Item D.
- May include either, neither, or both of Items E and F, depending on the rules associated with Option Group C.

FIGURE 11-2. *Bill explosion for a configured item*

Option groups may appear within option groups, and ATO items may appear within PTO items. The system is extremely flexible—and complex. Powerful as it is, the Bill of Materials feature alone does not have enough scope to define all option combinations or to present them in a way that an untrained user can grasp intuitively. Oracle's Product Configurator adds rule-processing logic. It can, for example, add the power requirements of boards within a computer to determine which power supply must be configured to drive the system.

An analysis of a company's Order Entry business processes needs to determine whether Order Entry is sufficient or whether Bill of Materials, Engineering, and the Product Configurator modules are needed as well. Oracle Bill of Materials defines the structures of bills and the resources required in manufacturing; Oracle Engineering manages the change in bill structure over time, reflected in engineering changes and item revisions; Oracle Product Configurator provides rule-based logic to support the selection of options in Configure-to-Order bills for both ATO and PTO.

The analysts need to look at recognized PTO and ATO operations, and also at kitting. *Kitting,* the process of assembling groups of items so they can be stored and shipped under a single part number, can often be eliminated by redefining the kits, as PTO items. Changing to PTO saves the labor of assembling the kits and frees the inventory space that would otherwise be used for fully assembled kits.

Available-to-Promise

Order Entry's Available-to-Promise (ATP) feature analyzes all transactions of a particular item in Inventory, Purchasing, and Manufacturing to answer one of the most fundamental questions of Order Entry: "When can the customer have it?" Oracle provides a lot of processing to provide the answer, and at times the logic is complex. An individual order exists as part of a stream. For resale items, the ATP logic must go upstream from items in the warehouse and open orders that are already committed to determine whether uncommitted units are available when the customer wants them.

ATP does an abbreviated Bill of Materials explosion to compute the availability of Pick-to-Order and Assemble-to-Order items. The availability of the product depends on the availability of its components. In the case of an ATO item, the time for final assembly must be factored in as well.

The ATP process follows rules that you establish as part of setup. These are similar to the forecasting rules described in Chapter 10. They define the sources that can be used to satisfy an order and order timing, such as whether an item available one week can be used to satisfy demand the next week.

Complex as it is, the ATP process operates online to provide real-time information as you accept and enter orders. Your ability to provide and honor firm commitment dates is essential to maintaining customer confidence.

Standard Value Rule Sets

Defaults on the Sales Orders window make the process go faster because less information needs to be filled in. Defaults that cannot be changed enforce your business rules. Standard Value Rule Sets are defined to provide default rules as part of your setup. Many order entry fields can be defaulted based on the first three fields entered on the Sales Orders form: Customer, Order Type, and Agreement.

A Standard Value Rule Set maps to the structure of the Sales Orders window: field within screen. For each order type, it can specify default rules for each field where defaults make sense. Your company may have different order types for each channel. Telemarketing would need to capture full shipping address data, which is information that could be defaulted for a standard order from an existing customer.

You may specify more than one source for the default value. The program searches in the order you specify until it finds a non-null entry.

You may specify in Rule 1, for instance, that the salesperson comes from the Agreement record, in Rule 2 that the salesperson comes from the Customer record, and in Rule 3 that the salesperson has a constant value of "RSmith."

If the salesperson is defined for the Agreement record, that is what Oracle will pick. Otherwise, it will take the salesperson from the Customer record, and if none is there also, RSmith will get credit. The rules control which defaulted fields can be changed. Specifically, you can indicate whether users can modify defaulted values to uphold contractual agreements.

Security rules restrict the changes allowed after an order has been entered. Oracle is generally quite flexible. Without rules to the contrary, the user might change the order type, price, or other terms. These rules, defined at setup, govern what can be changed at entry time, after booking, after the demand has been interfaced to Inventory, after an ATO item is in manufacture, and at other points that are meaningful in your order cycle. To ensure the integrity of the data, some system security rules come seeded and cannot be overridden; for example, you cannot cancel an order once it has been shipped.

Inquiries

The inquiry process provides for queries by means of almost all meaningful identifiers, including customer, customer location, order number, purchase order, ordered item, and order status. The process works for all order types: customer orders, RMAs, and internal orders.

The order inquiry form provides a single point of reference to view nearly all information associated with an order and its lines. Cycle status tells you who has the action on an order. Does it need approval? Is it on credit hold? Has it been invoiced? Has it been paid? It displays information on individual lines, indicating which are on backorder, in manufacture, on hold, and already shipped. It displays shipping information, including the date shipped, quantity, carrier, and waybill.

Shipment Scheduling

Shipment scheduling endeavors to give customers what they want, when they want it. Precise shipping dates are important: some customers will reject shipments that do not arrive close to the specified date, and others will at least note the inconvenience. Plan to use either Order Entry's ATP inquiry feature or the link from the Order Entry screen to an Available-to-Promise query screen to ensure that you can satisfy the customer's request. If you are using ATP, you usually should enable reservation logic, so you can make sure the material is available to satisfy the customer order. A reservation directs the Oracle Inventory to hold enough stock so the order can ship on time. In practical terms, it means protecting the stock if necessary by refusing it to orders that attempt to reserve that same item later, even if they could ship earlier.

Customers may specify different shipment dates for different lines on an order, or multiple shipment dates or ship-to addresses for a single line. This results in a kind of matrix. On each of several different shipment dates, the customer wants some fraction of the ordered quantity of some subset of the order lines. Use shipment schedule lines to break the order line quantity out into the quantities to ship on different dates. It is most economical in terms of shipping costs, and most satisfactory to customers, if you ship everything they want together and schedule it to arrive on the day they want it. Yet there are other scheduling options available.

One option is to ship what you have and back-order the items that are not available. It probably increases your shipping costs. From the customer's perspective, it certainly increases the costs of receiving and handling the order. A partial shipment may not even be of use to your customers if the items are related. To meet your needs and the customer's, you may specify groups of lines that must ship together. In Bills of Material, you may specify that kits and models for Pick-to-Order operations need to ship together.

Sales Credits

Order Entry's default is to assign the credit for an order or return to the primary salesperson assigned to the customer. The Enter Orders form allows you to override the default by explicitly assigning sales credit to one or more salespeople. The total sales credit within Order Entry must equal 100 percent. Oracle Sales Compensation allows you to apply more complex credit assignment algorithms by accessing your own PL/SQL modules through its APIs.

The sales credit data captured by Order Entry flows to Oracle Receivables through the AutoInvoice interface. Oracle Sales Compensation bases its commission computations on the records in Oracle Receivables. This process provides an important level of control: commission payment depends on realizing the revenue through billing or actual collection.

Notes and Attachments

You often need to exchange information with your staff and customers that is outside the formal data design of Oracle Order Entry. You can attach your customers' correspondence to you as text, images, and linked documents. You may, for example, attach a scanned image of a purchase order or attach a recording of a telephone order.

You may also enter your notes to your customers, dealers, and staff at the order and line levels. You can add free-form text to your orders, order lines, returns, and return lines. These notes are available online to provide additional information about an order. They are included on standard reports, such as the sales order acknowledgment, pick slip, pack slip, bill of lading, and commercial invoice.

Internal Orders

Internal orders originate as requisitions in Oracle Purchasing. The requisitioner does not need to distinguish between stock items, which will be satisfied from inventory via an internal order that goes through Order Entry, and items sourced externally from suppliers. The cycle for internal orders is as follows:

1. An employee (or an application) enters a requisition for a stock item.

2. The requisition goes through any necessary approvals in Purchasing.

3. The Purchasing system passes an internal sales order to Order Entry.

4. Order Entry imports internal sales orders through the Order Import process. Since the approvals have been done in Purchasing, internal sales orders move through without human intervention. They are processed at Inventory cost—there is no price list—and they are not open to changes. Order Entry creates a pick release when the item is available in the warehouse.

5. If the requisitioner is at another location, Order Entry handles packing and shipping to that site.

6. The item is delivered to the requisitioner.

Internal sales orders are invisible to the requisitioner, who theoretically should not be concerned whether the material is being shipped from a vendor or from another warehouse within your own company. Passing these orders (however quietly) through Order Entry fills several functional requirements. The orders use Order Entry's picking and shipping logic, whether items are being released across the street or across the country. Order Entry consolidates internal and external demand for the purposes of replenishment. It handles the accounting for the release from Inventory and Purchasing handles the accounting for the issue to the requisitioner.

To state this from Inventory's perspective, Purchasing handles material supply. Its logic validates requisitions from within the company. It needs to see the order so that it can decide whether the order can be handled from Inventory or must go to an outside supplier. Order Entry handles demand. It needs to see internal orders to make sure that the system orders or makes more of an item and to be sure that internal users do not consume materials that are reserved for manufacturing or customer use. Order Entry generates the warehouse release and handles shipping.

Inventory balances supply with demand to determine when the item needs to be replenished. It needs an aggregate view of all internal and external demand, and all sources of supply, to determine when to reorder.

Although it may seem unduly complex to thread through Purchasing, Order Entry, and Inventory, one should consider the processing necessary to support internal consumption and the benefits of having each piece of functionality handled by only one application.

RMAs (Return Material Authorizations)

Order Entry gets material out the door; Return Material Authorizations (RMAs) brings it back in. Customers return material for a variety of reasons: the item was shipped on consignment, it was a demo; it needs service, it is defective and needs to be replaced; the customer got too much, the wrong item shipped, and so forth. Item attributes can define whether an item is returnable.

Oracle's RMA cycle basically reverses the order cycle, getting material in the door, putting it back in stock, and issuing a credit. There is also a corresponding Return to Customer transaction for getting the needed repair or replacement back to the customer. However, you will need to create a new sales order manually if you require a packing list or want to invoice for the repair/replacement. Dividing the process into a return and a reissue simplifies processing significantly. It does, however, require some work on the user's part to retain the connection between the return and the reissue parts of a transaction.

Oracle Order Entry facilitates the link back to the original order through a Reference Source field on the return form that ties to a sales order or invoice line. Once the link is established, all the relevant information from the original order that shipped the item will be defaulted to the RMA. The Copy Orders form is also useful in RMA processing, because with the exception of the order type, an RMA is very similar to the original order. The Copy Orders form can provide the link forward by copying the RMA to the sales order that ships the repaired/replaced item back to the customer, or it can provide the link backward by copying an entire order to be returned.

Return receipts are handled by Inventory. An RMA interface step in the RMA order cycle notifies Oracle Inventory of expected returns. As returns arrive, they are processed through the Receive Customer Returns form rather than the receiving function of Purchasing. If you receive the return into your Inventory, you can retain it or ship it to your supplier. If you pass the returned item to your supplier, you should notify the buyer and authorize the return by generating an RMA between your company and your supplier. The related Inspect Customer Returns form comes into play when returns are conditional based on the state of the returned goods.

You may have to interface Order Entry's RMA process with custom-written or third party software to handle back-end processing. Configured items are, by definition, Assemble-to-Order. Your company will have its own undoubtedly unique rules for deciding the extent to which you want to disassemble configured returns and put the parts back in stock instead of putting the configured item into inventory. Rules you establish for granting credit upon the return of individual components of a Pick-to-Order item will certainly be unique; some components may not even carry sale prices.

Your setup and testing have to ensure that RMA items are not treated as regular inventory. After defining your RMA business process for configured items, test and verify that Manufacturing does not see these units as demand and attempt to rebuild them. Also, you need to separate RMA items from regular finished goods by assigning them to a separate subinventory, for example, *REPAIR,* to hold them until they are certified for reissue.

Oracle Service provides post-sales support for the products sold through Order Entry. Service picks up product details such as the serial number and warranty when it ships. Order Entry sometimes has a role as service is delivered. It handles orders for maintenance agreements and per-call orders for customers without agreements. It forwards invoicing information to Oracle Receivables. Customer returns for depot maintenance (that is factory repairs) are handled by the RMA process.

RMA activity generates credits and charges to be passed through to Receivables. You have to define business processes to deal with shipping charges (both ways) and parts and service charges for maintenance.

Oracle Web Customers

Oracle's Self-Service Web Applications enhance Order Entry rather than replacing it. Web Customers feeds orders to Order Entry through the standard open Customer and Order Import interfaces. The order cycles you define for Web orders will probably hasten them through the system with minimal holds or approvals, offering maximum productivity and responsiveness. See Chapter 13 for a more complete description of the Self-Service Web Applications.

Report Output

Several of the Order Entry documents will form an integral part of your business, whether they are internal (used by warehouse personnel) or external (viewed by your customers). These include the Pick Slip, Pack Slip, Mailing/Shipping Labels, and Sales Order Acknowledgments. While Oracle does provide these documents as standard components of the software, it is likely that you will need to customize them to meet your needs. At a minimum, they need to bear your company name and logo and present information in as clear and concise a manner as possible. They should highlight the important data and eliminate fields on the standard Oracle documents that are irrelevant in your business. Often data segments you capture on Descriptive Flexfields will be used in warehouse or customer documents. You should design your external documents early in the process so they can be developed and fully tested for your conference room pilot.

You may want to change the means by which you deliver the documents, using e-mail or fax, for instance, to send order or shipment confirmations. You may also want to alter the process by which the output is produced and expand on the Picking and Shipping Document Set, which allows you to automatically print reports at the appropriate time. Chapter 15 describes the steps you take to do so.

Electronic data interchange (EDI) is now supported in Order Entry. EDI is a powerful tool for accepting orders and order modifications, and for sending order confirmations and shipment notifications. It is not uncommon to need custom scripts to filter incoming and outgoing transmissions.

The Order Cycle

You associate an order cycle with each order type. The order cycle defines stages that orders and order lines can go through, and what actions are allowed at each stage. Oracle Order Entry predefines all the steps most businesses need, from Booking through Demand, Picking, Ship Confirm, Inventory, and Receivables interfaces and closing the order. Its open design leaves room for you to add extra stages, unique to your business, while taking advantage of all the processing associated with the predefined steps.

Not all actions apply to all orders. An order cycle defines the actions appropriate to a given type of order. To offer some examples from the computer business:

- An order for freeware that has been downloaded already requires entry and billing, but does not require approval or shipment.

- An order for a free upgrade requires order entry, booking, approval, and shipment, but does not require invoicing.

- A drop-ship order has a Purchase Release action in place of the warehouse actions of Pick Release, Ship Confirm, and Inventory Interface.

- A phone order for hotline support service requires booking and invoicing, but not approval or shipment.

- An internal order that will ship from one location within your company to another does not require Receivables Interface.

At each point in the order cycle there is a predefined next step if all goes well, and one or more alternatives in the case of exceptions. The order cycle may ensure that an order is booked before being invoiced, or approved before being shipped. You can set up an order cycle that specifies that the only possible outcomes of an approval step are Pass or Fail, and that a Pass is required before the order can be booked. Order cycles are composed of distinct cycle actions. A cycle action indicates a processing step such as entering the order, reviewing the order for legal approval, or pick-releasing the order. Cycle actions produce specific results; for example, the action of entering the order can result in the order being partially entered or being booked. An order cycle is created by linking cycle actions together in a sequence. The results of a cycle action determine when an order should proceed to the next cycle action in the order cycle.

You can define as many order cycles as you need to match your business processes. You can insert approval steps for lines or orders that represent processes handled within Order Entry or outside the system. Once a customer has requested a sale, orders are available immediately, even if they remain unapproved in the order cycle for a short period. By taking unapproved orders into account you can get a more realistic demand forecast earlier on in the cycle.

The design for order cycles support is highly generalized. Different order types have different cycles, some of which may include approval processes. These are set up through Action/Result combinations. The cycle defines an action and possible outcomes. Those results may lead to further actions or to cancellation of the order or line. Typical question pairs have to do with legal review (can we export this?) and manufacturing (do we have the capacity to handle it?). Standard reports show where orders are in the cycle. You can use the reports, or better, implement your own alerts to make sure that orders do not get stuck in the pipeline.

Many companies add a user-defined credit approval step to certain order cycles instead of using Oracle's credit hold mechanism. Credit holds are designed to work on an exception basis. If your business processes define every order of a given type as an exception, it becomes easier to define a new cycle step, and then use the order cycle step approval process rather than the hold release process to move an order through the system.

You may use additional actions and results to support your own business processes. Oracle's own processes use less than a third of the thirty actions that have been defined for order headers, and it uses only half of the thirty available for order lines.

Delivery-Based Shipping

Your objective in shipping is to achieve the optimal balance between customer satisfaction and your own financial objectives. Delivery and departure planning gives you the tools to minimize shipping costs and maximize profit as you meet your commitments.

A *delivery* is one shipment to a customer. It may represent any number of order lines across several different orders, or partial deliveries against some lines. A delivery involves one waybill and one carrier. You may associate a shipment priority with a delivery, because you are committed either to use a given class of delivery service or to meet a promised delivery date.

Imagine a delivery van as a departure. It may include deliveries to any number of destinations. You may have to consider the following factors in planning a departure:

- Honoring delivery date commitments to customers

- Using as much as possible of the delivery vehicle's capacity, which is usually measured by weight and *cube* (volume, measured in cubic feet or meters)

- Loading the vehicle in the reverse order of deliveries, so the first order to be delivered will be closest to the door

The factors will be different, but similarly complex, for departures by freight forwarder, rail, air, ship, and other modes of transportation. Oracle provides information about the customer, delivery commitment, and the material. Oracle Order Entry uses the results of your manual or automated process for defining deliveries to create pick slips in the most useful way possible.

Pick Release

Warehouse pick slips are generated through a batch process. Pick Release matches open order lines that are within the date window to be shipped against available inventory, instructing the warehouse to prepare for a shipment. An exception is produced if Pick Release fails to pick an item because it was not available. Among the things that determine whether inventory is available are whether it has been reserved against this order or any other order, and whether it is in an appropriate subinventory to satisfy customer orders.

You set rules to have the pick-release process support your shipping and financial objectives. Releases can be sequenced by order, schedule, or delivery date, or they may be sequenced by shipment priority. You can also have them ordered by outstanding invoice value, if your objective is to drive money in as quickly as possible.

Pick slip grouping rules minimize the work involved in assembling shipments. You can group pick slips by subinventory, so you can pick up all the material from one area of the warehouse in one pass. Alternatively, you can group pick slips by destination, order, customer, ship to, carrier, departure, delivery, or priority. The rules mechanism is powerful enough to combine these factors.

Shipping is an expensive, labor-intensive operation. There are likely to be inefficiencies in your present process because you don't have the information at hand to improve it. Make sure you examine your business processes as you convert to take full advantage of this extensive functionality.

Ship Confirm

Ship Confirm informs Order Entry of what was actually shipped and instructs Inventory to decrement its balances accordingly and to count items that could not ship because they were not available.

The confirmation process captures the data you need to track and pay for the shipment, including waybill, container, and carrier. It can also accept efficiency statistics, such as the percentage of the container or vehicle actually used for the shipment, and give warnings if the shipment is over or under the pre-established capacities.

When you close a pick slip, the Ship Confirm form automatically initiates a concurrent job to print the shipping documents you have specified through your setup, such as packing lists and mailing labels. The shipping documents represent what is actually shipped, not what was ordered (any difference between the two owing to the item's unavailability).

Customers use the packing slip in their receiving operations to compare what they receive against what they ordered. This is especially important in the case of Pick-to-Order lines, which expand through the bills of material into several different lines on the shipment documents. Keep customs requirements in mind when you design packing slips for international use. The inspectors need to be able to physically match what they find in the container against the packing slip, regardless of the way in which the customer ordered the items.

Your business procedures have to deal with the fact that confirming a shipment is final. You need a high level of confidence in the manual process that confirms the materials picked for shipment, because you cannot undo or correct a shipment once it has been closed. The best recourse, using RMA for returning items marked as picked that actually were not, is rather cumbersome.

The online Ship Confirm records an outgoing shipment. The Update Shipping Information process, running in batch mode, updates orders to reflect shipments and to back order items that did not ship. Another batch process, the Inventory interface, writes records to the Material Transactions Interface table. The Inventory Transaction Worker process finds them there, edits and imports them, and updates inventory balances accordingly.

Backorders

Backorders can be entered at ship confirm time. If the warehouse can not satisfy the entire amount on the pick slip, it may elect to ship what is available and back-order the rest. Whether to do so is a matter of setups and business procedures. Back-ordered items can be released by the standard batch pick-release process, under the control of runtime parameters at a later time when the product does become available.

Drop Shipment

Drop shipment allows you to reconsider the role of your warehouse in the supply chain and, possibly, bypass it by shipping directly from your suppliers to your customers. Sometimes the advantages of having material in your own warehouse are not worth the maintenance costs. A warehouse operation does provide the following benefits:

- You can quickly satisfy customer orders for a variety of goods from different suppliers in one shipment.

- You can control quality by inspecting items before shipment.

- You can handle customs, tariffs, and taxes at a wholesale level.

At times a warehouse is essential, particularly if you need to provide storage for materials you manufacture. On the other hand, having your warehouse handle goods en route from your supplier to your customer can add considerable expense, such as:

- Occupancy costs for the warehouse itself.

- Labor in receiving, storing, and shipping goods.

- Inventory carrying costs, shrinkage, and obsolescence.

- Additional time to satisfy a customer order, as the merchandise passes from your supplier through you to the customer.

- Inability to receive and forward nonstock items, which may limit what you can sell.

Drop shipment is an attractive alternative when the costs of warehousing outweigh the benefits. You can even mix warehouse and drop shipments to satisfy a single customer order, drilling down to the point of splitting a single order line.

This new functionality available in Release 11 provides a direct automated link between your suppliers and customers. The drop shipment model is useful for intangibles and for brokered and consignment arrangements. Your organization may deliver service to your customers through an agreement with a third party. You convert the customer's order into a purchase order to the third party, and then invoice your customer upon your receipt of the bill from the third party.

Oracle Order Entry lets you specify by order type whether an order can (or must) be for drop-ship items. It converts a drop-ship line into a purchase requisition, which it forwards to Oracle Purchasing through the open interface. The requisition carries the customer information needed to satisfy the order.

The full mechanics of Oracle Purchasing are available to satisfy drop-ship orders. To minimize the time and labor involved in purchasing, set up blanket purchase orders and autosourcing so the requisition is converted automatically into a PO release to a supplier.

Drop shipment depends on the supplier and customer for correct shipping and receiving information. The most automated approach is to have the supplier send an Advance Shipment Notice (ASN) with information about the carrier and expected delivery date via EDI. The ASN may trigger an invoice. However, your business processes may make do with the supplier invoice or telephone calls from the supplier or customer. Make sure you record any information you need for customer service, such as the serial number(s) and warranty.

The drop-shipment business process must address any exceptions. What happens when the shipment is over or under, or when the customer wants to return it? Chances are you don't want it coming back to your warehouse. Spell out the details in advance with the supplier and the customer.

Pricing

Pricing is a complex art. Oracle Order Entry gives you the tools to price goods and services with precision to meet your corporate objectives. The price a customer pays for an item is a factor of the applicable list price and discount. Table 11-1 shows the computations and logic that take place at setup time and as an order is entered.

Price List Setup Tasks	Order Entry Tasks
Set the item price on a price list; base the price on the item cost, obtained from Inventory, and a percentage or absolute monetary adjustment to the price list.	Choose the applicable price list for an order and then find the list price for the item or the secondary price list it designates.
Set up pricing rules for computing the list price of items with variable pricing, such as software licenses.	Accept any variables (such as number of seats and CPU size) that, in addition to quantity and units of measure, are applied by the pricing rules to identify the list price.
Set up automatic discounts as percentages, absolute monetary adjustments, or fixed prices.	Identify the best available discount.

TABLE 11-1.   *Timing of Price Development and Application*

Applying Prices

Order Entry determines the price list and discount schedule at an order level. Upon entry of an order, the price list will be defaulted from the Order Type, Customer, Invoice to, Ship to, or Agreement level. Depending on the setup, the specialist may override the price list for the order. In any case, one price list applies to the whole order. Prices on the price list can also be overridden by order line.

A specific price list may not cover every item offered for sale. Each price list specifies an associated secondary price list. Unless there are items that cannot be sold to some customers, this backup should have a price for every item. In general, the primary price list covers the items a given customer or set of customers is expected to buy, usually offering favorable prices. The secondary list includes the entire product line, but carries the item at higher prices. Order Entry uses secondary prices only for items that are not on the primary price list.

Discounts

Discounts are structured to apply to individual price lists rather than across the board and serve as a mechanism to reduce the selling price. You may effectively discount an order by specifying that the discount for one line is spread across multiple order lines for revenue purposes. This level of control protects you from booking unprofitable business. Several discounts may be associated with one price list. They can be made applicable to specified customers, agreements, items, order types, purchase orders, or pricing attributes (see the upcoming section on, *pricing rules*). Release 11 adds item categories and customer class to the discount drivers.

Discounts may be automatic, in which case they are applied immediately, or they may be applied only when the clerk specifies the discount. If more than one automatic discount is valid for an order line, the Sales Orders window logic locates the most favorable one.

Discounts at the order level are distributed across lines. This must be so since, due to the flexibility inherent in the system, all lines on an order do not pass through the system as a group. The sequence of events is as follows:

1. An order is priced in Order Entry, using the appropriate combination of price lists and discounts.

2. Each order line is passed to Oracle Receivables via the AutoInvoice Open Interface as it is ready to be recognized as revenue, then invoiced and collected. The fact that some lines are backordered, canceled, or scheduled for future shipment does not affect the invoicing of lines that have been shipped.

3. Oracle Receivables composes an invoice from the lines that have been passed from Order Entry. An invoice can include lines from multiple orders.

The effect of this is that Order Entry spreads order-level discounts down to the lines on the order.

You will often include implicit discounts when pricing Pick-to-Order items. The price of a complete set of chinaware will be less than the combined prices of the plates, cups, and serving dishes when sold separately. Careful consideration should be given to your return policy when this is the case. Customers should usually be able to return any part of the order for a replacement, but you do not want to allow them to return individual components of the PTO item for credit at the list price.

The functions provided by Oracle in the price list and line-by-line discounting structure are powerful enough to help you achieve almost any pricing objective. However, they may not accommodate the way your firm has handled discounting in legacy systems. This area warrants thorough analysis; it may mean changing your current business process.

Discounts can be set up either as absolute amounts or as percentages. A volume discount can specify a schedule of discount amounts or percentages based on unit or currency volume.

You can easily propagate a discount from one price list to another by copying it, then changing the price list name. The Copy function drags the customer, item, agreement, and other data associated with the discount to the new schedule, at which point you modify it as required.

Price List Elements

A price list is made up of item numbers and prices associated with them. Price lists are a feature of Order Entry and are not directly recognized in the other modules.

Price list lines carry the following elements:

- Item.

- Unit price. Service items may be priced as a monetary value, like a new car warranty, or as a percentage of the item being serviced, as is typically done for licensed software.

- Selling unit of measure.

- A pricing rule and pricing attributes, if the list price varies depending on usage factors.

Except for service items, price lists carry monetary values, not percentage figures. The formulas that update them may be expressed in terms of percentages, but a price on a list is fixed. The only computation at order time is discounting.

TIP
Inventory and other modules have the capability to capture costs in enough detail that costs can be allocated down to the item level with a good degree of confidence. Inventory can carry all the components of item cost at the item level. You can improve control of your margins by having your business procedures use Inventory costs as a major determinant of Order Entry prices.

Pricing Rules

The list price for items for which volume or usage is an issue, such as software licenses or communications services, may be expressed as a formula to avoid having to make a separate price list entry for each combination of factors. The single formula ensures that prices for the many saleable items it represents are derived uniformly.

Pricing rules can involve any number of factors and any combination of arithmetic operators. One restriction is that the values used by the formula must be entered through a Descriptive Flexfield (DFF). DFFs have limited capability for table lookup (one DFF segment can reference a previously entered segment in an SQL statement), but in most cases the formula will work when the values are entered directly by the operator.

Effective Dates

Price lists can be made effective for a restricted period of time, and price list lines on a price list can likewise have an effective date range. The date ranges cannot overlap; only one price is effective at a time. Oracle will only use currently valid prices.

Oracle Order Entry's mass update feature does not set effective dates. A mass update applies to the prices currently in effect, overwriting the previous values. Past and future prices are unaffected.

Maintaining Price Lists

Once it has been determined which group or individual within your organization will maintain the price lists, it is important to establish an approach to retain consistent data. A common set of steps for maintaining price lists follows:

1. Create categories in Oracle Inventory to group items for the purposes of creating cost lists. Oracle categories are very flexible. They do not have to be mutually exclusive, nor must every item be assigned to a category.

2. Choose an Inventory organization to serve as the basis for pricing. In Oracle's Multi-Org scheme, there may be many inventory organizations, each with different costs, within the scope of one Order Entry organization.

3. Use Order Entry's Add Inventory Items form to create a base price list carrying all items at cost for the current period. You might name it *COST_JUN_99*. This list will serve as the basis for other price computations, perhaps also as the price list for internal orders. Because there is no way to add items to or delete items from a price list en masse, you need to create one base price list corresponding to each price list you will eventually offer to customers.

4. Use the Copy Price List function to create target price lists.

5. Update the target price lists with the desired markups, by category and item range.

6. Manually update Customer, Agreement, and Order Type records to point to the new price lists.

TIP
Compute standard prices as a function of cost and markup. It helps to have a relatively uniform markup, since other price lists and discounts will typically be set as percentages of the standard list cost. Uneven markups could result in setting sales prices below cost.

Item Groups

Item groups are predefined sets of items, with list prices, that can be added easily to a price list. They are a convenient way to add new items to price lists. First, put the items into a group, and then add that group to every affected price list, adjusting by an appropriate percentage as you go. Groups are not an appropriate vehicle for managing large numbers of items, because items in a group must be added and deleted individually.

Price List Arithmetic

Price lists are easy to use if you want to key in the items and prices individually. But Order Entry's power is in productivity—it gives you the ability to work with groups of item prices at one time. Prices will be easier to administer and more consistent if you align your business processes with Oracle's price list administration mechanisms. Consider the following factors in setting up your business procedures.

■ **Starting point** The only external basis for price generation within Oracle is the Inventory Frozen Standard item cost. Any other point of departure, such as commodity market quotes, requires a custom script to load the price tables.

■ **Pricing adjustments** Adjustments do not create new price list lines; they update existing ones. The new price (for a range of items) can be expressed as a percentage or absolute monetary adjustment to the old price.

- **Ranges of items** You use Item Identifier ranges and categories to specify the items affected by an update.

- **Copy, not merge** You can copy all or part of a price list to create a new one. However, price lists cannot be merged.

It is prudent to return frequently to the baseline, actual costs, instead of allowing successive updates to bring you to the point where the relationship between the markups and the underlying costs is no longer clear. Oracle has recognized the impossibility of anticipating every user's pricing needs. Its table structure, as described in the following section, is very accessible to programmers.

Using Scripts to Maintain Price Lists

Oracle's design makes it easy to use custom scripts to update price lists. Whereas scripts take better advantage of effective dates, the Update Price Lists form affects only the current price. An SQL routine can use start and end dates to set future prices. Using effective dates means that you do not need to change the price list references in Customer, Agreement, and Order Type records.

Another advantage of a custom script to update price lists is that you can refer to any pricing baseline. You can compute prices based on commodity pricing schedules, dealer price lists, competitors' prices, or any other such basis. You can use the five cost elements and infinitely granular cost subelements carried for each item in Oracle Inventory. A price can be updated on the basis of underlying pricing factors—cost and margins—rather than simply the frozen item cost.

It can be a lot of work to set up discount schedules for individual items. In many cases it is useful to apply decision logic. For example, instead of specifying a 10-percent, across-the-board discount on small appliances to a group of customers for the month of February, you may want to compute the actual discounted prices to be the higher of (a) 10 percent off, (b) the GSA price, or (c) cost plus a 20-percent margin. You could compute these figures in a spreadsheet and enter them manually, but if you go through this kind of operation often, it would make sense to put the code into a concurrent process written in SQL. As described here, the price list would reflect the discounted prices, so no additional discounts would be needed.

Scripts can write directly to the SO_PRICE_LIST_LINES table. They should ensure that only one price is valid at any point in time. If there is more than one price for a given item and price list, the ending effective date for one price should exactly equal the beginning effective date for the next price. Use TRUNC(SYSDATE) to store only the day, month, and year, leaving hours, minutes, and seconds off the date. The best practice is to save the truncated date in memory so that every row you update gets exactly the same value, even if your process runs over midnight.

GSA Pricing

The federal government's General Services Administration negotiates government-wide contracts annually with its major suppliers. The GSA sets a price list for the year, which contractors usually publish in book format and distribute to all potential customers within the government. One of the conditions the government imposes is that the vendor may not offer more favorable prices to any other customer.

Order Entry enforces this rule by comparing the discounted price on an order line against the GSA price. Order Entry will prevent the order or, depending on the setup parameters, at least issue a warning to the effect that the GSA terms are being violated. GSA prices serve as a floor.

Companies with customers who are eligible for GSA prices allow these customers to order from the GSA price list. Even companies that do not do business with the federal government may want to put GSA pricing in effect to warn of sales being made with substandard margins.

Multicurrency Pricing

You can carry price lists in as many currencies as necessary. You can handle currency conversion and rounding as you establish the list—offering your customers abroad price stability—or you can do spot conversions to set the foreign currency amount at invoice time. Oracle Receivables has the complementary logic to account for multiple currencies, such as variance accounts for gain and loss on exchange.

Accounting

Order Entry is not a financial application; that is, it has no direct interface with General Ledger. It passes records of its revenue-generating activity with customers and items to Oracle Receivables via the Receivables Interface and

AutoInvoice open interfaces. Receivables is the eventual source of the revenue accounting logic that creates ledger journal entries. Receivables uses the Account Generator (AutoAccounting prior to Release 11) to determine the appropriate flexfield values for the revenue transaction. (See Chapter 2 for a discussion of the Account Generator and the modules it replaces, AutoAccounting and Flexbuilder.)

Revenue comes at a cost. Order Entry uses the Account Generator (formerly Flexbuilder) to create an Accounting Flexfield for the Cost of Goods Sold (COGS) Account. It passes the COGS Account via the Inventory interface program. Inventory uses the information to create a GL journal to debit the Inventory Asset Account and credit the COGS Account.

Users define income reports using the General Ledger's Financial Statement Generator by subtracting COGS and other expenses from income. Most companies measure income by business unit, so it is important to have the Account Generator assign Accounting Flexfields in such a way that they can be easily compared. The item attributes for Sales Account, Expense Account, and Cost of Goods Sold Account are major inputs in determining the Accounting Flexfield associated with a transaction. To measure income accurately, expenses should be placed against cost, department-by-department and product line-by-product line, so that comparisons make sense across the organization.

The same logic used by the Account Generator is used to credit the appropriate organizations and locations with revenue through Oracle Receivables. It is critical to profit and loss computation that expense systems use parallel logic. Cost accounting FSG reports lose their value as a management tool if one region receives credit for a sale but another is charged with the expense of servicing it.

Oracle provides considerable flexibility to define and control the interface process through various setup options. Since the interface is open, it is fairly easy to customize by updating the data in the open interface tables between the Receivables interface and AutoInvoice steps.

The same elements of information are generally available to the Account Generator for revenue and cost of goods sold. These include the customer, salesperson, item, order type, and many others. You should ensure that the rules for generating all except the natural account and subaccount are consistent. The account values will naturally reflect revenue on one side and expense on the other.

In terms of timing, the order cycle establishes the point at which an order is sent to Receivables for invoicing and revenue recognition. The accounting rule passed from Order Entry establishes when to accrue revenue and post it to the ledger. In computing income, the financial reports may have to recognize that there is a timing difference between expense and the associated revenue. This is a major issue in companies with small numbers of large orders, and such institutions as universities in which revenue (tuitions) may precede expenses (faculty salaries). Use General Ledger accruals as necessary to put revenues and offsetting expenses in the same period.

Integration with Other Modules

Order Entry communicates with other systems by sharing master data and exchanging transaction data through open interfaces. Figure 11-3 shows the most commonly shared master tables, and Figure 11-4 shows the major transaction interfaces.

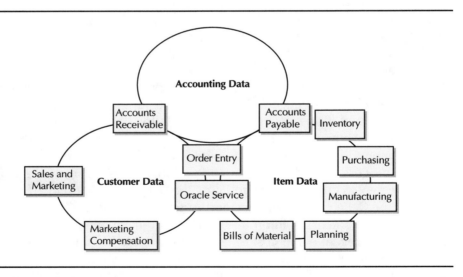

FIGURE 11-3.   *Shared master data in Order Entry*

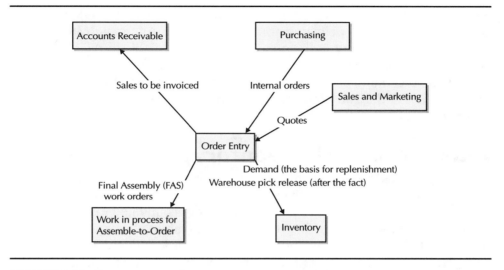

FIGURE 11-4. *Major Order Entry transaction interfaces*

Integration with Receivables

Oracle Receivables shares customers with Order Entry, Sales and Marketing, Sales Compensation, and Service. The Applications share the function of maintaining these master tables. Order Entry has the capability to import data to set up customers, a plus when integrating Oracle with third party systems that manage presales and sales activity. It is common to allow users to enter and maintain customer data through Order Entry responsibilities, since customer data plays a major role in determining the order defaults. Even if you do not have Oracle Receivables installed, Order Entry will require use of its base tables.

Order Entry passes Receivables the information it needs to bill the customer and collect. In a reverse process, it passes RMA information so customers can be credited for returns. This interface to Receivables is one-way. Adjustments to the invoice do not find their way back to Order Entry. They flow to the ledger through adjustment accounts defined in

Receivables. Order Entry will never find out if a Receivables clerk gives the customer a credit for a defective or missing product. A formal RMA, which originates in Order Entry, is the only mechanism available to register an adjustment in Order Entry. Receivables, because it deals with money actually invoiced and collected, is the authoritative source for completed sales activity. Order Entry reports are the source for reports on future revenue from open sales orders.

Integration with Inventory

Inventory defines the stock items and their related costs that Order Entry has available to sell. When order lines are demanded and reserved through the order screen and Pick Release process, Inventory is updated to reflect the item's availability (effecting the MTL_DEMAND table). Once an order has been Ship Confirmed and Inventory Interfaced, Order Entry will write to the MTL_TRANSACTIONS_INTERFACE table, thereby allowing Inventory to decrement its on-hand quantities. Order Entry can also take significant advantage of the categories defined in Inventory to ease data entry and reporting requirements.

You may be able to achieve a smoother workflow by using bar code scanners in the pick confirm process. The Ship Confirm Open Interface offers a batch-mode alternative to the Confirm Shipments window.

Integration with Purchasing

Order Entry links with Purchasing for internal orders and drop shipments. A requisition for internally sourced items will create an order through the Order Import open interface, then be processed through the full Order Entry cycle. The Purchasing locations are translated into shipping and receiving warehouses. Requisition information is viewable in the Order Inquiry screens in these situations.

Integration with Sales and Marketing

Sales and marketing manages presale contacts with customers. A sales analyst incorporates transaction-based data into management information. Sales compensation allots sales credits to marketing personnel.

Conversion Issues

In a phased implementation, the Customer and Inventory master tables that Order Entry needs may have been put in place already for Receivables, Purchasing, and Inventory. It is up to the architects of those conversions to ensure that the attributes that Order Entry needs have been loaded properly into the shared tables. Refer to Chapter 10 for conversion issues related to the item master and catalogs.

To minimize your work, plan for Order Entry as you implement the earlier systems. It can be difficult, for instance, to convert items to Pick-to-Order if they are being transacted already as prepackaged kits. Resetting the Order Entry attributes on established items can be time consuming. It takes extra effort to compose a full implementation plan at the outset, but ultimately it saves a lot of time.

Order Import

Order Import greatly simplifies the conversion of orders by loadng them into the five major Order Entry tables that hold them. The open interface is as complex as the relationships among those five tables, and it can accommodate a wide variety of data conditions, although it does not support all of the function that are available when data is entered through the screens. However, few organizations really need all of the features available in Order Import. Oracle Consulting, or another group with conversion experience, can often streamline an implementation by adapting conversion scripts that they originally developed for other customers.

You will need a strategy for handling conversion of incomplete orders. Good as it is, the open interface may have difficulty in dealing with backorder situations or partially filled orders. It raises questions of invoicing: What has the legacy system passed to Receivables, and what should Oracle do? It is best to eliminate as much complexity as possible before the conversion. An optimal strategy may involve the following steps:

- At some date just prior to conversion, complete booking and order-confirmation activity on in-process orders, and hold off entering new orders until after conversion. This will put all orders to be converted into booked status.

- Complete all open warehouse activity in the legacy system: picking, shipping, and ship confirmation.

- Use the legacy system to invoice for completed activity.

- Use an automated process to convert booked, and approved orders for which there has been no shipping activity. These are the majority of the orders, the easy ones. Load them through the open interface. If the volume is enough, it may be sufficient simply to rekey every open order. The issues are labor and the time the operation can afford to be down for conversion.

- List the exceptions for manual entry into Oracle. These will include partially shipped orders and held orders. Implement a manual procedure to deal with invoicing and cash application for orders that are satisfied under both legacy and Oracle.

Responsibilities

Order Entry is a large product covering functions that usually fall within several different departments. Most commonly the responsibilities are divided as follows:

- Order entry is usually a department of its own, working closely with the sales department to enter and correct customer sales.

- The order entry department enters price lists, discounts, and prices, with input from many departments throughout the company.

- Credit checking and approval is a financial function, often found in the accounts receivable department.

- The item managers in the inventory department usually add new sales items and establish bills of materials for PTO and ATO items.

- Fulfillment is usually a warehouse function.

All constituencies should be represented among the Superusers who compile the Order Entry setup. The department heads of each area need to define the different responsibilities within their areas.

Conclusion

Productivity, flexibility, accuracy, and control are the major issues in Order Entry. Oracle's product satisfies them well. Its integrated links through Inventory to Purchasing and Manufacturing ensure optimal availability of goods to satisfy customer demand. Its close relationship with Receivables means that customer invoices will be timely and accurate and that each sale will be accounted correctly for the purposes of sales compensation and the ledger.

Order types and order cycles give Order Entry the power to address virtually any type of order, while defaults minimize the number of keystrokes required during data entry. The hold mechanism and the approval steps you build into the order cycle ensure that orders that need special attention receive it, while routine orders move swiftly through the system.

Pick-to-Order, Configure-to-Order, and catalog functions make it easier for customers to decide what they need. They can make their choices on the basis of descriptions meaningful to them, not just your internal part numbers. They don't have to concern themselves with the details of what components you require to satisfy their needs.

The pricing and discounting tools are designed to leverage the cost data captured in Payables and Manufacturing and carried in Inventory. With Order Entry you can easily implement strategies to meet your competitive and margin objectives.

Order Entry is a customer-oriented system, and Oracle is using the Internet to bring it closer to the customer. Web Customers gives them the ability to enter orders and inquire about order status. You can use the Web to offer your customers the access and flexibility they need, while you retain the levels of control and confidentiality essential to your business.

CHAPTER
12

Using Multiple Currencies

oday, many companies are operating and competing in the global marketplace. For example, a company may have its manufacturing plant in Mexico and pay its employees there in pesos, but it may purchase parts from its parent headquarters in Germany using deutsche marks. In addition, the company may sell to customers located in the United States, thus receiving income in U.S. dollars. The presence of these multiple currencies creates an added level of complexity for companies trying to maintain accounting records and manage accounting information systems, especially when performing consolidations. When companies operate in such environments, terms such as *revaluation, conversion,* and *translation* become commonplace.

Oracle Financials offers a complete multicurrency solution to help companies that routinely operate on a global level. Oracle General Ledger and other Oracle Financials subledgers allow you to define unlimited currency types with varying exchange rates, enter foreign currency transactions, and report on foreign currency balances at the subsidiary level as well as the consolidated level.

Multicurrency Accounting

Multicurrency accounting has been developed as a way of dealing with business activities denominated in different currencies. The following situations require companies to restate the value of foreign currencies:

- Entering foreign currency transactions.

- Consolidating foreign currency balances from foreign subsidiaries.

- Operating in countries with unstable currencies.

- Operating in European countries that are members of the European Monetary Union (EMU), requiring them to adopt the single currency, the euro.

Oracle General Ledger allows you to define as many different currency types and exchange rates as you need. Oracle Financials includes specific features to accommodate European countries' currency needs, such as non-ISO (International Standards Organization) currencies and the new euro currency.

Foreign Currency Transactions

A transaction that requires settlement in a foreign currency is called a *foreign currency transaction.* The most common of these involve the importing and exporting of goods and services, with the payable and receivable amounts denominated in foreign currency. Such transactions are recorded in the subledgers and converted to the functional currency using a specific exchange rate. Your *functional currency* is the one you use to record transactions and maintain your accounting data within Oracle Applications. The functional currency is generally the currency in which you transact most of your business, and the one you use for legal reporting.

A Foreign Currency Transaction Example

Oracle Receivables allows you to enter transactions such as foreign currency receipts, debit memos, on-account credits, invoices, deposits, and guarantees in any currency. It automatically converts foreign currency amounts to the functional currency using the exchange rate you specify.

Consider a sale of goods by a U.S. company to a French company for 125,000 French francs. You have defined the exchange rate in Oracle General Ledger as 5.388 French francs (FRF) to one U.S. dollar (USD). Oracle Receivables uses the exchange rate you entered in Oracle General Ledger to convert the invoice amount from francs to dollars. When you post the invoice in Oracle General Ledger, the following entries will appear:

Account	Original Currency	Functional Currency (USD)		Foreign Currency (FRF)	
		Debit	Credit	Debit	Credit
Accounts receivable	FRF	23,199.70		125,000.00	
Revenue	FRF		18,559.76		100,000.00
Freight income	FRF		4639.94		25,000.00

Exchange Rate Strategies

Oracle uses a single set of currency exchange tables as a reference for all products. You are responsible for entering the appropriate exchange rate data into the table. It is important that you use a consistent methodology to enter exchange rates, especially when the Applications must tie in to other systems.

Exchange rates are held in two Oracle General Ledger tables: GL_TRANSLATION_RATES and GL_DAILY_CONVERSION_RATES. The rates are available to all other applications whenever they are needed. In most circumstances you can override the default exchange rate on a journal or transaction at the time of entry. Multiple exchange rates are held for distinct purposes within General Ledger:

- Daily rates
- Average rates
- Period-end rates

Daily rates are used during data entry to crystallize a specific exchange rate for foreign currency journals (in General Ledger), supplier invoices (in Payables), and customer invoices and receipts (in Receivables). Average and period-end rates are used when you translate your actual and budget account balances. Revaluation rates are used when you revalue foreign-denominated account balances.

Revaluation

Revaluation reflects changes in conversion rates between the date of journal entry and the date of receipt or payment of the foreign currency amount. The purpose of revaluation is to adjust balance sheet accounts (asset and liability accounts) that may be materially under- or overstated due to significant fluctuations in exchange rates between the time when the transaction was entered and the end of the period. General Ledger posts the change in converted balances against the unrealized gain/loss account you specify.

Using the earlier example, suppose it is December 31, the close of the U.S. company's accounting year, and the invoice remains unpaid. The exchange rate is no longer 5.388. It has moved to 5.200—the franc has strengthened in relation to the dollar. The 125,000 FRF receivable amount should be revalued to 24,038.46 USD, and the following revaluation entry should be made in the U.S. company's books to reflect this adjustment:

Account	Currency	Debit	Credit
Accounts receivable	USD	838.76	
Unrealized gain	USD		838.76

Notice that the revaluation adjustment is made in dollars, the functional currency, and does not affect the foreign currency account balances. Journal entries like this one can be generated automatically in Oracle General Ledger by running a revaluation program.

Conversion

Oracle General Ledger converts your foreign transaction at the point of entry, without having to run the revaluation program. At the time of entry, the conversion program immediately converts the foreign currency transaction to the functional currency using an exchange rate that you supply. Oracle General Ledger maintains separate balances in the foreign currency amounts as well as the functional currency amounts for each transaction.

Balance Translation

Translation is the act of restating the balances of a company's entire set of books from the functional currency to a foreign currency. It is used to consolidate the results of foreign subsidiaries. Normally, translation is done after you have completed all your journal activity for a period. Oracle General Ledger allows you to translate your actual and budget account balances from your functional currency to another currency. For example, if you are a U.S. company that wants to report financial results in euros, you can use General Ledger's translation feature to translate your account balances from your functional currency (U.S. dollar) to the foreign currency, the euro.

The Euro

In May 1998, the European Commission published a schedule for the introduction of the European Monetary Union. This schedule states that the initial fixed exchange rates between the national currencies and the euro will be set and that the European Central Bank (ECB) will be established. Countries within the European Union that agree to join and comply with certain economic standards have formed the European Monetary Union. Under this schedule, this initial group of countries started using the euro (make settlements, issue documents, and so on) on January 1, 1999. The relationship between their existing currencies and the euro was fixed on that date. During the three years up to January 1, 2002, both the national currencies and the euro itself will be valid units and expressions of the euro, but no euro coins or bank notes will be issued. On January 1, 2002, euro coins and bank notes will become legal tender. On July 1, 2002, the national currency units will be discontinued, and the euro will remain as the only legal tender.

The euro cannot be treated as just another currency; it will have two monetary units in an EMU country: the euro unit and the National Currency Unit (NCU). Transactions in euros will not be considered foreign currency transactions because the national currency will have a fixed relationship to the euro, just as one cent has a fixed relationship (100:1) with one dollar. In practice, this means that transactions initiated in either euro units or NCUs can be denominated in either the euro or local currency. In any member state, bank transfers, electronic funds transfer (EFT) payment runs, and checks need to specify whether they are in euro or NCU or both. Conversely, invoices issued in the national currency could be paid using euro units without any possible currency fluctuations. Oracle Payables, Oracle Receivables, and Oracle General Ledger allow you to process cross-currency settlements for invoices. Cross-currency settlement is necessary for companies that invoice in euro and receive payment in French franc, or Italian lire, for example. Oracle has catered for euro-zone transactions by creating a new currency infrastructure in the Applications. The infrastructure incorporates the special parent-child relationship between euro and NCUs, adheres to the European Community's regulations, and supports euro-zone settlement logic for invoices and receipts. The new currency infrastructure underpins all Oracle Application modules—all business processes have been revised to exploit it.

In contrast to EMU countries, where the former national currencies have a fixed-rate relationship to the euro, organizations outside EMU countries that want to comply with euro requirements will have to maintain and support floating exchange rates between their national currency and the euro.

Oracle Applications has minimized the conflicts between filing and accounting requirements with the euro. It allows you to maintain national currency books when you are required to file in the national currency, and to maintain books in euro units when you are required to file in euro units. All transactions from your subledgers and General Ledger can be recorded in both national currency units and euro units; this arrangement allows you to prepare comparative reports analyzing the value of your business and the results of your operations in both the national currency and euro units. One way to do this is to use the Multiple Reporting Currencies (MRC) feature, which is new in Release 11. Expressly designed to meet euro requirements, MRC enables you to monitor your business simultaneously in the old and new units of currency, both for detailed transactions and for financial reporting.

Reporting in Multiple Currencies

As previously mentioned, Oracle General Ledger's translation feature is used to translate amounts from your functional currency to another currency at the account balances level. If you want to convert amounts from your functional currency to another currency at the transaction level, you can use the Multiple Reporting Currencies feature.

Multiple Reporting Currencies allows companies to view and report on transaction-level detail in an unlimited number of alternative currencies. MRC automatically replicates journals from your primary functional currency set of books into one or more foreign currency sets of books used for reporting purposes. This process ensures that your primary set of books is always synchronized with each of the reporting sets of books.

MRC is specifically intended for use by organizations that must regularly and routinely report their financial results in multiple currencies. MRC is not intended as a replacement for General Ledger's translation feature. For example, an organization that needs to translate its financial statements to its parent company's currency once a year for consolidation purposes, but that has no other foreign currency reporting needs, should use General Ledger's standard translation feature instead of MRC.

Conclusion

Oracle Financials gives you the ability to manage your multicurrency accounting needs and helps you account for foreign currency transactions. You can consolidate foreign companies and operate in countries with unstable currencies that force you to maintain transactions in both your local currency and a foreign currency. You can also operate in European countries. Many trading processes have been re-engineered to accommodate the accounting demands of the new European single currency.

CHAPTER
13

Oracle Self-Service
Web Applications

racle Corporation, driven by founder and CEO Larry Ellison's vision, stands out among its competitors. This evolving vision has led to Oracle's domination of the database market and features the relational database concept itself, total portability, a tool suite based on the database, distributed and linked databases, and exponential growth. The Web has allowed Oracle to expand that vision even further, delivering powerful enterprise-level databases and tools, with a full graphical interface, to any desktop throughout the world.

The Web has allowed Oracle to improve the Applications offerings in two ways:

- As a delivery mechanism for the Oracle Applications features that were previously available in Smart Client and in character-based implementations. This is the Internet Computing Model, formerly known as the Network Computer Architecture (NCA) implementation of the Applications.

- As a trigger for new modules that push access to the Applications beyond the core of trained, regular system users to casual users inside and outside the corporate world. These are the Self-Service Applications for the Web.

Oracle's Self-Service Web Applications are being rapidly enhanced and augmented—the current product range includes Oracle Web Customers, Web Suppliers, and Oracle Web Employees. These products are described later in this chapter.

Oracle's Vision and Direction

Growing the Oracle Corporation by providing increased value for the customer is a constant thread. The Applications have added tremendous value. The Internet offers a new world of opportunity, and the Web Applications offer you the ability to:

- Provide untrained users with universal access to applications, inside and outside your company, within the security limits you establish.

- Support secure financial transactions on a worldwide basis.

■ Relieve desktop users and network administrators of the need to maintain desktop systems on a one-by-one basis.

■ Provide high-level integration with other vendors' applications, third party "black box" modules, desktop software, multimedia products, multiple host machines, networks, desktop environments, and browsers.

■ Make complete and timely extracts of transaction data accessible to desktop decision support tools.

Oracle's database and tools support these functions, and its Financials product releases bring them closer to the user. This book addresses a number of product-specific improvements within the relevant chapters. More general enhancements that do not fit easily within the context of a single application are addressed in this section.

Expressing the Vision Through the Applications

Oracle Applications affords a technical integration that is unique among database and tools vendors. While other database companies have to anticipate what developers are going to need, Oracle hears directly from its Applications division. Conversely, because its Applications do not have to be portable across databases, Oracle can fully exploit the features of the underlying database and tools. New Applications features, layered on top of built-to-order tools, make its corporate vision concrete.

Web Customers, Web Suppliers, and Web Employees are Oracle's first three Self-Service Web Applications. They leverage the features of Order Entry, Receivables, Purchasing, and Payables, pushing it closer to end users using the Web and workflow technologies.

Overview of Oracle Workflow

A premise of Web operations is that the person using an Internet browser can be almost anybody. Oracle defines it as the four Ws: Web Without Workflow is Worthless. The most obvious implication is that the system needs to be secure: you cannot expose yourself to financial loss, the compromise of confidential data, or to hackers. Oracle's Self-Service Web Applications add their own security atop that which is integral to the Web server tools.

The other major implication is that users will need help. You can expect users to know how to use an Internet browser (more or less), and what they want to accomplish (more or less). Therefore, you need:

- Intuitive applications built for the untrained, casual user.

- Oracle Workflow, to guide users through Web transactions and to guide transactions to those who need to act on them.

Workflow supports non-expert users while protecting the integrity of your system. It provides a roadmap, leading users step-by-step through a transaction. It gives you the opportunity to route their transactions according to business rules. You can make the data entry process quick and painless for frequent, trusted users of your system, yet provide help to unsophisticated users. You can have Workflow invoke human judgment when it is needed for complex transactions, for uncertain users, or for parties who have not yet earned a high level of trust. It can engage users at various levels, appropriate to who they are and what they know.

Oracle Order Entry and Purchasing have long employed different processing cycles for different combinations of customers, products, vendors, and transaction types. The ability to tailor an approval cycle gave these applications a great deal of power. Programming support for user-defined cycles represented a major investment on Oracle's part, and setting up parameters to use it is a big investment for Applications users. Oracle drew on this experience in designing Workflow. It provides robust and easy-to-use support for a number of recurring themes in transaction processing:

- Different transaction types have different information requirements. For example, an order for material requires a mode of shipment. An order for services does not.

- Different types of transactions require different approvals, but the elements of the process are always the same. There is a hierarchy of approvers, with different levels of authority, who can give different types of approval (financial, technical, scheduling, and so on).

Anybody in the chain can disapprove a transaction and send it back. The particulars of a transaction dictate how high up it has to go for final approval.

■ Ongoing process evaluation is part of the workflow process. It has to do with quality in transaction processing. Late payments, late shipments, faulty goods, and incomplete information are typical problems. Workflow activity monitors can trigger action in response to exceptions. Workflow captures Oracle Quality, Oracle Service, and Oracle Engineering transactions.

■ A company must constantly evaluate the cost of transactions in light of their value to the business. Minimizing, automating, and eliminating transactions can mean major savings to you and your business partners. A workflow process can identify your transaction processing costs, element by element. You can use this information to streamline your processes, building relationships of trust that replace transaction processing with macro-level activities such as periodic audits.

■ Being an effective partner means monitoring the status of ongoing agreements. Are you fulfilling your obligations to your partners? Are you within budget?

Oracle recognized the workflow aspects common to transactions across all applications and devised a single architecture to address them all.

Workflow Architecture

Oracle Workflow is an enabling piece of systems-level technology, like flexfields, that Oracle is embedding throughout the Applications suite. It is fundamental to all the Self-Service Applications. Oracle has also implemented its Automatic Account Generation module in Workflow. This module permits your systems staff to define company-unique logic for selecting flexfield segments, and at the same time give high-quality guidance to ensure that users don't get frustrated and that they choose accurately. There are four components to Oracle Workflow, which will now be described.

Graphical Process Designer

The Oracle Workflow product uses a graphic drag-and-drop screen to lay out how transactions will flow between workstations and what will happen at each station. It manages the business rules, routings, and controls that characterize workflow, and it makes the necessary links to the application-specific code that processes transactions. In this sense Workflow is a high-productivity development tool, one that the business process owners may not need the help of professional programmers to understand and use. It employs a user-extensible set of familiar or intuitively obvious flow diagram symbols.

You can change your Workflow processes without changing the application code. For example, the dollar level of an approval authority or the transaction routing can be changed right in Workflow. The application logic that is applied to the transaction once it is approved does not need to change.

Extensible Server-Based Process Engine

A Workflow Engine running on the database server tracks all activity. The presentation-level Workflow tools hosted on the Web server invoke PL/SQL routines to notify the Workflow Engine of changes in the state of a transaction. The Engine examines the rules and initiates whatever activities are eligible to run on the basis of the change. The Engine supports a variety of logical constructs, including branching, looping, simultaneous activities, and subflows.

You can program your own arbitrarily complex rules in PL/SQL through the Application Programmer Interfaces (API) built into the product. The API makes the procedures significantly easier to customize, because your modifications are applied at a plane above the Oracle Applications. The implications for your modifications are as follows:

- They are placed in a predefined location, associated with predefined APIs, instead of scattered throughout the Oracle-provided source code.

- They function in an upstream direction from the Applications open interfaces. The transactions will be thoroughly validated by standard Oracle code before being imported into an application.

Notification/Messaging System

Workflow notifies people by electronic messages when their participation is required in a transaction, usually for an approval. You instruct Workflow to notify a specified *role* of the required action. One or more people may be assigned to a role. As they log into the Oracle Applications, workflow notifies the person or persons who occupy the role of all transactions awaiting their action. The notice for a transaction will remain in the Personal Inbox for everyone assigned to the role until someone has taken care of it.

Although the Web is a medium that absolutely demands Workflow, the opposite is not true. Workflow within the Applications does not rely on the Web. Oracle has designed the function to be portable, to be delivered through many different media:

■ You can use the Web.

■ You can notify people of exceptions with e-mail, similar to Oracle Alerts.

■ The Applications can deliver notification. For example, Oracle Purchasing can notify approvers of pending actions when they sign on.

Graphical Activity and Analysis

Speedily moving their transactions through your system makes you a good partner for both suppliers and customers. The Workflow Analyzer allows you to monitor individual transactions as they flow through and to analyze your overall activity. It is a great device for spotting bottlenecks, which Workflow allows you to quickly rectify at the Workflow level without affecting the underlying application.

Improved Relationships

Whatever savings it yields as a programming tool, the major benefits Workflow can bring is in improved relationships. It allows you to:

■ Identify and eliminate activities that add no value.

■ Manage by exception.

- Program predictable decisions, calling on human judgment only for exceptions.

- Empower users to control business rules and modify automated processes.

- Monitor the performance of your business partners, and follow a series of preplanned actions to remedy their shortcomings.

In short, you stop wasting people's time. You develop long-term, trusting relationships with your partners, so a transaction created by one party can satisfy the others' automation needs. You don't bother people with predictable decisions. You provide partners with the information they need to serve you efficiently and well. You gently advise partners so they can take action when their level of service is falling below expectations. You and your partners both save money and aggravation.

Integration with Other Financials Modules

Oracle Workflow feeds the underlying Oracle Applications through open interface tables. The integration points include:

- *Master table references, on a read-only basis.* The Self-Service Applications validate input data relating to customers, products, and accounting distributions against the master tables shared with Oracle Applications. Some Self-Service Applications download master data in advance, so the user can check against it in "disconnected" mode. Any errors caused by outdated validation tables will be trapped in the next step.

- *Open interface tables.* Various transactions that are initiated from the Web place data into open Applications interface. Modules then process the data as they would from any external source, creating transactions within the standard application. Erroneous transactions are tagged and left in the interface table. The Self-Service application can present errors back to users the next time they access the system, or by e-mail.

Central Control

Self-Service Applications, like the Web Applications, should be administered centrally. All the modules reside on shared Web servers. This structure gives the Web Applications the advantages of centralized security management, by which one set of security policies can be applied to all users. It means universal and uniform extensibility: Every user has access to the same Oracle features.

Consistent with their design objective of universal availability to untrained users, the Self-Service Applications do not require user setup on the client side. It happened first in Self-Service; now the Internet computing model has nearly eliminated client-side issues for all the Applications. All the user needs is a Java-enabled browser. The server handles everything else, such as downloading the necessary applets behind the scenes. The Oracle 8 database is designed to carry all types of objects. Most of the objects of interest to the Self-Service Applications come from applications within the desktop environment. These present some client-side configuration considerations. The particular office suite on the client is an important factor in desktop integration, and it will remain so until word processing, spreadsheet, and other desktop functions can be delivered over the Web. If your users choose to use the disconnected expense spreadsheet to do their expenses, and attach spreadsheets to their expense reports, it matters whether you support Lotus or Excel.

Browser hardware selection is also a factor in setting up Web Applications. Although HTML is designed to be hardware independent, there is a certain window size at which Web Applications screens look and work their best. The level of Java support will matter as more and more programmed functions are executed at the browser level.

Oracle Self-Service Web Applications

Self-Service Applications are central to Oracle's Internet vision. They give great value to Applications customers by pushing the boundaries of the applications outside the corporation. They give Oracle great leverage on their investment in the building blocks: Applications open interfaces, Web Server, and Workflow products. More packages have followed quickly on the success of Web Customers, Web Suppliers, and Web Employees. Like the first three, they involve broad communities of users, with different levels of training and involvement, who need to share data inside and outside the company.

Oracle Web Customers

In this do-it-yourself age, the biggest obstacle between you and your customers is often you. Customers want to do it themselves. Direct PC manufacturers are an excellent example of organizations empowering their customers, allowing them to configure and order products over the Web.

Marketing

You probably already market through a Web site that tells prospective customers who you are and what your products are. A link to Web Customers will let your prospects browse the catalogs that you have compiled under Oracle Inventory and Order Entry. You can even invite them into a closer relationship through self-registration. Netscape, for example, accepts a registration online, then e-mails back a confirmation and a password that gives customers entry to the next level of marketing. It might be access to a priced catalog, authority to download trial software, or access to technical product literature.

Orders and Payment

Customers, along with your own salespeople, can enter orders through Web Customers. Web Configurator can be used to simplify the ordering of complex products. This real-time configuration support saves time for the customer as well as your order acceptance group. It shortens the order cycle, increases customer satisfaction, and takes less of your peoples' time in the bargain.

Speaking the customers' language is good business, and Web Customers lets them order using their own part numbers. Web Customers' integration with Oracle Context lets customers make intelligent searches of your online literature. Oracle Context is much more than a mere keyword search product. It is able to abstract and index the "sense" and "content" of documents in a way that can lead your customers reliably to the information they need.

Regardless of whether your customers are invoiced or they simply pay on receipt, they can now view their entire order totals online, including sales tax and freight calculations and other charges that can affect the total invoice amount.

Configuration

Product configuration can be a difficult task, and Oracle Web Configurator does an excellent job of simplifying the procedure. Order Entry supports it through Oracle Bill of Materials, in which the available options are expressed as option groups within a model bill of materials. It requires people trained in the structure of products and options and the order entry process. The Java-based Web Configurator's ergonomics and workflow support now make it possible for untrained customers to configure their own orders. The multilevel, indented-list presentation makes the option choices easier to visualize. The rule-based logic of the underlying Oracle Product Configurator can apply programmed logic to guide customers through more complex configuration decisions.

It is a natural application for Oracle Workflow. Workflow can evaluate the order and require approval steps to protect you against all sorts of difficulties. Among them, the product might not fit the customer's need, it might not be possible to build, it might not be available as required, or the customer may be a credit risk. The approvers can be anywhere in the company. The rules as to who needs to see which orders, what to do when the first-choice approvers are not available, and how high a given order needs to go in the approval chain can be quite complex.

Forecast

You and your customers can both save money when you share forecast information. They can be confident you will provide what they need when they need it, so they do not lose sales. You can be confident you will not be saddled with the cost of carrying, or disposing of, excess inventory. Web Customers can accept your customers' forecast information to feed your inventory and manufacturing systems' Material Requirements Planning (MRP) logic. Their projections will describe their business better than your guesses, and in most cases both parties want to maximize their service level.

Service

Do-it-yourself support offers major benefits in customer service. Customers can often solve problems directly with information from your support knowledge database. They can enter service requests when they need service, they can query the status of a service request and review the history of an individual service call, a product, or their whole relationship with you. Service was another natural application of Oracle Workflow. The longer a problem goes unresolved, and the more critical it is, the more you probably want to escalate its visibility within both your organization and the customer's.

A customer may return an item for service, credit, or replacement—or for a refund at the end of a trial or lease period. You provide the customer with an RMA (Return Material Authorization) number in advance, so your receiving dock knows what to do when a shipment arrives. Knowing the RMA number, your customer can use Web Customers to check the status of depot repair orders being managed by Oracle Service.

Customer Relationships

You can measure the quality of a customer relationship by the success of individual transactions. You can use Web Customers to measure their performance: how often do they change and cancel orders? Do they pay you quickly? How good are their forecasts? It can also measure your performance in filling their orders and satisfying their service requests. Web Customers gives you a handle on these relationships, which are the life of your business. You can use data tools, like Oracle Express, to download the workflow it provides for comprehensive analysis. The Workflow features let you devise special processes to address the unique needs of special customer relationships and at the same time give equal treatment to customers who enjoy equal standing.

Web Suppliers

The benefits you derive from high-quality business relationships apply to you both as buyer and seller. Being a reliable customer by keeping your suppliers informed of your needs in a timely fashion reduces their costs and ultimately the prices they charge you.

Web Suppliers supports every phase of developing a relationship. Through online registration, you can tell who vendors are and what supplies and services they provide. You can have Workflow automate some decisions with regard to new suppliers, then call them to the attention of buyers for further action. You can provide approved suppliers with password access to projected requirements and upcoming RFQs.

Purchasing products and services from your suppliers involves complex judgments, balancing the quality and number of relationships you manage, any personal relationships, prices, and service. Web Suppliers can provide more information to support those judgments. It helps you maintain relationships with more suppliers, manages price and delivery information from more sources, and provides meaningful data on performance under your existing contracts.

Competitive Solicitations

Requests for Quotations (RFQs) are useful Web tools. Posting them publicly and e-mailing potential suppliers invite the broadest participation. You can let respondents download templates in word processor or spreadsheet formats or a format to be sent back through the Oracle EDI Gateway.

Orders, Receipts, and Returns

Web Suppliers does not alter the fact that Purchase Orders originate in Oracle Purchasing. You may still send them to the supplier in paper, fax, or EDI format. Web Suppliers enters the picture after the Purchase Order has been created. It gives your suppliers the ability to look up the requirements you expect them to fulfill.

Using Advance Shipment Notices (ASNs), suppliers can inform you exactly what is in a shipment and when you should expect it. This information means your receiving dock can process against an expected receipt, with no exceptions, instead of against an order, where the normal types of exceptions are encountered, including backorders, short shipments, and substitutions. ASNs make the process more accurate and efficient.

Web Suppliers supports your merchandise returns, usually controlled by an RMA number from the supplier. You share visibility of the return process until it is resolved by a replacement, repair, or repayment action.

Building Efficient Supplier Relationships

It is traditionally your responsibility as the buyer in a purchasing relationship to let the supplier know what you want via a Purchase Order and to keep them apprised of changes in your needs via Change Orders. You sometimes lose track of your requirements, and suppliers may misplace an order in a complex and fast-changing environment. By providing online access to open Purchase Orders for your suppliers, they can see the status of open orders, recent PO changes, shipping schedules, and receipts. They can take the initiative in meeting your changing requirements.

You may even structure your Purchase Agreements in such a way that your online posting represents your sole notification: your supplier's obligation is to meet the requirements you have posted through Web Suppliers and to notify you if there is a problem. You can almost totally eliminate paperwork if you combine this approach with Oracle Purchasing's payment-on-receipt feature. Equally important, this approach offers your suppliers the most up-to-date information for planning purposes. Using Oracle Supplier Scheduling, they can be with you step-by-step as your requirements change over time and as their participation moves in from the planning horizon to the moment of delivery.

Forging tight links with your suppliers gives a new meaning to quality in a relationship. You elevate transaction-related measures such as timeliness and quality to the level of statistical measurement. Other measures, such as the accuracy of POs and invoices, become moot when both parties are working from the same database. You can add new parameters to your evaluation of quality, such as the vendor's resourcefulness in satisfying your changing requirements and in passing its transaction economies through to you in the form of favorable pricing.

Some manufacturers, notably car makers, have their suppliers retain ownership of parts up to the moment they are consumed on the assembly line. The supplier accounts for the assets financially, but the manufacturer has to account for them physically. In such cases, Web Suppliers can provide suppliers a window into a manufacturer's inventory operations so they can see and manage their own stock.

If you outsource manufacturing you must inform the suppliers not only what you need but how to build it. They keep their manufacturing bills of materials in step with your changing engineering bills of material. This arrangement works best as a collaborative process, because you need the suppliers' input to maximize profits. The total cost of the product includes component costs, which your engineering department can assess, and the costs of the resources your supplier will use in manufacturing. It is the kind of requirement Oracle's Concurrent Engineering workflow product is intended to support.

Web Suppliers provides links that can give you a significant competitive advantage. Proactively providing your suppliers with information adds value to their relationship with you. Sharing information and eliminating redundant transactions up and down the supply chain, from manufacturer to consumer, significantly reduces overall costs. You and your business partners benefit in proportion to the trust and support you offer one another by sharing information through the Oracle Web products.

Oracle Web Employees

Most employees today are assumed to have at least occasional access to the Internet. It has taken its place alongside computers, telephones, faxes, and copiers as an indispensable part of the corporate infrastructure. Web Employees uses this new medium, along with Workflow technology, to improve communications between employer and employees. Web Employees currently supports supply requisitions and purchase cards, expense reporting, and human relations issues.

Personal Expenses

Procurement cards give employees authority to "just do it," using a company credit card to buy supplies they need, within their credit limits, from authorized suppliers. For accounting employee expenses usually takes place after the fact. Oracle Payables imports a list of transactions in electronic format with the invoice from your card issuer. You distribute them to the individuals who made the purchases. These individuals confirm the transactions and provide whatever accounting data is needed. They may identify some transactions as personal and make provisions to reimburse the company.

Oracle Payables can assemble much of the necessary accounting information from the transaction itself using Automatic Account Generation. It will usually determine which department to charge by the procurement card number. It may be able to deduce other accounting flexfield entries, such as the GL account, by applying logic to information provided by the card issuer. For instance, you may let the system assume that expenses on a corporate Exxon card have to do with cars, and hence go to the GL account for employee auto expense. On the other hand, there will be times when you need to provide account and organization data. Oracle Payables is able to pay the card issuer's invoice on time whether or not all the accounting distributions have been collected. As with all Workflow applications, you have the ability to monitor the process. You can spot bottlenecks in the process and identify people and departments who are slow to identify their expenses.

Expense Reporting

Expense reporting can be a major burden, both for employers and for administrators. Expenses usually need to be entered very soon after they are incurred, so they can be accounted in the appropriate period and reimbursed. They need to be accurate, and at least some expenses will need to be approved.

To meet the timeliness requirement, your employees can fill out their expenses in disconnected mode on any computer with a spreadsheet. A laptop on an airplane will work. Web Employees validates accounting distributions against information stored on the laptop, then double-checks it against the live database as the data is imported into Oracle Payables. You may ask employees to use Descriptive Flexfields to identify or categorize expenses below the level required by accounting. You may want to identify the mode of transportation (taxi, metro), or airline ticket number, or meal (breakfast, lunch), or type of personal service (dry cleaning, health club use). For VAT recovery, the expense process can capture the tax amount for an expense item.

The employee has to make some network connection, usually over the Internet, to upload the spreadsheet expense report into Oracle Web Employees. The system does its own check against the live database and follows Workflow procedures to have somebody resolve any errors. After they are entered, whether online or in disconnected mode, expense sheets flow through a Workflow approval process. Your business rules will determine what levels of approval are required by the type and amounts of expenses.

You need to integrate Web Employees into the business procedures for managing receipts. You can set a threshold below which the employee need not bother with receipts, or define items that need no receipt. When receipts are required, the Workflow process has to define the form they will take:

- OLE objects, such as spreadsheets or scanned images, that are attached to the expense report

- References to hard copy in a filing cabinet

Your Workflow design has to take into account how receipt documentation will be used. Do approvers need to see every receipt or merely be able to look them up as needed? How will they be made available to auditors? Will any auditors need access to the hard copy? The answers to these questions will determine whether and where in the cycle to scan in hard copy receipts and what to do with the paper after it is scanned.

In one of the relatively infrequent instances of overlapping functions, Oracle Project Time and Expense, a separate product in the Project Accounting family, also handles expense reporting. You'll need to use PT&E if you have a project orientation, or if you account for time utilization as well as expenses. Oracle has eliminated the redundancy by integrating project functions into Web Employees.

Requisitioning

Web Employees offers real-time support for creating Purchase Requisitions through an Internet browser. It guides employees through the simplified steps needed to create a requisition, then puts the finished requisition in the Requisitions open interface. Oracle Purchasing's workflow approval process takes it from there.

The requisitioning process offers several features to speed the process. *Requisition copying* lets them copy, modify, and resubmit a requisition. You can have multiple accounting distributions if necessary.

The major catalog features of Oracle Purchasing are available through Web Requisitioning. Context-based catalog searches enable employees to find items using descriptive attributes. There is an open interface to load catalogs. Employees can enter special orders for items that are not in the catalog. They can put together "templates" for frequently ordered items. A template acts as a reminder and saves a lot of time. The employee simply enters quantities next to the items they need and adds lines for items that are not on the template.

The budget can act as a control on requisitioning, especially in the public sector. *Encumbrance accounting* can prevent you from ordering something you don't have the budget to pay for. Web Employees can perform the budget check through its integration with Oracle Purchasing and General Ledger. It will advise an employee when the total of expenditures to date, open purchase orders, and open requisitions exceeds the budget.

Personnel File Maintenance

Web Employees gives your people the ability to directly update their personnel data. You can give them the authority and responsibility to keep their records straight regarding marriages and divorces, births and deaths, and changes in address and telephone number. They can also participate in maintaining career-related information such as their résumés, classes they have taken, qualifications and awards they have earned, and skills they want considered in matching them with assignments.

Employees can use Web Employees to initiate a variety of actions, such as applying for a posted position, enrolling in a training class, or seeking tuition reimbursement. Workflow processes manage approval and resolution of these transactions.

Line Manager Direct Access

Line Manager Direct Access gives your managers and executives the ability to analyze records and initiate activities that affect their employees. Some of the processes include:

- Managing job applications

- Creating appraisals and participating in group appraisals

- Initiating awards, granting certifications and licenses, and recording education

- Profiling employee skills

- Managing applications for training classes

Workflow processes handle the flow of transactions that have to pass through several people, such as job applications and appraisals.

Managers can search the personnel database for skills, employment history, personnel characteristics, or other data. Search results can be useful when it comes to making staffing decisions, evaluating individual employees, and evaluating the performance or the impact of policies on groups of employees.

Conclusion

Web Applications serve as a front end to many of the Oracle Applications. They group functions as much by the type of user they support as by the back-end package. Two premises underlie their design:

■ They must support unlimited, universal access by untrained users and therefore...

■ They require Oracle Workflow to make users productive and to protect the company from routing mistakes.

The Web and Workflow dramatically extend the reach of the Oracle Applications with a relatively modest investment on your part. Expect Oracle to implement Web Applications to support most types of activity by people who may be remote from major corporate centers.

PART III

Managing and Customizing an Applications Environment

CHAPTER
14

The Oracle
Financials Environment

racle Corporation is unrivalled when it comes to creating the environment in which its applications run. Its control of the technology stack, illustrated in Figure 14-1, extends from the database itself through to the application programming. The only major components it does not include are the hardware, operating system software, and network.

The unmatched level of integration in an Oracle solution offers significant benefits. You can be confident that the technologies needed to support the Applications will evolve with them. Internet Computing and the Web Server are good examples; they were designed with the needs of the Applications in mind. Oracle's Business Intelligence System and Activa products use the Oracle Express analysis tool and data warehouse to mine strategic information from the transaction data captured by the Applications.

Much of the power of the Applications is realized through foundation features that are available to all through the Applications Object Library (AOL). These include built-in devices such as flexfields, folders, quickpicks, and the Concurrent Manager, along with other tools such as Alert and Workflow. The foundation software makes it possible for Oracle to make across-the-board improvements to the Applications, increasing your ability to significantly customize the Applications without programming.

Because Oracle has created the languages in which the Applications are implemented, it can provide the well-defined integration points and interface specifications a programmer needs to modify or enhance the packages. Custom (bespoke) modules created by the Designer and Developer 2000 tools integrate naturally with Oracle Applications' standard modules, since they were developed with exactly the same tools. However, to customize the GUI versions of Applications forms, you must have a special version of the forms, which is included with the Applications software distribution.

Oracle Applications are among the most significant suites of software in almost every organization that uses them. For this reason, most users have comparative freedom in selecting the hardware and operating system environment used to support them. Oracle's open design means there are always a number of vendors competing for your business; it is important to appreciate the significance of different factors in the process of making decisions about hardware and software.

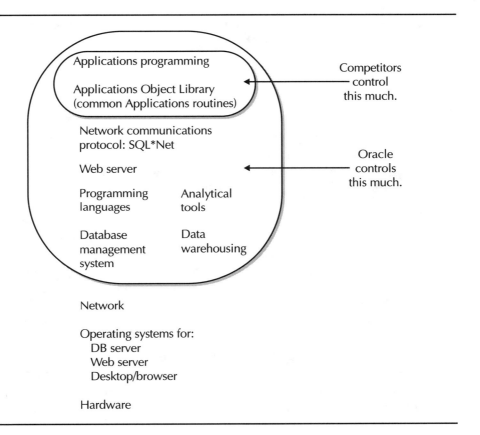

FIGURE 14-1.   *Oracle Applications' place in the technology stack*

The topics touched upon here are covered in depth in the *System Administration User's Guide, Flexfields Guide, NLS Installation Guide, Oracle Applications User's Guide,* and *Developer's Guide.* This discussion introduces the topics and relates them to one another. It provides the high level understanding of system features you need in order to make the best use of the Applications.

Online Operations

Oracle Applications' user interface is handled through Oracle Forms programs. The forms' two basic modes of operation are *query mode* and *data-entry mode.* You use query mode to fetch data that has previously been stored in the database to be displayed or modified; you use data-entry mode to insert new data.

Query Mode

Oracle has designated query blocks in many of the Smart Client/Internet Computing forms. This reduces the confusion that may arise from the fact that the appearance of the form does not change between query and data-entry modes. Even experienced users stumble on error messages as they attempt to enter data when they are in query mode. You know you are in query mode when you are looking at a query block. The forms take you automatically to a data entry block when the query completes, but the query block remains in an open window waiting for your next query.

Forms that include a query block usually allow you to query within the data entry block. You press the Enter Query function key, enter data matching the record you want to find into the corresponding fields on the screen, and press the Execute Query function key. All rows that match your query show up in the screen.

The underscore (_) and percent sign (%) are wildcard characters representing, respectively, one character and any number of characters. To query all customers whose names start with "AB," you would enter **AB%** in the Customer Name field and execute the query. To find all manufacturer's part numbers with a "2" in the second position you would enter **_2%** in the Part Number field. You can have as many wild cards as you want in a query. Entering **A%B%C** would fetch all rows having the letters A, B, and C in sequence.

Oracle*Forms recognizes a distinction between uppercase and lowercase letters, but the Applications are sometimes programmed to ignore it. You generally have to query by upper- and lowercase in a field, such as a description, where you would commonly enter upper- and lowercase values. Queries on fields such as Warehouse Location do allow lowercase values, but they will usually translate for you.

You can recall the last query you made by pressing the Enter Query function key a second time. In one practical application of this feature, you will find that the system responds much faster if you provide a concurrent request number than if you do a blind query in the View My Requests form.

The next time you want to check, press the Enter Query key twice. The job number will come back, and you can press the Execute Query key.

Oracle*Forms offers a powerful programmable query feature to users who know the names of the database columns. If you put a single colon (:) in one of the query fields, Oracle*Forms will prompt you to enter the text of an SQL WHERE clause. You can then make your query as complex as you like, within the limited size of the edit window they give you. You can query on attributes that are not otherwise available, such as the user attributes behind Descriptive Flexfields. For example, to query all invoice line rows in Oracle Receivables that have been imported from your employee expense system and reference customer ABC, you might enter the following in response to the prompt.

```
INTERFACE_LINE_CONTEXT = 'EXP'
AND INTERFACE_LINE_ATTRIBUTE3 LIKE 'ABC%'
```

NOTE
*The colon query is an Oracle*Forms feature. You can look in the* Forms Operators' Guide *for full details.*

Data-Entry Mode

You enter data into a form by putting the cursor in a field and keying. Oracle accepts data at the field level. It reads what you enter and provides immediate feedback in the form of validation error messages and lists of values to choose from.

Many fields offer a limited number of valid entries. For example, when you enter a sales order it must be associated with a valid customer. The form gives you a visual clue that a list of values is available by highlighting a list icon in GUI[6] and lighting a lamp at the bottom of the screen in character mode. It presents your choices when you press the List of Values function key.

Some lists of values are programmed to use an auto-completion function. When you have keyed enough that the form recognizes that there is only one valid entry, it automatically fills in the rest of the field. It saves you keystrokes. Some forms are programmed to pop up a list of values automatically as you enter the field, others if you enter an invalid value. List

---

[6]Graphical User Interface, which Oracle uses in its Smart Client and NCA implementations.

of values entries almost always handle case translation; you can key in "YES" when it is looking for "Yes."

In data entry fields where you are choosing from a list of values, there is no need to enter to the entire value. Simply type only enough to make your value unique, and Oracle will fill in the rest for you. Using the Yes/No example again, enter in only **Y**, and since "Yes" is the only value in the list that meets the criteria, the word "Yes" will be filled in as you move to the next field.

Messages

The forms use the message presentation system embedded in the Applications Object Library (AOL). Any routine, including stored procedures invoked by a form, can set a message. Processes native to forms management determine when messages have been set and must be presented, and whether a message is merely informational or indicates a condition that must be remedied. The most common use of messages is in field-level edits, when you receive an error message for entering an invalid value.

There is a national language indicator associated with each online session. AOL's message presentation routines select the appropriate message text, substitute variable data into the message if necessary, and display it at the bottom of the screen. The message stays until the user acknowledges seeing it.

Field-level edits can sometimes seem to trap you in a data screen. Even though you want to leave the form, it may not let you exit without entering a valid value. This is a frequent problem for new users in character-mode operations. Here are some strategies for escaping:

- Try to erase the field.

- Try to erase the screen.

- If it is a new row, which is usually the case, try to delete the current row.

- Enter a valid value for the field, even though you want to leave the screen. Then exit when you get to a field with more forgiving edits.

- When all else fails, leave the Applications and return.

Oracle Applications use a standard exit to present error messages. This device keeps the messages external and supports multiple national languages. Source text is kept in an AOL table, updated through the Define Text form in the "Application Developer" responsibility. However, for the sake of execution speed, the generated message text for character-mode operations is kept in an operating system file in the /mesg subdirectory of the Application's root directory.

Navigation and Special Functions in Forms

The mouse has changed the nature of navigation. Character-mode forms use function keys for navigation: Next Block, Previous Block, Next Field, and Previous Field. In GUI you usually use the tab key to go from one field to the next, but otherwise use the mouse to get to the field or block you want.

Both GUI and character-mode forms use function keys for functions such as clear screen, delete row, enter query, execute query, and commit. Both offer alternatives. In GUI there are icons to perform most of these functions. In character you can select most of them from the menu.

Function keys are a convenience in GUI. In character mode, they can be essential. While Oracle Forms 2.4 was designed to work with dumb terminals such as the VT220, by now almost every user accesses it using terminal emulation on a PC. There is little standardization among either PC keyboards or emulator programs. Unless the DBA has been diligent in puzzling out the keyboard mappings, there are likely to be some functions that are only accessible through the menus.

REMEMBER
In character mode using a terminal emulator the Execute Query command must be assigned to a function key. You cannot access the menu in query mode, so unless you have a function key there is no way to execute a query. This is not an issue if you use the Business Manager front-end, nor is it with the GUI products.

Display Formats

Oracle has applied consistent design standards to give forms throughout the Applications a consistent look and feel. Although you will develop an intuitive feel for how they work in short order, the rationale behind the design merits some discussion.

Single-row and Multi-row Displays

Forms can display one or multiple rows per region. The formats are quite different. Oracle uses an entire region to display one row when there are a number of data fields to display. It puts the field description just to the left of the field itself. Labels go above the columns in a multi-row display.

The multi-row format provides information in a format that is extremely easy to grasp at a glance. It is so useful that Oracle uses it even when there is more information than can be displayed at once. It displays the key information on the left, and allows you to scroll through the remaining fields on the right side of the window. Some screens allow you to define custom folders for the scrolled fields, eliminating fields you never need to see and shrinking the display width on others so they just fit your requirements.

Correspondence to Underlying Tables

Users see the applications as a collection of *displays*, or *screens*, which, under Internet Computing are actually collections of free-floating *windows*, each of which (*display* or *window*) can have a number of *regions*, which are called *zones* in character mode, and which contain a number of *fields*.

Figure 14-2 illustrates the concept. A display or window incorporates one function—one entry on a menu. In rare cases one screen may call another. A region frequently but by no means always corresponds to one database table, and there is never more than one base table to a Region. A field within the region may be for display only, or it may be part of the base table.

Navigation, the process of moving around among menus, displays, regions and fields, differs depending on whether the user interface is character, GUI, or Internet Computing.

The organization of data displayed within an Oracle form corresponds to database tables. Within a form, each window (previously called zones and regions; Oracle*Forms calls them blocks) usually corresponds to a database

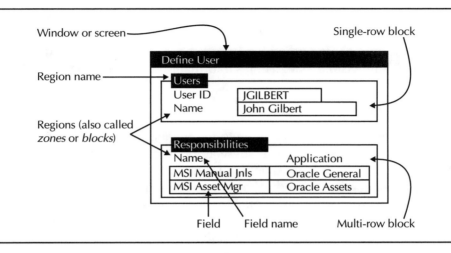

FIGURE 14-2.   *Windows, regions, and fields*

table, and fields in the zone correspond to table columns. There are some exceptions. A zone may not have a base table if none of its fields are stored in the database. An inquiry zone may correspond to a view that joins more than one table. Finally, the master table zones may correspond to views that restrict the user's access to one organization within the underlying table on which the view is defined. The names of these tables end in _ALL, such as PO_HEADERS_ALL, and the view name is the same but without the ALL. So the Multi-Org view for the PO_HEADERS_ALL table is PO_HEADERS. The _ALL tables are owned by module schemas (i.e., Purchasing in the case of PO_HEADERS_ALL) and the views (such as PO_HEADERS) are owned by the APPS schema.

Forms are organized to present master data zones followed by as many layers of detail as are needed. For example, the Order Workbench form (Enter Orders in Release 10) includes windows for querying orders, entering order master data, and entering order line data. This is the essential information: who is placing the order and what do they want? There are supporting windows to capture pricing information at the header and line levels and shipping information at both levels; tax and payment information at the header level; and scheduling, project, and release management information at the line level.

The zones are arranged such that you always see the context of your actions. Essential header information—such as order number and customer and line information, including the line number, item number, and description—are visible as you enter information about a shipment against that line.

One of Forms' strongest features is block coordination, a behind-the-scenes feature that manages context for you. Block coordination queries up only those detail records that belong to the higher level records already displayed. Sometimes it does the query automatically as you bring up the master, and sometimes it waits until you enter the block. Block coordination preserves the integrity of the database. It usually allows queries only within the context of a master record. You cannot, for instance, query the open order lines for an item across all orders through the Orders Workbench. You may come across block coordination activity in the process of navigation. When Oracle asks you if you want to commit your work, the most common reason is that it wants to save the detail records associated with one master before moving on to the next.

Multiple Open Windows

Since productivity is one of the major reasons to use Oracle Applications, users find it aggravating when the online system works slower than they do. It is a fact of life, however, that some operations take time. By their design, concurrent processes leave you free to do other things as they execute. With a little planning you can achieve the same with online processes.

It is easy to keep multiple windows open in character mode. All you need is to have your Systems Administrator permit multiple logins at the operating system level. Having several sessions open can save a lot of navigation and keep several activities going simultaneously. It works because all the processing takes place on the host machine, which is designed to do several things at once. It is common to have one window open for submitting concurrent processes, another for querying concurrent processes, and a third for making changes to the records used by concurrent processes. Updating standard costs is one example of an activity where multiple windows are useful.

Multiple open windows are a problem in Smart Client mode under Windows 95 or Windows 98. You can have more than one window open, but the active window ties up your desktop machine until it is done with a process. If you do a blind query for every item in the database, your machine may be locked up for minutes. True multiprocessing is the way around the problem. If you use Windows 2000 on your desktop, or do your processing remotely through a system like Citrix, you can get more than one process going at one time.

Oracle's Internet Computing architecture inherently supports multiple simultaneous processes. The real work is done on Web Servers, each of which is intended to support a large number of users. The Web Server does not know or care if two or more of those processes represent different sessions for the same person.

Although many users can read a database record at the same time, only one at a time can update a record. Oracle*Forms locks a queried row for the exclusive use of a user the moment that user changes a field. Other users are not allowed to update the record until the first user releases it. Since the system views you as more than one user when you are logged on multiple times, you have to be aware that what you are doing in one window may prevent you from doing something in another.

Batch Operations

Online processes take place (ideally) in real time. They progress at the user's pace, accepting data, updating the database, and presenting information as requested. An online process requires a full-time monitor that runs under control of the operating system to respond to everything a user does.

A user kicks off a batch process saying in effect "Here's what I want. Let me know when you're done." Different operating systems vary in how they dispatch batch jobs and handle their output. The Concurrent Manager provides a standard user interface within the context of the Applications. It also imposes security and manages access, operating system resources, and batch process outputs. The Concurrent Manager is built to the lowest common denominator of operating system function. It does not employ any features that are not common to all the operating systems it supports.

The Concurrent Manager

The Concurrent Manager oversees batch processes in Oracle Applications. It proceeds according to the following steps; Figure 14-3 illustrates how it works.

1. A display screen in the Applications gathers all the information needed to run the batch process. The Run Reports form captures runtime parameters from Descriptive Flexfields.

2. The online program submits the job by writing a row to the FND_CONCURRENT_REQUESTS table.

3. The Concurrent Manager searches the table every few seconds. It determines

   ■ Which jobs are eligible to run

   ■ Which of the eligible jobs should be executed

4. The Concurrent Manager initiates job execution.

5. The Concurrent Manager uses operating system-specific calls to track the status of its executing jobs until they terminate. It posts status changes to the table.

6. Users can submit queries to find the status of their jobs.

7. Users can have output printed or view it on their desktops.

TIP

Instead of constantly navigating to query the status of batch jobs, keep a second session of the Applications open to the query screen (Navigate Other Concurrent). Reduce query time and clutter in the returned screen by querying on your user id or, better yet, the concurrent job number itself. Press the Enter Query function key twice to automatically retrieve your last query.

Experienced Forms users sometimes enter a colon in one of the query fields. SQL*Forms then displays a window where the user can enter a precise query, as in this example:

```
REQUEST_ID > 943124 AND (STATUS_CODE = 'E' OR PHASE_CODE = 'R')
```

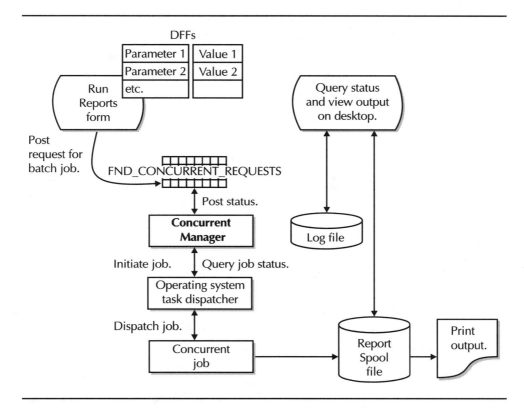

FIGURE 14-3. *The Concurrent Manager oversees batch jobs.*

This query would combine with any other query criteria (such as user id) and return only jobs greater than 943124 that were running or had errored out. (See the AOL technical reference for the column names.)

The Systems Administrator can define multiple concurrent managers with different characteristics, all driven by a single Internal Concurrent Manager (ICM). Each of these individual concurrent managers is allowed to run no more than a set number of jobs at any time. The number of jobs that the ICM can handle depends on the number of CPUs available. Typically it is two jobs per processor. So just increasing the number of jobs in the ICM does not translate into more jobs processed by the ICM.

A concurrent manager may be specialized to run only certain jobs or to operate in a given work shift. The System Administrator can use concurrent managers to control allocation of system resources, permitting more batch jobs to run concurrently at night than during the day, when they would take resources from online users. A concurrent manager may be specialized to run only certain high priority tasks, so they do not have to wait in the queue with standard report requests.

The Concurrent Manager takes into consideration the characteristics of individual jobs and job steps as it determines which ones can be initiated. It uses information provided in the Define Concurrent Job and Define Request Sets screens to identify:

■ **Incompatibilities**   Jobs that cannot be run at the same time as other jobs, or can only have one copy running of the job at a time.

■ **Sequencing**   Steps within a Request Set that have to run in a specified order.

■ **Job priority**   Jobs are normally scheduled according to the priority profile option for the user. The priority can be set, however, in the job definition.

The Internal Concurrent Manager manages all of the existing concurrent managers, waking up periodically (as defined by an operating system clock function) to ensure that everything that should be running is running. It identifies the jobs that are eligible to be started for each concurrent manager, then decides which, if any, will be started. "Eligible" means that there are no conflicts, such as a dependency on an uncompleted job or a conflict with another job currently in execution, and that there is a concurrent manager eligible to run the job. There is a target number of jobs for each manager, representing the maximum number of jobs it can run concurrently, subject to the limitations on the Internal Concurrent Manager, as discussed earlier. The manager will initiate eligible jobs, based on priority and time-in-queue, until it reaches its quota of active jobs.

AOL does not manage the computer's internal dispatching priority. All active batch jobs have equal access to CPU resources. This architecture reflects the fact that all the major operating systems do not function in the same way. Oracle's approach is to recommend that you define special concurrent managers for long-running or resource-hungry jobs, so they can be run in off-hours, or to limit the number of such jobs that can run simultaneously.

AOL spawns batch jobs as independent processes. It assembles the parameters in the FND_CONCURRENT_REQUESTS row into the standard operating system format and includes them on the command line it passes to the operating system. The command line includes the schema name and password that Oracle processes need to access the database. AOL invokes the process under an operating system user id associated with the current instance, so the environment variables are set appropriately. It uses standard operating system procedures to pass the names of the log and print files to the background process.

The concurrent manager updates the appropriate row in FND_CONCURRENT_REQUESTS to show job status, setting a completion status when it finishes. Jobs may end on their own, successfully or not; the user may terminate them; or they may be terminated due to the failure of another related job. You specify when setting up a report set whether the success of the set depends on the success of each individual job. Often, one job will spawn other jobs. Update Standard Cost in Inventory spawns reports showing changes in inventory, WIP and in-transit inventory; AutoInvoice Import in Receivables spawns a report on the success of the import process. The success of the parent jobs depends on the success of the jobs they spawn.

Third party vendors, such as AppWorx, offer support for users who need to program complex intra-step dependencies and dependencies with non-Oracle systems or for users with sophisticated load-balancing requirements. The third party software usually interfaces seamlessly through the use of database triggers.

Concurrent Program Parameters

A concurrent job needs a group of parameters specific to the type of process, and another group specific to the job itself. All Oracle*Reports jobs need a schema name and password, the name of the .RDF file to run, and the name of an Oracle*Reports profile file. AOL provides these parameters to the operating system—the user is oblivious to the detail. Each individual report needs the parameters that were specified by the programmer. They are specified in the Define Concurrent Program screen. Different program types accept the parameters in different formats:

■   SQL*Plus and Host programs accept positional parameters. The parameters must be specified in the Concurrent Program Details zone of the Define Concurrent Reports form in the same sequence they are expected by the program.

■ Oracle*Reports accepts keyword parameters. The token name you give as you register the report must match the one the programmer used within the actual report as the user-defined parameter.

■ SQL*Loader accepts all its parameters as a string in the Execution Options field of the Concurrent Program zone. You don't use the Details zone at all.

The parameters you specify in the Details zone are carried as a special form of Descriptive Flexfield, with each parameter acting as a DFF segment. There is a value set associated with each parameter, which prevents free form entry and limits input to a predefined list of values. Each parameter can have a constant, profile option or an SQL statement to generate a default value. You can also use the current system date or system time. The SQL code for value sets and default values can reference previous parameters, as described in the upcoming "Flexfield Definition" section. You could, for example, specify an item category in one parameter, then restrict the user's choices to replenishment orders for items within that category in a subsequent parameter.

Report Sets and Report Groups

It is common to need groups of reports to all run at the same time, especially for period closings and related processes. Report Sets satisfy the need for reports to be produced and distributed together. They provide the sequence in which reports are to run, and they pass appropriate parameters to each report in the set.[7] Report sets are assigned to responsibilities in the same way as individual reports. A user may have access to a report not by itself but only through a report set.

As you set up a report set, you specify the sources for the parameters for each separate step. You may set up defaults, so the user who runs the report set does not have the same range of options as if they had run the report by itself. You can specify shared parameters, so that the same value is passed to two or more programs in the set.

Report sets are a convenient way to satisfy other common objectives. You can provide a given responsibility with access to a report it does not

---

[7]Reports within a set should always represent data in the same state. In other words, there should be no posting or update activity going on as the report set is running. This depends on administrative controls; Oracle does not generally prevent database activity while reports are running.

otherwise have and limit the uses to which it can be put by predefining certain of the parameters. You can join a SQL*Loader step and a SQL*Plus step in tandem to load an interface table. The alternative, invoking them both from a Host script, is unattractive: you could compromise security either by hard-coding the password into the script or by passing the password to the script as a plain-text parameter. It would also require several lines of shell script coding to attain the same results you automatically have by using a report set.

The parameters for batch processes within a report set can be fixed at three points in time:

- As defaults (constants or profile parameters, or through SQL) when the report itself is registered.

- As defaults when the report set is established.

- At run time.

The parameters for each report are presented separately, in the same DFF format that is used when initiating individual reports. Those that cannot be changed at run time can be set up to be displayed or hidden.

The Concurrent Manager treats a report set as a single job until it is initiated. At that point it creates one concurrent job for each step in the report. The report set is the parent of all. The report set job does not complete until all children are complete. You can set up rules to make its success dependent on the success of its children, to make the children run in sequence, and to have the failure of one job cause all subsequent steps to abort.

Printing and Other Means of Output

An Applications environment can include many different kinds of printers. Some users don't want paper, at least not immediately; they want to preview report output online. The Applications incorporate the output flexibility built into the Oracle*Reports and SQL*Plus programming tools. The user can specify printer characteristics at execution time. In character mode, the user can control page height and width. GUI mode gives greater flexibility and more choices, such as between PostScript and PCL.

The user may have the Concurrent Manager print any number of copies of the report automatically, as the job is executed, or after reviewing the report online. The character-mode report reader offers a 24 × 80 window to look at reports that are often as large as 60 × 180. This is at best only marginally adequate. Improved online report viewing is one of the immediate advantages of Smart Client and Internet Computing. Smart Client routes your output to whatever desktop viewer you prefer. The Web Server puts report output into HTML for Internet Computing.

Most of the Oracle Applications reports are written in Oracle*Reports. Reports is a fully GUI capable tool, with a word processor's flexibility working with fonts, text placement, and graphics. This GUI, or bitmapped mode of operations, is standard in desktop operations. For compatibility with older types of printers, however, Oracle*Reports offers a character mode of operation.

Oracle distributes its Applications reports using the character mode option in Reports. Every platform is capable of handling character mode, and even though most modern printers can support some form of GUI operation, Oracle does not assume that every user installation will have GUI capabilities. Character-mode operations are the lowest common denominator. You will probably want to customize documents that go outside the company, among them Payables checks, Purchase Orders, Order Confirmations, Packing Slips, and Invoices. You can take the opportunity to improve their appearance.

If you require graphics, such as logos, to appear on reports produced from Oracle Applications, you have several options available. You can add graphics directly to Oracle*Reports, through preprogrammed printer cartridges or third party software. Printer-level graphics can execute faster and be easier to implement. The Evergreen check print program that Oracle delivers uses this approach to put MICR (magnetic ink) printing on checks. The character-mode report embeds HP PCL (Printer Control Language) control sequences in its text output. The printer interprets the control sequence to change fonts, in this case to MICR. Depending on the make of the printer, such control sequences can be used to include graphics or to invoke background masks that give the appearance of preprinted forms.

The limitations to printer-level graphics are:

■ You can't include graphic objects selected from the database.

■ You generally can't mix fonts, or use proportional fonts, because Oracle*Reports assumes fixed space formatting when it operates in character mode. In other words, you can send font-change commands to the printer, but no Oracle process applies logic to protect you against running over the margins. You are on your own.

You can produce beautiful output with Oracle*Reports, but there are a few general limitations:

■ You must use a PostScript printer, and execution is usually a bit slow at the printer level.

■ If you want to see the reports on your client computer, the report-viewing agent on your desktop must able to present PostScript files.

■ You have to load the host machine, which generates the reports, with fonts corresponding to those on the desktop where you develop the reports. Since Oracle*Reports uses the font size to determine how much data will fit on a page, the fonts have to be available on the machine where the report is generated.

Concurrent processes, including reports, run on the Database Server, which may be a mainframe, VAX, Unix, or Windows 2000 machine. Though almost all servers will support GUI printing through PostScript, it is a facility that may not be commonly used. You may need to locate an operating system consultant to set up the environment for bitmapped printing. Many companies are put off by these setup issues and choose the other options instead. But it may be worth looking into this alternative and its long term cost savings, depending on how many documents will need the graphics and how often those documents will need to be altered.

Flexfields

A flexfield is a segmented identifier, like a phone number. An international number could include Country Code, Area Code, Prefix, Calling Number, and Extension segments. Each segment has its own meaning and may have its own rules controlling the entries that are valid for the segment.

Oracle defines Key and Descriptive Flexfields. Key Flexfields are used as unique identifiers and are predefined by Oracle and require only you to finalize the specific setup details. Ledger accounts, Inventory items and Fixed Assets are Key Flexfield identifiers. Descriptive Flexfields are Oracle's way of letting users add, fill, and view columns of their own data within the Application database tables. Key flexfields are usually required data elements within the application; Descriptive Flexfields are optional.

Key Flexfields

Key Flexfields allow Oracle to use a single internal value to bind related records together, while giving users maximum flexibility in assigning external identifying numbers. For every Key Flexfield there is one master table with columns named SEGMENT1.SEGMENT*n* and a key column named *something*_ID. In General Ledger, the column is CODE_COMBINATION_ID in the GL_CODE_COMBINATIONS table; in Inventory, it is the INVENTORY_ITEM_ID in the MTL_SYSTEM_ITEMS table. Every other table that refers to an Accounting Flexfield carries a column, frequently also named CODE_COMBINATION_ID, that joins as a foreign key to GL_CODE_COMBINATIONS. It would be unwieldy in the extreme to have thirty-segment columns in every table that joins to GL_CODE_COMBINATIONS, such as those carrying balance, budget, and journal details!

Oracle uses number generators, called *sequences,* to generate unique ids. Sequences are a feature of the RDBMS. There is a naming convention for sequences—the sequence name is the table name suffixed with "_S." In several instances, however, a single sequence is used to generate primary keys for multiple tables. Oracle numbers can be up to 22 digits long, enough to enumerate the grains of sand on the earth. The size of the generated key is not a limiting factor.

Using generated keys makes it easy to change the external identifier. An inventory user can correct a part number without concern for any issue, receipt and balance records that reference the part. The major issue in changing a part number is whether it still makes sense to the buyers and warehousemen. Figure 14-4 shows that the flexfield values are stored in the master table, but the juncture to a detail table is done via the generated key.

The Applications usually do not allow users to delete the records that define Key Flexfield combinations. Deleting them could orphan detail records, destroying referential integrity. Instead, many tables carry an END_EFFECTIVE_DATE or some similar column to indicate that the master record cannot be used for new transactions. Users sometimes rename items

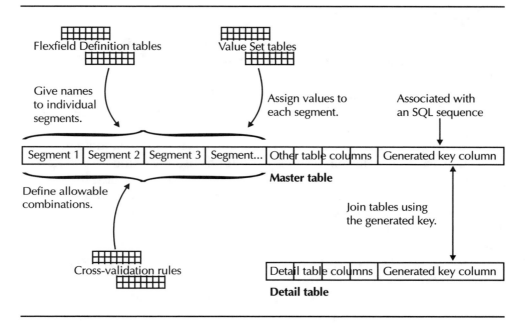

FIGURE 14-4. *Key Flexfield structure*

that are obsolete or have been entered by accident, giving them a Z- prefix or other flag to indicate that they do not represent real items.

You define a structure for each Key Flexfield, naming the segments that make up the flexfield, indicating their length and format (alphabetic or numeric) and the value sets used to validate them. A single master table may include rows with different structures. For example, the ledger tables may support several sets of books, each with a unique chart of accounts structure. Each Inventory Category usually has its own structure. The master table that carries the individual segment values also carries a flexfield structure identifier that tells AOL how to interpret the segments.

General Ledger's Accounting Flexfields make the most extensive use of the key flexfield structure of any application. It is the only package to use three features of key flexfields, namely parent-child relationships, rollup groups, and compiled value attributes. Chapter 2 describes these features in the context of implementation concepts.

Descriptive Flexfields

Descriptive Flexfields (DFFs) allow users to define custom fields into standard forms without modifying the system. Oracle includes a one-column [ ] "beer mug" device in regions that correspond to tables capable of carrying DFF data. When you navigate to the "beer mug" in a form where the DFF is active, a window pops up to display and capture DFF segments. Your DFF specification includes text to identify both a user-defined field in the DFF pop-up and a specification of the value set used to validate it.

A DFF exists as values in a series of columns usually named Attribute 1 through Attribute n in the underlying table. There are exceptions; the Receivables interface uses two DFFs, a standard DFF on the Attribute n columns, and another on a set named INTERFACE_LINE_attribute$n$. Since there is no generated key before the rows are imported, Oracle Receivables uses the interface line DFF to provide the foreign key link among the interface tables: RA_INTERFACE_LINES, RA_INTERFACE_SALESCREDITS, and RA_INTERFACE_DISTRIBUTIONS.

Oracle has established in advance which tables support Descriptive Flexfields. They include the Attribute n columns in the table layout, along with a field for the DFF on the forms that maintain the table. Use the Define Flexfield Segments form to activate the DFF by defining how the segments will be used.

Programmers can populate DFF columns by other means, such as database triggers and stored procedures, which totally bypass the DFF validation. The concept of a Descriptive Flexfield is immaterial to pulling data out of the tables for character-based reporting; including them requires bespoke programming in any case. Smart Client/Internet Computing desktop reporting includes features for adding DFFs to standard reports.

A typical use of DFFs is in purchasing. Federal law allows contractors to request expedited delivery of materials to be used on defense contracts. The contractor passes the contract number and defense rating down to the supplier, who then lets them jump the sequential delivery queue for hard-to-get items. A Federal Contractor might define the following DFF in the Header block of the Enter Purchase Orders form:

Column Name	Description	Format	Value Set
ATTRIBUTE1	Contract Number	Alpha, 20 char	None
ATTRIBUTE2	Government Priority	Alpha, 2 char	DODX

The value set DODX would contain two entries: "DO" and "DX." As a result of this definition, a block containing the following fields would appear when the user entered the DFF field of the input form:

Contract Number _____
        Priority _____

If the DFF were defined as mandatory, the user would not be able to exit the block without making an entry. Contract could be anything, but priority would have to be "DO" or "DX." The entered values would be stored in Attribute 1 and Attribute 2 of PO_HEADERS, the base table for the Headers zone.

Oracle's standard report submission form uses the Descriptive Flexfield device to accept runtime parameters, a usage that taxes the DFF architecture to its fullest. A range of value sets prompt users for beginning and ending values, such as a range of inventory items to include in a cost rollup. You can use special validation to have the user enter a key flexfield value as a parameter. It pops the Key Flexfield, guides the user through the entry of a valid value, and captures the generated key column as the parameter.

Contexts

Contexts give you the ability to redefine the flexfield structure based on the type of record or the value of another field. In setting up Inventory, you may want the Purchasing category to carry flexfields naming the normal procurement vehicle and normal safety stock percentage for new items in the category, but Order Entry might carry the normal order ship time you quote for products in the category. As another example, Oracle Receivables handles invoicing for Order Entry and for Oracle Projects. Each system tags the invoices it passes to Oracle Receivables for billing with system-unique data fields. Projects uses a Project Number, and Order Entry uses a Pick Slip Identifier. Receivables is *context-sensitive,* meaning that it uses the context to determine what the fields mean. The DFF will react differently depending on the value of its Context field.

Flexfield Validation

Some segments in a flexfield may need to be validated. It may be necessary to make sure that the country or area code in a telephone number is valid, or that Department 739 exists within a company. The list of valid values for a given segment is called a Value Set. They can be handled in two ways. Oracle provides tables and update screens for users to maintain smaller, not-so-volatile value sets. Alternatively, the System Administrator can define a link into a column in a table anywhere in Oracle, inside or outside the Applications, in which valid values are to be found. A second column can be identified as the description, to help the user choose a value.

Cross-Validation Rules

There are usually flexfield combinations that do not make sense and should not be allowed. The department number associated with Asset and Liability accounts in an Accounting Flexfield must usually be all zeroes. If the country code for a phone number is 011 (for the U.S.), then area code 911, or prefix 555, is not valid. Cross-validation rules can prevent users from entering these combinations. Figure 14-4 shows segment validation and cross-validation for a key flexfield.

The values in a dependent value set depend on the value of another, independent segment. General Ledger subaccounts are commonly dependent on the account segment. Assume, for example, that the meanings you give for accounts 1001 (Cash in banks) and 1002 (Money Market Assets) are always the same within the value set. However, in your subaccount value set you might define 01 to mean Citizens Bank when the account is 1001, but Rushmore Fund when account is 1002.

TIP
Make flexfield segments as independent as possible of one another. Most dependent segment relationships, such as department within division, change over time. You have more flexibility if you use parent-child relationships on a flexfield segment instead of defining hierarchies into the flexfield structure itself. It is tedious to constantly maintain dependent value sets or cross-validation rules.

Cross validation and dependent segment validation are complicated to manage. They work best when the segment values do not change often. A flexfield that includes complex, volatile and difficult to validate segment values merits reexamination. It may be possible to exclude segments or control them by administrative procedures rather than by automated validation.

Cross-validation rules follow INCLUDE/EXCLUDE logic. A simple rule that most companies use is to force the Department number to the default on asset and liability accounts. Assuming a very simple three-segment Accounting Flexfield, the rules would be:

Action	Company Low	Company High	Department Low	Department High	Account Low	Account High
INCLUDE	00	99	000	999	00000	99999
EXCLUDE	00	99	001	999	00000	19999

These rules are applied in sequence. The first one here says that all accounting flexfields are valid if the company is between 00 and 99, the Department between 000 and 999, and the Account between 00000 and 99999. That's everything: if you were to use Rule 1 only, there would be no invalid combinations.

The second rule excludes combinations in which the Department is anything other than 000, for all values of Company and for values of Account between 00000 and 19999. In other words, combination 01-010-05555 would be invalid. Though it is in the INCLUDE range for the first rule, it is also in the EXCLUDE range for Rule 2, since 010 falls between 001 and 999, and 05555 falls between 00000 and 19999. The effect of both rules together is that only department 000 is valid with any account in the range 00000 to 199999.

Though these INCLUDE/EXCLUDE rules could be applied differently, Oracle recommends that you stick with their convention of defining one INCLUDE followed by a series of EXCLUDES. It is harder to debug and harder to maintain if you do cross-validation with a series of includes, such as the logically equivalent:

Action	Company Low	Company High	Department Low	Department High	Account Low	Account High
INCLUDE	00	99	000	000	00000	19999
INCLUDE	00	99	000	999	20000	99999

The recommended approach favors leniency in that errors would result in failing to exclude invalid combinations rather than excluding valid ones. You can usually trust the system users to know their data. Their own caution usually keeps them entering bad values, and you can be sure you will hear from them when they cannot enter a good one.

The Applications apply different edit mechanics as rows are created, updated and queried. As you create a master record with a Key Flexfield identifier, all the segment values must be valid and the combination must pass the cross-validation check. This is the only time cross-validation rules are used. Changing them later has no effect on records you have already created.

If you create a row with a combination of valid segments, but later disable an individual segment, the master record remains in the database and can be transacted. General Ledger allows you to disable account and department values, preventing their use in new code combinations, while still accepting journals to be posted against existing code combinations using those segments. The point to remember is that disabling an individual segment value does not prevent transactions against existing records. To prevent all transactions against a given GL account value, you would need to disable every existing code combination that uses the value.

Flexfield Security

Flexfield Security gives you the ability to control access to Key and Descriptive Flexfield combinations at the Responsibility level. It is often applied to the Accounting Flexfield to define different responsibilities for different GL companies and prevent companies from making entries in each other's books. You might apply it to the System Item flexfield to reserve a range of item numbers for the engineering department and prevent manufacturing from creating or referencing items within the range, or to the Asset Flexfield if you want to distribute responsibility to different organizations.

You write the exclusion rules in the same format as the cross-validation rules shown earlier. You give each set of rules a name, and associate the names with responsibilities. As a flexfield is presented to the user, AOL filters out the values that the rules prevent the user from accessing.

Flexfield Definition

There are several reasons for having any complex flexfield structure laid out in a document. First, doing so documents the flexfield usage. Second, it provides a single source from which the flexfield can be copied identically into multiple instances. Last, because flexfield definitions persist in memory even after they have been changed in the database, flexfields are easier to debug if they are entered afresh for every test.

When you have multiple contexts for a flexfield, you usually need a separate series of segment definitions for each context. Though different contexts may have the same segment, the edits are often different. It is generally easier to define two distinct value sets, each of them simple, than to define a complex one to do double duty. The spreadsheet (or word processor) columns for each segment within a context should include the following:

Flexfield information

- **Segment name**   This is the label that will appear when the flexfield is presented.

- **Security flag (Y/N)**   Do you want flexfield security? If you define access rules, security can restrict the users who can access a flexfield. You can also use security merely to prevent users from changing values in a flexfield that is meant only to display information. For example, Oracle Payables gives the option of importing the DFF values from employee expense reports as you convert them into the invoices used for reimbursement. You might want the DFF values to be visible on the invoice, but if you allowed users to change them, they would become inconsistent with the expense report values.

- **Segment format: Char or Number**   This refers to the entered value, not the hidden value that will eventually be stored. Char is appropriate most of the time even when the values are numeric, such as for General Ledger accounts. You do need to define the format as number for numeric range validation: 10 is lower than 2 in an alphabetic comparison but not in numeric.

- **Segment length**   How many characters do you want entered? It is best to make segments equal to the length defined for the column returned by the validation and the default WHERE clauses. The flexfield presentation routines will encounter errors that users cannot bypass if the results exceed the length you give. Even in GUI, the size of the description plus 150 characters maximum for the value exceeds the width of the screen. Sometimes you have to specify a display length less than the segment length in order to fit the flexfield on the screen. In that case the segment will scroll.

- **Validation type**   This is usually None, Independent, Dependent, Special, or Table. Value pairs are used for specifying ranges, primarily as parameters. Special validation is useful for entering Key Flexfield values as parameters.

- **Value set name**   This will tie the DFF to an existing value set, limiting the values available to only those in the quickpick. Because value sets can be difficult to debug because of the persistence of their values in memory, it is useful in debugging to define new value sets rather than fixing old ones. At least in your test instance, it is convenient to give value sets a suffix like _00, so you can change them globally within your word processing source document, including all :$FLEX$.value_set_name references, as you debug them.

Value Set Information

- **For table validation**   Make a list of the tables referenced in the validation SQL, each with a one-character alias. (It is important to economize on name lengths, as you'll see later.) You can leave the Source Application field blank. Tables can actually come from multiple Applications, or even from outside the Applications.

■ **Name the value column**   This is what the user will see.

■ **Name the description column**   This is what the user will see as confirmation. This can be handled by "Additional Columns" as well, with the small difference that the Description is presented even when the value is filled by default, which is not the case for Additional columns.

■ **Hidden column**   If you make an entry here, this column, rather than the Value column named earlier, will be stored in Attribute *n*. This is useful for picking up generated keys or code values.

■ **Additional column**   These are values that will be shown to help the user make a selection when he or she is presented a list of values for a segment. For instance, it may help when asking a user to select a customer number to present the customer name and marketing contact.

■ **WHERE clause for the value set**   Use the table aliases established earlier to keep this as short as possible. You may reference the value selected in value sets associated with prior segments by :$FLEX$.value_set_name.

Additional Flexfield Information

■ **SQL default for the flexfield definition**   The format for selecting the default value in the flexfield closely parallels the WHERE clause of the value set that validates it, so it is convenient to keep them side-by-side. Economy is important: the length of the SQL phrase is limited to 200 characters in the Default Value field of the Define Flexfield and Define Parameters screens. As with the WHERE clause earlier in the value set, you may refer to the values selected in prior segments by :$FLEX$.value_set_name.

Often, once an Oracle Form or Responsibility has loaded a value set, the value set definition will persist in memory even after its definition has been changed in the database. The WHERE clause in a value set definition often presents this problem. You will find it difficult to perfect your code by changing it in place and retesting, even if you navigate out of the form and change responsibility. You will usually find it easier to abandon and reenter unsuccessful value sets than to try to fix them. The work goes faster if you are able to create a new value set for each test by updating the value set names in a reference document, as described here, then copying and pasting them into the Applications.

National Language Support (NLS)

Many companies that use Oracle Applications are multinational. Oracle's national language support (NLS) satisfies the need to fully operate your Oracle database and Oracle Applications in a foreign language. There are two distinct parts to NS/LS, and you can install one or both parts. The database NLS extension allows you to store data in a language other than American English. The application NLS extension provides screens, reports and seed data that has been translated into a language other than English. The following sections describe these NLS functions in detail.

AOL-Level Language Determination

A user's national language is established at the very beginning of a session. In NCA, each listener on the Web server operates in one language. A user determines the language of a session by the URL he or she chooses at login time. In Smart Client, the desktop software is language-specific; in character mode, it is established as part of the user's environment when he or she logs into the Applications. This approach makes national language independent of security considerations, such as responsibilities, and it means you do not have to confine a multilingual user to one language.

Internally, the language is carried as a session variable. SQL's USERENV function can return the national language attribute of an Oracle login session and the current form. Programmers can take language into consideration in PL/SQL routines and even SQL*Plus code. Specifically, it gives Oracle Applications a device to determine the language in which to communicate with any given user.

Literals in screen canvases are compiled into Oracle forms and reports. Oracle handles the translation centrally; the installation provides forms generated in the necessary national languages. The Applications server directory structure includes sublibraries for each language; a structure to support American English and French would look something like the following:

```
APPS161
  BOM60
   forms
     us
       BOMxxxxx.fmb  (interpretive forms 4.5 file)
       BOMxxxxx.fmx  (interpretive forms 4.5 file)
     fr
       BOMxxxxx.fmb  (interpretive forms 4.5 file)
       BOMxxxxx.fmx  (interpretive forms 4.5 file)
   mesg
 us.msb  (English messages)
 fr.msb  (French messages)
```

The Applications use their own message format. Instead of having all possible messages and help text hard-coded into the forms, Oracle puts in subroutine calls that name the message to be presented. The forms find the message in the appropriate national language library. Oracle's device of staging the messages in operating system files on the server, rather than storing them on the database server, makes the presentation more efficient.

Character-mode forms use a similar scheme. The messages, however, are stored on the server side, in a subdirectory named $*APP*_TOP/mesg, and the Forms 2.3/2.4 code is stored in a subdirectory named $*APP*_TOP/forms.

National Language Support for Reports

Separate versions of reports programs are required for the same reason as they are for forms. Their boilerplate includes compiled literals in headings and field identifiers, they need to select the appropriate translations of lookup codes, flexfield values, and data fields, and they need to use the right display format for numbers and dates. National language versions of report programs are stored using the same directory scheme as for forms.

National Language Support for Flexfields

Flexfields are used to capture variable data and report runtime parameters. The prompts for each segment are in the forms user's native language. As part of your setup you need to translate your custom flexfields and value sets for the countries to be supported by your implementation. A user profile option controls whether Flexfield entries are keyed left to right or, as in Arabic or Hebrew, right to left.

National Language in Data

Data is defined here as information that your organization stores in the database; it is directly affected by the character set. With any character set, you can store American English, and—as long as they are the same character set that you enter—store multiple other languages in your database. You may only have one character set defined for your database. So you could not store English, German, and Japanese in the database. In the future with the use of the UTF8 character set, you will be able to achieve this.

Perhaps the language is French, and you enter a description such as **Marteau.** When you click the translation icon on the toolbar, a form will pop up the languages available for translation and allow you to make entries for those you wish. You might want to enter the English translation as **Hammer**, and the Spanish as **Martillo.**

The form presents the translation that corresponds to the language of the session. If the user were connected via a session in French in the previous example, bringing the record just entered up in a query form would only display "Marteau."

Alerts

Oracle*Alert is licensed as an Application, but it functions as an extension of AOL in that it supplements the features of all the Applications.

An alert is essentially a single SQL statement or PL/SQL block and instruct what to do with the rows it returns. The most common action is to e-mail them to the people who need to take action. You can have an alert generate one e-mail per row or put all rows into a single e-mail. You can have multiple recipients. Alerts can be used in place of reports, with the following benefits:

■ Alerts send information only when it is needed, whereas reports are usually produced on a periodic basis, and may not always be promptly read.

■ Alerts send just the relevant information, not a whole report.

■ Alerts target just the people who need to know.

■ Alerts are easy for programmers to implement. They justify their cost by making the business more responsive and reducing paper costs.

There are two types of alerts, periodic and event. Periodic alerts are fired by the clock, Event alerts by a predefined change in a database table. Event alerts usually require more system resources than periodic alerts because they have to execute every time the database changes. Unless the recipient needs to respond extremely fast, and you can count on the recipient to actively monitor his or her e-mail, a periodic alert that runs a few times a day should suffice.

The periodic alert mechanism has a clock at its core. It wakes up on the schedule you set to see what needs to be checked. It executes a check for each alert whose time is due.

If the check comes back positive, it takes an action. Sending an e-mail message is the most common action, but alerts can kick off virtually any kind of process within Oracle or the Operating System shell, such as the following:

■ Check the age and number of completed concurrent requests on the system. If the number is too great, kick off a job to delete the oldest ones or send a message to have the DBA do so.

■ Initiate an operating-system level process to send or receive electronic data transfers. Though alerts have the power to handle such operations, most users implement them through the Concurrent Manager.

■ See if any tables or indexes are close to being out of space. Make a quick fix by allowing more extents and alert the DBA.

■ Check for data exceptions such as a missing field value that may be optional in Oracle but required by your business practice. You might choose an alert as an inexpensive alternative to modifying a form for the purpose of tightening the edits.

■ Notify a manager that a purchase order is awaiting approval.

The real-time nature of event alerts triggers generally dictates that they work one row at a time. Periodic alert triggers can be written either way. In general, a single message with multiple actions is easier for a user to deal with than many messages with one action apiece. You don't want to flood inboxes.

Because they are written in SQL and not highly formatted, alerts are generally quicker and easier to write than custom reports. Oracle Alert is an end-user tool, and so individual alerts enjoy support from Oracle at the same level as, for instance, FSG reports in Oracle General Ledger. Oracle does not assume similar responsibility for bespoke code you write in Oracle*Reports or SQL*Plus. Nonetheless, Alerts do require knowledge of programming. The people writing them need the level of understanding of the Applications tables that is provided by the *Technical Reference Manuals*.

Event alerts can be CPU-intensive, so you should weigh the gain versus the cost involved in developing these types of alerts for active tables. If used effectively, alerts are a great tool, but if used excessively they become a drag on the system and fill up users' mailboxes with unimportant notifications.

TIP
Programming staff should consider whether an Alert would do the job before undertaking a bespoke report.

Application Management

All the standard applications are preregistered in AOL. New applications that you build and install yourself are registered under AOL using the same conventions. Knowing what and where things are makes the system easier to debug, and makes it easier to communicate with Oracle in resolving problems. This knowledge is essential to developers writing enhancements to the system.

When upgrading or applying patches, the process may, at times, alter or completely delete and re-create AOL data that is owned by the standard applications. However, these processes will never affect data that is owned by your custom applications if it has been set up correctly.

Users and Responsibilities

In setting up an Oracle Applications user, you define the person in terms of their role in the business. They need, of course, a user id and a password, the same kind of access control as for a network, an operating system, or Oracle. You also provide the user's name and e-mail address.

A person is linked by his or her name to the Human Resources system, which places the person in the hierarchy of organizations and managers. Systems like Purchasing may require managerial approval for some type of transactions. The Applications maintain a link between people in the HR master table (PER_PEOPLE_F) and system users (FND_USER). This link frequently determines access to Purchasing, Payables, and Human Resources functions.

Oracle Alert and Workflow processes use the e-mail address to notify a user of actions that need attention. E-mail is an especially convenient medium for getting the message to those users whose jobs do not require that they log onto the Applications frequently.

Responsibilities are Oracle's device for giving and controlling access. Granting control user-by-user and process-by-process would be unworkable. Instead, the System Administrator can do the following:

- Assign multiple functions to a form. (This is possible only in GUI or Internet Computing mode.)

- Put every needed form on one or more low-level menus.

- Put low-level menus on one or more higher-level menus, working up to a top-level menu.

- Create a Responsibility name associated with that top-level menu.

- Assign one or more users to the Responsibility.

Any user with the Responsibility can get to any process in the associated menu structure. Each user can have as many Responsibilities as necessary. As a matter of convenience, however, it is useful to put all their commonly used functions into a single Responsibility, saving users from the effort of constantly changing Responsibilities.

The Responsibilities that Oracle delivers provide maximum access—and minimal control. The System Administrator's best course is to leave them alone and define new, more limited Responsibilities that suit the business and to deactivate the original Responsibilities, at least in the production instance. Creating new responsibilities can seem complex at first and involves developing new high-level menus to be associated with them. The most common need is to offer a more limited number of lower-level menu choices. However, you can also broaden menu choices, even including functions from multiple applications in the menu structure of a single Responsibility.

Your custom high-level menu will usually use the lower-level Oracle menus as delivered. For example, you will usually want to take the ability to create and update inventory items away from most users. However, users who have the privilege can usually both create and update items. Oracle's low-level menu offers those choices. You would place it, as is, on the higher-level menu you create for the inventory item definition and Responsibility.

The wide-open Responsibilities that Oracle delivers with the system remain useful to the developers. They don't need to be restricted by the administrative controls imposed over production. The primary reasons that a System Administrator may limit developers' activity to the development instance are to control system functions and protect sensitive data, both of which can be managed by granting or withholding Oracle Responsibilities. Since the only easy way to create a test instance is to copy production, and production Human Resources/Payroll is bound to contain sensitive personal and salary data for each employee, it makes sense to provide access to those systems on a need-to-know basis. The System Administrator may need to withhold Systems Administration privileges from developers to prevent them from modifying system security and from granting themselves access to HR/Payroll.

However, when you design your new menus and Responsibilities, it is imperative that they be owed by your custom application and that all profile options that have been defined for the same standard application also be defined for your custom application. Without this your custom Responsibilities will not work as expected.

Security

Encrypted passwords at the Applications user id and Oracle user-id levels form the basis of security within the Applications. The System Administrator assigns Applications user ids and initial passwords (by convention, "WELCOME") to new users. The password assigned by the Systems Administrator is immediately expired. The new user is prompted to change it when he first logs on, after which it is known only to him. The System Administrator can change it but cannot read it.

Figure 14-5 diagrams how a user goes through the two levels of security to get to the database. From left to right:

1. The user presents his user id and password to AOL at logon. This logon is done after the user has logged onto the operating system and network, which may or may not be password protected.

2. AOL presents a list of the responsibilities authorized to that user. Each responsibility is associated with a top-level menu, which branches down to a menu tree of Applications functions. The Systems Administrator custom-tailors the top-level menus to meet the needs of the installation. Most organizations stick with the submenus that Oracle distributes.

3. Each menu entry represents a lower-level menu or an Oracle Form. The bottom level is always a form (though it may be the form that invokes reports and other batch processes).

4. AOL looks up the Oracle user id and password appropriate to the Application to which the process belongs. In Releases 10.7 and later, there is a common view, shown in Figure 14-5 as the APPS schema, that has been granted the appropriate permissions on all the application schemas. AOL fetches and decrypts the password for the appropriate user id, then activates the form in a session with that Oracle user id. The form may go through this process again to kick off batch jobs such as reports.

5. The Application's user winds up using a form or batch process that has access to the Oracle RDBMS. Changes the user can make to the database are limited by the functions programmed into the process and the permissions the Oracle Application has on database tables.

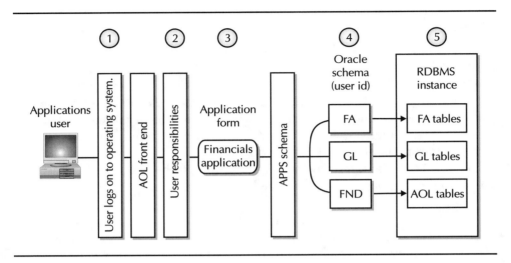

FIGURE 14-5. *Applications security*

There is an added need for security with Internet Computing because with the Internet you have no control over who will attempt to access your system. Information exchanges between clients and the Web server under Internet Computing are all encrypted using 40- or 128-bit algorithms. When communications are encrypted, security depends on controlling the cryptographic keys. Oracle maintains control over the client machines, which cannot be physically secured, from the platforms that can be secured, namely the Web server and database server.

Internet Computing's digital signature security uses public key encryption techniques. The keys to encrypt and decrypt the data are different, and one cannot be derived from the other. The Oracle host can provide the desktop client with keys to decrypt inbound messages and encrypt outbound messages without disclosing the encryption scheme itself. The exposure is small even if one key is compromised, because they change from session to session.

The challenge, then, is to authenticate a desktop as it logs into the Applications. Oracle manages this by maintaining a positive control of the desktop from the very start. There is an encrypted digital signature in the applet that Oracle Applications downloads to the desktop browser of an Applications user. The desktop client also contains the identity of a "trusted source" and a public key that can be used to decrypt messages from that source. The browser matches (a) the digital signature in the desktop applet, and (b) the digital signature in the certificate file using (c) the message from the trusted source, as decrypted by the public key in the certificate file. The browser will not accept the download of a new applet without this authentication.

Once a user is validated to Applications, the process is the same for all users. The menu structure provides functional security, preventing unauthorized access to processes. Oracle responsibilities have the following two mechanisms to control access to data:

- **Multi-Org**   Restricts users to a single Organization or operating unit.

- **Flexfield Value Security**   Blocks access to ranges of flexfield values.

Multi-Org, described in Chapter 2, cleanly segregates data through the use of views defined on major tables. Only a minority of the tables, mostly at the master level, have views defined. Those views automatically limit access to subordinate tables, because there is no way to get to the detail except through a join on the master table. The tables on which views are defined have names ending in _ALL.

The view definitions use an interesting device in the Oracle RDBMS itself. The Applications set the organization ID as an RDBMS-level environment variable. Whereas views in the past have referenced only data in the database, these Multi-Org views apply this environment variable to determine which rows are included. Because the views are 1:1 with the underlying tables, the Applications can insert and update through them.

Flexfield Value Security operates at a lower level, within an organization. You set up rules to apply to individual Key Flexfields, such as the Accounting Flexfield or System Item (inventory part number) Flexfield, and assign the rules to Responsibilities. AOL filters the rows it presents, on screens or in batch processes, through the rules for the current Responsibility. Here are some examples of the types of problems that Flexfield Value Security can help you prevent:

- One organization creating ledger journals using another organization's accounts.

- Unauthorized persons seeing budget and actual journals for personnel expenses.

■ Manufacturing using a range of part numbers restricted for Engineering.

Some Applications, notably character-mode Order Entry, can be customized at setup time to restrict access to regions and fields on forms. The Order Entry controls are intended to enforce a freeze on order attributes after a given point in the order cycle, booking in particular, rather than to restrict access to predefined groups of records, such as items or customers.

Instances

The Applications are built on the Oracle Relational Database Management System (RDBMS). A high-level overview of the database structure is essential to understanding the Applications and to provide a basis for communicating with DBAs and Systems Administrators.

Figure 14-6 gives a high-level view of the elements in the RDBMS. An *instance* is a complete Oracle database. There is usually more than one instance per environment. In fact, four is a common number for the Applications: Oracle's Demo instance, the Conference Room Pilot, a Test instance, and Production.

The database is only for data storage. The Oracle software modules that manage the instance are not part of it; they are kept in operating system directories just like other programs. The system tables that keep track of database objects, such as tables and users, are themselves data and therefore within the instance.

Keeping the Oracle database in sync with the software, which is maintained at an operating-system level and may support several instances, requires good configuration management on the part of the DBA. Quite often a patch will include changes to both the database schema and program modules that use it.

Bringing the database up or down takes place at the instance level. Oracle expects all of the Applications data to reside within a single instance. For the purposes of the Applications, either all tables are available or none are. The Order Entry process should never hang up, as an example, because Inventory is not available to validate the product number. There is a device called a *database link* that makes it possible to join tables across instances and interface data from remote systems. It is possible to distribute the

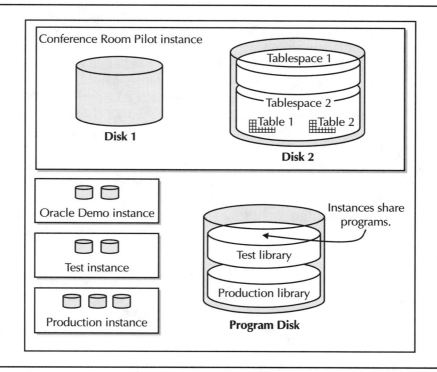

FIGURE 14-6.   *Oracle's Relational Database Manager System (RDBMS)*

processing across nodes in a network system, but Oracle Financials does not support databases distributed across machines.

The disk space for an instance exists in operating system level files, usually several files spread on more than one hard disk. To Oracle, these are *tablespaces*; to the operating system, they are files. A tablespace can consist of more than one disk file. This allows for large tablespaces, spread over more than one hard disk, and for expanding tablespaces. Table placement in tablespaces and on disks can be independent of schemas. Tablespaces represent the outer limit of objects recognized by Oracle and inner boundary of those recognized by the Unix, MVS, VMS, or NT operating system. DBAs manage tablespaces. Users have no need to be aware of them.

Tables are at the heart of the relational concept. A table is made up of a number of *rows*, all of which have the same *columns*. A table is like a spreadsheet, which is why they are usually shown symbolically as grids, as in Figure 14-6. *Relationships* make the difference between a database and, say, a collection of spreadsheets. Two RDBMS tables can be related to one another by a common column. The PO_HEADERS_ALL and PO_LINES_ALL tables in the Purchasing application have the header_id column in common. The database can use the relationship based on this shared column to find the customer associated with a purchase order line, or the items associated with a purchase order header. Spreadsheets don't do that.

Each table exists within one tablespace and belongs to one of the users defined to that instance of the Oracle RDBMS. A user is known by a user id, or *schema*. Database users are distinct from the AOL users described earlier. The original notion was that a schema was a group of related tables—a database design. That concept became outdated, as the Financials design now integrates a large number of schemas. In any case, one schema, or user, can give permission for other users to read and/or modify data in tables it owns.

Oracle Applications concepts function at the table level. Keys to the Applications architecture are that:

- Each Application is known to the Oracle RDBMS by one Oracle user id or schema. Records of individual Applications users are stored within the Applications themselves, and the Application users will not have corresponding database user ids.

- Each Application owns tables through its Oracle user id. The Applications achieve their integration by sharing tables with one another. They are written with the assumption that all tables are available all the time, that is to say, in the same instance.[8]

- In Releases 10.7 and higher, every Application grants full permissions on all its objects to a single schema, named APPS. With more than 40 products now in the suite, this simplification is essential. Every form and Concurrent Manager process initiated within the Applications uses the APPS schema.

---

[8]There may be reasons to spread Applications across multiple instances. The DBA has to make sure that all the instances and the links between them are available whenever the Applications are in use.

File Storage

Each application has its own root within the operating system directory structure, and each kind of code and operating system data has its own home within that root.[9] Internet Computing and Smart Client use two directory structures, one on the database server and another on the client side, either the desktop or (preferably) a LAN or Web server. The structure for the database server is outlined in Table 14-1.

The client-side directory structure is similar but simpler. For most Applications, forms are still the only code executed there. Look for them to expand as more and more Applications get desktop integration, data analyzers, and other client-side tools.

You usually need at least two directory structures on both the client and server side—one for production and another to test patches. Figure 14-6 shows two on the server side. The DBA handles the association between program libraries and the instances they support, and makes sure that the data is compatible with the software assigned to it.

Quickcodes and Lookup Types

Oracle keeps data in the database, external to the programs. For the most part, Oracle-written programs use code values instead of literals. For example, an mrp_planning_code value of 3 means MRP planning; 6 means not planned. Using codes is a tenet of a properly normalized data architecture, and it is the only reasonable way to handle multilanguage implementations. It prevents data redundancy. The delivered databases are seeded with a number of such Oracle-provided data values.

Quickcodes support *quickpicks,* standard sets of user-defined values. They offer users a choice of codes for values such as invoice type or payment terms. There are separate quickcodes tables in each application that uses them. Users are generally expected to modify and add to the delivered quickcodes.

A *lookup* is a combination of a code and a description. The code is stored in the database, the description in a lookup table. Descriptions are carried in the user's national language. The lookup tables are generally populated by the scripts in the application's /install/odf directory. Whereas

[9]There are also subdirectories for things other than code, among them reports and logs from the concurrent processor and regression test output.

Class of Subdirectory	Name	Contents
Runtime code	bin	C programs, SQL*Loader, and operating system shell scripts. (These are relatively uncommon.)
	forms	Oracle*Forms source and interpretive code.[10] In Smart Client, this directory is on the desktop or LAN server. In Internet Computing, it is on the Web server.
	srw	Oracle*Reports interpretive code to be invoked by the Concurrent Manager.
	sql	SQL*Plus and PL/SQL interpretive code to be invoked by the Concurrent Manager
Install-time code	install/odf (prior to 10.6) admin/odf (10.7 and later)	Install scripts to set up database objects such as tables, views, indexes, grants, and the like.
	install/sql (prior to 10.6) admin/sql (10.7 and later)	Install scripts to create database triggers, packaged procedures, and the like. Unlike the modules in the /sql subdirectory, this code is run only once, at setup. Forms and concurrent processes will invoke these triggers and stored procedures repeatedly.
	install/drv (prior to 10.6) admin/drv (10.7 and later)	Driver scripts to install the application. These modules invoke the ones in the /install/sql and /install/odf directories.

[10]The Applications are written primarily in Oracle*Forms, Oracle*Reports, and PL/SQL. These are interpretive languages. The real executable modules are the interpreters; they reside in the Oracle Tools instead of in the Oracle Applications directory structure. The only true executables in the Applications directory structure are in the /bin subdirectory. Everything else is really data to a runtime engine, such as runforms or runreports.

TABLE 14-1. *Database server directory structure in NCA and Smart Client*

Class of Subdirectory	Name	Contents
Other operating system files	mesg	Compiled message files needed at runtime by forms. In Smart Client or Internet Computing it is on the same host as the forms.
	out_*instance*	Subdirectories with names starting with "out" hold concurrent process output. *instance* is optional; the default name is simply out. This directory may not be present. Instead, DBA can have all output go to the directory pointed to by the $APPLCSF environment variable.
	log_*instance*	Subdirectories with names starting with "log" hold concurrent process logs.
	regress	Regression testing results. Testers create this directory only if it is needed. It exists in character mode only.

TABLE 14-1.   *Database server directory structure in NCA and Smart Client* (continued)

users are expected to customize quickcode values, you usually do not modify lookup table values except to support custom extensions.

Managing the Applications Environment

Any group of Oracle Applications users will invariably have a number of copies of each package installed. Production always takes one copy. Obviously, developers and DBAs should never jeopardize production by testing their patches and improvements there; they need their own copies. Fixing what is and creating what is to come are two different jobs that usually need different environments. Successfully managing software multiplicity can be a challenge, but DBAs and implementers have a number of strategies available:

- Multiple host processors

- Multiple database instances on one processor

- Multiple versions of the Oracle Applications software on one processor

- Multiple installations of a product within one database instance

- Multiple organizations within a single installation of a single product, via the Multi-Org feature

- Multiple front-ends (Smart Client, Internet Computing, Web server, character mode) to the same data. (There remain some patching issues when SC and Internet Computing coexist as front-ends.)

- Multiple Currency Reporting for a single package

REMEMBER
Just as there are different types of users, there are different paths to multiplicity. The strategies that succeed with one group may not be appropriate for another.

Multiple Environments for Development

DBAs use separate machines, database instances, and program directory structures to separate testing and development from production. The issues with Oracle's distributed program code are different from those dealing with the database. Several database instances—that is, several copies of a Financials Application—can share a common code library. The reverse is not true. The Oracle seed data within the database must match the code.[11] Figure 14-6 shows a typical environment, with four instances and two library structures.

---

[11]To give an example, Oracle performs lookups to find the appropriate text to display for Yes/No parameter settings in the database. That is, Yes/No, Ja/Nein, Oui/Non, Si/No, etc. The codes in the database are now 1 = yes and 2 = no. Previously, they were Y = yes and N = no. In one situation a customer error in applying a patch resulted in an Inventory screen program that was looking for 1 or 2 while the database values were still set to Y and N.

Code

The DBA and developers need separate code libraries and directory structures to test Oracle distributions of new versions of applications before putting them into production, and to test patches before applying them in production. Oracle builds the software release level into the directory tree name at the operating system level. For instance, all the code for Release 11.0.3 of Purchasing will be in this directory:[12]

```
/oraappl/po/11.0.3
```

By this convention the Oracle install scripts will know exactly where to put Version 11.1.2—and will create the new subdirectory.

```
/oraappl/po/11.1.2
```

Patches are a different issue. Oracle patch distributions modify the code within a distribution library. Oracle stresses, and we stress, that patches must be tested before putting them into production. The only way to do that is to have a separate copy of the code libraries for test purposes. Apply the patch in the test library (and the associated test instance), test the patch, and then use the same Oracle patch procedure to reapply it in production once it works.

Custom development does not require the same kind of separation because it does not carry the same kind of release dependency as do Oracle's distributions. Oracle's convention is to have users define custom applications to own custom modules. Doing this works because:

- The Applications are designed to share your data and custom tools with each other. It is easy; for example, say that you've designed an inventory form to use within your custom inventory application. You can easily include that form in a menu of standard Oracle inventory forms. It is just as easy to incorporate your customized reports.

- Oracle's upgrade scripts touch only standard applications. Putting bespoke code in a separate application protects it from upgrade and patch activity.

---

[12]The DBA decides on the top-level directory name (in this case, oraappl). Oracle's install scripts create the rest of the tree.

Database Instances

The high level of integration within the Oracle Applications can lead to unexpected consequences in development. Repeatable results have been an essential part of testing philosophy since Roger Bacon pioneered the scientific method. With the Applications, however, a tester will often alter the database in a way that cannot be undone. Moreover, a tester cannot know, or take time to figure out, the full impact of his testing. A functional test that generates Purchase Orders to test EDI, for instance, can affect the General Ledger, Accounts Receivable, Inventory, and manufacturing.

The ideal solution would be to create separate database instances in which each developer could test in isolation. The disk space this would require makes it unfeasible, precisely because of Oracle's high level of integration. Each test instance requires data for all the Applications. To stick with the previous example, Purchasing requires items from Inventory, code combinations from the Ledger, and vendors shared with Accounts Payable.

The reality is that Oracle Financials developers have to establish conventions that let them work effectively within compromised environments. These safeguards usually include the following:

- Keeping two or three Oracle Instances for development, corresponding roughly to development, integration testing, and patch testing.

- Periodically refreshing the test instances, usually by restoring copies of production. The copy populates the test instance with "real" data, as distinguished from "live" data. It is no longer "live" because it is not being used to run the business. Real data is essential for test purposes. Users understand the real data, and they explain their problems in terms of real data, and of course it would be a huge task to generate representative test data for all the Financials.

- Using custom scripts as necessary to sanitize the real data by scrambling salary, medical, budget, and other sensitive data.

- When possible, having developers use rollbacks or SQL scripts to reset the database to its initial state prior to their testing.

- Allocating ranges of data to different testing purposes. For instance, Accounts Payable testers might restrict themselves to Vendors starting with "A" and stock numbers starting with "1." Purchasing testers might then use "B" and "2."

Whatever the compromises, the developers will always work with fewer instances than they would like. Two instances are the least number that is at all workable.

Many organizations keep the Global Manufacturing demonstration instance that Oracle delivers available for developers to experiment with. It is easier to try screen processes with a fully populated system than a new one, which would require setup and generation of master data before it could accept transactions.

Conference Room Pilot instances are a useful testing device for setup scripts and data. A CRP is usually an uncontrolled environment, allowing developers and users alike to conduct experiments without having to be concerned about the impact their transactions may have on testing. Because CRP is uncontrolled, usually using the wide-open Oracle responsibilities, it is important to maintain external documentation for the setup values used. You can use Oracle's AIM methodology, or the approaches outlined in Chapter 15.

Multiple Use of the Applications in Production

Most of the Applications were initially designed to support a single organization with a single set of setup parameters. It became common in earlier versions of the Applications to see multiple installations of Fixed Assets or Accounts Payable within a single enterprise, each one supporting some portion of the organization. Oracle's Multi-Org feature now supports multiple organizations within a single install of a package.

Multiple Product Installations

Each Application gets its own schema, or Oracle user id, to identify it within the instance. Doing multiple installs of an application within one instance is then a matter of setting up multiple schemas. They share the same executable code because the operating system-level environment variables are set identically for all of them.

The System Administrator gives each install within the instance a unique application name. He or she groups Applications into data groups, each of which cannot have more than one install of any given Application within it. Each responsibility is assigned a data group, so the responsibility resolves the issue of which installation of a package is associated with a given user.

It was easy to have one install of General Ledger support multiple installs of packages such as Accounts Payable, because the data flow is one way. AP posts to GL, not the other way around. AP references GL master data (i.e., code combinations) and not the other way around.

Packages other than GL usually have a two-way data flow. These have to be one-to-one. For example, Oracle Payables cannot deal with two purchasing or two inventory systems. It is not prepared to decide which of two identical PO numbers, or two identical stock numbers, are referenced on a given invoice. The decision to use multiple installs of these systems would atomize the business, depriving a company of a unified view of operations, uniform application of policy, and consistent dealings with vendors and customers. In practice, multiple installs worked best with Applications such as Fixed Assets that are largely independent of other modules.

DISTRIBUTED DATABASE   As of Release 11, the Applications do not require distributed databases, but the Applications can handle them in a limited fashion if the DBA chooses to implement them. The DBA may desire some forms of distribution or replication for the purposes of performance and data integrity. Partitioning tables by ORG_ID in a Multi-Org implementation appears to be an attractive alternative. The Applications have no programmed awareness of distributed database concepts: to them it is all one. Users too will do better to visualize the database as a monolith rather than a collection of isolated files. Logically it is an integrated whole, the physical siting of which is a matter of convenience for the technical people.

Oracle's Multi-Org feature uses an ORG_ID column as a high-level key to split master tables by Operating Unit. This suits it to the Partitioning feature of Versions 7.3 and up of the RDBMS. Partitioning facilitates geographic splitting of tables, even across multiple machines. Multinational users can look for further developments in this area.

Multi-Org

Applications using Oracle's Multi-Org feature (described in Chapter 2) are able to physically combine the records of logically separate business units. Keeping all the records in a single installation of the Applications is easier from an administrative perspective. It also makes it possible to draw from different groups' information to produce higher level reports, such as a summary of customer or vendor activity across the entire company. Online users, however, are confined to working only with data that belongs to their own organization.

The user's login responsibility is associated with a single organization. A PL/SQL function, created especially for the Applications, sets an environment variable to indicate that organization. The environment variable can be referenced by an SQL/PL/SQL function call. Specifically, it can be included in the WHERE clause of a view.

Most processes as of 10.7 reference the master tables through a view instead of directly. They can update through the view because it uses only the one table. The WHERE clause will restrict the view to records belonging to the user's organization.

Some tables, such as the customer master, may contain rows that are available to all organizations. The convention in that case is to leave the ORG_ID (or ORGANIZATION_ID) column NULL. The view uses convoluted logic with a series of nested NVL functions to select rows with either a NULL or the right organization code. The code that generates the views is available in the /install/odf subdirectories of the various Application directories.

Multi-Org poses a setup rather than an installation question, something for the functional users more than for the DBA to decide. It adds somewhat to the complexity of using the packages. Users are frequently prompted to tell the system which organization they are in. Moreover, they can become frustrated looking for a Purchase Order or an item that they know is in the system but cannot find. The Applications will not let them receive a shipment that is not due in to their organization or look at an item that is not defined to their organization. Using Multi-Org requires very well thought out business procedures.

Multiple Inventory Organizations

It is possible to use multiple inventory organizations even without using the Multi-Org feature. A company may have inventory locations for manufacturing, sales and distribution. The same items appear in each, but the item attribute settings vary. One location holds items for sale, another holds them as manufacturing finished goods, and the distribution warehouse does neither. One can receive the item, another can order it.

Inventory provides the essential ability to define an item globally. This means that the 8 × 3/4-inch screw used to build tractors in Peoria and trailers in Tucson has the same part number in each operation. Or, the waffle iron built by an overseas subsidiary carries the same item number there as in the U.S., where it is sold. Managers can use the global definition to ask global questions: "How many screws do we need to buy next month, and how many waffle irons must we make?" At the same time it can leave lower-level decisions, such as stockage quantities, make-or-buy, and manufacturing processes, to lower-level organizations within the company.

Profile Options

Applications programs need to know a lot about specific users. What printer do they use? What print style do they prefer? How many copies do they usually want of reports? Which set of books do they use? What menu style do they prefer? Rather than tediously asking each time, the Applications keep a set of defaults for each user, maintained at different levels.

The System Administrator is responsible for setting appropriate higher-level defaults, so the users only have to deal with real choices. If there is only one printer in the Fixed Assets department, the user should not be bothered having to name it. There are four levels of defaults within the Applications:

- Site
- Application
- Responsibility within an application
- User

The System Administrator sets profile options at all four levels; however, users can update some of their own, less critical profile options themselves. Because users are at the lowest level in the default chain, whatever is specified in their personal profiles overrides all the other levels. Otherwise, what the System Administrator specifies for a Responsibility overrides the specification for an Application, and those for an Application override the defaults for the instance of the Oracle Applications (site).

AOL gives you the ability to set up profile options to be referenced by bespoke code. This is a convenient device for the communicating characteristics of individual users. There is no Descriptive Flexfield defined on the FND_USER table, so this feature can be used instead. It is a convenient way to give specific instruction to a generalized module. Some users of a bespoke form may be allowed to update it, while others may have view-only capability. Some responsibilities under which a report is registered may be restricted to viewing reporting data within a single organization. Profile options are straightforward to implement and well supported in PL/SQL. You pass the FND_PROFILE.GET procedure two parameters: the names of the profile option and the name of a field to put the profile value.

If you are using custom responsibilities and applications, which is very likely, you must define all the profile options that are set up under the standard Applications and responsibilities for the custom application and responsibilities as well. Without this setup, you may experience inconsistencies and data problems.

Oracle's Application Implementation Methodology (AIM)

Even the most limited implementation of Oracle Applications is a major undertaking. Whether or not you plan to change them, you have to define your business processes to Oracle as a part of setup. The information you assemble about your business processes will be in the hands of many people scattered throughout your organization. A lot of it will never have been committed to writing. Once in hand, you use this information to establish setup parameters for the Applications, devise tests to ensure that they execute your business processes correctly, convert your data over to Oracle, and train your users.

Oracle Consulting Services developed AIM for their installation teams to meet this challenge. They have packaged their expertise as AIM Advantage. Features of the package include:

- Planning and management of the implementation project

- Predefined business process workflows that can serve as your starting point for defining your company's operations

- Tools that will help you analyze and document your business requirements

- Design and development standards

- Conversion and bridging modules

- Test plans

Release 11's Workflow-based Application Implementation Wizard further automates the process of creating setup parameters. It operates within and supports the AIM Advantage methodology. The Wizard guides you through a multipackage installation process, displaying the setup screens within each Application as appropriate. It recognizes the interdependencies between Applications, the sequence in which your setups have to be done, and which setup steps are not necessary based on previous setup decisions.

Oracle Consulting Services remains closely associated with the AIM products. Their consultants use AIM to achieve consistent results and high productivity across a highly diverse client base. Buying the products means you can make optimal use of Oracle Consulting Services to support your implementation and use their work products to maintain the system after they have completed. Conversely, other technical services firms often favor their own tools. You should have *some* methodology, and preferably only one. Your project manager will have to assess the productivity and training cost trade-offs among your existing methodologies, AIM, and other contenders.

Hardware Considerations

Hardware selection for the Oracle Applications is a multitiered affair. All users must decide on desktop and database server hardware. Internet Computing and most Smart Client users have to decide on a middle tier as well. Figure 14-7 shows the major patterns for distributing processing in multitiered architectures.

The database server is the largest machine in every configuration and needs to be the most reliable. The best rule of thumb is to choose a platform already used by a large number of Applications customers, such as Sun and HP Unix platforms and Windows 2000. These are the ones for which Oracle

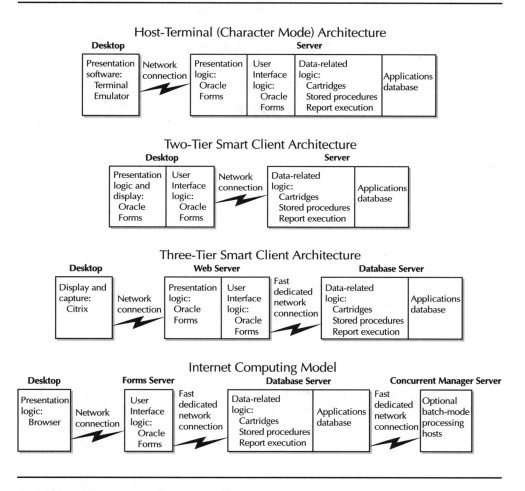

FIGURE 14-7. *Multitiered architecture in Oracle Applications*

first tests the combination of hardware, operating system, RDBMS release and Financials release.

Equipment from the Unix hardware manufacturers is quite scalable. A new user's objective should be to get a platform big enough to start with and capable of growing with the Applications. Capacity planning is a difficult and inexact science that has been made largely obsolete by Moore's law. Machine capacity is cheap enough, and machines are scalable enough, that it is not worth spending lots of money analyzing the requirement. When you need more capacity, and you cannot wring much more out of your existing system by tuning, you simply buy what you need.

Database Server Sizing: Your Processor, Memory, and Disk Space

The Applications are similar to other Oracle systems when it comes to main memory and processor power requirements. It is a function of the number of online users.

TIP

For more in-depth coverage of the topics presented here, check out two excellent references available from Oracle Press: the Oracle8 DBA Handbook *by Kevin Loney, and* Oracle8 Tuning *by Michael Corey, Michael Abbey, Dan Dechichio, and Ian Abramson (both 1998, Osborne McGraw-Hill).*

The host machine, or database server, cedes increasing amounts of processing to other processors under Smart Client and Internet Computing. In character mode, the host handles everything. Under Smart Client the host cedes the presentation function to desktop (or Citrix) machines, but retains database management and concurrent processing. Internet Computing goes even further, with the option of pushing concurrent processing onto smaller servers. Oracle's design allows the largest machine, the database server, to focus more exclusively on the database processes that require concurrent support for a large user community. Web servers and concurrent process servers handle tasks that, because they support a single user at a time, can be handled by multiple, smaller servers. These smaller servers offer better prices and performance, and built-in redundancy.

Oracle provides estimates of the minimum machine performance required to support its desktop software requirements in all three modes of operation: business manager for character mode, the client in SC, and a browser for Internet Computing. In character mode, the software will run on nearly anything. Running Oracle*Forms on the desktop in Smart Client takes a midrange Pentium-class machine with lots of memory, and running Java under the browser in Internet Computing takes a Pentium-class machine with a moderate amount of memory.

Processing power is the key factor for the middle tier. The amount of disk space needed for storing forms and messages is static, and there is not a tremendous need for temporary storage. You multiply your estimated number of simultaneous users by the estimate that Oracle provides of the processing power required by each user.

Estimating requirements for the database is more difficult. Equations exist to compute memory and processor requirements, but they are rather arcane and they assume more knowledge about the application than a beginning user ever possesses. The best rule-of-thumb is to talk to others who have their packages in production in a similar environment. The Oracle representative or the local Oracle Applications User's Group is a good place to start. Use their experience as a starting point, then factor in measurable differences such as the numbers of users, items, customers, journal postings, and the like.

Disk space requirements are easier to compute. Oracle's seed data takes up very little space. The majority of tables in each application are temporary or are smaller tables used for reference purposes, containing setups, value sets and lookups. Each application has a handful of major master and transaction tables that can be used to size the whole application. Two master tables in General Ledger are the Code Combinations and GL Balances; Journal Lines is the most populous transaction-level table. A user can make a rough-cut estimate of journal storage requirements by computing the number of characters in a journal line record and multiplying by the estimated number of rows. Doing the same for balances and code combinations provides a baseline for estimating all of General Ledger. Multiplying the space taken by the major tables by a factor of three to account for Oracle's overhead, the space taken by other tables, reserves for growth, and the DBA overhead of padding tablespace allocations to allow for table growth will yield a very rough estimate

This offhand method exceeds the level of planning actually done in most shops. For large, sophisticated users it becomes worth the effort to make more accurate projections of space requirements. Oracle provides a space planning spreadsheet (named sizr10.wk1 in Release 10) for this purpose.

The ability to carry BLOBs (binary large objects) in the database with Internet Computing or Smart Client radically changes the equation. The storage required for images, sound bites, and movies will almost always eclipse that needed for character-mode data. There is nothing in the

Financials to predict the size of a BLOB—each shop will have to make its own estimates. Many users use a two-tier disk storage approach for BLOBs. They store pointers instead of the BLOBs themselves in the database. That way the BLOBs can reside on cheaper, slower storage devices. Factors that make magnetic disk storage less expensive are bigger devices, fewer controllers, and less built-in redundancy. A writable optical disk is a very inexpensive alternative if the volumes are large. Assuming there are no BLOBs in the database itself, the major factors that drive sizing in each application are shown in Table 14-2.

Other factors that expand the total amount of disk required include:

- The amount of RDBMS overhead space needed in each instance. This requirement includes temporary tables, sort areas, rollback segments, unrecovered extents, and space lost to inefficiencies in tablespace allocations and the like.

- The number of database instances required for development, testing and maintenance. Except for large shops, each test instance needs to be the same size as Production because they will be populated with copies of Production. There is no easy way to reduce the space required in a test instance by deleting data; records within the database are too interdependent. Large shops may manage it to some degree by partitioning transaction tables by date. After you size Production, multiply by at least three or four to account for test and development instances.

- The amount of operating system storage space required for the Oracle distribution (at least two copies), for patches and bespoke code, and for Concurrent Manager reports.

- The file space required to hold concurrent job output and log files. Some reports run to thousands of pages. Bitmapped reports, especially if they include graphics, are many times bulkier than character reports. The space requirements mount up quickly if you allow them to remain on the disk more than a few weeks.

In deference to users who need a rule of thumb on which to ground their initial estimates, a small installation on a single database server will need four instances at 10GB per instance, plus about 20GB for library, temporary

Application	Sizing Factors
Oracle Assets	Number of assets Number of depreciation periods for each asset
Oracle General Ledger	Number of Accounting Flexfield combinations Number of historical periods kept online, each of which requires balance and may have budget data for each active Flexfield combination Number of lines posted to budget and actual Number of periods for which journal detail is kept online
Oracle Inventory	Number of transactions (primarily issues and receipts) per month Number of months' transactions online Number of items Number of storage locations per item (average) Whether or not items have to be tracked individually, by serial number
Oracle Order Entry	Number of order lines, including configurations, per period Number of shipments per order Months of historical transactions kept online Number of customers and sites
Oracle Payables	Number of invoices and invoice lines per period Number of historical periods kept online Number of vendors (shared with Purchasing)
Oracle Purchasing	Number of requisitions Number of PO lines per period Number of historical periods kept online Complexity of receiving operations (inspections, partial shipments) Number of vendors (shared with Payables)
Oracle Receivables	Number of invoices Volume of collection activity Amount of online invoice and payment history Number of customers and customer sites (shared with Order Entry)

TABLE 14-2. *Major Factors Determining Disk Space Requirements for Representative Applications*

and other space—or a total of about 60GB on the database server. Be skeptical of numbers much smaller than that.

Windows 2000 and Unix Operating Systems

Though many platforms will support the Oracle Financials server requirements, the two primary alternatives for users without a prior commitment to an operating system are Unix and Windows 2000. They generally offer the most performance per dollar.

The three-tier Internet Computing architecture exploits the strengths of both operating systems. Unix, with its greater reliability and scalability, is usually the best choice for the database server.

Windows 2000 and Unix both work well as Web and concurrent process servers. The greater reliability of Unix can be offset by redundant Windows 2000 machines. It is not a disaster if a Windows 2000 system crashes or must otherwise be rebooted. Assuming that there are several Web or concurrent servers to choose from, the Release 11 load-balancing mechanism can simply bypass the failed machine until it is available again.

Host/Terminal and Smart Client configurations are more dependent on a single server, which supports both the database and concurrent processing. The reliability of that single server is an important factor in the success of the whole implementation. Oracle does not support Windows 2000 for character-mode operations.

Windows 2000 has appeared to offer savings over a more traditional enterprise operating system, largely because of the reduced cost of the hardware it runs on. That hardware cost equation is changing as Unix systems vendors are supporting Intel-compatible platforms and bringing down the costs of their own hardware. The cost of ownership associated with the architectures of the two operating systems is the increasingly important issue in choosing between Windows 2000 and Unix. Estimate the cost of your support staff, focusing particularly on the assumption that Windows 2000 will require less maintenance than Unix. Both operating systems are nuanced pieces of software that will not perform well in the hands of amateurs. There are several significant areas for comparison.

User Interface

The Windows interface is a major attraction of Windows 2000. The whole thing is windows. There is a vestigial remnant of the MS-DOS command language, but Microsoft hides it fairly well.

The Windows format is excellent for running desktop software. A Windows 2000 machine is (almost) identical to a Windows 98 system as far as desktop applications go. The Windows 2000 architecture offers a significant benefit in that it is designed to run multiple jobs concurrently.

Windows tools can handle all systems setup and operations, but the fact is, a Windows-based setup can be frustrating. While the graphical interface does make the product relatively attractive to work with, the far more crucial issue is that many Windows functions are just as difficult to execute as they would be if you had to type them in as command lines. It can be aggravating to try and guess which obscure path to take through the "intuitive" Windows icons to get to the function you want. To make matters worse, Windows' online help is frequently not that helpful, offering scattered fragments of the answer but no body of text to explain the whole scheme.

The more pedestrian approach that you take in Unix, reading the many excellent hard-copy references and researching the online manuals to find a utility you can execute from the command line, is still easier for most programmers than navigating the Windows maze. In fact, even though Unix systems offer windowed interfaces, most systems programmers still perform setup and management through the command-line interface.

Utility programs in the Unix world show their origins. Those such as backup/restore usually have more features, and are more powerful, but they tend not to be consistent from vendor to vendor and are often more complex than their Windows 2000 counterparts. Windows 2000 has nothing to match the powerful command-line, character-mode tools, such as grep, sed, awk, and vi. On the other hand, the tools require precisely the kind of operating system guru that Windows 2000 buyers want to avoid hiring.

Unix has the most powerful shell language of any common operating system. In contrast, the command line is antithetical to Microsoft's philosophy. Its shell language, inherited from MS-DOS, is comparatively weak and poorly documented. This will not affect "plain vanilla" users much, but it is often convenient to use operating system shell scripts for custom programming. Some things are just not better with GUI.

Connectivity

The ability to communicate with desktop browsers is not an issue with Internet Computing. All servers offer equivalent desktop connectivity using Internet/intranet facilities.

Oracle Applications installations require other kinds of connectivity for which the different operating systems have varying levels of support:

- Unix can work with dumb terminals and terminal emulation, whereas Windows cannot. Only Unix (and other traditional operating systems) can support the applications in character mode. Unix provides lowest-common-denominator communications with almost any other platform using FTP and Kermit.

- Windows database and Web servers handle networking seamlessly among Windows client machines. While the Windows tools are more limited outside the Windows environment, within it they are more robust and easier to use than their Unix counterparts. If you have a mix of different operating systems in your environment you will find in general that Unix offers more connectivity.

Device Support

Device support is a major operating system function. Printers and disks are the most important devices for an Applications server. To be as universal as possible, the Applications use printers in character and PostScript modes. Windows does a great job with printers generally. Unix always works, but it takes a bit more effort to install and maintain bitmapped printers. Unix has the advantage when it comes to disks. The industry trend is to intelligent disk arrays, like the EMC Symmetrix, with built-in redundancy and backup. These still remain somewhat more widely available in Unix.

Reliability

What does it mean that Unix is more reliable than Windows? It is not uncommon to find Unix systems that have not been rebooted for a year or more. NT 4.0 systems tend to go down, or need to be brought down, quite a bit more often. Improved reliability is a major design objective of NT 5.0. Not only is the Windows operating system not yet as stable as Unix, but the hardware it runs on has traditionally been engineered to PC and LAN server standards, which have been somewhat less exacting than those for enterprise servers. The differences are reflected in price. Windows systems have generally offered better price performance than Unix.

These generalizations are rapidly becoming less true. The two operating systems are both becoming available on the other's traditional platforms, and Microsoft is making great efforts to improve Windows reliability. Whatever the balance point, the Internet Computing architecture will continue to make the best use of both Unix' reliability and Windows' price advantages.

Redundancy is easiest to engineer for individual users or tasks. If a desktop browser fails, you can exchange the failed machine for a good one. Most users can afford to be out of business for the hour or so it takes for the exchange. Likewise, most shops can accept the delay as Oracle Applications reassign a task after its concurrent server goes down. The machines that host these individual tasks can afford to be less reliable, and thus less expensive, because the impact of their failure is limited and local.

Tasks on the database server support all users simultaneously. The entire organization suffers when they go down. Because keeping the database in a consistent state is imperative, recovering from a failure can take a significant amount of time. Redundancy and reliability therefore has more value in a database server. Redundancy may be built into the disk subsystems, in disk mirroring, in multiple processors, in multiple paths between processors and disks, and in multiple links out to the networks. Each element increases reliability and cost. And yet, even the most redundant system can never be 100 percent reliable. They all need tape backup systems to guard against the worst case.

The Unix operating system and the hardware designed to run it are generally more reliable than Windows. The Unix file system is simpler than the one used by Windows, and simpler is better when it comes to Oracle. It does not need much operating system support for disk storage. The RDBMS takes big blocks of disk space from the operating system and does its own formatting and allocation. Having an additional layer of disk space management at the operating system level just confuses the issue. Windows systems programmers have observed that the best way to keep disk usage straight on Windows is to reformat and reload the systems every few months.

Scalability

There are so many variables in any Oracle Financials environment—the number of applications, the size of master tables, the number of transactions, and the number of other processes on the machine—that it is impossible to calculate machine requirements. The alternative is to take out insurance, in the form of scalability. You can afford to start with less hardware than you need as long as you know you can expand.

Unix systems from Sun, HP, Compaq and other major vendors can be configured large enough to handle the largest enterprise's Oracle Applications database server requirements. Windows solutions remain more limited, both in terms of the number of processors in a single box and the ways in which multiple boxes can be strung together to increase power and reliability.

The number of Unix and Windows systems that can be linked via a network is limited primarily by bandwidth. You can add Web and concurrent processor servers as necessary. The tradeoff between using Windows 2000 or Unix processors in these server functions is a matter of the price and performance of individual boxes—keeping the total number of boxes to manage at a workable number—and the productivity of the network administrators, DBAs, and systems programmers managing them.

Available Talent

Oracle Applications users need systems programmers for the server, LAN administrators, client-side systems programmers, Oracle DBAs, and Applications Administrators. Depending on the installation these may be one or several people, and they may be employees or contractors.

The skills tend to come in groups, and it is common to find DBAs with Unix and Oracle experience. It is less common to find people with Applications experience as well. It is desirable to have these skills combined in one person, since those who have them need to communicate closely with one another.

On the other side, Windows, LAN and client-side experience are often found together. It is less common to find extensive Oracle DBA experience in a Windows expert, because larger Oracle implementations have favored heavier platforms. Applications experience is still rarer, because Windows is such a new platform for the Applications.

Vendor Support

Unix vendors have historically been geared to support their customers' mission-critical applications. Microsoft has had to evolve its customer support model as Windows moves into the enterprise. It is now a serious matter when a Windows machine crashes.

Microsoft's support model has historically been passive, commensurate with the low price of the Windows 2000 operating system. They put bug information and patches on the net for customers to find and apply themselves. This level is inappropriate for Oracle Applications installations, which need a high level of support when their production systems crash. On the other hand, Microsoft's mass market, passive support model has forced them to engineer a relatively high level of reliability into their product. Now that HP, DEC, and even Sun support Windows 2000, it is reasonable to expect that they will provide that customer base the same level of support that they do for Unix.

The Bottom Line

Windows' best feature is price. The software and the hardware it runs on are inexpensive. Oracle's Internet Computing architecture is designed to accommodate its weaknesses and allow users to take advantage of its strengths.

Windows' GUI interface has no significant advantage over the Unix command line for the DBA who supports the Financials. The supposed advantage that Windows requires less systems programming support may not prove significant. Any server, no matter who the vendor, will require tuning, backup and restore, disk space management, user management, and a host of other functions. They are conceptually and practically not much simpler under Windows 2000 than Unix. It is just a different interface.

Unix has more proven reliability and scalability and more universal networking capabilities. Most Unix vendors offer a level of technical support appropriate to the Oracle Applications; Windows users may have to make sure they contract for what they need. In the final analysis, small users will probably find the costs of ownership more or less comparable between the two operating systems.

Distribution of Platforms

Personnel and telecommunications considerations drive the placement of platforms. A few people still need to physically get their hands on the machines, and everybody else has to access them over the network. They need to be somewhere with reliable telecommunications links.[13]

---

[13]Now that frame relay is replacing point-to-point telecommunications, the most vulnerable part of most networks is usually the connection between the host computer and the network "cloud." The computer should have enough redundant network connections that one daydreaming backhoe operator can't knock it offline by cutting the phone cable.

Continuity of operations is a major consideration in considering where to put the computers. Two or more separate physical installations are advantageous: so when a hurricane knocks out the East Coast, or an earthquake the West, the company can stay in business.

The Client Side

Oracle's Application product line has completed the transition from the host-terminal through Smart Client to the Internet Computing model. Customers are still using all three models, however, and may continue to do so for some time. At one end of the spectrum, many installed clients are happy with the speed of character-mode operations, pleased with the reliability of the system, glad that it is Year 2000-compliant, and unwilling to buy the additional system resources required for Internet Computing or Smart Client operations. At the other end are customers who are upgrading their entire data processing operations using the essential technologies of Release 11: Oracle Web Server, Workflow, data warehousing, and OLAP (*Online Analytical Processing*).

Character Mode

Oracle Applications is written in SQL*Forms 2.4 to support the standard 24 × 80 character-mode displays. VT220s were the most common. Most users have migrated to PCs as terminals. Oracle's character-mode applications are reliable and perform well. Power users like the fact that there is no mouse involvement—data entry goes faster because they never have to take their hands off the keyboard. Release 10.7 Smart Client shops may benefit by keeping the character-mode interface as an alternative for users who prefer it over GUI.

Terminal emulators are frustrating to Financials users. Almost every terminal emulator implementation leaves some function keys unmapped. Users have to use a three or four keystroke menu sequence to do what a function key can do in one. Emulators have other bad habits. Sometimes they lock up. They get out of sync. The displays get garbled. Oracle's Business Manager offers a better solution.

Business Manager is the lightest of light clients. It is Oracle's own custom-built terminal emulator for the Applications, running under Windows and Mac. It interfaces to the same Forms 2.4 translation hooks as any other terminal. Business manager provides something of the look-and-feel of a GUI interface. It lets a user navigate using the mouse and cut-and-paste to other desktop applications. It has the added advantage of being more attractive.

Oracle still provides extended application support for character-mode operations, but quit enhancing it a while ago. For example, Order Entry's powerful Delivery Based Shipping and function level form access control are not available in character. All new applications since the availability of Release 10.6 have been offered in GUI only. There will be no upgrades to character mode past Release 10.7. You will need to check with Oracle for the published cut-off date for character mode support. Given the installed base of character-mode users, the authors expect it to be through the end of the year 2000.

Smart Client

The forms reside and run on the client side in a Smart Client implementation. Traffic to the database server is cut down to mainly commands and data. Though the software can reside on each user's PC, it usually sits on a LAN server close to the user. The LAN traffic, mainly Forms 4.5 programs, can be heavy.

It is significant how much processing remains on the server even under Smart Client. Reports and other batch processes are unaffected. Database tables remain centralized. The design of Release 10.7 allows all three client-side modes of operation against a single database. In all three models, the server handles stored procedures.

By its nature the Smart Client architecture requires a good deal of bandwidth to operate effectively. Users with 10MB Ethernet LANs notice the wait as Smart Client loads forms and returns large queries from the server. Installing a faster LAN is one way around the problem. The other alternative is to implement a more efficient three-tier architecture.

Citrix Corporation offers the best three-tier architecture in a client-server operating mode. The Oracle*Forms modules of the Oracle Applications are executed on the middle-tier Citrix server, which is a Windows NT machine. The server sends the display to Citrix client software on the desktop, which presents it to the user. The Citrix desktop then accepts keystroke and mouse movements to send back to the server.

This three-tier mode of client-server operations can offer improved performance by using a high-speed network connection between the middle tier and the database. It can offer economy by making use of desktop machines that would not be powerful enough to support the Applications directly. Nevertheless, because there is no intelligence on the desktop it still involves a lot more traffic between the desktop and the middle tier than does Internet Computing. A Citrix solution requires almost continual communication, sending each keystroke and mouse movement to the middle tier as it is entered. Internet Computing's communications are much more terse. It can wait until it needs to perform an edit, often first accepting several data fields, before it needs to communicate with the Web Server.

Internet Computing

The Web implementation of the Applications also uses Forms 4.5. It runs on the Web Server, a middle tier in the architecture, generating Java windows to be viewed through a browser on the client machine.

The Forms Client applet that runs on the browser supports screen and local data management functions for all Oracle Applications. The browser downloads the applet and caches it locally. Thereafter, the traffic exchanged between the browser/applet and the Web Server is quite succinct: Java presentation displays data from the server to the browser, and captures data going back.

Oracle initially provided its own browser to ensure adequate Java support on the desktop. The Internet Computing Applications now work with both Netscape and Internet Explorer; Oracle simply downloads any additional Java classes it needs.

Just as with Smart Client, forms presented by the browser can access the database as required on a field-by-field basis to fetch lists of values and to validate field entries. Whereas the browser/applet will have the programmed intelligence to validate a Yes/No entry, it will need to perform a query to determine whether a customer number is valid.

Oracle adds the necessary Java classes to run whatever browser you choose. The dominant ones in the Windows environment are Netscape and Internet Explorer. The desktop machine must be powerful enough that running the Java applet does not slow users down—a 200MHz Pentium or better.

Network Links

Network speed is a major factor in the performance of the Oracle Applications. While they work adequately through a dial-up Internet connection, performance will be better on a proprietary Wide Area Network (WAN).

Encryption is essential for traffic that may go over the Internet. Internet Computing uses the 40-bit RSC-RC4 encryption standard. Most companies provide connectivity for regular users over Wide Area Networks rather than simply the Internet, more for reasons of performance than security.

The heaviest network traffic in a three-tier architecture is over the links used by the database server. It takes a significant amount of bandwidth to support the traffic between it, the Web server and any concurrent process servers. Communications companies offer your network engineers a number of options for making these high-speed network connections.

Conclusion

Oracle Applications under Internet Computing represent the realization of a sweeping vision. Oracle developed general purpose programming languages and communications, analysis, network, and database components to be sold in the market for custom development tools. At the same time the company is its own best customer, making Oracle Applications a showcase for what can be done with their database and tools. Control of the technology stack gives Oracle significant advantages in product reliability and performance as well as the speed with which it can incorporate new technologies.

Oracle is taking advantage of the high level of productivity afforded by its tools to expand the features provided by its Applications suite. The new package extends the number of business areas it addresses, specializes the Applications for the needs of specific industry segments, and makes Oracle solutions increasingly possible for businesses that have few staff available to manage an implementation.

CHAPTER
15

Customization and Modification

T he Oracle Applications modules offer great value, given the range of functions built into them and the ease with which you can extend them to meet your special needs. Establishing custom applications is the first step in adapting Oracle to your business. The installation process allows a remarkable degree of manipulation. Beyond that, the environments in which the Applications are written and execute are open to modifications at the program code level. Oracle includes complete source code and technical documentation with your software purchase.

The challenge during implementation is to derive maximum value from the Oracle system. Meeting this challenge means making the best use of the standard features within each package and considering the most advantageous trade-offs between modifying your business processes and modifying the Applications.

The architecture of Oracle Applications is open to customization or modification at a number of levels. It is useful to start with a definition of terms:

- *Customization* is the process of setting parameters within the Applications to make them operate in accordance with your business rules. Part II of this book addresses the customization tasks involved in setting up each major application.

- *Modification* involves writing or changing code and tables. Some modifications, very minor relative to the massive body of code that makes up each application, are usually necessary. Extensive modification is costly and risky, and may warrant writing a totally customized subsystem.

- *Custom code*, known in Europe as *bespoke code*, is what you write in order to achieve a modification. To reduce confusion, we have used the expression *bespoke code* throughout this book to describe programming you do yourself.

The size of your company weighs in the economic trade-off between modifying business procedures to fit the code, and modifying the code to fit business procedures. Smaller companies, with fewer people to train and fewer resources to modify the package, tend to adapt to Oracle as it is. They may find the cost to alter an existing process to be very low. Larger companies find it cost effective to invest in modifying the software in order to minimize the impact on their business practices, since larger numbers of employees and customers will be effected. Chapter 14 describes the customization devices provided by Oracle. They include flexfields and value sets, menus and Responsibilities, Alerts, profile options, and Workflow. Individual products have Application-specific customization features, such as the Financial Statement Generator within General Ledger and the approval hierarchies within Purchasing.

Modifications are characterized by programming. Whereas all of Oracle's customization features are supported directly through specialized online setup processes, you implement modifications by programming in standard tools, outside of the Applications. Some bespoke code, such as custom forms and reports, is programmed using Oracle Applications conventions and tools and is registered with Oracle Applications.

Other bespoke code, such as database triggers and stored procedures, are totally outside the Oracle Applications architecture, although they operate on Applications data.

Oracle's architecture anticipates modification better than that of its competitors. The code is well documented and accessible. The applications are characterized by a generally thorough and robust data model that is capable of representing, or being easily extended to represent most real-world situations. While the applications always include forms written to capture transaction data, they cannot, and could not, be optimally adapted to every business and work flow situation. Likewise, the standard reports provide a prototype of every report you are likely to need, but it would be impossible for Oracle to anticipate which fields are essential and which have no meaning for your business as they work within the design limit of 180 columns maximum. The architecture and documentation make it possible to create your own bespoke versions of Oracle's forms and reports to meet your business needs, in a controlled fashion, with minimal risks to data integrity and with minimum effort required for version upgrades.

Anticipating and Planning Customizations and Modifications

Executives who buy Oracle Applications are almost all of one voice: "Don't change the code!" It often takes the MIS shop a number of months to soften that stance, in which time they and the users may be forced into poor business decisions to avoid "changing the code." Here is what Oracle says:

Do Not Use Database Tools to Modify Oracle Applications Data

"Because Oracle Applications are interrelated, any change you make using Oracle Applications can update many tables at once. But when you modify Oracle Applications data using anything other than Oracle Applications, you may change a row in one table without making corresponding changes in related tables. If your tables get out of synchronization with each other, you risk retrieving erroneous information and you risk unpredictable results throughout Oracle Applications.

"When you use Oracle Applications to modify your data, Oracle Applications automatically checks that your changes are valid. Oracle Applications also keeps track of who changes information. If you enter information into the databases using database tools, you may store invalid information. You also lose the ability to track who has changed your information because SQL*Plus and other database tools do not keep a record of changes.

"Consequently, we STRONGLY RECOMMEND that you never use SQL*Plus or any other tool to modify Oracle Applications data unless otherwise instructed."

This standard disclaimer (taken from the preface to the *Oracle Inventory User's Guide*) is as interesting for what it says as what it does not.

- It says, "Do Not Use Database Tools to Modify Oracle Applications Data."

- It adds, "if you enter information into database tables using database tools, you may store invalid information."

- It does *not* say, "Don't modify the code, or add your own code."

Rather than forbidding system modifications, it implicitly establishes a commonsense ranking, from those changes that are expected and pose little threat to those that are ill advised because of the risk. Oracle Applications implementers need to establish, from the inception of the project, that they have the authority to perform the implementation in the most effective way. It may at times include modifications and bespoke code. By the same token, management needs to make sure that each bespoke module is cost-justified and carefully managed, as described in Chapter 16.

There are predictable ways in which users modify the applications. The following sections examine them individually.

Risks and Costs in Customization

The database integrity risks involved in the types of customization described earlier sort themselves out easily into minor and major threats, depending on whether they update the database. Figure 15-1 gauges the potential impact of different types of modifications.

Here are some guidelines for assessing the risks from various types of modification:

- *A module that does not update the database can imperil only itself. The risks are easy to bound.* The example would be a report or query screen. A programming error can do no more harm than to produce incorrect information or possibly cause poor database performance from a long-running query.

- *A module that only updates user attributes (Attribute 1 to Attribute n) can affect only modules that use those attributes.* This limits the impact of the Descriptive Flexfield (DFF) features and the reports that incorporate user attributes. Problems manifest themselves quickly, but without much serious impact. For example, the user may query a row on which a DFF has been defined, change something other than the DFF, and then not be able to resave the row because the value set imposed on the DFF does not allow a value that had been previously inserted by a bespoke module. Problems at this level are certainly annoying to users, but they do not compromise the system.

- *A module that inserts rows into database tables as if Oracle had done so can affect the whole system.* The potential impact may even extend to Oracle-created rows in the same tables. Oracle has provided Application Programmer Interfaces (APIs), in the form of open interface tables, to enable you to safely load major transaction

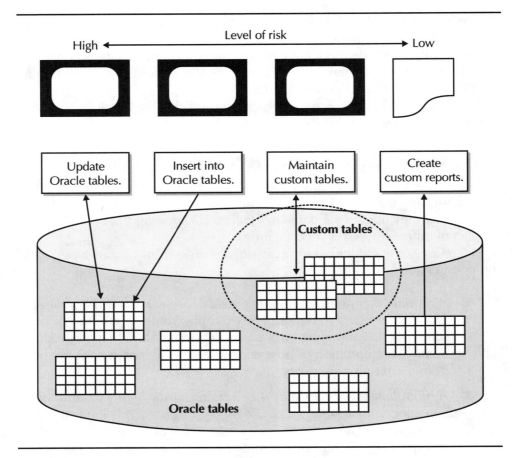

FIGURE 15-1. *The impact and risks of modification*

tables and those master data tables with complex relationships. However, there inevitably will be some data you wish to interface that does not have an existing open interface. In these cases you should study records entered through the forms, their tables and columns, using the trace utility.

■ *A module that updates Oracle's attributes in rows created by native Oracle modules can imperil every process that uses the updated material.* The risks are harder to assess. These modifications require thorough analysis to determine where the values are used, backed up by extensive testing to prove the underlying hypotheses. For example, there is no batch device to update inventory item attributes. All Oracle provides is the Define Items form, which would be impractical to use when there are thousands of items to update. Oracle's form does extensive cross-checking to protect against inconsistent attribute settings. You would have to test any batch script to make sure you don't load attribute combinations that Oracle would not have allowed.

The most obvious advice is to do a thorough job of analysis before updating anything. Include a test plan as part of the analysis or design document, and make sure your programmers and users execute that plan thoroughly. Programmers must not modify code they don't understand. Developers often overlook the WHO columns (CREATED_BY, CREATION_DATE, LAST_UPDATED_BY, LAST_UPDATE_DATE) in a custom script, but they should always be set. It goes without saying that one should be extraordinarily careful deleting rows.

Bespoke code always involves a degree of development risk. The history of data processing is one of slipped schedules and cost overruns. Every implementation that involves an automated cutover from a legacy system requires some bespoke code just to handle conversion and bridging. The task may appear easy, given the existence of well-documented open interface tables. Looks are deceiving. Do not overestimate the quality of the data in your legacy system, or underestimate the complexity of mapping legacy data to Oracle. Populating the interface tables in a way that is acceptable to Oracle is not a trivial task. For accomplishing this you will want to use your most experienced in-house staff, or hire some good consultants. It is not a task for those inexperienced with the Oracle Database, tools, or applications.

Writing the modules that are essential for cutover presents you with more than enough risk. Project managers are wise to keep functional modifications to a minimum at cutover. A good argument for postponing all but the most obvious requirements is that the users cannot know exactly what they need until they have operational experience with the system. A large percentage of the developers' time after cutover will be spent fixing and writing bespoke extensions to the system. The implementation project manager has to balance the risks of the users' not being able to run the system because they don't have an essential modification at cutover against the risk of making unnecessary modifications because the users don't appreciate how they can do their job using Oracle's native capabilities.

Dealing with the expected but unpredictable requirements for system modification argues strongly in favor of a phased implementation approach. Even if they were able to communicate perfectly, users could never adequately voice their full requirements without having actually used Oracle Applications. Chapter 16 addresses the benefits of breaking a project into phases.

The Applications are wonderful in that they come almost fully programmed— and very well programmed. They are problematic in that an organization can never know exactly how this preprogrammed package will actually meet its needs. Oracle Applications customers have to acknowledge the nature of the bargain they make in buying licensed software. In exchange for the massive amounts of programming you avoid, you must be cautious about the effects of the minimal programming that you do perform, so as not to interfere with Oracle-designed functions.

Changing Oracle's Table Definitions

A cardinal rule is that you never change Oracle's table definitions. There is no assurance that Oracle will not change them from release to release, or even through the distribution of of patches. A corollary is that you may break a lesser rule of database design. . That is, if you need additional columns beyond what can be satisfied using the user-defined attributes, you may implement a custom table with a one-to-one relationship with the Oracle table.

The Framework for Modifications

Bespoke code has to be kept separate from Oracle's standard code distribution to keep it from getting overlaid by patch and upgrade activity. It is also convenient for the developers to keep their code in a separate place and to know that place contains all the code for which they are responsible.

The best approach is to place your bespoke code in custom applications. Doing this does not limit access; any menu can be customized to include forms programs that belong to any other application. In a similar way, the report groups for one application can include custom reports and batch programs from all applications. Locating your bespoke modules in custom applications makes them easy to identify, without restricting the way you use them. It makes configuration management easy. Because all the code within your newly defined application is bespoke, you can easily compare the state of modules in your development and test environment against those in production.

Planning a User-Defined Application

An application has its own library directories and its own Oracle schema, as described in Chapter 14. The schema, also called a user id, owns tables and other database objects. As of Release 10.6, all applications share their objects with the APPS schema. Giving a custom application the APPS schema gives it full access to the Oracle tables.

Creating a custom application accomplishes one key objective. It keeps bespoke program modules separate from Oracle code. Users who are doing extensive modifications may want to define several custom applications, each one corresponding to an Oracle standard application. Others may find that one custom application is enough. Then all custom AOL objects (forms, reports, menus, Responsibilities, and so forth) will be assigned to that custom application.

Creating an application of your own requires that you define the following elements:

- **Name** Oracle's application names all start with "Oracle"; yours will probably start with a company or division name. Watkins-Johnson, for instance, has defined the application "WJ Purchasing" for the extensions they have made to purchasing.

- **A root directory** This directory must reside in the database or applications server operating system, and should meet the conventions for Oracle Applications described in Chapter 14. The directory names should be lowercase, as Unix is case-sensitive (although other operating systems generally won't care). A typical root directory for bespoke code would be:

    /oraappl/custom/ap

    where */oraappl* is the root directory designated at installation time for all applications, including Oracle's distribution; */custom* is the root for all bespoke code; and */ap* is the application being modified

(Accounts Payable). This directory would have the standard subdirectories for bespoke code: /bin, /forms, /srw, and /sql.

- **For bespoke forms, a root directory on the Web server**   The directory scheme will be similar to that on the database server.

- **A basepath**   This is an operating system-symbolic variable name for the root directory. The reference to the basepath is usually of the form $*co_ap*_TOP, where *co* is a company abbreviation and *ap* is the application in question. By Unix conventions it is in uppercase. Most other operating systems are case-insensitive, so it might as well be uppercase. Watkins-Johnson, for example, has defined the basepath $WJ_PO_TOP for its bespoke purchasing modules.

- **Short name**   This is used by programmers to identify modules, messages, and other components. Oracle Applications uses two or three letters, such as INV for Inventory or PO for Purchasing. The best bet is to add a one- or two-letter prefix to the Oracle short name and abbreviation.

- **Abbreviation**   This is used to prefix custom table names and other database objects. Form it using the same prefix as the application's short name.

- **A message prefix**   This will be important if you write custom forms using Oracle's message presentation facilities. The major benefit of a message prefix is translation among multiple national languages. Use the application abbreviation as a default.

Registering a Custom Application

To register an application follow these steps:

1. Have the system programmer create the planned root directory with all the subdirectories described in Chapter 14. Make sure that the developers and the Concurrent Manager user are given the necessary read-write-execute permissions to access the directories. The Unix command for assigning full permission is:

   chmod 777 *directory_name*

In Windows NT you predefine groups of users, then, after selecting the directory, navigate File Sharing Security Permissions to grant access to those who need it.

2. Have the systems programmer modify the Applications login script to add the assignment statement equating the basepath symbolic variable to the directory named earlier.

3. Log in using the System Administrator Responsibility.

4. Navigate to the Register Applications form and enter the data and enter the values, as previously planned.

5. Navigate to the Security menu and assign your new application to an Oracle schema. In 10.6 or later you want the APPS schema, which gives you access to all Oracle Applications tables.

Bespoke/Custom Code Conventions

The registration process starts with the operating system file name for a form or report. The module name should do the following:

■ Uniquely identify the module within the Oracle Applications universe.

■ Identify the module as bespoke code.

■ Have an appropriate suffix for the module type.

■ Fit within operating-system limits on name length.

■ If possible, associate the code module with its design document.

The eight-character limit on DOS file names does not apply in Windows, but it may still affect your developers as they transfer modules using e-mail and file transfer programs. Most modules that Oracle delivers still adhere to an eight-character naming standard. You need to decide whether the eight-character limitation affects you. If you are free of it, the best bet is to use the 30-character convention that applies to database objects within Oracle. Even though some operating systems such as Windows are less restrictive, it is a good idea to require that module names start with an alphabetic character and do not include any special characters other than the underscore.

Modules have multiple names within the Oracle Applications. A form has its module name, names(s) on menu lines to select it, and the name displayed by the form as it executes. The naming convention applies to the module name, the file with the .fmx suffix, or in character mode, .frm). A report has three module names: the name of the operating system file containing the report definition (with the suffix .rdf for Oracle*Reports, or .sql for SQL*Plus), the registered name of the executable module, and the registered name of the combination of a report and a set of parameters. It also has a name to select from the report menu and a report title. It saves confusion if you use the same name for the operating system file, the executable, and the short name you give in registering a process, unless an executable will be tied to more than one process.

It is usually best to name modified Oracle modules with their eight-character Oracle name plus the prefix that announces bespoke code. Totally new modules can have a unique name within the same convention.

It helps if the names of your design and user documents for a module can have the same name or at least start with a set of characters that relates them to one another. The .doc suffix will identify program documentation as such. It is convenient to keep the documentation close to the code. Some shops put documents in a LAN directory structure that parallels the Applications directory structure. Others actually put it in the same directories.

If you use configuration management, you will want to control release levels of the documentation by the same means as the modules it describes. The documentation should reflect each change you make to the code.

Custom Output

Reports top the list of essential modifications. Every business uses uniquely formatted external paper documents. Most Applications users find that the Oracle-designed reports are adequate, but there are instances in which it is worth a small investment to tailor them to the business.

Documents

The formatting possibilities of documents are endless. Oracle*Reports has the flexibility to print these documents in exactly the format any user needs. Oracle delivers stock print programs in the expectation that customers will use Oracle*Reports' flexibility to modify the output to correspond with their exact needs. This usually includes documents that will be distributed externally. Following are programs that are commonly modified from Oracle's standard output:

- AP Check Print
- PO Purchase Order Print
- AR Direct Debit
- AR Invoice Print
- AR Dunning letters
- AR Statements
- SO Sales Order Acknowledgment
- SO Bill of Lading
- SO Pick Slip

These external documents usually carry the company logo and other stylized entries. They were traditionally produced on preprinted forms, or generated with laser printers capable of flashing boilerplate text and images onto the forms.

Reports run on the database server, independent of the three client-side modes of operation. Oracle*Reports is a graphical, bitmapped tool. It is intended to design reports in a WYSIWYG (what-you-see-is-what-you-get) environment. Character mode operation is no more than an overlay on its native GUI operation. Nevertheless, Oracle distributes its standard reports in character mode—the lowest common denominator— thus ensuring that all customers will be able to run them. Your customization will usually involve modifying the programs to change fonts and include appropriate graphics.

Chapter 14 describes the alternatives for bitmapped printing. One is to print to a PostScript device using the full GUI features of Oracle*Reports. The more common approach is to embed printer command escape sequences in character mode reports. Such embedded commands can invoke report masks to overlay the character printing and font changes within the print output. Though the escape sequence approach is not as technically appealing as PostScript, it is well supported by Hewlett-Packard's PCL language and by a large number of third parties such as

Evergreen. The escape sequence approach is fast and reliable; it is relatively cheap to get a third party to set it up for you.

Reports

Reports present information derived from data in the database. Oracle expects users to modify the standard reports and add their own. The facilities and documentation it offers for writing bespoke reports are excellent.

There is little risk in modifying the reports delivered by Oracle. Though the Oracle*Reports language has the ability to update data, few standard reports actually do so. As part of the analysis of the Oracle*Reports modules you plan to modify, look for update code in the PRE- and POST-REPORT triggers.

If there is not a standard report that satisfies your needs, there is usually one that comes close. It may lack a column or have the wrong sort order, or it may need to accept another parameter. The most common solution is to modify Oracle's program to meet the custom requirement. The usual approach is to do the following:

1. Analyze Oracle's code. Many reports are quite complex and appear to be case studies in the flexibility of the Oracle*Reports product. Some, such as the Bill of Materials Report, use PRE-REPORT triggers to populate temporary tables used in the report. Make sure you do not clutter such tables by failing to do a rollback in the post-report trigger. SQL*Plus reports can do the same, populating tables in one step and reporting in another.

2. Decide whether to modify Oracle's code or simply borrow its SELECTs to incorporate in a totally new module. The reports that Oracle delivers follow a consistent design. The PRE-REPORT trigger reads the parameters, performs any additional validation, sets internal processing flags, and performs any preprocessing required for the report. Oracle usually incorporates major bodies of function in stored procedures rather than in the report trigger itself. It frequently composes WHERE and ORDER BY clauses as program variables in the PRE-REPORT trigger and references them as bind variables in the SELECT statements for the queries. It is often easier to deduce the essence of what they are doing, and then incorporate

queries based on their SELECT statements in new modules, than to modify and debug code you do not fully understand.

3. Modify or create the report in a development instance. Compare the output of your custom report with the native Oracle report to make sure you are picking up the right rows and running the computations correctly.

4. Follow the procedures described in the upcoming "Registering Custom Processes" section to put the report into the development instance, define the runtime parameters, add it to a report group, and test it concurrently.

5. Migrate the tested report into the custom application in the production instance.

Almost all of Oracle's reports are written in the Oracle*Reports tool. However, SQL*Plus is adequate for most custom reports. The trade-offs for SQL*Plus are:

Advantages	Disadvantages
Every Oracle programmer knows how to use SQL*Plus, whereas many do not know or are not proficient in Oracle*Reports.	SQL*Plus cannot handle complex formatting. It is limited to printing columns across the page, with data directly under the column headings.
SQL*Plus reports are quick to write and simple to debug.	SQL*Plus cannot handle master-detail reports, except in a very limited way by doing page breaks at the master control break.
SQL*Plus reports execute quickly.	SQL*Plus does not have any bitmapped logic for handling fonts and graphics.
SQL*Plus reports have access to the operating system shell via the HOST command.	SQL*Plus reports are plain, sometimes unattractive in comparison with Oracle*Reports.
SQL*Plus modules can invoke PL/SQL routines. They can perform DDL (data definition language) commands such as creating and dropping tables.	The SQL*Plus devices for computing sums and showing control breaks are primitive. They make poor use of the column width available within a report.

Advantages	Disadvantages
SQL*Plus is all in ASCII. It is easy to scan your code to apply across-the-board changes.	Since most of Oracle's standard reports are written in Oracle*Reports, a custom modification may be easier than rewriting the report in SQL*Plus.

The cost-benefit equation usually favors using SQL*Plus for custom reports that are within its architectural reach. More complex reports require Oracle*Reports.

Registering Custom Processes

You register batch programs with the Application Object Library (AOL) to make them eligible for AOL services. AOL will accept runtime parameters, initiate and manage program execution, spool print and log file output, and present output to the users at their desktop or in hard copy. The steps to register a report are as follows.

First, make the program available to the AOL by copying it into the directory structure for the application to which it belongs. The module name should conform to the naming standards discussed previously. Copy Oracle Reports modules to the /srw subdirectory of the application root, SQL programs to the /sql subdirectory, and HOST programs to the /bin subdirectory.

Second, register the process executable in the development instance through the Define Concurrent Program Executable form. Registration establishes an internal database name that corresponds to the external, operating system file name for the executable program. It is easiest to manage if they are the same. The executable registration form also asks for the application, which is your custom application, and the execution method (that is, executable type: SQL*Plus, Oracle*Reports, shell script, or C), and a description.

Third, register the process through the Define Concurrent Program form. Registration associates a printer format with the executable module defined earlier. It allows you to define other programs (including itself) that cannot be run at the same time. An update process, especially if it commits its changes by stages, often should not run at the same time as another process that updates the same tables. Lastly, define runtime parameters through the Define Concurrent Program form. Because you can use a single executable module in many concurrent program definitions, you can provide different parameter settings for different sets of users.

Usually the original reports you write will have relatively few parameters. If you copy from Oracle, though, you will need to copy over Oracle's parameter definitions. Some reports have as many as 40 parameters. Oracle provides a facility to do this within one Oracle instance, but copying parameter definitions between instances as a manual process can be quite a chore. You have to either copy again from the native Oracle report in the new instance or create the parameters manually. The best way to copy parameter definitions is to open one window of Define Concurrent Process for the new report and another for the existing report, then manually copy from the old to the new. You have to bounce back and forth between zones in each screen. As an alternative, have your DBA adapt and test the authors' copyparm.sql[14] script available on the McGraw-Hill Website (www.osborne.com).

The Define Concurrent Program form captures runtime parameters. You specify a prompt, a value set, and optionally, a default for parameters that the user is allowed to enter. Parameters they cannot change may be displayed or not. The default value can be a constant, a profile value, a system value such as the date, or derived from a SQL statement you provide. You can validate one parameter based on the entries for previous parameters. Oracle uses the Descriptive Flexfields device to validate and manage runtime parameters, as described in Chapter 14.

If you are defining an Oracle*Reports process, you provide a keyword (or token) for each parameter. The sequence of the parameters does not matter, except to the extent that the value set you use to validate one parameter refers to the entry for a previous parameter. SQL*Plus and HOST programs don't use keywords. The Concurrent Manager passes a list of parameters in the same sequence that you define them. In SQL*Plus, substitution variable &1 is the first parameter, &2 the second, and so on. For HOST programs in Unix, the variables are $1 through $9, with the others available after you execute a shift command.

Registering parameters for SQL*Loader are different. You enter its runtime keyword parameters, such as DATA =, CONTROL=, and ERRORS=

---

[14]copyparm.sql is on the margins of what conflicts with Oracle's "Injunction Against Modifying the Applications." It inserts values into tables that belong to AOL. On the other hand, those values are used only by the one report process to which they apply, so the consequential damages are limited if it does not work. Testing is the key. Make very sure the parameters work before you put them into production. Then you will find that copyparm is as useful for migrating reports from one environment to another as it is for copying parameters from one report to another.

through the Execution Options field. It does not require any entries in the Parameters block of the form.

Lastly, use the Define Report Group form to add the report to one or more report groups. This makes it accessible from the Run Reports form for every Responsibility associated with the report group through the Define Responsibility form.

The Execution Environment

Oracle's concurrent manager makes the bridge between online and batch operations. The Run Reports form writes a row to the FND_CONCURRENT_REQUESTS table as you submit the job. The operating system activates the concurrent manager at intervals to check the table. It initiates your request when it has worked its way to the head of the queue and there is an initiator ready. The concurrent manager submits the job to the operating system for background processing. The background process belongs to the applmgr user, just like the concurrent manager that spawned it.

The environment variables for your background process are established by the profile commands for applmgr. In most Unix systems the .profile command file establishes the environment. Environment variables include the instance ($ORACLE_SID) and the top directories for each application ($AP_TOP, $GL_TOP, and your custom application root directories).

TIP
*It is useful to register SQL*Plus and Host utility modules with a name such as TEST to the System Administrator Responsibility. You can then substitute any test code you need for these modules named $FND_TOP/sql/TEST.sql and $FND_TOP/bin/TEST. For example, when your concurrent jobs do not even start due to a file not found condition, check the environment. If you are in a Unix environment, put the env command in the TEST script, or HOST env in the TEST.sql script, to verify the environment settings being used by the concurrent manager.*

As applmgr executes your module, the default directory is the log file directory. Depending on your installation options, this directory is usually either $APPLCSF/out*SID,* where *SID* is the name of your instance, or $*app*_TOP/log, where *app* is the name of your application. See the Oracle Applications installation references for more details. The log file (named l*request_no*.log, where *request_no* is the concurrent request number) is written to this default directory.

The Concurrent Manager directs your spooled report to a subdirectory named /out or /out*SID* in the immediate parent directory of the log file just described. It uses different devices to get it there. For Oracle*Reports modules, the Concurrent Manager specifies this as the report output file name on the command line used to invoke Oracle*Reports. This is not an option on the command lines to execute SQL*Plus and HOST programs. Instead, under SQL*Plus, the Concurrent Manager will redirect the output to a SPOOL file as it invokes SQL*Plus. You cannot change it. Though you do not get the file name directly, you can use AOL stored procedures to get your concurrent request number and reconstruct it. If you direct output elsewhere through another SPOOL command, you cannot return to having it sent to the concurrent manager's intended file.

As the Concurrent Manager invokes a SQL*Plus routine it runs a prolog that includes the following commands:

```
SET TERM OFF
SET PAUSE ON
SET HEADING OFF
SET FEEDBACK OFF
SET VERIFY OFF
SET ECHO OFF
WHENEVER SQLERROR EXIT FAILURE
```

It sets the LINESIZE according to your report style: 80 for Portrait, 132 for Landscape, and 180 for Landwide. It also invokes whatever SQL*Plus login script has been established for the applmgr user. This is the place to look if your SQL*Plus programs do not work consistently in all database instances.

Once your module has control you can override the initial settings with a SET command. Two of the most common settings to override are PAGESIZE and NEWPAGE. If the output is going to a laser printer you usually want SET NEWPAGE 0, to force each new page to go on a new sheet of paper.

It's a good idea to convert positional parameters in SQL*Plus into keywords immediately after the header block in your script. This will make your code easier to understand, as illustrated in this example:

```
DEFINE P_USER_ID          = &&1
DEFINE P_REPORT_HEADING   = '&&2'
then
SELECT
  user_name
FROM
  fnd_user
WHERE
  user_id = &&p_user_id;
```

The Concurrent Manager uses the same spooling device for HOST (operating system level) programs as for SQL. If you could see the Unix command line used by the concurrent manager it would look something like this:

```
your_program parm1 parm2 parm3 parm4 \
parm5  & > orequest_id.out >2 lrequest_id.req
```

In Unix, you can reconstruct the spool file name using the request id parameter within the command line, which is available to you as parameter $1. If you redirect the output, the concurrent manager will not be able to find it to print or display to the requester, unless you bring it back into the spooled output for your session with the Unix command

cat

or the Windows command

type

Overview of the Open Interfaces

Oracle does not want users bypassing the edits in its forms by using scripts to directly update the Applications tables. This had been a problem in earlier versions of Applications, in which the online processes were the only means available for loading the database. Users had to decide between disregarding Oracle's stricture against modifications and rekeying data. Since rekeying destroys the integrity of the data in any case, not to mention being slow, most users chose to ignore the warning and load Oracle's tables through a batch process.

Recognizing the problem, Oracle has put emphasis on enhancing their Application Programmer Interfaces (APIs) in Releases 10 and 11 of Applications. The Open Interface APIs serve as bridges between the Oracle Applications modules themselves and external systems, they serve installers in the conversion process, and they serve you in building bespoke extensions to the system.

Oracle's own applications communicate with each other via the APIs. The Financial applications place journals in the GL_INTERFACE table. Purchasing and Order Entry place transactions in MTL_TRANSACTIONS_ INTERFACE to notify Inventory about receipts and shipments. Order Entry, Projects, and Service place invoice data in RA_INTERFACE_LINES and its related tables.

The applications often have to interface with your company's third-party service providers. Those vendors, rather than either Oracle or the customer, define the interfaces. Oracle provides the generic programs or Application Programmer Interfaces (APIs) so you can modify the programs they provide or write code to load the open interface. Here are some examples:

■ AR Lockbox

■ AP and Payroll Bank Reconciliation

■ AP Electronic Funds Transfer

Oracle's documentation is reasonably explicit about the values that need to be loaded, column by column, via the Open Interface tables. There is even more to be learned by referring to the Technical Reference Manuals (TMs). They tell you what lookup tables join to code columns. Often the value displayed in the screen or in a report is not the actual value stored in the base table. Instead, the base table stores a code that ties to a lookup table that has the full description of the value. You can use homemade lookup scripts, such as the one shown here, to find the valid lookup code values.

```
COL lookup_code FOR 999 HEAD 'Code'
COL lookup_type FOR a25 HEAD 'Lookup Type'
COL description FOR a40 HEAD 'Description'
SET HEAD ON PAGESIZE 6000
SELECT
```

```
    lookup_type,
    lookup_code,
    description
FROM
    po.po_lookup_codes
WHERE
        lookup_type LIKE '&1'
    AND lookup_code LIKE '%'||'&2'||'%'
REM
REM:  Use similar code for MFG_LOOKUPS, FND_LOOKUPS and SO_LOOKUPS
```

The seeded values in the lookup tables rarely change, but the documentation describing seeded values is somewhat scattered within the reference manuals. Use the techniques described in the following sections to research the actual contents of rows inserted via the online processes.

Populating the Open Interfaces

The strength of the Open Interfaces is in their complexity. They are designed to validate and load every possible attribute value and data relationship. The major interfaces will use data from three or more interface tables to populate a half-dozen or more Oracle Applications tables. Their weaknesses also arise from their complexity. Their performance may be slow and the error messages difficult to decipher.

Interface Program Execution

The open interface programs are executed as concurrent processes. You explicitly submit jobs to run most interface processes. Some, like the Material Transactions interface, don't have to be started because they are handled by worker processes that resubmit themselves every few minutes.

The interface tables include process flags to indicate the status of a row: not yet processed, in some state of being processed, and in-error. Some interface processes will operate on every eligible row within a table; others will take no more than a maximum number you have established with a parameter. The first thing they do is to set the process flags of the selected rows to indicate that they have been selected. You are then free to continue inserting rows into the interface while the interface program processes those that have been selected. Normally the rows will be deleted from the interface table once they have been successfully imported, unless otherwise stated.

You will discover that some interface processes, despite the fact that they will select every row in the interface table, work more efficiently with small numbers at a time. Some even run out of system resources and end abnormally when they attempt to process too many records. In these cases you can write your scripts to load a given number of records at a time into the interface tables. An easier alternative is to load all the records to the interface, but set the pending flag to a value the interface program does not recognize, –1,000,000 in the following example. You can then release rows in the interface table a few at a time with a script like this one:

```
UPDATE mtl_system_items_interface SET process_flag = 1
WHERE process_flag = -1000000 AND ROWNUM <= 100;
```

Interface Errors

The open interface programs process all the records they can and mark the rest with error messages. The messages may be in the failed records themselves or in an errors table linked to the interface.

The message system is designed to indicate the column in error and the nature of the problem. One error may cause several messages, in which case you will need to investigate them all to determine which is the original problem. It is important to isolate the original error message and not waste time with messages that are only byproducts of the original problem. Some messages will be too obscure to lead you to the problem. Some strategies for debugging your interface load script are:

- Develop your script in a test instance so you don't load invalid data into production.

- First get it to work for a simple case. If you are loading customer master records, start with the simplest possible customer, one with one site, no ship-to or bill-to addresses, contacts, or other related records. Add in the complexity one element at a time.

- Load one row at a time until the script works. Until you understand the process, plan to totally clear the interface tables after each unsuccessful test instead of trying to fix the failed rows in place. You can safely DELETE rows from the interface without destroying data integrity.

- Reduce the processing that the interface program has to do. Look up and insert the primary keys yourself. Translate codes yourself. By doing this you encounter problems such as trailing spaces in a VARCHAR2 column in your own code.

- Once the interface works, use an online process to query, update, and then commit the records you have inserted. This will cause the form to revalidate the record you created. In some instances, the online edits are different from the open interface edits. You want to be sure the rows are acceptable to every module that will use them.

Occasionally, when you present them with a data condition they are not equipped to handle, the open interface programs may experience an RDMBS-level error such as "Numeric or Value Error." In that case they do not give you any help identifying the individual row in error, and every row selected will remain in the interface table. The problem is usually a data error on your part. You can usually find it by reducing the number of rows you are inserting and eliminating complexity until it does work. A careful examination of the most recently removed attributes should lead you to the cause.

It can be helpful to check with Oracle Support prior to using the open interface and obtain the latest version of the interface code. This can save time and frustration, as the initial versions of open interface programs may contain bugs, and Oracle Tech support is likely to have patches that will resolve any performance problems.

In extreme cases, you can go to the code. Most open interface programs are written in C, which makes them appear—on the surface—to be inaccessible. Their table processing logic, however, is most often in PL/SQL stored procedures. Use a Unix grep or a Windows Find command to search the $Appl_TOP/admin/sql directory (/install/sql for 10.5 and earlier) for modules that work with the interface tables in question. Your programmers will find most of the modules under 20 pages in length and fairly well commented. If need be they can copy the modules, insert their own debugging code, regenerate the stored procedures, and then run the interface program again. Incidentally, the easiest way to log debugging data is to write your messages to a custom table.

Checking Interfaces

The applications use many of the open interfaces—among them, MTL_
TRANSACTIONS_INTERFACE, GL_INTERFACE, and RA_LINES_INTERFACE—
for internal communications in daily operation. Though they rarely
experience problems, your DBA needs to respond when they do. It is a good
idea to monitor them with periodic alerts, reporting to the DBA when there
are error rows in an interface or when records seem to be accumulating in
the interface.

Most of the errors you experience in the interface tables will be due
to data errors. Some of the interface tables are directly accessible through
forms within the applications, thereby providing you a generic ability to
update rows in the interface. Often, though, you need to do more. The best
business practice is usually to fix data in the feeder system and resubmit
records to Oracle. Doing that keeps the records in the two systems
consistent. You need to consider systems and business processes for
dealing with errors. Some elements to consider in a more extensive error
handling process are:

- An alert or a bespoke program, usually something simple written
  in SQL*Plus, to display the error record in the context of the
  originating system.

- A Descriptive Flexfield defined on the interface table to display
  pertinent data from the source system in a useful format.

- An established procedure for remedying the problem in the system
  that is feeding the interface.

- A standard Oracle process or bespoke program to clear erroneous
  records out of the interface.

- Instructions and processes for resubmitting transactions to Oracle,
  ensuring that each transaction is submitted once and only once.

The open interfaces are a powerful tool for communicating between other
software packages and Oracle, but it takes a little planning to keep the
channels open.

Scripts For Inserting Rows into Standard Tables

Even the Release 11 APIs do not satisfy all requirements for loading Oracle master and transaction tables. Some users will still have to write scripts. Here are some common-sense rules for writing these scripts:

1. Use the defined Oracle sequences to generate unique ids. (This process is described in Chapter 14). By doing this, you can be sure to avoid duplicating the identifier of a row generated by Oracle. For most tables, the name of the sequence is formed by adding "_S" to the name of the table. A typical script to get a sequence would be:

```
SELECT mtl_system_items_s.NEXTVAL from dual;
```

2. Research the actual contents of the tables by using the online screens to add the kinds of records you want the script to insert, and then printing them out. You can use the upcoming printtab.sql utility to display them in a useful format.[15] Write your SQL or PL/SQL scripts to make entries similar to the ones that already exist in the database.

3. If you are using SQL, create master table records first, so the detail records will have generated keys available to reference. You need your own, external unique key (such as the PO number) to relate master to detail records. It may be helpful to carry that unique external key in one of Oracle's user attribute columns, whether or not it is defined for use in a Descriptive Flexfield. If you are adding sets of related records using PL/SQL, put the master and detail records in the same commit group, so there is no chance of destroying data integrity by getting only some of them. Oracle Applications prior to Release 11 makes little use of database constraints; consider adding constraints yourself to ensure the integrity of tables you address with bespoke code.

4. Use the System Administrator Responsibility to create an Oracle Applications user-id with no function other than to identify batch

---

[15]The standard SQL statement "SELECT * FROM tablename WHERE ..." is not especially helpful for displaying Applications tables. If you set headings on, the headings run forever and you cannot relate them to the content. If you set headings off, there is nothing to indicate which column is which. Even in a browser, which can produce an infinitely long line with the headings and contents properly aligned, it takes a lot of scrolling to get a sense of the contents of a complete record.

insertions. Populate the CREATED_BY and LAST_UPDATED_BY fields with the user-id associated with that user in the FND_USER table. Pull the date into a substitution parameter, so that all transactions created in the script have the same CREATION_DATE and LAST_UPDATE_DATE values, as shown here. This process has a very important side effect. It rounds dates. Without rounding off the hours, minutes, and seconds it is more difficult to construct a SELECT to locate the rows your process has inserted or updated.

```
COL c_date NEW_VALUE p_date NOPRINT
COL c_uid NEW_VALUE p_uid NOPRINT
SELECT
  user_id,
  TO_CHAR(SYSDATE)
FROM
  fnd_user
WHERE
  user_name = 'BATCH_USER'
/
INSERT INTO application_table (
  creation_date,
  created_by),
. . . . . . . . . . .
VALUES (
  TO_DATE('&&p_date'),
  &&p_uid),
. . . . . . . . . . .
/
```

5. Make sure you back up the tables that will be affected by your script, so you can restore the database to its original condition to rerun the test. Let other people who are testing in the same instance know what you are doing.

6. Do not leave legacy data behind as you convert to Oracle. If the staging tables you load from the legacy system include fields that do not map to Oracle columns, either plan to retain your staging tables permanently or concatenate the data fields and place them in one of the user-attribute columns. Doing this protects you against the risk that after conversion the users will recognize an oversight and refer to that data in straightening it out. It is common, for example, to need to modify the planning, lead time or WIP supply type attributes in the inventory master table based on legacy settings. It is most convenient if the data is readily available.

7. Insert and commit the records.

8. Use Oracle screens to display and report on every record type and every relationship that should be observed among the newly added rows and between them and existing rows. Set up regression tests to do this automatically for large-scale modifications.

9. If there are any problems with the newly loaded data in your test instance, delete it all. The new rows will be uniquely identifiable by the WHO column values. You must never, of course, delete any rows other than the ones you added, and you hope never to have missed a problem in testing that would force you to delete from production.

10. The following script prints rows from a table, one column at a time.

```
REM printtab.sql.script ====================
PROMPT Enter table name
DEFINE table_name=&1
SET PAGESIZE 0 VERIFY OFF FEEDBACK OFF LINESIZE 100
SPOOL printtab1.sql
/* Generate SQL to read Varchar, Date and Number columns */
PROMPT SELECT
SELECT
  '"'||RPAD(column_name,30)||'=>"'||'||'||column_name||' ||CHR(10)||'
FROM
  fnd_columns c,
  fnd_tables t
WHERE
    c.table_id = t.table_id
  AND t.table_name = '&&TABLE_NAME'
  AND column_type <> 'L'
ORDER BY
  column_sequence
/
/* Generate SQL to read LONG column (if present)  ====================*/
PROMPT "
SELECT
  ',"Long:",'||column_name
FROM
  fnd_columns c,
  fnd_tables t
WHERE
    c.table_id = t.table_id
  AND t.table_name = '&&table_name'
  AND column_type =  'L'
/
/* Run the generated SQL to print the table ===================== */
```

```
PROMPT FROM &&TABLE_NAME
PROMPT WHERE
SPOOL OFF
SET VERIFY ON PAGESIZE 14 FEEDBACK ON
START printtab1

REM You may want to SPOOL the output of this utility and use a Unix sed
REM script to eliminate null columns.
```

This generates SQL that is missing a WHERE clause. You need to add a WHERE clause to select the one or two rows you are interested in. The script pauses just where you need to key one in. SQL*Plus cannot deal with a concatenation of more than about 60 columns, so you may need to edit the intermediate printtabl.sql. This script assumes only one LONG column per table; CHR (10) is a new line character.

Updating Standard Tables

Using Oracle programming tools to directly update the Applications tables goes directly against Oracle's injunction against modification, discussed earlier in this chapter. It is a risky alternative, but sometimes the only one. It may be essential, for example, to use an automated procedure to update lead time attributes in Inventory or to set computed shrinkage factors. The volume would make it impossible to post such data manually through the screens. If you must "SQL the database," here are some essential precautions:

1. Look in the Technical Manuals (TMs) to see how each column is used. Do not ever update a foreign key column.

2. Keep it simple. If possible, confine the update to a small number of related columns. Read the functional references as well as the Technical Manuals. The TMs are not intended to document the interdependencies among columns.

3. As part of your analysis process, use the Trace facility to see what SQL statements are executed in the course of the online update transaction you are replicating through batch codes. The DBA can set up Trace for you.

4. Read the SQL*Forms source code to see how each attribute you are updating gets edited by the native Oracle update or entry process.

The following section on analysis describes how. Make sure you do not change data so that it would not pass the edits on the forms field. When necessary, trace the validation logic through to C-code exits and PL/SQL routines.

5. Check the DBA_TRIGGERS table to see if any database triggers set or test the column value. Remember that it is possible that another, related module can use or be dependent on data in other modules, so you must check them all.

6. Do not delete rows unless the Oracle forms you have analyzed allow them to be deleted and you are sure you understand the process. Use the Oracle purge process if there is one, or at least read that code to be sure you understand all the integrity constraints that Oracle observes in deleting records.

7. Use the WHO columns to show how the row was changed. Set the LAST_UPDATED_BY and LAST_UPDATE_DATE columns as described earlier for insertions into the database.

8. Save the old values in an unused user attribute in the table. If you have the old values, and you can use the WHO columns to identify the rows that were updated by your bespoke process, you can reverse your update if necessary.

9. Thoroughly test every usage of the updated attribute, and every online form in which it appears, to make sure the forms behave exactly as if the values had been set by native screen processes.

Batch scripts that update the Applications database are often one-time affairs used to correct oversights in setup or conversion. If the changes are at all extensive or the implications of the change cannot be fully assessed, consider creating Regression Tester scripts, as described in the upcoming "The Analysis Process" section to apply the changes through the forms. That will give you the benefits of Oracle's native edits.

Deleting records is permanent. Recovering from an accidental deletion may mean restoring the database. As an alternative, consider moving the "deleted" records out of the way by changing the sign of the organization_id and generated key values to negative. You can wait to confirm that getting rid of the records had no adverse effects before truly deleting them. A common example would be moving inventory locations from one subinventory to another. Oracle does not allow you to make such a move once there are transactions in the locations. This restriction makes sense; the subinventories could have different material accounts, and moving locations could affect the ledger accounts. The following four-step script will accomplish the move.

1. Put ZZ prefix on Segment 1 of the MTL_ITEM_LOCATIONS records to be moved from the old subinventory. This will identify them as old. Changing Segment 1 does not affect system integrity because the system uses the generated key (inventory_location_id) and not the segment values for foreign key references. The ZZ prefix, incidentally, gets the old values out of the way by sorting them to the end of list-of-values selections.

2. Create new locations in the new subinventory by copying the old locations in the old subinventory, less the ZZ prefix. Use the sequence defined for the table (here, MTL_ITEM_LOCATIONS_S) to generate the primary key. The new records are accepted because they do not cause duplicates in either the primary key index or the Key Flexfield index (on the segment values).

3. Insert transactions for the subinventory move into the MTL_TRANSACTIONS_INTERFACE table so that Oracle will make the moves and take care of the accounting considerations.

4. Once all the transactions for the old locations are complete, the balances are zero, and the period has been closed, get the ZZ prefix locations out of the way so they don't appear in lists of values or on reports. Do this by making organization_id and inventory_location_id negative. If you later find you have made a mistake in your analysis and these old locators are needed, you can put them back by making the key values positive again. You can delete them later when you are confident they are no longer needed.

You need to exercise several levels of caution in making a change like this. Start with a thorough analysis of the requirements. Then test thoroughly in a development instance. Take a backup of the database before you run your update script in production. After your update, query the changed records immediately to ensure that they can be read and updated online. Then run concurrent processes against the changed records. Lastly, keep your old data in the database, to ensure that the process is fully reversible at every step in case you find you made a mistake.

This cautious strategy is effective for applying templates to existing items through open item interface. The interface does not directly allow you to update existing records. However, you can do the following:

- Tag the existing items with the name of the new template. You usually put it in the item_type attribute or one of the user attributes.

- Use the Open Item interface to create new records in the master inventory organization for the items you want changed. You can prefix them with some special character like an asterisk or pound sign to avoid creating duplicate records; because they are new they are automatically assigned new inventory_item_ids. Using the open interface assures you that the new attribute settings are valid and consistent.

- Once the records are in place in the master organization, use new templates to create new records for the changed items in the other inventory organizations.

- When all the new records are in place, move the old records out of the way by making their organization_id and inventory_item_ids negative and putting a prefix such as ZZ on Segment 1. Then put the newly created records in their place by updating their inventory_item_ids and dropping the special character prefix from Segment 1.

Any time you update inventory items you run the risk that you may not be able to complete processing open transactions. As part of your analysis, you need to test every type of template change online to see what warning messages you get.

There are two primary reasons that this approach is less risky than simply applying SQL to the inventory master table. First, it takes advantage of Oracle's native edits built into the open interface. Second, it is fully reversible if you find you have made an error, in that you can reverse the script to put the old records back.

Using Descriptive Flexfields

Oracle Applications gives you all the flexibility you need to capture and carry data that is specific to your needs. The major Oracle tables include user attribute columns (attribute1-attribute*n*) for your use. You can define Descriptive Flexfields to them, as described in Chapter 14, or populate them directly with bespoke conversion, bridging, or forms modules you have written. Going further, if you need whole new record types, you can define your own tables to the applications and integrate bespoke modules to populate them.

It is good practice to define all uses of Attribute *n* columns on the Define Descriptive Flexfields form, even those you don't use as Descriptive Flexfields. Define them, but set Enabled = No. This provides a placeholder, which will prevent the next developer from defining a Descriptive Flexfield and overwriting an attribute*n* column that is being used behind the scenes.

Getting data into your tables and attributes is more of an issue. The advantages and disadvantages of using Descriptive Flexfields are as follows:

Advantages	Disadvantages
Easy to implement.	DFFs are limited to the validation checking provided through format checking and value sets.
Fit into existing screens, zones, and tables.	Querying DFF values is an involved process. You do so by entering a colon in one of the enterable fields on a query screen, then typing the WHERE clause for SQL.
	DFF values are always stored as alphabetic.
	DFF attributes are limited in number (usually 15) and in size (usually 160 bytes).

Custom input forms, however, come with a significant trade-off of their own:

Advantages	Disadvantages
Can handle any input requirement.	Require significant programming effort.
	May damage database integrity if they populate native Oracle Application table columns other than user-defined attributes.
	Must be integrated into the responsibility/menu structure.
	Usually become release-dependent.
	Must be implemented independently for each client environment (character mode, or GUI).

It is usually easier to work around the shortcomings of Descriptive Flexfields than to create and implement custom forms. Chapter 14 describes how to set up a Descriptive Flexfield. Refer to Figure 15-2 in considering the following approaches to data entry:

■ *Use DFFs, and accept the level of validation available through value sets.* It may not be necessary to go beyond the native capabilities of the Descriptive Flexfields. It is often not worth the effort. As you know from legacy experience, users can be good at following procedures even if they are not enforced by the system. It works best, of course, when those users are the ones who have to live with the results of their own mistakes. As an example, it is usually not necessary to apply an edit to ensure that users do not embed special characters in part numbers. The few users allowed to create part numbers are smart enough to do it right.

You can apply a separate edit to a segment within a DFF for each context you define for that DFF. Micros Systems uses a DFF defined on Employee Expenses to capture customer data when the expenses can be recovered. The context indicates whether the employee is providing a sales order number or just a customer name. With a sales order number there is nothing else to add; the SQL statements defined to generate DFF defaults automatically look up and display

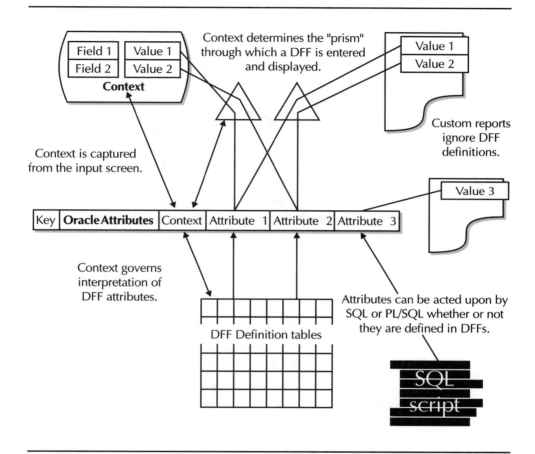

FIGURE 15-2. *Populating and validating user-defined attributes*

the customer, ship-to, bill-to, order type, and sales representative. With just a customer name, however, the ship-to, bill-to, order type, and sales representative segment values have to be entered and validated. The DFF captures the same fields in either case, but the value sets used to edit them depend on the context.

■ *Use the DFFs, but write alerts or batch reports.* Do this to perform editing beyond what is possible with native value set features. This approach is sometimes an acceptable compromise. It requires users to revisit their errors. Catching errors after the fact requires good procedures and discipline. It leaves a gap in time in which the system can continue to process with incorrect data in the database, and it leaves open the possibility that users will never bother to correct the errors.

- *Modify the Oracle screen.* You should add your own edits to the DFF fields and your own error messages. This approach does not require extensive analysis because it does not touch Oracle's logic. It does, however, make the form release-dependent. .

- *Define custom database triggers to operate on DFF data.* Modify the Oracle forms. You can add your won edits and error messages for validating the DFF fields. Such triggers can modify the data, populate user-defined tables, or set user attribute values in other Oracle tables.

  Database triggers cannot easily pass error messages clear back to the form. It is a matter of timing. Users need feedback as they enter data, but the triggers fire only at commit time, when the user presses the SAVE key. Moreover, the database trigger applies to every row that is being committed. A standard error message cannot tell the user which row had the problem, or if multiple rows were in error.

  The exception comes through the fact that database triggers can fail. When a trigger fails it sends the user a message to the effect that the commit failed because of a trigger error. You can write a user-defined error code in PL/SQL that will provide a useful message. Because it is a database-level error, though, users have to know to ask for it to be presented. Nonetheless, despite these shortcomings and given the effort involved in modifying forms, database triggers are sometimes an attractive alternative for implementing custom edits.

  Debugging database triggers can be frustrating. Until you become accustomed to Oracle's logic, "Mutating trigger" errors will often come up as a trigger working on one row attempts to select or update data from another row within the commit group. To give a simple example, you could not write a PRE-INSERT trigger on the PO_LINES table to keep the total PO value in attribute1 of the PO_HEADERS table. If you tried to commit two PO_LINES rows at the same time, the RDBMS could not decide whether to use the value computed by the first or the second execution of the trigger (row 1 or row 2 in PO_LINES). For the sake of consistency, the database trigger mechanism will not ever let you do it, even in instances where you are only committing one PO_LINES record.

Customizing Workflows

Oracle is integrating the power of its Workflow tool to provide more and more flexibility within the applications. Workflow manages the interaction between users and the automated system in the course of processing a transaction. It handles transaction routing and lets you capture and attach information to a transaction in all media formats, including scanned images, voice, and video.

Workflow Builder is a separate Oracle product. It is not essential that you buy it with Applications. However, you will find it very useful if you see a need to modify online processes. The predefined workflows that Oracle provides allow you to provide parameters, such as approval hierarchies and threshold amounts, but the workflow decision logic within them is fixed.

Decision logic is an integral part of transaction routing. It is implemented in the Workflow Builder and can be supported by PL/SQL modules. This gives you all the power you need, in most instances, to customize the data entry function. Workflow has the PL/SQL ability to query the database to validate data, the decision logic to test data conditions, and the ability to route the transaction to a user with an appropriate message when it finds an error.

Using Workflow to modify the applications makes modification of the online processes a much more attractive proposition than otherwise. It protects database integrity because your modifications do no affect the integrity of the "lower level" validation within the Applications code itself. Configuration management is easier because you place your bespoke code in a predefined location, Workflow's PL/SQL API.

Bespoke/Custom Forms

There is less need to develop bespoke screens, or forms, than to develop bespoke reports. Descriptive Flexfields handle most users' needs in the way of entering additional data fields, and as described earlier in this chapter, data can be manipulated after the fact by custom code, alerts, triggers, or even reports. Despite all this, there are often good reasons to write bespoke forms, and Oracle delivers all the machinery and instructions necessary to do so.

Here are some typical uses for USAGE custom forms:

Requirement Solution	Requirement Problem	Example
Control	The Oracle-provided form gives the users power to see too much data or alter too many fields.	The Define Item screen in Inventory lets any user update all attributes in a group. A custom form may let users update only one field, such as lead-time.
Efficiency	Standard Oracle forms require users to navigate through a number of screens, keying the same data multiple times.	Adding a new inventory location, moving all stock from an old location to the new one, and making the new location the default for issues and receipts.
Additional Fields	Standard Oracle forms may not display or accept all of the needed data.	Modification of the Bill of Material Inquiry form to display cross-references and reference designators on the indented BOM explosion.
New Subsystem	Write totally new functions, in a new application, against a combination of new and Oracle Application tables.	A Proposal pricing screen to enter prices, component sources, and modifications to standard Bills of Material for a custom bid.

Oracle Applications makes a distinction between inquiry and update screens. The worst a bespoke inquiry screen can do is confuse the user by displaying incorrect data. A form that only updates the user attributes (DFF segments) and custom tables does not jeopardize the integrity of standard Oracle data. The only forms that present major risks are those that affect the columns whose values Oracle sets and references within tables that belong to the applications. The updates they perform are on a par with scripts that "SQL the database."

The costs of analysis and testing mean there must be a significant business justification for writing a bespoke forms process that updates Applications tables. The Analysis Process section later outlines the essential steps in analysis and design. The program design documents should specify extensive testing.

Oracle*Forms programmers (using Forms 4.5, for Smart Client and NCA, but not character-mode Forms 2.3/2.4) have the ability to customize any form according to their own needs without changing the form itself. Forms trigger-code is stored in a series of external libraries that are searched in sequence. Changing the code is a matter of placing your modification in the custom trigger library ahead of the standard library.

Custom form developers can use all of the AOL library routines in their bespoke code. These include flexfields, folders, quickpicks, and zooms. The AOL Reference manual describes the use of each. Client/server and NCA users may want to use Designer 2000 to lay out their screens, especially to take advantage of its ability to generate both Oracle*Forms and Web-based forms.

Modifications to Applications forms are release dependent because the tables they reference and the database triggers on those tables are release dependent. Their design documents should address the analysis requirements associated with release upgrades. You may want to specify regression tests in the design documents for more complex forms to confirm that their operation has not been affected by an upgrade.

Any custom tables used in a screen have to be registered prior to registering the screen itself. Registration populates AOL's tables with the essential data needed to support field-level help. Use the Register Tables menu process within the Application Developer Responsibility.

You invoke the screen registration process as a batch process under the Application Developer Responsibility. Information about the screen, zone and fields is placed in AOL tables. That makes the form available for the context-sensitive help, the EXAMINE function, and other internal uses.

One of the best references in Oracle's documentation suite for Smart Client/NCA is modestly entitled *Coding Standards*. It is more than that. It describes how to modify Oracle's Designer 2000 code and how to work with Flexfields, Zooms, and other AOL devices.

Messages

Message service routines in the Applications present messages in the users' own national language (English, French, and so on). The program module, be it in Forms, Reports, or PL/SQL, invokes the Applications message routine, passing the message name as a parameter. The presentation subsystem returns the message in the appropriate language.

Predictably, the messages are stored in a database. Less predictably, AOL compiles them for use by the forms, according to national language, into an operating system file on the client or Web server machine in the $app_TOP/mesg subdirectory. This approach eliminates the need for a trip to the database. The forms program invokes a message by a subroutine call (i.e., a user exit in C in Forms 2.3/2.4, or a stored procedure in Smart Client/NCA). It passes the internal name of the message to be presented and in some cases variables to be substituted into the message text. The message subroutine determines the national language, searches the operating system file for a match on the internal name, fetches the associated natural-language text, substitutes in the replacement parameters, and presents the message.

You need to use Oracle's architecture if you are designing a bespoke form to be used in a multilanguage environment. You must do the following:

- Give each message an internal name.

- Translate each message into each national language.

- Maintain versions of the forms boilerplate text in each national language you use.

It is simpler if you use only one national language. When messages don't need to be translated, you can embed them directly in the form itself and use the standard Forms 4.5 messaging services to present them.

If you do use bespoke/custom forms and they are registered under custom applications, you will need to take a step that allows your form to read Oracle's standard message file. To do this, in the Define Profile Option form, assign your custom application the profile option Message: Shared Application to have the value of the standard Oracle application it is matched to. For example, WJ Receivables will share messages with Oracle Receivables.

Sometimes highly used forms are called by another form, into which the application and form name are hard-coded. If you wish to let users access your custom form from the native forms that include hard-coded references, you will need to create a link between your custom form and the Oracle form it replaces. Follow these steps:

1. Create your own module, giving it an appropriate custom name to distinguish it from modules written by Oracle.

2. Rename the Oracle distribution form according to your local convention. For instance, rename OEXOEMOE.frm to OEXOEMOE.frm.original. This makes the original name available for your use.

3. Create an alias using the appropriate operating system feature, such as a soft link with the ln command in Unix or a shortcut in NT, linking the original Oracle module name in its native directory to your module in the custom directory.

This procedure satisfies the objective of separating Oracle from custom code without creating excessive work dealing with additional customizations.

It is often useful to set and retrieve messages in PL/SQL. The AOL reference manual describes the process reasonably well. However, the best way to understand the message process is to read Oracle's source code for the message service routines. These, along with the Concurrent Manager routines and many others that are useful in modifying the system, are in the $FND_TOP/admin/sql directory. Find the message routines by navigating to that directory and giving the following command (in Unix):

```
grep -i get_message *
```

A Windows NT user, or any other user with NFS access to the server directory structure, can locate the files using the Word for Windows advanced file find facility, under File/Open/Advanced.

Performance Tuning

Database performance tuning is a specialty unto itself. Performance depends on table size, table placement, indexing, activity, and many other factors. The most significant factor in the performance of an individual program is usually how the SQL within the program is coded.

Most of the DBA's tuning activity takes place at the RDBMS level, invisible to the applications. The Application Designer's capacity planning will tell the DBA how much space is needed for each application and what the major tables are within each. The technical manuals provide the needed information about indexes.

The DBA may add indexes on the Oracle tables to meet local needs. It is common, for instance, to add indexes on the user attributes populated by DFFs. Non-unique indexes can improve performance, and unique ones can constrain users from making duplicate entries.

Sometimes the Oracle indexes wind up missing after an upgrade or a patch. It is a good idea, when performance seems to have degraded significantly on a given table, to check to see that the indexes are all there. The technical manuals list the indexes that are supposed to be on a table. The following script will read the metadata to do the same:

```
SELECT
    i.index_name,
    i.uniqueness,
    c.column_name ,
    ic.column_sequence
FROM
    fnd.fnd_indexes i,
    fnd.fnd_index_columns ic,
    fnd.fnd_columns c,
    fnd.fnd_tables t
WHERE
    t.table_id = i.table_id and
    ic.index_id = i.index_id and
    ic.column_id = c.column_id and
    t.table_name = '&1'
ORDER BY
    i.index_name,
    ic.column_sequence
/
```

Your DBA can compare this list with the indexes that are found through the USER_INDEXES view to determine if any are missing.

Online Processes

Network speed and tuning is very important in Smart Client. In NCA the issues are the speed and placement of the middle tier or Web server, the speed of its links back to the database server and forward to the client, and the speed of the desktop machine itself. Oracle recommends at least a medium speed (200MHz +) Pentium to drive the Applications applet running in your browser.

The performance issues with online processes often have more to do with user productivity than network or computer speed. The preceding section discussed situations in which it may be desirable to create one form that combines the function of several native Oracle forms. Workflow can be a very useful tool for streamlining the data entry process, allowing you to eliminate unneeded steps and providing default information.

Batch Processes

Oracle*Reports is a much more powerful tool than SQL*Plus, but it executes somewhat more slowly. There may be reports that run so frequently in the course of a day that it makes sense to speed them up. It can be a simple matter to pull the queries you need from an Oracle*Reports module and re-implement them in SQL*Plus or a simplified Oracle*Reports program.

Compiled programs, usually written in the Pro-C language, offer more programming flexibility and better performance than any other tools. They are also an order of magnitude harder to code, debug, and manage. Oracle itself is committed to replacing all the Applications logic now implemented in C with PL/SQL by Release 12. Only large organizations doing major modifications will find it worth the effort to use compiled code.

The Analysis Process

You can't modify a system without understanding it. You need a minimal understanding just to describe your problems to Oracle Support so they can fix them. How do you find out what goes on behind the scenes?

Analyst/Designers fill the same role with the applications as they do in custom development. They present user needs in a requirements document, then design a solution to the problem. The solution may be any combination of business procedures, customizations, and modification. An Applications designer starts with a fully functioning, integrated system made up of a massive number of modules, whereas the designer of a bespoke system starts with no more than a legacy system and a concept of what might be.

Learning what the Oracle system does, and how it does it, is a challenge to which no analyst can fully respond. The packages are intricate, and the documentation about how they work internally is limited. The analyst always has to judge how much knowledge is enough for a particular job and to weigh the risks associated with what he or she does or doesn't know.

The User Reference Manuals

The user reference manuals frame the discussion between users and analysts about the requirements. Users describe what they want in terms of what the delivered system can and cannot do. Both the users and the analyst should read the relevant overview sections of the user references (Release 11) or Topical Essays (Release 10 and prior) and the screen and report descriptions carefully. The analyst needs a test instance in which to practice using the native Oracle features before giving any thought to changing them.

The Technical Reference Manuals (TMs)

The TMs describe each module in the system that has Application functions. They tell you how to use AOL, and they tell you how Oracle built Payables or Purchasing. Chapter 14 describes how information is organized in the manuals. Each contains a data module of that module, providing a good starting point in understanding relations between the tables.

The analyst can use the TMs to find the names of the modules involved and the subroutines they call, what the modules do, and what tables they use. The TMs are reasonably accurate about which tables and subroutines are involved. They describe the functions of each module only at a very high level. As is usual, the source code itself is the most authoritative documentation. The TMs are the key to the source code.

Reading Code

The only way to know for sure what a piece of code does is to look at it. The various applications are written in different tools, with different characteristics. This section explains how to read the code.

SQL*Plus and PL/SQL Routines

These are written in ASCII text. They are totally accessible and Oracle does a good job of commenting the code. The Applications use these languages for relatively few reports. However, they have migrated more and more of the complex logic for routines such as Bill of Material explosion from Pro-C to PL/SQL. PL/SQL is the source language for database triggers, packaged procedures, Oracle*Forms triggers, and Oracle*Reports triggers. Stored procedures, triggers, and other PL/SQL routines that are executed at setup time are in the $app_TOP/admin/sql directory for each application. $FND_TOP/admin/sql contains the AOL routines for concurrent process submission, messaging, and the like.

SQL*Forms 2.4 (Character-Mode Screens)
These have been replaced by Forms 4.5 in Client/Server and NCA. Oracle has implemented all newer Applications, and certain new forms in the older ones, only in Forms 4.5. Where both character and GUI versions of a form exist, they typically have the same module name and the same features. The edits, though they are implemented in different languages, are intended to work identically.

Forms 2.4 Programs
These can be viewed through the *iad* design program available from the command prompt. They are displayed block by block (Forms blocks equate to Applications zones) and field by field. A programmer can examine all the triggers associated with a given field by using iad's display mechanism to read the code at the field, block, and form level and simply an ASCII editor to view the source code.

Alternatively, the analyst can take advantage of the fact that Forms 2.4 uses an ASCII source code format. It takes a while to get used to reading the source programs. They are decidedly nonsequential and the .INP files run several hundred pages in length. Top to bottom, the code is organized as shown here:

> *Form header*
> *Form-level triggers*
> *Block 1*
> > *SQL code to query rows into Block 1*
> > *Block 1 triggers*
> > > *Field 1 name*
> > > *Field 1 type, position and characteristics*
> > > *Field 1 triggers (within code for each field)*
> > > *Field 2 - Field n in the same format as Field 1*

Block 2 - Block n in the same format as Block 1
Boilerplate for form pages 1 to n

For purposes of analysis, Forms 2.4 code offers one major advantage over Forms 4.5 code. All the source code is in one ASCII module, accessible by an editor, whereas Forms 4.5 logic is scattered through a large number of PL/SQL Load Libraries (PLLs) that have to be searched individually. Even Smart Client users may find it convenient to keep the 2.4 code around for reference. Start by using the \ Other Examine menu sequence in Applications to find the name of the form, block, and input field.[16] Then bring the .inp file up in an editor and search on that name. You will find where the field is defined and everywhere that it is referenced. From that information you should be able to determine what edits and processing are imposed on it within the form. Also pay close attention to the user exits. Exits are coded as a pound sign followed by an exit name (usually three characters) and a number of parameters, like #BOM or #MSG. Look at the following sections for a discussion on deciphering this compiled C code. #PLSQL exits invoke stored procedures, the source for which is easy to read.

Forms 2.4 triggers predate PL/SQL. They combine SQL with a macro language that is unique unto itself. Because most navigation in the Applications forms is handled by AOL triggers, there are only a few macro commands you need to understand in order to read the code. CASE and END CASE control decision logic. GOSTEP handles branching; you will usually find the target label a bit further down in the code. ENDTRIG terminates the trigger. COPY assigns values to form variables, including globals. One block of trigger code can call another using the EXETRG macro function. Called triggers that belong to AOL are almost always defined at a form level, whereas most of the calling triggers are application-specific, and occur at the block or field level. With that introduction you should be able to follow trigger logic in the .inp file of a character-mode form.

Developer 2000 Code: Oracle*Forms and Oracle*Reports

This code has to be viewed through the appropriate Developer 2000 tool. Forms are organized into blocks, each one based on a database table.

---

[16]DBAs are often reluctant to enable the Examine function, since you can alter the database tables directly with this tool. They are right as far as production goes, but it is a valuable tool in development.

Reports are organized into groups based on SQL queries. Each provides a number of ways for users to add asynchronous triggers where the most interesting code is often buried.

Your desktop environment may not enable you to view all reports. The PL/SQL buffer in Windows is only 64K. Several PRE-REPORT triggers, among them the ones for Bill of Materials explosions, are too large to display. A quick-and-dirty workaround is to bring a Forms or Reports module up in a word processor. Most of it will be unintelligible, but the SELECT, INSERT, and UPDATE statements are readable because they remain in ASCII. You may be able to do a find on a table or column name and get a quick idea of what the module does with it without laboriously examining its component parts in Designer 2000. Some editors are better at this than others. Microsoft Word seems to pick up everything, whereas the Unix vi editor appears to impose a limit on the length of the lines it can handle. It drops material when the distance between carriage returns is too great.

C Code

C is still used throughout AOL as of Release 10.7, though Oracle is phasing it out. Application-specific C code is pretty much confined to Forms exits and concurrent processes. Oracle does not provide the source. The only way to figure out what the code does is to bring it up in a word processor and scan to find the embedded SQL code. This task is especially difficult for Forms exits because all the logic for an entire application is compiled together into one module. If you are dealing with attributes whose names appear in the C code, in a context that suggests they are being updated or they serve as the basis for decision logic, you will probably never fully understand exactly how the code works.

Laboratory Method

Working with the Applications is a science. Some source code simply isn't available, and much of the rest will be just too complex, or at least too voluminous, for your programming staff to reasonably understand. After reading the documentation and as much code as possible, the analyst needs to apply classic laboratory methods to confirm theories as to how the various "black boxes" function.

The laboratory process generally encompasses these steps:

1. Define the process to be analyzed. Modules of most interest are those that update the database, both batch and online processes.

2. Determine by reading the User References, TMs, and source code which tables are affected by the process and its subroutines.

3. Comb through the tables to see if any database triggers defined on them affect yet other tables. For example, inserting new items into the MTL_SYSTEM_ITEMS table can fire a trigger that populates CST_ITEM_COSTS and CST_ITEM_COST_DETAILS.[17]

4. Take a "before" image of the tables used by a process. You can usually confine yourself to the rows you know will be affected. The easiest way is to create a side table of just those rows with a CREATE *yourtable* AS SELECT * FROM *Oracletable* WHERE...You may want to use the printtab.sql routine shown previously to display the values in these rows beforehand. Needless to say, you do this in a test instance.

5. Execute the update process. This usually amounts to keying data into the screen and committing.

6. Compare the values in the tables before and after execution. The printtab.sql routine is useful for a visual comparison. If the data volumes are large, you may want to write a custom script to compare the before and after images of the database.

7. Establish why each changed value was changed, and determine the significance of each change.

8. If you are going to repeat the analysis process, use a script to restore the test instance tables to their original condition or pick another master record for the next test.

---

[17]"Combing" is a science unto itself. The Unix command `grep -i MTL_SYSTEM_ITEMS 'find . -name "*.sql" -print' > $HOME/msi` will look for the table name MTL_SYSTEM_ITEMS, in all files with a .sql prefix, in all subdirectories of the current directory, and put each instance found into a file called msi in your home directory. You can then look there to find database triggers affecting the table. Microsoft Word's advanced FIND facility (under the file open menu) will do the same thing.

Some processes, especially database triggers, are easy to overlook. The database trace function is useful for determining exactly which tables are affected by an operation.

Detailed Table Analysis

The Applications' metadata tables can tell you more than Standard Oracle RDBMS functions. It is worth learning how these foundation tables can tell you what you need to know.

- **Columns in a table**   The DESC function displays columns and datatypes. The fnd_col script shown here is a SELECT joining the FND_TABLE and FND_COLUMNS tables. It includes the column description text used in the TMs. It has the added virtues of presenting only columns that satisfy a LIKE clause, weeding out the predictable Attribute *n*, Segment *n*, and WHO columns and presenting the descriptions. It helps you cope with the large number of columns in the Applications tables.

```
REM fnd_col.sql script====================
COLUMN table_name   FOR a20   HEAD Table
COLUMN column_name  FOR a20   HEAD Column
COLUMN col_type     FOR a4    HEAD Type
COLUMN descr        FOR a30   HEAD Description
SELECT
  t.table_name   table_name,
  c.column_name  column_name,
  c.column_type||SUBSTR(LTRIM(TO_CHAR(c.width)),1,4)  col_type ,
  c.description descr
FROM
  applfnd.fnd_tables t,
  applfnd.fnd_columns c
WHERE
      t.table_id = c.table_id
  AND t.table_name LIKE  '%&fnd_table%'
  AND c.column_name LIKE '%&COL%'
  AND c.column_name NOT LIKE 'ATTRIBUT%'
  AND c.column_name NOT LIKE 'SEGMENT%'
  AND c.column_name NOT EQUAL 'LAST_UPDATED_BY'
  AND c.column_name NOT EQUAL 'LAST_UPDATE_DATE'
  AND c.column_name NOT EQUAL 'CREATED_BY'
  AND c.column_name NOT EQUAL 'CREATION_DATE'
 /
```

■ **Tables where a column is used** Using the LIKE feature and reading the column descriptions provided by the fnd_col.sql script make it fairly easy to find all the foreign key joins on a column like inventory_item_id. It would be a lot of work to dig that out of the TMs. Want to know which tables use po_header_id? Do a select entering that value for the column and leaving the table name blank.

You should be aware of some the weaknesses of this approach. Corresponding columns are not always named the same in every table in which they appear. In some cases, such as more than one-column joins to a single foreign key, they could not be named the same. For example, 17 columns within MTL_PARAMETERS join to code_combination_id within GL_CODE_COMBINATIONS. In other cases nomenclature has changed as the system evolved. The primary key of MTL_ITEM_LOCATIONS is inventory_location_id. Most foreign key columns that join to it are named locator_id. The likely explanation is that the base table was in place prior to Oracle's decision to use the word locator to denote inventory stock locations and the word location to mean a business location.

■ **Forms that use a table** The form registration process creates a record of the tables and columns used by a form in the FND_FORM, FND_BLOCK and FND_FIELD tables.

■ **Menus on which forms appear** Oracle's standard reports show a menu structure from the top down. It is sometimes handy to look from the bottom up, to find where a given form is used. The following is an example of a script to do this.

```
COLUMN menu_name for a20
COLUMN form_name for a14
COLUMN prompt for a11
COLUMN description for a30
SELECT
   fm.menu_name,
   fme.form_name,
   fme.prompt,
   fme.description
FROM
   fnd_menu fm,
   fnd_menu_entry fme
```

```
WHERE
      fm.menu_id = fme.MENU_id
  AND (UPPER(fme.prompt) like '%'|| UPPER('&1')||'%'
      OR UPPER(fme.form_name) like '%'|| UPPER('&1')||'%'
      OR UPPER(fme.description) like '%'|| UPPER('&1')||'%')
/
```

Regression Testing

New software releases are supposed to offer new functions and fix known problems without introducing new complications. Making sure that the old features still work requires significant effort. Oracle provides Forms 2.4 character mode users with the automated Regression Tester (RT), which they can use in-house to test the operations of forms created in prior versions of the product.

The problems are more complex in the windowing environments of Smart Client and NCA. Oracle decided to buy a regression testing suite from Mercury rather than build one for its own internal use. The Regression Tester can still be used in character mode by customers with 10.6 and 10.7 GUI installations.

The purpose of a regression tester is to apply identical tests to different modules of code, usually new and old versions of one module, and to compare the results. Most regression testers have similar architectures. Their major features include:

■ A means of capturing keystrokes and mouse movements. Most systems use operating system files. Oracle's Regression Tester uses a combination of database and flat files.

■ A device to edit the keystroke files so that tests can be copied and altered.

■ A device to play back the keystrokes, simulating online operation, and to save the results of the simulated online session. Two forms of output are of interest. There is a log file showing the interaction: the data provided by the Regression Tester and the response from the module being tested. The log file is the place to look when a test goes off track because the tested module does not receive data and commands in the sequence it expects. There is also a file containing effects of the program's execution, which in Oracle's case are changes to the database.

■ A program to compare the changes to the database resulting from different runs of the Regression Tester.

The objective of regression testing is to prove that the new, improved version of a program performs its old functions exactly as it did before. Each new release of a module should be accompanied by new regression tests to serve as the baseline for testing yet later releases.

Even though very few Oracle Applications shops are rigorous enough to implement automated regression testing, testing is important in managing release upgrades. Even though Oracle thoroughly tests its software prior to release, it is a good practice to execute all your major system functions in a test instance before putting them into production. Doing so protects against your own oversights in implementing the upgrade, against Oracle's in testing it, and against misunderstandings as to how the code has changed. The better defined the tests, the more successful they will be. All good tests are:

■ Defined in advance

■ Repeatable

■ Thorough

Whereas you regression test Oracle's code at an application level, you need to regression test each module of bespoke code individually as you do an upgrade. Examine the code, then run a test to see if it has been affected by changes to Oracle's schemas and code. Rather than use an automated regression tester, most shops can manage by including a written description of the tests to be performed as part of the design documentation for bespoke code.

Using Regression Tester for Mass Updates

Regression testers, because they invoke Oracle Applications' online edits in a batch mode, can be very useful for applying complex changes to the system. Say, for instance, that you need to apply a new template to each of 1000 items in the Inventory Master. The approach would be as follows:

1. Capture the keystrokes as you apply the change to one item through the online process.

2. Write a script to read the keystroke file, change only the item number, and rewrite it under a new name.

3. Run the script for each of the 1000 items to be changed, creating 1000 test files.

4. Run the 1000 tests.

This method usually involves significantly more work than just "SQLing the database." It is also significantly safer because it uses Oracle's native edits and processing. Depending on the features of the Regression Tester, you can program each individual test to abort if it encounters an unexpected condition such as an error message returned from the online form.

Even GUI users of versions 10.6 and 10.7 of Applications may find the character-mode Regression Tester valuable for making mass changes to the database. See the Osborne McGraw-Hill Web site at **www.osborne.com** for a paper on the subject.

Document Control

More is written and less done about methodology than any other topic in data processing. Documentation? Coding standards? Logs? Records? Most Applications shops do not see themselves as developers. They have little in the way of development procedures and do even less in the way of observing the ones they have.

Deadline pressure is the most frequent culprit. Consultants and employees scramble to get the system up, telling themselves that they will document after the fact. They are surprised to find themselves inundated with maintenance and enhancement requests long after the implementation, by which time even the people who are left on the project remember little about the implementation.

Minimalism is the key to success. People will adhere to methodologies if they are reasonable and understandable. Here are some general guidelines:

- Decide on your own methodology. A packaged system from a large consulting firm is almost always too complex, and usually is not appropriate to Oracle Applications. The best that can happen is that it will be honored in the breech. Second best, it will be totally ignored. Worst of all, some well-intentioned administrator will doom the project to generating nothing but shelfware by enforcing it.

- Let the programmers and analysts decide what they need. Journeyman team leaders and independent consultants are often the best guides.

- Keep it simple and quick.

- Remember that quality has to be built in, not grafted on. Let the senior developers and consultants establish the culture and set a model for their peers.

- Keep standards and documentation close to the code. Programmers appreciate well-structured and well-commented code because it is useful to them as they maintain it. They don't care about what they don't use—and it shows. Paper documents have a tendency to stay in the filing cabinet. A better approach is to keep word processing documents available over the network, if possible in the same directory structure as the code they describe.

The standards and procedures described here are minimal but yet more rigorous than most organizations manage to sustain. Anybody who takes the issue seriously will find yards of shelf space devoted to books on the subject of standards in a computer bookstore.

Log Maintenance

It is essential to know what is in the Applications environment in order to maintain it. The key logs are discussed here.

Oracle Release History

The DBA needs to keep a log of when each instance is updated to each new dot-point release. There are relatively few entries for each instance because release upgrades are major events, occurring only every year or so. The log should indicate the levels of the RDBMS and operating system. Applications upgrades involve scripts to migrate data to new table structures. Keep the output logs for the most recent upgrade. Since most test instances are created as copies of the production instance, be sure to copy the patch log as part of setting up the new instance.

Oracle Patches

DBAs apply patches with some regularity, and Oracle support always needs to know which ones have been applied. DBAs are usually very conscientious about keeping records of their activity. Each patch generates a log as it is applied. Hang onto the output logs for patches to the current release in each database instance.

Setups (Reference Document Used for Manual Setup)

Each application has a series of setup screens for the parameters that control its operation. The "setups" are in constant flux as the system's Superusers work out the business procedures appropriate to their installation. The setups invariably have to be keyed in a number of times, as in the experimentation phase of the project. Setup parameters should be organized according to the screen on which they are captured. Use one word processing table per application, with these columns:

    Screen Name
    Field Name
    Value
    Reason
    External reference

The reason column is essential. The users should note why the parameter value was chosen and what other parameters are related to the setting. The external reference will link to spreadsheets where you keep those setups that involve a large number of values, such as Inventory Templates and Fixed Asset Categories.

Screen prints, often used to document the setups, fall short of doing the entire job for several reasons. The most obvious is that they can only be created after the fact. They take a lot of time and effort to create. Their natural medium is hard copy; embedded in word processing documents they are bulky and slow to print. Most significantly, they do not carry the intelligence as to why a value was selected, only what it is.

The Superusers of the individual applications most often key in the setups. This can be a lot of work, but it gives them a chance to review the values, and they can ensure they are keyed accurately. You can cut the work down using Oracle's Application Implementation Wizard. Power users may even consider using scripts or a regression tester to automatically key in the setups for multiple installations.

The word processor document describing the setups used in each Oracle instance should be referenced in the DBA's documentation for that instance.

Value Sets

Value sets are part of setup. Some, especially GL accounts and organizations, can be fairly large. You can choose to document small ones in the word processor document in line with other setups. The best way to handle large value sets is in a separate spreadsheet. Some of these you can load through the Applications Desktop Integration tool. You may need scripts to load others from the spreadsheet into the FND_FLEX_VALUES and FND_FLEX_VALUES_TL tables. (See Osborne's Website for a prototype script for loading value sets.)

Users may define value sets to validate Descriptive Flexfield (DFF) segment values and report parameters. Most such values are rather static and should be entered as part of setup. They deserve their own documentation. Larger and more volatile value sets are usually handled by, and documented as, user-defined tables.

Application-Specific Setup Documentation

Some applications have setups unique to themselves. Inventory uses item templates to facilitate setting up new items. Purchasing and Inventory share lists of buyers. GL uses Financial Statement Generator reports.

Oracle is designed to require users to key this customization into each new instance, except where it is propagated by the backup/restore process. The documentation should describe the entries and how to set them up.

Alerts

Alerts do not have source code per se. They exist only within the Oracle Applications tables. It is useful to keep a one-page document describing each alert and a list of alerts that relates their Oracle name to the document that describes them.

The Alert description should include:

- The purpose and type of the alert

- The SQL code in the alert, which can be cut-and-pasted right into the document

- What the alert does: send e-mail, initiate a process, or whatever

The best practice is to set up and test alerts in a development environment. You key them into Production after they are debugged. They then migrate back to your test environments as they are periodically refreshed with copies of production.

Alerts are a common suspect when system performance slows. The documentation will help the DBA in that regard. Aside from that, the documentation is useful in maintaining the alert and propagating it to new environments. The creator will almost always put it together in a test environment, document it, and then use the documentation to rekey it into production.

CHARACTER-MODE ZOOMS   A one-page document for each Zoom can describe the need it serves, the screens that it links, and the "context," or variable data, it takes back and forth between the two. Complex Zooms may involve a number of execution steps to query and populate fields. Copying those steps into the documentation can be a big help in implementing the Zoom in new environments. The documentation for an instance should reference a list of all Zooms within the instance.

RESPONSIBILITY SETUP   The security plan for each instance deserves a document. It should name the different Responsibilities and specify who is expected to use each of them. It should name the top-level menu and report group. If the high-level menu structures you develop are not documented elsewhere, this is a good place for them.

You administer flexfield security at a Responsibility level. The documentation for the Responsibility should include the rules that restrict access to key and descriptive flexfields. It can be useful to include printouts of the reports within the report group and the menu tree under each

Responsibility. However, in many environments these change quite frequently. The best approach is to pull menu and report group reports off the system as needed.

USER ATTRIBUTE USAGE BY TABLE   Though the only support Oracle provides for user attributes is as Descriptive Flexfields (DFFs), you are free to use them any way you want. You can populate them through DFFs, database triggers, custom-written forms, or batch processes. You may put them to temporary use as a record of changes to the database, as described in "The Analysis Process" section earlier in this chapter.

The best practice is to define a DFF for each attribute field you use, whether or not you actually need to display it on a screen. Make the DFF segment inactive, but define it. This marks the attribute as taken, so no other programmer will attempt to put it to a different use. A DFF usage document also helps programmers to know which user attributes are in use and which are available. For debugging they need to know which processes set and use the attribute values. The table of attribute usage should include columns for:

- Table name

- Attribute name (attribute1 through attribute*n*)

- Narrative description of the way the column is used. Occasionally there are multiple uses, controlled by a DFF context segment.

- Name of the DFF using this attribute, if any.

- Context of the DFF using this attribute, unless it is global.

- DFF segment names for this attribute (if any). There can be one per context.

- The name of the value set associated with the segment and context, if it is used in a DFF and is validated.

- Column format as used. User attributes are almost always defined to Oracle as VARCHAR2(150) to VARCHAR2(240), but the DFF or other module that populates it determines the actual length and format of the contents. It is common, for instance, to put the numeric values of generated keys in user attributes. Oracle Receivables links back to Sales Order Lines by this device.

■ Modules and processes that set the value, such as DFFs, triggers, bespoke forms, inbound bridges, and conversion routines.

■ Modules and processes that use the value, such as reports and outbound bridges.

USER-DEFINED DATABASE TRIGGERS BY TABLE   Database triggers have to be reestablished every time a new instance is set up. The DBA needs a list to make sure they are all present as needed. In fact, in most development instances, and all production instances, it is the DBA who will implement the triggers using the developers' scripts.

Database triggers are also the frequent cause of data corruption problems. There are tools to show the trigger names and whether or not they are enabled. It takes documentation for the DBA to decide whether a given trigger has anything to do with a given bug.

The list of database triggers should include the following elements for each trigger:

■ Trigger name

■ Table name

■ Brief purpose of the trigger, including reference to the design document that specified its need

■ Columns referenced by the trigger

■ Tables and columns updated by the trigger

■ The applicable design document

There should be a design document supporting each database trigger. Triggers often do not have separate documentation when they exist as part of a larger suite.

USER-DEFINED STORED PROCEDURES   PL/SQL code in Oracle*Forms, Oracle*Reports, database triggers, and SQL*Plus modules can all call stored procedures. They represent "black box" procedures that can be separately tested and debugged, then used as needed.

The DBA needs to be able to implement stored procedures in each new instance, and certainly needs to know what they do to the database. The table of stored procedures should include these details for each procedure:

- Owning subsystem

- Procedure name

- Purpose (two-sentence narrative)

- Tables and columns updated by the procedure

- Reference to the design document that specifies the stored procedure. Each stored procedure usually belongs to a suite. It doesn't each need its own design document, but it should be covered by some design document.

CUSTOM INDEXES ON NATIVE ORACLE TABLES   Users sometimes put their own indexes on Oracle's tables to improve system speed or to enforce uniqueness. The DBA needs a list of such indexes.

USER-DEFINED TABLES AND VIEWS   Users often define their own tables in adding custom functions to the Oracle Applications. The DBA needs a list of these. The columns should include:

- Owning schema. There should be only one, or at most a few. Many organizations name it CUSTOM. At any rate, the objects you create should not be owned by the Oracle Applications schemas.

- Table name

- Usage, in two sentences or so

- Design document name. The design document will list the attributes within the table.

- Indexes

- Grants and synonyms

- Registration (i.e., is the table registered to Oracle Applications, or not?)

- Whether or not the table holds a value set defined to the applications.

USER-DEFINED REPORTS AND OTHER CONCURRENT PROCESSES   The AOL tables include entries for each registered report and concurrent process. The documentation lists what should be there rather than what is, and names the design document for each of them. The custom concurrent processes list needs columns for process name, owning application, purpose, and design document name.

Design documents for the individual processes tell what the report or process is for. They also describe the runtime parameters—how to set them up and which value sets are used to validate them.

USER-DEFINED FORMS   The list of user-defined forms is similar to that for reports. AOL's tables have entries for all registered forms. The documentation list indicates which ones should be there and names the governing design document.

CUSTOMIZED WORKFLOWS   Maintain a list of your modifications to the workflows delivered by Oracle and those you have designed to support bespoke processes. Reference the design documents.

THIRD PARTY SETUPS   Keep a record of the objects in Noetix Notes, Business Objects, Microsoft Access, Vertex, and other packages that reference and modify Oracle Applications tables. You need to apply regression tests to revalidate the integration after an upgrade of either Oracle or the third party package.

Configuration Management

Matrixed into each of the lists of database objects is the concepts of configuration management: what version of each module is in each of the different instances. Oracle Support, the DBA, and the developers need to have version information in order to support users in each environment.

Developers usually implement the Applications modules a suite at a time. They will put in a DFF, a database trigger, and two reports that use the newly defined user attributes all at once. To tell what is where, they need a matrix showing when each change is applied to each environment, with the following:

■ The suite name, such as "Add Pick-to-order unit pricing functions"

■ A list of the modules within the modification suite

- References to the design documents
- The implementation date
- The name of the person doing the implementation
- Implementation notes

The production environment needs tight control, imposed by the DBA and/or Data Administrator. The developers and DBA together can determine how much configuration management they need in the development and test environments. It depends on the size of the shop, how much modification there is, how many environments there are, and how likely the developers are to confuse themselves as to the state of their code in the multiple places it exists. They need to deal with the fact that the database typically migrates backwards, from production to development and test, while code migrates forward, from testing to production. The code can get out of step with the database in a development instance.

There needs to be one master library for all source code. Bespoke code exists as operating system files, but the setups exist only in documentation and the database itself. Other customizations, such as DFF definitions, value sets, and Alerts, also exist as Oracle Applications objects for which there is no flat-file representation. A LAN server is usually best suited to host the mix of program documentation, source code, and code that exists only in documentation format.

Conversion code is generally not subject to configuration management. Its primary use after conversion is as a reference, as in "How did we get into this mess?" Putting conversion code in separate libraries keeps it available but out of the way. Sharing it may make you some friends within your local Oracle Applications User's Group.

A number of vendors offer configuration management software. Be cautious. A packaged solution may be overkill, and it may not fit the requirements. Older CM packages are designed to handle source programs in text format, like COBOL. Not many modules in Oracle Applications fit this description. Start with a discipline of setting up a library structure in which there is a place for everything, and get the developers in the habit of putting things where they belong.

A major function of an automated CM system is to force programmers to check software modules out before they change them, then put them back before they can be migrated into production. This is not terribly effective when much of what is being controlled is in the form of documentation—specifications, setup documents, instructions for setting up descriptive flexfields, test scripts, and the like. Build a foundation of good manual procedures, then move to an automated system only when you see where administrative procedures fall short.

Programming and Documentation Standards

Each shop has its own approach to documentation and programming.[18] The universal rules are few. Each piece of documentation should be self-explanatory, stating what its own purpose is and naming the other documents and the code modules it references.

Code is an individual thing. The code examples here demonstrate standards used in one Applications shop, Watkins-Johnson, at one point in time. One of WJ's best traits is that it never stops improving its development process. The following section of code and the subsequent analysis exemplify the kinds of issues you may wish to address.

```
l_variable                          VARCHAR2(30);
l_counter                           NUMBER := 0;
CURSOR
  variable_cursor
IS
  SELECT
    substitution_constant,
    variable_name
  FROM
    wj_fnd_rt_constants
  WHERE
    regression_test_name = '&&regression_test_name';
BEGIN
 FOR parm_rec IN variable_cursor LOOP
   l_counter := l_counter + 1;
   v_constant (l_counter) :=
               CHR(39)||parm_rec.substitution_constant||CHR(39);
   v_variable (l_counter) := parm_rec.variable_name;
 END LOOP;
END;
PROCEDURE insert_quotes (
```

---

[18]For a more extensive discussion of documentation and programming standards, see *Oracle Data Processing : A Manager's Handbook* by Graham Seibert (Windcrest/McGraw-Hill, 1993).

```
      l_in                          VARCHAR2,
      l_index                       NUMBER)
  IS
      l_open_bracket                NUMBER;
      l_close_bracket               NUMBER;
      l_length_in                   NUMBER;
      l_out_db                      VARCHAR2(500);
      l_out_char                    VARCHAR2(500);
      l_work                        VARCHAR2(500);
  BEGIN
      l_open_bracket := INSTR(l_in,'[');
      l_close_bracket := INSTR(l_in,']');
      l_length_in := LENGTH(l_in);
      IF (l_open_bracket = 0) OR
         (l_open_bracket >= l_close_bracket)
      THEN
          l_out_db := """||l_in||"""; /* Whole entry is a literal */
          l_out_char := insert_pounds(l_in);
      ELSE
        IF l_open_bracket > 1
        THEN                    /* ============ Do the opening literal */
          l_work := SUBSTR(l_in,1,l_open_bracket - 1);
          l_out_db :=''''||l_work||''''||;
          l_out_char := insert_pounds(l_work);
        END IF;
        /* ========= Do the bracketed command ============= */
        l_work := SUBSTR(l_in,l_open_bracket,
                      1 + l_close_bracket - l_open_bracket);
        l_out_db := l_out_db || l_work;
        l_out_char := l_out_char||xlate_brackets(l_work);
        IF l_close_bracket < l_length_in
        THEN                    /* ====== Do the closing literal */
          l_work := SUBSTR(l_in,l_close_bracket + 1,
                      l_length_in - l_closing_bracket);
          l_out_db := l_out_db || '||''''||l_work||'''';
          l_out_char := l_out_char||insert_pounds(l_work);
        END IF;
      END IF;
      v_action_table_db (l_index) := v_out_db;
      v_action_table_char (l_index) := v_out_char;
  END;
```

Every piece of PL/SQL or SQL*Plus code has a header, similar to the following, that explains what the code is, where the specification is, who wrote it, and when it was written.

```
/*============================================================================*/
/*                                                                          */
/*    Name:           Regressi.sql                                          */
/*                                                                          */
/*    Description:    Meta-code to extract regression test actions and create */
/*                    source code to include in custom programs to use RT   */
/*                    for mass updates to the DB.                           */
/*                                                                          */
/*    Reference:      regressi.doc                                          */
/*                                                                          */
/*    By:             Graham Seibert                                        */
/*                                                                          */
/*    Date                                                                  */
/*                                                                          */
/*============================================================================*/
/*    Parameters: 1: Regression Test name, also constant name              */
/*                                                                          */
/*                                                                          */
```

This C-code remarks format works in other programming languages as well. Similar headers will work for Unix shell scripts, Windows NT BAT files, and SQL*Loader control files.

Watkins-Johnson, has standard document templates for programs:

- The template they used to generate the preceding code sample specifies 9-point Courier to get 80 characters in a 6" wide document (8½-inch paper with 1¼-inch margins). The code is easier to format when the word processor line length is the same as that for the Unix vi editor. 80 or 132 characters are standard.

- As shown in the preceding fragment of code, keywords are capitalized and variables put in lower case. It makes the code easier to read.

- PL/SQL and SQL statements are indented for greater readability. No universal rules can be written for indentation; these are complex, free-format languages. Generally speaking, though, the code is easier to read when loops and IF statements are indented to show levels of nesting, and SQL statements are indented to put the keywords on one plane and the variables on another.

- Comments are placed throughout the code. This author uses arrows made of equal signs and less-than signs to highlight the comments, making them easier for the eye to locate.

- In this code, standard variable names and variable types are aligned, to make it easy to find variables. You may use a word processor to sort variable names so they are easier to find in a listing.

Code should never be data-dependent. A statement like the one following

```
IF organization_id = 202 THEN
   v_switch1 := 'Y'
ELSE
   v_switch1 := 'N';
```

represents a long-term risk, because it exposes the code to a change in organization codes. It would be tedious to locate every place where such data-dependent code appeared. A better approach is to set parameters externally or in a prolog to the module, as in this example:

```
DEFINE BEM_ORG_ID=202
...
...
IF organization_id = &&BEM_ORG_ID THEN
   v_switch1 := 'Y'
ELSE
   v_switch1 := 'N';
```

This approach lets you collect all parameter settings at the beginning of a module, where they are easy to find and modify; their definitions are easy to find with a global search command. It also ensures that you give the variables a meaningful name.

Each shop needs to establish standards to suit their background, tools, and needs. The examples here are only meant to show the kinds of things you want to consider in establishing standards.

Conclusion

There is no "Plain Vanilla." Bespoke code for conversion is part of virtually every implementation of Oracle Applications. Most implementations also involve some number of custom reports and bridges. There is virtually no way to do an implementation without performing some customizations or modifications. Your implementation will go more smoothly if the project managers acknowledge the need for bespoke code and work with the data processing shop to establish policies and procedures to manage it.

There is a spectrum of risk in modifying the applications. Reporting and inquiry modules are at the low end. Even if they produce incorrect results they have no impact on other processes. Open interfaces require somewhat more analysis because they do bring new data into the system. While you often need to write bespoke forms, bridge and conversion processes that directly insert rows into Oracle tables, invalid data you introduce by this means can affect other modules. Directly updating data in Oracle tables, and especially deleting rows, offers the most risk. Before writing scripts or forms that directly update Oracle's tables you need to thoroughly analyze the native Oracle processes that create, reference and further process the row.

There are circumstances that justify every one of these types of modification. They require an appropriate level of analysis, familiarity with Oracle's implementation tools and the Applications architecture, and testing commensurate with the level of risk involved. Analyzing and designing bespoke code is one of the best uses for consultants on an Applications project.

Development methodologies and disciplines are just as important for an Applications implementation as for locally written systems. The forms that testing, configuration management, and documentation take are somewhat different, but their importance is in no way diminished.

The open design of the Oracle Applications, the accessibility of the code, and the top-to-bottom integration of Oracle's technology stack tremendously enhance their value to you. Not only do you acquire the vast majority of features that your company needs with the price of purchase, you also get the industry's best architecture, tools and resources for extending and molding what you have purchased to meet your exact requirements.

CHAPTER
16

Project Organization
and Management

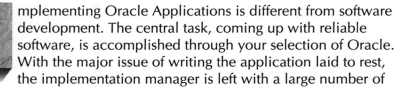

mplementing Oracle Applications is different from software development. The central task, coming up with reliable software, is accomplished through your selection of Oracle. With the major issue of writing the application laid to rest, the implementation manager is left with a large number of smaller but still significant tasks: installing, configuring, testing, and maintaining the Applications.

Functional users, often without much data processing experience, lead or play a dominant role in an Applications implementation. Success depends on their extended team. On the users' side, it extends far into each of the affected functional areas. On the technical side, it usually reaches beyond the Data Processing developers, systems experts, database experts, and communications experts to include outside consultants and vendors' technical support.

Most project participants from the user community are less than full time. They still have their assigned jobs to do. The Project Manager's task is to earn their goodwill, craft a mutually agreed plan, and provide the team with the direction and support it needs to succeed.

Tasks in an Oracle implementation are less dependent on one another than in a custom developed system. The code Oracle delivers will be sufficient to support setting parameters, installing networks and clients, writing bespoke extensions to the system, and developing business procedures, test scenarios, and training materials. With some restrictions, these tasks can proceed in parallel. Unlike the case in custom development projects, resource constraints are far more often the limitation than scheduling dependencies.

TIP

The limiting factor in an Applications implementation is experienced people—ones who can effectively combine knowledge of your business, Oracle Applications, and programming methods in an Oracle environment. Scheduling dependencies and critical path management are seldom major issues.

Oracle Software as a Step Toward Corporate Maturity

The move to Oracle often coincides with a critical growth phase in companies with a billion dollars or less in sales. Young companies are often built around personalities and have limited need for systems and written procedures as long as the founding experts are available to answer questions as they arise.

The personality model stretches thin with a few hundred employees. The experts cannot be everywhere at once, cannot train every new employee, and cannot wrap themselves around every new development in the business. They need to free themselves from tactical decisions so they can focus on strategic directions. Tactical decision-making has to be systematized, by written procedures and by policy built into enterprise software.

Oracle Applications is the catalyst for both. Placing a value on software's ability to enforce policy and procedures begs the question: what are the policies and procedures? Employees and managers of a young company often resist the imposition of such "bureaucracy." Cut-and-dried systems appear to cut down the company's flexibility. Reducing decision making to paper and code can be a personal threat: it makes the company veterans less essential for day-to-day operations. They may not appreciate that it becomes essential for the growth of the company to apply their knowledge at a strategic instead of a tactical level.

Installing the Applications represents an essential growth step. A foundation of sound systems must underlie its future growth, but getting there is the problem. The project manager will find that the small circle of company veterans, whose knowledge and support are key to success, are at the very least highly occupied with operational issues. At worst they may be indifferent to the project in the first place. Moreover, their lean staff usually does not allow lending of people to the Oracle project.

Smaller companies are also characterized by some significant strengths. They are nimble and enthusiastic, and tend to make decisions quickly. Their lack of bureaucracy can be a decided virtue, with no organizational hierarchy to distance the Applications implementation team from the functional users.

Certain critical success factors, applicable to all Applications installations, are especially important to the manager in a younger, growing company:

- The Executive Sponsor, who is often fairly accessible in a company of this size, and the Steering Committee have to show visible support for the project.

- Management and data processing methodologies must be simple enough for the in-house client to appreciate and understand.

- Each individual on the MIS team must be strong enough to earn the respect of his or her functional counterpart. Success will depend on personal relationships.

- The strongest functional people need to be named as Superusers, to define how the Applications will work in their areas.

- You must respect the Superusers' time. Most Superusers have two jobs: running the company and setting up Oracle. The MIS department and outside implementers must do their homework before any meeting and relieve the Superuser of as many writing, testing, and other "functional area" tasks as possible.

When all is said and done, implementations at young, growing companies can offer the greatest satisfaction to the Oracle project team. Their flexibility insures that all team members will be used to the maximum extent of their talent, learn a lot outside their assigned area, and be visibly associated with the success.

Spreadsheets versus Project Management Software

When the Data Processing department takes the lead, its first mistake is often to see the Project Management job as a technical rather than a management challenge. Project management deserves tools appropriate to the task and appropriate to the sophistication of the broader team, but not just software tools for their own sake. Applying project management software such as Microsoft Project to an Oracle Applications implementation without a commitment to the associated management disciplines is a misuse of technology. The best tools are those with which the project manager is comfortable, even if they are as simple as spreadsheets.

Critical path scheduling is a key design feature of project management tools. You enter an elaborate definition of the tasks to be done, the ways in which the tasks depend on one another, and the resources available to do them. The project management software uses this information to compute when the project will complete, on the basis of the given assumptions and how busy each resource will be at each point in the project.

Project management tools depend for their success on several assumptions, most of which are met in prosaic projects such as home construction, but few of which are consistently met in an Applications project. Among the assumptions built into a critical path scheduling package are:

■ *Tasks are well-defined.* It works in construction: experience is a good indicator of how many resources, and how much time, it will take to roof a house. It is much harder to determine how long it will take a committee to decide on a chart of accounts structure, or how many people are needed to clean up a legacy vendor file, or how much work it will be to normalize the legacy bills of material.

■ *Task sequencing is a limiting factor.* In home construction, the foundation must precede the framing, which must precede plumbing and electrical, which must precede drywall, which must precede painting, and so forth. A separate type of craftsman does each task. In the Applications, however, there are many more things that can be done in parallel, and each Applications implementer is generally versatile enough to handle multiple tasks. Though there will be dependencies, the lack of a particular resource is much less often a limiting factor than a shortage of total resources.

■ *The project plan is updated frequently.* Project management systems are built to provide management information. They assume you can and will adjust the schedule periodically to reflect progress to date and your revised estimate of work remaining to completion. A construction project manager cannot afford self-deception. Even if it means acknowledging that the project is behind schedule, he or she cannot afford to have roofers show up when there are no rafters to nail shingles to. Applications projects admit more self-deception. Regardless of the schedule, most of the project staff members will be flexible enough that they will find something to do. It is possible to avoid updating the plan until it confronts the reality of cutover, which includes fixing schedules for training and implementation team travel.

In practice, project management systems often turn out to be no more than a device to develop Gantt charts, which represent early hopes more than present reality. If you are going to use Project Management software, which should be the case for an effort involving ten or more people, be sure to commit the resources it takes to manage the software. That means defining and redefining tasks as the project evolves and, most important, updating the plan with actual data and accepting what the tool computes as an estimated completion date.

Spreadsheets are appropriate for projects too small to justify the effort involved in using project management software. All you need to do is identify the tasks to be done, estimate how long each will take, and assign someone to do the work. These are essential first steps in any system. Use the spreadsheet to total the work assigned to each individual and make sure there are enough people to do the job. If there are no major dependencies among the tasks, it may be all the management information you need.

Update the spreadsheet periodically, reducing the figures to reflect work actually performed, and recompute the amount remaining. This is easy enough to do, and it will accurately reflect the impact of decisions not made and tasks that go over budget.

Using any project management tool at all is a hard enough discipline. The project is better served with a simple tool used well than a sophisticated tool used haphazardly. In any case, simple tools are the best place to start.

Developing the Project Plan

Any project plan, whatever the tool, is based on a Work Breakdown Structure or WBS. The steps for developing a WBS are:

1. Outline high-level tasks on scratch paper. Include external tasks even if they are not part of the budget. Typical external tasks are installing computers, upgrading networks, putting browsers on desktops, conducting company reorganizations, and developing strategic business decisions.

2. Key the tasks into a word processor using the outliner feature. Keep reworking the outline until there is consensus among the business and technical leaders that it represents the tasks to be done. You may have to agree on which of several valid ways is best to structure a WBS for a project. For example, you may choose between defining similar tasks for your different locations or putting all your locations under each task.

3. Put the project into a spreadsheet to do resource loading and estimating. Use the spreadsheet to produce Gantt charts if they are needed, or for the sake of convenience use a Project Management package to paint and print Gantt charts. Figure 16-1 shows an excerpt from a project management spreadsheet. The outline structure, indicated by indentation, is carried over from the work processor outline. The number of days to be spent by the people in the project budget (PW and Prog) is shown against each task. Other resources, in this case user personnel who are outside the budget, are shown as notes. Project Management needs a view of the project that covers resources beyond their control that nevertheless are essential to the schedule.

The computed duration of the effort shown in Figure 16-1 would be about 1.4 months, the figure obtained by dividing the greatest amount of work (27 days, by the programmer) by the work days per month (20). Such a figure would typically be about right for a "bottom-up" budget spreadsheet

Task	Effort	Description	Days			
	Resource (initials or type)		PW	Prog	User	User Name
	Quantity of Resource	PW = Pete Prog = Sam or Carol	1	2		
1	Oracle Assets					
1.1	Assets Business Model					
1.2	Assets Mapping Leg. to Oracle					
1.3	Assets					
1.4	Oracle Assets Setup					
1.4.1	Asset Category Flexfield		2		2	Bobbie
1.4.2	Location Flexfield		2		2	Bobbie
1.4.3	Asset Key Flexfield		2		2	Bobbie
1.4.4	System Controls		1			
1.4.5	Locations	Develop spreadsheet of locations (or extract them from legacy); load to Oracle.		1	2	Bobbie
1.4.6	Asset Key Flexfields Combinations					
1.4.7	QuickCodes	Set up quick picks to use for manual entry of assets.	1		2	Bobbie
1.4.8	Fiscal Years		0.5		1	Bobbie
1.4.9	Calendars	Define the calendars over which items have been depreciated. These go back 30-40 years.	1		2	Bobbie
1.4.10	Journal Entry Sources	Done in GL.				
1.4.11	Journal Entry Categories	Done in GL.				
1.4.12	Book Controls		1			
1.4.13	Flexbuilder	Rules for automatically generating flexfields.	2		3	Bobbie
1.4.14	Depreciation Methods	Define methods to Oracle.	3		5	Bobbie
1.4.15	Depreciation Ceilings	Included in above.				
1.4.16	Investment Tax Credits	Included in above.				
1.4.17	Prorate Conventions	Included in above.				
1.4.18	Price Indexes	Don't use.				
1.4.19	Unit of Measure Classes	Use EA throughout.				
1.4.20	Units of Measure	Use EA throughout.				
1.4.21	Asset Categories		1		2	Bobbie
1.4.22	Financials Options					
1.5	Assets Scenario Development					
1.5.1	Develop asset scenarios.	Add assets, retire assets, adjust assets. Leases, expensed assets, capital assets, construction-in-process. Flow from FA through to GL, report from GL.	1		5	Bobbie
1.5.2	Test data to support scenarios.		0.5		2	Bobbie
1.6	Assets Conference Room Pilot I					
1.6.1	Set up (restore from clean setup).			1		
1.6.2	Run the scenarios.		1		3	Bobbie
1.7	Fixed Assets Conversion Dev.					
1.7.1	Map legacy asset fields to Oracle.			1	1	Bobbie
1.7.2	Write COBOL extract from MSA.			1	4	
1.7.3	Write Oracle Loader to staging table.			1		
1.7.4	Clean-up and Load	Write and test scripts to systematically clean up legacy data (duplicates, abbreviations, missing data, translations, etc.), and load to Mass Additions interface.		20	5	Bobbie
	TOTAL DAYS		20	27	43	

FIGURE 16-1. *Excerpt from a project management spreadsheet*

like this. It usually works out that the individual task estimates, such as three days to define depreciation methods to Oracle, are high. It all works out, however, because the excess time is eaten up by unforeseen tasks and by the unbudgeted overhead costs of meetings and project coordination.

The Project Budget

A budget is a planning and measurement tool. It justifies the line items in your capital and operating budgets associated with the Oracle Applications project. The accuracy of your budget depends on several factors, among them:

- Your level of experience with large data processing projects, and especially package implementations

- The level of confidence you require of the budget

- The effort you invest in developing the budget

- The political realities of your company

Your experience developing custom software will not apply directly to the Oracle Applications. The good news is that package installation is cheaper and less risky than developing custom software. The bad news is that most of the tasks that remain are those involving users; these are even less predictable than software development. An experienced project leader can be of great help in developing a budget.

A budget is a tool for achieving your planning objectives, and planning objectives vary widely from organization to organization. Public sector organizations tend to budget conservatively because it is difficult to get more if funds run out, and project managers tend to be measured by how well they succeed within the plan rather than whether the project is done in a cost-effective manner. Private sector project managers may accept more risk in the hope of achieving a lower overall cost. Given two proposed budgets, a $3 million budget with a 90 percent chance of success or a $1.2 million budget with a 75 percent chance of success, a conservative agency would have more incentive to choose the former, whereas an aggressive company would more often choose the latter. Both approaches are valid; you need to know how much confidence is required in your environment.

The reliability of a budget reflects the effort you put into it. As always, it helps to have an experienced project manager familiar with the cost elements of a typical project. You can learn a lot by soliciting bids for the integration work from technical services firms. Some companies need a detailed budget to cost-justify the decision to implement Oracle. Others see the conversion to Oracle as a strategic imperative and commit on the basis of a high-level estimate. The amount you want to invest to achieve an acceptably accurate budget depends on your situation.

The best approach would be to recognize the unpredictability of the process and budget incrementally, by six-month periods, basing each step on the results and findings of the one before. Most organizations, however, do annual budgets and fix them a few months prior to the budget year. The Oracle project manager's strategy is usually to build a case for the maximum budget that won't kill the project. Few projects wind up giving money back. Users always come up with out-of-scope needs, such as custom reports, Internet access, and the like, that are truly worth doing and manage to take up any slack in the budget.

The planning horizon for Applications projects is quite short. It is difficult to predict what people will be doing even six months in the future. It is important to apply actual figures to the schedule and budget spreadsheet at least monthly, to maintain an up-to-date estimate to completion. Expect this figure to change significantly as you learn more about the project. The most enlightened management approach is to be open about how much is unknowable and to be able to react quickly as more becomes known.

The ultimate questions are how much will it cost and how long will it take. The answers depend on many factors, but among them are the amount of conversion and customization necessary, the company's ability to make decisions, the data processing department's facility with Oracle, and the general level of talent among the business and data processing staff. With all those caveats, start with an expectation that a $1 billion company will take at least four staff-months of the functional area users' time and four of consultant time per package. Start with an estimate of $100,000 to $400,000 per package if you are using consultants. The best average would be six months calendar time from the time the team is in place until the first group of applications goes into production. Companies and packages are highly variable, however. The authors have experience with packages being installed in as little as two months with little outside help and, on the other side, with a six-package Applications suite for a domestic company with two locations taking over $20,000,000 and more than two years using a Big-5 integrator. There is no substitute for doing your own planning.

The Project Management Hierarchy

Applications software implementations apply data processing equipment and disciplines to business requirements. Who should manage the effort? The business area owners of the requirement, or the MIS owners of the methodologies to apply the solution? Either approach can be successful. The key factor is that the technical and functional people have to work as a team, regardless of who is in charge.

Rarely is there a "natural" project leader within the company who has experience in the business areas as well as data processing and installing packaged software. There are several alternatives when no natural leader is apparent:

- Put the best person within the company in charge, trusting that he or she will learn on the job.

- Hire someone who has managed integration before.

- Entrust an integrator with project management responsibility.

Using somebody within the company has major advantages. A solid manager, with knowledge of the business and the trust of people within the company, will usually be able to learn enough to manage an integration project. This manager should usually plan to engage consultants to bring the needed functional area and project management expertise.

Hiring an experienced manager can be risky. It is difficult to learn a new business and a new company. Moreover, a new hire is likely to lack either management experience or detailed product knowledge; it is difficult for a candidate to have learned both on one project. Hiring to fill the project management role involves risk, but it makes sense when there is no strong manager available internally.

It is tempting to offload the heavy responsibility onto one who has done it before, such as a partner in an integration company, creating a reporting structure like the one shown in Figure 16-2. This alternative carries risks as well. It isolates company management from intimate familiarity with the project. It also creates a potential conflict of interest. The systems integrator may be tempted to let his or her own corporate goals, such as training new

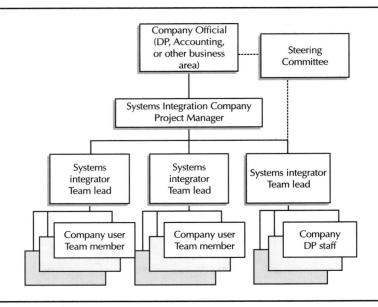

FIGURE 16-2. *Systems integrator management model*

employees, overshadow the client's interest. Placing responsibility with an outside firm requires a good management oversight plan.

In fact, there is no way for a company to totally pass off project responsibility to an outsider, whether that person is a new hire or an integrator. It can hire or contract for the functional, technical, and project management skills needed to make the project succeed. However, applications software invariably defines the way the business works, and the business' management has to be closely involved in those decisions.

As noted, Applications implementation is really an exercise in management. The project manager has to get cooperation from an extremely broad group of people inside and outside the company. The manager needs to establish a vision and generate commitment if that critical part-time involvement is to materialize. The people behind the decision to use Oracle need to follow it through implementation.

Team Formation

The implementation team is a two-headed affair. If a functional area person chairs it, the deputy should be from data processing. If a business-savvy data processing manager leads the effort, the seconds in command have to be from the business area. Balance is critical.

Because integration is one of the major benefits of a packaged solution, most implementations involve more than one package. Figure 16-3 shows a typical project organization for a 5000-employee, billion-dollar corporation.

Your corporate officer in charge of an Oracle Applications project, often called the Executive Sponsor, is typically one of the three top people in the financial organization, with a title such as Comptroller, CFO, or Director of Finance. Chief Operating Officer, and Director of Manufacturing are common titles for the nominee to head manufacturing and distribution

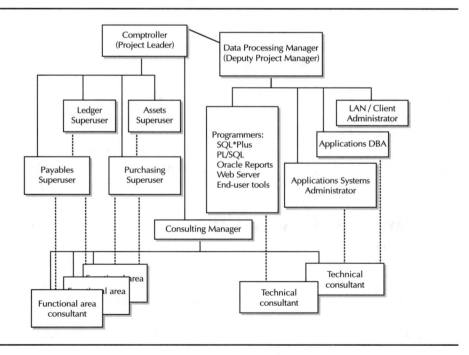

FIGURE 16-3. *Typical Oracle project team organization*

implementations. Their data processing counterpart is either the Chief Information Officer/Director of Data Processing or a direct report to that position. It is important that these leaders carry enough rank to command resources and force decisions within the company and that the two of them be of more or less equal rank.

The company project manager needs knowledge to act with authority. In addition to the MIS staff, it helps to have an experienced consultant aid with budgeting, staffing, scheduling, and the tradeoffs between customizing the software and modifying business procedures.

Functional Team Leads

Few companies have enough staff to name dedicated team leads in each functional area. The work of the company must go on as Oracle is installed. The most common arrangement is to have "Superusers" in each area commit half their time to Oracle setup. The Superusers attend Oracle classes, experiment with the Demo instance of the Oracle products, work closely with outside consultants, act as the representative of their department, and coordinate with other area Superusers. These Superusers must be well chosen; they drive the project.

There is no substitute for experience. It is much more efficient to engage people who have worked with the Oracle Applications before than to learn the system through trial and error. A company can use business-area employees with Oracle experience, data processing analysts with that experience, or outsiders. The need is for highly talented people for a short period of time—a definition that favors consultants. The organization charge shown in Figure 16-3 includes consultants in the project team structure.

Database Administrator

Management Information Systems will bring technical talent to the team. The most obvious requirements are for programmers, a systems administrator, LAN and desktop experts, and a database administrator. Equally important, and often overlooked, are development disciplines. Testing, configuration management, security administration, and continuity of operations are vitally important to the success of Oracle Applications projects. Many MIS shops have to improve their maturity levels in these areas to support the Applications.

An *Applications DBA* is an Oracle database administrator who is familiar with the special requirements of Oracle Applications. The DBA needs to be familiar with what is known as the Application Object Library (AOL), or Applications Foundation. AOL is the way Oracle has integrated proprietary C-language routines with programs written in the Forms, Reports, and PL/SQL developments tools.

A capable Oracle DBA on your staff can quickly absorb the Applications from a knowledgeable consultant. Technology transfer works well at the technical level.

TIP

The DBA's job is to create an environment in which other people can be successful, not one in which nothing ever goes wrong. An occasional failure is the price of success. The Project Manager must ensure that the developers have enough access and resources to get their job done. An overly controlling DBA, in eliminating risk to himself, can doom a project.

There is nothing unique about the programming tools used in the Applications. Oracle programmers can write interfaces and enhancements without special training. The requirements for specialized knowledge are as follows:

- It takes more programming talent to understand and modify complex programs such as those Oracle delivers in the Applications than to develop new programs.

- It takes detailed knowledge of the Applications modules to write specifications for programs that will interface to Applications tables and processes.

- Someone, not necessarily the programmer, must know how to bring custom code into the Applications.

Programmers

Not all Oracle developers are Oracle Applications developers. They may be familiar with the tools for building the customizations, but will likely not know how to implement their changes within the application. The team may be staffed with Oracle Reports and PL/SQL programmers with no Applications experience. You will get better results if you support them with a consultant or senior programmer with experience writing code in an Applications environment. The programming team as a group will be most effective with the following types of expertise:

- Host Operating Systems: Unix, NT, Linux, VMS, or mainframe

- Client Operating Systems: Various flavors of Windows, Mac OS, Linux, and others

- Browsers: Netscape or Internet Explorer

- LAN server software: Novell, NT, and others

- Local Area Networks

- Forms and Reports (Developer 2000)

- Oracle Application Server

- SQL*Loader

- SQL*Plus

- PL/SQL for Reports, Forms, stored procedures, and database triggers.

- Oracle Applications "programming" skills: Key and Descriptive Flexfields, report parameter definition, Oracle Alerts, interface programming, and related skills.

- Editors and utilities. In Unix these include vi, sed, and sort.

- Shell language programming (Unix, NT, VMS, or mainframe).

- Applicable end-user tools (Oracle Express, Business Objects, ODBC interfaces to spreadsheets, and third party reporting tools).

- Applicable desktop software, including word processor macros and templates, spreadsheet macros, and presentation packages. While not essential, these tools can greatly improve programmer productivity.

Sources of Staffing

Oracle's success is reflected in the marketplace. Oracle people are hard to find, and Oracle Applications people doubly so. This presents problems in staffing with employees, and the supply/demand equation makes consultants expensive.

It is almost always most efficient to staff with fewer and better people. Communication difficulties increase factorially with the growth of your team's size. It is easier to know who is responsible for each task on a small team, and to assess each individual's contribution. As every MIS manager knows, a good programmer can be ten times as productive as a mediocre one. The issue is where to find the good people.

Finding good employees is a matter of paying them and giving them incentives. The first issue is salary. You need to be sure your Human Resources department's salary structures reflect the realities of the marketplace. Non-cash incentives are important in hiring and especially in keeping your staff. Professionals want to be respected, and they want to work on successful projects. The job you do in managing the implementation will have a strong bearing on your employee retention.

There are similar issues in assigning strong people from within the business to the Oracle project. They become attractive to other companies, especially consulting firms, as they gain Oracle experience. The best place to look for functional-area talent is within your company, but you need to be willing to recognize the market value of the Oracle skills they will gain on the project.

Most projects need some outside consulting support. Here are the usual sources:

- Oracle Consulting Services (OCS)

- Technical services firms (such as CSC or Cap Gemini)

- Accounting firms (such as Touche or PriceWaterhouseCoopers)

- Regional technical services firms (such as CMSI or Noblestar)

- Oracle Applications implementation specialty firms (such as Allen-Sauer Consulting, Margaret Coleman Consulting, Seibert & Costantino, or Cornerstone Systems)

- Independent consultants

The larger firms tend to charge higher hourly rates for a given level of experience. The rates may be justified by the completeness of their offering: extensive marketing support prior to the engagement, experienced project management, and in the case of Oracle, outstanding training and a direct pipeline into the best sources of expertise.

Smaller firms and independent consultants offer the most experience for the dollar. They are also somewhat harder to find. Whereas the larger firms will actively advertise and market to you, you may have to look to find small, new firms that are more focused on technology than marketing. Go to Oracle's Web page **(www.oracle.com)** and search its lists of business partners. Try the search engines under keywords "Oracle" and "Applications." Alternatively, contact the Oracle Applications User's Group (c/o Meeting Expectations in Atlanta, **www.oaug.org** or phone (404) 240-0897) to find a local user's group chapter and ask informally for recommendations. You can also ask through the local chapter of the International Oracle User's Group (IOUG). Contact them at **www.ioug.org**, or phone (312) 245-1579.

Choose a consulting firm appropriate to the size of your business and a consulting team appropriate to the size of your project. An inappropriately large firm or team can swamp a project by outnumbering and overwhelming the company employees assigned to the project or by reporting at a level above the decision-makers within the client company. Conversely, too small a firm may be unable to bring in additional resources when they are needed and may be unable to work essential communications channels within your company because it reports at too low a level in your management hierarchy. Your project manager as well as your programmers will benefit from outside advice. Your organizational structure may almost require that it come from different people.

In general, larger firms such as Baltimore Gas and Electric, use larger integrators, like Oracle Consulting, and smaller enterprises use regional firms and independent consultants. Your business should be significant enough to the consulting firm that they cannot risk giving you poor service.

Staff Size

Each company has to evaluate the trade-offs involved in project staff size, some of which are listed next:

Advantages of Larger Staff Size	Advantages of Smaller Staff Size
Reduced opportunity costs. Quicker implementation means quicker realization of benefits.	Reduced cost. Greater use out of employed staff, reduced use of consultants keeps costs down.
Operational impact. More outside staff means less disruption to continuing business operations.	Training. More employee participation means more knowledge transfer. Employed staff gains and retains Oracle knowledge.
Business tempo. Demonstrate results within a matter of months of the commitment to Oracle.	Control. Intimate involvement in implementation decisions ensures that setup is appropriate to the company.
	Esprit. Employees enjoy being empowered to define business procedures that affect them, playing significant roles in a major team effort.

Regardless of its eventual size, a project team should grow incrementally. It is important for a core group to establish the project plan, environment, and methodologies before the main cadre comes on board. Overstaffing, evidenced by short workdays and the lack of a sense of urgency, makes project members feel superfluous and undermines their commitment. A team working overtime is more effective, and certainly cheaper, than an underworked one.

Types of Contracts

Cost and risk are key issues in contracting. What will it cost, and who bears the risk? There are several risks in an Applications implementation. The most obvious is that the implementation is never completed. Your company spends money for the software, for implementation services, and on the costs of its own staff, and your implementation team can never bring it to the point of being installed. The other risk is that the business suffers damage because you have not set the software up correctly.

It is tempting to try to push the risk onto a contractor, the possessor of expert knowledge in Oracle Applications, through a fixed-price contract. Oracle, its competitors such as SAP and PeopleSoft, and major integrators are moving in that direction. They are all developing ways to make package implementation a more straightforward process. The Application Implementation Methodology used by Oracle Consulting includes a project plan and techniques for managing setup, conversion, training, and all other steps in an implementation. The Workflow-based Application Implementation Wizard product, available in Release 11, leads you and your contractor together through the setup process. Oracle has products that handle data mapping for conversion and bridging.

It is possible for contractors to deliver all the components of a working system on a fixed-price basis: software installation, setups, conversion programs, bridges, training, and user documentation. They are reluctant, however, to guarantee will work. The contractor may not always be able to prevent or offset failures on your part. Success depends on your ability as the client to define your business processes, test the system, absorb training and operate the system. The contractor's technical knowledge may be essential to success, but it cannot guarantee success.

Vendors that do offer fixed-price contracts for Oracle Applications implementations usually word them in such a way that the client still bears the ultimate risk. The scope of the contract may extend through setup but stop short of cutover. It will not include post-cutover support. The contract will specify a maximum number of reports to be modified. The terms will require that your key people be available to meet with their team for a given number of hours within a specified number of days of contract start. The terms are such that only a well-organized company can realistically meet them. However, a strong company that appreciates the risks will usually opt for a time-and-materials arrangement to save money.

You usually do best to recognize the need for a partnership between you and the contractor and to contract the work on a time-and-materials basis. Time and materials contracts can be structured to foster partnership. The client pays for services as they are needed, and the contractor serves at the convenience of the client. The contractor works knowing they will be replaced if they are not delivering value.

You need to manage a time and materials contract closely to ensure that it does not get away from you. The data processing press is full of horror stories about out-of-control projects in which the client no longer knows what is happening with a project, is bleeding money to a consulting firm, and is scared or unable to rein in the contractor. Some strategies to retain control are the following:

1. Although a contractor may provide most of the project management expertise, make sure that the de facto project manager is a company employee, not a consultant.

2. Develop a detailed project plan, with a work breakdown structure and budget. Have the contractor report progress against the budget. Make sure there is an employee or independent outsider knowledgeable enough to assess the contractor's justification of budget overruns and slippages. Dedicate the resources it takes to make effective use of project management software.

3. Define and enforce data processing methodologies. Keep track of all contractor work products, so that in the worst case they can be given to another contractor.

4. Use two or more consulting firms, or incorporate independent consultants into the team, to obtain the benefit of independent points of view. Becoming dependent on a single source makes you vulnerable. No company owns any "magic bullet" technology without which other project members would be ineffective. Professional respect, not company loyalties, is the essential bond among members of your team.

5. Have the consulting firm staff up gradually. Make sure that you, the client, control when each new member joins the team and that you understand what he or she will be doing.

6. Staff the project with employees to the extent possible, to ensure that they learn the system for which they will be responsible and that the solution is based on employees' knowledge of the business rather than consultants' second-hand understanding.

7. To the extent that you can, use consultants for advice and have employees do the work. This is especially important in the functional areas. After the consultants leave, somebody has to understand why the system is set up as it is.

8. Ensure that contractors document their work. Because of their productivity, independent consultants usually offer good value as developers. You can afford to let outsiders do more in the realm of programming, so long as you can maintain what they produce.

9. Schedule deliverables frequently enough (every four months, for example) that the contractor has to show demonstrable progress.

Project Phasing

Most Oracle Applications projects involve more than one module. There is often a question of whether to cut them all over at one time—a "big bang" conversion—or to convert in phases. There is no preferred approach, only a set of pros and cons that will vary from company to company. They are as follows:

Advantages of a "Big Bang"

Less wasted effort. Converting all at once eliminates the need for bridge-backs to legacy and puts all testing and cutover processing into one conversion.

Quicker total implementation. The full benefits of Oracle are available earlier.

Better integration. Thinking through all system requirements at once eliminates reengineering in later project phases.

Advantages of a Phased Conversion

Lower risk. There is less impact on MIS and the company at cutover.

Maintaining management attention. A phased plan can show progress every four months, building confidence along the way.

Full testing. It is easier to test with a limited set of logic paths.

Quick stabilization. The first packages in a phased implementation (GL, FA) typically affect few users. The impact of a rocky conversion is localized, and can be corrected before moving on.

Lower overall cost. A longer implementation schedule means employees can shoulder more of the work.

Managing Your Relationship with Oracle

Oracle has a vested interest in your success. A successful customer is an ongoing source of business and of positive referrals. Just as Oracle will continue to sell you on the value of its new products, you need to sell

Oracle on your value as a customer. Customers who develop a genuine partnership with Oracle have more say in how the products evolve, early access to products as beta testers, and more leverage in picking the Oracle people to provide them with support.

Oracle Releases and Versions

The Oracle products continue to improve over time. Oracle has a vested interest in seeing that you continue to invest the time it takes to stay up to date. Oracle can provide better technical support to users of current-release software. Better support means that you are more likely to be pleased with the product—and more likely to buy more Oracle software.

Oracle assigns Release numbers to the Applications taken as a group and each application individually. The scheme is universal; it also applies to the Oracle tools in which the Applications are implemented, the Oracle database on which they run, the operating systems that run the databases, and the hardware that runs the operating systems.

A software Release is a set of modules proven to work together by design and testing. In the Applications they are identified by triple-segmented numbers, such 11.0.2. The first number represents a major change in functionality, with new screens, reference manuals, training materials, and table structures. The second number, called a dot-point release, represents a smaller increment in design, such as the introduction of a few new programs, without any profound change to the architecture. The third number identifies a maintenance release. The higher the third digit, the more bugs it fixes in the base release.

The triple-segment system applies to individual Applications as well as the Applications as a group. Version 11.0.2 of the Applications will be made up of all the Applications, each at its own release and version level, proven to work together as an integrated unit. It could include General Ledger 9.2.1, Oracle Assets 5.2.3, and Sales Compensation 2.0.3. Users are generally unaware of the individual application release levels; the documentation references levels only for the whole Applications suite.

Each release of each Application, and thus of the Applications, is certified to work on one or more releases of the Oracle RDBMS. The Applications exploit new database functionality as it comes out, and they depend on fixes to the RDBMS.

The RDBMS in turn has a release-level dependency on the host operating systems that support it. Newer releases of the RDBMS require newer operating system releases.

The interdependencies among the release levels of the Operating Systems (server and client), the RDBMS, and the Applications often force a stepwise upgrade path. Users who fall well behind may be forced into interim upgrades to achieve their final goal. Fortunately, the Applications are always available on at least two versions of the RDBMS, and an RDBMS version is usually proven on more than one release of the Operating System. The best practice, however, is to remain current within the past year. A shop should plan to hit every major Applications release level (9, 10, 11...), which come out every two years or so. Users who fall too far behind sometimes find it easier to reconvert, treating their old installation as a legacy system, than to go through an extended stepwise upgrade process.

Oracle's customers are responsible for upgrading the operating system and the RDBMS to the version levels required to install the delivered version of the Applications. It is a job for their DBA or a consultant filling the DBA role. The entire combination of Oracle Applications, RDBMS, and Operating System version must be certified by Oracle Support. The DBA keeps a log of software upgrade activity in order to be able to provide release-level information to Oracle support in reporting problems.

Resolving Errors: TARs and Patches

Servicing its customers is one of Oracle's most challenging tasks. The channels through which the company delivers technical support is under constant reorganization, yet is never as responsive as customers would like. The good news is that Oracle customer support (along with IBM's) is usually ranked best among the major software vendors. It is a tough job.

Oracle's help desk logs Technical Assistance Requests (TARs) from supported customers. They may resolve a TAR by an explanation of how to use the native features of the package, by providing a workaround for the bug or shortcoming, or by changing the software to fix the problem.

Oracle creates patches to fix bugs. A patch may affect any number of modules, and may involve seed data within the database as well. Oracle usually has to apply the same correction in multiple release levels of the software and on multiple platforms. It is a major configuration management issue for them. It is not cost effective to maintain an excessive number of back versions of the software. Oracle will often ask users to upgrade to a more current software release rather than commit Oracle resources to fix a bug in an old release.

Oracle maintains an internal database cross-referencing TARs, patches, and release levels. Its technical support staff researches this database to see if there is an existing patch to address any new TAR. Most can be resolved through a previously identified patch or workaround.

It is important to understand that patches do not come with ironclad guarantees. They are unit tested, to make sure they fix the stated problem in the stated module(s). Some patches don't apply to all users. A patch that applies to a standard-costing inventory operation, for example, might induce errors in an average-cost shop. That is not a problem so long as Oracle controls who uses the patch.

Oracle cannot regression-test to make sure each patch does not create problems in other modules. That is the reason Oracle is reluctant to provide patches on a wholesale basis. Applying them willy-nilly often creates more problems than it solves, and the problems are even more difficult to resolve because the patched software no longer agrees with Oracle's baseline.

Certain patches have widespread applicability. Oracle periodically assembles the important ones into "mega-patches" or "maintenance packs," which it does subject to regression testing. It distributes these maintenance packs widely and incorporates them into new shipments of the software. They are often available on Oracle's proactive patch ftp site. A mega-patch often implements the fixes that are being shipped in newer dot-point releases.

In terms of direction, expect Oracle to make increasing use of the Internet to allow users to research problems and to distribute patches. It is likely that Oracle will permit keyword searches of the TAR database, by problem and module, and will send out patches in response to specific inquiries. It is less likely, for competitive reasons and simply to protect itself from idle inquiries, that Oracle will make full lists of TARs and patches available for general browsing. It is also unlikely that it will allow users to download patches without their being formally released: the risks of users' misapplying them are simply too great.

Managing Bug Fixes

Oracle takes seriously its responsibility for making its software work correctly. It is organized to support a mix of weak and strong customers. It is no secret, however, that stronger customers, those who earn the respect of the Oracle help desk by making good use of their time, are more satisfied with Oracle support. They generally have more success overall.

Chapter 15 recommends that you maintain logs of Technical Assistance Requests (TARs) that you place with Oracle and of patches you apply to fix problems. You need to actively manage your open issues, making sure that Oracle understands the priority of each reported problem. It is a relatively unusual occurrence to report an unknown bug to Oracle Support. In most cases the problem has already been identified and corrected. When contacting support, it is important to be concise and do your own research first. Has your organization customized the process that is erroring? Has the process executed successfully in the past? Does the process error only in production, or on your test and development instances as well? You should always have the log file available, and the exact program name, executable, and version available.

Oracle's help desk is much more responsive when your DBA is able to define a problem precisely as he or she reports it. Compare this:

The PO Print program ended abnormally with error ORA-1800, Format Error

with

Program POXPRPOP got error ORA 1800 when it was executed under Concurrent Manager, where it was executed with the Unix command

```
ar25runb PROG=POXPRPOP VERSION=2.0b P_PO_NUM='123' COPIES=3
                    DESFORMAT=PSHPL.prt.
```

It executed successfully from the command line after the following parameter change:

```
DESFORMAT=vinprn01.
```

The first message does not provide Oracle much information to go on; their recommendation may be only a guess. The second definition of the same problem is much more likely to exactly match a known bug, and bring an immediate, correct response. The difference is the DBA's ability to communicate with Oracle, which requires knowledge of the architecture of the applications.

You have no contractual responsibility to diagnose or fix Oracle's bugs. You will eventually get a resolution from Oracle even if you do nothing to help yourself. However, shops that take a more holistic view are usually more successful. Taking into account the time you will spend on the telephone with Oracle tech support educating them about your unique situation, the time you spend testing the solutions they propose, and the costs to your business of waiting for a solution, it makes business sense for you to invest some of your resources to help Oracle. Your DBA and programmers are familiar with the programming languages Oracle uses, and you have the source code for most of their modules. With four hours' work a good programmer will be able to positively identify perhaps half of the bugs you experience, and will at a minimum be able to provide Oracle with detailed information about those he or she can't find. You'll have more success if you cast yourself as Oracle's partner in resolving problems.

Reference Sources for Oracle Applications

Applications implementers need an overwhelming number of reference materials to do their job. Every project needs a librarian to make sure the necessary materials are on hand. The following sections outline the materials that should be available through the library.

Oracle Corporation takes pains to ensure that their documentation is easy to get. They distribute books and CD-ROMs of documentation with the software. They sell and sometimes hand out the CD-ROMs for Releases 10 and 11, each of which includes a complete set of user documentation for the Applications and a copy of Oracle*Book with which to read the Release 10 version. Their automated fax-back service (800) 252-0303 will send ordering procedures and pricing for all their documents on demand. Their Website (**http://www/oracle.com**) provides links to products and documentation.

Applications User References

There is a set of reference documentation for each application. Depending on the complexity of the application, they run from one to four volumes. All of the product documentation is organized the same way, though it is different between Releases 10 and 11. Release 11 documentation generally places the chapters in this topical sequence:

- Setup
- Descriptions of major functions
- Reports
- Batch processes

Release 10 (character) arranges topics in this order:

- Introduction
- Forms used to run the application, transactions first, then master table maintenance
- Reports, including sample reports and a description of the runtime parameters
- Setup forms, used to set the parameters and value sets that govern operation of the application
- Topical Essays, describing the use of major features of the application

It used to be that the Topical Essays gathered into one chapter at the end of the reference described the major functions, while the rest of the reference focused more narrowly on individual forms and reports. In Release 11, the discussions of application logic have been moved to the chapters on Setup and individual system functions. The new organization appears better adapted for delivery by an online help system.

Delivery of documentation is a major concern for Oracle. It charges $95 (U.S.) apiece for most of the hard copy reference manuals, yet makes the complete set of 100 or so documents available in HTML and PDF format at a nominal cost. This pricing provides a strong incentive for you to make the documentation available on your Web servers.

Online delivery has many advantages besides cost. It is easily shared. It doesn't get lost. It is easy to do a keyword search of one or more documents. The HTML versions of the documentation include hot links. You can integrate Oracle's documentation with your own. It is possible to produce hard copy printouts of individual sections as needed. The major advantage of hard copy references is that they are easier for reading long passages. In the final analysis you may need only about two sets of the books for each Application, one for the developers and another for the Superusers. Everybody else can work from the soft copies.

The HTML and PDF document formats in Release 11 are so universal as to present no problem. You can probably assume that desktop users can read them. Oracle*Book, the presentation mechanism for the Release 10 CD-ROM, has to be installed on your users' desktops if you plan to make documentation available over the network. You will need to include installing Oracle*Book as a task in your project plan.

AOL References

There are a number of reference manuals that describe the technical architecture underlying all the applications. These are included on the CD-ROM, though the DBA and development shop will usually want to have hard copies. They include:

- *Oracle Application Object Library* (deals mainly with customization and testing)

- *Oracle Applications Implementation Manual* (roadmap for installing the Applications)

- *Oracle Applications Open Interfaces* (how to import data into the Applications)

- *Oracle Applications Developer's Guide*

- *Oracle Applications User Interface Standards*

- *Oracle Alert Manual* (how to set up alerts)

- *Oracle Workflow Guide*

- *Oracle Applications Systems Administration Reference* (user and application management)

- *Oracle Application Flexfield Manual* (structure and use of flexfields)
- *Oracle Applications User's Guide* (the user interface)
- *Oracle Applications Messages Manual*
- *Multiple Organizations in Oracle Applications*
- *Multiple Reporting Currencies in Oracle Applications*

The first six are primarily of interest to the MIS staff; the user community needs access to the rest.

Online Help Within the Applications

The Applications offer an online version of the reference manuals through Windows help. Users can add their own text to Oracle's context-sensitive help messages for the Forms, Regions and Fields in the system. Larger users may find this degree of customization worth the investment.

The best approach for smaller users is to develop a comprehensive User's Guide in document format. Such a guide can lead users through all aspects of a transaction, which may thread through many screens. Typical transactions would be adding a new item or ordering from a new vendor. Such a document can be delivered in document format via a file server or HTML format over the intra/Internet.

Custom help, however it is delivered, has to be included as part of the test plan. It usually points to the logic paths that should be included in test scenarios in the first place.

Applications Technical References

Oracle publishes a set of Technical Reference Manuals (TRMs) for each Application. They describe the databases and modules: forms, reports, packaged procedures, and compiled C code. Because this documentation represents Oracle's proprietary architecture, and because it provides information that makes it possible to get in trouble by modifying the applications, Oracle does not make its availability known in the same way as the User's Guides. The Technical Manuals are available only to customers and only in hard copy.

Every shop should have copies of the technical references. Even users who have no intention of modifying the delivered code need them as an aid in debugging and understanding how the application works. Outside consultants will expect to find a copy when they come to help.

The Technical References all follow the same outline:

- An introduction and disclaimer. The disclaimer makes it clear that Oracle will not assume responsibility for supporting modified code or data.

- Entity-relationship diagrams showing the foreign-key relationships among tables supporting the major functions within the Application. This is essential knowledge.

- A catalog of the modules within the Application.

- Machine-generated descriptions of the major tables and views within the system. The reference also shows the Oracle-created indexes on each table and the Oracle sequence (if any) used to generate the primary key of the table.[19]

- Functional overviews of the modules named in the catalogs listed earlier, with CRUD[20] diagrams and the names of called subroutines. The overviews are a guide to the source code. The comments in the code itself are the only reference available for most of the decision logic.

The Technical References are the key that relates what the users see on screen to the underlying Oracle objects. The user sees the external name of a form in its header; the Technical Reference provides the name of the form as found in the forms subdirectory. The user sees a record within a block on the form; the Technical Reference gives the name of the table.

TIP
The Examine function on the Applications menu is a quick way to find the name of the current table and column.

---

[19]Oracle distributes the tables from which the hard-copy table layouts are printed. See Chapter 15 for a discussion of the tables.

[20]CRUD = Create, Read, Update, Delete. A CRUD diagram indicates, at a column or a table level, which functions a module performs on the tables it uses.

Oracle Tools and RDBMS References

It is essential for the DBA and programmers installing Oracle Applications to use Oracle*Loader, SQL*Plus, data export, PL/SQL, and other utility products. The library must include copies of the appropriate reference manuals. Every user will need to have his or her own copy of the major ones. The essentials are the following:

For Each Developer

- *SQL Reference Manual*
- *SQL*Plus User's Guide and Reference*
- *PL/SQL User's Guide and Reference*
- *Server Utilities Guide* (Loader, Import/Export)

In the Library

- *Server Administrator's Guide*
- *Application Developer's Guide*
- *Server Messages*
- *Server Reference*
- *Server Tuning Guide*
- *Oracle*Forms Library Set*
- *Oracle*Reports Library Set*
- *SQL*Net Library Set*
- *Oracle Web Server Library Set*

Oracle8 versions of all the Oracle tools documentation are available in both HTML and PDF formats on a CD-ROM. By far the least expensive and most convenient way to provide library access to this material is online.

Third-Party Oracle References

Third-party books can never duplicate the detail of the Oracle references. They can offer insight into how the many pieces of Oracle's product line fit together and on making the best use of the features described in Oracle's references. They also collect essential reference material into a more compact format. The most useful references usually include:

- Database Sizing and Tuning, such as Oracle Press's *Oracle DBA Handbook* by Kevin Loney (Osborne McGraw-Hill, 1998)

- SQL and basic Oracle, such as *Oracle: the Complete Reference* by George Koch and Kevin Loney (Osborne McGraw-Hill, 1997)

- Production operation, including backup and recovery

- Web server/HTML references

Operating System References

The Applications make extensive use of their host operating systems. The systems programmer, DBA, and programmers need good reference materials on:

- Command and shell languages

- Editors, such as vi in Unix

- Printers and PostScript Printing (a tough subject in Unix)

- Utilities, such as sed in Unix

User's Group Materials

The Oracle Application User's Groups[21] hold meetings about twice a year in each major geographic region worldwide. The proceedings offer a wealth of practical information on installing the applications. The best investment is sending people to the conferences, where they can bring themselves up-to-date on Oracle's future directions as well as gain tips and techniques for the here-and-now. Second best is to buy a copy of the proceedings to put on the shelf.

---

[21]Contact Meeting Expectations in Atlanta, (404) 240-0999, for information. Oracle Corporation will gladly provide user's group contacts worldwide.

The North American OAUG supports a forum on CompuServe, which serves users worldwide. It offers a lively exchange on Applications-related topics. The volume is growing at a great pace. The forum is likely to have changed form when you read this, but it will surely still exist. Its Website is **http://www.oaug.com**. To subscribe to the mailing list, send a message like the following:

> To: listproc@cpa.qc.ca
> Subject: *(Blank if possible)*
> SUBSCRIBE OraApps-L *Your real name goes here.*

The list sees a lot of traffic—it can flood a mailbox. You may want to check with Meeting Expectations or the list manager at **owner-OraApps-L@cpa.qc.ca** before signing up.

Managing Implementation Activities

A project manager is constantly called upon to make trade-offs between meeting the deadline and doing a thorough job. Doing a thorough job means adhering to the essential data processing methodologies of written analysis and design documentation, testing, coding standards, quality control, problem-management, and configuration-management. Though you pay in the long term for short-term expediency, a manager cannot successfully defend a systematic approach unless he or she knows the disciplines.

The right decision does not always favor more methodology. The PM will be called upon to arbitrate between competing interests. Oracle Corporation and many large technical services firms protect themselves by defining methodologies that may be more rigorous than is required. Clients sometimes complain about contractor methodologies that take large amounts of time and generate volumes of documentation that they, the client, can scarcely use or understand. Because they must apply a consistent standard to all customers, Oracle's position for even its most sophisticated clients is that they must wait for Oracle Support to fix software bugs rather than do it themselves. An experienced independent consultant, on the other hand, might just fix the problem and move on. The PM has to weigh cost and business necessity against the benefits of the methodologies. He or she has to know the methodology well enough to be its advocate most of the time, and well enough to know when it can be abbreviated.

TIP
Applications software is no exception to the rule that poor methodologies cause software implementations to fail. These prosaic disciplines are more significant than hardware, staffing levels, or budgets. Good methodology answers the most essential question: "How do I know that it works?"

Written Business Procedures

Testing and training are based on business procedures that describe how the business works using Oracle Applications: "This is how we process orders from established customers"; "This is how we process orders from new customers"; "This is how we handle customer returns"; "This is what we do when a longtime customer owes on invoices more than 90 days old"; "This is how we define tasks within a project."

The procedures for Oracle are based on the needs of the business, which are represented by existing procedures. These are just as often embodied in company culture, handed down by oral tradition, as they are written. Even in companies that do have written procedures, as encouraged by ISO 9000 and modern management science, actual practices often elaborate on or differ from the written procedures. The analyst's challenge is to define current business practices, then how they will be done in Oracle.

The greatest part of the business procedures usually addresses exceptions. It is relatively easy to describe the normal flow of a transaction such as a customer order. The complexity is in the exceptions. What orders should go on credit hold? Who releases them? When? What if it is not in the warehouse? Can we honor an order for an old release level? When do we partial fill an order? Can we fill a Pick-to-Order order from multiple warehouses? One of Oracle's great strengths is that it will apply your business rules for you. To take advantage of Oracle you have to define policies that may have always been made on an ad hoc basis.

Testing

Business procedures describe how the Oracle system will be used. Each procedure needs to be supported by test scenarios to prove that it does work. The system is supposed to accept prepaid orders in foreign currencies? Manufacturing should be able to handle assemble-to-order jobs with outside processing in the final assembly step? Prove it!

Levels of Testing

Testing is a traditional data processing discipline, which Oracle of course performs extensively before shipping its software. Steps in the testing process take on somewhat different meanings for the Applications:

UNIT TESTING   Making sure that individual modules of code work, applies to custom programs written as extensions to the system or for purposes of conversion and bridging to outside systems. Unit testing is the best description to apply to shaking down Applications setups, flexfield rules, Oracle Alerts, and the like in test instances.

INTEGRATION, OR SYSTEM TESTING   Also known as string testing, confirms that individual modules of code work together as a unit. In the case of bespoke code, such testing demonstrates that the custom code interacts properly with the native Oracle code. At a pure Applications level, it means making sure that transactions flow through all the Oracle Applications as expected. As an example, the testers need to confirm that accounting data entered on a sales order or requisition results in the expected ledger postings.

ACCEPTANCE TESTING   Part of a process in which the users agree that a system is ready to put into production. If the system implementers are outside contractors, bonuses or contingency fees may be tied to passing the acceptance test.

PARALLEL TESTING   An old data processing shibboleth that needs to be raised in order to be dismissed. It is the concept that the Oracle Applications will run live in parallel with the legacy systems for a period of time, after which it will be decided whether or not Oracle "meets the test." Here are the flaws in the parallel testing concept:

- There is never enough time, or enough staff, to run two systems at the same time, keying in all the transaction twice.

- Business processes invariably change with Oracle. It is unreasonable to expect that the accounting flexfield, item numbers, invoicing policies, replenishment computations, and so on will be identical. It is a given that the outcomes of the two systems will be different— and it would take an impossible amount of time to reconcile the two.

- Some transactions can only afford to take one path, such as warehouse releases. Whose pick slips would the warehouse recognize—legacy or Oracle? Items could not be double-shipped. Inventory records would be bound to disagree with the actual warehouse counts.

The best use of "parallel processing" is prior to cutover. It is entirely appropriate to convert legacy balances for the General Ledger, as well as prior months' journal postings, in order to confirm that Oracle's ledger reports agree with those from legacy. This is a totally adequate test of the Oracle ledger, but with crucial differences from real parallel processing. Testing with historical data removes the need for dual input, removes the time pressure of closings, and guarantees that the results are indeed comparable because the transactions are identical. It amounts, in fact, to running test scenarios that happen to use real, historical data.

REGRESSION TESTING   A rigorous discipline to prove that the software still performs old functions properly after being enhanced with new features. The test system maintains a set of test data and test results, as described in Chapter 15. The expectation is that the enhanced software should produce exactly the same results as the original.

Oracle developed its own regression tester for use with their character-mode system, and made it available as part of AOL. It could not continue this host-based approach with client/server or NCA systems. Instead, Oracle has standardized on Mercury Corporation's tester, and recommends the same to those users who have developed enough custom code to warrant an automated approach to testing. Because they are the most difficult modules to test, forms are the primary focus of Oracle's regression testing. Both systems employ scripts to simulate keyboard input and capture the impact on the database. They are set up to execute multiple scripts in batch-mode processes to probe all the logic paths in a form. Because they execute on the client side, Mercury's products can be used to "stress test" Oracle by loading the system with high volumes of transactions.

Test Scenarios

A test scenario is a sequence of related tasks, not necessarily automated, each of which is described by business procedures. For instance, there may be procedures to describe how to:

- Enter requisitions in Oracle Purchasing

- Approve requisitions

- Generate internal orders for release from the warehouse

- Pass internal orders to Order Entry

- Release the material to the requisitioner

- Replenish inventory

A typical test scenario would require a series of related transactions to test all these procedures. Create a requisition, approve it, get it issued, and replenish to replace the materials that were issued. Another scenario would specify a requisition for a stock item with zero on hand. Yet another would specify a requisition for a non stock item. Another would specify a requisition for a magazine subscription, for outside services, for a high-dollar item requiring special approvals, and for a purchase that requires competitive bids. Each scenario would trace the transaction through several business procedures: requisitioning, purchasing, receiving, and whatever else is relevant.

The test scenarios specify expected results: requisition denied, replenishment order generated, overshipment refused, and so forth. The scenarios need to be specific about financial outcomes. Automatic Account Generation includes some of the most complex setup logic in Oracle. If you have defined rules to have the cost-of-goods-sold account use the warehouse's company and location, the product line segment associated with the item, and the natural account associated with the customer, you need to confirm that the system is generating what you expect.

Your Superusers should start to develop test scenarios as they test Oracle's functionality in the Conference Room Pilot. Testing will confirm their understanding of the effects of setup parameters on system operations. Keeping formal test scenarios will make it possible for them to confidently repeat a test after they have changed the parameters. Take, for example, a company that deals mainly in prepaid orders and receives a small volume of customer returns. Is it worth using Oracle's RMA (Return Material Authorization) feature, or should the business procedure simply specify a miscellaneous receipt into inventory and miscellaneous payment through Payables? The Superuser can test the alternatives, then write up the most logical approach as the agreed business procedure.

Test Data and Test Scripts

Test data and scripts give substance to a test scenario. The test script for the preceding test scenario might be:

1. Log in with the Responsibility CATALOG_MANAGER.

2. Create an item with the identifier TEST_ITEM*nn*. The *nn* makes the item unique; this way the test can be repeated. Use template EXPENDABLE_SUPPLY. Give it a requisitioning objective of 8.

3. Do a miscellaneous inventory receipt to give TEST_ITEM*nn* an onhand balance of 6.

4. Log in with Responsibility ENGINEERING_USER.

5. Create a requisition for 10 of TEST_ITEM*nn*.

6. Allow the Order Entry import concurrent process to run as scheduled for the test, every minute.

7. Run the Pick/Release process.

8. Process the partial issue.

9. Run the Demand Interface process.

10. Run the Inventory replenishment process.

11. Confirm expected results: Issue of 6, backorder of 4, replenishment requisition for 12 sent to purchasing, issue charged to engineering department—expendable supplies.

Test data and test scripts need to run against master data. In this instance one master record (the part) is entered as part of the script. Doing this ensures that there are no open orders against it. The other master data (requisitioner) is assumed to be in the system.

Testing has to be repeatable. The test scenario needs to specify the initial and final states of the database. A test scenario may restore the database to its initial state. This one might require canceling the backordered portion of open requisitions before it is run. Alternatively, the script may be repeatable through slight variations. You can repeat the preceding script, for example, by changing the part number.

Acceptance tests are the most thorough applications of the testing methodology. They precede the trial cutovers described in Chapter 17; the base process is the same for both acceptance and cutover:

1. Create a new instance, keying in fresh setup parameters for each application.

2. Convert data into the new instance.

3. Run a full suite of test scenarios in the new instance.

4. Confirm the expected outcomes of the test scenarios.

Consider the test unsuccessful if the expected outcomes are not achieved or if the discrepancy cannot be explained. If a test reveals flaws in the setup parameters or conversion processes, it generally means that the whole test needs to be run again. This is hard medicine, but it is the only way to demonstrate conclusively that the setups are consistent.

Unscripted testing is one factor that distinguishes acceptance testing from trial cutovers. The functional users perform acceptance tests. After they confirm that all the tests in the test design work as expected, they usually want to enter transactions of their own to logic paths they may feel were not addressed by the test scenarios and just to get the feel of the system.

CAUTION

Testing is inherently destructive. Test data corrupts a database. That is why testing has to be done in a test instance, prior to cutover. Spot-checking live data after conversion is never an adequate substitute for testing.

Configuration Management

An Oracle Applications environment is made up of a tremendous number of objects. Oracle delivers thousands of modules and tables; there are usually three or four database instances. Including a minimal amount of bespoke code, you add thirty or forty different types of objects to those databases and program files. If you follow any development discipline you will also develop a large number of specifications documents, test scripts, and other documentary support for the implementation. Configuration Management is the discipline that keeps you from getting swamped.

Chapter 15 addresses configuration management for custom code. It boils down to version control—knowing what versions of programs and setups are current in which environments.

Configuration management for implementations without custom code boils down to controlling:

- Business procedures
- Test scenarios
- Test scripts and data
- Setup parameters for each application
- Value sets for each application
- Flexfield setups
- Attribute usage
- Alerts
- Responsibilities and menus

Almost all exist in document format. The major need is for a shared document library on a LAN server, with a subdirectory structure that gives a home to every document type.

Problem Management

The project manager's job can be defined as problem solving. Most projects have a systematic treatment of:

■ **Logging and resolving user problems**   Prior to cutover these are problems that the functional users have setting up and testing Oracle software. Afterwards, they are live production problems—some processes will not do what they need to do. These problems may be resolved by the Superusers, the programmers, or the DBA. They are linked to Technical Assistance Requests (TARs) when they require Oracle's help.

■ **Logging problems reported to Oracle through Technical Assistance Requests (TARs)**   The TAR log will show when the problem was reported, the phrasing used to report it, when Oracle responded and what they recommended. The actions can be implementing a patch, using a work-around, or the discovery that it is not a problem but a misunderstanding.

■ **Logging project issues that require management decisions**   An issues log should give the issue a short name, indicate who is managing the issue, give the status, show a deadline date, and reference an issue paper that goes into the details. The setup document for the application in question should also reference the issue paper.

Open issues on these logs are perennial agenda items for project status meetings, along with tasks from the WBS that are started, completed, and stalled for one reason or another.

Quality Assurance

Quality is built in, not added on. You assure quality by adhering to established processes that yield predictable results. Some hallmarks of quality are an established planning process, well-defined methodologies, metrics for measuring performance against the plan, and a system for improving methodologies based on measured results.

One of the project manager's roles is to make sure that the team agrees on adequate and appropriate sets of standards and methodologies. The team members are the ones who will live with them, so they should be the ones to develop them. The project manager's job is to encourage, lead, and sometimes push them to get it done. Quality assurance is making sure that the project team agrees about quality, what it is and how to create it, and that they are committed to producing it.

Conclusion

The project manager cannot mandate success. He or she has to provide the leadership and environment in which his or her team can succeed. The success of an Applications project always depends on outsiders and people who do not fully belong to the project. The project manager needs to convince the team that installing Oracle is worthwhile, that there is a workable plan, and that the project will be a success.

The project manager needs the discernment to recognize appropriate methodologies and the discipline to apply them. It takes leadership as well as a fair knowledge of data processing. The de facto methodologies are whatever the team implements in its work products. The project manager needs to convince the team of the need for a systematic approach and lead the team to select techniques that they can apply successfully. Approaches adapted from the mainframe, or custom code development, or even other Applications implementations may not be appropriate. The team will not understand them, much less buy into the concepts, unless they contribute their own ideas.

Testing is the most important of all the disciplines. Each component of the system, and the system as a whole, has to be proven to work before it goes into production. You know the Oracle software works, but that fact is of no value unless you have defined the business processes you need to make it work for you. The consequences of going into production without proving that you know how to execute all major business functions can be disastrous.

The project manager's responsibilities span the range of classical management functions. He or she must have management adopt achievable plans and budgets. The project manager must bring together a staff with the best mix of functional area specialists, data processing staff, implementation contractors, and consultants. He or she must lead by vision and decision-making. Lastly, the project manager must see that the methodologies essential to quality, and hence success, are defined and observed.

CHAPTER
17

Data Conversion, Training, and Cutover

T he entire Oracle Applications implementation project focuses on the "go live" date. Time is critical; the business is at a standstill while the conversion team scrambles to switch software and hardware and ensure that the new system data files are completely up-to-date. Though the entire project requires good planning, timing is especially critical at cutover. It has to be planned and managed like a military operation.

Data conversion is as essential to planning as to live operations. Real data makes the system real to the Superusers who set it up. You write the data conversion programs to populate the Conference Room Pilot, then constantly test and improve them up until cutover.

Before planning the setup, the implementation team needs training in what Oracle can do. During implementation the system users need training in what it will do. Their use of the system is a matter of the system setup and your unique business procedures, including manual processes that may not even be tracked in the automated system. You need an appropriate training plan for each phase of the project.

The cutover date is the last milestone on the critical path. A slip in any of the setup, training, data conversion, infrastructure implementation, and customization tasks can cause it to slip. Pre-cutover tasks such as training and hardware installation must be scheduled well in advance. Setting an achievable cutover date and ensuring that all of the prerequisite tasks are completed by that date are the Project Manager's main objectives.

Training Requirements

All participants in an Oracle Applications implementation need training to become familiar with the products. Their needs differ widely, depending on the roles they play and the phase in the project life cycle. The agencies and means of delivering training are also varied. Acquiring appropriate training at an acceptable cost is an ongoing task for the project manager.

Introductory Training

Users acquire a superficial understanding of the Applications' capabilities during the sales cycle. They attend demonstrations, evaluate proposals, and read company literature in the course of selecting Oracle as the package vendor.

Getting down to work requires fuller knowledge. The Superusers and MIS professionals on the teams need to find out how the packages function. They need this knowledge before they can start planning the implementation, which is to say before the Applications are configured for their installation, and often before they are even installed. The class has to be taught by outsiders; the question is by who, and whether it will be on- or off-site.

Oracle Corporation offers scheduled classes on the Applications projects on a regular basis throughout the world. Oracle has excellent resources. The classrooms are well appointed, the computer hardware is first-rate, the teaching materials have been professionally prepared, and the instructors have the benefit of Oracle in-house training and support. The major drawbacks are the cost and the fact that the training is general, not tailored to any customer's specific needs.

At this time, Oracle has little competition from third parties offering scheduled classroom training in Oracle Applications. It would be difficult for another firm to put together the critical mass of equipment, software, training facilities, and schedule to offer a credible alternative. Outside of Oracle classroom training, the alternatives are:

- Standard Oracle training delivered on-site, by Oracle

- Custom training delivered off-site, by Oracle or others

- Custom training delivered on-site, by Oracle or others

Standard Oracle training on-site can be cheaper per seat than attending off-site classes if there are many attendees, as it eliminates travel costs. However, your facilities may not be as good as Oracle's, and the infrastructure will almost surely be inferior. On-site training also eliminates the major hidden benefits of off-site training. First, travel and training are enjoyable. Going away for class is usually a pleasure and it sets a good mood. Secondly, removing people from the office eliminates interruptions and ensures that they can concentrate on the subject at hand. Finally, Oracle training throws people from different companies facing a common requirement together. They learn from each other and can support each other later on. Your Superusers and team leads will usually benefit most from Oracle classroom training.

Custom training makes sense after your company's requirements have been defined, once the analysis and setup phases are complete. At that point you can teach exactly what your company will do with the Oracle packages instead of the general package capabilities. Custom training for the end users is essential just before cutover, but not usually appropriate at the beginning of a project.

Self-teaching can be an effective tool with the Applications. Oracle delivers a fully populated demonstration instance for the fictitious Global Manufacturing Company as part of the product. It is a good idea to make this instance available to developers and users as an example of a valid setup. Your Superusers will find it useful to refer to the demonstration database as they experiment with setup options in the Conference Room Pilot. Chapter 16 describes the different instances and the reference books that are available to users who wish to teach themselves.

Technical Training

The installation of Oracle Applications imposes new training demands on the data processing staff. They must become familiar with elements that are new to their environment including the Oracle RDBMS and tools, as well as Oracle communications and Internet products, such as SQL*Net and the Oracle Web Server (for NCA installations). They need to learn to use the components of Oracle Applications that resemble programming languages, such as flexfields and value sets, Workflow, Alerts, setting up concurrent processes and parameters, managing printers, and defining responsibilities and menu structures.

Classroom and self-study instruction courses are widely available for the Oracle database and tools. Most shops will want their permanent programming staff to be trained in SQL, PL/SQL, Discover 2000, and the current version of Oracle Forms and Reports. The DBA and network administrators will need training in database administration, tuning, and networking software.

Most Oracle Applications programmers usually make only limited use of operating system commands. They can usually pick up what they need to know from reference books and consultants. There are a number of topics that are not included in any curriculum; the only ways to learn are by trial and error or from someone who has experienced the need before. One of the most valuable services of outside consultants is to bring this seed knowledge into your organization.

It is frequently useful to have experienced employees and consultants teach mini-sessions on specific topics, such as "Using the vi editor," "Writing efficient SQL," "Using Word Perfect as a program editor," "Basic Unix commands," "Writing Oracle Alerts," "Uses of the ed and sed editors," "Batch scripts in Windows NT," and the like. Oracle Applications User's Group meetings, both regional and national, are also great places to look for this sort of presentation. Old conference proceedings are a good place to look for teaching materials.

Cutover Training

The end users who will interact with Oracle every day need to be trained by the time of your cutover. The training they need is not specific to Oracle, but rather how to do their jobs using Oracle. Training should be customized to address:

- Using the applicable Oracle Applications interface (character, smart client, or NCA)

- Adopting organization-specific business procedures in each functional area

- Carrying out individual job responsibilities within the organization using Oracle Applications

Superusers, people already familiar with the business, are in the best position to deliver training. If they have done a good job of defining business procedures and executing test scenarios, they should know how to use the system to accomplish the company's business. Second best, if the Superusers do not have time to put a class together, is to have analysts or consultants deliver the training with a Superuser at hand to address user questions.

User training usually affects a fair number of people. It should be short and to the point. The attendees need to feel that their time is well spent. It should be delivered in a hands-on environment, so the users get the feel of the system as they process real-world transactions. Training is most effective if the users have a chance to put it to use shortly after you deliver it. People will quickly forget what they don't use. If you have enough people to do it, the optimal time to train is while operations are shut down for the cutover.

The Data-Conversion Approach

Data conversion is one of the earliest considerations in an Oracle Applications implementation, both because cleaning up your legacy data can be very time consuming and because the mapping of legacy data into Oracle is relatively independent of your Applications setup. It is also important in testing. Superusers find it much easier to decide how they will use Oracle when they have real data to experiment with in the Conference Room Pilot instance. Programmers put together data conversion scripts first to populate the CRP and test environments, then to cut over into live operation.

Oracle provides open interface programs for most of its master tables to facilitate conversion and integration. The open interfaces subject imported data to the same full edit that would be applied if the data were entered online. Most open interfaces are designed to load a number of related tables at the same time, which assures that the data you load is complete as well as consistent. Other alternatives for getting data into the system are:

- Manually keying data into the system.

- Using Desktop Integration, for example, to load budgets into the General Ledger. Oracle is rapidly extending desktop integration throughout the Applications at this writing.

- Using a programmable tool to feed data in through the Oracle forms. Oracle's regression tester handles this in character mode. Programmable emulators and visual basic work in NCA and Smart Client environments.

- Writing SQL scripts to directly load the database.

Though Oracle's APIs handle an increasing percentage of the task, conversion invariably involves some custom-written, one-time code. Even when you use the open interfaces, you need bespoke code to load the interface tables. Chapter 15 suggests standards and approaches for writing conversion code.

Data Mapping: Legacy to Oracle

The first step in data conversion is to map legacy data to Oracle. Legacy records and fields seldom equate neatly to Oracle. In most cases, the Oracle tables are more highly normalized than the legacy files. Oracle makes some distinctions the old system may not, such as between a customer and a customer site, between an asset tag number and an asset number, and between a default and an actual inventory storage location for an item. The conversion to Oracle sometimes forces choices. You may have traditionally used several part numbering schemes in different inventory operations; consolidating inventory operations under Oracle will require a common part numbering scheme.

There are open interface tables to handle most of your conversion requirements. The *Oracle Manufacturing, Distribution, Sales and Service Open Interfaces,* and *Oracle Financials Open Interfaces* manuals describe these requirements column by column.

- The data columns in the interface tables correspond to fields you can enter through the screens. The data entry form documentation provides the best descriptions of the columns.

- It is desirable to fill most columns from master setup sources such as item templates and customer profiles. Functionally, these devices allow you to set attributes and administer policy at a group level. They simplify data conversion by reducing the number of columns you need to populate and validate.

- You often have a choice of entering the external item identifier, such as the segment numbers of a key flexfield, or a quickpick value, or the corresponding internal number. You reduce the chances for errors in the interface if you do the lookups in your own code and put the internal numbers in the interface table.

- The reference manuals indicate which columns are mandatory. You will usually leave most of the others null. Many of them do not correspond to legacy data columns, and many others will be filled automatically from master setup sources.

- Oracle uses key identifiers, usually from your legacy system but sometimes generated by you, to join the master and detail rows you place in the open interfaces. Make sure the program that populates the interface checks that they are unique and in the right format.

You may need to do a bit of analysis to determine how the target tables need to be populated. The Technical Reference manuals describe the Applications tables. Chapter 15 offers scripts to determine the valid values for standard code columns implemented as quickpicks. It is sometimes difficult to know which columns you can safely leave null. You may want to enter a few test transactions through the online system, then use the printtab routine shown in Chapter 15 to show how data you entered is stored in the database. Your objective will be to create the same results through the open interfaces.

The best legacy system sources are user and system documentation, file layouts in legacy programs, and printouts of the actual files. In mainframe systems there are often many different record types mixed within one file. The field names offer a clue as to the contents, but they are often cryptic. The analyst often needs to assemble all available clues: field names, user-documentation descriptions of input fields, user reference materials, and actual field contents seen in file dumps, to deduce the data available from legacy.

Create a spreadsheet for the mapping from legacy to Oracle. Use the SQL*Plus DESCRIBE command to list all of the columns in each of the interface tables, then cut and paste. It is a good idea to include every column in the spreadsheet even though you will leave most of them blank. The spreadsheet columns are:

- Destination table name

- Destination column name

- Flag to indicate if the column must not be null

- Destination data format

- Source file or table name

- Source record type, if there are multiple types in a data file

- Source field name

- Source field format

- Conversion and lookup rules. Describe how the program needs to manipulate the input field to get the output field. Indicate what to do with null values on input. If no source field is used, name the setup master source (such as a template) that will provide data.

Some legacy fields will not map directly into Oracle. Their use may be unclear, or they may just seem irrelevant. Because it is so much easier to save data than to re-create lost data, it is a good strategy to keep the unused fields all together in comma-delimited format, in one or more of the user-defined attributes (attribute*n*) in the target Oracle table. They will then be available if live operation reveals that they need to be used to update Oracle attribute settings or referenced in bespoke reports. As an alternative, plan to retain the staging tables used in conversion until well past conversion.

Oracle provides the option of using generated numbers as transaction and master record identifiers in a great many areas, among them for customer number, supplier number, purchase order number, and sales order number. You can optionally provide your own unique keys. Though you will usually find it most convenient to let Oracle make up new numbers after conversion, the legacy system numbers are an essential link with paper files and existing customers, suppliers, and other outsiders. The most common approach is to set automatic numbering off and retain existing numbers through conversion. After conversion, the DBA can set the internal sequence generator higher than any existing number at the same time you set the automatic numbering parameter on, so that new suppliers, customers, POs, etc. are numbered sequentially starting with a number greater than any already in use. In most cases, Oracle accepts alphabetic numbers from your legacy system, though the ones it generates are numeric. If you start automatic numbering at a round number, such as Purchase Order 1000001, your users will be able to quickly distinguish Oracle from legacy documents.

The Applications have a modern appearance. They present data in upper- and lowercase, in proportionally spaced fonts. Legacy systems frequently forced data to be in uppercase only. Considering that appearance is a major attraction in converting to a graphical system such as Oracle, it makes sense to convert data to upper- and lowercase. Here are some pointers:

- Test to determine which conversion function works best for your data. Usual candidates are the SQL INITCAP function and word processor case conversion facilities.

- Use outside reference tables as much as possible, such as Vertex or PostalSoft, to get valid spelling and capitalization of city and county names.

- Plan to write custom scripts to address identifiable language rules (e.g., in names that start with "Mc," the third letter should be capitalized; and "St." as a prefix in a city field means "Saint," while in an address line it means street).

- Use this opportunity to convert to the preferred national language usage. Convert "Mueller" to "Müller," "Renee" to "Renée," and so forth.

- Don't worry if the data conversion isn't perfect. Most upper/lower-case fields are descriptive. In most cases, Oracle Applications will permit users to fix the fields when they spot errors.

Besides being more appealing, upper- and lowercase reports are easier to read. The additional visual clues and improved use of white space make the information easier for the mind to absorb. The improvements in productivity, and in the image you present to your customers and suppliers, are impossible to measure but very real. You can use modernization of your software as an opportunity to look modern.

Conversion Processing and Cleanup

The completed data mapping will show a source for every needed Oracle column and the processing required to generate it. Common conversion steps include reformatting dates, changing names (separating or combining first and last names, stripping out the "Mr." and "Mrs."), and inserting the implied decimal into a numeric field.

Your old data may be flawed to the point that it causes problems in legacy system operations. There may be inconsistent usage of fields, sometimes including a title like "Dr." with the first name, sometimes not; sometimes recording the first name of "J. Jack Johnson" as "J. Jack" and other times as simply "J." The same company may appear multiple times in the same file, with variations on the same address or different addresses, some valid and some old. City names may be inconsistent with ZIP codes.

Conversion is the time for cleanup. Oracle will reject some invalid data outright. Other data will cause the same problems and inconsistencies in Oracle that it does in legacy. Experience demonstrates that:

- A company that cannot find time to clean up data before conversion is likely not to find time afterwards.

■ Fixing data once it is in Oracle is several times harder than fixing it in flat files en route to Oracle.

A hybrid cleanup process usually works best. Automated scripts do the bulk of the work, but individual reviewers need to review and make final corrections. There are no hard-and-fast formulas, only rules of thumb:

■ Have the users clean the data up as much as possible in the legacy system before they export it to Oracle.

■ Do as much format conversion as possible in the legacy extract. In particular, handle binary and packed decimal conversions in the data's native environment.

■ Export into a format that will be easy to import. Fixed-length, tab, and comma-delimited fields, with one record format per input file, are easiest to work with.

■ Have the legacy extract processes normalize records to match Oracle's table relationships. If you can, for example, create separate vendor and vendor site records for export. It goes without saying that the relationships will be easiest to determine at the source of the data rather than in Oracle, after it has been filtered and converted.

■ Generate control totals on the legacy side, primarily record counts and monetary sums, which can be used as controls throughout the process. In the case of inventory conversion, you need to make sure that the total number of inventory items is the same between legacy and Oracle, and also that the total inventory value has not changed.

■ Use desktop tools to clean up files of only a few thousand records or so before sending them to Oracle. The global search-and-replace capabilities of a spreadsheet or word processor are useful for making mass changes, after which the user can fix individual errors. Spreadsheets can export comma-delimited files, which are perfect as input to SQL*Loader.

■ Write the simplest possible SQL*Loader script to put data into staging tables you define in Oracle. Do not have SQL*Loader do any date or number conversion—bring all data in as characters, so the load process will not experience any errors. Problems are easier to find and fix with PL/SQL. Never load the Oracle Applications interface or master tables directly—leave data in staging tables until you clean it up and validate it.

■ Use PL/SQL routines running under SQL*Plus to handle field conversion from character to numbers or dates. Plain SQL diagnostics are weak when dealing with individual rows. For example, when there is a letter in a numeric field, SQL*Plus will not indicate which row or which column experienced the error. On the other hand, PL/SQL can be written to work with one record and one field at a time. Its BEGIN.. EXCEPTION.. END structure allows you to trap and examine individual conversion errors. A programmer can write meaningful error messages using PL/SQL or even automatically clean up fields that do not convert properly.

■ Provide users with the tools they need to clean up the data in your staging tables. There are a great number of alternatives, some of which are:

　■ Write scripts to extract erroneous records into spreadsheets, then re-import and re-edit the corrected data.

　■ Write reports to list possible error conditions, and provide the users with bespoke forms to clean them up.

　■ Give the users desktop access to the staging tables through ODBC links into spreadsheet products, so they can clean the data up themselves.

　■ Identify potential problems, and have the users clean them up with Applications forms after they are loaded to the Applications but prior to cutover.

■ Follow the custom code standards given in Chapter 15 in writing SQL and PL/SQL scripts to load the data. The same standards apply for loads to the open interface tables and directly to the Applications master tables.

■ Load one record at a time at first to test the scripts. After the record has loaded successfully, run transactions against it to make sure the settings are appropriate as well as acceptable to Oracle. Weigh the risks of deleting records from the Applications tables (normally a very bad practice) against the benefits of reusing the same record until it loads correctly. As an alternative, alter the script for test purposes to suffix certain data fields to make them unique each time you test the script.

■ When the conversion process works for one record, try it with different record types a few at a time, and then finally with the whole staging table.

The Oracle open interface programs are written to validate every possible data condition. The user documentation does not, and could not, fully explain the validation logic built into them. The error messages they produce are often quite cryptic, more useful for programmers than for end users. The developers of the scripts that load the interface tables can gain significant insights from reading the Oracle code that processes them. Though most of the top-level programs are written in C and therefore hard to decipher, the bulk of the logic to validate the data, load the tables, and generate error messages is implemented in PL/SQL stored procedures. If your programmers get stuck, have them use the techniques in Chapter 15 to find and read the interface code.

It is a good idea to document your conversion code to the same standard as production modules. Although conversion is theoretically a one-time affair, most users find themselves executing conversion scripts tens and hundreds of times in the course of perfecting them. The scripts are needed to populate the Conference Room Pilot instance months before the actual cutover, and they will be constantly improved during that time. You may later want to adapt the conversion logic for mass table loads in support of acquired companies, new products, corporate reorganizations and other one-time activities.

Conversion Strategies

The objective of conversion is to make the state of the Oracle database agree closely with the state of the legacy system data at the time of the cutover, and to be able to reconcile any differences. That is, if a project is in the legacy system, it should be in Oracle. If a purchase order is open in legacy, it should be present and open in Oracle. There are different ways to achieve this objective.

If your operations will allow it, freeze master tables in advance of cutover, giving yourselves time to clean up and convert the data. The accountants have total control over the Chart of Accounts. Human resources may control the mutation and recombination of departments. Manufacturing controls the definition of resources. These groups need to agree on a date preceding cutover to freeze their master tables and value sets so they can be converted and tested. They can accumulate changes to be applied after cutover.

Tables with low volatility can sometimes be converted ahead of time, then updated in parallel in Oracle and legacy. In the case of Inventory, the sheer volume of items may require this approach; there may not be time at cutover and the complexity invites complications. Not only does the item have to be in both systems, but its attributes have to be the same. If there are open Purchase Orders due in to Inventory, the item must be defined as a stock item. If there are open sales orders, the item must be a sellable item. If it is in stock, the bin locations should be the same. You may find it necessary to build a bridge program to keep the two masters in agreement.

Transaction tables that cannot be frozen for the last few weeks of operation in the legacy system have to be converted during the cutover phase. The two major approaches are called *runout* and *flash conversion.* Flash conversion involves moving transactions from legacy to Oracle. Runout entails processing old transactions to completion in the old system and entering only new transactions in Oracle. Runout works best for transactions with a short cycle time, such as accounts payable. Payables systems generally complete payment within a week or two of receiving an invoice. Change the parameters and they can clear the backlog of unpaid obligations. Many AP conversions therefore do not involve converting transactions. Old obligations are paid out of the old system, and new ones out of the new system. For some systems runout can quickly reduce the number of active transactions in legacy to a small number, at which point those few can be rekeyed into Oracle.

Flash conversion is useful for tables of transactions with longer cycles. Lead times in Purchasing and Order Entry run into months and sometimes years. It may be impractical to run the legacy and Oracle systems in parallel for a long enough period to flush out all old transactions. The standard approach is to convert open transactions. Some systems, such as Order Entry, have open interfaces to make this easy. Others, such as Purchasing, require direct loading of the Oracle tables by the methods outlined in Chapter 15.

Flash conversions require preparation of your data. Before conversion you need to move open transactions into states that can be reproduced in Oracle. It makes sense to complete as much processing as you can on each transaction, then do a freeze prior to a purchasing conversion so there are no open requisitions, purchase orders in the approval process, or in-process receipts at cutover. The system should have to deal only with purchase orders where the action is in the suppliers' hands.

Many companies change accounting structures in conversion to Oracle. The legacy system may have nothing comparable to Oracle's multisegment Accounting Flexfield. The Oracle setups may require you to establish new accounts. For example, Oracle forces you to designate items as stockage if they are ever put into inventory, regardless of your intent to reorder them. You need a General Ledger asset account for them. Open purchase orders for them must be tagged as due-in for inventory, rather than expense. It is often necessary to translate accounts, and sometimes necessary to change transaction types as part of the conversion.

The conversion plan needs to insure against double postings to the ledger, and to confirm that clearing accounts are in fact cleared. Purchasing accrues a liability upon receipt, which Payables then reverses upon payment. If any open receipts are converted, the process needs to create the liability postings for Payables to relieve. Encumbrance accounting involves even more of these kinds of considerations. In short, testing has to include accounting implications of the conversion process. You must be able to reconcile the Oracle ledger with the legacy ledger.

The Cutover Plan

Cutover is the subset of the Work Breakdown Structure tasks that needs to be executed in the short period of time between shutting down the old system and bringing up Oracle. Because your business cannot process transactions during cutover, you have to make every effort to ensure that the process is fast and reliable. Cutover is supported by less time-critical pre-cutover tasks that prepare the organization, and post-cutover tasks to clean up afterwards.

Because they are time-critical, cutover tasks need to be tested multiple times, carefully scripted, and rehearsed so that they come off flawlessly in their final, live performance. Module and integration testing per se is a prerequisite to, not part of, the cutover plan. The pre-cutover tasks begin where development leaves off.

The characteristic that distinguishes the actual cutover from testing is that it cannot be validated by running test transactions; they would corrupt the live data. Instead, the cutover process is validated by record counts and account value comparisons and queries to make sure that all the converted data is accessible in the Oracle tables.

To determine whether or not Oracle Applications is now prepared to run your business, you must run live transactions through key business processes. The transactions should be chosen ahead of time—a batch of invoices to enter into Payables, a stack of orders to enter into Order Entry, a pick/release cycle to confirm activity against inventory, and perhaps a replenishment and a warehouse count cycle.

The go/no-go decision point is a critical part of cutover. The plan should define the criteria for success, and define a contingency to fall back to legacy in case it fails. The fallback has to include re-entering the transactions in legacy, and may involve reactivating old hardware, business procedures, communications links, and other elements of the legacy setup.

Typical Pre-Cutover Tasks

- Develop and test data cleanup and conversion routines.

- Prepare the client systems:

  - Install desktop systems (NCs, PCs, LANs, etc.).

  - Install desktop software.

- Prepare application servers:

  - Install client-side software.

- Training:
  - Prepare training.

    Compose courseware.
    Schedule classrooms.
    Set up training hardware and software.
    Prepare class examples.

  - Deliver training.
- Complete all possible transactions in the legacy system:
  - Complete material receipts and shipments.
  - Perform monthly closings and postings.
- Create control reports to validate the conversion:
  - Inventory valuation report
  - General Ledger reports
  - Record counts
- Develop a suite of live-operation transactions to be used to confirm that the system works.
- Develop a contingency plan to fall back to the legacy system if cutover fails.
- Load configuration-managed program data to a new operating system file system for production:
  - Load Oracle software.
  - Apply proven patches from Oracle.
  - Copy configuration-managed custom code into custom directories.
- Create an empty instance for production:
  - Create RDBMS objects:

       Custom tables and views
       Database triggers

- Perform application setups from configuration-managed setup documentation:

       Key in Setup Parameters.
       Define Responsibilities and Menus.
       Custom report and form registration
       Oracle Alerts

- Load static setup data:

       Value Sets
       Reference tables (Vertex)

- Load historical transaction data:

       Prior months' GL balances and journals
       Closed purchase orders, shipments, and other data that must be available in Oracle for reference purposes

- Announce changes in business procedures:

  - Externally, to customers and vendors.

  - Internally, to departments affected by the new systems but not involved in the Oracle implementation.

Typical Cutover Tasks

- Set up user environments:

  - Provide access to the production instance.

- Reroute automated communications into the Oracle system:

  - EDI communications

  - Bank reconciliations

- Perform Data Conversion:
  - Perform legacy system extracts after legacy shutdown:

    Master data
    Transactions to be converted automatically

  - Run cleanup and conversion scripts.

  - Import legacy data:

    Through APIs when possible.
    Directly to Oracle tables when necessary.

  - Key in legacy transactions in cases selected for manual conversion, frequent examples of which are:

    Invoices to be paid after conversion
    Customer orders to ship after conversion

- Make go/no-go decision based on the success of initial live operation.

- Execute the contingency plan to fall back to legacy, if necessary.

Typical Post-Cutover Tasks

- Provide user and system support for the baseline system:
  - Superuser and consultant presence in user departments as needed

  - Help desk

  - Problem tracking for custom software, setup, and Oracle TAR problem resolution

- Respond to new user requirements that surface in live operation:
  - Incomplete business procedures

  - Additional custom reporting requirements

- "Sunset" the legacy system:

    - Catalog and save the programs...

      So the logic is available for reference.
      So the whole system can be restored as a deep fallback.

    - Archive master and transaction files at the point of cutover.

    - Activate custom systems that make historical transactions available to Oracle Applications users.

    - Shut down legacy hardware.

Phased Cutover

Multiplant and multinational organizations usually find it efficient to convert one country or organization at a time. The conversion unit usually equates to an Oracle set of books or Operating Unit.

The more autonomous the operations, the better a phased cutover will work. Assuming the business units communicate with each other in the same arms-length way they work with outside customers and suppliers, one unit's conversion will not affect another unit's operations. Where they are more highly integrated it may be necessary to build bridge programs to support the phased conversion.

Post-Cutover Activity

The weeks after cutover are typically the most hectic of the entire project. The Project Manager's top priority has to be supporting the users. It is essential to maintain a help desk and a problem log. The help desk is there to answer users' questions and field their complaints. Responsiveness is critical—the initial users' experience can make or break the system.

If the system has been thoroughly tested, more help-desk calls will require helping the users with their understanding of the system than fixing the system itself. The help desk should be able to coordinate with the

Superusers to provide support to people in their areas. Access to the Oracle system is often an issue. There is usually a fair amount to do getting users' Windows and browser environments and Oracle responsibility assignments set up right.

Managing problem logs are one of the critical methodologies outlined in Chapter 16. You should have logs for user-reported problems, Oracle TAR reports, and patches set up well before cutover. You need to actively manage the logs, making sure you know the status of each open item and who is responsible for following through.

There is usually more work to do than time to do it prior to cutover. The Project Manager almost always has to put off less critical tasks such as custom reports until after cutover. The programming team will split their time between urgent fixes to the operational system and the enhancements that had to be postponed.

Budget pressure leads many companies to end their consultants' engagements rather abruptly after cutover. However, phasing them out over time is usually more prudent. As conversion ends, you will have made a significant investment in training your contractors in your business. The consulting team is often in the best position to help you respond to problems related to setups and data conversion, and to requirements for bespoke reports that you may have postponed until after cutover.

Cutover gives you an opportunity to improve productivity. You can retain the strongest members of your team, who already know your staff and your requirements, to address the backlog of tasks that could not be accommodated prior to cutover. You may want to use this period to deepen the relationship with independent consultants, local people you will be able to call back periodically and whose knowledge of the conversion can be a corporate asset.

Sunsetting the Legacy System

The legacy system will have lost its usefulness as an operational system within a month after cutover. Whatever the deficiencies in your Oracle operation, the point of no return will have been passed.

It is important that you archive the major files from the legacy system. There is an occasional need to research those records for audit purposes and, less often, to go back and retrieve information that may be needed by the Oracle system.

Legacy system tape files often cannot be read by anything other than legacy hardware. Beyond that, the backup data only makes sense to the software systems that wrote it, and the software can't be run without the old hardware. It is a good idea, when planning the future uses of old data, to do some triage:

- Master file data as of the time of cutover had to be available in Oracle format to do the conversion. You usually want to retain the versions that were loaded to Oracle staging tables.

- Plan how long you will need to retain master files in their original format for audit purposes. Tag them appropriately.

- Keep the old source programs that include descriptions of the old master files as long as you retain the files they describe. The old executable programs, on the other hand, can be discarded with the old machine. They become useless once you reach the point of no return.

- Transaction files at time of cutover usually include both active and closed transactions. Make sure users can retrieve old transactions if they need them. A common approach is to put them in user-defined Oracle tables, in spreadsheets, or on optical disk storage that can be accessed from the desktop.

You will probably migrate all the legacy data that is of any operational interest over to Oracle in your first year of using Financials. Thereafter, the primary reasons for keeping the old data are legal ones. Some companies maintain a records retention office; others have their legal counsel determine how long the old data must be maintained. It is a good idea to mark it with a destruction date; the people who know the data may leave before its time is up. Magnetic tapes deteriorate in a matter of years. If you need to keep the data indefinitely you will need to find special tape storage or migrate the data to a more permanent medium.

Conclusion

The cutover date is the focus of your Oracle Applications implementation. Your users need to be trained before the new system comes up, but not so far in advance that they forget how to use it. You need to convert and purify master file data in advance of cutover, but not so far that users are forced to maintain two systems for a length of time.

Oracle forces you to purify and normalize your data to some degree. It is wise to take the opportunity of conversion to remedy as many of the shortcomings as possible in your legacy data. This is a much easier task to do en route to your new application than once the data has been loaded.

Oracle's open interface processes guarantee the quality of the data you convert. It takes a solid knowledge of the legacy data, the Oracle tables, and the Oracle defaulting processes to make the best use of them. Data conversion is usually the major programming task in an Oracle implementation. It should be done early in the project for two reasons: Real data is essential in Conference Room Pilot testing, and the conversion code should be as thoroughly tested as possible for cutover.

Cutover has to be rehearsed because it has to go right. Your business is at a standstill between the time you shut down legacy and you bring up Oracle. Each step has to have been tested and proven. There must be a set of criteria, including matching record counts and ledger balances, to determine that the file conversion is a success. You need to pre-plan the live operation activities you will execute to determine that the system is operational.

CHAPTER
18

Live Operation
Considerations

nce testing and cutover have been completed and your system is live, the users will need special attention for the first few weeks and months. The considerations associated with supporting a live system are quite different from those associated with implementation. This chapter discusses what you will encounter, and provides tips, suggestions, and workarounds. The material is set out in the following order:

- Guidelines for closing periods and tracing transactions back to their origin

- Accounting workarounds

- Troubleshooting common problems

- Optimizing application performance

Closing Accounting Periods— Month-End and Year-End

Each Application module in Oracle Financials controls its period statuses (Open, Closed, Permanently closed) independently. Period statuses must be maintained for each separate set of books. The number of period statuses to be closed does multiply quite quickly. An organization with three sets of books, running Receivables, Payables, Fixed Assets, and General Ledger (a fairly modest configuration) will have 12 (3 × 4) period statuses to close. Having each Application module close independently of the others allows the closing process to proceed incrementally through the organization in a wave. The wave starts with the subledgers, like Inventory and Purchasing, and flows inwards to close General Ledger last. GL has to close last since, until all other modules are closed, there is a risk that unposted transactions will not be transferred to GL and will need to be posted. The closing sequence, depending on which of the modules you have installed and the setup of your organization, will follow this sequence:

1. Inventory

2. Purchasing

3. Payables

4. Receivables

5. Fixed Assets

6. General Ledger

Closing procedures are built up from daily (and sometimes weekly) procedures. The first step of a period-end is to do the day-end. Then there are some additional steps that are only done at period-end. Similarly, a year-end is composed of a day-end, then a period-end, and some additional steps that are only performed at year-end. It is not possible to be dogmatic about what needs to be done during a period-end or a year-end, because it partially depends on the business activities that are routinely done each day. Some companies reconcile their bank statements on a daily basis, while others on a monthly basis. Clearly if done monthly this is normally considered part of the month-end routine.

Before closing each module the business will want to do the following:

1. Confirm that all period transactions have been entered.

2. Confirm that all interfaces have been run and any period exception records have been corrected and successfully imported.

3. Run housekeeping processes such as Approval in Payables and Revenue Recognition in Receivables.

4. Run the data transfer programs in all the subledgers and ensure that all resulting journals are imported into and posted in General Ledger.

5. Close the subledger. (Set the period status to closed.)

At this point, you will typically perform other period-end tasks, such as producing period-end reports, perform reconciliations between modules, and running consolidations.

 TIP
Typically a company will first soft-close a period (to prevent additional transactions from being posted). Doing this allows the company to perform reconciliations while the period is still open and—if any corrections or adjustments are required—to post these immediately in the correct month.

Closing the period in each module is simply a matter of changing the period status in each to Closed. Period statuses are stored in the table GL_PERIOD_STATUSES. When you initiate a period close, Financials looks for any unposted transactions in that period. It is also possible that transactions will get stuck. When this happens, you first need to identify which specific transactions are the source of the problem, then correct the transaction in a way that allows it to be selected and transferred. The rogue transactions may show up when you run one of the "unposted" reports. However, it is possible that corrupted transactions will not show up. Refer to the upcoming section on finding rogue transactions for help in identifying unposted (or indeed, unpostable) transactions.

Year-End

Year-end has no special relevance except in General Ledger. In all of the other Applications, the first period of the new year is opened, and the last period of the old year is closed, in an identical manner to all other periods. In General Ledger, opening the first period of a new year triggers the calculation of the retained earnings figure. When you open the first period of the new year, Oracle General Ledger calculates the profit or loss, sets all revenue and expense account balances to zero, and posts the difference to the account defined in General Ledger setup as the retained earnings account. The application does this for each company segment in the entire chart of accounts. It recalculates the retained earnings if prior periods are open, and transactions are posted to prior period revenue or expense accounts.

NOTE
There is no year-end journal entry created by the open-period process. The account balances are modified, but no record is created of the account movements in the GL_ JE_LINES table. Why this is has always been somewhat of a mystery, as it undermines accounting convention and best practices.

Subledger Drill-Down and Audit Trails

A significant constraint imposed upon accounting systems is the ability to trace transactions from the General Ledger back to the subledger and from there to the source document (invoice, receipt, or whatever). Tracing can be facilitated by using the GL import references table. The audit trail itself can be made more explicit by using the Global Accounting Engine (GAE). Discrepancies between the General Ledger and feeder systems can be eradicated by freezing journals imported from external systems.

The Import References Table

The GL Import References table (GL_IMPORT_REFERENCES) is a bridge between journal lines and the subledger module or feeder system where they originated. The references are particularly useful if you import in summary mode, as they can then be used to trace back the group of feeder system records that were summarized into one single journal line. To make use of the GL Import References table, you must switch the feature on—this is controlled by an option (Import Journal References Yes/No) on the Define Journal Entry Sources window. If you transfer postings from Oracle Receivables or Oracle Payables in summary mode, it is vital to keep the GL import references; otherwise, you are missing a crucial part of the audit trail from General Ledger back to the subledgers.

NOTE
By default, the sources Payables and Receivables have the option Import Journal References set to No.

The data retained in the GL_IMPORT_REFERENCES table is used by standard reports such as the Account Analysis with Subledger Detail. The information is also accessed by inquiry zooms in order to drill down from a journal entry line to a transaction in the subledger.

The information stored varies according to the type of subledger transaction. Essentially the GL_IMPORT_REFERENCES table takes the columns REFERENCE_1,…,REFERENCE_10 as whatever was in the GL_INTERFACE columns REFERENCE21,…REFERENCE30. When you import data from a feeder system you are at liberty to choose how you populate these columns. The choice, however, is predetermined for data derived from subledgers. Table 18-1 shows the population rules for transactions transferred from Oracle Payables and Oracle Receivables.

The Global Accounting Engine

The Global Accounting Engine (GAE) is an optional plug-in for Oracle Financials that was developed to counter some perceived weaknesses in the base product. These features are not an issue for American or U.K. companies, or any company that operated Anglo-American accounting practices. Other countries, notably Italy and France, impose stronger audit requirements which cannot readily be met by the standard features of the software. Italy requires sequential document numbering, while France imposes a statutory chart of accounts. The GAE has been introduced to cope with such issues.

The GAE enhances the controllability of subledger postings to General Ledger and provides a complete audit trail from journal entries back to the originating subledger detail transactions, even for transferred summary transactions. The main features of the GAE are as follows:

- **Control Accounts** Allows control accounts to be secured so that only the subledgers can post journals to them. This prevents direct manual entry on control accounts from General Ledger and thus ensures that the control account balance in the subledger matches the account balance in General Ledger. Manual entries in General Ledger to subledger control accounts was one reason for discrepancies between General Ledger and its associated subledgers.

- **Transaction Control** The journal entries created by the subledgers may be protected against update and deletion. This feature prevents users from interfering in the transfer process until the journal is posted in GL.

- **Audit Trails** A more robust audit trail from the journal entries in General Ledger back to the source subledger transactions.

App	Type	REF 1	REF 2	REF 3	REF 4	REF 5	REF 6	REF 7	REF 8	REF 9	REF 10
AP	Invoice liability	Supplier name	Invoice id	Distribution line number		Invoice number	AP INVOICES	Set of Books id			LIABILITY
AP	Invoice distribution	Supplier name	Invoice id	Distribution line number		Invoice number	AP INVOICES	Set of Books id			
AP	Payment liability	Supplier name	Invoice id	Check id	Check number	Invoice number	AP PAYMENTS	Set of Books id	Invoice line number	Payment id	LIABILITY
AP	Payment bank	Supplier name	Invoice id	Check id	Check number	Invoice number	AP PAYMENTS	Set of Books id	Invoice line number	Payment id	CASH
AR	Invoice	Posting Control id	Customer_trx id	Cust_trx_line_gl_dist id	Invoice number	Customer number	CUSTOMER	Customer id	INV/CM/DM/CB for invoices, credit memos, debit memos chargebacks		RA_CUST_TRX_TRX_LINE_GL_DIST
AR	Receipts	Posting Control id	Cash Receipt id	Cash Receipt history id	Receipt number			Customer number	MISC/TRADE		AR_CASH_RECEIPT_HISTORY
AR	Adjustments	Adjustments Posting Control id	Adjustment id	Adjustment id	Invoice number	Adjustment Type number		Customer number	ADJ		AR_ADJUSTMENTS

TABLE 18-1. *Information Held in the GL_IMPORT_REFERENCES Table*

How Does GAE Work?

Once GAE has been installed and set up, new GAE programs replace the standard subledger transfer programs from subledgers to General Ledger. The replacement programs create journal entries in General Ledger in a way that is defined by the user, that is to say, the content and format of journal entries transferred from subledgers can be customized. The principle behind the engine is that all accounting transactions (called *Events* in the Oracle documentation) can be classified and individually programmed by the user to create journal entries according to user-defined rules.

Enhanced Auditability Between General Ledger and Subledgers

General Ledger provides the ability to freeze journals that were imported from subledgers. If you choose to freeze journal entries that were transferred from a specific feeder system, then those journal entries will be unchangeable in General Ledger. This makes it easier to maintain an audit trail between the journal entries in General Ledger and the transactions in the feeder system.

Useful Accounting Workarounds

There are a variety of accounting transactions that are not immediately available in Oracle Financials. Most of these instances can be classified as annoyances rather than serious defects—the following sections are intended to describe the situations and provide tips on workarounds.

Cross-Ledger Transactions

In the base product, Receivables and Payables do not interact directly with each other. For example, customer and supplier master files and transactions are separate. This arrangement is an inconvenience when accounting for refunds because the cash is flowing in the opposite direction than normal. A supplier refund means that cash flows into the business, whereas Payables is designed to handle only the cash flowing out of the business. Another complication occurs when your suppliers are also customers.

Refunds to Customers

Customers who overpay an invoice, or pay one invoice twice, are due a refund. Many companies will absorb the overpayment as income if it is a small amount, but if customers demand refunds, as they will no doubt do for larger amounts, companies must be able to pay them. There are essentially three approaches for handling customer refunds:

- To issue a manual check, to record it in Receivables as a Debit Memo, and match the memo to the cash receipt.

- To persuade the customer to leave the cash "on-account" and apply it to the next open invoice.

- To create cross ledger postings to Oracle Payables, set the customer up as a supplier in Payables, and issue a check out of payables in the normal way.

Which approach you choose will depend on considerations like the volume of refunds you have to administer and the impact on your bank reconciliation. The third option is more labor intensive, but it will make bank reconciliation a good deal easier, as all checks will be found in the same place. In order to create the cross ledger postings you will need to create a pair of transactions, one in Receivables and the other in Payables. Be sure to nominate a suitable cross ledger clearing account to post through. Imagine starting off with an overpayment in Oracle Receivables. This would appear as follows in the customer Account Inquiry:

Receivables Transaction	Debit	Credit
Cash receipt		12,000

The next step is to create a correlated pair of transactions, a Debit Memo in Receivables to clear the customer's account, and a quasi-invoice in Payables to represent the fact that the customer (who must also be set up as a supplier) is owed $12,000. The Account Inquiry would now appear as follows:

Receivables Transaction	Debit	Credit
Cash receipt		12,000
Debit memo	12,000	
Payables Transactions	**Debit**	**Credit**
Invoice		12,000

Finally, the Payables invoice would be picked up and paid in the normal way by Oracle Payables.

REMEMBER
The Debit Memo/Invoice combination must be created in pairs. This requirement can be enforced by posting the contra posting of each through a clearing account. The clearing account should always show a zero balance.

Refunds from Suppliers

Care must be taken with supplier refunds, as there are many circumstances that lead to their creation. For instance, the supplier may decide to give you a discount after you have remitted your payment and sends a refund. Other reasons for supplier refunds are as follows:

- The invoice has already been paid. (This implies that the same invoice exists twice in Oracle Payables.)

- The payment amount was too high. (This implies that the invoice amount had been incorrectly keyed.)

- The payment was sent to the wrong supplier. (This implies that the invoice was incorrectly entered.)

There is no single application screen designed to record supplier refunds in Payables, but there are two possible workarounds. Refunds can be simply entered as credit memos in Oracle Payables or as a receipt in Receivables, with a cross ledger transaction to be applied to the appropriate supplier account.

Although the second method is more lengthy, you are normally forced to follow this route because the incoming check payment is processed by the accounts receivable department, which will often enter it first and only later establish that it is a supplier refund rather than a customer receipt.

A credit memo entered into Payables would create these postings:

Account	Derivation of the Account Flexfield	Debit	Credit
Liability	You take this from the invoice that was paid twice.		35
Distribution	The bank cash account where the check was cleared.	35	

Netting of Supplier and Customer Accounts

Netting occurs when a trading partner is both a supplier and a customer. If this is a one-time occurrence, it will typically be ignored—the receivable and the liability can be treated separately. There are industries where netting is normal practice and the sums involved can be significant. Agency-type businesses typically perform netting. An agent sells a product on behalf of the manufacturer and in doing so receives a commission. When the product is shipped, the company bills the agent for the product in Receivables. When the product is sold, the agent invoices the company and this liability is recorded in Payables. The net of the payable and receivable is the agent's commission.

The ability to link a supplier and customer through reporting was made available in Release 10.6. Currently, the only function of this feature allows you to run a Supplier/Customer Netting Report. The report determines like suppliers/customers based on the Join Criteria you provided at runtime. The options are name (where your supplier and customer names must be identical), NIF Code, and VAT/Tax Code.

While not a complete solution, the netting report at least provides you with a list of suppliers/customers eligible for netting along with the associated payables and receivables balances and the net amount. Check your accounting policies—some companies do not net supplier liability and customer receivables as a matter of principle.

Transfer to Doubtful Debt

Most companies track their overdue receivables diligently, requesting that customers provide full payment on the overdue amounts. Sometimes payment is unlikely, and the debt is classified as *doubtful*, meaning there is good reason to believe it will never be collected. Alternatively, it will be written off completely as a bad debt. In Oracle Financials, handling bad debt is straightforward: you create an AR adjustment against the invoice, reducing the amount due on the invoice to zero, and then select an appropriate Bad Debt Write-off expense account to which you post the amount.

TIP
Set up a Bad Debt customer profile with a zero credit limit. Then, whenever you must write off a customer's invoices, immediately change his or her profile to "Bad Debt" to prevent further credit sales to that customer.

Doubtful debt on the other hand is somewhere between a healthy receivable and a bad debt write-off. Doubtful debt accounting—invoices remain open and show on the customers account, no longer posting to the normal Trade Receivables account, but rather to a Doubtful Debt account—is hard to mimic in Oracle Financials. Some companies are content to change the customer profile to Doubtful Debt Customer and then use reports to track these customers. Doing this does not of course move the receivables from Trade Receivables to Doubtful Debt in General Ledger. One way to move the receivables to Doubtful Debt is to close the original invoice with a credit memo and enter a new debit memo for the customer with the Doubtful Debt receivables account. Manual controls must be put in place to ensure that the credit memo and debit memo are always created in pairs and that the same revenue account is used for both memos.

Segment-Level Security

The recognized standard technique for restricting user access to specific accounts involves the use of *segment-level security*. This technique works on ranges of Accounting Flexfield segment values and blocks out forbidden ranges for Responsibilities that are not authorized to use those accounts. Segment-level security is a powerful technique that is often overlooked. Security rules can be used to prevent keying errors. A Responsibility is associated to a set of books, and a set of books is associated with one or more company codes. Without segment-level security, it is theoretically possible to log into the ACME U.S. Corporate set of books and enter a journal with the company code ACME Switzerland S.A. Such cross bookings can easily be prevented using segment-level security.

Segment-level security is not just active for online work. Standard reports running in the Concurrent Manager observe the same segment-level security rules. In that context, the report will include financial data only for the segment values that you can access. The GLDI product also fully supports and enforces segment-level security rules.

Flexible Date Format

The standard date format in Oracle Financials is dependent on the value of the NLS_DATE_FORMAT (which is set in the Oracle.ini file). The value will be set to either DD-MON-YY or DD-MON-RR. This setting controls the default date setting within the database and the application. In some circumstances you would like to be able to change the date format—doing this, though, is not possible. A format like DDMMCCYY can be entered quickly and thus increases user productivity. This restriction on date formats is imposed by the application and not by the database. In fact, the Oracle Database is very accommodating when it comes to date formats. People have mistakenly thought that changing the database date format variable will magically change the application date format, but, sadly, this is not true. If you alter the NLS_FORMAT_DATE you risk encountering application code errors. Oracle Development and Support have clearly stated that they do not support any date formats other than DD-MON-YY or DD-MON-RR.

If you are a Forms 2.3 character mode user, your forms will simply not work. If you use Forms 4.5 10SC, the forms may appear to work, but intermittently return obscure Oracle errors. The worst scenario is that the application will silently misinterpret the date values entered. This result is often the case since many forms within Oracle Applications have their date fields defined to nine characters, or they attempt to apply a date mask of DD-MON-YY or DD-MON-RR.

Automatic Job Submission

Often you want to be able to resubmit a report on a daily basis and have an input parameter in the report automatically populated with the current date at runtime; today's date today, and tomorrow's date tomorrow, and so on. Unfortunately, despite some powerful Concurrent Manager features that come very close to achieving this, it is not possible using the standard features alone. Two features partially meet the requirement: automatic resubmission and the parameter $SYSDATE$.

Automatic Resubmission

Whenever you submit a concurrent program you have the option of specifying resubmission options, which include a date or interval when the concurrent program will be resubmitted. The resubmitted program will inherit the parameter values from the original submission to the Concurrent Manager. (The resubmission process is explained in Chapter 5.)

Defaulting the Current Date

When registering a concurrent program in the Application Object Library, you may set the default value of an input parameter to be the current date. The value returned is the current system date, similar to "select sysdate from dual," and the format depends on the length defined for the parameter. A length of 9 returns *DD-MON-YY,* and a length of 11 returns *DD-MON-YYYY.* If this default is used in combination with the option to hide a report submission parameter so the user cannot modify the parameter value, you can ensure that the date parameter is always the current date. There is, however, one caveat. The default value type of current date placeholder derives its value when the program is first submitted by the user, and not when the program executes. As a result, if you use current date as a default value and automatic resubmission together, each subsequent resubmission of the program uses the date of the first submission as the date parameter. There seems no way to coax the application into taking the execution date as the date parameter so that each day the program runs it will use the actual date as a parameter.

An elegant solution to this problem involves building a custom extension to the Application Object Library that allows specific concurrent program parameters to be registered as recurring date parameters. A background program (itself a concurrent program that is resubmitted daily) would look through all the jobs waiting on the queue, and, if any were recognized as having recurring date parameters, the parameter string in FND_ CONCURRENT_PROGRAMS would be incremented to set the date appropriately.

Matching and Carry-Forward in GL

Matching and carry-forward are accounting processes that in specific situations can be very important. Matching and carry-forward are particularly critical in a manual bookkeeping system but are not entirely superfluous in a computerized accounting system. Indeed, some of the features in General Ledger come very close to accommodating this process. The GL Account Reconciliation, provided as part of the Regional Globalizations, is aimed at journal line matching. However, none of the features convey the elegance or simplicity of the manual equivalent. Fundamentally, there are two types of accounts in bookkeeping. Some accounts carry forward their balance at period-end, others carry forward all open postings that make up the balance.

Accounts That Carry Forward Balances

At the end of each period, the account is closed by totaling all the debits and credits in the account and entering a journal, either a debit or credit, that will ensure that the debits equal the credits and thereby bring the account balance to zero. The counter entry to this journal is the first entry in the next period for that account, that is, the opening balance for the account.

Accounts That Carry Forward Open Items

The alternative to carrying the balance forward is to carry forward all entries that are not matched. A matched entry is one that has been matched to a corresponding debit or credit. A constellation of matched entries has a combined balance of zero. The actual balance of an account is the same whichever of the two methods you choose to apply.

There is no concept of *matching* in General Ledger. Period-end works as a modified combination of both "carry-forward balances" and "carry-forward open items." In Oracle General Ledger all accounts have a carried-forward balance, and all previous journal entries in previous periods are retained to justify that balance.

Much of the time, the absence of matching and carry-forward for open items is not a problem. However, for some specific accounts, like a check clearing account, such a feature would be very useful.

Troubleshooting Common Problems

Rogue data—records that have become corrupt, are stuck in an interface, or simply cannot proceed to the next step—can be extremely difficult to locate. If the data exception is not listed on a standard report or cannot be queried in a standard screen, the only way to identify the problem data is to develop an ad-hoc SQL*Plus script to pull out what is needed. Almost every consultant who works with Oracle Applications has a toolbox of scripts that have built up over the years. Many of these are on-off and unique to a specific set of company data and therefore of limited appeal. Those described here are more generic and have universal appeal. In the majority of cases, these scripts are needed only to locate the rogue data. Once the data has been identified, the cause can be rectified using the normal screens. Before you consider modifying Financials data you must consider carefully the consequences, both for data auditability and for the integrity of the system.

Some setup data simply should not be altered—the referential integrity of the whole database may be broken, producing unpredictable results. Should you need to change these settings, your best option is probably to re-implement the system in a fresh database. Re-implementation of a live system cannot be taken lightly, and this option normally rules itself out as being too extravagant.

Some other setups can be modified even if they resist update by conventional techniques. In the same way that a safe *should* not open without a key, an experienced locksmith can crack a safe. Similarly, some application setups *should* not normally be changed, but if the circumstances warrant, unconventional action can be justified. For example, you might need to add an extra segment to the Accounting Flexfield, or you might want to change from 12 to 13 calendar periods. These are legitimate requests from dynamic companies that are continually seeking to restructure their organization and improve their internal operations. They crop up from time to time—the ethos of this section can be summed up as "I'll look into that" rather than "It cannot be done." The scripts provided in this section do not modify any data.

Identifying Customizations Prior to an Upgrade

Chapter 15 describes the difference between customization and modification. Customizations relate to setting parameters within the Applications. However there are two ways to go about customization:

- **Customization by Extension**   You add new applications, responsibilities, menus, forms, reports, etc. to the base package.

- **Customization by Modification**   You modify an existing seeded component (responsibilities, menus, reports, etc.).

On the whole, extensions are to be encouraged, and modifications are to be discouraged. Modifications earn the accolade "quick and dirty" and, apart from a few special cases, can be avoided. The distinction is particularly relevant when you come to do an Applications upgrade. Extensions will survive the upgrade while modifications will not and will likely be completely deleted from the system. The drastic behavior of the upgrade process results from the way Oracle Applications populates seed setup data when the Applications are installed. Simplistically stated, the seeded rows are given low value row ids, and the sequence for the row ids is set to some high value.

When Oracle Applications is upgraded from one release to a higher release, all the seeded setup data from the source release is deleted and replaced with the new seeded data of the target release. That is to say that modifications to the seeded data can get wiped out. There is no simple way to identify seeded data when you review setup through the application forms. One way is to access the Row Who information for each row— seeded data will be created by a user called AUTOINSTALL.

The traditional technique for identifying the modifications prior to an upgrade was to perform a test upgrade with a copy of the production system, then comb through the upgraded system to see what has been overwritten. The laboriousness of this technique was the motivation to develop the upcoming script. It sifts through every table in the database looking for data created by AUTOINSTALL and updated by someone else.

The script works by selecting table names from the system tables. (The script has to be run by the system database user, on a pre-upgraded database.) A dynamic SQL file is created containing the necessary select statements. The full script is available on the Osborne Web server; the SQL statement at the heart of the process is listed here:

```
COL user_id NEW_VALUE autoinstall_user_id
SELECT user_id
FROM    applsys.fnd_user
WHERE   user_name = 'AUTOINSTALL';
SELECT 'PROMPT '||owner||'.'||table_name||CHR(10)||'SELECT * FROM
'||owner||'.'||table_name|| ' WHERE created_by = &autoinstall_user_id and
last_updated_by != &autoinstall_user_id;'
FROM    all_tab_columns
WHERE   column_name = 'CREATED_BY'
AND     (owner, table_name) in (SELECT t.owner, t.table_name
                                FROM   all_tab_columns tc, all_tables t
                                WHERE  column_name = 'LAST_UPDATED_BY'
                                AND    tc.owner = t.owner
                                AND    tc.table_name = t.table_name)
ORDER BY 1;
```

The script is extravagant in that it blindly selects from all tables in the database, whereas we know that some transaction tables never contain seeded data; this factor is more than compensated for by the fact that the script is independent of any particular release of Oracle Financials. It will work on Release 9, Release 10, or Release 11, or any dot release in between.

Inability to Close a Period

It can happen that after all the pre-close steps have been followed up and the GL transfer program has been run, when you attempt to close the period you cannot, because there remain unposted transactions. There could be legitimate reasons for this happening: In Oracle Payables, invoices will not be transferred if they have certain holds against them. In Inventory, uncosted transactions will prevent the period for a specific organization to be closed. These transactions need to be reviewed, modified, and transferred. Through an unknown series of events, transactions can get stuck and remain unpostable. When this happens, you first need to identify which particular transactions are causing the problem, then correct the transactions in a way that will get them picked up and transferred. In many cases, the rogue transactions will show up when you run one of the unposted reports. However there are certain situations where corrupted transactions do not show up. The next few sections show specific examples with SQL scripts for finding rogue transactions.

Identifying Unposted Journals

Before a period can be closed in General Ledger, the application checks to see that there are no unposted journals outstanding for that period. However, there may be data sitting in the Journal Import interface table (gl_interface) that is destined for the current period but has not been loaded yet. The following script summarizes all accounting transactions broken down by the accounting date, so that you can assess whether there are any journals pending before you close the period.[22]

```
select    USER_JE_SOURCE_NAME,ACCOUNTING_DATE,count(ACCOUNTING_DATE),
          sum(ACCOUNTED_DR),sum(ACCOUNTED_CR)
from      gl_interface
group by  USER_JE_SOURCE_NAME,ACCOUNTING_DATE
order by  ACCOUNTING_DATE,USER_JE_SOURCE_NAME;
```

Identifying Unpostable QuickCash

Batches of Receivables QuickCash receipts are entered, individual receipts applied and then posted within Receivables. Posting a QuickCash batch updates the customer account with the applied receipts and prevents the batch from being modified. Occasionally, when two users work on the same batch, one can have the batch open on screen while the other selects the batch for posting. Doing so will invariably leave orphaned receipt records in the AR_INTERIM_CASH_RECEIPT_LINES table. The following script will recover these:

```
select    PAYMENT_AMOUNT,LAST_UPDATE_DATE,BATCH_ID
from      AR_INTERIM_CASH_RECEIPT_LINES
where     CASH_RECEIPT_ID not in
          (select CASH_RECEIPT_ID from ar.AR_INTERIM_CASH_RECEIPTS);
```

---

[22]This and the other scripts that follow in this chapter should be run from the *apps* database schema.

Identifying Unposted Invoice Distributions

The following script will list all Payables invoices that have unposted distributions:

```
select    'Unposted invoice distribution' , ai.INVOICE_NUM
from      ap_invoice_distributions api,
ap_invoices ai
where     api.period_name = '&&period_name'
and       api.accounting_date between '&&start_date' and
'&&end_date'
and       api.accrual_posted_flag = 'N'
and       api.invoice_id = ai.invoice_id
order by  ai.INVOICE_NUM ;
```

Invalid Bank Accounts and EFT Programs

The Payables EFT programs look at the supplier tables to find the supplier's bank details. Increasingly, the globalized application validates bank details according to local rules to check the number of digits, or trailing check digits. Despite this practice, invalid bank account numbers can creep into the system, and invalid bank account numbers can cause the EFT program to error. This process is unable to write the error records to an exception file and continue processing the remainder. Instead, it fails the entire payment batch. Rather than cancel the batch and start again, it is possible to rescue the situation without repeating the entire payment run:

1. Correct the supplier bank account details.

2. Reset the status of EFT payment batch using the following script:

```
update    AP_INVOICE_SELECTION_CRITERIA
set       STATUS = 'BUILT'
where     CHECKRUN_NAME = '&batch_name' ;
```

3. Rerun the EFT formatting program.

NOTE
The AP_INVOICE_SELECTION_CRITERIA.STATUS column progresses through SELECTED, BUILT, FORMATTED, and CONFIRMED. On no account should the status of a batch be modified other than as in the script provided. Doing so would have unpredictable results, since all the other status changes are associated with related updates to invoice and payments. The payment batch control screen should be used for cancelling batches in a controlled manner.

Mass Update of Customer Information in Receivables

The following example shows how a standard Oracle interface, in this case the Receivables Customer Interface, can be used to do a mass update of incorrect customer information. The background to this script is that customer information had been loaded from a legacy system, but the customer profile information had been incorrectly mapped. The system had been live for several weeks when this was first noticed, so there was no chance to delete what they had and to repeat the data conversion from legacy. The script was a fast and efficient solution which, by making use of the customer interface, did not require any data modifications directly into the underlying Receivables tables. Thus, you are using the standard Oracle features.

```
insert into ra_customer_profiles_interface
(orig_system_customer_ref, insert_update_flag, CREDIT_HOLD,
customer_profile_class_name, orig_system_address_ref,
last_updated_by, last_update_date, created_by, creation_date)
select    ORIG_SYSTEM_REFERENCE, 'U', 'N',
'INTERCOMPANY', null,
172, sysdate, 172, sysdate
from      ra_customers
where     CUSTOMER_NUMBER like '99999%'
```

The intercompany customers had been loaded with an inappropriate profile class. The local convention was that all intercompany customers had customer numbers starting with 99,999. The following script identifies all such customers in the ra_customers table, and inserts a record in the Customer Interface table to signal that the customer's profile class should be updated to the desired value INTERCOMPANY.

The beauty of this approach is that the updates to the Receivables base tables are performed by the Customer Interface program and not by an SQL script, so that all the necessary validation and integrity checks are performed.

Mismatched Account Types

Account types (A = Asset, L = Liability, O = Owners Equity, E = Expense, R = Revenue) are held in two places: against each account code combination and against each account segment value. Two data problems can arise. Firstly, account segment values can be set up with an incorrect account type, and, secondly, there can be a mismatch where the account type on the combination does not match the account type of the account segment. The Oracle *General Ledger Reference Manual* contains a topical essay on how the misclassified accounts can be corrected.

The following script can be used to identify all mismatches of the second type. These mismatches will, if they do nothing else, lead to confusing behavior at year end when the profit and loss for the year is calculated and brought forward into the new financial year as retained earnings. The full script is available on the Osborne Website (**www.Osborne.com**); the extract here shows how a SQL script is built dynamically to correctly format the account code combination segments. Doing this is necessary because each implementation can have a different number of segments, and the segments can be stored in any order.

```
COL concatenated_segments format a55
SPOOL account_temp.sql
PROMPT SELECT code_combination_id, account_type,
SUBSTR(compiled_value_attributes, INSTR(compiled_value_attributes, CHR(10),
1, &account_segment_num-1)+1, 1), SUBSTR(''
SELECT '||''-''||''||application_column_name
FROM fnd_id_flex_segments
WHERE id_flex_code = 'GL#'
AND id_flex_num = &coa_id
AND enabled_flag = 'Y'
ORDER BY segment_num
```

```
/
PROMPT ,2 ) concatenated_segments FROM gl_code_combinations cc,
fnd_flex_values fv WHERE cc.&account_segment_name = fv.flex_value
AND SUBSTR(compiled_value_attributes, INSTR(compiled_value_attributes,
CHR(10), 1, &account_segment_num-1)+1, 1) != account_type
AND fv.flex_value_set_id = &account_value_set_id ORDER BY 1
PROMPT /
SPOOL OFF
SET HEAD ON
SET PAGES 60
SPOOL account_types
@account_temp
SPOOL OFF
```

Once all the misclassified accounts have been identified, they can be rectified in the way described in the reference manual.

Correcting Data Problems

Oracle strongly recommends that you never use database tools to modify Application tables or data. However, as a last resort in unique situations, you may have to update data directly in the database using SQL*Plus. Although we advocate this on occasion, it should always be a last resort, when all other avenues have been exhausted. As an alternative to SQL*Plus updates, consider doing the following:

■ Use the Examine tool to modify database columns.

■ Delete the incorrect data (using a form if possible) and rekey it.

Sometimes an SQL*Plus update is the fastest, most accurate and easiest way to correct data. If you do resort to SQL*Plus database updates, consider these pointers:

■ Use the Trace tool to find out what updates the application makes in a similar circumstance.

■ Perform the updates on a test database first.

■ Always have a good series of backups before updating a production database.

■ Obtain Oracle Support go-ahead for each individual script.

TIP
When making updates or inserts directly into the database, provide meaningful values for the who/when columns on the table. By doing this you will retain an accurate audit trail.

Improving Performance in a Live System

Oracle performance tuning in general and Applications tuning specifically are extensive subjects. This section does not attempt to cover these topics comprehensively—for an excellent overview refer to *Oracle Performance Tuning (Nutshell Handbook)*, by Mark Gurry and Peter Corrigan (O'Reilly & Associates, 1996).

This section itemizes some specific actions that can be taken to improve the performance and effectiveness of an Oracle Financials implementation.

Boosting the Hit Rate of Receivables Lockbox

Lockbox works by importing customer receipt information into Receivables from a bank file provided by your bank. The receipts are loaded into Receivables as QuickCash batches, but more often than not, Lockbox has been unable to identify the customer number or the invoice number. That condition leaves the receipt unidentified or unapplied in Receivables—there is still a considerable manual workload involved to first identify the receipt and to then go into Receivables and apply each one. The reason for the poor success rate is that the Lockbox has to find the reference field in precisely the right place or it will not be able to interpret the records correctly. Usually, the bank does provide the relevant identification data (customer number, invoice numbers), but the text is free format and cannot easily be used by Lockbox.

One effective way of increasing the hit rate is to preprocess the Lockbox bank file to sift out the good reference data and place it in a fixed format place in the file ready for the automatic Lockbox program to pick it up and interpret it. The following case study is of a German company working with a file from the Deutsche Bank. The hit rate was increased from 0 percent to 60 percent, and up to eight invoice numbers could be applied with one receipt. This one program was a great success and over the long term allowed three people from a department of fifteen to be reassigned to more valuable work.

Program Descriptions

The essence of the design is that the bank file is preprocessed using Unix shell commands to increase the readable data in the free form text fields, loaded into the Receivables Interface tables, and then post-processed to remove as many exception records as possible before the standard Lockbox interface is run to import the records. This is shown schematically in Figure 18-1.

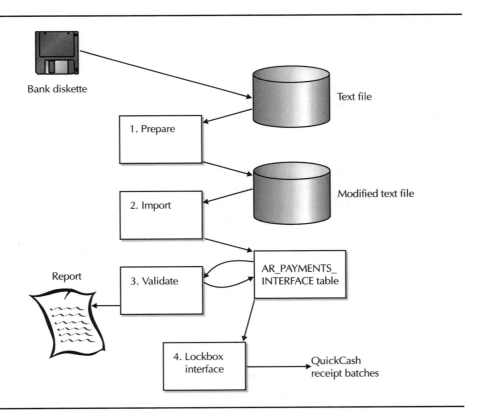

FIGURE 18-1.   *The extended Lockbox process*

In addition to the standard Receivables Lockbox load and import programs, shown as Processes 2 and 4 in Figure 18-1, there are two supplementary processes: one to preprocess the data file (Process 1) and the other to post-process (Process 3). In combination, these two processes recover and clean up as much useful data from the bank file as is possible. In detail, the four processes are:

- **prepare.sh**   A Unix shell script that works on the data file.

- **import.ctl**   An SQL*Loader control file that loads the data file into the ar_payments_interface database table.

- **validate.sql**   An SQL*Plus script that removes invalid invoice numbers and produces a listing of the data records that have been imported.

- **Lockbox**   The standard Receivables Lockbox process, which creates receipt information from the data in the interface table.

After each banking day a data file is received from the bank. This could be either on disk or transmitted via modem or the Internet to the receiving computer. The data file contains all incoming bank transfers and all outgoing checks from the company's main bank account.

The customer may have provided his or her customer account number or the invoice numbers of the invoices he is paying. The customer may be paying several invoices with one receipt. The Lockbox interface can deal with an unlimited number of invoice applications for each receipt. This particular implementation was designed to cope with up to eight invoice numbers. This considerably simplified the work involved, as all eight invoice numbers can be formatted on the same ar_payments_interface record without needing to have multiple extension records for one receipt.

The text that the customer provides is free-format text; no reference that they might provide will be in a fixed position within the file. We do not know what we are looking for, and we do not know where it will be in the file. The human eye is generally very good at scanning data files and picking out numbers that might be, say, customer numbers or invoice numbers. The computer has to be taught the hard way. The purpose of the Prepare script is to find all numbers that could be candidates for customer number or invoice numbers. It marks each customer number by placing a < (less than) symbol immediately before them in the file; each invoice number is marked with =

(an equal sign). In this particular implementation of Lockbox, the patterns listed in Table 18-2 can be recognized. (Clearly, at any other site, the length and format of the numbers you are looking for will be different, and the script will have to be modified accordingly.)

Once these candidates have been identified, one customer number and up to eight invoice numbers are moved to fixed positions within the file, so that these can later be picked up by SQL*Loader. At this stage the numbers identified are only candidates; validation later on will determine if they are indeed recognized as customer numbers or invoice numbers.

The sed script reproduced here (part of the prepare program) is the brains behind the entire process and works by performing a series of exhaustive character matches.

```
s/[^0-9]\(3[0-9]\{7\}[^0-9]\)/<\1/g
/[^0-9]\([1-46][0-9]\{6\}[^0-9]\)/<\1/g
s/[^0-9]\(9[0-9]\{7\}[^0-9]\)/=\1/g
s/[^0-9]\(2[0-9]\{8\}[^0-9]\)/=\1/g
s/[^0-9]\(1[0-9]\{9\}[^0-9]\)/=\1/g
s/^\(.\{13\}\)\(.\{18\}\)/\1                         /g
s/^\(.\{13\}\)\(.\{8\}\)\(.*\)\(<\)\([0-9]\{8\}\)/\1\5\3\4\5/g
s/^\(.\{13\}\)\(.\{8\}\)\(.*\)\(<\)\([0-9]\{7\}\)\([^0-9]\)/\1\5 \3\4\5\6/g
s/^\(.\{21\}\)\(.\{10\}\)\(.*\)\(=\)\(1[0-9]\{9\}\)\([^0-9]\)/\1\5\3\4\5\6/g
s/^\(.\{21\}\)\(.\{10\}\)\(.*\)\(=\)\(9[0-9]\{7\}\)\([^0-9]\)/\1DE\5\3\4\5\6/g
s/^\(.\{21\}\)\(.\{10\}\)\(.*\)\(=\)\(2[0-9]\{8\}\)\([^0-9]\)/\1\5 \3\4\5\6/g
```

The syntax for a sed search-and-replace can be visually confusing because so many characters have to be escaped with a backslash (\) in order to give them a special meaning in the search string. Details of sed and awk can be found in the excellent reference *UNIX Power Tools* by Jerry Peek, Tim O'Reilly, et al (O'Reilly & Associates, 1993).

Length	Characteristic	Type of Number	Marker
8 Digits	Starts with a 3	Customer number	<
7 Digits	Starts with 1, 2, 3, 4, or 6	Customer number	<
8 Digits	Starts with a 9	Invoice number	=
9 Digits	Starts with a 2	Invoice number	=
10 Digits	Starts with a 1	Invoice number	=

TABLE 18-2. *Numeric Patterns That Can Be Recognized*

Once the markers are in the file, it is a straightforward process to move the candidate numbers to fixed positions within the file. Only then can they be picked up and processed by SQL*Loader.

The validate program is quite lengthy, so it has not been reproduced here, although a copy of it can be found on the Osborne Website. It essentially validates the candidate invoice and customer numbers against the Oracle Receivables base tables and removes those that are invalid.

Rebuilding Interface Tables

Rows are continually being inserted into and deleted from interface tables (and some other tables within the Applications). Unless the DBA has taken permanent steps to avoid it, this practice will result in fragmentation. Check interface tables for fragmentation, and if there is a problem, get the DBA to rebuild the table by exporting and importing it. This needs to be done offline. The following tables should be routinely monitored:

GL_INTERFACE	Journal Import table
AR_PAYMENTS_INTERFACE	Lockbox table

Running the GL Optimizer

Optimizing General Ledger is particularly important after creating a significant number of new account code combinations. The GL Optimizer gathers information about the number and range of account code combinations. It might determine that the account and cost center segments are very selective, whereas the company segment is not. This information is stored and then later used to improve query performance for long-running processes like FSG report generator and consolidation. These programs are cleverly written to produce dynamic SQL based on the data statistics unearthed by the Optimizer. If you don't run the Optimizer, these programs may be running suboptimally. The GL Optimizer is a primitive cost-based optimizer that the Oracle Financials developers created several years before a cost-based optimization option was introduced into the Oracle RDBMS (first introduced in Version 7). The GL Optimizer, as with all Financials code, is intended for execution with the RDBMS running in rule-based optimization mode.

Concurrent Manager Queue Design

A production environment with the default Concurrent Manager set up will have one Concurrent Manager queue, with a limit of, say, eight jobs that can be running at any one time. It's possible that the queue may become backed up with eight long-running reports that are all at the top of the queue. Long-running programs tend to monopolize the top of the queue precisely because they are long running. Once they get there they stay there. They may take several hours to complete (this is not at all unreasonable for some long-running analysis reports, like the Receivables Aged Trial Balance, or a complex General Ledger FSG report—it is not necessarily indicative of a poorly tuned system or underpowered hardware). However, during their running time no other jobs, even if they are short-running, can advance to the top of the queue and be processed. A bottleneck is particularly irksome for time critical jobs—the user typically waits for the job to finish and then checks that it has completed successfully before moving onto the next activity. A delay at the top of the Concurrent Manager queue can be totally unacceptable.

The solution is to set up a separate queue for quick-running programs and then apply specialization rules to allow only specific jobs to process in that queue. Such jobs as Receivables Post QuickCash, the Payables Approval program, and Pick and Pack Slips, for which the users need to see the results in a short turnaround, are ideal candidates. You may also want to create a queue for reports, such as FSGs, that will process only after-hours. This will allow users to submit the reports all day, but they will wait to process, freeing up system resources during critical business hours. This procedure can be accomplished by setting that queue's workshift to process only outside of normal hours.

Conclusion

Live operation brings sharply into focus operational issues that receive low priority during implementation. A finance system is not truly bedded in until it has been through the first year-end. The systems emphasis then shifts towards support and the database administrator. Over time, a business becomes familiar with the day-to-day processing, and interest shifts to less frequent activities such as year-end procedures and audit. Users' know-how increases rapidly and demand builds up for improved systems performance, cutting out unnecessary manual effort and generally streamlining the accounting operation. This chapter has sought to show that expertise and know-how is important for some time after an Oracle Financials system has been put live. We have seen concrete examples of database scripts that can be used to locate hard-to-access data, how interfaces can be implemented to drastically reduce manual workload, and how the database can be tuned to improve online response times and systems performance.

APPENDIX

Overview of Other Oracle Applications

The focus of this book is the Financial Applications, the more mature products at the core of the product line. Since two of the major attractions of Oracle are integration and a common architecture, the other packages merit a brief discussion. The Oracle Applications share data internally and present a common look and feel to the user. The incremental cost of ownership of an additional Applications module is low. All the Applications make use of the same Oracle development tools, and Applications upgrades can be applied to the entire integrated system. Support and maintenance costs are thereby reduced. Most of the products described here are new. With the exception of Manufacturing, these modules were developed from their inception to take advantage of Smart Client, Web, and Workflow.

The Customer Suite

Oracle Receivables and Order Entry are the cornerstones of the customer-oriented product series. They maintain shared customer master data and handle customer transactions from the point of order entry through billing and collection. Sales Analysis and Marketing Compensation use sales transaction data to drive other corporate processes.

Oracle Sales Compensation

The compensation plan drives your sales force. You structure the plan to put differing emphasis on different classes of business, and the salespeople respond by putting their efforts into bringing in the business that is most lucrative for them.

Sales Compensation tags each sales order line with a revenue class category. You can define these on the basis of any combination of customer, product, service, industry, and market. Many companies, for example, give greater credit for sales to new accounts, for sales of strategic new products, or for sales in a strategically important industry. Such plans give salespeople the incentive to develop their knowledge of new products and new sets of customers. At its simplest, the quota credit for a sale equals the monetary amount of the sale times the compensation factor associated with the revenue class.

You can use a variety of sales agents, including a direct sales force, distributors, and external agents, each with their own plan. Representatives from more than one channel may participate in a given sale. The credit can be shared. For example, a matrixed sales organization may team an industry representative, a product specialist, and a territorial representative to land one sale. The three could share credit by splitting the revenue among themselves, or each of the three could get full credit for it, or the sales plan could specify some other formula for assigning quota credit.

A company can recognize revenue at different points in the sales cycle, usually when an order is booked, when it is shipped and invoiced, and when the invoice is paid. Salespeople can likewise be credited with commission at these points, or the commission can be made payable in fractions at all three stages. The decision depends on the level of follow-through required from the salespeople.

Sales plans give money, but they can also take it back. The plan may pay salespeople a base salary or may pay a draw against future commissions. It may deduct commissions for sales that are canceled, returned, or not collected.

Most organizations set sales quotas for their representatives and pay commissions on the basis of quota attainment. A sales representative may have several quotas, such as new accounts, product lines, and services. A given sale may apply to more than one quota. Compensation under each quota is a factor of the size of the sale and the plan for rewarding quota achievement. There may be sliding scales. A plan might state that each percentage of quota attainment up to 100 percent is worth $100; each point between 100 percent and 125 percent is worth $150, and all points over 125 percent of quota attainment are worth $200.

Oracle Receivables transactions drive sales compensation. Order Entry collects the applicable data, such as the price list, salesperson, and revenue class, by the time an order is booked. It passes the data through to Receivables for invoicing and collection, and Receivables passes it to Sales Compensation. Since Oracle Receivables is the system that feeds the General Ledger, making it the gatekeeper ensures that sales compensation ties out to actual revenue flows.

Tuning a sales compensation plan is a tricky business, and often the problems are legion. Salespeople are notorious for exploiting ill-conceived compensation schedules. Representatives who are paid on business volume can "give away the store" with large amounts of unprofitable business. Ross Perot supposedly left IBM one January after attaining his maximum possible compensation for the year in the first month (he went on to build EDS and to found Perot Systems). Oracle Marketing Compensation has a powerful, graphic modeling facility that allows you to visualize the results of different sales scenarios. You want to be sure your salespeople are paid well enough, but not more than necessary, and that they are motivated to carry the company towards its strategic product goals.

Sales Compensation turns the complex rules you give for computing sales commissions into PL/SQL code, which you can access. It gives you the opportunity to review and modify the programmed logic to be sure you get exactly what you want.

CAUTION

If you do modify the generated code, you have to reapply your changes each time you change the compensation rules and regenerate it, and complex plans can take a while to execute.

Oracle Sales and Marketing

Sales and Marketing handles presales activity, generating leads, identifying prospects, and managing and tracking contacts. It supports telemarketing, team selling, and customer base management. The system is designed for disconnected client operations. Your representatives can enter their call notes and plans on a laptop, then upload them later. Oracle Sales and Marketing lets you target qualified prospects, manage demand-creation, fulfill literature requests, and track campaign effectiveness. Qualified leads are automatically transferred to your salespeople for immediate action.

The relationships among prospects are varied and complex. You deal with different people and departments within the same organization and with organizations that are related to each other in any number of ways. Sales territories are defined along these imprecise boundaries. Sales and Marketing's schema for managing prospects not only handles prospect relationships, it also offers constructive support in sorting them out.

Contacts are the lifeblood of a sales organization. You need to know who they are, how they are related to each other, who all has called on them, what the results were, what you have promised them, and what your next steps are. It is essential for all members of a sales team to share what they know, so they present a common face to the prospect. There is an automated link with Order Entry's shipping module to ship materials such as literature, kits, and trial packages.

Other systems are affected as prospects turn into clients. Sales and Marketing carries the information that will be needed by Order Entry and Sales Compensation when an order is booked. It draws on product availability information from Oracle Shipping

Sales drive the rest of your business, whether you provide products or services. The company makes its plans for future periods on the best estimates from the sales force. Sales and Marketing rolls up data on opportunities–how much, when, what, and how probable—into forecasts that can be used by Oracle Inventory and Manufacturing.

Oracle Call Center

Call scripting is a requirement unique to telemarketing. Traditional scripts exist on paper, but a database is a much better tool to follow the various paths a call may as determined by a prospect's responses. Oracle Call Center can guide representatives through incoming and outgoing calls, collect information along the way, and fulfill requests for literature and follow-up.

The Oracle Call Center suite features a new application, Oracle Telephony Server, that provides telephone access to all information contained in the Applications for inbound or outbound calling functions. Users can manage high-volume centralized or distributed call center environments and can also operate blended-function, service and sales call centers.

The Human Resources Suite

Oracle's Human Resources suite turns a prosaic record keeping function into an area of strategic advantage. People represent the most significant element of cost for most companies, and their performance is essential to success. Oracle applications manage all aspects of hiring, training, managing and compensating your staff. Because organization and personnel information is used by almost all Oracle applications, elements of Oracle Human Resources are present in every installation.

Payroll is the transaction-oriented system that handles the financial side of personnel—paying them. It also handles the financial side of deductions.

Oracle Payables, the other payments system in the Applications family, also does payments to people. It commonly handles expense reimbursements and sometimes commission checks and benefits payments, such as tuition payments to educational institutions. Payroll may need to account for the tax liabilities due on payments through Oracle Payables, and it may be used as a vehicle for expense reimbursements.

Oracle Human Resources

HR sees people in the context of the jobs and positions they fill within organizations. It maintains the Multi-Org hierarchy used throughout Oracle Applications. HR does a thorough job of tracking the time dimension. It is able to reconstruct the organizational structure, and the way it was staffed, at any point in history.

The way in which people are mapped to the organization becomes increasingly bureaucratic as an organization grows. Jobs in a large concern are usually described generically—"Payables Supervisor" or "Warehouse Manager," for example. Job classifications are necessary for relating similar functions in different parts of the organization, and for standardizing job requirements and pay grades. Positions are instances of jobs within a given organization. They figure into headcount and salary budgets. Your organization may have positions for three Payables Clerks. Lastly, people fill positions, and not always exactly. The HR system has to accommodate the fact that the job title of an incumbent may differ from the job description for the position.

Not all organizations make careful distinctions among jobs, positions, and people and it is not required to do so in Oracle Applications. You can, for instance, define an approval workflow either by people or positions. The term "role" is used in this broader context. As one example, you need to tell Web Customers who it is that fills the role of removing orders from a credit hold. You determine in advance whether you will assign the role using a person's name or a position name.

Self-Service Human Resources extends the power of Oracle Human Resources to managers in the field and their employees. It provides workflow control over major HR activities such as hiring and performance appraisals. It also offers self-service support so employees can take control by updating their own records and arranging their own training.

You define qualifications, grade, and pay structures for jobs and positions. This standardization, to the degree you implement it, offers objective criteria for hiring and for rewarding employees with raises and promotions. Records of individual employees show their past, present, and projected salaries, benefits, and monetary awards.

Salary administration is the immensely sensitive matter of determining each employee's worth to the company and compensating them appropriately. Oracle Human Resources provides the tools you need to compare and plan employee compensation based on job descriptions, performance, geography, seniority and a host of other variables.

Regardless of the merits of individual employees, proposed salaries are constrained by budget considerations. Oracle Human Resources provides the base figures needed to feed the General Ledger budgeting process, and the tools to apply whatever adjustments are dictated by the budget. You can do detail-level salary planning in a spreadsheet.

Competency Management is the process of matching skills to requirements. Oracle Human Resources is able to match people's skills, training and experience against job requirements. Storing definitions of the organization's goals and core competencies, Human Resources supports hiring, assessments and appraisals, and individual development to enable the company to grow the talent needed to support its strategic directions.

The first impression a candidate has of your company is through your recruiting. You have to evaluate a candidate, assess the fit between him and the company, and sell him on joining. Oracle Human Resources manages candidates' applications, resumes, referrals and other data. It keeps a record of contacts you have had with the candidate. It keeps the data you need to statistically evaluate your recruiting efforts.

Each organization within a company may be slightly different with regard to personnel policy. Certainly each country has different laws and customs. Acquired organizations may retain some of their own character, but may in other ways be made to conform with the parent. Different divisions and departments may have their own characteristics. Oracle Human Resources has the subtlety and flexibility to manage your company it is. Virtually all Oracle applications use organization data from HR, even if HR is not installed and used by your company. A great many use information about specific people. Purchasing identifies buyers; Order Entry, Sales Compensation, and Sales and Marketing have salespeople; Bill of

Materials uses the hourly rate for people in defined positions to set standard costs; WIP captures the actual costs of human resources consumed in manufacturing. Projects computes project cost on the basis of the actual salary paid to an employee and standard costs for a position. Payroll pays people. All workflow processes have to identify people or positions in the approval process. Human Resources has more integration points than any system besides General Ledger.

Government takes a major interest in issues of employment. Human Resources produces a wide range of statutory reports. In the U.S. these include COBRA, OSHA, ADA, EEO, AAP, and Vets-100.

Oracle Payroll

Payroll applies Human Resources data to salaries and benefits to compute how much to pay and how to get the payment to the employee. Payroll management is an extremely demanding business function, highly complex, highly visible, and time-critical. The tax rules encoded in a payroll system are country specific. Oracle Payroll is supports national tax codes and regulations throughout the world.

Gross pay can be determined by salary, timecards, and payments such as commissions and awards. There can be any number of deductions to arrive at net pay. Many different types of rules govern deductions. To name a few obvious ones: income tax is proportional to income; medical insurance is usually a fixed amount; social security tax has an annual cap; loan repayments end when the obligation is fulfilled; garnished wages may be governed by rules specific to a jurisdiction. Deducted money has to be accounted for, consolidated for all employees, and sent to the agency on behalf of which it was deducted.

Income tax levels are set by different levels of jurisdiction: federal, state, and local. The rules can get complex, with factors such as reciprocity between the workplace jurisdiction and the employee's residence. Oracle Payroll is integrated with Vertex™ Payroll Tax to keep the rates and rules up-to-date.

Vacation, paid time off, and sick leave are quasi-monetary benefits with their own rules. They can be paid for in cash upon termination, but most of the time they are accounted as hours. Accumulated vacation appears on the books as an accrued liability, a benefit the employees have earned but not yet drawn.

Mistakes can be corrected through restatements of pay and recomputation of payroll deductions for one or more past pay periods. The system has to make an appropriate accounting to the employee and the taxing bodies or benefit providers. It prepares quarterly and annual tax returns, including U.S. forms W2, W3, W4, 940, and 941.

Employees can be paid by check or direct deposit, from any number of bank accounts. Payment can be split. You can also use the payroll process to liquidate other obligations to employees, such as expense reimbursements.

Labor distribution rules let you split the payroll expense among ledger accounts, organizations, and other Accounting Flexfield segments to any level of detail you need. You can combine payroll accounting with Project Time and Expense, in the Oracle Projects family, to reconcile the way you compensate labor with the projects and tasks that use it.

Oracle Training Administration

Oracle Training Administration supports the entire training function and can be implemented for both internal and commercial training purposes. With Oracle Training Administration, you can schedule and track training events and manage course enrollments. Updated employee skills information is immediately available in the career management functions within Human Resources. Oracle Training Administration is integrated with the Oracle Financials Applications to administer the financial aspects of the training business.

The Projects Suite

Businesses such as construction companies or consulting firms have traditionally operated on a project basis. They have developed specific techniques to manage, schedule and organize a project. Such organizations want to measure profitability on a project-by-project basis by capturing the true costs and revenue of each assignment. Many industries, though not traditionally project-driven, are adopting project techniques and financial management practices to better manage their own businesses. The need for a complete activity management solution, integrated to a company's core financial systems, has become more critical. The Oracle Projects product suite includes:

- Oracle Project Time and Expense
- Oracle Project Costing
- Oracle Project Billing
- Oracle Activity Management Gateway

The "project dimension" is time. Oracle's other applications assume more or less continuous business processes. General Ledger budgets and reports by periods: months, quarters, and years. Period-to-period comparisons make sense because, with some moderate evolution, the same activities figure in each. The other systems are the same way. Individual transactions exist in time, but Purchasing, Payables, Order Entry, Receivables, Inventory, Manufacturing, and the others assume there will be a continuous flow of transactions year in and year out.

A project has a beginning and (usually) has an end. Each project is made up of a number of tasks or activities. Although similar tasks and activities will figure into multiple projects, the usual reason to recognize a project is that each one is unique and requires individual tracking and management. Here are some examples of projects, ranging from the obvious to the perhaps not so obvious:

- An internal construction project, such as building a new plant
- A contract to build custom software, with a statement of work specifying tasks and deliverables
- A manufactured product, from inception through manufacture, support, and obsolescence
- A marketing campaign
- A program to provide technology training to your employees

The things that characterize a project, concepts which are not found in other Oracle applications, include:

- A work breakdown structure that decomposes the project into as many levels of tasks and subtasks as needed to manage the work. Though most tasks have start and end dates, some may be ongoing for the life of the project.

- A project schedule, giving planned dates for project milestones and showing how tasks are related to each other and to the achievement of the milestones.

- A budget for the life of the project, which may be time-phased to tie it out to accounting periods and operating budgets. Oracle Projects, unlike any other application besides General Ledger, can deal with both income and expense.

- The need measure earned value: how much benefit have you received to date for the investment you have made to date.

Direct Projects are ones that are billable to clients. Oracle Projects manages both the expense and revenue sides of the project. The major expenses include labor, materials, and usages, charges for services, and the use of plant and equipment. Revenues are computed directly in a Time-and-Materials contract. They amount to reimbursable labor and expenses. Labor may be charged at pre-established rates or as actual costs burdened with the contracted amounts of overhead, general and administrative expenses (G&A), and profit. Direct expenses are more commonly billed at cost plus the applicable burdens.

Time is a major issue in T&M contracts. You need to identify all expenses for a period, close the period, and get the bill to the client as quickly as possible. Expenses that get reported late will be paid late, confuse the accounting, and may not be eligible to be reimbursed at all.

Revenue and expenses are more independent in fixed-price contracts. In most cases your expenses are your own concern, for you to pay as you incur them. The customer will accept an invoice to pay you when you reach a contractually stipulated milestone, such as the delivery of a design or a finished project. Fixed price work is generally more risky than time and materials. Earned value is a critical measurement for fixed price. Is the progress you have made commensurate with the amount you have expended? You may be behind schedule, and you may have spent millions: the key question is whether you will get it back, and with what profit. Earned value answers that question.

Indirect projects represent internal expenses. They have no revenue component. Moving to a new location and installing Oracle Applications are typical indirect projects. The project view is useful for budgeting and management. Earned value can be a more useful measure than a GL budget line for indirect projects. Low expense, which looks good on the budget, could equate to little progress.

Rules for the business processes controlled by Projects can be infinitely variable. Oracle has written the basic logic in PL/SQL stored procedures. The user manuals tell you how to modify the routines to meet your own unique business needs. It is the best of both worlds. Oracle has designed the database and written code to ensure its integrity, but you can fit the logic to your own needs in such vital areas as time and expense accounting, overhead accounting, and invoice generation.

Oracle Project Time and Expense

Project-oriented employees charge their time and expenses against projects. Oracle Project Time and Expense handles accounting for employee-reimbursable expenses and expenses such as airfare that are incurred by employees but paid to third parties. It verifies project and ledger accounting data in either online or disconnected mode, then uploads expense data to an interface table. A workflow process handles approvals.

Project Time and Expense's expense functionality overlaps that of Oracle Self-Service Human Resources and Oracle Payables. Projects users will generally choose to use Project Time and Expense for all employee expense processing. Project Time and Expense may share employee time accounting data with payroll. Subcontractor labor often needs to be reconciled with subcontractor invoice payments made through Oracle Payables.

Labor costing is not a straightforward exercise. It can be costed at a standard rate for a position, or as the actual cost of the person doing the work. The charge for overtime premiums is usually spread over the week, so Friday's client doesn't pick up the full burden. Extra hours worked by exempt employees are cheaper, because only 40 hours per week are paid. The standard business rules allocate the benefit among all accounts charged for the week. You might want to change them, maybe leaving time charged to overhead projects out of the equation as long as billable hours exceed 40. Oracle tells you how it coded the logic to handle these situations, giving you the power to change it if you want.

Oracle Project Costing

There are predefined paths for cost information to flow into Oracle Projects from most Oracle modules that can record expense:

- Project Time and Expense (labor and employee expenses)

- Purchasing (purchase commitments, to be paid later by Payables)

- Payables (invoices of project expenses)

- Manufacturing (resource and material costs)

- Inventory (issues and receipts of project assets)

There is an open interface to accommodate any other expenses, such as third-party travel management packages and those recorded by non-Oracle systems handling functions that could be satisfied by Oracle Applications. The drill-down functionality of Projects can take you back to the system in which an expense originated.

Encumbrance accounting can count money as spent from the moment Oracle Purchasing processes a requisition or a purchase order for a project expense. This level of control is very important to projects, which operate against a project lifetime as well as an accounting period budget. Project encumbrance is independent of, and does not require, General Ledger encumbrance accounting.

Oracle Project Billing

Oracle Receivables handles invoicing and collections using invoice detail generated by Oracle Projects. The cost buildup includes varying combinations of direct labor and material expenses, direct (project-related) overhead, indirect overhead, and General and Administrative expenses and profits. Overhead rates are usually pre-established, but they can vary depending on the type of expense, location, and task.

One client may have many ongoing projects. Conversely, one project may have multiple clients. For example, the jurisdictions at either end of a bridge usually share the cost of a project, with federal money included if it is an interstate highway. Each client may have its own percentage of the billings and its own budget. It is often the case that different billings are split according to different algorithms. Oracle's data design can handle almost every type of client relationship.

Oracle does not apologize for the fact that the cost development logic it delivers is rather basic. To take one instance, multiple overhead rates are all applied to direct labor, instead of to one another. Oracle does, however, provide an Applications Program Interface to a PL/SQL routine that you can adapt to fit your business needs. You feed Oracle Receivables as much detail as it needs to present on the invoice.

You have a lot of latitude in choosing when to bill and when to recognize revenue. You usually accrue revenue as you perform the work, even though the contract may specify payment by milestones or you may withhold a fraction of T&M payments until completion. Oracle Projects billings also tend to experience a fairly high level of adjustments. Taxes, late-reported hours, disputed expenses, and a host of other changes can come up. Oracle provides a powerful workflow process and requires approval of trial billings, to ensure that all these factors are considered before the interface to Oracle Receivables. It also has the tools to apply changes when they are needed.

Oracle Projects expects you to do Gantt charts and critical path scheduling using an external project management tool. The most powerful is Artemis, the most ubiquitous is Microsoft Project. The usual sequence of events is:

1. Outline the work breakdown structure in a word processor, spreadsheet, or project management tool.

2. Load resources against the tasks and develop the critical path in a project management tool. Associate budget and GL account figures with the tasks.

3. In Projects, define the clients, agreements, terms and conditions, billing cycles, project types, and so forth needed for the project in question.

4. Upload the data into Projects.

5. Use Projects to collect actual expenses, report project status, report project budget performance, compute estimates-to-complete, handle billings, and otherwise manage the project from a financial standpoint.

6. Periodically export actual data to the project management software and re-import the updated plan.

Projects links with Payables and Fixed Assets to capture the costs of creating a capital asset. Treating capital expenditures as projects provides benefits in terms of budgeting and management. Projects, unlike Payables, is able to group expenses, associate internal expenses such as labor with external expenses settled through Payables, and associate related expenses into meaningful units of Construction in Process (CIP) for Oracle Assets.

Oracle Activity Management Gateway

The Activity Management Gateway (AMG) makes it possible for project management (and other) external packages to create and maintain projects and budgets, including actual and committed expenses and revenue, and to manage earned value, following business rules maintained in Projects. It is an enhanced API, a two-way bridge.

Oracle Projects lets you manage each project as a separate undertaking. At a higher level, cross-project analysis can be an extremely useful tool for measuring projects against each other, extracting standards and developing estimating techniques, examining profitability by activity type, and any number of other such applications. It leverages the investment you make in capturing transaction-level data to provide you a powerful management tool.

Projects, like Manufacturing, is more often the application that drives the business than a mere accounting adjunct to it. It is central to Oracle's Applications' strategy and is integrated up and down the Applications suite. It represents a major investment, the least of which is buying the software, and can produce a major improvement in the way in which you manage your business.

When implementing Oracle Projects, be sure your plans include engaging Oracle Consulting or experienced outside consultants for assistance. Prepare yourself to incorporate the concept of projects across the major sectors, if not the entire extent, of your business processes.

Oracle Project Connect

Oracle Project Connect delivers seamless integration between Oracle Projects and Microsoft Project. Projects, tasks, and budgets can be created and updated in Microsoft Project, and sent to Oracle Projects. Actuals collected and summarized in Oracle Projects can be sent back to Microsoft Project for status reporting and plan updates. Resources defined and managed in Oracle Projects can also be sent to Microsoft Project. The intuitive graphical user interface of Oracle Project Connect is an extension of existing Microsoft Project menus and toolbars, and each function and process preserves the enterprise business rules and function security defined in Oracle Projects.

The Oracle Project Analysis Collection Pack

The Oracle Project Analysis Collection Pack enables you to utilize the enterprise-wide project information collected in Oracle Project Costing and Oracle Project Billing and perform multidimensional analysis of project information across projects and organizations. This tool provides a business solution that allows high-level corporate managers to view data in a wide variety of ways using standard or user-defined parameters. For example, you can use some of the standard parameters to analyze cost, revenue, and budget data across projects, time periods, and organizations. Alternately, you can freely disable standard parameters or create your own to fit the analysis and reporting needs of your company. The Oracle Project Analysis Collection Pack offers flexible and extensible analysis capabilities limited only by the information that your company records.

The Manufacturing Suite

This book has already covered many of the Manufacturing applications in detail including Purchasing, Inventory, and Order Entry.

The basic manufacturing cycle is as follows: Customers enter demand for items through an order entry application. *Material Requirements Planning* (MRP) translates that demand into requirements for parts at all levels— purchased parts, assemblies, and end items. MRP uses the Bill of Materials to determine what parts are needed and how long it will take to manufacture the products. MRP takes into account current inventory quantities when determining what needs to be manufactured or purchased to meet the customer demand. MRP recommends Work Orders to manufacture the needed assemblies, and creates Purchase Requisitions to buy parts from suppliers. Work in Process manages work orders on the shop floor; routing them through the manufacturing process, issuing parts as they are needed, and keeping track of the resources and parts consumed until an assembly is finished and received into Inventory.

Other manufacturing applications are outside the flow of the shop floor. Oracle Engineering manages changes to Bills of Materials, such as the approval and timing of item revision levels. These represent changes in how the item is built. Capacity Planning uses resource restraints, such as machine capacity, work cells, and people to determine how much can be built and what is the best use of plant capacity in terms of profit and satisfying customers. Cost Management collects labor and material costs, which become available in the General Ledger for making more informed decisions about whether to make or buy products.

Oracle Bill of Materials

Oracle's Bill of Materials (BOM) manages the master files that describe how to make products. The item may be something that is made, or it could be something that is never actually made, such as a Pick-to-Order item, a model, an option, or a phantom assembly. *Phantoms* are an engineering convenience. A phantom represents a part that is consumed in a higher-level assembly as soon as it is manufactured. The items are called phantoms because they are never stored in inventory.

Each BOM includes:

- The item number and revision level of the product being made.

- A BOM name: there may be more than one way to make the same product.

- Routing records to show the work cells involved in making the item.

- A row for each component on the BOM. Components are parts, though it is convenient to include drawings, which are not consumed on bills. Options, option groups, and phantoms also appear as components. The row indicates the routing step where it is used.

- The resources used in manufacturing and the standard usage of those resources.

A Bill of Materials, or BOM, describes how to make something, for example 3 wheels + frame = tricycle. The item being made can be a product for sale (tricycle) or an assembly that will go into something else (wheels to put on the tricycle). The raw materials for the assembly step (wheels and frame) and the product (tricycle) are all described as Inventory items.

The process can get more complex. The make-up of a bill can change over time (after July we use stamped plastic wheels instead of metal ones with rubber tires). It can have options (tricycle = frame + wheels + [optionally] decals). It may use other manufactured items: the frame could be made in-house (frame = body + fork + seat). In this case, the bill of materials has to be "exploded" through multiple levels to determine the raw materials that go into the final product.

It takes more than just materials to make a product. Assembling the tricycle takes labor, tools, and a place to work. Building the wheels takes a plastic stamping machine and labor. Bill of Materials works together with a routing to specify the kinds and quantities of resources needed to make an item. The item's routing also specifies the time needed to set up, produce, and clean up after making an item. The Order Entry application can add these times up to compute an Available-to-Promise (ATP) date that can be quoted to a customer. The Master Scheduling/MRP application will use routing information to figure out when raw materials need to arrive for the manufacturing process. For example, if it takes 2 days to make the wheels, the plastic is needed on Day 1 but the frame components can arrive on Day 3.

The Order Entry process uses bills of materials in two ways. When the customer orders a Pick-to-Order (PTO) item (a phantom with a sale price), Order Entry explodes it into the components on the bill of materials—which can go more than one level deep. Order Entry then demands the piece-parts from Inventory and does the picking and shipping by piece-part, printing a reference to the ordered BOM item on the packing slip so the customer doesn't get confused.

Configure-to-Order (CTO) items present options to the customer, enabling them to choose the options they prefer. PTO items can also be CTO. An example would be a great-books set: Order the basic product and you get Locke, Hume, and Adam Smith. Order the French option and you get Voltaire and Rousseau thrown in; the German option includes Goethe and Kant. This set would be structured as a three-level bill. Great Books, the top level, would be a model bill—for ordering only. The next level would include a standard bill for the English authors and an option group specifying that the product can include either, neither, or both the French and German groups. The third level would be two standard bills, one for the French and one for the German group.

Assemble-to-Order (ATO) items are things that are not made until the customer orders them. They can be standard or Configure-to-Order. Their distinguishing characteristic is that a Final Assembly (FAS) Work Order is created to make precisely what the customer orders.

Oracle Engineering

Engineering and Bills of Material both work with the BOM tables, but the emphasis in Engineering is on product development while that of BOM is on production.

Engineering manages Engineering Change Orders. Whenever either its constituent items or the way an assembly is made changes, the change needs to be planned and approved. Will the new bill of materials go into effect immediately? On some specified date? When the factory runs out of a particular component item? Purchasing needs to know what kind of items to buy, and customers may need to know what they bought.

Both Engineering Change Orders (ECOs) and Item Revisions are put into effect by date. The BOM exploder uses the composition of the bill as of the effective date of the explosion. It uses the same effective date to find the applicable item revision level. Oracle Engineering manages ECOs such that the item revision and the bill changes to make it have the same effective dates.

Oracle Inventory can track items down to the revision level. It gives you the ability to move old products out of your inventory and to record in Oracle Service exactly what you have shipped to each customer.

Oracle Master Production Schedule

Master Scheduling supports the high-level decision of what products to make, feeding Material Requirements Planning so it can support the low-level decisions: which assemblies to make, what parts to buy, when, and in what quantities.

Both processes are driven by demand, represented by forecasts and orders. The Master Production Schedule (MPS) determines what high-level assemblies are possible to make, and when they can be made, by matching the resources available with those required to satisfy demand. Some constraints are absolute, but some can be bent. You may not be able to expand the factory overnight, but you can schedule a second shift or rent additional equipment. You execute the MPS process iteratively, trying different demand and resource assumptions in an attempt to optimize profits while still meeting commitments.

The MPS drives Material Requirements Planning, which plans the lower-level bill of material components. MRP, like MPS, checks resources and capacity to ensure customer demand can be met with the existing resources.

Oracle Material Requirements Planning

MRP looks at requirements over time, out to a planning horizon. It projects material needs by time buckets. It takes into account the cumulative time that it takes to manufacture each item. That computation includes the time to get materials from suppliers, time to set up for manufacturing, time to make however many layers of subassemblies are needed, and time to assemble the final product. It recommends what to make, and when to start making it, by backing off how long it will take to make an assembly from when it is needed. MRP generates requisitions to ensure that there will be enough parts to supply the manufacturing process at the time each job is scheduled. It will recommend expeditious action on parts whenever it projects a shortage.

The Bill of Materials is critical to both MPS and MRP planning. MPS balances the resource requirements associated with high-level items against total capacity. MRP explodes these high-level item BOMs to find which components go into each item, then compares the date they are needed with the lead time to determine when it will have to place an order with the supplier. This is an area where close relationships with suppliers are useful. When they are allowed to see the plans MRP generated for you to drive your organization, they can do a better job of anticipating your needs.

Oracle Work in Process

In discrete manufacturing, Work in Process (WIP) creates work orders to initiate and track the manufacture of a given number of a given item. Work orders describe how many of what assembly to make, when the assembly is supposed to be complete, and where to put it upon completion. Work orders use items issued from inventory for the parts and assemblies needed as input at each step.

The BOM and routing serve as a budget in creating a work order. Together they provide standard values for the material and resources to be consumed in the manufacturing process. WIP collects the actual data. There can be a budget for attrition due to parts getting lost, breaking or not meeting the appropriate standards. Although a standard amount of labor is budgeted via the routing, WIP can capture the actual amount of labor used. The difference will be charged to variance accounts. Cost Management collects the actual figures, making it possible to update the standard costs as things change. The objective is to keep variances to a minimum and, of course, to continually improve the efficiency of the manufacturing process.

Oracle Flow Manufacturing

The Work Order concept does not adequately support all methods of manufacturing, especially the assembly line-style repetitive or flow methods. A major issue in all manufacturing methods is setup. The objective is to find the optimal trade-off between the carrying costs of the inventory that results from long production runs versus the setup costs involved in short runs. Part consumption has to be recorded without waiting for the job to end. It is usually handled by backflushing; when 100 televisions roll off the assembly line, you know to decrease inventory by 100 tubes and 300 knobs.

Repetitive manufacturing is used to make long production runs of the same item, without incurring the long cycle times associated with items snaking their way through the factory from operation to operation and waiting in queues before each one of those operations. Repetitive manufacturing greatly reduces cycle time but limits the flexibility and responsiveness of the factory.

Flow manufacturing is used for mixed-model manufacturing, where any number of items can be produced in any sequence. Flow manufacturing is very flexible and combines the efficiency of repetitive manufacturing with the flexibility of a work-order based job shop.

Oracle Process Manufacturing (OPM)

Process manufacturing (or *continuous manufacturing*), such as petroleum refining, is very different from the discrete manufacturing we have been discussing. Raw materials and finished product are constantly flowing with varying potencies. Measurements and minimization of downtime become major issues as the production process must be continually adjusted. As the ingredients change potency, the ratio of one ingredient to another may change to ensure consistency. Oracle Process Manufacturing (OPM) supports continuous manufacturing. Specific process manufacturing techniques, such as formula and recipe management, are supported for food, drink, pharmaceutical, and chemical companies.

Oracle Service

Oracle Service manages the installed base you create as you ship products. It maintains a database of "customer products," or items you have shipped. Service on these shipped products can then be delivered over the telephone, on site, or by having the customer return the product for "depot" maintenance at your site. The service can be covered by warranty, invoiced as delivered, or handled under a number of types of service contracts.

Service characteristics are one of the eight major attributes groups that Oracle Inventory carries on an inventory master item. Serviceable products have flags to indicate how service applies (it is serviceable, service is billable, and so forth), and the services themselves have product numbers. Oracle Inventory and Oracle Service manage the links between services and the products to which they apply—forming a two-way relationship.

Order Entry populates the installed base interface as it ships orders. It picks up the item number, service characteristics, serial number if applicable, the customer, and the location. At that point, the customer's product and the inventory item take on lives of their own. The inventory item can continue to evolve and improve, through engineering changes and new item revision levels. The customer's product may or not be improved through field upgrades, and its configuration may change through field maintenance. Oracle Bill of Materials can recreate the "as built" configuration to support the service engineers.

Service can record changes that take place in the field. If five identical, non-serially numbered items are shipped, the installed base will group them together. You need to update the record if the customer sells one and keeps the other four on maintenance. If there is a warranty replacement, it will record the fact that there is a new serial number. It can change most meaningful data at the customer product item level and can provide the necessary information in cases where you need to track components within the product. It maintains the concept of a "system," a group of customer products (like a computer) that work together as a unit.

Order Entry also manages customers and orders for service. Its Return Material Authorization (RMA) process handles customer returns for replacement, warranty service, and billable depot maintenance. Order Entry sends billing data to Oracle Receivables over its standard interface. This tight integration means customers, serviceable items, and services are defined only once within the Applications universe, and there is no duplication of the shipping, receiving, billing and collection functions. An integrated view of sales and service is an essential tool in measuring customer relationships.

Warranty Service and Service Agreements provide a vehicle for product maintenance. There are usually terms and conditions covering the length of the service, days of the week and hours in the day for service, whether or not repair parts are covered, shipping costs, and similar consideration that affect the cost of delivering service. Oracle Service matches service requests against the terms of the agreement, so it can deliver what the customer is authorized to receive.

Delivering service is a workflow process. The steps differ according to the product, but it may move through several levels of telephone support, then to onsite service, and finally to depot service or replacement. Workflow gives you the ability to apply business rules in routing service requests and to raise warnings when a problem remains unresolved for too long. Workflow can also help you keep up-to-date, by confirming customer data as you log a call. This is often the way you learn who is the ultimate customer of one of your dealers, that customer names and locations have changed, or that a customer resold one of your products. You need this information to deliver service, but knowing who your customers are is also useful to marketing.

Depot maintenance, the heavy-duty repair you do in your own facilities, is a kind of manufacturing job. The common steps for depot-level repair of a single customer return are:

1. Estimate the cost of repair and decide whether the item is economical to repair.

2. Get a decision from the customer whether to repair, replace, or do nothing.

3. Create a nonstandard Work Order, routing the job through the necessary work stations to remedy the diagnosed problems.

4. Collect parts and resource usage data at each station.

5. Put the repaired item back into inventory, and let Order Entry ship it back to the customer.

The depot repair model, using WIP functionality, is able to collect very detailed data on the costs of maintenance. Engineering can use the database to assess mortality rates at a component level to improve quality, and you can use experience as the basis for your repair estimates and charges. The Army develops bills of materials to use for depot-level maintenance. In planning to fix 100 tanks, it might order 20 new barrels, 50 new treads, and 30 fuel injectors, based on past experience regarding the parts it expects to be consumed.

Oracle Quality

Oracle Quality unifies your company's quality specifications, processes, measurement results, and analysis at a corporate level. It is a valuable aid in developing complete and consistent procedures across the business, as required for ISO 9000 certification.

Quality applies to several elements of other Oracle applications. It manages the results of physical testing of items in the receiving and manufacturing processes. The results can be associated, among other things, with suppliers, receipts, WIP jobs, item revision levels, subinventories and finished goods that incorporate tested items.

Quality can also apply to business processes. You can assess how many overshipments your suppliers make; how many timesheets fail because they have improper accounting distributions; or how many newsletters are returned for invalid addresses. All it takes to measure quality are:

■ A way to identify the item being measured, such as item and serial number, or department and month.

■ The property being measured, called the *collection element*. For items it might be weight, for a department the number of unplanned absences.

- A collection procedure. Procedures may involve test equipment, they may be applied to every item or on a statistical basis, or they may be derived from other automated systems. Oracle lets you implement database triggers to collect quality records throughout the Applications.

There is no point in collecting quality data without a plan to use it. Employing what you collect involves:

- Specifications to establish acceptable values for the collection element and severity levels for departures from the standard.

- Prescribed actions to take in response to deviations from the standard, adjusted according to their severity. Oracle Quality makes extensive use of Alerts to launch actions that range from sending a message to executing a concurrent job. You can force the system to take immediate action, such as returning a shipment or putting a hold on a payment.

Quality data is sometimes more useful for analysis than for immediate action. You may want to develop reports comparing your suppliers' success in meeting quality standards, or business departments' success in submitting timesheets by the deadline. Comparisons do not imply an absolute standard, and there could be reasons for the observed differences. There may be no need to take remedial action at a transaction level, such as bringing an issue up with your supplier. However, you may use your knowledge of the quality problems to change your procedures. You might reassess your product engineering or provide your suppliers with more frequent feedback.

Cost is a constant consideration in measuring quality. Some costs of quality deficiencies can be measured. You can put a price on rework and returns to vendor. Opportunity costs such as customer dissatisfaction can only be estimated. However inexactly, you can estimate the value of improved quality to be some fraction of the costs associated with defective quality.

The costs of implementing quality procedures can be measured more easily. The major elements are the effort to put collection procedures in place, the costs of capturing quality transactions, the costs of acting on quality problems, and the costs of analysis. Oracle is a very efficient mechanism for determining the cost elements. Using Oracle Quality will tip the cost/benefit equation in favor of increased quality control in your enterprise. Using Oracle to take an enterprise-level view of quality provides you a number of benefits:

■ You can use the Applications' built-in tools, such as Alerts, triggers, and Workflow, to create and act on quality transactions very economically.

■ You have automatic access to Oracle's powerful analysis tools, such as the data warehouse and graphical presentation tools.

■ You can propagate quality information throughout your process. The quality measurements for a batch of parts, for instance, can be associated with the finished item shipped to a customer.

■ You can use an enterprise view to compare the quality of comparable processes throughout your organization.

■ You can relate quality measurements to standards and procedures kept in documentary form, such as ISO 9000 processes.

Oracle Quality is a large concept. Unlike most other applications, you can implement it gradually by bringing more and more processes under its control as your business matures. Just as surely as quality is central to the ISO 9000 and to the goal of reducing nonvalue-added work, Oracle will continue to extend Quality until it becomes a cornerstone of the Applications architecture.

Index

D

V

W

X

Y

Z

Think you're
smart?

Get Your **FREE** Subscription to Oracle Magazine

Stay informed and increase your productivity with every issue of *Oracle Magazine*. Inside each FREE, bimonthly issue you'll get:

- Up-to-date information on Oracle Data Server, Oracle Applications, Network Computing Architecture, and tools
- Third-party news and announcements
- Technical articles on Oracle products and operating environments
- Software tuning tips
- Oracle customer application stories

Three easy ways to subscribe:

1 MAIL Cut out this page, complete the questionnaire on the back, and mail it to: *Oracle Magazine,* P.O. Box 1263, Skokie, IL 60076-8263.

2 FAX Cut out this page, complete the questionnaire on the back, and fax it to **+ 847.647.9735.**

3 WEB Visit our Web site at **www.oramag.com.** You'll find a subscription form there, plus much more!

If there are other Oracle users at your location who would like to receive their own subscription to *Oracle Magazine,* please photocopy the form and pass it along.

☐ YES! Please send me a FREE subscription to Oracle Magazine.   ☐ NO, I am not interested at this time.

If you wish to receive your free bimonthly subscription to *Oracle Magazine,* you must fill out the entire form, sign it, and date it (incomplete forms cannot be processed or acknowledged). You can also subscribe at our Web site at **www.oramag.com/html/subform.html** or fax your application to *Oracle Magazine* at **+847.647.9735.**

SIGNATURE (REQUIRED) ✓		DATE

NAME _____   TITLE _____

COMPANY _____   E-MAIL ADDRESS _____

STREET/P.O. BOX _____

CITY/STATE/ZIP _____

COUNTRY _____   TELEPHONE _____

You must answer all eight questions below.

1 What is the primary business activity of your firm at this location? *(circle only one)*
- ○ 01 Agriculture, Mining, Natural Resources
- ○ 02 Architecture, Construction
- ○ 03 Communications
- ○ 04 Consulting, Training
- ○ 05 Consumer Packaged Goods
- ○ 06 Data Processing
- ○ 07 Education
- ○ 08 Engineering
- ○ 09 Financial Services
- ○ 10 Government—Federal, Local, State, Other
- ○ 11 Government—Military
- ○ 12 Health Care
- ○ 13 Manufacturing—Aerospace, Defense
- ○ 14 Manufacturing—Computer Hardware
- ○ 15 Manufacturing—Noncomputer Products
- ○ 16 Real Estate, Insurance
- ○ 17 Research & Development
- ○ 18 Human Resources
- ○ 19 Retailing, Wholesaling, Distribution
- ○ 20 Software Development
- ○ 21 Systems Integration, VAR, VAD, OEM
- ○ 22 Transportation
- ○ 23 Utilities (Electric, Gas, Sanitation)
- ○ 24 Other Business and Services ____

2 Which of the following best describes your job function? *(circle only one)*
CORPORATE MANAGEMENT/STAFF
- ○ 01 Executive Management (President, Chair, CEO, CFO, Owner, Partner, Principal)
- ○ 02 Finance/Administrative Management (VP/Director/ Manager/Controller, Purchasing, Administration)
- ○ 03 Sales/Marketing Management (VP/Director/Manager)
- ○ 04 Computer Systems/Operations Management (CIO/VP/Director/ Manager MIS, Operations)
- ○ 05 Other Finance/Administration Staff
- ○ 06 Other Sales/Marketing Staff

IS/IT Staff
- ○ 07 Systems Development/ Programming Management
- ○ 08 Systems Development/ Programming Staff
- ○ 09 Consulting
- ○ 10 DBA/Systems Administrator
- ○ 11 Education/Training
- ○ 12 Engineering/R&D/Science Management
- ○ 13 Engineering/R&D/Science Staff
- ○ 14 Technical Support Director/ Manager
- ○ 15 Webmaster/Internet Specialist
- ○ 16 Other Technical Management/ Staff

3 What is your current primary operating platform? *(circle all that apply)*
- ○ 01 DEC UNIX
- ○ 02 DEC VAX VMS
- ○ 03 Java
- ○ 04 HP UNIX
- ○ 05 IBM AIX
- ○ 06 IBM UNIX
- ○ 07 Macintosh
- ○ 08 MPE-ix
- ○ 09 MS-DOS
- ○ 10 MVS
- ○ 11 NetWare
- ○ 12 Network Computing
- ○ 13 OpenVMS
- ○ 14 SCO UNIX
- ○ 15 Sun Solaris/ SunOS
- ○ 16 SVR4
- ○ 17 Ultrix
- ○ 18 UnixWare
- ○ 19 VM
- ○ 20 Windows
- ○ 21 Windows NT
- ○ 22 Other ____
- ○ 23 Other UNIX ____

4 Do you evaluate, specify, recommend, or authorize the purchase of any of the following? *(circle all that apply)*
- ○ 01 Hardware
- ○ 02 Software
- ○ 03 Application Development Tools
- ○ 04 Database Products
- ○ 05 Internet or Intranet Products

5 In your job, do you use or plan to purchase any of the following products or services? *(check all that apply)*

SOFTWARE

	Use	Plan to buy
01 Business Graphics	☐	☐
02 CAD/CAE/CAM	☐	☐
03 CASE	☐	☐
04 CIM	☐	☐
05 Communications	☐	☐
06 Database Management	☐	☐
07 File Management	☐	☐
08 Finance	☐	☐
09 Java	☐	☐
10 Materials Resource Planning	☐	☐
11 Multimedia Authoring	☐	☐
12 Networking	☐	☐
13 Office Automation	☐	☐
14 Order Entry/ Inventory Control	☐	☐
15 Programming	☐	☐
16 Project Management	☐	☐
17 Scientific and Engineering	☐	☐
18 Spreadsheets	☐	☐
19 Systems Management	☐	☐
20 Workflow	☐	☐

HARDWARE

	Use	Plan to buy
21 Macintosh	☐	☐
22 Mainframe	☐	☐
23 Massively Parallel Processing	☐	☐
24 Minicomputer	☐	☐
25 PC	☐	☐
26 Network Computer	☐	☐
27 Supercomputer	☐	☐
28 Symmetric Multiprocessing	☐	☐
29 Workstation	☐	☐

PERIPHERALS

	Use	Plan to buy
30 Bridges/Routers/Hubs/ Gateways	☐	☐
31 CD-ROM Drives	☐	☐
32 Disk Drives/Subsystems	☐	☐
33 Modems	☐	☐
34 Tape Drives/Subsystems	☐	☐
35 Video Boards/Multimedia	☐	☐

SERVICES

	Use	Plan to buy
36 Computer-Based Training	☐	☐
37 Consulting	☐	☐
38 Education/Training	☐	☐
39 Maintenance	☐	☐
40 Online Database Services	☐	☐
41 Support	☐	☐
42 None of the above	☐	☐

6 What Oracle products are in use at your site? *(circle all that apply)*
SERVER/SOFTWARE
- ○ 01 Oracle8
- ○ 02 Oracle7
- ○ 03 Oracle Application Server
- ○ 04 Oracle Data Mart Suites
- ○ 05 Oracle Internet Commerce Server
- ○ 06 Oracle InterOffice
- ○ 07 Oracle Lite
- ○ 08 Oracle Payment Server
- ○ 09 Oracle Rdb
- ○ 10 Oracle Security Server
- ○ 11 Oracle Video Server
- ○ 12 Oracle Workgroup Server

TOOLS
- ○ 13 Designer/2000
- ○ 14 Developer/2000 (Forms, Reports, Graphics)
- ○ 15 Oracle OLAP Tools
- ○ 16 Oracle Power Object

ORACLE APPLICATIONS
- ○ 17 Oracle Automotive
- ○ 18 Oracle Energy
- ○ 19 Oracle Consumer Packaged Goods
- ○ 20 Oracle Financials
- ○ 21 Oracle Human Resources
- ○ 22 Oracle Manufacturing
- ○ 23 Oracle Projects
- ○ 24 Oracle Sales Force Automation
- ○ 25 Oracle Supply Chain Management
- ○ 26 Other ____
- ○ 27 **None of the above**

7 What other database products are in use at your site? *(circle all that apply)*
- ○ 01 Access
- ○ 02 BAAN
- ○ 03 dbase
- ○ 04 Gupta
- ○ 05 IBM DB2
- ○ 06 Informix
- ○ 07 Ingres
- ○ 08 Microsoft Access
- ○ 09 Microsoft SQL Server
- ○ 10 Peoplesoft
- ○ 11 Progress
- ○ 12 SAP
- ○ 13 Sybase
- ○ 14 VSAM
- ○ 15 **None of the above**

8 During the next 12 months, how much do you anticipate your organization will spend on computer hardware, software, peripherals, and services for your location? *(circle only one)*
- ○ 01 Less than $10,000
- ○ 02 $10,000 to $49,999
- ○ 03 $50,000 to $99,999
- ○ 04 $100,000 to $499,999
- ○ 05 $500,000 to $999,999
- ○ 06 $1,000,000 and over

OMG